VIOLENCE AND TERRORISM

Third Edition

Editor

Bernard Schechterman
University of Miami

Bernard Schechterman is a professor and former chairperson in the Department of Politics and Public Affairs at the University of Miami. He received a B.Soc.Sci. from the University of Wisconsin (Madison) in 1948, an M.A. from Indiana University (Bloomington) in 1950, and a Ph.D. from Indiana University (Bloomington) in 1973. He is Chief Editor of *The Political Chronicle*, an editor with *The Journal of Political Science*, and an editorial consultant with *The Middle East Review*. He co-authored the book *Multidimensional Terrorism* (1987) with Martin Slann.

Editor

Martin Slann
Clemson University

Martin Slann is a professor of political science at Clemson University. He received an A.B. from the University of Miami in 1964, an M.A. from the University of Connecticut in 1966, and a Ph.D. from the University of Georgia in 1970. He is co-editor of *Morality and Conviction in American Politics: A Reader* and co-author of *The American Republic: Politics, Institutions, and Policies*. He is also the author of *Eight Nations: An Introduction to Comparative Politics*, and the editor of the *Journal of Political Science*.

Cover illustration by Mike Eagle

Annual Editions
A Library of Information from the Public Press

The Dushkin Publishing Group, Inc.
Sluice Dock, Guilford, Connecticut 06437

The Annual Editions Series

Annual Editions is a series of over 55 volumes designed to provide the reader with convenient, low-cost access to a wide range of current, carefully selected articles from some of the most important magazines, newspapers, and journals published today. Annual Editions are updated on an annual basis through a continuous monitoring of over 300 periodical sources. All Annual Editions have a number of features designed to make them particularly useful, including topic guides, annotated tables of contents, unit overviews, and indexes. For the teacher using Annual Editions in the classroom, an Instructor's Resource Guide with test questions is available for each volume.

VOLUMES AVAILABLE

Africa
Aging
American Government
American History, Pre-Civil War
American History, Post-Civil War
Anthropology
Biology
Business Ethics
Canadian Politics
China
Commonwealth of Independent States and Central/Eastern Europe (Soviet Union)
Comparative Politics
Computers in Education
Computers in Business
Computers in Society
Criminal Justice
Drugs, Society, and Behavior
Dying, Death, and Bereavement
Early Childhood Education
Economics
Educating Exceptional Children
Education
Educational Psychology
Environment
Geography
Global Issues
Health
Human Development
Human Resources
Human Sexuality

India and South Asia
International Business
Japan and the Pacific Rim
Latin America
Life Management
Macroeconomics
Management
Marketing
Marriage and Family
Microeconomics
Middle East and the Islamic World
Money and Banking
Nutrition
Personal Growth and Behavior
Physical Anthropology
Psychology
Public Administration
Race and Ethnic Relations
Social Problems
Sociology
State and Local Government
Third World
Urban Society
Violence and Terrorism
Western Civilization, Pre-Reformation
Western Civilization, Post-Reformation
Western Europe
World History, Pre-Modern
World History, Modern
World Politics

Library of Congress Cataloging in Publication Data
Main entry under title: Annual editions: Violence and terrorism. 3/E.
     1. Terrorism—Periodicals. 2. Violence—Periodicals. I. Schechterman, Bernard, *comp*.
II. Slann, Martin, *comp*. III. Title: Violence and terrorism.
303.6′25′05   ISBN 1–56134–133–9

Third Edition

Manufactured by The Banta Company, Harrisonburg, Virginia 22801

Printed on Recycled Paper

Editors/ Advisory Board

To the Reader

In publishing ANNUAL EDITIONS we recognize the enormous role played by the magazines, newspapers, and journals of the *public press* in providing current, first-rate educational information in a broad spectrum of interest areas. Within the articles, the best scientists, practitioners, researchers, and commentators draw issues into new perspective as accepted theories and viewpoints are called into account by new events, recent discoveries change old facts, and fresh debate breaks out over important controversies. Many of the articles resulting from this enormous editorial effort are appropriate for students, researchers, and professionals seeking accurate, current material to help bridge the gap between principles and theories and the real world. These articles, however, become more useful for study when those of lasting value are carefully *collected, organized, indexed,* and *reproduced* in a *low-cost format,* which provides easy and permanent access when the material is needed. That is the role played by *Annual Editions.* Under the direction of each volume's *Editor,* who is an expert in the subject area, and with the guidance of an *Advisory Board,* we seek each year to provide in each *ANNUAL EDITION* a current, well-balanced, carefully selected collection of the best of the public press for your study and enjoyment. We think you'll find this volume useful, and we hope you'll take a moment to let us know what you think.

Terrorism is an international curse of the late twentieth century. Its causes are as varied and as complicated as its manifestations. Governments and citizenries have come to accept the phenomenon of terrorism as one of those hazards of life that is not completely resolvable.

The articles in this reader were chosen in an effort to represent the several categories of terrorism and the multiplicity of terrorist organizations. One primary criterion for their selection was succinctness. There are simply too many ways to track and analyze terrorist groups and activities to concentrate at length on particular facets in one introductory reader.

The readings are authored by reputable journalists and academicians, most of whom have written extensively on terrorism. Their views are not always in agreement with one another and some of their suggestions or analyses may not be agreeable to the student. They are, however, both informed and informative. These articles should stimulate thoughtful inquiry into the subject of terrorism.

However disconcerting political terrorism may be, it remains a constant in international and often domestic politics. Terrorism may not be an indefinite reality, but it is one that certainly has demonstrated staying power. For this reason it is of singular importance that we learn what terrorism really is, what motivates terrorists ideologically, and how the goals of terrorism as well as its outrages can be understood and countered.

This volume is organized into 9 units. Unit 1 is devoted to the difficult task of defining and conceptualizing both "terrorism" and "terrorists." Unit 2 introduces and explains the more pronounced reasons for terrorism. Indirectly, this unit's articles also make the point that terrorism may have no realistic termination; hatred is a long-term as well as a destructive emotion. Unit 3 explores the different categories of terrorism, with a particular emphasis on the most effective and lethal type: state-sponsored and state-supported international terrorism. Unit 4 on state terrorism naturally complements unit 3. State terrorism is a mass killer, and during this century it has destroyed more lives than any other human endeavor. Unit 5 deals with both the actuality of and the potential for terrorism in the United States. The United States is neither immune from nor totally open to terrorism. Unit 6 is a brief but pertinent consideration of the relationship between terrorism and the news media. The emphasis here is on the dilemma every free society faces: although the coverage of terrorism is newsworthy, it also encourages future terrorism. Unit 7 emphasizes one of the more frightening characteristics of terrorism: as the articles in this section reveal, terrorism is frequently well financed and organized to maximize resources through networking, intimidation, and even illicit drug trafficking. Unit 8 is the largest collection of articles and attempts to assure the reader that something is being done about terrorism's threat and to explain what the limits and successes are in countering terrorism. These articles identify and analyze what individuals as well as governments do and can do to thwart those who would harm them. Terrorism will remain a permanent and dangerous threat to international peace and political stability. In light of this fact, the articles in Unit 9 are devoted to potential and projected trends in terrorism.

We hope that this volume acquaints the student with terrorism. Ideally, it will be an acquaintance that will foster further inquiry into this omnipresent global phenomenon.

Your comments have produced an improved third edition of *Annual Editions: Violence and Terrorism.* Your further opinions and suggestions are still welcome and will help shape future editions. Please fill out and return the article rating form on the last page of this book. Any anthology can be improved; this one will continue to be.

Bernard Schechterman

Martin Slann
Editors

Contents

Unit 1

The Concept of Terrorism

Three articles examine the phenomenon of terrorism in the context of today's world security.

Unit 2

The Causes and Scope of Terrorism

Four articles discuss the more prevalent lethal causes and scope of contemporary terrorism.

The concepts in bold italics are developed in the article. For further expansion please refer to the Topic Guide and the Index.

Unit 3

The Terrorists: International, State-sponsored, and State-supported

Nine selections examine the vicious forms of violence generated by state-sponsored terrorism, and the extent to which a government can go to put pressure on its citizenry.

The concepts in bold italics are developed in the article. For further expansion please refer to the Topic Guide and the Index.

Unit 4

State Terrorism and Dissent (Revolutionary) Terrorism

Fourteen articles consider the extent to which a nation's government can exercise terrorism.

The concepts in bold italics are developed in the article. For further expansion please refer to the Topic Guide and the Index.

Unit 5

Terrorism in America

Four articles examine how terrorists impact on American domestic society.

Terrorism and the Media

Four selections examine the critical connection between terrorism, the media, and the audience.

Tactics, Strategies, and Targeting

Eight articles discuss how terrorists share tactics and strategies. Terrorist organizations, if they are to be successful, need logistical and financial support.

Unit 8

Countering Terrorism

Eight articles examine methods used to counter
terrorism, from legalistic to retaliation through force.

Unit 9

Trends and Projections of Terrorism

Four articles discuss the possible future of terrorism.

Topic Guide

This topic guide suggests how the selections in this book relate to topics of traditional concern to students and professionals involved with the study of violence and terrorism. It is useful for locating articles that relate to each other for reading and research. The guide is arranged alphabetically according to topic. Articles may, of course, treat topics that do not appear in the topic guide. In turn, entries in the topic guide do not necessarily constitute a comprehensive listing of all the contents of each selection.

TOPIC AREA	TREATED IN:	TOPIC AREA	TREATED IN:
Abu Nidal Organization (ANO)	12. Abu Nidal Organization 49. Economic Analysis Can Help Fight International Terrorism 58. Middle Eastern Terrorism in Europe	**Hostage-taking (cont'd)**	42. Kidnapping and 'Taxes' Transform Guerrila Inc. 53. Terror and Negotiation
African Terrorism	4. Violence Against Violence 6. Terrible Toll of Human Hatred 10. Horn of Misery 18. Genocide: An Historical Overview 30. War and Peace Advance in Sudan 39. Emerging Iranian-Sudanese Relationship	**Irish Republican Army (IRA)**	15. Triangle of Ethnic Struggle 32. Domestic Terrorism in the United States 46. Terrorism and Public Opinion 58. Middle Eastern Terrorism in Europe
Airline Hijackings/ Bombings	3. Unmasking Terrorism: The Fear of Fear Itself 9. Terrorists' Payoff in the Hostage Deal 38. Terrorism and the Media 48. Terrorism and World Order 49. Economic Analysis Can Help Fight International Terrorism 50. Closing Our Eyes 55. Terrorist Threat to Commercial Aviation 58. Middle Eastern Terrorism in Europe	**Latin American Terrorism**	16. Peru's Rebels Buck Trend as Troop Strength Grows 22. Travesty of Justice 32. Domestic Terrorism in the United States 41. Peru's Maoist Drug Dealers 42. Kidnapping and 'Taxes' Transform Guerrilla Inc. 43. Fugitive Leader of Maoist Rebels Is Captured by the Police 44. Colombia's Bloodstained Peace 46. Terrorism and Public Opinion 57. Terrorism in the United States
Biological/Chemical Weapons	40. Hidden Threats 45. Will Terrorists Use Chemical Weapons?	**Lebanese Groups**	2. Is Symbolic Violence Related to Real Violence? 9. Terrorists' Payoff in the Hostage Deal 11. Israel's Deadly Game of Hide-and-Seek 12. Abu Nidal Organization 36. Media Dilemma and Terrorism
East Asian Terrorism	2. Is Symbolic Violence Related to Real Violence? 4. Violence Against Violence 6. Terrible Toll of Human Hatred 23. China's Black Book 24. Tibet's Shattered Hopes 25. India Under Fire Over Rights Abuses 26. Ethnic Conflict in Sri Lanka 27. Burmese, After Years of Terror 28. Nature of the Genocide in Cambodia 29. Violence, Like Punjab's Wheat, Finds Fertile Soil	**Left-Wing Groups**	16. Peru's Rebels Buck Trend as Troop Strength Grows 21. Decline of the Red Army Faction 26. Ethnic Conflict in Sri Lanka 28. Nature of the Genocide in Cambodia 32. Domestic Terrorism in the United States 41. Peru's Maoist Drug Dealers 42. Kidnapping and 'Taxes' Transform Guerrilla Inc. 43. Fugitive Leader of Maoist Rebels Is Captured by the Police 57. Terrorism in the United States 58. Middle Eastern Terrorism in Europe
Ethnic Rivalry	4. Violence Against Violence 6. Terrible Toll of Human Hatred 13. Europe's New Right 15. Triangle of Ethnic Struggle 16. Peru's Rebels Buck Trend as Troop Strength Grows 18. Genocide: An Historical Overview 24. Tibet's Shattered Hopes 26. Ethnic Conflict in Sri Lanka 28. Nature of the Genocide in Cambodia 29. Violence, Like Punjab's Wheat, Finds Fertile Soil 30. War and Peace Advance in Sudan 32. Domestic Terrorism in the United States 39. Emerging Iranian-Sudanese Relationship 56. Specific Trends and Projections for Political Terrorism 57. Terrorism in the United States 58. Middle Eastern Terrorism in Europe	**Media**	35. Manipulation of the Media 36. Media Dilemma and Terrorism 37. Media Coverage of Political Terrorism and the First Amendment 38. Terrorism and the Media 46. Terrorism and Public Opinion 47. 10 Steps Against Terrorism
Hostage-taking	9. Terrorists' Payoff in the Hostage Deal 31. Structure of Counterterrorism Planning and Operations in the United States	**Narco-Terrorism**	11. Israel's Deadly Game of Hide-and-Seek 16. Peru's Rebels Buck Trend as Troop Strength Grows 33. Bombs Over America 34. Plague of Our Cities 41. Peru's Maoist Drug Dealers 43. Fugitive Leader of Maoist Rebels Is Captured by the Police 44. Colombia's Bloodstained Peace 57. Terrorism in the United States

The Concept of Terrorism

This section of the book has two primary goals: (1) to place the phenomenon of terrorism in some context of political modes of violence, and (2) to shed light on the actual meaning and boundaries of this form of activity.

There is a continuing controversy among those who study terrorism as to how to define it. There is widespread concurrence on the general characteristics of terrorism, and there are divisions on certain factors beyond these basics. The minimalist approach focuses on three ingredients: perpetrator, victim, and an audience deliberately affected by the violent act. Of the three, the victim remains the subject of the most contentious debate. The official U.S. concept of terrorism stresses that an assault against a noncombatant civilian victim is clear-cut evidence of a terrorist act. The maximalist approach, favored by the Israelis and others, includes the presence of passive military targets alongside civilians as a basis for labeling an attack a terrorist act. The definition becomes crucial to statistical compilations, especially trend and geographic pervasiveness analysis, as well as to the question of countering terrorism (see unit 8).

The article "Defining Terrorism" reviews the ongoing debate and variations in the attempt to define terrorism (and the terrorist act). Drawing upon the comprehensive literature on the subject, the author delineates the contentious issues and helps to facilitate the defining process.

Article 2 focuses on a widespread debate on the relationship between religious ideas and the avoidance versus the need to choose violence as a response to social circumstances. The Girardian focus has both religious and secular connotations.

"Unmasking Terrorism: The Fear of Fear Itself" places great stress on a critical ingredient of terrorism and terrorist objectives—the creation of a climate of fear, in which the ultimate goal is the intimidation and coercion of the public, especially in open and democratic societies. Aside from the personal fears of physical harm, the most dangerous ramification is the disruption of the ordinary life-styles of citizens in free societies.

Looking Ahead: Challenge Questions

Why are there basic difficulties in reaching agreement on the characterization and definition of terrorism?

What ideas are central to the American definition of terrorism? Which of these may be misleading?

Where does terrorism fit on a continuum of organized modes of political violence in today's world?

Unit 1

DEFINING TERRORISM

Peter C. Sederberg

Peter C. Sederberg, Ph.D. is professor of political science at the University of South Carolina.

A weary cliche, yet a most persistent myth in the study of terrorism stresses the subjectivity that supposedly afflicts efforts to define the phenomenon. The aphorism "one man's terrorist is another man's freedom fighter" suggests that all attempts to formulate the concept will be hopelessly compromised by essentially arbitrary personal or political bias. Consequently, any analysis based on such dubious conceptual foundations will be distorted and most likely vacuous.

The emotional baggage attendant on the term leads it to be used more for condemnation rather than clarification. To successfully attach the label "terrorist" to one's opponent constitutes a moral and political victory (Jenkins, 1985). Such victories, though, are purchased at high cost for critical discourse on the problem. Christopher Hitchens (1986, p. 68) argues that the terrorist label "disguises reality and impoverishes language and makes a banality out of the discussion of war and revolution and politics." Little wonder, then, that some conclude that the "very word terror is a hindrance in the investigation of violence" (Bell, 1978a, p. 39).

This lamentable condition induces some commentators to abandon the quest for a working definition. Laqueur (1977, p. 5) argues that a comprehensive definition is unlikely to be found in the foreseeable future but asserts that "to argue that terrorism cannot be studied without such a definition is manifestly absurd." On somewhat similar lines, Geoffrey Levitt (1988) suggests that the deductive approach to terrorism may produce a certain political satisfaction but is too vague to serve as a basis for practical responses to terrorism. As a pragmatic alternative, he suggests a inductive approach that simply identifies a series of criminal acts to be addressed. From a different ideological position, other critics assail terrorist definitions as simply rhetorical weapons used to castigate opponents

of the established order (Chomsky and Herman, 1979; Herman and O'Sullivan, 1989).

While the critics of the concept make valuable points, we need either some kind of working definition in order to delimit the boundaries of terrorism from other forms of conflict behavior (Gibbs, 1989; Provizer, 1987; Wardlaw, 1982, 1989; Weinberg and Davis, 1989) or else be prepared to abandon the term to the mindless pleasures of the politicians. Unfortunately, the lack of consensus produced by the combination of inherent ambiguity and polemical pressure results in a plethora of definitions. Alex Schmid (1983), in a comprehensive review of the literature at the time, identifies over a hundred competing definitions. When he published a second edition (1988), the situation had worsened, ironically, in part, in response to a survey on the definitional problem he conducted.

To sort through this morass, we first review several problems afflicting various definitions, thereby suggesting some means for assessing comparative worth. We then suggest a kind of "middle range" strategy that allows us to distinguish terrorism from other forms of coercive conflict, though not without a certain degree of irreducible ambiguity. Somewhat paradoxically, if we can be clear about the areas that lack clarity, we will possess a better understanding of the terrorist phenomenon than we would if we embraced a definition that obscures its own obscurities.

Perhaps the most easily recognized definitional flaw consists of the failure to distinguish between presumed terrorist activities and other forms of coercive action not normally (or usefully) considered terrorist. Brian Crozier (1974, p. 4) suggests that terrorism is " 'motivated violence for political ends' (a definition that distinguishes terrorism from both vandalism and non-political crime)." Unfortunately, it doesn't distinguish it from any other tactic of internal or external warfare. Similarly, a CIA study (1978, p. 1) defines international terrorism as "the threat or use of violence for political purposes when (1) such action is intended to influence the attitude and behavior of a target group

From *Terrorism: Contending Themes in Contemporary Research*, by Peter C. Sederberg, 1991. From *Annual Review of Conflict of Knowledge*, published by Garland Publishing, New York, NY.

wider than its immediate victims, and (2) its ramifications transcend national boundaries." The blunt edge of this instrument eliminates the distinction between a PLO hijacking and the Battle of Midway in World War II. Other examples of the tendency to conflate terrorism with a variety of other forms of coercion include Russell, Banker, and Bowman (1979), Lodge, (1981a), U.S. Department of Defense (1986; quoted in Schmid, 1988), and Falk (1988).

A second definitional shortcoming arises when terrorism, however characterized, is primarily associated with one side or the other in a political struggle. Not surprisingly, given the nature of the dominant political agenda, terrorism is often identified with revolutionary dissent. Take, for example, the effort of the U.S. Department of Defense (1983, p. 1220) to confine terrorism to "the unlawful use or threatened use of force or violence by a revolutionary organization against individuals or property with the intention of coercing or intimidating governments or societies, often for political or ideological purposes." This definition manages to be both vague and tendentious. Other definitions that seem to be compromised by too close an identification with the established order are those of Lodge (1981a) and Buckelew (1986).

Given the polemical purposes frequently served by the terrorist label, those identifying with various dissident struggles castigated as terrorist have attempted to appropriate the term for their own purposes. Falk (1986, pp. 135–137) argues that the manipulation of political language serves to disguise the indiscriminate violence of what he calls "First World Terrorism." Noam Chomsky (1988, p. 1) makes a somewhat similar point when characterizing the Fifth Freedom; "the freedom to rob, to exploit and to dominate, to undertake any course of action to ensure that existing privilege is protected and advanced." Finally, Goren (1984, p. 13) quotes a definition of terrorism offered by an ad hoc group of nonaligned nations which condemns, among other things, "acts of violence and other repressive acts by colonial, racist, and alien regimes against peoples struggling for their liberation. . . ." Proponents of this definition clearly intend that the actions of the South African and Israeli regimes be considered as terrorist.

Somewhat less contentious than explicitly defining one side or the other in a political struggle as terroristic are those definitions that single out the nature of the victims as being central to the understanding of the terrorist act. Unfortunately, the definitions stress different characteristics such as being "innocent" (Friedlander, 1980; Netanyahu, 1986), noncombatant or civilian (Francis, 1981; Sederberg, 1989), symbolic (Crenshaw, 1981; Singh, 1977; Thornton, 1964), or arbitrarily chosen (Kupperman and Trent, 1979; Wilkinson, 1974). Whatever the superficial similarities, these traits are not equivalent to one another. A civilian victim may not be "innocent" (whatever that means). Non-

combatants may not be civilians; they might be prisoners of war. Symbolic victims might be combatants, and if they are symbolic, they cannot be chosen arbitrarily, but for their symbolic value.

If the pitfall of political identification is avoided, definitions sometimes slip into circularity. For example, Crelinstein (1987) defines terrorism as "the deliberate use of violence and the threat of violence to evoke a state of fear (or terror) in a particular victim or audience." Other definitions that stress the fear-inducing character of the act include Duvall and Stohl (1988), Mickolus (1980), and Wardlaw (1982). Now the question of why acts considered terrorist are often capable of inspiring a state of terror in disproportion to their actual threat is an important area for research (see below), but to define terrorism as action causing (or intended to cause) terror fails to provide much of a basis for distinguishing terrorism from other forms of coercive conflict. Such definitions obscure the many purposes beyond brute terror for which terrorism is used or make the character of the action dependent on the success it achieves in causing terror in the target.

In all, Schmid (1988) identifies twenty-two elements that appear in the 109 definitions he analyzes. In an effort of cumulation, if not synthesis, he (p. 28) offers a definition that incorporates sixteen of the twenty-two elements:

> Terrorism is an anxiety-inspiring method of repeated violent action, employed by (semi-) clandestine individual, group, or state actors, for idiosyncratic, criminal, or political reasons, whereby—in contrast to assassination—the direct targets of violence are not the main targets. The immediate human victims of violence are generally chosen randomly (targets of opportunity) or selectively (representative or symbolic targets) from a target population, and serve as message generators. Threat- and violence-based communication processes between terrorist (organization), (imperiled) victims, and main targets are used to manipulate the main target (audience(s)), turning it into a target of terror, a target of demands, or a target of attention, depending on whether intimidation, coercion, or propaganda is primarily sought.

Although an impressive effort at summarization, the definition's convoluted and somewhat contradictory nature diminishes its utility.

A variety of problems, then, impede our efforts to develop an analytically useful definition of terrorism. First, an understandable, but confusing, tendency to intermingle explanation, justification, and condemnation mars many definitions. Second, the confusion between the action (terrorism), the actor (the terrorist), and the effect (terror) detracts from the ability to distinguish between terrorism and the larger class of coercive behavior of which it is a part. In this regard, definitions should focus on the act, and recognize that issues of actors and effects are areas for inquiry, not definitional attributes. Finally, the option of focussing on various subspecies of terrorism fails to specify what it is about these subspecies that make them terrorist. Though we may be able to formulate some policy response to particular activities, we would be forced to abandon the search for a more general understanding.

If we are to rescue the concept of terrorism from the polemicists, as well as address the concerns of those who believe it to be an empty category, we must specify those characteristics that distinguish terrorism from other coercive tactics used within or between political communities. Two traits, each drawing upon fairly well-established rules of war, seem to hold some promise (Walzer, 1977). The most well-established limits on the conduct of warfare involve the targets selected and the means chosen to attack those targets. Specifically, the targets of attack should be combatants, and the weapons used against these targets should be highly discriminating.

The principle of noncombatant immunity and the ban on indiscriminate means are certainly interrelated; nevertheless, they raise distinct issues. Terrorism may be seen as a tactic of severe coercion that deliberately violates these two rules of war: Noncombatants are the targets, and the means used to attack these targets are relatively indiscriminate. These two criteria, then, suggest two propositions and two qualifying exceptions (Sederberg, 1989, p. 37):

Proposition One: Discriminating acts of coercion aimed at combatants are not terrorist.
Exception One: At some point, attacks on combatants may become so indiscriminate (counterforce nuclear war) that they become terrorist in effect, if not intent.
Proposition Two: Undiscriminating and severe coercive attacks deliberately aimed at noncombatants are terrorist.
Exception Two: At some point, attacks against noncombatants may become so discriminating in choice of target (e.g., a tyrant) and means, that they are not usefully labeled terrorist (George, 1988).

The value of this definition lies both in its clear specification of what tactics are or are not terrorist and in its explicit identification of the areas where disputes are likely to arise (i.e., indiscriminate attacks on presumed combatants; highly discriminate attacks on noncombatants). Moreover, by treating terrorism as a tactic, it incorporates recognition that all contenders in a political struggle may yield to the terrorist temptation. Two key questions remain open, however: Who is a noncombatant? and, how indiscriminate is too indiscriminate? These probably cannot be convincingly resolved by definitional fiat, but although they remain open to debate, provisional determinations need not be arbitrary, but should be supported by reasoned elaboration.

The characteristics we have suggested for distinguishing terrorism from other coercive tactics, however, suggest why terrorism has the common consequence of spreading fear far in excess of the concrete damage done or the probabilities of being a victim. The distinction between combatants and noncombatants is, perhaps, the last firebreak of a civil order. Once breached, no one can feel secure. Terrorism, moreover, often involves innocuous targets, such as airplanes, railway depots, and department stores, places that people normally consider safe. Terrorist acts cause not only substantive damage, but also they undermine the confidence people have in the familiar. Now every place must be viewed with suspicion, if not alarm.

If we abandon the concept of terrorism to the ideologues or ignore the differences between terrorism and other forms of coercion, we hamper the possibilities for successful political action to contain this particular tactic. Only if we have a sensible and reasonably clear idea of the distinctive traits of terrorism can we pursue questions of who uses it and why.

Editor's Introduction:
Is Symbolic Violence Related to Real Violence?

Mark Juergensmeyer

Mark Juergensmeyer is a Professor of Religious Studies and Political Science at the University of Hawaii, where he is Dean of the School of Hawaiian, Asian and Pacific Studies. Previously he served as Director of the Religious Studies Program at the University of California, Berkeley. His writings include Religion as Social Vision *(1982),* Fighting with Gandhi *(1986), and a chapter of* Inside Terrorist Organizations *(edited by David C. Rapoport). He is completing a book on religious violence and nationalism sponsored by the Harry Frank Guggenheim Foundation and the U.S. Institute of Peace.*

Violence has always been endemic to religion. Images of destruction and death are evoked by some of religion's most popular symbols, and religious wars have left through history a trail of blood. The savage martyrdom of Husain in Shiite Islam, the crucifixion of Jesus in Christianity, the sacrifice of Guru Tegh Bahadur in Sikhism, the bloody conquests in the Hebrew Bible, the terrible battles in the Hindu epics, and the religious wars attested to in the Sinhalese Buddhist chronicles indicate that in virtually every tradition images of violence occupy as central a place as portrayals of nonviolence. This raises two haunting questions: why are these images so central, and what is the relationship between symbolic violence and the real acts of religious violence that occur throughout the world today?

To explore questions such as these, the Harry Frank Guggenheim Foundation convened an exploratory conference of scholars at Sterling Forest, New York, in September 1989. Most of those taking part were social scientists and scholars of comparative religion who have studied incidents of religious violence and terror caused by militant Muslims, Jews, Christians, Sikhs and Sinhalese Buddhists. One scholar, however, brought a more theoretical and literary perspective to these contemporary cases. This scholar, René Girard, has formulated theories about the social role of symbolic religious violence that have been widely discussed in his own field of comparative literature and throughout the humanities; they have been especially influential in the field of religious studies. But despite the wide readership that his ideas have attracted,

Girard has rarely come face to face with social scientists and other investigators of cases of religious violence in modern society. One of the significant moments in the conference was the dialogue among Girard and these scholars over the applicability of his theories to the contemporary world.

The dialogue that began at Sterling Forest continued in written form in 1990, culminating in a series of essays written by several of the participants on the relevance of Girardian themes to their own analyses of contemporary cases of religious violence. It is these essays, with Girard's written response, that are presented [in *Terrorism and Political Violence*, Volume 3, Autumn 1991]. The essays contain much more than a discussion of Girard—one will find useful information and penetrating analyses of a variety of situations in contemporary Lebanon, Israel, Egypt, Sri Lanka, India, Indonesia, and elsewhere—yet the themes that Girard has enunciated tie together the disparate interests of the authors.

The authors gratefully acknowledge the support of the Harry Frank Guggenheim Foundation for launching them on this venture, and the involvement of its president, James Hester, and its program officer, Karen Colvard, in the lively discussions that led to this book. Although this volume was not commissioned by the Foundation, nor does it contain the papers prepared for the 1989 conference in their original form, the conversation which the conference stimulated is appropriate to the Foundation's primary concern: understanding, and ameliorating, the forces that lead to conflict and violence in the contemporary age.

The Girardian Themes: Sacrifice and Mimetic Desire

Perhaps one of the reasons that Girard is regarded with such interest, especially in the field of Religious Studies, is that he supplies a straight-forward answer to a question that has vexed thoughtful observers of religion for centuries: why violence is so central to religion. In looking for an answer, Girard turns toward certain aspects of human relations that are potentially violent, and suggests that religion provides mechanisms for defusing their violence.[1]

In saying that violent symbols and sacrificial rituals evoke, and thereby vent, violent impulses, Girard follows the lead of Sigmund Freud, who also wrote about the importance that religion holds in symbolically displacing feelings of hostility and violence. Freud is, in fact, the major theorist with whom Girard wrestles in his pioneering theoretical work, *Violence and the Sacred*, and Girard is sometimes congratulated for rescuing an interesting Freudian explanation for religious violence from its ties to the controversial theory of the Oedipal complex.

Similar to Freud, Girard is fascinated with religious myths of violence and sacrificial rites. Girard, like his famous mentor, regards such myths and rituals as recollections of original violent acts that must be controlled. Girard and Freud both regard these incidents and their symbolic responses as ubiquitous in religious traditions; understanding them is critical to an understanding of the meaning of religion *per se*. If one can decipher their importance for the human condition, one can understand what lies behind religion; and in doing that one deciphers the puzzle behind all forms of culture.

Common to both Freud and Girard is the notion that sacrifice is the primary sacred act. It is primary, they assert, because those who conduct a rite of sacrifice are projecting onto the sacrificial victim qualities that relate to some of their own most intimate concerns. In demolishing the victim they are symbolically annihilating aspects of themselves. What is destroyed is destructiveness itself: the feelings of violence and hostility that lie behind attempts to carry out violent activities. Such feelings are antithetical to the ties of friendship that bond a community together, and feelings of violence toward one's peers and associates must be banished if a closely-knit community—such as a tribal brotherhood, a spiritual fellowship, or a modern nation—is to survive.

Insofar as sacrifice is a mechanism for helping to banish intracommunal violence, it plays an important social role, one which both Freud and Girard see as positive. It allows adherents to release feelings of hostility towards members of their own communities, thereby 'purifying' these feelings and allowing for the social cohesion of affinity groups. 'The function of ritual', claims Girard, 'is to "purify" violence; that is, to "trick" violence into spending itself on victims whose death will provoke no reprisals'.[2] Of course, those who participate in rituals of violence are not consciously aware of the social and psychological significance of their acts, for indeed 'religion tries to account for its own operation metaphorically'.[3]

Thus far, Girard and Freud are in agreement, but Girard parts company with Freud over the question of what causes these destructive urges. Freud, in a famous hypothesis extracted from the myth of Oedipus, suggests that instincts of sexuality and aggression aimed at parental figures lie behind the desire to destroy, and these are the traits projected onto the scapegoat foe. Girard rejects this, and attributes the root cause of violence to what he terms 'mimetic desire'.

Mimetic desire, according to Girard, is 'a desire imitated from the desire of a model who thereby runs the risk of becoming a rival for the same object of desire'.[4] One identifies with an idealized image of another person. Yet this identification can also lead to competition and hatred of the other. For this reason, posits Girard, it is important to have symbols of the rival that one can conquer, and therefore assimilate. Hence the centrality of the rite of sacrifice: it offers up a scapegoat of the rival that one can literally devour. It thereby fulfills not only the cultural and community-building functions that Freudian theory implies, but also personal goals, such as controlling one's feelings of competition and aggression. Without it, mimetic desire can run amok, and violent urges can become focused on scapegoat enemies rather than on symbolic victims. Such is the situation a society confronts when it no longer has convincing symbols of sacrifice to dispel violence. The society then faces a 'sacrificial crisis', as Girard puts it.

The two central aspects of Girard's theory—sacrifice and mimetic desire—are regarded by him as inextricably linked. But they are conceptually distinct. One can appreciate much of what Girard has to say about the function of sacrifice in symbolically displacing feelings of violence without accepting that mimetic desire is the villain that motivates the feelings. Similarly, one may see how mimetic desire plays a potent role in situations of conflict without looking for evidence of sacrificial displacement or even a 'sacrificial crisis'—the situation of violence that occurs when rituals are inadequate to displace violent urges.

In some of Girard's later writings there is yet a third aspect to his theory: the uniqueness of Christianity. According to Girard, among the world religions Christianity is alone in its understanding of the sacrificial victim. Nowhere else is God perceived as having played this role. Christ provides all humanity with a 'perfect model': one who, having no appropriate desire, does not run the risk of triggering mimetic rivalry.[5] He thereby ends the cycle of sacrifice by allowing himself to be the sacrificial victim. As a result Christianity gives to the world an enduring message of pathos and peace. Like other aspects of Girard's theory, however, one can accept or reject this aspect of it without disturbing the rest of his theoretical design.

Looking at Contemporary Cases of Real Religious Violence

What, one might ask, do these various aspects of Girard's theory have to do about *real* acts of religious violence in the contemporary world? The death squads of Sikh and Sinhalese revolutionaries, the Muslim terrorists of Lebanese and Egyptian movements, and the extreme elements of militant Jewish and Christian activists are all engaged in violence in a direct and significantly non-symbolic way. It might appear that their actions do not fit Girard's theories: their sacrifices do not result in the peaceful displacement of violence that ritualized forms of religious violence are supposed to produce, nor are Christian activists less vicious than religious warriors of other faiths. Yet it is the conviction of most contributors to this volume that some of Girard's ideas about symbolic violence can be applied to these real cases as well, making symbol and reality not so removed from one another as first they might appear.

The essays [presented in *Terrorism and Political Violence*, Volume 3, Autumn 1991] explore Girardian themes in relation to real contemporary cases. Each of the authors has taken Girard seriously as an analyst of sacrificial violence, and they have looked at their own case studies to see which of Girard's theories apply. Some of the authors have found quite a bit of correspondence between what Girard says about symbolic religious violence and what occurs in the real world. Others have found less. In both cases they differ in what they regard as Girard's most significant contribution: some have found the notion of mimetic desire to be Girard's most suggestive idea; others have found to be more appealing his understanding of the role of sacrifice in displacing violence. Still others have replaced parts of Girard's theories with other theories, or found that his work, to be appreciated, must be understood in a broader theoretical context.

Among the authors in this volume, Mark Anspach, in 'Violence Against Violence: Islam in Comparative Context', has made the greatest use of Girard's theories. After looking at a number of instances of violence in pre-state societies, Anspach concludes that, like many traditional cultures, Islamic communities often resort to vendetta and punishment to deal with expressions of violent feelings, rather than relying solely on the mechanism of sacrificial ritual. He agrees with Girard that such a situation can create 'a sacrificial crisis', where ritual is confused with history. Without an adequate sacrificial lamb, violence is pitted against violence, as Girard has sometimes said, in a spiral of reprisals. The violence of contemporary Islam shows what happens when the mechanism of sacrifice does not work.

Martin Kramer, in 'Sacrifice and Fratricide in Shiite Lebanon', is also concerned with the sacrificial motif in contemporary Islamic violence. Kramer focuses on the recent cases of 'self-sacrifice' of those young members of the Hizbollah and Amal terrorist groups in Lebanon who have given their lives in suicide missions aimed against the American and Israeli military. What

Kramer has found is that these young people bear many of the characteristics of sacrificial victims in traditional religion: they are physically and spiritually pure and yet in some ways socially marginal. They are of marriageable age, for instance, but not yet married; and some lack family ties. Kramer concludes that these agents of 'self-sacrifice' are in fact chosen by society, or at least by social pressure: they are victims. He goes on to claim that there is a sacrificial competition between the Hizbollah and Amal groups, creating what amounts to a 'mimetic rivalry' as each attempts to outdo one another in acts of self-sacrifice.

It is not Girard's notions of sacrifice, but his ideas about mimetic desire that initially interest Ehud Sprinzak in his essay, 'Violence and Catastrophe in the Theology of Rabbi Meir Kahane: The Ideologization of Mimetic Desire'. Here Sprinzak examines the writings of one of modern Israel's most strident religious ideologues, and finds within the late rabbi's thinking a pattern of mimetic rivalry, involving a desire to be like the Gentiles and to supersede them. The main purpose of God's creation of Israel, according to Kahane, is vengeance: to be a 'fist in the face of the Gentile world'. Yet Kahane rejects the symbolism of sacrifice that might (in Girard's reckoning) save Israel from the violent implications of this mimetic desire. According to Kahane, Israel must repudiate the sacrificial role that history—and the Hebrew Bible—would seem to force upon it. It must not be the willing lamb. But in abandoning the image of sacrifice, Kahane loses one of the resources that Judaism offers for symbolically displacing violence. As Girard's theory would leave one to conclude, Kahane is left with a strategy for confrontation that is based on vengeance, power, and violence. His is mimetic rivalry in its most raw form.

The theme of mimetic desire is also explored by Emmanuel Sivan in 'The Mythologies of Religious Radicalism: Judaism and Islam'. The rivalry that interests Sivan is the curious one in the Middle East between fundamentalist Muslims and fundamentalist Jews. Although they are, in a sense archenemies, the conservatives aim their arrows of degradation at the apostates in their own religious communities rather than at their Muslim or Jewish counterparts. In certain ways they seem to respect and even emulate one another. The Muslim censuring of Salman Rushdie, for example, was met with a certain approval by orthodox Jews; and Sivan implies that in many ways they compete in their attempts to out-orthodox each other. The sacrificial consequences of this mimetic desire are also noted by Sivan. He quotes a Jewish rabbi as having suggested that the *Intifadia* could be handled by Israel sacrificing 'a scapegoat'—in this case, the Gaza strip—in order that bloodshed might be avoided.

The last three essays . . . take a somewhat different tack. Rather than applying aspects of Girard's themes to specific cases, they use these cases to evaluate some of Girard's basic assumptions. Bruce Lawrence, in 'The Islamic Idiom of Violence: A View from Indonesia', deduces from his study of the Indonesian case that what might appear to be religious violence in many parts of the world is in fact political violence. It is a part of (or a rejection of) the violence implicit in the construction of the modern nation-state. Taking cues from the British sociologist Anthony Giddens, Lawrence finds that Islam occupies a subordinate role in the modern world, and the violence attributed to it is in fact an aspect of modern nationalism. In Lawrence's view, Girard's theory, which initially emerged from the analysis of classical literary images, is not so much wrong in its own terms as irrelevant to the modern social situation.

My article, 'Sacrifice and Cosmic War', based on insights gleaned from case studies of Sikhs in India, Sinhalese Buddhists in Sri Lanka, Christians in Nicaragua, and Muslims and Jews in the Middle East, also questions some of Girard's assumptions. I begin, however, by agreeing with him in many basic respects. I concur that ritualized violence is important to virtually all religious cultures, and that violence conducted by religious actors in the real world often exploits those images. I question, however, the necessity of the concept of mimetic desire for explaining the origins of these symbols, and the notion that sacrifice is the fundamental religious image. Instead, it seems to me, a case may be made that what stands behind virtually all religious activity is the quest for order. This quest involves a struggle between order and disorder that is often exemplified in the grand metaphor of cosmic warfare. Sacred war is a dominant motif in the rhetoric of modern-day religious activists engaged in violent endeavors, and this metaphor, I suggest, is more seminal to their thinking than sacrifice.

David C. Rapoport's essay is not so much an application of Girard's theory, nor a critique—although he is disappointed at Girard's failure adequately to deal with the conscious use of violence by religious actors—as it is an attempt to put Girard in context. In 'Some General Observations on Religion and Violence', Rapoport outlines five reasons to think that religious revivals will always be associated with violence. The first has to do with the capacity of religion to command loyalties and enlist total commitment—a line of reasoning that is employed by political theorists, including Machiavelli. The second, which incorporates my point of view, focuses on the language of religion and the way that it is by its nature suffused with violence and images of sacred war. The third reason—which encapsulates Girard's perspective—emphasizes the violent origins of religion, and the aspects of these origins that help to keep violence in check. The fourth reason, the study of the role of revivalist and apocalpytic doctrines in fomenting religious violence, is the one with which Rapoport himself is most closely identified. A fifth

reason stresses the connections between religious and political communities and the lure of religion for the secular political actor. In presenting each of these reasons, Rapoport draws on a variety of sources, and suggests that many of these points of view are more compatible and intersecting than they may first appear.

At the conclusion of the book, Girard himself has an opportunity to respond. In doing so he confronts some of the theoretical challenges made directly by the contributors to this volume and indirectly in the case studies to which they refer. Girard restates and defends many of his basic positions, and shows their relevance to contemporary issues. Yet at the end of the book the reader is faced with many of the same questions with which the book began. Among them is a central one: does an understanding of the origins of the symbols of religious violence help in understanding actual instances of religious violence in the modern world?

The essays . . . do not give a definitive answer. They do not prove that Girard's theory is intrinsically true or consistently useful; nor do they prove the opposite. They do demonstrate, however, that in some cases, aspects of Girard's theory are not only useful but directly applicable. And in all cases they demonstrate that the themes that have exercised Girard's imagination—the motifs of sacrifice, rivalry and religious violence—are of enduring, and pointedly contemporary, concern.

[Editor's Note: This article reviews the essays that appear in the special issue on Violence and the Sacred in the Modern World, *Terrorism and Political Violence*, Autumn 1991.]

NOTES

1. The major work to which the authors of this volume refer is René Girard, *Violence and the Sacred*, trans. by Patrick Gregory (Baltimore; MD and London: The Johns Hopkins University Press, 1977), orig. published as *La Violence et le Sacre* (Paris: Editions Bernard Grasset, 1972). See also his *'To Double Business Bound': Essays on Literature, Myth, Mimesis, and Anthropology* (Baltimore, MD and London: The Johns Hopkins Press, 1978); *Things Hidden Since the Foundation of the World* (Stanford, CA: Stanford University Press, 1987), orig. published as *Des Choses Cachées depuis la Fondation du Monde: Recherches avec Jean-Michel Oughourlian et Guy LeFort* (Paris: Grasset, 1978); *The Scapegoat*, trans. by Yvonne Freccero (Baltimore, MD and London: The Johns Hopkins University Press, 1986), orig. published as *Le Bouc Emissaire* (Paris: Grasset, 1985); and *Job: The Victim of His People* (Stanford, CA: Stanford University Press, 1987), orig. published as *La Route Antique des Hommes Pervers: Essais sur Job* (Paris: Grasset, 1985); and Walter Burkhert, René Girard, and Jonathan Z. Smith, *Violent Origins: Ritual Killing and Cultural Formation*, edited by Robert G. Hamerton-Kelly (Stanford, CA: Stanford University Press, 1987).

2. Girard, *Violence and the Sacred*, p.36.

3. Girard, *Violence and the Sacred*, p.36.'

4. Correspondence to me from Girard in response to an earlier draft of this introduction (4 Feb. 1991).

5. The wording in this description of Christ as 'perfect model' was provided by Girard (correspondence to me in response to an earlier draft of this introduction, 4 Feb. 1991).

UNMASKING TERRORISM

THE FEAR OF FEAR ITSELF

Rushworth M. Kidder

Boston

WHEN "The Color Purple" went to the Cannes Film Festival in France this month, director Steven Spielberg and star Whoopi Goldberg stayed home.

The Italian Open tennis tournament began yesterday in Rome, but there were no junior players from the United States: The US Tennis Association had decided not to send any.

A trade delegation from the state of Washington canceled a European trip just days before it was to have begun.

TWA is closing down its Cairo-Athens and Cairo-Rome connections; Pan Am has laid off 212 employees and canceled new services planned for the Chicago-Frankfurt and Los Angeles-Paris routes; and US travel agents are reporting 20 to 30 percent declines in trips to Europe.

The reason in each case: fear of terrorism.

In the past year, terrorism has made its mark on America as never before. A relatively small number of committed terrorists, operating thousands of miles from America's borders, have succeeded in changing the way the most influential nation on earth lives, works, and relaxes.

The present upsurge in concern began, perhaps, with the 17-day ordeal of TWA's Flight 847 in the Middle East last summer. Watching the hijacking unfold in lurid detail on network television, ordinary Americans were reminded once again how much they, too, were susceptible to terrorism.

Americans had seen plenty of terrorism before, of course. But much of it had been directed at government officials and other obvious targets. The takeover of the US Embassy in Tehran, Iran, in 1979, although

> Terrorism, so often sponsored by nations and magnified by the media, plants seeds of fear throughout the world. And fear can imprison free men and women more surely than the stoutest walls.

of much longer duration than the TWA incident, involved diplomats, not ordinary folks. The truck-bombing of the Marine barracks in Beirut in 1983, though far more lethal, involved uniformed servicemen.

But TWA 847 seemed different. Ordinary Americans from places such as Indianapolis, Little Rock, Ark., and Albuquerque, N.M., became hostages. The terrorists, given plenty of television air time, explained their deadly purpose with new force.

So the nation was already primed with concern when, in October, New York passenger Leon Klinghoffer was brutally murdered by the Palestinian hijackers of the Italian cruise ship Achille Lauro. The spiral of fright rose another notch when, in December, five Americans perished in the wanton massacres by Palestinian gunmen at the Rome and Vienna airports.

Could not *something* be done? Must the Western world stand by helplessly while trained terrorists strike out at will against innocent people?

The occasion for response came after a discothèque frequented by US soldiers in West Berlin was bombed April 5. US intelligence traced the cause to Libyan agents in East Berlin. On April 14, US planes bombed Libya.

Never before in the Western world's two-decade-long battle against modern terrorism had military force been directed against a government. Terrorism had moved into the big leagues.

Historians will long debate the wisdom of the Reagan administration's decision to send in the bombers.

Will the strike help limit terrorism, by sending messages that states supporting ter-

ter'ror-ism:

n. [Fr. *terrorisme*] **1.** the act of terrorizing; use of force or threats to demoralize, intimidate, and subjugate, esp. such use as a political weapon or policy **2.** the demoralization and intimidation produced in this way

— **Webster's New World Dictionary**

"...the unlawful use or threatened use of force or violence by a revolutionary organization against individuals or property with the intention of coercing or intimidating governments or societies, often for political or ideological purposes."

— **Department of Defense, 1983**

"...the unlawful use of force or violence against persons or property to intimidate or coerce a government, the civilian population, or any segment thereof, in furtherance of political or social objectives."

— **FBI, 1983**

"...premeditated, politically motivated violence perpetrated against noncombatant targets by subnational groups or clandestine state agents."

— **State Department, 1984**

"...violent criminal conduct apparently intended: (a) to intimidate or coerce a civilian population; (b) to influence the conduct of a government by intimidation or coercion, or (c) to affect the conduct of a government by assassination or kidnapping."

— **Department of Justice, 1984**

"...the unlawful use or threat of violence against persons or property to further political or social objectives. It is usually intended to intimidate or coerce a government, individuals or groups or to modify their behavior or policies."

— **The Vice President's Task Force on Combatting Terrorism, 1986**

T errorism's central weapon is fear itself. It consists of an attempt by the weak to gain dominion over the strong.

And since its ultimate target is not the victim but the public at large, terrorists seek access to channels of communication.

rorist groups cannot escape without penalty? Or will it provoke new fury and new attacks on Americans?

Will the attack drive wedges between America and friendly nations, or will the unified stand against terrorism articulated at the recent Tokyo summit prove to be a bellwether for tougher stands in general?

Is terrorism best fought with military force? Or does it take better police work, tougher security, and more preventive intelligence?

Should Americans seek to emulate the successes of the British and the Italians, who have managed to diminish the incidents of Irish Republican Army (IRA) and Red Brigades terrorism by strict adherence to the law? Or is the world now fighting a new kind of terrorism — masterminded by puppeteers controlling suicidal operatives and sweeping across international borders — that demands a new kind of response?

Finally, can terrorism be fought without altering the fabric of free democracies? Or must protection of liberty involve curtailment of individual freedoms? These questions have been the subject of scores of Monitor interviews conducted over the past five months in London, Belfast, and Aberdeen; Bonn, Cologne, Bremen, and Hamburg; Paris, Milan, and Rome; Tel Aviv and Jerusalem; and Washington and Boston.

From discussions with politicians, government officials, past and present intelligence analysts, police and military officers, counterterrorism specialists, academics, security consultants, clergymen, journalists, terrorist sympathizers, and ordinary citizens, the following points come to the surface:

● Terrorism's central weapon is fear itself. It consists of an attempt by the weak to gain dominion over the strong. And since its ultimate target is not the victim but the public at large, terrorists seek access to formal or informal channels of communication.

● Terrorism stems from some of the basest elements of human nature — hatred, revenge, and territoriality. Yet it often comes in the guise of religious or political movements, a just attempt to gain a homeland or a remedy for past injustices.

● It is essentially a problem affecting the free world, not the communist bloc. The US State Department conservatively counts 695 terrorist incidents worldwide in 1985. Only one took place in Eastern Europe. And although only four occurred in North America, American targets overseas were involved in about 25 percent of all terrorism. Of the 695 total, the vast majority took place in the Middle East (310), Europe (184), and Latin America (125).

● Terrorists are becoming more sophisticated in weaponry, selection of targets, use of intelligence, and manipulation of the news media. The gunmen themselves are beginning to use home video equipment to make tapes for release to commercial networks. The terrorist of the future, writes expert Neil C. Livingstone, "may more likely be armed with an Apple II home computer than a Polish-made WZ63 machine pistol."

● Terroists are building new alliances. Isolated groups are beginning to come together in what John Newhouse, a New Yorker writer, has dubbed "a freemasonry of terrorism." A meeting in Tripoli in early February at which Libya's Col. Muammar Qadaffi was host brought together 22 Arab terrorist groups. An unrelated meeting, in Frankfurt, West Germany, from Jan. 31 to Feb. 2, brought together several hundred participants from 11 European countries to discuss "anti-imperialist and anti-capitalist resistance in Western Europe" and to review strategy with "comrades" from the Middle East and Central America.

● Terrorists are shifting to a new target: the tourist. Robert Kupperman of the Center for Strategic and International Studies at Georgetown University in Washington, D.C., notes that "the real story in terrorism [these days] is the tourism business." In the 1970s, embassies and military installations were frequently attacked. These targets, subsequently "hardened," may soon become even more secure: The US State Department is proposing to spend $4.4 billion to build 79 new embassies and renovate 175 others. A second source of targets, the international business community, has also hardened itself: A Rand Corporation terrorism expert, Brian M. Jenkins, notes that businesses in America spend $21 billion a year on security. So terrorists, seeking softer targets, increasingly look to tourists. Estimates are that countries around the Mediterranean lost $1 billion

in canceled bookings in 1985, with Greece alone losing $300 million.

● Much of modern terrorism is tied to the Arab-Israeli conflict — involving two cultures whose dominant religious teachings both make room for revenge. But many observers agree that the solution to terrorism does not lie simply in resolving the Palestinian problem. Even if that problem were solved tomorrow, they say, Middle Eastern terrorism would continue at the hands of militant Shiite fundamentalists. Terrorism would also continue from other groups: Sikhs, Tamils, Basques, Irish Republicans, the Boricua Popular Army in Puerto Rico, the Red Army Faction in West Germany, and the M-19 in Colombia, to name a few.

● Terrorism appears to be more than a passing phenomenon. "It's a problem to be managed, not to be solved," says Ambassador Edward Marks, a counterterrorism specialist on leave from the State Department

The Rand Corporation's Mr. Jenkins cites new sources of frustration and new levels of state sponsorship as reasons for the rise in terrorism. He also notes a widening arena: By the mid-1980s, terrorist incidents were occurring, on average, in 65 countries each year — up from 29 countries in the late 1960s.

● Most experts agree there is plenty of room for strong counterterrorist measures. Noting that terrorism is most effective when the public lets fear take over, many observers urge that it be kept in perspective — noting, for example, that the 23 American lives lost overseas last year in terrorist incidents are greatly overshadowed by the 18,000 murders in the US each year.

They note, too, that the presence of conditions in which political violence seems to flourish does not mean that terrorism will necessarily occur. "People who have lost their homelands don't automatically turn to terrorism," notes Rand Corporation scholar Paul B. Henze. "We have enormous groups of these people around the world who haven't gone to [terrorism] at all."

ACTS OF TERROR?

'**T**HE Boston Tea Party was a historical event or a terrorist act, depending on which side you sat." When he speaks to American audiences, former Italian intelligence official Franco

Ferracuti uses that line to point up the difficulty of defining terrorism.

From the gunman's point of view, "terrorist" is a dirty word. Journalists in Northern Ireland, seeking interviews with

1. CONCEPT OF TERRORISM

State terrorism
Acts of terror perpetrated by governments using their own military or police forces. The best-known example is probably Nazi Germany. More recent examples include the slaughter of 20,000 Islamic fundamentalists by Syrian troops in Hama in 1982 and the widespread use of violence by several Latin American governments.

State-sponsored terrorism
Support of quasi-independent terrorist groups by sympathetic governments. Most terrorist groups receive some state support such as funds, training, arms, intelligence, or safe houses. Examples include the Palestinian Saiqa organization (largely controlled by Syria) and the Salvadorean FMLN (which gets support from Cuba).

Acts of war
Open military hostilities between governments, whether declared or not. Unlike terrorism, war usually avoids attacks on civilians and primarily involves conflicts between uniformed soldiers. Since few such wars are fought today, other terms have arisen, such as low-intensity conflict, involving a political-military struggle short of war.

Idiosyncratic terrorism
Disturbed individuals, acting without accomplices and without criminal or ideological motivation, can also terrorize. Examples include the San Ysidro, Calif., massacre at a MacDonald's restaurant in 1984 or even John Hinckley's attempted assassination of President Reagan. Such acts are not, however, usually considered "terrorism."

Criminal acts
A term reserved for acts of lawlessness where the motive is personal rather than ideological gain. Crime usually involves only the victim and the perpetrator, who usually wants to remain of sight. Terrorism involves a third party, the public. This distinction blurs in organized crime, where victims are sometimes shot in public to make a point.

FILE PHOTO/AP

Terrorist act? Grand Hotel, Brighton, England, after '84 bombing of British Cabinet members by Irish Republican Army: when targets are political, most experts call it terrorism.

FILE PHOTO/REUTERS

Act of war? US Marine barracks at Beirut International Airport after '83 explosion of a Shiite suicide truck-bomb: If the target is soldiers, is it terrorism or guerrilla warfare?

Provisional Irish Republican Army officials, are careful to use such terms as "paramilitary activist." Palestinians on the West Bank see themselves as resisting unlawful occupation, while rebels in El Salvador think of themselves as freedom fighters.

Among students of terrorism, the term lies somewhere on a scale stretching from crime to war. Most definitions (see box), include four elements: the method (force and violence), the perpetrator (a revolutionary or conspiratorial group), the target (governments and civilian populations), and the purpose (to coerce and intimidate for political ends).

Scottish scholar Paul Wilkinson, seeking to distinguish terrorism from crime, cites "the deliberate attempt to create fear, intensive fear, in order to coerce the wider target into giving in to what the terrorist wants." By "wider target" he includes the public at large.

Israeli scholar Eytan Gilboa, seeking to distinguish terrrorism from war, emphasizes "a deliberate policy of hurting civilians" as opposed to unintented injury.

And the Bush Commission report, noting that "terrorism is political theater," emphasizes the terrorists' need for publicity.

Despite such definitional efforts, there is still plenty of slippage. The mining of the Gulf of Suez in 1984, presumably by the Libyans, is usually called terrorism. But the United States administration does not use the term for the 1984 mining of the harbor in Nicaragua by Central Intelligence Agency-backed "contras."

FILE PHOTO/AP

Criminal act? Abortion clinic, Washington, D.C., after '85 bombing: because no "conspiratorial enterprise" can be found, the FBI does not define antiabortion attacks as terrorism.

Such definitional difficulties sometimes stem from ideological differences: Both the United Nations and the Bush Commission reportedly spent inordinate amounts of time trying to define terrorism.

Different definitions can lead to practical problems. Italian officials say they know of 290 left-wing and 65 right-wing Italian terrorists who are still at large, and complain that the majority live openly in France. But France, citing a tradition of asylum dating back to the French Revolution, is loath to extradite any "terrorist" who might, in fact, be a political exile.

The Causes and Scope of Terrorism

This section assesses the overall scope of contemporary terrorism and examines its most prevalent, as well as most lethal, causes. Terrorism, in its modern sense, is the result of both excessive resentment and extreme self-righteousness. Many terrorists are genuinely convinced that their cause (which is usually associated with their ethnic or religious community or ideological convictions) has been systematically betrayed and exploited by powerful and nefarious forces. They consequently feel justified in victimizing others with similar atrocities. According to their beliefs, they have been left no choice in the matter by a cruel and insensitive world.

It is this perspective that eliminates the possibility of compromise or flexibility. Terrorists view the world in terms of good and evil. One does not negotiate or "work through the system" with evil; one can only destroy evil, root and branch.

Terrorism, then, represents an absolutist approach to resolving political problems. It is also indicative of a decidedly anti-Western bias. A great deal of contemporary terrorism is motivated, justified, and inspired by fundamentalist religious doctrine. Article 4 provides an explanation of the theological rationale for simultaneously being antithetical to violence while serving as the very basis for the resort to violence. Despite the paradoxical views of religion, it would be deficient to overlook its inspirations in recent times for religious zealotry.

The perception of being morally wronged, sometimes passed on for generations, is compounded by the fact that terrorists are simply unpleasant individuals. "Unmasking Terrorism: The Terrorist Mentality" characterizes them as aggressive, lonely, frustrated, and dogmatic people who tend to oversimplify issues. Terrorism for such individuals is the ultimate expression of a chip on the shoulder. Whether religiously or ideologically motivated, a sense of self-righteousness can be a powerful catalyst for violence.

"The Terrible Toll of Human Hatred" reveals how terrorists can easily take advantage of ethnic and religious distrust and suspicion to completely wreck a country. The ability of terrorists to take advantage of human misery should not be underestimated by any society desirous of avoiding Lebanon's fate.

Finally, "Explaining Terrorism" helps to explain what we are up against in terms of the social psychology of terrorism. Destructive behavior is a complicated and frightening phenomenon.

Looking Ahead: Challenge Questions

Why does the religious fundamentalist surge that has inspired much of the political unrest in the Middle East and elsewhere over the last several years involve an antagonism toward the West? How is it that this antagonism also has secular roots?

How can a terrorist be profiled? What are the more pronounced personal, ideological, and psychological characteristics?

Why does terrorist violence seem relentless and endemic in several societies across the globe? What are the historical, ethnic, and religious dimensions of this violence?

What is the more or less current status of international terrorism? Which countries assist terrorism, and which attempt to frustrate it?

Are terrorist acts so abhorrent to the entire world community that assassination of terrorists is actually justified, even for democratic societies?

What do terrorist organizations realistically expect to achieve? Do they understand their limitations? Can they be expected to resort to future violent acts if they receive at least some of what they want? What if they do not?

Unit 2

Violence Against Violence: Islam in Comparative Context

Mark R. Anspach

Mark R. Anspach, currently a research scholar at the Centre de Recherche en Épistémologie Appliquée, École Polytechnique, in Paris, has recently completed his Ph.D. at Stanford University under the guidance of René Girard. He is a member of the editorial board of the Journal of Violence and Religion, *and is a founding member of the Colloquium on Violence and Religion.*

To study violence within religion is to confront a paradox, the definition of which depends on one's perspective. From a vantage point inside the Western religious tradition, religion may be perceived as inherently antithetical to violence, making religious violence a paradox from the point of view of the religion itself. But an observer surveying religions in general will find that such an internally-recognized antithesis is far from universal. For this outside observer, the real paradox is that religion can play a vital role in controlling violence *without* being antithetical to it. Indeed, from this point of view, the role of violence in religion constitutes perhaps the central paradox not only of religion but of social order itself.

In this article I explore the nature and implications of this paradox, focusing for the most part on the place of violence in the religio[n] of 'primitive' or pre-state societies. Ritual sacrifice is the one kind of violence we all identify as religious since it has no apparent secular function. My argument is largely devoted to showing that other violent institutions that are not generally regarded as primarily religious—vendettas, leadership battles, the punishment of transgressors—can in pre-state societies be understood as extensions of sacrificial ritual which, together with sacrifice proper, form a unified system. I address the question of violence in a non-Western 'world religion', Islam, within the comparative context established by the preceding discussion.

Durkheim identified religion with the principle of social cohesion, and social cohesion requires in turn that a check be imposed on the centrifugal force of social violence. René Girard's contribution has been to demonstrate the paradox that religion controls violence *through* violence—it 'contains' violence in both senses of the word, employing 'good' violence against 'bad'. 'Good'

violence is the controlled, inoculatory dose of violence directed against a scapegoat held responsible for the outbreak of uncontrolled 'bad' violence that like a plague threatens to engulf society. Religious ritual re-enacts the transition from the undifferentiated state of generalized violence to the differentiated state of social order through the sacrifice of a victim by the group. The opposition between the victim and the group is the primordial cultural difference; it is the foundation of the religiously sanctioned system of differences that defines the culture.

Differences keep the peace. This may seem an odd notion when we are accustomed to the language of 'overcoming differences', but it follows from Girard's observation that imitation—the attempt to be the 'same as'—leads to conflict if it is allowed to extend to the realm of desire: 'Two desires converging on the same object are bound to clash'.[1] In pre-state societies, individuals are assigned different objects by kinship regulations, 'totemic' obligations and prohibitions and what might be called the 'ritual division of labor'. In fact, as the anthropologist A. M. Hocart emphasized, where economic division of labor, and Durkheim's 'organic solidarity', are lacking, the 'only differentiation of function is in the ritual'.[2] It would be misleading to speak of the economy—or the family, or politics—as independent spheres of activity in a pre-state society, since not only are all these interrelated, they are also organized within a common religious framework. Religion furnishes the Durkheimian web of social cohesion, but it does this in the first place by forging differences; in the words of Lucien Scubla, 'religion indeed contributes to weaving the social bond, but it unites men by separating them, by putting them at a good distance from one another and by keeping them from getting too close to each other'.[3]

The first part of what religion achieves is to avoid occasions for friction. This is not to say that primitive religion eliminates all freedom of choice and hence all possibility of competition. Even the most rigidly prescriptive kinship system will not tell a man exactly whom to wed. Nonetheless, by defining a relatively narrow category, it significantly limits the potential for conflict.

We can reformulate this first aspect of religion in positive terms by saying that it channels rivalry into

From *Terrorism and Political Violence*, Vol. 3, No. 3, Autumn 1991, pp. 9-29. *Terrorism and Political Violence*, published by Frank Cass and Company, Ltd., England.

different directions. That is what it does day in and day out. On periodic occasions, however, there is a ceremonial reversal of the usual taboos that culminates with the channeling of violence in a single direction. After being kept apart the rest of the year, people are brought together at last around the same object—but only by sharing in its destruction. Nothing generates 'collective effervescence' like a well-organized lynching. As we know, the fundamental rite for Girard is the unanimous murder of a lone victim.

The unanimity of the group and the marginal status of the victim are essential to ensure that no one will come forward to wreak vengeance on the sacrificers. The sacrifice must remain an isolated act. Isolation of violence is the whole point of the procedure. Like desire, violence is contagious; sacrificial violence is 'good' violence insofar as it does not spread. The problem with vengeance, Girard writes, is that it 'threatens to involve the whole social body' because it is an 'interminable, infinitely repetitive process' of violence hurled against violence: 'every reprisal calls for another reprisal', and the 'multiplication of reprisals instantaneously puts the very existence of a society in jeopardy'—which, he concludes, 'is why it is universally proscribed'.[4]

Some anthropologists have challenged this vision of vengeance as a phenomenon whose appearance automatically places the society in mortal danger. Raymond Verdier points out that while vengeance is always proscribed among the members of a group, it becomes a social obligation in the face of aggression. Avenging the victim is a sacred duty for the survivors, often a religious duty sanctioned by the authority of spirits. Verdier's collaborator, Joseph Chelhod, describes the Bedouin belief that a murder victim's soul 'is transformed into a screech-owl who clamors incessantly to drink his enemy's blood'.[5] Little wonder that the quest for revenge takes priority over everything else. 'So that he would not be tempted to evade this sacred duty, the anteislamic Arab solemnly swore to renounce profane pleasures and the enjoyments of this world as long as he had not accomplished his vengeance.'[6]

Girard is of course aware that vengeance can be a duty; more than that, he sees here once again the paradox that violence can only be controlled through violence: 'The obligation never to shed blood cannot be distinguished from the obligation to exact vengeance on those who shed it'.[7] Verdier observes, however, that this duality is normally correlated with a distinction between aggressors from within the group and those from without: 'the duty of vengeance without is the counterpart of the prohibition on vengeance within: duty and prohibition express the two faces, external and internal, of solidarity; one cannot avenge oneself on those whom one has precisely the duty to avenge'.[8]

Not only is vengeance theoretically limited to dealing with offenders from the outside, its proper execution is typically governed by a host of other restrictions, leading

Verdier to speak of it as a full-fledged 'system of regulation and social control having its rules and its rites' concerning the time, place, methods and targets of revenge. The kind of vengeance run wild that Girard depicts can only emerge when the system is not functioning: 'It is only when the system comes unhinged . . . or when it doesn't yet apply (as during the three days of the "boiling of the blood" after a deliberate murder, among the Bedouins) that vengeance goes wild'.[9] Verdier's own volumes are studded with sufficient fearsome examples of 'system failure' that we may suppose the threat of uncontrolled vengeance to be real enough.

It is clear, though, from his work and that of others, that the repetitive process of reprisals in a regulated vendetta may continue for generations without proving fatal to the society as a whole. Ernest Gellner recalls the astonishment of a field-worker observing negotiations for the settlement of a feud in southern Arabia upon learning 'that one of the deaths had been caused by an arrow—a weapon not in use in the region for a long, long time. In other words, the accountancies of reciprocal killing stretched back right into an age of long-past military technology, without straining anyone's arithmetic'. Still, while this suggests to Gellner 'an economical and relatively humane system', he cautions that at 'other times and places, feuds could escalate uncontrollably'.[10]

The stability of the feud requires that the adversary groups adhere to the same system of codes and rites. For this reason, a simple, twofold distinction between external and internal violence is inadequate. Verdier proposes a threefold distinction that situates vengeance in an 'intermediate social space' where the social distance between the parties involved is neither so small that it is forbidden nor so large that the conditions for its controlled application do not exist. In the world beyond the sphere of vengeance, the alterity of the other is 'such that any kind of recognition is ruled out and, for want of mediation, the affirmation of one party takes place through the negation of the other'. This is where vengeance gives way to war. While acknowledging that the two are often difficult to distinguish in practice,[11] Verdier stresses that the objective of vengeance is ideally restoration of parity among approximate equals rather than conquest or annihilation of an enemy; feuding parties seek to surpass but not destroy one another, defining each other through 'antagonistic complementarity' in a 'dynamic equilibrium'.[12]

The maintenance of a violent equilibrium among groups is itself a means of assuring the internal cohesion of each group. In his controversial reflections on Amerindian social structure, Pierre Clastres went so far as to present this type of chronic external violence as a way for tribal entities innocent of political inequality to keep the specter of coercive authority at bay: 'Primitive society is society against the State insofar as it is society-for-war'.[13] Alfred Adler notes a recent parallel tendency of some Africanists to treat endemic armed conflict as integral to the autonomous existence of the groups involved rather than as necessarily orientated towards territorial or other material aims.[14]

One need not see this form of violence as directed against the state to conceive it as an alternative to state organization. Expanding on the classic work of E. E. Evans-Pritchard, Gellner writes that, in egalitarian Muslim desert tribes lacking a central enforcement agency, order is maintained thanks to their segmentary social organization characterized by the institution of the feud:[15] 'The system works, without the benefit of political centralization, through the cohesion-prompting presence of violence at all levels'.[16] Segmentary groups are in horizontal juxtaposition and vertically nested so that at each level are found rival groups which are themselves subdivided into rival groups. Groups opposed at one level will nonetheless cooperate in defending the larger group to which they belong from a rival at the next level,[17] a pattern reflected in the Arab aphorism 'I against my brothers, my brothers and I against our cousins, my brothers, cousins and I against the world'.[18]

'The unifying effect of external threat is something which of course operates in all societies', Gellner comments, but in segmentary societies, he asserts, it is the dominant operating principle, 'or very nearly the only one'.[19] At this point we may ask whether Gellner is not overlooking a second and perhaps related principle at work in stateless societies—namely, the unifying effect of sacrifice, with which we began. In both cases exists the paradox of violence controlled through violence. Whether the violence is channeled outwards, towards a member of an external group, or inwards, towards a marginal member of the group who is isolated and made external, it is prevented from spreading within the group's own ranks.

Moreover, if the obligation of external vengeance is necessarily accompanied by a ban on internal vengeance, internal offenses can only be met with sacrificial measures. Either a purificatory rite is performed to cleanse the group of the pollution created by the transgression, or the transgressor is himself ritually expelled by and from the group. The Cheyennes did both, as A. Hoebel tells us in a passage of *The Law of Primitive Man* worth reproducing here for the enthusiasm with which it underscores the opportunity for cohesion-building provided by a murder within the tribe, an enthusiasm which can only be described as infectious:

. . . extrusion was necessary to cleanse the putrid infection from the body politic. The solution was exile. . . . Simple banishment of the offender was not enough, however. The tribe as well as the man was stained. Purification was called for, and this was done through the ritual of Renewal of the Medicine Arrows. . . . And by means of it the Cheyennes achieved a positive social result of tremendous value. As an integrator of the tribe nothing equaled it. The feeling of oneness was not to be escaped. So it was that the act which could shatter the unity of the tribe—homicide—was made the incident that formally reinforced integrity of the people as a people.[20]

In ancient Hawaii the purification necessitated by a transgression of the taboos entailed the sacrifice of the transgressor himself. So conscious were the Hawaiians of the unequaled value of such proceedings that they sometimes were not content to wait for an offense to be committed. 'Transgressions are often artificially provoked when a sacrifice is necessary', explains Valerio Valeri, citing the account of an early nineteenth-century voyager: 'Taboos were instituted, such as it were next to impossible to observe, and the first offender was seized and dragged to the morair [temple] for sacrifice'.[21]

Hawaiian society included a special class of future sacrificial victims, the *kauwa*, considered the family gods of the nobles with whom they maintained a close relationship. This class comprised not only transgressors and rebels against the king, but also enemies taken prisoner.[22] Here one is reminded of those Amazonian Indians who used to integrate captives into society, give them a wife and treat them royally until the day they were sacrificed and eaten, a practice faithfully depicted in the film *How Tasty was My Little Frenchman*.

Just as Valeri views the Hawaiian taboos as a ritual device designed to guarantee an internal supply of victims, Girard sees the constant warfare of the Brazilian Tupinamba as a way of arranging a steady external source of victims: 'it can be said that the tribes have come to an agreement never to agree; that a permanent state of war is maintained for the express purpose of providing victims for ritual cannibalism'.[23] 'A sacrificial cult based on war and the reciprocal murder of prisoners is not substantially different from nineteenth-century nationalistic myths with their concept of an "hereditary enemy"', remarks Girard. 'In both instances the basic function of foreign wars, and of the more or less spectacular rites that generally accompany them, is to avert the threat of internal dissension by adopting a form of violence that can be openly endorsed and fervently acted upon by all'.[24]

Along with the foreign captives adopted into the group, the native warriors sent to die abroad may also be conceived of as a category of sacrificial victims. The latter aspect of fighting in pre-state societies is the one most clearly preserved in contemporary wars which no longer openly feature the murder of prisoners, but in which calls to sacrifice oneself in battle are often heard. The sacrificial status of the warrior is highlighted by Alfred Adler. Where Girard compares the lavishly received Tupinamba prisoner to the African sacred king, another marginal member of the community destined for ritual killing,[25] Adler draws an analogy between the African king and the Indian warrior of the Americas, portrayed by Clastres as engaged in an enterprise which can only be crowned with death:[26] 'Each feat of arms hailed and celebrated by the tribe in fact obligates him to aim higher',[27] until, 'realizing the supreme exploit, he thereby obtains, with absolute glory, death'.[28]

The ultimate feat according to Clastres is that of the warrior who heads off by himself to attack the enemy camp, braving 'the most absolute inequality': *'Alone against all . . .'.*[29] Clastres' absolute inequality corresponds to Girard's original difference: that between the assembled group and the lone victim; 'alone against all' is an inverted but equivalent version of the sacrificial 'all against one'.

Similarly, Adler's analogy replicates Girard's while it is turned around. The warrior sent abroad to die in glory like a sacred king and the warrior captured and brought home to be maintained in royal splendor till execution are the same figure viewed from opposite directions. The arena may appear different depending on whether one is seated with the home crowd or the visitors, but the game is the same. It is Verdier's 'regulated game' of vengeance,[30] Girard's 'agreement never to agree'.

The tacit complicity between opposing sides in this kind of vendetta is demonstrated by the fact, reported by Clastres, that an Indian captive well understood he could not go home again: 'among the Tupi-Guarani a prisoner of war could remain for years safe and sound, free even, in the village of the victors: but sooner or later, he was inevitably executed and eaten. He knew that and yet didn't try to flee', for were he to do so, 'the people of his village would refuse to take him in: he was a prisoner, his destiny must therefore be accomplished'.[31]

An arrangement to obtain victims by exchanging prisoners in battle achieves the same purpose as one which makes prisoners of internal transgressors. As Valeri observes, a 'defeated and fallen' Hawaiian noble 'can be considered "transgressed"',[32] and the 'transgressed' Tupi-Guarani warrior is expelled from his own group as surely as if he were a transgressor: 'the captured warrior no longer belongs to the tribe', Clastres emphasizes, 'he is *definitively excluded from the community* which'—paradoxically—is only waiting to learn of his death in order immediately to avenge him'.[33]

A member of the group must be killed so that the group may wreak vengeance; another group is needed to carry out the killing so that the vengeance will be directed outward. Ritualized vengeance becomes an aim in itself when it makes it possible to keep vengeance from spreading within the group. In this way the sacred duty to avenge highlighted by Verdier can be reconciled with the prohibition on vengeance stessed by Girard, for whom 'the interminable vengeance engulfing two rival tribes may be read as an obscure metaphor for vengeance that has been effectively shifted from the interior of the community'.[34]

To the modern observer, sacrifice proper looks much more like a religious ritual than does an endless vendetta. True, we are accustomed to seeing both sides in military struggles draw on religion for an extra fillip of pious justification, and we realize as well that some people genuinely fight to achieve religious ends opposed by their adversaries, but we have more difficulty in understanding how warfare could be a religious requirement in itself—especially warfare between groups which share the religious values of the larger society to which both belong. Yet wars were 'of' religion long before there were any 'wars of religion'. Relgion provides the framework for forms of warfare which have nothing to do with struggles for power.

One of the purest examples of the displacement of internal violence on to external scapegoats in religious warfare is head-hunting. Renato Rosaldo, who lived with the Ilongots in the Philippines, calls their ritualized head-hunting 'very like sacrifice'. To take a head is a requirement of manhood. The young are led by older men whose prime motive for initiating an expedition is devastating personal loss. If . . . somebody close to them dies, they become enraged. . . . What these people say is that they need a place to carry their anger'.[35]

Rosaldo 'heard many reports of people learning of the death of somebody they've loved very much, being devastated by it, picking up a long knife, and just chopping up everything in sight', and he comments, 'When it's culturally available that one can go headhunting, that's the ultimate place to carry one's rage and anger. If it's not culturally available, then you hack up the furniture'.[36] In the absence of a culturally available external outlet, however, more than the furniture may be at risk—as Euripides reminds us in *Medea*. Girard quotes the lines spoken by the nurse, who vainly seeks to have the children kept out of Medea's sight: 'I am sure her anger will not subside until it has found a victim. Let us pray that the victim is at least one of our enemies!'[37]

Enemies are useful—so useful they sometimes must be invented, as any politician well knows. The modern state, with its monopoly of violence, renders unnecessary the prevention of internecine conflict through the violent unanimity of sacrifice. Nonetheless, a regime anxious to create consensus will still fall back on the unifying effect of internal or external threat. Even when the enemies designated are wholly secular, the language we use to describe the phenomenon betrays the religious origins of the technique: witch-hunting, demonizing opponents.

When the regime itself resorts to religious language to rouse the crowd against its opponents, we feel it is perverting religion by bending it to other ends—and so it is, in the case of a modern religion with a long history of separation of church and state behind it. The cynical exploitation of religion should not, however, lead us to believe that the religiously-couched designation of worthy victims is an invention of the state alien to the essence of religion. In fact, it is a unifying technique which is already part and parcel of religion in stateless societies like those analyzed by Clastres, where there can be no question of exploiting the technique to reinforce the power of the leaders because the latter do not exercise power as we know it. If anything, Clastres suggests, it is society in these groups which exercises power over the chief—the chief is the victim.

Like a social deviant, the chief or king is a marginal figure, often historically or mythically an outsider, who appears on the scene as an external threat which must be domesticated through the royal ritual, a process Marshall Sahlins describes in 'The Stranger-King'.[38] 'Kingship incorporates marginality as well as centrality', affirms Masao Yamaguchi, who notes, 'In the actual life of ancient Japan, princes were often executed for conspiracy and for incest'.[39] Incest is for Girard the typical example of a transgression 'that signifies the violent abolition of distinctions—the major cause of cultural disintegration'.[40] If cultural renewal and the reestablishment of differences are built on the sacrifice of a scapegoat blamed for provoking the dissolution of differences, it becomes clear why certain African kings destined for real or symbolic sacrifice are obliged to commit real or symbolic incest: 'The king must show himself "worthy" of his punishment'.

We saw that Girard likens the sacred monarch to the Tupinamba captive; indeed, he declares that the king 'reigns only by virtue of his future death; he is no more and no less than a victim awaiting sacrifice'.[41] Hocart believed that the wait was once very short. His comparative analysis of ceremonies from around the world led him to the conclusion that the original rite was at once a royal installation *and* a human sacrifice, implying that 'the first kings must have been dead kings'—a notion which only 'sounds absurd because we are accustomed to the idea of kings as directors of society. It sounds less absurd when we realize that the earliest kings did not govern'.[42]

In the case of kings who govern and retain a sacred character, it is sometimes found that the ritual pattern continues as a structural tendency even where actual sacrifice of the monarch is not institutionalized as part of the ceremonies. Sahlins explores the interface between myth and history in Fiji, where he correlates symbolic sacrifice in the rite of chieftainship with a historical trend noticed by one of Hocart's informants: 'Few high chiefs were not killed'.[43] According to Valeri, ancient Hawaiian succession regularly involves 'a violent confrontation among closely related pretenders. He who succeeds in sacrificing all the others becomes the only king', so that 'the kingdom is always *conquered* by its king, who, moreover, must constantly defend it from the "rebels", that is, from his rivals'. But, again, 'these rivals are not simply killed; they are sacrificed . . .'.[44] The succession struggle is 'real', the victory 'ritual', with the rivals or 'rebels' killed below the temple and their bodies offered up on the altars.[45]

Yamaguchi finds a similar conflation of ritual pattern and political history in Japan: 'The *Kojiki* chronicle tells us of the internal wars carried on between the fifth and seventh centuries, almost in a ritual way, every time a king died. Although *Kojiki* is a legendary record, it reminds us of the succession wars that were fought in the lacustrine kingdoms of East Africa, as well as of the ritual of rebellion of the Bantu kingdoms of southeast Africa . . .'.[46] Consideration of ritualistic succession battles in Africa prompts Girard to formulate the following

remarks regarding the difficulty one can sometimes have in distinguishing ritual re-enactments and political events, a difficulty which we will later encounter in the case of Islamic succession struggles:

. . . in a conflict whose course is no longer strictly regulated by a predetermined model, the ritualistic elements disintegrate into actual events and it becomes impossible to distinguish history from ritual. This confusion is in itself revealing. A rite retains its vitality only as long as it serves to channel political and social conflicts of unquestionable reality in a specific direction. On the other hand, it remains a rite only as long as it manages to restrict the conflictual modes of expression to rigorously determined forms.[47]

Let us return now to the segmentary society of the Muslim desert tribes and look at their feuding in this light. We suggested that the violence among groups as portrayed by Gellner could be understood as a ritual means of controlling violence through violence. The feud certainly channels real political and social conflicts, but in what way does the religious framework provided for the violence restrict it from getting out of hand? After all, as Gellner comments, 'observers are generally struck or appalled by the pervasiveness of violence', yet 'the system does not disintegrate into total chaos. How is this attained?'[48]

The answer Gellner proposes lies not so much in segmentary organization as such but rather in 'the religious style which it engenders or at least which it favours': 'The most characteristic religious institution of rural, tribal Islam is the living saint'. The saint enjoys a type of hereditary charisma, belonging to a lineage that typically invokes descent from the Prophet, and he fills a pacific role crucial to the smooth operation of the segmentary tribal system: 'At its many fissures it has a great need for arbitrators and mediators, and these can only function well if they are in it but not of it. Saintly status and, very often, obligatory pacifism, makes the mediators both viable and authoritative, standing as they do outside the web of alliance and feud . . .'.[49]

In his studies of the pre-colonial society of the Iqar'iyen, Moroccan Berbers of the eastern Rif, Raymond Jamous presents this mediation as the intervention of men of *baraka* or 'divine benediction' in the exchanges of violence among men of honor. Only a head of household protecting and exercising authority over a 'prohibited' domain, a domain of *haram*, can claim to be a man of honor. But the sense of honor is expressed most fully through violence and murder.[50] Indeed, participation in violence is required to maintain one's honor: 'Every man of honor knows that he risks death by wanting to engage in violence, but also that he must take this risk if he wishes to assert his value'.[51] An aggression also demonstrates that the object of attack is himself a man of honor worth challenging: 'Nobody would attack a musician or a Jew without dishonoring himself'. Honor is hence a value which rests on a paradox': 'it supposes the assertion of authority over the domains of "prohibition", and also the transgression of these prohibitions through challenge and counterchallenge'.[52] Thus, while Girard's theory would lead one to interpret the system of prohibitions as guaranteeing the differences that should constitute a bulwark against violence, the same system includes a built-in encouragement to violence.

This is where the men of *baraka*, the holy men or 'sherifs', enter the picture. As Jamous explains, 'The game of honor prevents the laymen from declaring their wish to interrupt the violence: that would be a demonstration of weakness. . . . Only the mediation of a man in whom non-violence is a virtue makes it possible to arrest—if only temporarily—the cycle of violence'. The success of a mediator's mission is what confirms his possession of *baraka*. As a tribute to his status, the victim's group consents to accept a payment in compensation for the murder instead of pursuing vengeance, which remains the more honorable course.[53] But the payment of blood money or the gift of a bride or servant in itself is not sufficient. The parties to the conflict must take part in a ritual of peace, a ritual centered on a sacrifice: the symbolic sacrifice of the murderer, displaced onto an animal victim.

The murderer's relations, accompanied by the sherif, bring the blood compensation and a sheep to the territory of his victim. They march in procession with the murderer at their head, 'hands tied behind his back and a knife between his teeth. He "offers himself in sacrifice"'. At the border of the victim's territory, a close relative 'removes the knife from the murderer's mouth and, instead of killing him, cuts loose his hands and cuts the throat of the sheep in his place'. The sherif then blesses the gathering, and everyone present shares in feasting on the meat of the sheep.[54]

The pivotal position of sacrifice in the transition from violent to peaceful relations can be understood as a logical corollary of Verdier's postulation that the 'sacrificial response to a crime within a community is the counterpart of the vindicatory reaction on the outside.'[55] Having the adversary parties share in a sacrificial rite indicates that they now form an association within which vengeance is forbidden, as it is within the group, where sacrifice takes its place. Sacrifice figures prominently in reconciliation ceremonies in many cultures. An example from the borderlands of the Islamized kingdoms of the central Sahel is particularly telling for what it reveals about the way in which sacrifice permits the participants to control violence by putting it into a form in which it can be externalized and hence expelled from the group.

Just as divine malediction will fall upon the party that breaks an Iqar'iyen pact of reconciliation,[56] the Moussey sought to assure peace by 'placing between the two enemy groups a magic barrier the trespassing of which would provoke the automatic punishment of the one responsible'. Note in passing the paradox that it is the creation of barriers, not their destruction, which brings harmony; this is consistent with what we said at the outset about religion's forging differences to keep people apart. Now, in one of the Moussey rites of peace, a slave—qualified to handle the dangerous power of sacrifice by virtue of his expendability—slices a live dog in two at the border dividing the two groups while intoning, 'Here *sulukna*, very powerful business, we slaughter an animal to you, that nobody may be killed any more!'[57] And '*sulukna*', the name of the occult force invoked, means nothing other than vengeance.

In this example the identity of violence and the sacred is particularly transparent and the import of that identity more easily traced. We can see that the representation of the violent reciprocity of vengeance as something transcendent makes it possible to externalize it, to put it at a distance, and to begin to manipulate it for the social good. 'Successful sacrifice prevents violence from reverting to a state of immanence and reciprocity', writes Girard, 'that is, it reinforces the status of violence as an exterior influence, transcendent and beneficent'.[58]

In Girard's version of history, the evolution of religion is the story of a progressive transcendence of violence: first, in the sense of a projection of violence out of society and onto a transcendent divine; then, in the sense of a divine injunction to rise above all violence, to renounce pitting violence against violence whether through vengeance or through sacrifice. In *Le désenchantement du monde*, Marcel Gauchet views human history as the story of the progressive transcendence of religion: first, in the sense of a projection of the divine out of society; then, in the sense of society's leaving the divine behind. In Gauchet's reversal of the usual perspective, the rise of the 'great religions' corresponds to a 'decline' of religion as the ruling force of terrestrial existence, for the more absolute the monotheism, the less absolute the domination of the divine over human action. It is in pre-state societies that one finds the most thorough submission to a sacred law beyond human control, so that 'religion in its purest and most systematic form is at the point of departure, in that world before the State . . .'.[59]

'From this angle', Gauchet asserts, 'the emergence of the State appears clearly as the major event of human history'[60] because the domination of man over man, even if despotic, even if legitimated by religion, wrests the locus of power from the grip of the radically other and brings it for the first time within human compass: 'The power of a few in the name of the gods is the beginning—O how timid and dissimulated, but irreversible—of a power of all over the decrees of the gods . . .'.[61] The separation of Church and State is another decisive step on the road to liberation from the sacred: 'The more the apprehension of the beyond is strictly controlled by a specialized hierarchy. . . . the more the terrestrial sphere displays its own sufficiency, freeing itself from the omnipresent preoccupation of a supernatural that is better and better defined and contained. A gaping breach thus opens into which the temporal power will leap in order to plead the necessary independence of its task in the world and to claim, in the face of this spiritual monarchy, complete mastery of its own domain'.[62]

In attempting to reflect on the relationship between Islam and violence in the pages that remain, I take as my starting point the complementary perspectives afforded by the visions of these two contemporary thinkers: Girard's, in which religion progressively distances itself from an original unity of violence and the sacred, and Gauchet's, in which society progressively liberates itself from an original submission of the social to the sacred.

Girard has been dubbed the 'Hegel of Christianity',[63] and Gauchet, for whom Christianity promises to be 'the religion of the exit from religion',[64] could be aptly styled the 'Hegel of secular humanism'. Neither one includes Islam in his *welthistorischer*. Girard has not written on the subject, while Gauchet only refers to it a couple of times in passing, although he offers a clue as to how it departs from the grand design in his brief allusions to 'submission in belief'[65] and to the 'revelation supplied by the *Koran*, the very presence, irrefragable and literal, of the transcendent in the immanent'.[66] What about Georg Wilhelm Friedrich himself? Gellner recalls that Hegel had to 'indulge in most painfully tortuous arguments in order to explain how an earlier faith, Christianity, nevertheless is more final and absolute than a chronologically later one, namely Islam'.[67]

My hunch is that Hegel's uneasiness holds the key to a theoretical neglect of Islam that is far from being confined to Girard and Gauchet. Fifteen years ago, sociologist Bryan Turner found the conscientious sociologist of religion to be 'in the embarrassing position of facing a massive gap in his knowledge of world religions':[68] 'In comparison with the established and flourishing literature on other world religions and their associated civilizations, the systematic study of Islam is a neglected field in sociology, phenomenology and history of religions'.[69] The problem, I suspect, is that Islam will not fit neatly into a preconceived evolutionary scheme.

In particular, Islam does not conform to expectations raised by the idea that it followed in the footsteps of the other religions of the book'. The theorist proceeding on the basis of this idea will be disorientated for a simple reason spelled out by Joseph Chelhod in a work that Turner deems one of the 'major land-marks in Islamic scholarship,' *Les Structures du Sacré chez les Arabes*:[70] 'the religious structures of Islam are better understood when one compares them to the ancient Arab cultural bedrock than when one seeks to illustrate them by borrowings, often undeniable, from Judaism and Christianity'.[71]

Chelhod acknowledges that 'the incontestable influence of the ancient Arab religion on Islam exerted itself essentially in the domain of beliefs, rites and institutions; it hardly affected the intransigent monotheism of Mohammad'.[72] Alongside this monotheism, however, 'it is in immanence which seems the dominant trait of the Islamic conception of the sacred, as to behavior'. God as the ultimate controlling agency is superimposed on an animist infrastructure; the divine transcends more manipulable forms of the sacred which nonetheless persist—*haram, baraka*—so that 'one of the essential aspects of the sacred is to be intimately bound to the profane activities of the believer'.[73]

Apparently, then, the terrestrial sphere is in Gauchet's terms still characterized by an ubiquitous preoccupation with the supernatural. Emmanuel Sivan reports the same finding after studying the religious weeklies published by Egypt's ruling party and by the moderate Liberal opposition: the world inhabited by the readers of these periodicals 'is one where the natural and supernatural are inextricably interlaced. A world populated by ghosts, the spirits of the dead, *jinn* (invisible beings) of the harmful and of the helpful varieties; a world haunted by the specter of the Tempting Satan and his demons, where the believer may be succored by holy men and angels and, if need be, by miracles; a world where communication with the dead (especially one's relatives) is an everyday occurrence, and where the presence of the supernatural is deemed quite real, almost palpable'.[74]

Religion and everyday activity are inevitably intermingled because the temporal power never carved out its own, secular domain. Indeed, 'the very notion of a secular jurisdiction and authority . . . is seen as an impiety', according to Bernard Lewis, who notes that until the nineteenth century the word 'secular' could not be translated into Arabic or Turkish, while even today these languages contain no equivalent terms for 'church' and 'laity'. For Muslims, Lewis emphasizes, religion is not a compartment of life reserved for certain matters, and separate, or at least separable, from other compartments of life'.[75] This is not merely the attitude of fundamentalists; it is also the diagnosis of a leftist critic:[76] 'Ours is a society which defines all its activities and the events occurring around it through ritual and relationship to God'.[77]

'Islam is the religion which has most completely confounded and intermixed the two powers', writes Tocqueville,[78] ' . . . so that all the acts of civil and political life are regulated more or less by religious law'.[79] Rather than speaking of 'confusion,' it would be more exact to say that secular power never differentiated and detached itself from the religious matrix. Conversely, as Sivan notes, 'Muslim civil society (led or educated by the *ulama*), 'while disdaining the political sphere and harboring precious few illusions as to its evil nature, tends on the whole to acquiesce with the way its masters control it'.[80]

What does all this imply for the relationship between Islam and violence? If opposition to violence as such is not internal to Islam, that does not mean religion plays no role in the control of violence. Insofar as the lack of separation between religious and (what to us would be) other spheres of life is also characteristic of tribal religions, we might well expect to find in Islam the ritual procedures studied earlier for channeling violence outside the borders of the tribe.

But was it not the achievement of Muhammad to substitute a universal religion for a kinship-based tribal cult? It is no doubt true, as Turner observes, that 'the universalism of the new Islamic community (umma) based on faith rather than blood cut right across' the particularism of the tribal system and its concomitant customs of blood feud and retaliation'.[81] However, it is also true that the Muslim community as a whole regards the universe beyond the Abode of Islam (dar al-Islam) much as a tribe would regard the world beyond its boundaries: it is the Abode of War (dar al-Harb).

It is a religious obligation to maintain a state of war with those outside the rule of Islam.[82] The standard Muslim greeting salam 'alakum, 'peace be upon you', is reserved for addressing fellow Muslims and must not be employed in addressing non-Muslims—rather as if peace within the Muslim community were made possible only by forbidding peace with those on the outside. In the same way, if the sherifs who are the peacemakers among the Iqar'iyen are the only men for whom non-violence is a virtue, it is not an absolute virtue even for them: the requirement for them to behave pacifically is lifted in the case of war against the infidel.[84]

This of course is the famous jihad or 'holy war'. The translation of the term is not beyond debate—literally meaning 'striving', it could be taken in a spiritual sense, and the tag 'holy' is redundant except as a reminder that all Islamic duties are ordained by God—but Lewis assures us that the 'overwhelming majority of classical theologians, jurists, and traditionists . . . understood the obligation of jihad in a military sense'.[85] More controversial, perhaps, is the use of 'jihad' for wars of aggression against unbelievers. Modern Muslim apologists have argued that jihad is in reality a purely defensive doctrine. It is worth noting the response that this approach elicited from the intellectual fathers of today's militant fundamentalism. According to Leonard Binder, both Abu'l-'Ala al-Mawdudi and Sayyid Qutb 'rejected this interpretation, finding in it an expression of false consciousness. Muslim apologists had been tricked into adopting an idea which not only conformed to the Christian religious doctrine, but one which also suited the political preferences of non-Muslim political leaders'.[86]

One might ask whether attributing to Islam a purely defensive military outlook would not in fact amount to an ethnocentric projection onto another religion of attitudes proper to the Western religious tradition. The ritual channeling of violence outward is a commonplace component of other religions—and is doubtless an equally common phenomenon in the West. The difference is simply that, as Gellner puts it, Christianity is 'ambivalent about its own bellicosity'.[87]

If, then, violence channeled outward against the infidels appears to be a ritual requirement in Islam, internal violence seems to accompany in ritual or quasi-ritual fashion the succession of a leader. Like the Hawaiian king, the sultan of traditional Morocco must conquer his throne and constantly defend it from rivals and rebels. The death of a sultan is regularly followed by a period of anarchy during which the pretenders fight it out to see which one has the superior baraka. The prosperity-producing sacrifice of the Hawaiian rivals or rebels by the victor also has its parallel in Morocco. As long as the future sultan hasn't vanquished his rivals and brought the rebels to submission', Jamous explains, 'his violence is the simple manifestation of his strength or weakness and places him on the same level as his enemies. But when his violence triumphs, it takes on another sense and becomes a sacrificial act in the course of which the hapless opponents of the new sovereign play the role of propitiatory victims offered for the reestablishment of the divine order and for the prosperity of the community of believers'. The violence that puts an end to the reciprocal play of violence against violence reveals its divine nature: 'The triumphant violence . . . is perceived as being of divine essence'.[88]

The baraka of the sultan only makes itself known retrospectively. Gellner sums up in like manner the way the ulama, or religious scholars, determine the legitimacy of Muslim rulers in general: 'the verdict of the ulama regarding legitimacy, like the flight of that much overrated bird the Owl of Minerva, takes place only after the event, and hence in effect ratifies the actual power situation, rather than sitting in judgment on it.'[89] Furthermore, while the Holy Law imposes limits on the power of the sovereign, Lewis notes a 'flaw': 'it established no apparatus and laid down no procedures for enforcing these limitations, and no device for preventing or challenging a violation of the law by the ruler, other than force'.[90]

But the overthrow of leaders by force seems to be built into the system. The survival rate of chiefs of tribal leagues among the Iqar'iyen is no better than that of high chiefs in Fiji. The chiefs of leagues in Jamous' historical survey were all exiled or killed by their own dependents,[91] as if they reigned by virtue of their status as sacrificial victims in waiting: 'Everything takes place in sum as if the Iqar'iyen chose men on whom they lavished praises before sacrificing them so to speak on the altar of honor, the supreme value perpetuated through offerings of the noblest victims'.[92]

The question I would ask in closing, then, is to what extent this model can be seen as paradigmatic of an Islamic political pattern rooted in the religion. A similar pattern seems to unfold at different levels with varying degrees of ritualization, beginning perhaps with the assassination of three of the first four caliphs to succeed the Prophet. In the absence of strictly determined forms, the sacrificial channeling of violence against violence is always in danger of spilling over into renewed revenge cycles of violence against violence, ultimately resulting in the confusion of ritual and history.

2. CAUSES AND SCOPE OF TERRORISM

NOTES

1. René Girard, *Violence and the Sacred*, trans. by Patrick Gregory (Baltimore, MD and London: The Johns Hopkins University Press, 1977), p. 146.

2. A. M. Hocart, *Kings and Councillors: An Essay in the Comparative Anatomy of Human Society* (Chicago, IL: University of Chicago Press, 1970 [orig. published in 1936]), p.40.

3. Lucien Scubla, *Logiques de la Réciprocité*. Cahier du CREA, No. 6 (Paris: École Polytechnique, 1985), p.76.

4. Girard, *Violence and the Sacred* (hereafter abbreviated as *VS*), pp.14–15.

5. Joseph Chelhod, 'Equilibre et parité dans la vengeance du sang chez les Bédouins de Jordanie' in Raymond Verdier, ed., *La vengeance*, vol. 1: *Vengeance et pouvoir dans quelques sociétés extra-occidentales* (Paris: Cujas, 1980), p. 125; see also Joseph Chelhod, *Les Structures du Sacré chez les Arabes* (Paris: Maisonneuve et Larose, 1964), pp. 151–2.

6. Chelhod, 'Equilibre et parité', p. 130.

7. Girard, *VS*, p. 15.

8. Raymond Verdier, 'Le système vindicatoire' in Verdier, ed., *La vengeance*, Vol 1 (Paris: Cujas, 1980), p. 21.

9. Ibid., p. 24.

10. Ernest Gellner, *Muslim Society* (Cambridge: Cambridge University Press, 1981), p. 97.

11. Verdier, 'Le système vindicatoire', p. 24.

12. Ibid., p. 30.

13. Pierre Clastres, *Recherches d'anthropologie politique* (Paris: Seuil, 1980), p. 206.

14. Alfred Adler, 'La guerre et l'Etat primitif' in Miguel Abensour, ed., *L'esprit des lois sauvages: Peirre Clastres ou une nouvelle anthropologie politique* (Paris: Seuil, 1987), pp. 98–9.

15. Gellner, *Muslim Society*, pp. 36–7.

16. Ibid., p. 40.

17. Ibid., p. 39.

18. Ibid., p. 69.

19. Ibid., p. 39.

20. Quoted in Verdier, 'Le système vindicatoire', p. 39.

21. Valerio Valeri, *Kingship and Sacrifice: Ritual and Society in Ancient Hawaii*, trans. by Paula Wissing (Chicago, IL: University of Chicago Press, 1985), p. 356.

22. Ibid., p. 164.

23. Girard, *VS*, p. 278.

24. Ibid., p. 280.

25. Ibid., p. 278.

26. Adler, 'La guerre et l'Etat primitif,' pp. 111–12.

27. Clastres, *Recherches d'anthropologie politique*, p. 232.

28. Ibid., p. 237.

29. Ibid., p. 234.

30. Verdier, 'Le système vindicatoire', p. 30.

31. Clastres, *Recherches d'anthropologie politique*, p. 236.

32. Valeri, *Kingship and Sacrifice*, p. 374.

33. Clastres, *Recherches d'anthropologie politique*, p. 236.

34. Girard, *VS*, p. 279.

35. 'Discussion' with Renato Rosaldo in Robert G. Hammerton-Kelly (ed.), *Violent Origins: Ritual Killing and Cultural Formation*, (Stanford; CA: Stanford University Press, 1987), pp. 242–3.

36. Ibid., p. 252.

37. Girard, *VS*, p. 9.

38. Marshall Sahlins, *Islands of History* (Chicago, IL: University of Chicago Press, 1985), pp. 73–103.

39. Masao Yamaguchi, 'Kingship, Theatricality, and Marginal Reality in Japan' in Ravindra K. Jain, ed., *Text and Context: The Social Anthropology of Tradition* (Philadelphia, PA: Institute for the Study of Human Issues, 1977), p. 165.

40. Girard, *VS*, p. 98.

41. Ibid., p. 107.

42. A. M. Hocart, *Social Origins* (London: Watts, 1954), p. 77.

43. Sahlins, *Islands of History*, p. 94.

44. Valeri, *Kingship and Sacrifice*, p. 160.

45. Ibid., p. 163.

46. Yamaguchi, 'Kingship, Theatricality, and Marginal Reality', p. 165.

47. Girard, *VS*, pp. 109–10.

48. Gellner, *Muslim Society*, p. 40.

49. Ibid., pp. 40–41.

50. Raymond Jamous, *Honneur et baraka: Les structures sociales traditionnelles dans le Rif* (Cambridge: Cambridge University Press, 1981), pp. 67–9.

51. Cécile Barraud, Daniel de Coppet, André Itéanu and Raymond Jamous, 'Des relations et des morts: Quatre sociétés vues sous l'angle des échanges' in Jean-Claude Galey, ed., *Différences, valeurs, hiérarchie: Textes offerts à Louis Dumont* (Paris: Editions de l'École des Hautes Études en Sciences Sociales, 1984), p. 493.

52. Jamous, *Honneur et baraka*, p. 69.

53. Ibid., pp. 210–12.

54. Ibid., p. 212.

55. Verdier, 'Le système vindicatoire,' p. 23.

56. Jamous, *Honneur et baraka*, p. 212.

57. Igor de Garine, 'Les étrangers, la vengeance et les parents chez les Massa et les Moussey (Tchad et Cameroun)' in Raymond Verdier (ed.), *La vengeance*, Vol. 1 (Paris: Cujas, 1980), p. 97.

58. Girard, *VS*, p.266.

59. Marcel Gauchet, *Le désenchantement du monde: Une histoire politique de la religion* (Paris: Gallimard, 1985), pp. x–xii.

60. Ibid., p. X.

61. Ibid., p. 31.

62. Ibid., p. 103.

63. Jean-Marie Domenach, *Enquête sur les idées contemporaines* (Paris: Seuil, 1981), p. 107.

64. Gauchet, *Le désenchantement du monde*, p. ii.

65. Ibid., p. 95.

66. Ibid., p. 102.

67. Gellner, *Muslim Society*, p. 7.

68. Bryan S. Turner, *Weber and Islam* (London: Routledge & Kegan Paul, 1974), p. 2.

69. Ibid., p. 7.

70. Ibid., p. 2.

71. Joseph Chelhod, *Les Structures du Sacré chez les Arabes* (Paris: Maisonneuve et Larose, 1964), p. 257.

72. Ibid., p. 261.

73. Ibid., pp. 255–6.

74. Emmanuel Sivan, *Radical Islam: Medieval Theology and Modern Politics* (New Haven, CT: Yale University Press, 1985), pp. 135–6.

75. Bernard Lewis, *The Political Language of Islam* (Chicago, IL: University of Chicago Press, 1988), pp. 2–3.

76. Nadim al-Bitar, 'Major Causes of Arab Political Physiognomy' in *QA*, May 1979.

77. Quoted in Sivan, *Radical Islam*, p. 185.

78. *Alexis de Tocqueville, Oeuvres complètes, vol 3.*

79. *Quoted in Gellner, Muslim Society, p. 1.*

80. *Emmanuel Sivan, Interpretations of Islam (Princeton, NJ: The Darwin Press, 1985), p. 109.*

81. *Turner, Weber and Islam, pp. 35–6.*

82. *Lewis, The Political Language of Islam, p. 73.*

83. *Ibid., pp. 78–9.*

84. *Jamous, Honneur et baraka, p. 193.*

85. *Lewis, The Political Language of Islam, p. 72.*

86. *Leonard Binder, Islamic Liberalism: A Critique of Development Ideologies (Chicago, IL: University of Chicago Press, 1988), p. 181.*

87. *Gellner, Muslim Society, p. 42.*

88. *Jamous, Honneur et baraka, p. 228.*

89. *Gellner, Muslim Society, p. 115.*

90. *Lewis, The Political Language of Islam, p. 113.*

91. *Jamous, Honneur et baraka, p. 170.*

92. *Ibid., p. 173.*

REFERENCES

Adler, Alfred, 'La guerre et l'Etat primitif' in Miguel Abensour (ed.), *L'esprit des lois sauvages: Pierre Clastres ou une nouvelle anthropologie politique* (Paris: Seuil, 1987) pp. 95–114.

Barraud, Cécile, Daniel de Coppet, André Itéanu, Raymond Jamous, 'Des relations et des morts: Quatre sociétés vues sous l'angle des échanges' in Jean-Claude Galey (ed.), *Différences valeurs hiérarchie: Textes offerts à Louis Dumont* (Paris: Editions de l'École des Hautes Études en Sciences Sociales, 1984), pp. 421–520.

Binder, Leonard, *Islamic Liberalism: A Critique of Development Ideologies* (Chicago, IL: University of Chicago Press, 1988).

Chelhod, Joseph, *Les Structures du Sacré chez les Arabes* (Paris: Maisonneuve et Larose, 1964).

_____ 'Equilibre et parité dans la vengeance du sang chez les Bédouins de Jordanie' in Raymond Verdier (ed.), *La vengeance. Études d'ethnologie, d'histoire et de philosophie*. Vol. 1. *Vengeance et pouvoir dans quelques sociétés extra-occidentales* (Paris: Cujas, 1980), pp. 125–43.

Clastres, Pierre, *Recherches d'anthropologie politique* (Paris: Seuil, 1980).

De Garine, Igor, 'Les étrangers, la vengeance et les parents chez les Massa et les Moussey (Tchad et Cameroun)' in Verdier, ed., *La vengeance*, Vol. 1. (Paris, Cujas, 1980), pp. 91–124.

Domenach, Jean-Marie, *Enquête sur les idées contemporaines* (Paris: Seuil, 1981).

Gauchet, Marcel, *Le désenchantement du monde: Une histoire politique de la religion* (Paris: Gallimard, 1985).

Gellner, Ernest, *Muslim Society* (Cambridge: Cambridge University Press, 1981).

Girard, René, *Violence and the Sacred*, trans. Patrick Gregory (Baltimore, MD: The Johns Hopkins University Press, 1977).

Hamerton-Kelly, Robert G. (ed.), *Violent Origins: Walter Burkert, René Girard, and Jonathan Z. Smith on Ritual Killing and Cultural Formation*, commentary by Renato Rosaldo (Stanford, CA: Stanford University Press, 1987).

Hocart, A. M., *Social Origins* (London: Watts, 1954).

_____ *Kings and Councillors: An Essay in the Comparative Anatomy of Human Society* (Chicago, IL: University of Chicago Press [first edition 1936], 1970).

Jamous, Raymond, *Honneur et baraka: Les structures sociales traditionnelles dans le Rif* (Cambridge: Cambridge University Press, 1981).

Lewis, Bernard, *The Political Language of Islam* (Chicago, IL: University of Chicago Press, 1988).

Sahlins, Marshall, *Islands of History* (Chicago, IL: University of Chicago Press, 1985).

Scubla, Lucien, *Logiques de las Réciprocité*. (Cahier du CREA No. 6. (Paris: École Polytechnique, 1985).

Sivan, Emmanuel, *Interpretations of Islam* (Princeton, NJ: The Darwin Press, 1985).

_____ *Radical Islam: Medieval Theology and Modern Politics* (New Haven, CT: Yale University Press, 1985).

Turner, Bryan S., *Weber and Islam* (London: Routledge & Kegan Paul, 1974).

Valeri, Valerio, *Kingship and Sacrifice: Ritual and Society in Ancient Hawaii*, trans. Paula Wissing (Chicago, IL: University of Chicago Press, 1985).

Verdier, Raymond, 'Le système vindicatoire' in Verdier, ed., *La vengeance*, Vol. 1 (Paris: Cujas, 1980), pp. 11–42.

Yamaguchi, Masao, 'Kingship, Theatricality, and Marginal Reality in Japan' in Ravindra K. Jain (ed.), *Text and Context: The Social Anthropology of Tradition* (Philadelphia, PA: Institute for the Study of Human Issues, 1977), pp. 151–179.

THE TERRORIST MENTALITY

THE Shiite suicide bomber who drove her explosive-packed Peugeo into an Israeli Army convoy in South Lebanon last year was 16 years old. The Jordanian who tried to assassinate the vice-consul of the United Arab Emirates in Rome in 1984 was 22. Of the four hijackers of the Achille Lauro, all of whom were sentenced in Genoa, Italy, last November the oldest was 23; the youngest, 19.

Rushworth M. Kidder

Tel Aviv

Terrorists, whatever their background or cause, have one thing in common: their age.

"Most of them are youngsters," says Prof. Ariel Merari, speaking of the Middle Eastern terrorists he has studied through the Project on Terrorism which he directs at Tel Aviv University.

Scholars looking at other parts of the world second his view. "The age of terrorism is the age of youth," says Jerrold M. Post, a psychiatrist who studies terrorism as director of behavioral sciences at Defense Systems Inc., a consulting firm based in Washington, D.C. "Apart from some of the leaders, you basically don't find middle-aged terrorists," he notes, citing research that puts the median age of terrorists at 22.5 years.

Dr. Lorenz Bollinger, a West German psychologist who conducted detailed interviews with imprisoned members of the Red Army Faction (RAF), sees elements of what he calls "adolescent crisis" among terrorists.

Experts remain divided about whether a particular terrorist mentality can be defined. On this one point, however, there is general agreement: The hand that actually carries the bomb or pulls a trigger is a young hand.

Why? In some cases, the answer is relatively simple. "In certain countries," says Prof. Paul Wilkinson of the University of Aberdeen, "whole families pass on to their children the message that this is the way you struggle for your rights, this is the way we work for the cause." The result, he says, is a "terrorist tradition" of inducting children into paramilitary activity at an early age.

Beyond that, students of terrorism can trace numerous threads.

Two broad types of terrorism

On one hand, Dr. Post points to the "nationalist-separatists," exemplified by the Spanish Basque group ETA and the Armenian Secret Army for the Liberation of Armenia. They live openly in their own communities — they are often lionized as heroes — and their goal is to establish a separate nation, usually as an act of loyalty to parents who have suffered under earlier political regimes.

On the other hand, says Post, are what he calls the "anarchic-ideologues," members of such groups as the RAF or Italy's Red Brigades. Living underground, often in rebellion not only against the state but against their own parents, they seek the wholesale destruction of the existing social order.

Increasingly, European specialists are finding it useful to add a third category: the spillover of terrorism from the Middle East. Often referred to as "international terrorism" (to distinguish it from the two domestic categories), it is characterized by state support and extensive training of commandos. International terrorism involves professional terrorists like Abu Nidal, who reportedly hires out his services to various states with little concern for ideology.

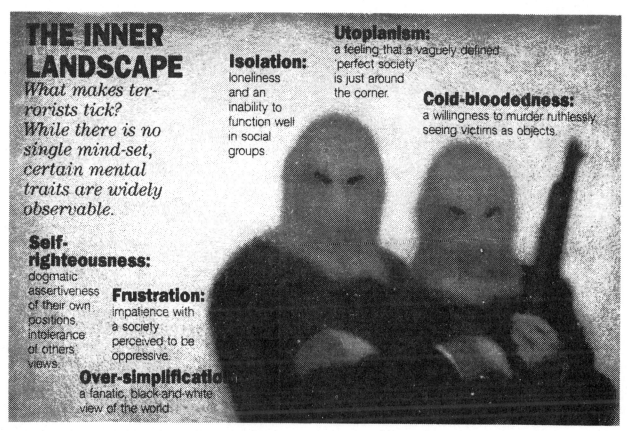

THE INNER LANDSCAPE

What makes terrorists tick? While there is no single mind-set, certain mental traits are widely observable.

Isolation: loneliness and an inability to function well in social groups.

Utopianism: a feeling that a vaguely defined 'perfect society' is just around the corner.

Cold-bloodedness: a willingness to murder ruthlessly, seeing victims as objects.

Self-righteousness: dogmatic assertiveness of their own positions, intolerance of others' views.

Frustration: impatience with a society perceived to be oppressive.

Over-simplification: a fanatic, black-and-white view of the world.

Because terrorists of these three types may resort to the same means, a bombing in Madrid may look much like one in Berlin or Beirut, and the perpetrators are often lumped together under the single label of "terrorist." The ensuing confusion illustrates the difficulty in finding a single definition for the term and leads to the adage that "one man's terrorist is another man's freedom fighter." The result is such a welter of differing behaviors and purposes that terrorist experts are often skeptical about identifying a universal mind-set.

"I don't see any reason to assume that there is more commonality among those that resort to *political* violence," says Dr. Merari, "than among those that resort to *criminal* violence." He adds that "even among terrorists of the same nationality, even among terrorists of the same terrorist group, there is not much reason to assume a common personality."

Nevertheless, he says, some common characteristics do emerge from studies of certain well-defined groups. His own research on Palestinian hostage-takers, for example, points to high levels of aggression, a disturbed family background, and early involvement in illegal activity.

Religious motivation

The difficulty, and the importance, of trying to define the terrorist mentality are illustrated by one key example: the influence of religion in terrorism.

Much of the recent violence generated in the Middle East is traceable to the brand of Shiite fundamentalism of the Iranian leader, Ayatollah Ruhollah Khomeini, especially to his approval of those who die for the cause.

Is the West, then, facing a particularly menacing threat in the form of suicidal terrorists? Dr. Merari plays down the threat. "Contrary to the image created by the media, and by the perpetrators themselves, religious fanaticism does not play a major role [in terrorism]."

Merari argues, and Israeli intelligence officials confirm, that much of the so-called suicide bombing is not carried out by fanatics who believe that by dying for a cause they will go straight to the presence of Allah. Interviews with would-be suicide terrorists who were captured alive indicate they were often tricked into believing they could escape before the bomb exploded or they were blackmailed into accepting the task, on threat of harm to their families.

Was the motive in attacking the US Marine barracks in Lebanon a religious one? In her recent book, "Sacred Rage: The Crusade of Modern Islam," veteran foreign correspondent Robin Wright offers one response. In Beirut a month after the bombing, Sheikh Fadlallah, perhaps the most influential Shiite leader outside Iran (and a man often accused of blessing young fanatics about to go forth on suicide missions), told her that "Suicide in such a way is forbidden in our religion."

Yet the extent to which religion plays a role remains a puzzle, even among the experts. One problem: inadequate understanding of the Muslim faith among Westerners.

"Don't underestimate the religious content of Islam," warns Franco Ferracuti, an Italian scholar and former government antiterrorism official. "That's the one variable that we seem to be losing sight of all the time."

Whatever the answer, one thing appears certain: Suicide attacks represent a new and challenging threat. Lord Chalfont, a former British Cabinet minister with antiterrorist experience in Cyprus, Malaya, and Palestine, observes: "The whole time that I have been involved in terrorist operations, which now goes back to 30 years, my enemy has always been a man who is very worried about his own skin. You can no longer count on that, because the terrorist [today] is not just *prepared* to get killed, he *wants* to get killed. Therefore, the whole planning, tactical doctrine, [and] thinking [behind antiterrorism measures] is fundamentally undermined." For example: The shootings last December at the Rome and Vienna airports were carried out by terrorists who had little if any thought of escaping.

A terrorist mind-set

Is there, then, a terrorist mind-set? From dozens of interviews over four months with longtime students of terrorist ideology and psychology, certain common characteristics begin to emerge. Not surprisingly, given the typical age of the terrorist, these characteristics are also often attributed to adolescence:

● Oversimplification of issues. Terrorists often reduce complex issues to black-and-white. Dr. Ferracuti points to the intensely intellectualized, inward-looking, and politically naive theorizing of many groups. The terrorist, he says, "no longer tests his ideas against reality by [engaging in] dialogue with people with different views." Instead, he lives out "a fantasy war," convinced that he has broad support from numerous like-minded followers.

● Frustration. Pent-up concerns about an individual's inability to change society figure strongly in this mind-set. Italian historian and journalist Giorgio Bocca notes: "They have no patience, these terrorists. They are totally absorbed in their cause. One of the slogans of one of these movements [I studied] was 'We want it all and we want it now.' "

● Self-righteousness. "They believe in [their] total rectitude," notes Professor Wilkinson, who adds that "intolerance, dogmaticism, authoritarianism, and a ruthless treatment of their own people who deviate from their own view are common to their mentality."

● Utopianism. Many terrorists seem to feel that a near-perfect future lies just around the corner, once the present order is destroyed. This utopianism, coupled with frustration at the slow pace of social change, often leads to political extremism on both the left and the right. "Unless you catch this utopian aspect," notes Professor Ferracuti, "it's difficult to understand the mind-set."

● Social isolation. Terrorists, says Dr. Post, are often "people who really are lonely." Terrorist groups use religious or political ideals to interest potential recruits. But those taking up political violence often share traits that are less religious or political than mental and emotional.

For many of them, Post says, the terrorist group is "the first family they have ever had."

● Assertion of their own existence. Terrorist actions are often laden with symbolic overtones, involving the choice of captives, locations, weapons, and timing. They are frequently meant to send messages — and the message, quite often, is simply "I exist! Pay attention to me!" French criminologist Jacques Léauté calls terrorism "a communication system" in which frustrated people are "trying to express through violence their own message."

● Willingness to kill. Perhaps the most startling characteristic, however, is the coldbloodedness of some terrorist murders. Students of terrorism relate this characteristic to a harsh oversimplification that allows killers to see victims simply as objects — a habit of mind observed among Nazi killers during the massacre of Jews in World War II. Researchers have noticed, however, that captors who hold hostages for protracted periods tend to develop a kind of bond with them that makes coldblooded murder less likely.

The Terrible Toll of Human Hatred

War may come and go, but ethnic rivalries are forever

Don Podesta

Lord Justice Maurice Gibson and his wife, Cecily, were returning to their home in Belfast from vacation in Britain in April when a bomb blew apart their car, killing them both.

The same week, half a world away in Colombo, Sri Lanka, a bomb at a bus station killed more than 100 persons and injured 300.

The attacks against Gibson, 74, the second-ranking judge in Northern Ireland, and against innocent patrons at the Sri Lankan bus terminal were but two instances of the most enduring form of human hatred: ethnic and religious rivalry, which has spawned more than two dozen violent conflicts across the world.

From Belfast to Beirut to New Caledonia, well over half a million people have been killed in the last quarter of a century because they belonged to one ethnic group or religious sect rather than another.

These simmering conflicts rooted in the most basic forms of human identity, often do not command the headlines that rivet world attention on international wars and guerrilla insurgencies, but they frequently prove more vicious and intractable.

Unlike conventional war between nations, these wars have no definitive time frame. And while the rival combatants often lack the weapons of destruction available to the major powers, they often disregard any recognized rules of warfare, killing and maiming civilians through indiscriminate car bombings, grenade attacks and mass shootings.

Invariably, furtive attacks evoke the timeless question of whether the perpetrators are terrorists or freedom fighters. The violence assumes different forms in different places:

- More than a decade of unabated civil war in Lebanon among Maronite Christians, Druze and Shiite and Sunni Moslems has taken 125,000 lives, police and relief organizations say. The cost of reconstructing the Lebanese economy is estimated at $100 billion.
- More than 1,000 members of the Dinka tribe in southern Sudan were reported killed in March after 6,000 of them had fled fighting in the south. A civil war between southern Sudanese, who follow traditional tribal religions, and Sudan's government, based in the Moslem north, has taken thousands of lives in the past 30 years.
- In the Philippines, the military now considers a Moslem revolt a more formidable threat than the communist insurgency because the Moslems—unlike the communists—control territory and are better organized and better armed, with a ready flow of weapons from patrons in Libya and other Arab countries.
- Basque separatists in Spain have been responsible for about 500 deaths since 1968, when a policeman reputed to engage in torture became the first victim of the ETA (Basque Homeland and Liberty in its Basque language initials).

Why so much bloodshed in so many, diverse places for apparently similar reasons?

There are several possible answers, but many originate in one emotion: fear.

"Fear, not aggression, is a prime motivator of conflict," says Gary Weaver, who specializes in intercultural communications at American University's School of International Service. This fear, Weaver and others say, arises out of a sense of vulnerability, the feeling that the ethnic group might not survive.

"Both sides in many of these conflicts see themselves as the persecuted minority," Weaver says. "This drives them to the feeling that 'if we don't stand up and fight, we're just going to disappear,' and leaders capitalize on that."

The idea that each side in a conflict feels vulnerable has striking parallels in Ireland and Sri Lanka. In each case, the island has a religious minority overall that predominates in the north of the island and that traditionally represents a more prosperous part of the society than the majority in the south. In both cases, the majority in the country is a minority in the north.

The Roman Catholic minority in Northern Ireland comprises a majority on the island of Ireland as a whole,

From *The Washington Post National Weekly Edition*, June 8, 1987, pp. 9-10. © The Washington Post.

ETHNIC AND RELIGIOUS VIOLENCE AROUND THE WORLD

Europe

1. CORSICA: Separatists seeking autonomy from France have attacked the homes, offices and businesses of French mainlanders since the 1960s. On March 21, at least 54 bombs exploded in 14 different towns and cities on the island, ruled by the French since 1796.

2. CYPRUS: Turkish troops occupied the northern part of the island in 1974 following a Greek-backed coup, later creating an independent republic recognized only by Turkey. Thousands of Greeks and Turks have been expelled from each other's side of the island.

3. NORTHERN IRELAND: British troops and Protestant paramilitary forces continue to battle Catholic nationalists seeking end to British rule and unification with Irish Republic. Provisional wing of Irish Republican Army continues terrorist activities. More than 2,500 killed since 1969.

4. SPAIN: Basques seeking independence in three northern provinces have been responsible for about 500 deaths since 1968. Government in Madrid also faces a less violent movement for regional autonomy by Catalans in the northeast.

5. YUGOSLAVIA: Ethnic Serbs, a minority in the southern province of Kosovo, have clashed repeatedly with majority Albanians. Thousands have fled the area—about 2,000 in 1986 alone—amid charges that the Albanians want to create an ethnically pure province.

Africa

6. ANGOLA: Union for the Total Independence of Angola (UNITA), supported mainly by South Africa (also covertly by the United States), opposes the Cuban-backed Angolan government. Although this is largely an East-West political struggle, UNITA leader Jonas Savimbi's power base is in the Ovambo tribe, of which he is a chief. Thousands have been killed, 2,000 in 1985 alone.

7. CHAD: Decades of violence between Moslem, Arabic northerners and Christian, black southerners. More than 21,000 killed since 1965.

8. ETHIOPIA: Four different rebel groups fighting for independence. The largest are the Eritrean People's Liberation Front and the Tigray People's Liberation Front. More than 45,000 killed since the conflict began in early 1960s.

9. NIGERIA: Repeated outbreaks of religious and tribal violence between northern Moslems, from regions traditionally less developed and poorer than the south, and the Christians who dominate southern life.

10. SOUTH AFRICA: Phase of increased violence between 90 percent nonwhite population and the white minority government began in 1984. Violence among blacks and among tribal groups has overtaken security force action as the main cause of fatalities. About 3,000 killed from 1984–1986.

11. SUDAN: Resumption of bloody civil war has pitted northern Arabized Moslems against black southerners who follow traditional beliefs and Christianity. Main rebel group is the Sudan People's Liberation Army, backed by Ethiopia. About 3,000 killed since 1983.

12. UGANDA: Decades of fighting between ethnic, tribal groups and private armies. National Resistance Army, which seized power in January 1986, continues to fight scattered forces of previous Ugandan leaders. Attacks on civilians resulted in 250,000 deaths from 1983 to 1985.

13. ZIMBABWE: Government of Prime Minister Robert Mugabe, whose power base is in the Shona tribe, continues to fight Ndebele guerrillas who support Joshua Nkomo. More than 1,500 killed since 1980.

Asia

14. BURMA: At least 14 separatist and revolutionary armed groups have opposed the government since Burma became independent from Britain in 1948. Heaviest fighting now with the Karen National Liberation Army which seeks an autonomous state for 2 million to 3 million ethnic Karen.

15. INDIA: Ethnic and religious violence has plagued India since independence in 1947. Sharpest conflict today is with Punjab Sikhs who seek autonomy or independence. Approximately 5,000 died in Sikh-Hindu violence from 1984 to 1986. Government also faces militant Hindu groups and separatist struggles in the northeast. More than 10,000 killed across the country from 1983 to 1986.

16. IRAN: Kurds (3 percent of the country's population) seek autonomy or independence in Iran's northwestern region. Largest rebel group is the Kurdistan Democratic Party. Thousands killed since 1979.

17. IRAQ: Kurds (15 to 20 percent of Iraq's population), seeking autonomy, have expanded antigovernment attacks on oil installations and military facilities since 1980. Iraqi Army controls only major towns and roads in northern region of Kurdistan.

18. ISRAEL: Israeli troops fight Palestinian guerrillas in southern Lebanon, and violence continues between Israelis and Arabs in the Israeli occupied West Bank.

19. LEBANON: Bloody civil war between shifting alliances of Shiite and Sunni Moslem, Druze and Christian militias and Palestinian guerrillas has continued since 1975. Shiites oppose the minority Christians who traditionally dominated political and economic life. More than 125,000 killed since 1975.

20. NEW CALEDONIA: Kanak separatists oppose pro-French settlers in their quest to end French rule of the South Pacific island. Approximately 30 people killed during two years of violence beginning in late 1984.

21. PAKISTAN: Periodic separatist guerrilla campaigns since early 1970s by Baluchis and frequent rioting by Pathans and Sindhis against the Punjabi-dominated central government. Approximately 9,000 killed since 1972.

22. PHILIPPINES: Moslem insurgency began about 15 years ago for separate homeland on the southern islands of Mindanao and Sulu. Conflict today is far less violent than during the mid-1970s. Rebel leaders say 100,000 have been killed; government estimates exceed 50,000.

23. SRI LANKA: Torn by violence between militant Tamils and the Sinhalese-dominated government. Conflict rooted in Tamil claims that Sinhalese discriminate against Tamils, their culture and language. More than 4,500 killed since 1983.

24. SYRIA: Government faces opposition from Islamic fundamentalist groups—notably the (Sunni) Moslem Brotherhood. Minority Alawite Moslems dominate politics and economics, but 72 percent of the population is Sunni.

25. TURKEY: Kurds (20 percent of Turkey's population) seek autonomy in southeastern Turkey. The Syrian-headquartered Kurdish Workers' party has escalated attacks on civilians recently, killing more than 40 in 1987 alone.
By Michael Drew and Clarice Borio—The Washington Post

which helps explain the Protestant fear of being absorbed into an all-Irish republic.

In Sri Lanka, Tamils represent only 18 percent of the population, but the majority Sinhalese consider themselves a minority, because Tamil separatist guerrillas receive support and sanctuary from the Tamil population across the Palk Strait in India's state of Tamil Nadu.

Academics and diplomats cite other factors contributing to violence among ethnic groups or by minorities against central governments, including the need to assert group identity, particularly among those who do not have a state of their own; economic disparity among groups, and disproportionate or lack of representation in government. These are often products of a colonial legacy. Colonial rulers frequently selected members of particular tribes to fill administrative posts, leaving behind ill will toward the privileged group when they departed.

Sri Lanka offers a laboratory for the study of ethnic conflict. The Tamil minority, which practices the Hindu religion, developed during colonial times into the preeminent business and bureaucratic class.

"The Sinhalese have incredible anxiety about cultural extinction," says Bryan Pfaffenberger, associate director of the University of Virginia's Center for South Asian Studies. "They have a unique culture at the tip of South Asia, and 20 miles across the strait they face 50 million Tamils."

This cultural anxiety drove the Sinhalese-dominated government to declare Sinhalese the official language in 1956 and sparked rioting in 1983 that destroyed 2,000 Tamil factories and businesses. "It was an act of consummate economic self-destructiveness, because most of these factories employed Sinhalese," Pfaffenberger says.

"They systematically dismantled the whole system of Tamil advantage," says Joseph Montville, research director of the Foreign Service Institute's Center for the Study of Foreign Affairs. Montville attributes violent behavior in such circumstances to "psychological regression . . . causing people to get more desperate" and seek the shelter of the ethnic group.

Among the Protestants of Northern Ireland, he says, "there has always been a very precarious world view, kind of like the Afrikaners in South Africa or the slave holders in the United States before the Civil War. The Protestants are conscious of having committed wrongs and are scared to death of being made to pay for it."

Another aspect of the colonial legacy is that boundaries frequently cut across tribal areas. After independence, most African and Asian nations kept those boundaries, lumping together tribes with little in common or leaving ethnic groups in more than one country with no homeland of their own.

The classic case of a people left without a homeland by its colonial masters is Kurdistan, a land that lies in parts of five countries—Syria, Iraq, Iran, Turkey and the Soviet Union—but nowhere on any political map of the world.

The Kurds, 20 million strong today, have been battling for years for some sort of autonomy. The first recorded use of aircraft to bomb civilian targets was carried out by Britain's Royal Air Force against Iraqi Kurds in the wake of World War I, when the British and French reneged on promises to create a Kurdish republic after the dismemberment of the Ottoman Empire. In May, the Iraqi army was accused of using poison gas against Kurdish villages to stop an Iranian offensive involving anti-Iraqi Kurds.

In other cases, such stateless groups are driven to form separatist movements by beliefs that they are bearing more than their fair share of the tax burden or carrying the rest of the country economically. The Basque and Catalan regions in Spain, for instance, are much more industrialized than the rest of the country. In India's Punjab state, called the breadbasket of India, militant Sikhs are agitating for independence.

Experts are divided on the degree to which economic factors influence ethnic and religious conflicts, but it is clear that they play a significant role. On the theory that "a rising tide lifts all boats," some experts argue that if more jobs, housing and other economic benefits are made available in countries wracked by ethnic violence, the various groups would have less reason to fight. Others take issue with this approach, pointing out that perceptions of inequality in the distribution of new economic benefits only exacerbate tensions.

The conflict in Northern Ireland, which goes back to the time of King James I in the early 17th century, is certainly between Catholics and Protestants, for whom a massacre 300 years ago and a shootout last year are equally infamous. But the real battle is over economic and political power and has little to do with churches. Religion, like language, takes on a symbolic importance, serving to identify people as members of a group, and thus can become a matter of life and death.

Communist countries, despite their traditional restraints on freedom of expression, are not immune to this sort of violence. The Balkan countries, and in particular Yugoslavia, have long served as the crucible of some of the world's most intractable ethnic conflicts, which have ignited local wars in this century and helped trigger World War I. National and ethnic tensions recently have gained significance as a force to weaken Soviet dominance among communist-ruled countries.

In Yugoslavia, ethnic tensions have threatened survival of the communist government. The most serious conflicts have involved the rivalry between Serbs and Albanians in the Yugoslav province of Kosovo; the persecution of ethnic Turks by Bulgarians in parts of southern and eastern Bulgaria; and pressure on ethnic Hungarians and Germans in Romanian-ruled Transylvania.

Another aspect of East bloc ethnic conflicts is that they have been stimulated by governments as part of subtle efforts to gain greater independence from Soviet control. In the years after World War II, national conflicts and national identities alike were suppressed by strict Stalinist rule. In recent years, however, Eastern European communist regimes have stressed national traditions and differences.

One effect of this trend has been a loosening of Soviet influence over domestic policies of East European countries. Recognition of "different roads" to socialism has become a key part of Soviet leader Mikhail Gorbachev's policy toward Moscow's allies. In a press conference in April in Budapest, Kremlin ideology chief Yegor Ligachev declared that the Soviets will no longer act as arbitrators in national-based disputes between allies.

At the same time, rising nationalistic sentiment in Eastern Europe must worry Gorbachev as leader of a country that has many ethnic and national groups, ranging from large Moslem populations in Central Asia to three once-sovereign Eastern European nations conquered by the Soviets only 40 years ago. Some observers believe that the recent riots in the Soviet republic of Kazakhstan may mark the beginning of an era in which Soviet national and ethnic groups begin to assert themselves in a way similar to what has occurred in Eastern Europe during the 1980s.

Washington Post correspondents Karen De Young in London, Jackson Diehl in Warsaw, William Claiborne in Johannesburg, Jonathan C. Randal in Paris, Richard M. Weintraub in New Delhi, Keith B. Richburg in Southeast Asia and special correspondents Nora Boustany in Beirut and Tom Burns in Madrid contributed to this report.

EXPLAINING TERRORISM

Peter C. Sederberg

Peter C. Sederberg, Ph.D. is a professor of political science at the University of South Carolina.

The lack of any consensus on a definition of terrorism or a typology of its significant forms hardly bodes well for the explanation of its occurrence. Indeed, the common characterization of terrorism as "senseless violence" suggests that no explanation is possible. No one, of course, really thinks terrorism is radically senseless; explanations emerge, if only of a conspiratorial or psychological sort, on the heels of every terrorist event. Nevertheless, respected commentators doubt whether true scientific explanations can be constructed for the myriad forms of terrorism (Laqueur, 1987; Wilkinson, 1976; 1979). Certainly, the absence of an accepted theory of civil violence in general does little to ameliorate the situation with respect to one of its particular forms (Rule, 1988).

Nevertheless, when explaining particular terrorist acts, analysts seldom content themselves with discrete, etiological interpretations; rather, comparisons and generalizations abound. These generalizations, unfortunately, cannot be facilely synthesized for at least three reasons: First, they focus on different levels of analysis; second, they reflect alternative, and somewhat incommensurate, methodological approaches; and third, they range from the essentially deterministic to the completely voluntaristic.

We cannot hope to resolve these incompatibilities; yet they can at least be organized and illustrated. Essentially, four broad types of explanation are drawn upon (in various combinations) to explain terrorist acts, whether dissident or regime: psychopathological, social psychological; sociopolitical; and strategic/tactical. These four also approximate a continuum from deterministic to voluntaristic positions.

Psychopathological Interpretations of Terrorism

Terrorist behavior, whether done in the name of change or preservation, certainly deviates from what we consider normal social interaction; therefore, we might conclude that some deviant personality could stand out from the background of "normal" people. From this perspective, certain people will be driven by their inner demons to engage in terrorism. In particular, the tendency to wreak havoc on the helpless seems to cry out for psychological explanation.

In his study of human destructiveness, Fromm (1973) distinguishes between defensive and malignant aggression; the former occurs in response to a threat to a vital interest, but the latter is simply bent on destruction. The two traits associated with malignant aggression are sadism and necrophilia. To illustrate the role played by such tendencies, Fromm explores in depth this century's three premier practitioners of terrorism: Hitler (a necrophilic), Himmler, and Stalin (both sadists). Similarly, Anthony Storr (1972; 1978) has developed an inventory of experiences that he argues contribute to the development of sadistic and paranoid personalities (again, assuming that these types possess the capacity to engage in terrorism for either regime or dissident). Billig's (1985) study of a leader of the Red Army Faction in West Germany hypothesizes that the inability to

identify with an adequate father-figure contributed to both antiauthoritarianism and a tendency to overcompensate in his own ruthless exercise of power. In interesting contrast with the Freudian position of Fromm and Storr, Hennelly (1988) develops a Jungian interpretation of how a destructive personality develops. Other psychological theories on the development of the "terrorist personality" are summarized in Schmid (1988).

People who commit acts of terrorism, however, need not appear as demented monsters outside of the context where they commit these acts. Both the "terrorist" and "torturer," to paraphrase Rubenstein (1987), may be like the person next door, indeed, it may be the person next door. Lifton (1986) develops the concept of doubling to explain how people can in one part of their lives commit unspeakable horrors, yet otherwise appear unexceptionable, even admirable. Doubling allows for the organization of "an entire self-structure (or self-process) encompassing virtually all elements of [a person's] behavior" (p. 418). One self commits terrorism while the other, semi-autonomous self participates in the conventional world.

While psychopathology may offer some intriguing insights, it tends to discount the significance of the social and political environment. Indeed, under certain conditions, such as those of the death camps, terrorist acts may become the norm, and the deviant personality may be the one who resists committing acts of terrorism. In response to such difficulties, Freedman (198, p. 6) observes that "a psychological profile of a model terrorist cannot be drawn. The personalities are disparate. The context and circum-

From *Terrorism: Contending Themes in Contemporary Research*, by Peter C. Sederberg, 1991. From *Annual Review of Conflict of Knowledge*, published by Garland Publishing, New York, NY.

stances within which terrorism . . . has been carried out are diverse in chronology, geography, and motive." On one hand, certain contexts may encourage the manifestation of destructive personality tendencies. On the other, the stresses and strains of particular social conditions may also encourage different forms of destructive behavior. A fuller understanding of terrorism involves both questions of social psychology and political context.

The Social Psychology of Terrorism

With the possible exception of the lone psychotic, terrorism must be placed in the wider political and social context of which it forms a part. Terrorism represents one form of severe coercion selected from among the alternative coercive instruments available to the establishment for repression or the dissidents for resistance. Coercive repression or resistance are themselves aspects of social control or protest, each of which, in turn, reflects some kind of discontent or fear. From this perspective, terrorism does not arise in a vacuum, but is one of many different responses to discontent. Social psychological explanations focus on the origins of this discontent.

Fundamentally, if rulers and subjects live in happy harmony, then there would be no terrorism. This observation doesn't carry us very far, since under these conditions, no forms of protest or social control, coercive or otherwise, would be needed. Nevertheless, though discontent may not be sufficient to explain the occurrence of terrorism, the argument that it is necessary seems plausible, and so do the social psychological theories that purport to explain the origins of discontent.

Discontent is generally seen as a state of mind, one related to experience, but not automatically determined by experience alone. Discontent, rather, arises from the interpretation we give to our experience; basically, whether we find our expectations met. Some of the classic work in this area includes that by Davies (1979), Feierabend and Feierabend (1972), Gurr (1970), and Schwartz (1973). Concepts such as "relative deprivation" or "alienation" suggest why members of the relatively privileged middle classes in Europe and America, as well as more obviously deprived sectors, might

be frustrated enough to resort to radical resistance, perhaps including terrorism. Recognition that members of the establishment might also find their expectations concerning the sanctity of privilege challenged by the dissidents and feel frustrated by a sense of relative powerlessness identifies a possible motivation for repressive terrorism (Duvall and Stohl, 1988; Rosenbaum and Sederberg, 1974). More recently, a number of studies focus specifically on the background experiences of those recruited into radical resistance (Crenshaw, 1981; Moxon-Brown, 1987; Thompson, 1989; Wasmund, 1986; Weinberg, 1986).

Socio-Political Influences on Terrorism

Deprivation, frustration, or alienation alone, however, cannot explain by themselves why people choose to respond with acts of severe coercion. Those alienated from the established order can, after all, withdraw, acquiesce, or engage in non-violent forms of protest. Those fearing the challenge of the dissidents have all the instruments of state control short of extreme coercion at their disposal. To address this issue, analysts identify a variety of socio-political factors which presumably encourage the choice of coercive responses, including terrorism.

A popular, but somewhat confused, explanation for internal terrorism of either dissidents or establishment blames external sponsors. The next section examines the complex issue of external manipulation and control. Here, we note only that this hypothesis continues a kind of determinism, in that although the external puppeteer presumably exercises deliberate choice, the perpetrators of terrorism are merely instruments.

Efforts to test various social psychological theories indicate that frustration by itself does not explain the choice of violence. Muller (1979) suggests a belief in the efficacy of violence, exposure to norms that validate violence, and alienation from the political system are more strongly related to the disposition toward dissident violence. Commitment to an ideology, either secular or sacred, provides a source for the validation of extreme coercion (Capitanchik, 1986; Drake, 1986; O'Sullivan, 1986; Rapoport, 1988; Wilkinson, 1986). Indeed, some evi-

dence suggest that identification with an ideology may be a factor of considerable importance in overcoming the "free rider" problem (Rose, 1987).

While the justifications for dissident violence receive most of the attention, similar values presumably exist to validate destructive behavior on the part of members of the establishment (Smelser, 1971; Duster, 1971; Walter, 1969). The validation of establishment coercion, however, might tend to be less explicit, because support values may well be taken for granted and need not be formally justified. Sometimes, however, rationales for destruction will be articulated, as in the case of the Nazi "bioideology" that consigned the Jews to their doom (Lifton, 1986).

A somewhat related proposition suggests that alienated elements may learn from the success other groups appear to have with violent tactics (Hacker, 1981). Such "contagion" presumably could influence members of the establishment as well as the dissidents. The media, unsurprisingly, is often identified as the medium of this terrorist contagion (Livingstone, 1986; Redlick, 1979; Schmid and de Graff, 1982; Wardlaw, 1982, 1990).

Political ideology may justify violence and the media may publicize such rationales and images of apparent success, but people must still have the opportunity to act on their intentions. Theories of collective action (McAdam, 1982; Tilly, 1978) argue that radical protest requires that the dissidents possess adequate resources and that something weakens the regime's instruments of social control. Although the notion that democracies are inherently vulnerable to terrorism, because their adherence to legal and political niceties opens up a space for terrorist abuses, has gained some currency, more credible research suggests that both dissident and establishment terrorism are more prevalent in relatively divided and unsettled states, whether democratic or authoritarian (Targ, 1988; Duvall and Stohl, 1988). On the other hand, terrorism may not develop out of the particular weakness of one side or the other in a political struggle; rather, there may be a "general tendency toward equilibrium in the severity of coercion used by all groups contending for power" (Gurr, 1986). Finally, changes in the political context appear to play a role in the decline of terrorism (Ross and Gurr, 1989).

The Terrorists: International State-sponsored and State-supported

Variations in the form terrorism takes include those that transcend borders and take place in other individual states. Transcending versions can include international state-sponsored or state-supported terrorism. In the last two instances, governments of particular states exert influence and seek to fulfill political objectives beyond their own territories by either directly sponsoring terrorist operations abroad or supporting those groups that parallel their goals. Sponsorship invariably means more than influence—it can translate into decision-making and control of the group's activities. Support usually refers to aiding and abetting existing terrorist groups that have degrees of independence or their own operational goals. Influence in the latter case moves both ways in the relationship. Admittedly, much of the literature fails to adequately differentiate the nuances between the two.

International terrorists may be territorially based but usually operate regionally or worldwide. Some have achieved nearly total independence, verging on a self-sustaining basis in their own right.

"What Constitutes State Support to Terrorists?" covers both versions of state sponsorship and state support, and it places special stress on motivational aspects of government involvement before turning to the instrumental nature of these activities.

Article 9 proves that state sponsorship and state support can be beneficial to both parties. The rewards for both Iran and Hezbollah appear to have been substantial upon the release of the American hostages. Though it does not portend immediate resumption of kidnapping as a terrorist tactic, the lesson cannot have been lost on the perpetrators.

As the article "Horn of Misery" describes, an estimated 23 million people in Somalia, Sudan, Ethiopia, and Djibouti are at risk from disease, epidemics, and starvation. The desperation of these peoples echoes across the area known as the Horn of Africa, as more than eight million people in the region have been forced from their homes during the last year.

Continued and further involvement by Iran in overseas support and sponsorship of terrorist activities are highlighted in the next article. In Lebanon there is a heightened intensification of the violent role by Hezbollah as the Iranian surrogate against Israel.

The international flavor of a terrorist organization, as well as its state-supported activities, are best typified by the Abu Nidal Organization (ANO). Contrary to numerous people's expectations that this phenomenon and the ANO are passé, they continue to function, shifting bases and affiliations as needed to survive.

Migrants from the Arab Near East and North Africa have now been joined in Western Europe by an influx of Eastern Europeans. Together they have inspired and intensified racism and xenophobic behavior within individual countries and across territorial boundaries by extremist groups, particularly on "Europe's New Right."

Europe's young neo-fascists share neither a particular goal nor specific creed, but something more dangerous: hatred. As "The New Sound of Hate" demonstrates, this youth movement has taken to music to get their message out. The music may not reach the Top 40, but it's still effective propaganda.

Though Glenn Frankel's article identifies three ethnic struggles taking place in different areas of the globe, the focus is mainly on Northern Ireland. A relentless struggle between two communities, each with extensive outside support, gravitates between efforts to reconcile and spasmodic violence. Most apparent is their inability to separate altogether.

Beyond the Middle East and Europe are various other regional examples of state involvements in terrorist activities—including cooperation with each other in such endeavors. The Shining Path in Peru seems to run counter to some of the trends in terrorism in Latin America by intensifying its efforts and successes. Its Maoist fanaticism joined to its increasingly important status in the world drug trade make them simultaneously one of the most independent and network-connected terrorist groups. Could they be the model for leftist terrorist groups in a future Latin America?

Looking Ahead: Challenge Questions

What are some prevalent reasons for governments indulging in state-sponsored terrorism? How is terrorism justified by the governments involved? How does religious extremism provide a motivation for state-sponsored terrorism?

How can state-supported terrorism be considered the most lethal and the most effective form of terrorism? How can the participation of states in terrorist activities be considered a rude reversal of the traditional purpose of the state?

How do governments contribute to and take advantage of other political systems? Through what means does state-supported terrorism accomplish this?

What are examples of some of the more notorious regimes that practice state-sponsored terrorism? How can terrorist groups benefit from the goals of such regimes?

Besides contributing to political instability and violence, how does a regime practicing state-sponsored terrorism benefit financially?

What are the characteristics of extreme right-wing and left-wing terrorist organizations? Do they have anything in common? How do their goals differ?

What Constitutes State Support to Terrorists?

Edward F. Mickolus

Despite the best efforts of governments worldwide to eradicate it, state-sponsored terrorism continues to dominate headlines. Whether we look at the scores of Afghan WAD/KHAD-supported attacks on Pakistani marketplaces,[1] or at almost two decades of Libyan-orchestrated depredations around the world, aid given to terrorists by governments continues to stymie our best efforts to protect ourselves. Indeed, many theorists have suggested that external support by governments is necessary to ensure the survival of terrorist bands, whose limited self-generated resources would otherwise cause these organizations to wither over time.[2]

Taking action to stop this official assistance to terrorists[3] has thus become a crucial component in legislative as well as non-traditional proposals to combat the overall phenomenon of terrorism. Many proposals as well as laws on the books call for actions against regimes which 'aid and abet terrorism'.[4] But where does one draw the line? If we are to go beyond mere name-calling, we need to determine what specific, observable actions draw our ire, and whether some actions are more reprehensible – and thus more critical to expose and combat – than others.

In addition to the policy question, the issue of state support raises methodological concerns which affect the conduct of our empirical research. As part of Vinyard Software's work in creating the ITERATE III dataset on international terrorist incidents,[5] we have wrestled with the issues of state support to terrorists: what constitutes evidence of support, and what constitutes a pattern of support? We have found in coding incidents that we may be faulted by some of our readers on criteria for inclusion. 'Some' evidence and 'overwhelming' evidence, as the US found when trying to get West European governments to move against Libya following the bombing of La Belle Disco in April 1986, is in the eyes of the beholder. If the US cannot get like-minded Europeans to agree on what a cancelled check and radio intercepts mean, it is doubtful that the far more disparate membership of the United Nations will take action against member states with goals parallel if not identical to their own.

The patron state issue also raises the broader question of what constitutes support for terrorists. Are we looking for specific-event assistance, or broader facilitation of terrorism without actually being involved in discrete incidents? Perhaps we (or the discipline as a whole) need a scale of types of behaviour/attitudes that governments can take which, volitionally or unintentionally, tend to make a terrorist's life easier. This article offers a scale of such actions, ranging from passive support to actual incorporation of the terrorist group into a quasi-official arm of a renegade government.

Motivations of Governments

As a first cut in constructing our scale, we can suggest several general degrees of government support/attitudes toward terrorists. In rough order of culpability/evil, there are:

- intimidated governments;
- ideologically supportive regimes;
- generally facilitative supporters;
- direct support in incidents by governments;
- official participation.[6]

To place regimes in any of these categories, we can examine specific observable behaviours made by governments which would lead us to infer the motivations of those governments. While we must always be mindful that these inferences can be faulty and we must consult multiple sources before feeling confident in these judgements, behaviours are, after all, what assist terrorists and what concern us here.

Refining our scale further to assign behaviours within each category, we can rank the behaviours in roughly ascending order of usefulness to the terrorists. One can quibble with the specific location of any given behaviour within these rankings; the scale is designed to be heuristic rather than theological.

Intimidated Governments[7]

In the first category we find governments which do not necessarily sympathize with the terrorists but whose actions, whether by inadvertence, inattention, ignorance, or intimidation, somehow assist terrorists. Examples of these acts appear below:

ACTS BY INTIMIDATED GOVERNMENTS WHICH DO NOT NECESSARILY SYMPATHIZE WITH THE TERRORISTS

1. Granting terrorist demands;
2. Refusal to sign/ratify bilateral/regional/universal anti-terrorist treaties;
3. Refusal to legislatively/juridically enforce #2;
4. Refusal to extradite on legal technicalities;
5. 'Quiet deals' by governments who permit terrorists to transit country in return for guarantee of no attacks on local soil.

Whatever one's rationale for granting terrorist demands, there can be little doubt that it directly assists terrorists. Indeed, such governments are giving the terrorists exactly what they request, a phenomenon almost unique among the behaviours along this scale. Wherever one stands regarding the debate on the merits of long-term deterrence versus short-term altruistic concern for hostages,[8] giving in starts governments on the slippery slope of terrorist assistance.

Other behaviours in this category are ones which the terrorists generally do not directly request, but which nonetheless assist them. Fence-sitting regarding anti-terrorist treaties, no matter how many other governments agree to them, tends to weaken the appearance of universal resolve to combat terrorists, and gives them the impression that if you attack the system at such vulnerable points, you can still win. We have put refusal to enforce such treaties, whatever the domestic political or constitutional excuses, higher on our list because this tergiversation gives terrorists the impression that perhaps all signatories were not really serious when they drafted the treaties.

Refusing to extradite on legal technicalities – vice political reasons, a greater offense on this scale – is similar to the previous entry on the scale, but gives more specific aid and comfort to the terrorists. Knowledge that they need not fear a probably tougher court in an aggrieved nation lessens overall terrorist fear of retribution.[9]

Quiet deals, while difficult to prove, are often cited by the Western press as explaining why terrorist attacks by foreign groups decline precipitously in certain countries. While the ploy does seem to buy a fragile peace for these countries, it bolsters terrorist resolve that their methods can work.

Ideologically Supportive Governments

Further along the scale are those governments whose motives are clearer. Far from being intimidated by the terrorists, they more openly embrace the

From *Terrorism and Political Violence*, Vol. 1, No. 3, July 1989, pp. 287-293. *Terrorism and Political Violence*, published by Frank Cass and Company, Ltd., England.

motives – if not yet the methods employed – of these bands. Their actions include:

ACTS BY IDEOLOGICALLY SUPPORTIVE GOVERNMENTS

6. Propaganda/rhetorical support to terrorist groups in media, international organizations;[10]
7. Permitting group to open office on local soil;
8. Refusal to extradite on political grounds;
9. Receiving visiting terrorist leaders on level normally given to heads of state;
10. Early release of incarcerated terrorists;
11. Failure to arrest hijackers who leave airplane on country's turf;
12. Granting of landing rights to hijackers;
13. Refusal to permit foreign hostage rescue squads into country;
14. Failure to arrest known terrorist transiting country.

Without belabouring the point with commentary on each entry, we shall simply note that these actions are more incident–specific than those earlier on the scale. Moreover, the given action requires a more formal decision by central governments which would more clearly understand the consequences of their actions in terms of assistance to terrorists.

Generally Facilitative Governments

Governments at this point on the scale have now decided that the actions of terrorist groups are in keeping with their own foreign policies. There can be no question of the sympathies of governments engaging in these actions. While not yet assisting in specific incidents, these governments are directly adding to the general capabilities of terrorists to conduct attacks. These actions include:

GENERALLY FACILITATIVE SUPPORT

15. Permitting group to set up safehouses/safehaven on local soil;
16. Permitting terrorists to conduct training on local soil;
17. General training by government of umbrella guerrilla bands which have terrorist appendages;[11]
18. Large monetary contributions to umbrella group's coffers;
19. Provision of arms to group or lax supervision of third party arms transfers.[12]

Incident-Specific Support

Governments engaging in these types of incidents are engaging in what Brian Jenkins has referred to as a type of surrogate warfare. While governments understand that they probably cannot win a conventional or nuclear battle with an adversary, they can conduct protracted conflicts with enemies through terrorist groups, which gives them the added benefit of deniability, however implausible. These actions include:

DIRECT SUPPORT TO TERRORISTS IN INCIDENTS

20. Providing false/true documents/passports/backstopping aliases/cover stories;
21. Providing diplomatic pouch to move terrorist items;
22. Provision of non-lethal operational assistance – maps, safehouses, communications;
23. Direct financing for specific operation;
24. Direct training for specific operation;
25. Provision of weapons for specific operation;
26. Adding to terrorist demands during incident;
27. Payment of insurance/bonuses to terrorists after the fact.

Joint Operations

Finally, we find governments which incorporate the terrorist methodology – and sometimes the terrorist group – into the government repertoire of official (if covert) action. These actions have included:

OFFICIALLY-SANCTIONED PARTICIPATION OF GOVERNMENT PERSONNEL IN INCIDENTS[13]

28. Participation of intelligence/security service personnel in planning of operation;
29. Government personnel joining terrorist attack squad

30. Joining terrorist attack squad once incident has begun
31. Incarcerating hostages
32. Shooting at hostage rescue squads

Concluding Remarks

Using the above scale, the ITERATE III project treats behaviours 20–32 as triggering our listing the incident as having state support. Acts lower on the scale, while we may be displeased with them, do not constitute the type of patronage which we would find sufficiently notorious for our purposes.

This scale, of course, is not meant to be exhaustive, nor need one agree with the absolute ranking given one action in comparison with another action. The intention of the scale is to determine the relative demerit of a pattern of actions – the broad category is key, not the numerical position.

The author hopes that this scale helps contribute to a more focussed policy debate on what constitutes state aid to terrorists and what we should do to stop it.[14] If we can agree on these definitional and typological preliminaries, we may be on our way toward a more effective policy response, and make the world just a little bit safer from further terrorist attacks.

NOTES

1. Consult, for example, *Patterns of Global Terrorism: 1987* (Washington, DC: US Department of State, 1988), as reported in John M. Goshko, 'World Terrorism up 7 per cent, U.S. Says', *Washington Post* (23 Aug. 1988), p.10, which notes in passing the increase in incidents is due to 'a wave of high-casualty bombings in Pakistan carried out by . . . the Afghan intelligence service known as WAD'. The report notes the WAD conducted 127 attacks inside Pakistan, killing 234 persons and wounding 1,200.
2. Consult, for example, the directory of terrorist groups, and their extensive networks of external supporters, in Alex P. Schmid, Albert J. Jongman, *et al.*, *Political Terrorism: A New Guide to Actors, Authors, Concepts, Data Bases, Theories, and Literature* (Amsterdam: North-Holland, 1988).
3. Our discussion is confined to regime assistance to terrorist bands, not the separate issue of terrorism (or other forms of gross violations of human rights, usually of the local citizenry) by repressive regimes, of whatever ideological persuasion.
4. For a fuller discussion of these proposals, consult the works cited in Edward F. Mickolus, *The Literature of Terrorism: A Selectively Annotated Bibliography* (Westport, CT: Greenwood, 1980), pp.297–301, as well as Edward F. Mickolus with Peter A. Flemming, *Terrorism, 1980–1987: A Selectively Annotated Bibliography* (Westport, CT: Greenwood, 1988), pp.67–81.
5. ITERATE III (International Terrorism: Attributes of Terrorist Events) is a follow-on to earlier numeric datasets on international terrorism. Available from Vinyard Software, 2243 Beacon Lane, Falls Church, Virginia, USA, it covers the 1980–87 time-frame. A numeric dataset, compatible with the ITERATE I and II coding schemes, is available, as is a computer-searchable textual version, which describes each incident. For a more detailed description of the datasets, consult Edward Mickolus, Todd Sandler and Jean Murdock, *International Terrorism in the 1980s: A Chronology, Volume 1: 1980–1983* (Ames, Iowa: Iowa State University Press, 1988), and the companion work, Edward Mickolus, Todd Sandler and Jean Murdock, *International Terrorism in the 1980s: A Chronology, Volume 2: 1984–1987* (Ames, Iowa: Iowa State University Press, 1989).
6. A similar scale of counter-terrorist actions could be constructed, with many of the entries the reciprocals of the items which will be described below.
7. As is evident by the opening sentence of this section, not all of the governments engaging in these behaviours are intimidated by the terrorists. Some may even be sympathetic to the terrorists, and engage in some instances in behaviours further along the scale. However, the vast majority of governments which engage in these behaviours are probably trying to avoid trouble for their nationals and believe that concession, rather than confrontation, is the easiest way out.
8. For a more thorough discussion of this debate, see Edward F. Mickolus, 'Negotiating for Hostages: A Policy Dilemma', Vol.19, No.4, *Orbis* (Winter 1976), pp.1309–25.
9. International narcotics traffickers, particularly members of the Medellin cocaine cartel in Colombia, show similar concern about being extradited to the United States, and go to extreme lengths – including million-dollar bribes to judges, hiring a terrorist group to kill the majority of the Colombian Supreme Court, and conducting a no-holds-barred media and lobbying blitz against extradition treaties – to throw a monkey-wrench into extradition efforts.
   Our ire with governments which refuse to extradite can be tempered somewhat by offers such as that given by Ireland when it refused to extradite to the United Kingdom an accused Irish Republican Army gunrunner. Although he held that Patrick Ryan could not get a fair trial in the United Kingdom due to media sensationalism, Irish Attorney General John Murray offered the British the option of using a 1976 Irish law to press charges in an Irish court. See Karen DeYoung, 'Ireland Turns Down Request by Britain to Extradite Priest', *Washington Post* (14 Dec. 1988), pp.A-27, A-32.
10. Paul Wilkinson would put this behaviour even further along the scale, under Generally Facilitative or even Direct Support. Personal communication, 6 Oct. 1988.
11. The Soviet Union, for example, was frequently cited in the late 1970s and early 1980s by Western observers for having trained and armed members of the Palestine Liberation Organization, some of whose members later turned up on terrorist missions. While many could argue that the Soviets did not intend for their arms and skills to be used by terrorists and that they were only assisting a revolutionary group which happened to have terrorist appendages, such aid did, even if arguably inadvertently and indirectly, build terrorist capabilities.

3. TERRORISTS: INTERNATIONAL, STATE-SPONSORED, AND STATE-SUPPORTED

12. While charges that Libyan leader Muammar Qadhafi has armed terrorists date back to his coming to power in September 1969, he none the less has continued these pursuits. The most recent evidence of Libyan arms collusion on a grand scale is the consignment of 150 tons of Russian-made SAM-7 ground-to-air missiles and other weapons destined for the Irish Republican Army which was intercepted in late 1987. However, senior Northern Ireland security chiefs believe that other shipments have been smuggled in. A senior Army official opined, 'We think it is almost certain they have the SAM-7's. I believe they are not using them at the moment because they do not have the sort of people of the calibre to use them and they are trying to do something about it.' The London Press Association article went on to say that 'A team of top provos is believed to be training in secret in one of Colonel Qadhafi's desert camps and others in isolated parts of the (Irish) Republic. The IRA may have already made an unsuccessful test firing in County Fermanagh. A helicopter pilot reported hearing a "woosh" and seeing what appeared to be a vapour trail.' 'IRA Believed to Have SAM-7 Missiles', *London Press Association* (21 Nov. 1988), reported in *Western Europe; FBIS-WEU-88–226* (Foreign Broadcast Information Service, 23 Nov. 1988), p.4.

13. The actions of the Iranian government during the takeover of the US Embassy in November 1979 to the end of the administration of President Carter come immediately to mind. The Iranians have kept busy since that incident, opening up camps for local and international terrorists at the Imam Hossein Post, the Manzarieh Camp, the Chamran Post, the Aqdassieh Post, the Qods Post, a Shiraz location, and the Najafabadi Camp. Consult Jack Anderson and Dale Van Atta, 'Khomeini Turns Attention to Terror', *Washington Post* (25 Nov. 1988), p.E5.

14. Two strategies immediately come to mind, based upon this scale. One is to attempt to prevent certain types of actions, for example, for openers, the 32 listed in this article. Another complementary approach would key on the categorization of governments, and hinge on attempting to work out appropriate sanctions for these patterns of behaviours.

The Terrorists' Payoff in the Hostage Deal

David H. Halevy

David H. Halevy is coauthor of "Inside the P.L.O."

WASHINGTON

What price did the United States really pay for the release of its hostages from Beirut? Administration officials deny, understandably, that they made a deal, but they seem to be oblivious to the deal cut behind their backs. That deal was struck at a secret meeting in Lebanon in the latter half of September, not long after Javier Pérez de Cuéllar, the U.N. Secretary General, had tea in Teheran with President Hashemi Rafsanjani.

President Rafsanjani and his intelligence minister, Ali Falahian, sent two high-ranking officials to the Bekaa Valley to confer with the operational and spiritual leaders of Hezbollah (also known as the Party of God), which is the covert arm of Iran's intelligence service, Sawama.

I know directly from one of the meeting's participants—who cannot be identified—that the full six-member command of Hezbollah attended this meeting called by Iran. Among them were some of the most feared names in the terrorist underworld—Haj Ihmad Mugneiyeh, Hezbollah's chief of security and mastermind of the 1983 bombings of the U.S. Embassy and Marine barracks in Beirut, and Sheik Mohammad Hussein Fadlallah, Hezbollah's spiritual leader and commander in chief.

Much earlier, the leaders of Hezbollah had concluded that all the Western hostages had become expensive and dangerous cargo. Throughout the Middle East, it was well known that fierce arguments raged in the terrorist organization over how and when the captives would be set free, and what would be given in exchange. There was no argument about the six Israeli prisoners of war held in Lebanon: they, or their bodies, simply would not be released.

Of immediate concern to Hezbollah at the meeting was protection for those engaged in hostage-taking and terror operations. Syria, which tightly controls the Bekaa Valley, was not the problem: as a result of the collapse of the Soviet Union, Syria's longtime ally, it was in no position to take on Iran. But neither Hezbollah nor Iran had much faith in quiet assurances offered by the British Government (or public hints from Washington and Jerusalem) that Hezbollah operators would not be gunned down after the Western hostages were freed.

Teheran soon put $86 million into the empty treasury of Hezbollah.

Thus, Ihmad Mugneiyeh and others demanded new identities and clean passports, even going so far as to ask for plastic surgery. I was told that he said: "Our faces are too well known by Western intelligence services and their bounty hunters, the Israelis. We need new faces." No surgery was scheduled, but Iran agreed to hide the Hezbollah operators from possible pursuit in other Iranian terrorist training camps near the holy city of Qum, south of Teheran.

According to the secret agreement, the last Hezbollah kidnapping unit in Lebanon would join comrades near Qum once two German hostages are freed, perhaps in January. They were kidnapped in May 1989 in reprisal for the arrest of two Hezbollah terrorists, the Hamadi brothers, in Frankfurt for the hijacking of a T.W.A. airliner in 1985.

Participants at the meeting say there was a second major item on the agenda: a renewed terror campaign. Hezbollah wanted to consolidate its organization, fragmented after the gulf war, and to reinforce its role as the dominant player in Lebanon's Shiite community. And neither Iran nor Hezbollah has given up the dream of turning Lebanon into an Islamic republic.

So it was agreed that Hezbollah would hit Israeli and U.S. targets throughout the Middle East, beginning as soon as possible and with the most serious attacks to start early in 1992. Iranian embassies and personnel stationed in Turkey, Greece, Jordan and Cyprus were designated to assist the operations with intelligence, logistics and escape routes.

Why would Iran, which reportedly hopes to normalize relations with the West, authorize and fund a terror campaign? While its motives for wanting to unload the hostages were simple—the settlement of outstanding cash claims with Washington and the hope of economic and technical assistance from Europe—its goals in the Bekaa Valley agreement were complex.

One aim, a member of the Iranian National Security Council told me, was to insure that Iran would not be sidelined in the Mideast peace process; it did not want any new postwar gulf security agreements orchestrated by Washington alone. Iran also wanted to cement its relationship with Arab fundamentalists by maintaining its transparently fictional identity as Hezbollah's sole beneficiary: Teheran hides the fact that it runs Hezbollah.

Also approved at a secret meeting: a new campaign against Israel and the U.S.

Iran's National Security Council had long been divided over how to bring about the release of the Western hostages held in Lebanon. Extremist mullahs led by Ayatollah Ali Husseini Khameini, the successor of Ayatollah Ruhollah Khomeini, were wedded to the conviction that dialogue with the U.S. would undermine and ultimately cause a complete reversal of Iran's Islamic revolution.

Opposition to the extremists was led by Ali Falahian, the intelligence chief, who sponsored the Bekaa Valley agreement and who thought a dialogue with the U.S. could serve Iran's purposes. The internal power struggle left Iran at an impasse, with President Rafsanjani pretending to remain aloof.

But on Oct. 4, according to a source on the Iranian National Security Council, President Rafsanjani approved a harsh anti-American sermon by Ayatollah Musavi Arbabili,

who said, "It is incumbent on all regional Muslims to attack American interests and take away their peace." Ayatollah Arbabili called upon Iranian youths to form cells for the purpose of attacking American interests and properties in the region. He denounced President Bush's "American peace conference," saying it was another secret plot to keep the region and its wealth under U.S. control.

Ten days later, at a stormy Iranian National Security Council meeting, the extremists consolidated their advantage. A tough stand on Middle East issues was adopted, spelling out Iran's intentions to play an active role in spreading "Islamic resistance"—terrorism—throughout the region.

In addition, the council decided to speed up Iran's trade negotiations with the European countries, which they felt posed no threat to the Iranian revolution, and to reject a dialogue with the U.S. Only then did it resolve to free all the remaining Western hostages at an accelerated pace.

Of course, Teheran also recognized Washington's readiness to compromise on three major issues. These compromises, which the Bush Administration dismisses as coincidental, were negotiated with the aid of the British Foreign Secretary and Mr. Pérez de Cuéllar, according to Iranian Government officials.

By mid-November, it was clear that the Israelis had been cut out of the deal. The sole possible survivor, Capt. Ron Arad of the Israeli Air Force, remains in captivity, with Israel demanding his return.

The Bush Administration agreed to compensate Iran $278 million for the military equipment the U.S. impounded following the takeover of

the U.S. Embassy in Teheran in 1979. Washington is also expected to lift its restrictions on the release of Iran's frozen assets—at least $7 billion held by American banks since 1979.

Furthermore, the U.S. Navy is now prepared to admit, albeit reluctantly that the Vincennes, a missile cruiser, was operating in Iranian territorial waters when it shot down Iran Air Flight 655 in 1988. In the works is a multimillion dollar settlement of claims resulting from the death of the 290 passengers.

In addition, the British Government signed trade and arms agreements with Teheran to the tune of $4.2 billion following the release of its three hostages, Terry Waite, John McCarthy and Jack Mann.

In short, the hostage-takers made out like the bandits they are. By mid-October, Iran had transmitted $86 million to Hezbollah's empty coffers. In the last week in October, Hezbollah launched its terror campaign in southern Lebanon, resulting in the deaths of six Israeli soldiers.

Over the past eight weeks, car bomb and hand grenade attacks have occurred in Ankara, Turkey, killing an American serviceman and an Egyptian diplomat. Moreover, Hezbollah operatives have been apprehended (and one Iranian was killed) while entering Israeli-occupied territory from Jordan and Egypt.

If the Bush Administration believes that the release of the hostages came out of the climate of a "new world order," it is sadly mistaken. Instead, once again the U.S. had been taken on an Iranian carpet ride, in a world more dangerous than ever.

Horn of Misery

In Akobo, a Sudanese town of 45,000 on the border with Ethiopia, relief worker John Jock Chol radioed a call for help to the projects director of an aid coordinating group in neighboring Kenya.

"Two thousand returnees arrived (yesterday) from Pochala," said Chol's March 23rd message. "Many are seriously wounded. They are in very bad condition. Thousands and thousands are still coming. If food is delayed, all the arrivals will die. Please try ways and means through the UN."

Three weeks earlier the Sudanese government had banned all UN flights to the refugee-swollen towns of Akobo, Nasir and Waat in southeastern Sudan. Many of the desperate people Chol saw were triply displaced by the region's shifting wars and had trekked back and forth across the Sudanese/Ethiopian border.

"These people have lost everything," Chol radioed March 25th. "They are staying under trees naked."

Two days later: "We are dying. Seven children died last night and more will die today."

April 10th: "Twenty-three people starved yesterday. Everybody is weak and waiting to die. The pastors' wives and others went to Gagwang nine days ago looking for food; they have not returned. We don't know if we will be on radio next week. It depends on God's will. We hope that some will remain."

The desperation in those pleas is echoed across the area known as the Horn of Africa. Chol's messages could just as well be the voice of a person in a forced relocation camp in the Sudanese desert, searching for food, water and shelter as the temperature rises; or the voice of a refugee in eastern Ethiopia, stranded in a strange city that relief organizations have abandoned to bandits; or that of a resident of the Somali capital Mogadishu, starving while watching ships loaded with food turn away from port because of shelling between rival militias.

At least 23 million people in Somalia, Sudan, Ethiopia, Eritrea and Djibouti are at risk from starvation, epidemics and disease, according to the UN Special Emergency Programme for the Horn of Africa (Sepha). Thousands have already died.

War and famine have forced more than eight million people in the region from their homes during the last year. More than a million have crossed national borders and at least seven million are on the move within their own countries.

Now the flood of refugees has spread to Kenya and as far south as Uganda, countries that are themselves experiencing drought and shortages. By late April, the number of refugees in Kenya had reached 180,000; that number is expected to rise to 340,000 by the end of June.

Humanitarian organizations warn that 1992–93 may be a repeat—or worse—of the 1984–85 famine that killed a million people.

While lack of rain contributes to the problem, it is the numerous and intractable armed conflicts that have displaced families, disrupted crop production, blocked relief supplies and spawned banditry.

In many ways, the misery is a Cold War legacy. Although feuds over land and cattle have been commonplace for generations, the deadliness of the current fighting and the widespread anarchy are new, fueled by proxy wars where superpowers vie for influence in the region.

Through the 1980s, the United States and the Soviet Union poured more than $13 billion of military assistance into the Horn, piling up arms and debts that will long outlast their own rivalry.

The complexity of the region's quarrels and the magnitude of events elsewhere have averted world attention from the creeping disaster. "People are talking about it, but there is no material response," laments Fesseha Tessema, a counselor at Ethiopia's UN mission. "People have to die on the television screen before something happens. After they die, to be on television, that doesn't help them."

And there is a measure of impatience in newsrooms or policy forums when the subject of famine in the Horn of Africa arises.

"There is a certain compassion fatigue which sets in," says U.S. Assistant Secretary of State for Africa, Herman Cohen. "Now, of course, we have the southern African drought, which is competing with the Horn on the humanitarian side. There's just not enough money to take care of every tragedy. And it seems to me that the natural disaster tragedies probably have greater priority than man-made. I think people who continue to make war with impunity have to understand that the West cannot just keep on feeding everyone indefinitely."

Aid agencies agree that farmers in the Horn need peace to feed themselves. But relief workers argue that, in the short term, emergency assistance is essential.

FAST FACTS

Ethiopia

Size: 483,123 square miles, about the size of California, Nevada, Utah and Arizona combined; Eritrea, a former Italian colony annexed by Ethiopia in 1962, is about the size of Indiana (36,183 square miles).

Population: 49,513,000; Eritrea, 2,614,699

Multiparty elections in Ethiopia and a referendum in Eritrea on the territory's independence are scheduled for next year. Hopes for peace and democracy are widespread following the overthrow of military ruler Mengistu Haile Mariam last year. But 30 years of war have left much of the country in ruins, and banditry and clashes over land and power plague the southeast. About eight million people need immediate aid. In some parts of the southeast, people are already starving. The hunger and deprivation threaten the transition to democracy.

Somalia

Size: 246,201 square miles, a little smaller than Texas.

Population: 7,339,000 (UN estimate, mid-1989)

Four and a half million people face hunger and disease in a country splintering along kinship lines after the January 1991 ouster of dictator Mohamed Siad Barre. Large-scale fighting threatens to break out in the northeast and a long-term national settlement is nowhere in sight. But a tense peace in the capital of Mogadishu has allowed the first major shipment of relief food in five months to reach the city, where 50 to 100 people were dying daily.

Sudan

Size: 967,500 square miles, about the size of the United States east of the Mississippi River.

Population: 20,564,364

Drought in the north and the biggest government offensive in the nine-year-old civil war against rebels in the south have left a third of the population in urgent need of aid. Hundreds in the south—where fight-ing and disputes over aid distribution cut relief routes—have already starved. Despite a string of government victories during the recent dry season, the country remains divided between the Islamic authorities in the north and two rebel factions in the Christian, animist south, with peace talks scheduled for later this month.

Djibouti

Size: 8,958 square miles, about the size of New Hampshire.

Population: 483,000 (1987 official estimate)

Djibouti is officially on the way to democracy, after 15 years under a single party dominated by one of the country's two main ethnic groups. But rebels in the north remain skeptical of the government's commitment to multiparty elections and will likely break a March cease-fire that ended four months of fighting. About one in 10 people in the country is a refugee.

Israel's Deadly Game of Hide-and-Seek

David Brooks

Mr. Brooks is deputy editorial page editor of The Wall Street Journal Europe.

ISRAELI-LEBANESE BORDER—The madness of southern Lebanon reached out across the globe Tuesday and touched down in Argentina. Islamic Jihad has claimed responsibility for the bombing of the Israeli Embassy in Buenos Aires, saying that attack is in retaliation for Israel's assassination of Lebanese terrorist leader Abbas Musawi. Why an Argentine priest—one of those killed in the blast—should die in connection with the Musawi assassination can only be explained by the twisted logic of Islamic Jihad.

Up here on the desolate security zone between Israel and Lebanon, that twisted logic constitutes a fundamental law of physics. The Israeli soldiers who patrol this region have somehow adapted to the insanity. They are an unusually animated group, who seem to be selected for their ability to make ironic remarks about fathomless situations. They play a deadly game of hide-and-seek with the Lebanese guerrillas. Driving around this region, one feels like Mel Gibson in "Mad Max."

MORAL COMPLEXITIES

That these soldiers would have personality quirks becomes more understandable as you learn about the moral complexities of their task of combatting the frequent border incursions and rocket attacks mounted by Mr. Musawi's Hezbollah, the Lebanon-based Islamic fundamentalist militia that applies a high degree of fanaticism to its mission of eradicating Israel. Over the past five years, according to senior Israeli officers, Hezbollah has attempted about 300 border incursions. Twenty Hezbollah bands made it through the security zone, which is three miles wide at its narrowest, to the Israeli fence. None reached their target. Of the members of those 300 raiding parties, one was taken prisoner and the rest were killed.

It is a bizarre and awful theater. The officers have no strategy textbooks to guide them, and report that they are given broad latitude by their higher-ups to carry out their mandate. The Israelis bombarded a southern Lebanese town one week, and then cut a deal with the town's leaders the next: Israel would rebuild the town if the townspeople would expel Hezbollah's bases. This week Reuters reported that the Israelis were using human shields, forcing Arab locals to drive in front of their patrols on a one-mile stretch of road in southern Lebanon that has been subject to Hezbollah raids.

Most of the firefights occur at random, when opposing patrols chance upon each other in open terrain. Israelis say that Hezbollah bands, unlike the Palestinian guerrilla groups, rush to engage in battle and fight enthusiastically.

Asked about the Musawi killings three days before the Buenos Aires blast, senior Israeli officers said that in the short term, the assassination is disrupting Hezbollah activity. But they admitted that in the long term, the effects would be counterproductive. But, they insisted, in southern Lebanon there is no long term. The constant rush of events and shifting alliances drowns out long-term considerations.

The region's anarchy did not happen by accident: it was created. On Oct. 13, 1990, the world turned a blind eye as Syria moved 40,000 troops into Lebanon and imposed a rough "peace." But Syria did not disarm Hezbollah. Syria's leadership does not share the religious fervor of Hezbollah, but Syria believes that its goal of extracting concessions from Israel and the U.S. is well served by having a non-Syrian army launch raids and rockets into Israel. Last April, Syria, as part of an agreement with its ally Iran, gave Hezbollah free reign to conduct anti-Israeli operations. Iran gives financial and technical assistance to Hezbollah and its members look to Tehran for guidance. Their immediate goal is to make normal life in northern Israel impossible.

According to Israeli intelligence, the Hezbollah military is divided into three branches. The first does technical work, devising the booby traps that dot the roads patrolled by Israelis and Hezbollah's Lebanese rivals. Some are simple land mines disguised as rocks, others are electronically detonated, using radio or telephone equipment. One type sets off a small explosion and then pauses, allowing the victims time to begin to flee their vehicle. A second explosion unleashes thousands of small pellets.

Most of the labor in this line consists of putting the booby traps in place. Instead of using maps, Hezbollah uses written narratives to guide their soldiers. Walk 50 paces to a bent tree, then 25 paces right to a large white rock, and so on. The painstaking work is in measuring out the distances between the various components of the trap, and then in camouflaging it properly. The Israelis admit they are perpetually one step behind in countering innovative Hezbollah traps and placements.

The second branch conducts intelligence work. The militia's membership is drawn from the Shiite community of southern Lebanon; intelligence agents tend to be native to the Lebanese towns in which they operate. The political splits within these towns are such that very often one brother will go to work for Hezbollah, another will fight for the Israeli-backed South Lebanese Army, and another will fight for one of the other private armies. Because of this integration, Hezbollah has been able to penetrate the other local forces. Israel coordinates its activities with the SLA, but assumes that any information given to the SLA immediately goes to Hezbollah.

Syria's leadership believes that its goal of extracting concessions from Israel and the U.S. is well served by having a non-Syrian army launch raids and rockets into Israel.

The final Hezbollah branch conducts operations. Several years ago, Hezbollah would stage raids with as many as 40 or 50 soldiers, but discovered that they could not succeed in any conventional clash.

U.S. Justice Department officials have privately charged that Hezbollah is engaged in trafficking in illicit drugs from the Bekaa valley, but some Israelis are skeptical, saying that Hezbollah is the only local militia that is not involved in the drug trade. Senior Syrian officers profit from Lebanon's $4 billion-a-year drug business, and there are private drug armies such as one finds in Latin America. But Hezbollah objects to drugs on religious grounds.

In fact, if there is a movement for social reform in southern Lebanon, it is Hezbollah. The leadership will not admit anyone into the organization who takes drugs, who drinks, who has debts, or who otherwise violates Islamic law. A few years ago, a leader of a rival secular

militia tried to defect to Hezbollah, bringing with him a captured Israeli airman. Hezbollah reportedly took the airman, but chased the captor away, on the grounds that he did not lead a religious life.

The military wing is but one aspect of Hezbollah activity. Like other militias, Hezbollah sponsors schools and hospitals for its members, and has its own police force. Terrorists are said to comprise a secret organization within Hezbollah. But the car bombings and other suicide attacks Hezbollah sponsors are believed to be conducted by emotionally unsteady individuals tangentionally connected to the organization.

The constant refrain in conversations with the Israeli soldiers on these fronts is that Westerners will never understand the complexities and absurdities of Middle Eastern warfare and life. They use this to explain and justify what would be outrageous behavior in normal military situations.

On a cold night last week, while gale force winds were whipping across the mountain, the Israeli patrols were using searchlights and night vision equipment to peer into the security zone. They patrol in oversized jeeps, five men to a patrol—a commander, a machine gunner, a radio man, a paramedic and a driver. They patrol for seven hours at a stretch, peering out into the darkness, and are not permitted to eat during that time. Some commanders make their crews periodically do push-ups to keep them sharp.

GRACE UNDER PRESSURE

Israeli soldiers volunteer for this sort of duty. The selection process is extremely competitive, emphasizing not so much overt machismo as grace under pressure. Tumbling out of their vehicle to meet a visiting reporter, they look like college freshmen on the first night of orientation week, some chubby, some scrawny, all eager to please.

Their commander, all of 21, explains that their orders are to shoot anything that moves in the security zone. They have a device that allows them to blow down the nearby fence if they need to pursue Hezbollah bands into the zone. They are bundled up in their flak jackets, the searchlights are blinding and there is no other life around.

But the final lasting impression of the visit is the drive down the hill from the other-worldly atmosphere of the security zone. You get in your car and by the time you settle on a radio station you're in Qiryat Shemona, driving past strip malls, pizzerias and the Burger Ranch. The contrast is jarring. Whatever one makes of the "peace" process, or of Israel's tendency to fight fire with fire, the geography is memorable. As Israelis see it, when it comes to security, that three-minute drive is their only margin of error.

ISRAEL GRAPPLES WITH TERROR WAR ON ALL BORDERS

Increasing Violence at Jordan Border

Figures for terrorist infiltrations into Israel have been released by the Spokesman's office of the Israeli Defense Forces (IDF) for 1988 through July 1991. [*Ed. Note: figures cited for the full year 1991 include data* **conservatively** *tabulated by the Security Affairs staff. Numbers refer only to each attempt, not to the number of individual terrorists involved in each attempt. Infiltrations include those attempts repulsed at the border, but not in the Israeli-maintained security zone in southern Lebanon. "Katyusha" rocket firings refers to terrorist firing of artillery rockets into Israel.*]

Jordanian Border
1991 14 infiltrations, including one Jordanian soldier captured.
2 Israelis killed.
12 Israelis wounded.

1990 5 infiltrations.
7 Israelis killed.
IDF forces are fired upon 3 times across border. Jordanian soldiers attack Israelis twice.

1989 5 infiltrations.
3 Israelis killed.
7 Israelis wounded.
Rocket fired from Jordanian territory. Exchange of fire with Jordanian patrol.

The Northern Border (Lebanon)
1991 At least 55 terrorist clashes with IDF and SLA.
4 infiltrations.
2 Katyusha firings.
4 Israelis killed.

1990 21 terrorist clashes with IDF and SLA.
1 infiltration.
11 Katyusha firings.

7 IDF casualties.

1989 22 terrorist clashes with IDF and SLA.
9 infiltrations.
4 Katyusha firings.
2 IDF casualties.

1988 40 terrorist clashes with IDF and SLA.
23 infiltrations.
18 Katyusha firings.
21 IDF casualties.
23 attempted infiltrations.

Egyptian Border
1991 1 infiltration attempt.
1990 1 infiltration by Egyptian soldier.
4 Israelis killed.
23 Israelis wounded.
1989 2 infiltrations.
1988 3 infiltrations.
3 Israelis killed.
8 Israelis wounded.

Reprinted from *Near East Report,* March 1992.

The Abu Nidal Organization

Carl Anthony Wege

Brunswick College, Brunswick, GA 31520

Abstract   *In recent years, the Abu Nidal Organization (ANO) has been politically marginalized. The [1990–91] Gulf crisis may serve to reinvigorate the ANO as a significant actor in the Middle East. As an organization with its raison d'etre rooted in violence, there is a paucity of literature concerning the ANO. It is, therefore, a useful exercise to collect and collate available information to construct a study of this organization.*

Keywords   Nidal, ANO, terrorism, Palestinian radicals.

INTRODUCTION

Terrorist groups may be categorized on a spectrum of violence, yet little literature exists concerning the most violent organizations. Comprehending the nature of such groups is fundamental to understanding the full spectrum of subnational political violence we commonly call terrorism. This paper examines the Abu Nidal Organization (ANO) as a prototype of the most violent terrorist organizations.

Organizations designated as terrorist are characterized by specific targeting of non-combatants to communicate political grievances. Nonetheless, there are gradations among such organizations. Some focus on diplomacy, some mix diplomacy and terror, and some focus on terror. The ANO is an example of the last type and is examined in this paper.

ORIGINS

The genesis of the ANO is in Fatah. Abu Iyad, the Black September chief, was an early Abu Nidal patron in Fatah. Nidal, like Iyad, was associated with the Black September Organization (BSO).[1] His first major diplomatic assignment occurred in 1969 when he was to open Fatah's Khartoum office. Difficulties there prevented that opening, and Nidal was transferred to Baghdad. As Fatah representative in Baghdad, Nidal began organizing operations immediately upon his arrival and, with Fatah approval, the Iraqis assisted Nidal's efforts.[2] He soon became enamored with the Iraqis and compromised by Iraqi intelligence.[3] Nidal subsequently argued for more systematic radicalization in Fatah. His initial following was among resident Palestinian students in Iraq.[4] This core was nourished by Nidal's financial support of the students[5] and was sustained by family ties.[6]

Another element of the incipient ANO were cadres from the National Arab Youth for the Liberation of Palestine (NAYLP). The NAYLP was led by one Ahmed al-Ghafour (Abu Mahmoud). Paralleling Nidal's rejection of the use of diplomatic tactics by the Fatah leadership, the NAYLP executed several operations in the early 1970s, which caused significant loss of American life. Owing in part to resulting diplomatic damage, Fatah sentenced al-Ghafour to death in absentia. A Fatah team managed to track down and execute al-Ghafour in Beirut. The remnants of his organization then made their way to Baghdad, where many of them linked up with the ANO.[7]

The embryonic Nidal organization flourished in Iraq. Initially, the ANO built a data base of Western publications. ANO staff used these both to monitor Western political developments and track business and political leaders. Some businessmen who traveled to the Middle East were subsequently kidnapped for ransom, which formed the seedbed of independent financing for the organization.[8]

The formal split between Nidal and his followers with Fatah occurred in October 1974. During that month, a Fatah revolutionary court sentenced Nidal to death in absentia on charges of attempting to mount

From *Terrorism*, Vol. 14, 1991, pp. 59-66. *Terrorism*, published by Taylor and Francis, 1101 Vermont Ave., NW, Suite 200, Washington, DC 20005.

armed insurrection within Fatah and conspiring to assassinate Fatah officials.[9]

The Fatah death sentence precipitated Nidal's overt efforts to establish a competing organization. Nidal argued that his new faction was the "authentic" Fatah, and included the aforementioned palestinian students resident in Iraq and cadres from three other sources. These were dissidents from al-Asifah (a Fatah commando organization), loyalists of the Fatah renegade Ahmad al-Ghafour, and some elements of the Palestinian Liberation Army's Qadisiyah Brigade (normally based in Iraq).[10]

Nevertheless, in the aftermath of the Fatah-ANO split, Nidal retained secret contact with senior Fatah officials.[11] Furthermore, while maturing over the years, Nidal's organization changed paymasters several times. It has, sequentially, contracted with the Iraqis, the Syrians, and the Libyans.[12] In 1990, the Gulf crisis resulted in the ANO coming full circle with its reestablishment in Iraq.[13]

ORGANIZATIONAL STRUCTURE

In examining the ANO, it is useful to begin with its financial structure. Financially, the ANO demonstrates reasonable management skills and access to resources. Major sources of ANO financing have included commercial operations, government subsidies (from Libya, Syria, and Iraq), and blackmail.[14] An account of commercial operations in Eastern Europe came to light in 1988.[15]

These commercial operations flourished in Eastern Europe prior to the democratic revolutions of 1989. In Warsaw, for example, a senior ANO financial adviser (Samir Najm al-Din) was responsible for SAS Trade and Investment. The basic operation of SAS was sales brokerage. Arms and other goods were traded between various governments (primarily between East Germany and Poland and Iran and Iraq). SAS would broker the sale and accept a commission on the same. In turn, SAS acted as an administrative center for several ANO front companies in Europe.[16] Other front companies also surfaced. A report from London noted that the London branch of the Bank of International Credit and Commerce (BCCI) was responsible for three front companies that moved money for the ANO.[17] If Poland and London have proved amenable to ANO financing, other areas of Europe have not. Samir Najm al-Din, the organization's chief financier in Europe, disappeared in Switzerland in the summer of 1988 — almost simultaneously with the breaking Polish story. Subsequently, the ANO kidnapped Swiss Red Cross workers in response to Najm al-Din's disappearance. It seems unlikely, therefore, that his disappearance was arranged under ANO auspices.[18]

Subsidies from various governments have also been important sources of ANO funding over the years. The ANO operated, in the mid- to late 1970s, on a budget of about U.S. $10 million a year, which was supplied by the Iraqis.[19] By the late 1980s, the ANO was estimated to control "... tens of millions of dollars."[20] Livingstone noted that much of this was in the form of an annual Libyan subsidy approaching U.S. $15 million, which constituted the bulk of the $20 million late-1980s budget.[21] It might be surmised that, with Nidal's return to Baghdad after falling out with the Libyans, Iraq was now paying the bills.

The role of blackmail is more problematic, although it is probably applicable to ANO actions against commercial companies and governments as well as individuals. Contributions to the Palestinian cause provide one with some political "fire insurance."

Conceptually, the ANO has been described as a staff of experienced agents insulated from, yet supplemented by, a stream of expendable recruits.[22] The hard-core staff numbered, prior to the Autumn 1989 purge, about 400 officials organized into cells that were scattered throughout the Middle East, Europe, and Asia.[23] The current Gulf crisis may precipitate activation of many such cells.[24]

Elements of these cells are found among some student populations. Significant numbers of Nidal cadres, according to Ariel Merari of the Center for Strategic Studies in Tel Aviv, pose as students in European universities.[25] Beyond Europe, centers of Nidal covert students organizations exist in Britain, Qatar, the United Arab Emirates, Kuwait, and Pakistan; there are also ANO functionaries in Algeria, France, and Belgium.[26]

The ANO's Lebanese base of operations during the late 1980s was near Tripoli (Lebanon).[27] The ANO had camps in places as disparate as the regions of Yanta (in the Bekaa valley), Hamara (once the Syrian-Lebanese border), and within a Syrian military installation at Nabi Zahour.[28] The late 1980s saw Lebanon serving as the ANO's main training venue with command structures in both Lebanon and Libya, although events in 1989 and 1990 altered the situation.[29]

With the onset of the Gulf crisis, the focus of ANO command structures were transferred to Iraq. The dramatic increase in Syrian influence in Lebanon, accomplished with the diversion of the Gulf crisis, can be expected to diminish the viability of ANO training facilities in Lebanon. The construction of additional training facilities may be expected in Iraq. The transfer of operational personnel from Lebanon to Iraq may be affected through the good offices of the Jordanians.

ANO operations function on the basis of cells. Individual cells are often congruous with family or clan times, or both, which allow significant operational security via simplified vetting procedures.[30] Such cells generally consist of three to seven persons,[31] and communication among cells is maintained with courier networks.[32]

A Central Committee serves as a basic ANO decisionmaking body. Its membership is partially elected and partially appointed by a politburo. Al-Banna controls the politburo and uses it as a mechanism to run the ANO. The politburo was constituted in 1985 with 10 members. Theoretically, it administers daily operations and executes Nidal's decrees.[33] The 1989 purge, however, shattered any pretense of independent decisionmaking within the politburo. An ancillary ANO body, the "Revolutionary Council," involves about 40 people who administer ideological matters.[34] In the aftermath of 1989, the Revolutionary Council was also reduced to pious servitude.

Organizationally, the ANO is a binary structure with a political and a military apparatus.[35] The ANO is constituted to mirror the original organization of Fatah. The U.S. State Department has noted six separate functional departments. These include the following:

1. Organizational Department: This department is concerned with relations with foreign governments and communications with private nongovernmental organizations (e.g., student unions). It coordinates with operational units in the field via six regional committees.
2. Finance and Economic Department: This department administers various commercial activities and manages accounting and payroll needs.
3. Information Department: This department is the main security organ. It administers intelligence and counterintelligence functions. It is also involved with planning operations.
4. Political Department: This department performs both liaison and propaganda functions. It publishes two periodicals. These are *Filastin al-Thawra* (an imitation of the Fatah organ), a newsweekly that is aimed at Palestinians, and *Al-Tariq*, an internal typewritten document reportedly written by Al-Banna. *Al-Tariq* contains information on ideological issues, personnel matters, and policy recommendations.
5. Lebanon Affairs Department: This department manages ANO activities in Lebanon and liaison activities with various Lebanese groups. The department was formed in 1986 to deal with Lebanon's increasing importance to the organization.
6. Administrative Department: This department deals with daily administrative functions.[36]

These functional divisions are, no doubt, paralleled by divisions of geographic responsibility. The resulting organizational network formed by juxtaposing functional and geographic lines allows bipartite support for any given set of objectives. This contributes to organizational strength and resilience through a series of operational cross-checks. The cell structure facilitates compartmentalizing functional and geographic responsibilities, which precludes complete organizational compromise while allowing the aforementioned dual tasking support.

The basic ANO training cycle for operational personnel apparently lasts about 45 days. It consists of the usual small arms and explosives training and political indoctrination. A special course was developed in the late 1970s on airline hijacking using foreign instructors—primarily Japanese, German, and Cuban.[37] This is noteworthy as there have only been a couple of known hijacking operations with ANO connections.

ORGANIZATIONAL DEVELOPMENT

During the late 1970s, Nidal's most significant training facilities were in Iraq—in Habbaniyah (near Ramadi) and near Hit.[38] Although much of Nidal's support came from Libya[39] in the late 1980s, most of the organization's personnel were either in Syria or Syrian-controlled territory.[40] Nidal's changing patrons necessitated ongoing relocation of training and command facilities. Until the summer of 1989, Nidal was closest to the Libyans, and the ANO opened a large facility there.[41] That camp was located near Rabta and could accommodate about 500 men.[42] The autumn 1989 purge, however, strained relations with the Libyans. Nidal's liquidation of incipient ANO moderates left him in control of a smaller, but ideologically more uniform, organization. His difficulties with Colonel Qaddafi required him to seek other accommodations for his command facilities. The ANO chief is thought to have looked first to Iran, but the Gulf crisis provided an opportunity to renew old friendships in Baghdad.

During the late 1980s, Lebanon was the most important venue for ANO operational facilities.[43] The most important operational site was then located near Tripoli (Lebanon) outside the zone of immediate Syrian control.[44] In 1987, about 300 ANO fighters were based in Lebanon.[45]

The ANOs activities in Lebanon in 1987 indicated continuing Syrian ties.[46] As late as 1989, the Syrians continued assistance to ANO personnel in Lebanon. In the spring of that year, the Syrians provided Lebanese identity cards, UNRWA identity cards, and Lebanese passports to the ANO.[47]

In the late 1980s, the ANO expanded its manpower base. In 1987, it sought arms on the black market to supply about 1500 men. Concurrently, it attempted to establish itself in southern Lebanon and open relations with Hizbollah there, although its main base of operations was north of Tripoli, Lebanon.[48] In 1988, ANO camps opened in the Bekaa valley and, combined with its men near Tripoli, the ANO approached 1000 men under arms.[49] Evidence of possible operational cooperation with Hizbollah surfaced after an attack in Khartoum on May 15, 1988.[50] The attack was later acknowledged as an ANO operation. The attackers, however, carried Lebanese passports with Shi'a names. One of the attackers was later found to be from a family with Hizbollah members.[51] However, with Syria's initial support for the anti-Saddam alliance and increasing Syrian influence in Lebanon, the ANO may experience decreasing operational flexibility in the Lebanese venue.

Although the ANO historically shunned close cooperation with other terrorist groups for security reasons, associations do exist. It was revealed in 1986 that the Marxist Kurdish Workers Party (MKWP) provided safe houses for ANO personnel over the preceding years. The MKWP has maintained cells in Germany, Holland, Sweden, Switzerland, and France.[52] The ANO has further cooperated with Action Directe in France[53] and maintained weapons caches as far away as Pakistan.[54]

Relations with a variety of extremist groups serve the ANO in two ways. First, it facilitates the seemingly easy movement of the ANO across hostile political frontiers (e.g., between Iraq and Syria by providing an insurance policy of sorts). Second, Nidal is said to want to create a "dynamic of terror" in the Middle East. This dynamic would consist of loosely affiliated terrorist organizations cooperating to destabilize the entire state system in the region.[55] The current Gulf crisis may provide an environment that facilitates such a dynamic, considering the consequences of outside intervention and the fragility of the existing state system.

CONCLUSIONS

In the autumn of 1989, there was a purge that again marginalized the ANO as a political actor. The origins of the purge appear in prompting by elements of the leadership to incorporate diplomacy into their activities.[56] The ensuing bloodbath resulted in the deaths of between 150 and 300 ANO cadres.[57] Liquidation of dissident elements of the leadership (numbering in the dozens) was concentrated in Libya; most of the other killings occurred in Lebanon.[58] One consequence of that purge was serious friction with Qaddafi in Libya,[59] which caused Nidal to consider moving his command structure to Iran; the Gulf crisis eventually precipitated his actual move to Baghdad.[60]

Politics requires nonviolent, as well as violent, communications. Consequently, the ANO is further marginalized as a political actor. Yet, the current Gulf crisis may reinvigorate the ANO as a regional actor. As the conflict plays out, however, the ANO simultaneously serves its own and Baghdad's interest in threatening Western and conservative Arab targets, which may result in its political rehabilitation among Palestinian moderates and the more radicalized Arab masses.

NOTES

1. Walter Laqueur, *The Age of Terrorism* (Boston and Toronto: Little, Brown and Company, 1987), p. 286.
2. *Philadelphia Inquirer,* January 5, 1986.
3. Laqueur, *The Age of Terrorism,* p. 286.
4. This initial cadre numbered about 200 persons according to Laqueur in *The Age of Terrorism,* p. 286.
5. Ibid.
6. Family ties are important to understanding Middle East politics generally and terrorist politics in particular. A general rule of thumb, noted by Laqueur in *The Age of Terrorism,* is the smaller the group the more important its clan politics. This is seen in Hizbollah factions (e.g., the Musawi clan), certain other Lebanese factions (e.g., the Lebanese Armed Revolutionary Faction [Abdallah clan]), and some of Nidal's operations (e.g., Hindawi brothers).
7. Christoper Dobson and Ronald Payne, *The Never-Ending War* (New York and Oxford: Facts on File Publications, 1987), pp. 230–231.
8. *U.S. News and World Report,* January 12, 1986, p. 31.
9. Defense Intelligence Agency *International Terrorism: A Compendium Volume II—Middle East* (Tehran Embassy 1979), p. 94.
10. Ibid.
11. *Foreign Report,* June 4, 1985, p. 7. As reported by Melman, Nidal's command structure is made up of four individuals. These are Mustafa Merad (reported killed in 1989 purge), Ghasan al-Ali, Muhammad Wasfi Hannon, and Abd al-Rahman Isa (until recently). *TVI Profile* notes this further information: Aataf Abu-Bakr was Nidal's deputy and the official spokesman for the organization (until his defection in 1989). Samir Najim al-Din is the director of the ANO's financial activities (until his disappearance in Switzerland in the summer of 1988). Ghasan al-Ali is the chief ideologist. Walid Halad is a organization spokesman and chief of foreign relations. Individual known as Hisnam is some sort of operations chief. *TVI Report* 8, no. 3 (1989): 5.
12. *Washington Times,* January 1, 1986.
13. *Washington Post* (National Weekly Editor, September 17–23, 1990), p. 16.
14. *New York Times,* November 28, 1989, p.6.
15. The account was based on a State Department document, which, in turn, was based on a Central Intelligence Agency report that used an ANO informant (possibly provided through the good offices of the Jordanians). *New York Times,* January 25, 1988.
16. *Wall Street Journal,* October 15, 1987, p. 24.
17. *Intelligence Newsletter,* April 26, 1989, p. 5. It might also be noted that the BCCI in Florida has been accused of co-mingling accounts of Contra rebels and cocaine traders.
18. *Intelligence Newsletter,* February 1, 1989, p. 7.
19. *Philadelphia Inquirer,* January 5, 1986.
20. *New York Times,* November 12, 1989, p. 26. In addition Abu Bakr noted in the *Washington Post,* November 20, 1989 that the funds existed in four bank accounts—three in Switzerland and one in Austria. A report in the *New York Times,* November 28, 1989 estimated the total amount of funds under ANO control up to $200 million.
21. Neil C. Livingstone and David Halevy, *Inside the PLO* (New York: William Morrow and Company, Inc., 1990), p. 243.
22. *Wall Street Journal,* January 2, 1986, p. 15.
23. *New York Times,* November 28, 1989, p. 6.
24. This activation may provide unusual collection opportunities for Western and other services further illuminating ANO organizational structure.
25. Ibid. It would appear, however, that these "sleepers" merely facilitate operations. Their professional utility is limited.
26. DIA *International Terrorism Compendium,* pp. 95 and 97.
27. *Foreign Report,* April 30, 1987, p. 5.
28. Livingstone and Halevy, *Inside The PLO,* p. 242.
29. *New York Times,* November 12, 1989, p. 26.
30. Yossi Melman, *The Master Terrorist: The True Story of Abu-Nidal* (New York: Avon Books, 1986), p. 80.

31. Ibid., 83.

32. Ibid. Most effective terrorist organizations use couriers to send messages. Any communication that uses an electronic medium can theoretically be intercepted. The smaller organizations in particular cannot put the resources into encryption devices secure against the resources of the major services. Using couriers is, therefore, their only safe means of communications.

33. United States Department of State *Abu Nidal Organization* (February 1989), p. 4.

34. Ibid.

35. Melman, *The Master Terrorist*, pp. 90–91.

36. State Department *Abu Nidal Organization*, pp. 5–6.

37. DIA, *International Terrorism Compendium*, p. 96.

38. DIA, *International Terrorism Compendium*, p. 95.

39. According to Melman, an aide to Nidal, one Shafiq al-Arida, established liaison with Libya through Naji Alush, a former member of the ANO. Alush had an excellent relationship with Abdallah Hijazi, Abdallah Sanusi, and Salim abu Sharukai the three lieutenant colonels who ran the Libyan intelligence services in the mid 1980s. This according to Melman, *The Master Terrorist*, p. 124.

40. *Philadelphia Inquirer*, January 5, 1986.

41. This is always a close call, the ANO is also currently cooperating with the Syrians and opening relations with the Iranians.

42. *Defense and Foreign Affairs Weekly*, May 8–14, 1989, p. 6.

43. *New York Times*, September 13, 1986.

44. *Foreign Report*, April 30, 1987, p. 5. It might also be noted that this same source indicated that the ANO may have been penetrated by Jordanian intelligence, since one of the ANOs senior members, Abdhul Rahman, had surfaced in Amman.

45. Ibid. This would change significantly by 1988.

46. For example, the ANO seized a pleasure yacht in the eastern Mediterranean in November 1987. The ANO claimed some of the passengers were Mossad operatives from France and Belgium. An ANO spokesman, Walid Khaled, held a press conference concerning the matter in Beirut. The conference was in a building housing some offices of Syrian military intelligence. If the Syrians had, in fact, cut ties with the ANO, it is unlikely they would allow ANO press conferences in buildings they used for official purposes. This was reported in the *Washington Times*, December 28, 1987.

47. *Intelligence Newsletter*, April 26, 1989, p. 8.

48. *Washington Times*, December 28, 1987, p. A9.

49. *Christian Science Monitor*, June 6, 1988, p. 32.

50. It might be noted here that folks always try to play games. There is a small, but quite effective, Palestinian group that calls itself 15 May Organization. Because this attack in the Sudan occurred on that date, the Palestinian faction is the first one investigators would look at, buying the ANO some time.

51. *Christian Science Monitor*, June 6, 1988, p. 32. Having noted the importance of clan politics to the smaller organizations if family members are involved in one organization, it greatly increases the probability of further clan involvement.

52. *Foreign Report*, December 10, 1987, p. 4.

53. Laqueur, *The Age of Terrorism*, p. 287.

54. *New York Times*, September 13, 1986.

55. *Wall Street Journal*, January 2, 1986, p. 15.

56. *New York Times*, November 12, 1989, p. 26.

57. *New York Times*, November 28, 1989, p. 20.

58. *Washington Times*, November 29, 1989.

59. *New York Times*, November 28, 1989, p. 1.

60. *Washington Times*, November 29, 1989.

Europe's New Right

With glib and presentable leaders, the extremists take their agenda into the political mainstream

The press calls him a "Yuppie fascist." Bronzed, handsome and eloquent, Jörg Haider, 42, heads the Freedom Party of Austria, a fast-growing right-wing movement that plays on the country's fears of being swamped by immigrants from Eastern Europe. "We talk about things that citizens don't have the courage to express openly and honestly," Haider tells a gathering of businessmen at a Vienna hotel. "We violate social taboos and create a climate for reform." For an hour he dazzles his audience with references to Max Weber, Henry Kissinger and Aleksandr Solzhenitsyn, among others. But in less polished moments, Haider's vocabulary might as well be drawn from Goebbels's dictionary. Political problems should be given a "final solution." His opponents face "total war."

In his mercurial way, by turns glib and menacing, Haider epitomizes Europe's new breed of upscale, far-right politicians. Compared with the bullies of the past, today's xenophobes like France's Jean-Marie Le Pen and Germany's Franz Schönhuber and populists like Italy's Umberto Bossi tend to be articulate and relatively presentable. Their message is authoritarian and sometimes racist. But they speak for great numbers of Europeans who have lost faith in more moderate political parties, who are disoriented by post-communist upheavals and who fear interlopers from other countries and other cultures. The threat of alien "otherness" is a potent right-wing message that has moved onto the agenda of mainstream politics.

In recent months, far-right parties have scored striking advances in city and regional elections in Germany, France, Italy, Austria, Belgium and Denmark. Moderate politicians don't know how to respond effectively. German Chancellor Helmut Kohl keeps insisting that "Germany is not an immigration country" when in fact it is deluged with refugees. Former French president Valéry Giscard d'Estaing, a centrist leader, complained recently about an "invasion" of foreigners and said the law should be changed so that citizenship would be given only to children of French parents, and not to children born on French soil to foreign parents. "The French Socialists are speaking like the French conservatives did five years ago, and the French conservatives are sounding like the ultra right did," says Anton Pelinka, director of Vienna's Institute for Conflict Research. "The whole political spectrum has shifted to the right."

Storm troopers: Even as their ideas move into the mainstream, some far-right politicians quietly maintain ties to the neo-Nazi "skinheads" who are responsible for widespread violence against outsiders (see box). In Germany, where the skinheads are most active, low-level functionaries of Schönhuber's Republican Party and the German People's Union, another far-right organization, hang out at skinhead clubs, organize and participate in marches, and offer odd jobs to the storm troopers. In Austria, Haider stays away from the neo-Nazis and professes a distaste for violence. But many officials of his own party have had contacts with the neo-Nazi National Party of Germany. Haider's confidant Andreas Mölzer, the Freedom Party political and ideology director, used to publish a magazine that described the Holocaust as "a lie without end." And Haider himself can find a kind word for fascism. When a parliamentary heckler compared his economic theories to those of Adolf Hitler, Haider slashed back: "Well at least in the Third Reich they had an orderly employment policy!"

One irony of the far-right resurgence in Europe is that many countries, including Germany and France, have largely closed the door on non-European immigration for more than 15 years. Apart from a small number of legal and illegal immigrants, most of the "aliens" who now arouse such complaints are citizens, the descendants of earlier immigrants and guest workers from the Middle East, Africa and Asia. So far, the main problem is race, not immigration. The "outsiders" look, talk and worship differently; Jacques Chirac, the conservative mayor of Paris, points out that they even have "smells" of their own.

Now, with the collapse of communism, Western Europe is battening down for a new round of immigration from Eastern Europe. The predicted tidal wave of refugees hasn't materialized yet. But at a time of economic stress and high unemployment, any new arrivals will be resented—even ethnic Germans who want to settle in Germany. This year Germany expects 400,000 would-be immigrants to apply for residence under a law that grants asylum to the victims of oppression. As in the United States, many citizens complain that the refugees are fleeing economic hardship, not tyranny, and should be kicked out.

Eventually, 95 percent of the applicants will be rejected, but many will stay on for years while their claims are processed. Because of widespread abuse, Germany is expected to scrap the asylum policy soon. Still, many people believe that fraudulent refugees benefit from favoritism. "People who claim to be politically persecuted get an apartment right away," insists Werner Rutschman, who lives in a Stuttgart suburb where 30 percent of the electorate voted Republican last month. "Our children will need apartments. Are they supposed to immigrate to the United States to find one?"

Most far-right voters are not fascists—or even right wingers, necessarily. "They are unhappy people, victims of cultivated fear," says Nazi-hunter Simon Wiesenthal. Few Italians want to bring back Mussolini; only about 6 percent of them voted for his granddaughter Alessandra's party this month. But many are fed up with the ineptness and corruption of Italy's coalitions. In Germany, the Federal Office for the Protection of the Constitution estimates that 35,000 people belong to extreme right-wing organizations, a figure that has increased only slightly in recent years. But in a single German state, Baden-Württemberg, 530,000 people voted last month for the Republican Party, which produced a racist campaign poster showing stereotyped Africans, Arabs and Chinese tumbling out of a boat labeled the "Ark of Germany."

Although there are politically significant far-right parties in most countries of Western Europe (Britain and Portugal are the most notable exceptions), their politics are less nationalistic than regional—sometimes almost tribal. Says Le Pen: "I prefer my daughters to my nieces, my nieces to my cousins, my cousins to my neighbors, my neighbors to my fellow citizens, my fellow citizens to foreigners. What's wrong with that?" Le Pen's National Front appeals mainly to the anti-big-government strain that has been a constant in French politics

for centuries. In Belgium, the Flemish Bloc, which won 25 percent of the seats on the Antwerp city council last November, is a new manifestation of the ancient hatred for French-speaking Walloons. Like Flemish separatists of the 1930s, the party is unabashedly anti-Semitic and authoritarian. Bossi's Lombard League, based in northern Italy, likes to take swipes at "foreigners" (including southern Italians), but its main demand is for regional autonomy.

'Unity Mensch': According to a recent French study, far-right voters are likely to live near, but not in, racially mixed areas. They may feel threatened by change they see bearing down on them. They complain about cultural diversity, which they think is being imposed upon them by their own central governments and by the European Community (EC). For some, America is a favorite whipping boy. They use "New York" as a code word for the supposed horrors of a multicultural society. Washington is assumed to be in the grip of the "Jewish lobby." Brussels, the home of the EC bureaucracy, is for them another symbol of what's wrong with the world. Haider rails

against the "European-unity Mensch," a homogenizing agent that he compares to the "multiethnic experimentation" in the former Soviet Union.

What the far-right parties and their supporters overlook is that even the most homogeneous European countries have long since crossed the multicultural Rubicon. Homogeneity ended when colonialism began and technology started to shrink the world. It is too late now for cultural purity, even on a local scale. "Europeans are used to sending émigrés out into the world, not accepting immigrants from elsewhere," says Willibald Pahr, Austria's commissioner for refugees and migration. "For European governments to undo centuries of practice and accept that there is immigration into Europe, and that it will continue whether they like it or not, requires political courage." The far right will continue to grind its ethnic ax, as it has done for decades. The courage to resist must come from leaders in the political mainstream.

KAREN BRESLAU *in Vienna with*
SCOTT SULLIVAN *in Paris and bureau reports*

Teaching Sensitivity to Skinheads

It's not exactly the neighborhood crowd from an Andy Hardy movie. These shaven-headed kids are in black pants and jackboots—a familiar sight these days in Marzahn, a suburb of east Berlin. They used to be far more likely to throw a Molotov cocktail than put on a show. Now, at 5 in the afternoon, they're sitting around drinking beer and schnapps. The club—a drab room with broken windows in a low concrete building, once the hangout of the local communist youth—offers them a place to reconsider and, perhaps, reform their lives. Progress is slow. "I'm against foreigners, against pseudo asylum seekers, against the German past being dragged through the dirt," says Michael Stegemann, 18, who claims he lost his job as a

shoemaker because he is a skinhead. Stegemann is one of about 30 young people, mostly teens, who are part of project Roots, a government-backed program to purge neo-Nazi violence through re-education.

It's a daunting job. "All of them have had encounters with the police," concedes Michael Wieczorek, 37, the social worker in charge of Roots. One club member tried to throw a man from Mozambique from a streetcar. Almost all are unemployed and undereducated, united in hatred for the guest workers and asylum seekers they blame for all their woes. But Wieczorek believes these kids are salvageable; he says few of them understand, much less hew, to extreme-right-wing ideology. That makes it somewhat easier to inch toward Roots's

goals: to stop the violence, find jobs or training and wean the kids from neo-Nazism.

After six months, Roots has had some success in curbing the worst savagery. "They used to drink from morning till night and beat up anyone they didn't like," says Wieczorek. "That would never happen here now." The threat of taking away the club is one deterrent. But Wieczorek has also tried to turn confrontation into communication. Recently, he brought a group of young Swedes to the club. At first a fight nearly broke out. But things calmed down, and the two radically opposed groups held a three-and-a-half-hour talk that ended with an invitation to visit Sweden. Local jobs, while scarce, can be had. Some kids earn three marks an hour gar-

dening around the clubhouse; others may find work sprucing up Marzahn.

Instilling a spirit of tolerance is proving a lot harder. "It has to be done in very, very small steps," says Wieczorek. Among the first: soccer tournaments against teams of Turks, Vietnamese and Russians. More ambitious is an upcoming trip to Morocco, where the kids will be forced to depend on an alien culture—and to defend *themselves* as foreigners. Some lessons are starting to sink in: last week the group voted not to celebrate Hitler's birthday and, instead, will host a festival for the children of Marzahn. Says Rene Noack, 16, "People will see that we are skinheads doing something constructive." That would be a first.

TOM POST *with*
THERESA WALDROP *in Berlin*

The New Sound of Hate

In Europe, a Generation of Neo-Fascists Use Music to Spread Its Message

Sharon Waxman

Special to The Washington Post

Ipswich, England, 1988: An unpredictable strobe illuminates a stage in what looks like a cellar; the flashing light veers wildly, and a spurt of white smoke clears to reveal the tops of four bald heads, faces tipped down at their instruments.

Interference, amplifier static—loud—then the music begins with a crash as all the instruments—lead and bass guitar, drums and Kev at the microphone with a vengeance—compete for attention to a post-punk beat with a heavy metal influence.

The music isn't very good, but at least it has a beat and some chords. It is Kev who makes the difference in the group Condemned 84; he grasps the microphone with two desperate hands and shoves it right up against his mouth, shouting through a series of songs, all with approximately the same lyrics:

"We must stay together," he howls. "We must stay together." Then: "We will fight—we'll never give in. We will win the fight. We will never die . . ."

Then: "The Youth . . . Go . . . March . . . Ing . . . In . . ." Here the skinheads in the audience grab the microphone to sing along: "The Youth Go Marching In!"

Kev is protected at the edge of the dance floor by two enormous skinheads, Stone-faced, they shove back members of the small crowd—maybe 30 people—who keep falling forward, dancing or drunk. There is one woman, shaved bald except for a few spikes of blond hair paralyzed upward, smoking near the stage.

Fans punch the air with excitement and chant along, "We will win! Never die!" Kev ends the concert hoisted on the shoulders of his stamping friends. "We will never die—die—die!"

The Condemned 84 concert is sold on video under the counter at a store near London's Piccadilly Circus; it is black-and-white, mostly out of focus. It looks as though it might be a forgotten newsreel from the 1940s. But people buy it—even at \$30. It is part of an underground neo-Nazi culture flourishing in the blush of a new Europe.

Bound by common dress, trademark music, symbols and signs, Europe's young neo-fascists share neither a specific creed nor any particular goal, but something far more visceral and, no doubt, more dangerous: hatred.

European police count the active members of the neo-fascist youth movement as no more than 10,000; watchdog groups say it's more like 100,000. But both agree that here in Europe, in the birthplace of fascism, it is both virulent and violent.

The movement has adherents in the United States, as well, with an estimated 3,000 racist skins. There are other American kids who shave their heads and call themselves SHARPS—"skinheads against racial prejudice."

In Europe, skinheads used to encompass rival political sensitivities, including kids who simply embraced punk rock or the ska music of the immigrant West Indian community. But today the movement has virtually been taken over by the neo-fascist right.

At skinhead concerts across the continent, the atmosphere is as tense as a tightly wound coil; the music lets loose a violence that rebounds against foreigners and symbols of things foreign. And sometimes the lyrics are more explicit than at the Ipswich concert, as in this song called "Bloodsucker" by the British skinhead band No Remorse:

> *Filthy little Asian*
> *With his corner shop*
> *Governmental help*
> *Gave him all he's got*
> *So do not buy his offers*
> *Burn them to the ground*
> *Ignore his pleas for mercy*
> *'Cause he puts you down*

Lyrics of this sort are illegal as incitements to racism in many countries, but recordings are widely distributed through catalogue sales by distributors in France, Germany and England.

Europe's two largest manufacturers and distributors, the German Rock O Rama and French Rebelles Europeenes, are also the main suppliers of music to the American neo-Nazi movement, whose members reportedly are not organized enough to produce their own.

Along with accompanying posters, neo-fascist magazines, T-shirts and other paraphernalia, the music is also sold at skinhead concerts, at stores around London's Carnaby Street and, increasingly, at rallies for extreme right political parties.

"It's a seller's market," said Tony Robson of Searchlight, a London based watchdog group. "When they're offering kids is a cultural scene. . . . The music is a way of bonding, and a way of bringing young kids into the movement. It's indoctrination, and it works. Every time there's a gig there's a spate of racial attacks."

"The role of skinhead music in the culture of skinheads is crucial," said Irwin Suall of the anti-Defamation League of B'nai B'rith in New York, which complains regularly to the German government about the production of such music.

"They don't go in for reading books and pamphlets, nor do they hold meetings as political organizations do. Their message is largely communicated through the music. It's the means by which they inculcate their views among their own people and among recruits, and in Rock O Rama there's an awful lot of antisemitism, racism and advocacy of violence," Suall said.

British police reported 70,000 racial incidents last year. At a 1988 skinhead concert in Brest, France, two Guadeloupans and two Indonesians were attacked, a pattern followed all around Europe. Several members of the band Skrewdriver are in Germany's Mannheim prison for attempting to murder someone in Cottbus in former East Germany after a skinhead concert late last year.

The same is true in the United States; two skinheads were convicted of first-degree murder for stomping a social worker to death in Pittsburgh in August 1989. Both men, James Brough and Richard Gribble, played in local skinhead bands.

There is nothing new in youth turning to music—loud, cacophonous music—as an expression of rebellion and frustration. But the sound of Europe's skinheads has ominous undertones.

With the collapse of ideology and the arrival of a borderless Europe, with the lack of economic opportunity for many East European youth and with Europe's historical precedents of fascism, experts say the time is ripe for the appeal of an ordered, illicit neo-Nazism.

Searchlight estimates that there is one skinhead concert a month somewhere in Europe, with several hundred in attendance. The dates, times and places are passed by word of mouth. Organizers rent halls under false names, and in England may spread the word to meet at London's Euston Station at a particular time; from there they leave to concerts outside the city where police surveillance is less prevalent.

It is in Germany and Eastern Europe where the movement, feeding on post-communist discontent, seems to be gaining the most adherents. While many skinheads are poor and unemployed—as in Dresden, where there are an estimated 2,000—much of the leadership tends to come from families of senior ex-communist officials. Police admit they have trouble monitoring neo-fascists in that part of the country, where the security apparatus is understaffed and underfunded.

In Germany, neo-Nazi groups include the German National Front and the German Alliance. "Wiking Jugend" (Viking Youth) is one non-skinhead, neo-Nazi faction. "They produce all kinds of propaganda material—Holocaust denial material, new fascist literature. They try to act like a new nationalist intelligentsia," said Michael Schmidt, a German journalist who investigates the pro-Nazi movement. Hitlerite material circulates freely in their circles, he said.

Hungary now produces one of the most professional of neo-Nazi fanzines, as they call their magazines. Panon Bulldog is a full-color publication, borrowing the name "Bulldog" from the youth wing of the British extremist National Front.

Searchlight, which says it has informants inside the neo-Nazi cultural scene, claims that orders from Eastern Europe for skinhead music has skyrocketed in the past two years to hundreds of thousands of recordings annually, mostly compact discs distributed by the Rebelles Europeenes, a recording and distribution company based in Brest. Rock O Rama is based in Hamburg and Frankfurt.

Others estimate sales Europewide at a much more modest several thousand.

Rebelles Europeenes, created in 1987 by the openly fascist Gael Bodilis, sells hate music in a half-dozen languages including German, Swedish and Italian. In one eight-page catalogue, you can order $18 compact discs by groups like the Klansmen ("Fetch the Rope"), Skrewdriver ("Boots and Braces" and "Hail the New Dawn") and the LP of No Remorse, "We Rise Again."

In an interview with the French magazine L'Evenement du Jeudi, Bodilis identified himself as "a nationalist revolutionary in battle against a multi-cultural society that is being imposed on us." He affirmed that he sold music because it was the best way to transmit his ideology.

French police said they knew nothing of Rebelles Europeenes, and the vice minister for rock and variety at the Culture Ministry, Bruno Lion, said he had tried to investigate the distributor, without success. "If the lyrics are openly racist it is against the law," said Lion. Repeated attempts to reach Bodilis were unsuccessful.

Music is only one part of the cultural scene. A recent issue of the British fanzine Blood and Honour, its cover emblazoned with a large swastika, featured pictures of a Skrewdriver gig in Stuttgart in 1991, notices for "an international meeting in memory of Rudolf Hess" in Wunsiedel, Germany, and "a Greeting from Polish skinhead band called 'Honour.' Another link in the chain of National Socialists spreading the word of White Power . . ."

Like other neo-fascists who have had brushes with the law, the brother of Blood and Honour's editor Neil Parish, David Parish, is awaiting trial for attacks against foreigners in Bedford, England, after a skinhead concert early this year.

Despite the differences in language and the tiny size of many of these groups, there are common codes and a uniform. Skinheads wear mainly black clothes, bomber jackets, and lace-up, leather Doc Martens boots. They often have swastika tattoos. The Viking Youth wear blueshirts, black trousers and Nazi symbols.

Increasingly bold youth now greet each other with "Sieg Heil," a sign of their growing confidence. In previous years they would say, "HH," for "Heil Hitler," or the even more obscure "88"—twice the eighth letter of the alphabet, H. Instead of a full hand salute, illegal in Germany, youth often use three fingers, forming a "w" for *widerstand*, German for resistance.

Instead of the swastika, their publications and T-shirts often feature arrows, fish or the Odal cross—rings with a cross—all Nordic, Teutonic symbols that recall warrior cultures. Other symbols include hybrids of the swastika, such as the three-sevens symbol of the pro-apartheid Afrikaner Resistance Movement.

Because of the obscurity of many of these signs, police say they can do little against such youths. "The groups are not illegal because we believe it is better to find them than to forbid them. We know where they are and who they are said Hans-Gert Lange, of Germany's Office of Constitutional Protection. "The songs are not normally forbidden, unless they are racially offensive."

Indeed, most of the songs use a sort of code language, talking about conquest, rising again and crushing the opposition. In Ipswich, it was a code that they all understood and sang together in blind, desperate faith: "We will never die—die—die . . ."

A Triangle of Ethnic Struggle

Northern Ireland's 'Troubles' Become A Fact of Life

Glenn Frankel

Washington Post Foreign Service

Freelance writer Malachi O'Doherty contributed to this article.

BELFAST, Northern Ireland—"Is that him?" demanded the Protestant gunman as he scrambled off the back of the motorbike one evening last October and took aim at Pearse McKenna's head.

The first bullet grazed McKenna's scalp. The second caught him in the lower back as he dived behind a parked bakery truck. He rolled under the truck and waited for the gunman to finish the job.

"I could see the feet of the man coming after me, walking around the lorry looking for me," McKenna would later recall. He escaped death only because the driver of the motorbike panicked and called the gunman back.

McKenna, who is Catholic, became yet another casualty in the bloodiest year of political violence here since 1982.

But McKenna's shooting also illustrated just how routine the killings have become and how embedded they are in the daily life of this province.

An outspoken union shop steward in a predominantly Protestant bakery, McKenna had objected to the display of British flags inside the workplace in violation of a local code. In many other countries, the dispute would have been settled on the shop floor or in court. But in Belfast, where word soon filtered to the neighborhood that a Catholic had insulted the Union Jack, it was settled on the street by a man with a gun.

After 23 years of political violence known here as "The Troubles," most people decry sectarian killing—including some of those actively involved in it. But many have become resigned to it as a permanent part of the status quo. And behind their acceptance is

Northern Ireland's darkest secret: that the status quo is tolerated because it serves, in some way, many interests in this messy but manageable little war.

Even in a bad year, the dead number only about half of those killed in car accidents. The violence provides the rationale for more than 20,000 jobs in the security forces here, most of which go to Protestants. It is at the root of more than $3 billion per year in subsidies that cushion Britain's poorest province from the vicissitudes of recession. And local leaders invoke it to hold together fraying constituencies by giving the people something to fear and unite against.

"You're safer here than you are on the streets of France or the sidewalks of New York," says Tom Hadden, a prominent political scientist and commentator. "For many people life is quite good, especially if you're a Protestant. The status quo is not comfortable, but it's livable. So there's no great hurry to do anything. Everyone says we don't have to make a deal now."

Northern Ireland has taken its place alongside Israel and South Africa as part of an Iron Triangle of protracted ethnic struggle. For years these trouble spots have seemed immune to efforts to resolve the fundamental conflict at the heart of each, even though political moves toward peace are now being pursued in South Africa and the Middle East.

Diplomats have devised peace plans, church leaders have bemoaned the violence, human rights groups have exposed abuses; but none has unlocked what writer Albert Camus called the "fatal embrace" of two peoples—Protestants and Catholics, Israelis and Palestinians, whites and blacks—sealed by history and hatred, unable to live together or apart.

With the end of the Cold War, this sort of intractable ethnic conflict seems, if anything, to be spreading. In places as far removed as Canada, Yugoslavia, Liberia, Sri Lanka and the now-defunct Soviet Union, rival ethnic and religious forces are ripping societies apart at their seams. In this sense, Northern Ireland, Israel and South Africa are not stubborn exceptions to the new global order but harbingers of things to come.

"We're in an era when proxy wars between the superpowers are coming to an end and the kind of communal violence epitomized by Northern Ireland, South Africa and Israel is taking their place," says Aryeh Neier, executive director of the New York-based Human Rights Watch. "In some ways it's a much more dangerous era because ideological conflict you can mediate, while communal conflict is often seen as non-negotiable."

As a foreign correspondent for The Washington Post, I have spent most of the past decade covering the triangle and been struck over and over again by the echoes among the three. The analogy is tricky because each is historically and sociologically unique. But their dilemmas and evasions, their sense of siege and of entrapment in a winner-takes-all contest, their dreams and their nightmares are all in a fundamental way the same. And they are not only political struggles but also personal ones, in which human emotions such as pride, anger, fear and humiliation play a crucial role.*

It begins in Northern Ireland, where Winston Churchill wrote after the end of World War I: "The integrity of their quarrel is one of the few institutions that has been unaltered in the cataclysm which has swept the world."

Churchill's words still echo down the grimy streets of West Belfast, the modern locale for a struggle between the British and the Irish that began centuries ago. Since 1969, when civil strife broke out anew between the Protestant majority and Catholics in the province, the IRA has waged a violent campaign to oust British forces and reunite Northern Ireland with the overwhelmingly Catholic republic to the south. Twenty-three years and nearly 3,000 deaths later, gunmen from the IRA and from their Protestant paramilitary opponents are still trading bombs and bullets with each other and with British security forces.

While the Berlin Wall and hundreds of miles of the former Iron Curtain have come tumbling down, the urban landscape in the working-class Protestant and Catholic neighborhoods here is still dominated by 60-foot-high watchtowers, reinforced concrete-and-steel security walls and razor-wire fences.

Security forces see the area as another country, enemy territory where death waits around the next corner. Soldiers patrol in "sticks" of 10, routinely aiming their automatic rifles at pedestrians and cars in anticipation of ambush. Police stations bristle with cameras and protective barriers, military helicopters hover overhead, and dozens of checkpoints spring up and disappear throughout the day.

Yet the bombers get through. The outlawed IRA recently launched a new bombing spree in downtown Belfast that featured a 600-pound car bomb that crumpled the front of the city's largest hotel and ripped the roof off the local opera house. It was the kind of explosion Belfastians had not seen for years, and Christmas shoppers strolled past Glengall Street for weeks for a glimpse of the gaping crater.

"The outlawed IRA recently launched a new bombing spree in downtown Belfast that featured a 600-pound car bomb.

A stream of bitter humor is also part of the landscape. The 20-foot-high barrier dividing Catholic Clonard from Protestant Shankill is called the "Peace Line." A pub near the spot where two British soldiers were dragged from their cars during a Catholic political funeral, beaten senseless and then shot in the head, is known locally as "The Corporals' Rest." Political views often are whispered even in the privacy of one's own home.

"Everything seems hunky-dory on the outside, but you scratch the surface and it's a real nightmare," says Peter Madden, a Catholic civil rights lawyer whose law partner, Patrick Finucane, was gunned down two years ago by a hit man who has never been arrested.

"The media try to portray this place as a normal society. The news bulletin starts with someone's killing but it ends with a funny anecdote. On the surface, people are living in modern times, but they're still passing down history from generation to generation. It's ingrained and it's frightening."

Sinn Fein president Gerry Adams, leader of the legal, political wing of the IRA, says people are too quick to dwell on what he calls "the politics of the last atrocity" and ignore the genuine political grievances of Catholics who constitute some 40 percent of the population. But the violence has its own momentum and its own justification. Gunmen kill because they've always killed—it's gone on for so long that many supporters don't even seem to think about it, let alone bother to justify it.

A constant flow of martyrs' blood drenches the ground. The IRA's newest tactic was to target a hospital; two months ago it bombed the military wing of a Belfast hospital, killing two soldiers and re-injuring a

[*Editor's note: Articles on Israel and South Africa can be found in the *Washington Post*, February 17–23, 1992, pp. 8–11.]

number of convalescing ones. A Protestant hit man revived an older method of attack three days before Christmas when he emptied most of his pistol into a crowded Catholic pub, then stood over a wounded 8-year-old boy and shot him in the head.

The conflict claims its victims not only among the dead and wounded but also among those traumatized by years of violence. People generally look older than their years. They smoke too much and drink too much, laugh too loudly and too nervously. "You have to look at Northern Ireland as an education in human nature," says Mina Wardle. "Otherwise, it'll drive you crazy."

"A Protestant hit man revived an older method of attack . . . when he emptied most of his pistol into a crowded Catholic pub.

Wardle lives on the Protestant side of the Peace Line in a tidy, red-brick row house on Argyle Street. Over the years she has been assaulted by armed men, cradled a dying taxi driver in her arms after a car bomb blew up his cab, and endured four armed robberies, a series of firebombs and the abduction of her husband by Protestant gunmen.

Outgoing and ebullient, Wardle became dependent on tranquilizers and developed severe agoraphobia—she refused to leave her house for seven months. "I felt if I sat in here for the rest of my life no one could harm me," she recalls, gently laughing at the notion.

On trips to the hospital she discovered dozens of other women suffering the same anxiety. Now she helps operate a counseling service that provides discussion groups and therapy for women whose life stories are a chronicle of human erosion: Many have had children killed or husbands jailed or lost limbs for a cause few understand and even fewer believe in.

Wardle says most of the people in her neighborhood feel betrayed, both by a British government that they believe finds Northern Ireland an unpleasant inconvenience and by their own leaders, whom they see as lacking the imagination or courage to take risks and make changes.

"You feel trapped between things," she says. "You're British but you're peculiarly Irish. Both governments deny you. The British would give this lot away tomorrow, but Dublin won't take it. We're an embarrassment to everyone."

It is only a few blocks from Wardle's home to the anonymous, whitewashed row house of Mary Nolan on Ballymurphy Road in one of West Belfast's Catholic public housing projects. This is one of the city's most "active" neighborhoods, where attacks on police and soldiers by the IRA are frequent and deadly. The male

unemployment rate here is estimated at 85 percent, and violence and poverty are so raw that at one time Mother Teresa felt compelled to leave the slums of Calcutta for several months to set up a mission here.

Mary Nolan and her husband, Kevin, are involved in republican causes and they estimate their house has been searched by security forces more than 25 times over the past decade. The searchers are looking for guns, batteries, tools or anything else that could be used to ambush a patrol or build a homemade bomb. They have pulled up floorboards, ripped open walls, dismantled the brick fireplace, torn open the staircase and the kitchen cupboard, even removed the upstairs toilet bowl and run sniffer dogs throughout the four-bedroom house. That they have never found any weapons does not seem to dull their ardor.

"It's not your home anymore," Mary Nolan says. "They come when they like. You have no safeguard and no protection. It leaves a mental scar. My nerves are always shaking."

At one point, she says, she threw out her rubber kitchen gloves because the police said they could be used to handle explosives. One day, when her 9-year-old son, Francis, came home with a toy walkie-talkie, "I jumped. I told him, 'Get that thing out of here.'"

Although they are both victims of the violence, Mina Wardle and Mary Nolan are sealed off from each other geographically and politically. There is no hatred between them, but neither is there much sympathy. Each is too busy coping with her own losses to heed those of someone living on the other side of the Peace Wall.

They are also sealed off from political leaders who could negotiate an end to the conflict. Wardle cannot compel Protestant politicians to talk with Catholics, and Nolan cannot persuade the IRA to suspend armed struggle.

"The politicians have bodyguards to protect them," says Mina Wardle. "Why should they care what happens to people like us?"

When it comes to the politics of violence in Northern Ireland, few hands are completely clean. The IRA clings to armed struggle because it says that is the only way of forcing the British to leave the province. But two decades of violence have not succeeded, and even some supporters admit that the armed struggle gives the IRA power and leverage within the Catholic community it otherwise would lack.

The moderate, predominantly Catholic Social Democratic and Labor party led by John Hume opposes the IRA. But it too enjoys political clout and attention in places like London, Dublin and Washington that it might not merit were Northern Ireland just another British province with ordinary problems.

Similarly, the two main Protestant parties led by Ian Paisley and James Molyneaux maintain much of their own leverage through frequent denunciations of the IRA. Hume often quips that if Unionists lost the word "no" from their vocabulary, they would be struck dumb.

The only major player who seems to draw little or nothing from the present arrangement is the British government. It pays out more than $3 billion per year in subsidies for security and economic development in the province and is frequently embarrassed when human rights groups, such as Amnesty International and Helsinki Watch, spotlight abuses by security forces and allegations of links with Protestant death squads. The British public is equally unimpressed: Although polls consistently show a clear majority in favor of military withdrawal, the issue hardly registers in electoral politics.

But Britain does not pull out. That is partly because of domestic politics; both the ruling Conservatives and opposition Labor Party would be badly split by such a move. And it is partly because the British fear that the army's departure could lead to a bloodbath much worse than the violence that brought troops there in the first place in 1969.

Instead, Britain works the diplomatic margins. Last year, Northern Ireland Secretary Peter Brooke succeeded in bringing together Protestant and Catholic political leaders, excluding IRA supporters, for the first formal talks in 16 years. Within weeks, the talks broke down over procedural issues. Nonetheless, Brooke is trying again. He has, officials contend, no other choice.

"Getting out is not really an option," says a senior civil servant. "Northern Ireland doesn't really impinge on the consciousness of the mainland. The costs are not unbearable. The British public is actually pretty stolid about the whole thing. Even when the IRA attacks targets in Britain, the response isn't, 'Let's rid ourselves of this problem,' but rather, 'Let's sort these characters out.'"

A recent edition of Republican News, the newspaper of Sinn Fein, the legal political wing of the IRA, contained a moving tribute to Patricia Black-Donnelly. She was one of two IRA "volunteers" killed last December in the English town of St. Albans when the bomb they were rigging went off prematurely outside a packed concert hall. British officials called them "evil and wicked" terrorists.

The article described her childhood in West Belfast, her hatred of Britain's "army of occupation" and her secret work as an IRA intelligence operative. It portrayed her as a warm, vibrant person: "She loved to laugh, she loved to dance and those who knew her recall her smile and her generosity of spirit."

But perhaps the most poignant fact was that Patricia Black-Donnelly was only 18 years old. She was born four years after "The Troubles" began. Her anger and her hatred were those of a whole new generation of Northern Ireland children who were born into the conflict and are just now coming of age. And her death was a warning, like a bell tolling in a graveyard, of a war without end.

Peru's rebels buck trend as troop strength grows

Sam Dillon

Herald Staff Writer

LIMA, Peru—For weeks, Shining Path guerrillas chipped away with sledge hammers and chisels at the underside of a bridge in a remote jungle northeast of Lima. Finally, the structure collapsed under a passing bus, killing the driver.

Often unorthodox, frequently bizarre, always fanatical, Peru's Maoist insurgents have been chipping away at the girders of power in this Andean country for more than a decade. Applying the same tactical pragmatism and strategic patience they brought to bear against that jungle bridge, they are advancing all across Peru.

"Shining Path is steadily building strength. The war is spreading," said Carlos Tapia, a former socialist congressmen who studies Shining Path.

With guerrillas laying down their arms elsewhere in Latin America and communism in collapse, Shining Path may be the only communist insurgency in the world that is gaining ground.

In Lima, Shining Path cadres are using political persuasion and murder to extend their control over thousands of shantytown dwellers. In the countryside, guerrilla columns have moved into vast new zones and are demonstrating destructive new combat proficiency. For the first time, they have claimed responsibility for shooting down a U.S. helicopter, killing three American contract drug agents.

In one two-week period in January, Shining Path combatants blew up a government convoy along a coastal highway, killing 14 soldiers; ambushed an army patrol in a northern jungle, killing six and wounding five; and razed an Andean military outpost, killing four soldiers. They also murdered half a dozen police, dynamited a freight train, a town hall and a government bank, and stole 150 boxes of dynamite in a raid on a mining town.

In recent weeks, President Alberto Fujimori has seemed to waken to the mounting threat. After taking office in August 1990, Fujimori devoted his first year to stabilizing Peru's chaotic economy and combating corruption, efforts that are beginning to bear fruit (monthly inflation is down from 30 percent to 4 percent) and has won broad support. In some mountain areas, Fujimori has recently armed civil defense patrols with shotguns, and they have appeared to drive the guerrillas back.

Now Fujimori is seeking legislative approval for dozens of presidential decrees that give sweeping—some say dictatorial—powers to the military for a nationwide counterinsurgency crackdown. That suggests that 1992, the 12th year of the *guerra popular* that has left 25,000 dead, could bring a climactic showdown.

Shining Path leaders have vowed to take power in Peru before the end of the century. Fujimori has sworn to defeat the insurgency before his term ends in 1995.

Conditions ideal for rebels

Abimael Guzman, a philosophy professor in the Andean university town of Ayacucho, founded the "Communist Party of Peru—Shining Path," modeling it after Mao Zedong's peasant-based Chinese party, and after years of underground organizing, sent it to war in 1980.

In the decade since, the 84,000 man Peruvian army has had little counterinsurgency success, despite repeated Draconian sweeps through the highlands. One reason is that Peru's sweeping expanses and rough terrain offer ideal conditions for guerrilla warfare: Peru is larger than America's entire eastern seaboard from Florida to Maine.

Last year, Shining Path's estimated 3,500 combatants moved into four new departments, including northern Piura, where they opened a corridor into neighboring Ecuador to match the transportation route they had already forged into Bolivia. Today they operate freely in 19 of Peru's 24 departments.

'Support bases'

In many zones they have destroyed the schools, clinics, postal agencies and other offices that once meant government to rural residents. They have murdered more than 250 mayors and other local officials in three years, according to government figures.

In two dozen "support bases," Shining Path has set up parallel provincial governments, where a estimated 4,000 full-time party functionaries arrest drunks, marry lovers and carry out other administrative functions. Most of these are tiny, remote pockets of Maoist control. But in the Huallaga Valley northeast of Lima—a region three times the size of El Salvador that is the world's largest coca producing area—Shining Path regulates the lucrative drug trade.

A correspondent for the Shining Path newspaper, El Diario, toured the Huallaga Valley recently and wrote of tilling the fields with guerrilla fighters, retreating into the jungle at the approach of a U.S. helicopter, attending an insurgent theater, and watching party executioners "annihilate" two men accused of theft and a woman accused of spying on the party by "sexually tempting" local cadres.

Academic dispute

Last year the party declared that its control of rural Peru was sufficient to warrant a new organizing offensive in Lima itself. That sparked an academic

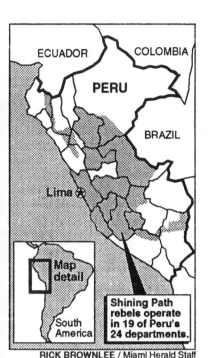

ECUADOR
COLOMBIA
PERU
BRAZIL
Lima
Map
detail
South
America
Shining Path
rebels operate
in 19 of Peru's
24 departments.

RICK BROWNLEE / Miami Herald Staff

dispute, with some who study Shining Path saying Guzman has radically altered his long-time strategy.

Cynthia McClintock, a political science professor at George Washington University, disagreed: "In their ideology they say they will build rural bases and use them to surround and asphyxiate Lima. And that's what they've done. They've fulfilled their geographic plan," she said.

In Lima, the insurgents aim to control slums surrounding strategic infrastructure—the high-tension electricity lines that drive industry, the rivers that channel water, the roads that deliver food. A journalist who writes for the party paper boasted in an interview that Lima's international airport is "very vulnerable" to a commando attack from the shantytowns surrounding it.

Swamp of despair

Why does anyone join? A reporter got a clue during a visit to the Miguel Castro penitentiary hugging a range of stony foothills at the edge of Lima. Built to house 900, the jail is packed with nearly 2,000 desperate inmates, some of whom sleep on the bare dirt for lack of bunks. A reporter had to elbow his way past pleading men with open sores and tiptoe across floors flooded with urine and feces.

But cellblock 1A, housing 120

women accused as terrorists, was a world apart. In a spotless dining hall, visitors were served a tasty meal of pasta and cinnamon tea. Outside, in a meticulously swept courtyard, 40 *camaradas* shook their fists toward a crimson flag, chanting "Long live the ideological grandeur of Marxism-Leninism-Maoism!" Later, a sober party cadre who is a former engineering student said of her incarceration: "Prison is just one luminous trench in a life of class warfare."

In a swamp of degradation and despair, cellblock 1A was an island of discipline and hope. And that's what Shining Path offers to residents of Lima's dirt-track slums, where United Nations officials estimate that three million of the capital's 5.8 million people live in "absolute misery."

Peru's per capita monthly income, about $56, is shrinking, despite the country's modest economic growth. Nine of 10 Peruvians can't find a job in their profession. Millions of poor pick through trash to survive. In this bleak environment, Shining Path recruiters are targeting grass-roots leaders who run soup kitchens and other slum survival programs—many of them women—as well as war refugees and embittered teenagers.

Threat grows

An American priest complained about recent desertions from the sports program he runs for slum teens. "In three weeks, Shining Path wooed away the entire cream of my crop," the priest said.

"They're growing, clearing they're growing," said an aide to a prominent congressman who lives in the Lurigancho shantytown and is frightened by the insurgents' recent gains. "We hear them every dawn—angry adolescents chanting slogans."

Recruitment opens with persuasion and favors. But community leaders who resist the party's advances are in trouble.

Since Sept. 1, when Shining Path gunmen burst into a soup kitchen and shot to death Juana Sanchez, 44, who ran a maternal feeding program in the port of Callao, the party has executed at least seven grass-roots leaders. One was Doraliza Espejo, a 35-year-old mother of five, the leader of a neighborhood "Glass of Milk" feeding

program, shot because she helped the army distribute food along her street.

One recent killing came Jan. 19, when Nelly Torres, a street vendor, was forced to her knees in front of her 12-year-old son in the El Agustino neighborhood and shot. Her masked killers dismembered her body with a charge of dynamite.

Brutality backfiring?

Some say this brutality is backfiring. "These murders are showing people that Shining Path terrorizes not only the government, but also the poor," said Grimaldo Rios, a community organizer in the Lurigancho district. He said an anti-Sendero backlash appears to be developing in Lima's slums.

A similar reaction seems to be under way in parts of Peru's countryside, with peasants in many zones joining self-defense patrols. Sen. Enrique Bernales, chairman of the Senate committee that monitors the war, said that nearly 800 villages in four Andean departments have formed their own patrols, while the army has conscripted farmers into more than 500 others.

The patrols have dealt Shining Path some costly recent defeats. "But I've learned not to minimize Shining Path's capacity to survive and grow," Bernales said.

PERU VIOLENCE

Total dead '80-'91 24,900

1991 death toll

Suspected rebels	1,522
Civilians	1,287
Armed Forces	334
Narcotics traffickers	37
Total	**3,180**

Source: Defense Ministry, distributed by the Senate Committee on Violence

Prisoners accused as terrorists

1985	974
1986	432
1987	739
1988	716
1989	951
1990	1,124
1991	1,507

Source: Interior Ministry, distributed by the Senate Committee on Violence

State Terrorism and Dissent (Revolutionary) Terrorism

The application by the state apparatus of terrorist mechanisms is perhaps the most devastating of all forms of violence. In this sense, the twentieth century is the most terrorized in history. It was in our own century that it became technologically feasible for a government, if it chose to do so, to acquire all the instruments required to wreak total havoc on its own population. Nor is a government bent on terrorism required to restrict its activities to its own indigenous citizenry. State terrorism can be transported beyond the borders of its jurisdiction to targets hundreds or thousands of miles away.

There is a tragic irony to state terrorism in all of this. The purpose of the state is, after all, to safeguard and enhance the lives of the citizens who, in effect, created the state in the first place. Thus, state terrorism is the opposite of and is in blatant contradiction to this crucial mainstream of Western political thought. Not that terrorist governments care about such niceties. In fact, a government employing state terrorism may be doing so not so much in ignorance of Western traditions as because of its defiance and hostility to such traditions.

The first two articles in this unit make the point that state terrorism has the capacity to ruthlessly destroy perceived enemies to the regime, a capacity that is frequently acted on without reservation. "The State as Terrorist" provides a capsule summary of the variants (they range from bad to worse) and gradations of state terror. It is not at all uncommon for governments to resort to terror to remain in power, but they then proceed to follow state terror to its horrifying and even logical conclusion—genocide. Examples in the last years of the twentieth century abound and show no inclination of disappearing. Article 18 concentrates on the history of genocide and emphasizes how our own century, supposedly the most enlightened one in history, is perhaps the most depressing of all.

Articles 19 through 27 reveal the "top-down" nature of state terrorism. They also suggest that state terrorism is not a phenomenon that is limited to a particular geographical or political region. Terror can be institutionalized by governments on the Left or the Right, on any continent, by any race or religious persuasion, and even within some societies that normally follow democratic practices. For example, these articles include mention of terrorist activities committed by current regimes in Iran as well as in Central America, and East and Southeast Asia. What they also reveal is that different terrorist regimes often have different targets: Iraq is well known for going after entire communities such as the Kurds with its full military apparatus, whereas death squads in Guatemala tend to restrict their murder to several individuals at a time.

Articles 28–30 suggest further complications on the subject of state terrorism. From these essays we learn, for instance, that as harsh as the genocidal policies of the Pol Pot regime in Cambodia were toward the majority population group, they were even more devastating when applied to the ethnic minorities that made up 15 percent of the population. We also learn that state terrorism can be at least a regional phenomenon even in a democratic polity, and that governments can displace hundreds of thousands of people from their homes to unfamiliar and desolate areas.

Looking Ahead: Challenge Questions

What explains the tremendous lethality of state terrorism? How do governments get away with so much violence?

What are the different circumstances for state terror in Africa, Latin America, and East and Southeast Asia? In particular, what are the characteristics of groups that are singled out for terror?

How do governments justify their usage of extremely harsh repressive measures, and how can they be termed terrorist?

The State as Terrorist

Martin Slann

Various social sciences have sought to identify and characterize the psychology, ideology, and goals of political movements using terrorist activities. Usually, those activities seek to undermine and discredit a society's governing process by making millions of individuals aware that, even as political innocents, they are vulnerable to violence. What is often unclear or overlooked is that the government itself may be utilizing violence, at least partially, to achieve its goals. As John McCamant has put it, "One searches in vain through the thousands of articles and books written by political scientists, political sociologists, economists, and anthropologists for references to the awful and bloody deeds of governments and for explanations of how and why these deeds are done."[1] This chapter attempts to illuminate the more brutal and sustained features of state terrorism.

Characteristics of State Terrorism

The most notorious historical examples of state terrorism—Stalin's purges in the 1930s and the Nazi regime's atrocities (1933–1945)—are especially frightening because they are so recent and because they were among the most lethal: coercion by the state was unchecked even by the usual norms of common sense and political prudence.[2] In these, as in numerous other instances, terror became so politically useful it seemed to develop a reckless permanency of its own.[3] State terrorism becomes institutionalized when this occurs.

Even though, predictably, terrorist organizations have often referred to the governments they oppose as "terrorist"—for example, the IRA in Northern Ireland and the Basque ETA in Spain consider their targets to be aggressors and occupiers of an exploited nation—for the purposes of this essay, however, an acceptable definition of state terror is "the more precise and deliberate act of inflicting harm on an individual or group in order to change the nature of their behavior and/or instill fear in other individuals or groups."[4]

This definition was first applied to South Africa, and for good reason. The psychological dimensions of the South African government's apartheid policies are obvious and have been most pronounced in the country's educational system, where the African school-age population is made aware in numerous ways years after year of its inferior social and political position. Certainly, the government prefers this form of "psychological terrorism" to more violent forms of pressure. State terrorism, then, does not always manifest as physical violence, although the threat is always present. This is an advantage that terrorists operating without government sanction conspicuously lack.

The state as terrorist is not a new concept or phenomenon. Anarchists (who often take on the appearance of terrorists themselves) have argued for centuries that the state, in any form, is an unmitigated and unnatural evil; and that physically and psychologically, it is an intimidating apparatus capable of any outrage.[5] The anarchists' message, however, is difficult to publicize, in part because the state most often controls the communications network. After all, "when state terrorism surfaces the government is usually quick in censoring the media. The net effect is an imbalance in the news coverage of terrorism. Informed only by the mass media, the average news consumer gets the impression of a unilateral upsurge in mainly left-wing insurgent terrorism,"[6] even though state terrorism is both more pronounced and more effective.

The state obviously has great potential to do harm. This is especially true if a government has at its disposal the tremendous resources offered by modern communication and transportation systems, which it usually does. The state ultimately controls or at least monitors extensively the exchange of information at all levels of society. Antistate terrorists have long appreciated this fact and have imitated the state's use of ruthless example to intimidate.[7] When a crowded marketplace is blown up or a plane hijacked, millions of people know about it within minutes. However, they are only temporarily horrified and intimidated; that is all any terrorist organization, even the most resourceful and well funded, can hope to accomplish. The apparatus of the state, however, can perpetuate continuing, relentless intimidation because of its maximum and often monopolized resources.

Certain forms of state terrorism actually enjoy a genuinely popular base. Iranian enthusiasm over the seizure of U.S. diplomatic personnel in 1979 is a case in point. When the hostages were seized, the students who took over the U.S. Embassy compound had only the most tenuous connection with the government. When the revolutionary regime realized the popular support for the act, it quickly condoned and eventually completely dominated the proceedings. The original act became an activity of state terrorism with widespread domestic support.[8]

A terrorist government can also seek to increase its influence abroad or sustain its effectiveness at home by exporting its version of revolutionary justice. In October 1986, for example, the Syrian Embassy in London became a virtual base for a terrorist effort to blow up an El Al flight. And less than two years earlier, the British had ordered the Libyan Embassy closed when a member of the embassy's staff (with full diplomatic immunity) shot and killed a British police officer. This transforming of a diplomatic headquarters into a terrorist enclave, which has become known as the "terrorist embassy,"[9] is almost without precedent in international relations. Embassies of rival states include spies on their staffs and even secret police detachments; however, even the tactics of Germany's embassies under the Nazis were more subtle and less violent than those of the terrorist state today. The Western political democracies, in particular, are now seeing in effect an outpost of the terrorist state established within their own capital cities. Using such means to extend its influence and presence, the terrorist state perpetuates its power and programs.

State terrorism is typically perceived by its perpetrators to be justified. "Government violence and even unjust violent policies are exempt from a definition of terrorism as long as we accord a legitimate monopoly of violence to the state and its duly authorized functionaries."[10] In other words, governments can get away with more violence than can any other institution in society, because of unrivaled resources, and because there is usually either some popular support for even the most brutal political regime or legitimization of the government from outside by the recognition of international law.

Gradations of State Terrorism

There are, of course, gradations of state terrorism, ranging from bad to worse. These are summarized below:

1. Intimidation—government attempts to anticipate and discourage dissent and opposition. Current noteworthy examples include Chile and South Africa, where intimidation occurs usually through control of the media and the widespread presence of police.
2. Coerced conversion—government seeks a complete overhaul of a national life-style, usually following a revolution. Nicaragua and Iran are obvious examples.

3. Selective genocide or autogenocide—government seeks to eliminate physically an entire class, ethnic or religious group, or other minority for ideological reasons. Two of the most pronounced examples are the Stalinist purge of the Ukrainian kulaks and the Nazi-perpetrated annihilation of European Jewry.

Obviously, there can be and often is some overlap among these categories. There is, for example, the charge that the Sandinistas of Nicaragua are pursuing a determined policy of near genocide against the Miskito Indians even as they attempt to indoctrinate the remainder of the population in Marxist ideology. And certainly the Nazi regime engaged in all three gradations of state terror.

Intimidation is almost universally used by terrorist governments. Conversion, on the other hand, appeals to those regimes that seek a profound change in a population's social and political environment. When conversion is coerced, of course, its effects can be brutal and even lethal. At least, though, conversion of a political or religious doctrine allows physical survival, which cannot be said of genocide. Here conversion is not considered a viable alternative. This most extreme form of state terrorism offers victims no hope at all of survival. When physical elimination of an entire community is the avowed purpose of a regime, the terror state can pursue the policy methodically and without interruption and usually without opposition. Moreover, a compelling ideology or charismatic leadership can be so persuasive that genocide assumes for its perpetrators a noble and even historically inevitable act.

A most lethal derivation of selective genocide is autogenocide, where the government is intent on destroying a large portion of its own citizenry. A recent example is Cambodia between 1975 and 1979, when the Pol Pot regime brutalized and starved between one and two million of the country's seven million inhabitants.[11] Had the regime endured, it is unlikely that any element of the population would have been able to oppose it.

Variants of State Terrorism

Once in power, a regime can indulge in a variety of terrorist enterprises. Besides settling old scores within the state, a regime can, as we have seen, export terror to foreign enemies and can also visit revenge on dissidents who have gone into exile. Examples of state sponsorship of terrorism are suggested in Table 1.

Obviously, state terrorism can become undifferentiated from the sporadic activities of terrorists' groups not aligned with the state. This is certainly the case in the second and third categories given in Table 1. In the first category, however, state involvement is immediate and direct. And all three types illustrate the fact that state terrorism is capable of assuming any sort of ideological posture, whether of the extreme right or left or of religious fundamentalism.[12]

TABLE 1
State Terrorism

Type	Description	Example
State-directed	Reign of terror	French Revolution, 1792–1794; Iran, early 1980s
State-tolerated	Private death squad	El Salvador and Guatemala, 1970s
State-exported	Selective assassination	Trotsky's murder in Mexico, 1940; Qaddafi exiles abroad

Primitivism and Zealotry

In some instances the terrorist state's goal is in essence to return to a purer, more primitive situation from the past. Many terrorist regimes have expressed such a desire. They regard the present as decadent and corrupt, and their attempts to return to an idealized past, while awkward and occasionally suicidal, are sincere. Some terrorist states have been criticized by their own advocates for not being firm enough in this regard. Julius Evola, for example, considered Mussolini's Italy to be a step in the right direction, but not fully committed to restoring the pristine values of the pre-Christian Roman state.[13]

In the 1980s, religious zealotry has become the most familiar characteristic of terrorist movements. This new terrorism is marked also by increasingly overt state sponsorship. The combination is both effective and frightening. Peter Merkl has written that "religious fanaticism and ethnic prejudice apparently can make the more selective *brigatisi* [Italian terrorists] and Baader-Meinhof terrorists look relatively humane."[14] Given the spectacle of a fully equipped state apparatus supporting theologically inspired terrorist acts, this is not an understatement.

This fundamentalism has become the primary motivation of contemporary terrorist states and has profoundly influenced their foreign policies as well. There are frequent references to the United States, Israel, and the West in general as "satanic." The more pronounced features of these "purist" regimes may be summarized as:

1. Compelling ideological or theological message
2. Total intolerance of dissent
3. Antipathy toward normal interplay of democratic polities
4. Extremist harassment of political, ethnic, or religious minorities
5. State inseparable from, and the self-designated enforcer of, the "truth"
6. Perennial conflict with external foes
7. Frequent denigration of and lack of concern with standard of living

As irrational as these may seem from a western viewpoint, it is important to keep in mind that even the most extreme form of fanaticism has, for the terrorist state, its own rationale. Terrorists do not see themselves as irrational and neither do terrorist states. Sartre implied a disconcerting parallel when he questioned whether, as repulsive as Palestinian terrorism may be, the Israeli state's destructive power is any less so when visited on Palestinian refugee camps?[15] Governments that sponsor or indulge in acts of terrorism have consistently claimed that, at best, they are simply vanguards in the fight for freedom and human progress and, at worst, they are engaging in the historically respected option of retaliation.

Moreover, the terrorist state seeks to preserve itself and assume legitimacy by joining the world political community and participating in its exchanges. It does not directly declare war against its perceived enemies, because it is not equipped to do so. Instead, like Libya, Syria, or Iran, the terrorist state opts for a policy of constant harassment against its foes.

The rational agenda of a terrorist regime should not be misunderstood or underestimated. Such an agenda may be hostile to democratic concerns and values, but it is supposed to be. The Iranian government or Iranian-inspired fanatics in Lebanon kidnapping or killing journalists, diplomats, or scholars is considered to be a legitimate method of bringing attention to a particular issue or securing compliance with a demand. Fundamentalist-based terrorist governments, after all, invoke a "higher" law than the international code that most countries accept as binding. It should be remembered that "terrorist-supporting nations will not surrender seriously held ambitions to expand their power and influence simply because the law is against them. Legal argument alone will not protect lawabiding nations and peoples against Quaddafi or Iran's Khomeini."[16]

Conclusion

In essence, state terrorism challenges, as well as departs from, the Western tradition of political philosophy. Possibly the terrorist state is simply a new formulation of the old conflict between despotism and democracy; between the point of view that the state precedes and is superior to the individual and the classical concept of individual sovereignty.

There is also the complementary concern that the most notorious terrorist states are also those most inspired by an absolutist, usually religious-based ideology. Fanaticism, however, in any form has never been compatible with political democracy and has consistently been in relentless opposition to it. Thus, state terrorism, regardless of the ideological direction of the regime, is basically antithetical to a Western political tradition that disavows extremism and insists on constitutional government. As authoritarian regimes headed by political or religious zealots become more plentiful than democratic polities,[17] it is incumbent upon democratic societies to fully understand the myriad dimensions of all forms of state terror.

NOTES

1. John F. McCamant, "Governance Without Blood: Social Science's Antiseptic View of Rule; or, The Neglect of Political Repression," in

Michael Stohl and George A. Lopez, eds., *The State as Terrorist: The Dynamics of Governmental Violence and Repression* (Westport, Connecticut: Greenwood Press, 1984), p. 11.

2. Stalin's purges, for example, decimated hundreds of thousands of loyal and talented communists; the Holocaust that consumed both Jews and non-Jews used up substantial amounts of German personnel and materiel needed for Germany's war effort.

3. It also developed a bureaucracy of its own, as suggested by the thousands of Nazi SS clerks who kept meticulous records on daily genocide.

4. Robert A. Denmark and Howard P. Lehman, "South Africa: The Costs of Containing Repression," in Stohl and Lopez, *The State as Terrorist,* p. 184.

5. However, before states developed, terrorism was practiced extensively in primitive societies by members of one clan against victims captured in conflict with another clan.

6. Alex Peter Schmid and Janny de Graaf, *Violence as Communication: Insurgent Terrorism and the Western News Media* (Beverly Hills, California: Sage Publications, 1982). p. 85.

7. For an example of this point, see Schmid and de Graaf, *Violence as Communication.*

8. An excellent account of this unusual sort of terrorism is found in Warren Christopher, et al., *American Hostages in Iran: The Conduct of a Crisis* (New Haven and London: Yale University Press, 1985).

9. See the commentary by Yoram-Eytan Ettinger, "Is There a Way to Find the Root Cause of International Terrorism?" *The Houston Post,* 19 September 1986, p. 3E.

10. Peter H. Merkl, "Approaches to the Study of Political Violence," in Peter H. Merkl, ed., *Political Violence and Terror: Motifs and Motivations* (Berkeley, Los Angeles, London: University of California Press, 1986), p. 20.

11. No one will ever be sure of the numbers. Some good guesses are made by Elizabeth Becker, *When the War Was Over: The Voices of Cambodia's Revolution and Its People* (New York: Simon and Schuster, 1986).

12. Religious fundamentalism itself is capable of springing from a variety of religious persuasions. Most, if not all, religions have the unpleasant and often contradictory ability to inspire both fanaticism and violence. See, for example, David C. Rapoport, "Fear and Trembling: Terrorism in Three Religious Traditions," *The American Political Science Review,* vol. 78, no. 3 (September 1983), pp. 658–676, and Bernard Schechterman, "Religious Fanaticism as a Factor in Political Violence" (Coral Gables, Florida: The International Freedom Foundation, 1984).

13. See Richard H. Drake, "Julius Evola and the Ideological Origins of the Radical Right in Contemporary Italy," in Merkl, *Political Violence and Terror: Motifs and Motivations,* pp. 61–89. Evola even traced the decline of the West from pagan times, where free inquiry helped to undermine traditional values and belief systems.

14. Peter H. Merkl, "Conclusion: Collective Purposes and Individual Motives," in Merkl, *Political Violence and Terror,* p. 361.

15. For a discussion of how confusing the sources of terrorism are, see Haim Gordon, *Dance, Dialogue, and Despair: Existentialist Philosophy and Education for Peace in Israel* (University, Alabama: University of Alabama Press, 1986).

16. Abraham D. Soafer, "Terrorism and the Law," *Foreign Affairs,* vol. 64, no. 5 (Summer 1986), p. 922.

17. See, for example, Juan J. Linz, *The Breakdown of Democratic Regimes: Crisis, Breakdown, and Equilibrium* (Baltimore, Maryland: The Johns Hopkins Press, 1986).

Genocide: An Historical Overview

Frank Chalk and Kurt Jonassohn

Montreal Institute for Genocide Studies, Concordia University, 1455, de Maisonneuve Boulevard W., Montreal, Quebec H3G 1M8.

The word genocide evokes the memories of several mass killings in the twentieth century: Hitler's Germany, Stalin's Russia, Pol Pot's Cambodia come readily to mind. However, although the word was coined only in the 1940s, the events it is meant to describe have been taking place since the dawn of history.

There are several reasons for taking a closer look at the historical origins of genocide. First, few people appreciate that it has been practiced throughout history in all parts of the world. Second, it is the ultimate violation of human rights. Third, it now produces far more than half of all refugees. We shall return to these points after we have dealt with some definitional matters.

EARLIER DEFINITIONS

International lawyers and scholars in the social sciences have their own legitimate sets of objectives when laying out the boundaries of a subject. For international lawyers, defining genocide means defining a crime. Like any criminal offense, the definition of genocide must be appropriate for legal prosecution and it must withstand review by judges and lawyers for the accused. Social scientists have a different set of objectives. When defining genocide, they are outlining the boundaries of a set of cases which they want to study for the purpose of discovering their common elements and analyzing the processes that brought them about. Perhaps these differences in objectives account for the differences in breadth and focus which one finds in the several definitions of genocide that have appeared since the concept was first elaborated by Raphael Lemkin in 1944.[1]

Lemkin, a Polish Jewish jurist, defined genocide as the coordinated and planned annihilation of a national, religious, or racial group by a variety of actions aimed at undermining the foundations essential to the survival of the group as a group. For a time, the General Assembly of the United Nations seriously debated adding a new category of victims—"political and other groups"—to Lemkin's list, but it gave up the effort when delegates from the Soviet and Eastern bloc argued that "because of their mutability and lack of distinguishing characteristics" the inclusion of political groups would blur and weaken the whole convention.[2]

On December 9, 1948, the United Nations adopted the Genocide Convention, incorporating the following definition:

Article II

In the present Convention, genocide means any of the following acts committed with intent to destroy, in whole or in part, a national, ethnical, racial or religious group, as such:

   (a) Killing members of the group;

   (b) Causing serious bodily or mental harm to members of the group;

   (c) Deliberately inflicting on the group conditions of life calculated to bring about its physical destruction in whole or in part;

   (d) Imposing measures intended to prevent births within the group;

   (e) Forcibly transferring children of the group to another group.[3]

The narrow definition of the victim groups which lies at the heart of the UN definition of genocide was the direct result of a political compromise designed to preserve the remainder of the Genocide Convention. It answered the practical needs of governments as well as the strictures of international lawyers. Since 1944, several alternative definitions of genocide have been advanced by social scientists. Among the most important for the field are those advanced by Pieter N. Drost, Irving Louis Horowitz, and Helen Fein.[4]

In 1959, Pieter N. Drost, a Dutch law professor with extensive experience in the Dutch East Indies, wrote a major work assessing the UN Convention. Drost assailed the omission of political and other groups from the UN definition of genocide, accurately predicting that governments would thoroughly exploit the obvious loophole in the convention. Rejecting the notion that the victims of genocide were limited to racial, religious, national, and ethnic groups, Drost proposed that the United Nations redefine genocide as "the deliberate destruction of physical life of individual human beings by reason of their membership of any human collectivity as such".[5]

In the early 1970s, Hervé Savon voiced his skepticism about the utility of the UN definition as a tool for sociologists, noting that it really belongs to the language

Revised version of the article as it appeared in *Social Education*, Vol. 55, No. 2, February 1991, pp. 92-96. Copyright © 1991 by Frank Chalk and Kurt Jonassohn. Reprinted by permission of the authors.

of law and ethics, not the realm of sociological analysis.[6] In 1976, the sociologist Irving Louis Horowitz addressed this same issue but proposed to view genocide as a fundamental policy employed by the state to assure conformity to its ideology and to its model of society. He amended the UN definition to emphasize that genocide was "a structural and systematic destruction of innocent people by a state bureaucratic apparatus".[7] Since then, Horowitz has concluded that a totalitarian society is a necessary precondition for the genocidal process, but it is not a sufficient one. Horowitz believes that national culture plays a much more important role in genocide than the ideology of the state. A totalitarian ideology may make class, race, or religion lethal sins, he contends, but the decision to eradicate these sins by committing genocide is largely a function of culture.[8]

In the 1980s, Helen Fein, another sociologist, focused her attention on developing a broader and deeper sociological definition of genocide. She arrived at the conclusion that:

Genocide is a series of purposeful actions by a perpetrator(s) to destroy a collectivity through mass or selective murders of group members and suppressing the biological and social reproduction of the collectivity.[9]

Fein's explanation of her definition shows that she has decided to include political and social groups as victims and to exclude deaths resulting from warfare.

Leo Kuper has contributed more to the comparative study of the problem of genocide in the twentieth century than anyone since Raphael Lemkin. In *Genocide* (1981) and *The Prevention of Genocide* (1985),[10] Kuper presents a comprehensive analysis of genocidal processes and motivations and confronts the difficulties of defining genocide. After delivering a devastating critique of the UN definition, the political compromises that shaped it, and the organization's morally bankrupt record of nonenforcement, Kuper reluctantly accepts the UN handiwork on the grounds that its definition is internationally recognized and may one day become the basis for more effective preventive action by the United Nations. Kuper does not ignore the groups excluded by the UN definition. He discusses the victims of state-organized, politically-motivated mass killings in Stalin's Soviet Union, in Indonesia, and in Kampuchea (Cambodia) under the heading "related atrocities". He suggests that each of these cases would have been labeled a genocide if the UN definition had included political groups.

OUR DEFINITION

The definition of genocide contained in the United Nations Convention on the Prevention and Punishment of the Crime of Genocide, adopted in December 1948, was quite unsatisfactory for one very simple reason: none of the major groups of victims of the genocides that have occurred since its adoption fall within its restrictive specifications. The crux of this problem is contained in Article II of the UN Convention which limits the term genocide to " . . . acts committed with intent to destroy, in whole or in part, a national, ethnical, racial or religious group . . ." Other victim groups— whether they be economic, political, or social ones—do not qualify as the victims of genocide because they were omitted from that definition. The reasons for that omission have been discussed by Leo Kuper[11] and are less relevant here than our need for a definition that would cover the planned annihilation of any group, no matter how that group is defined and by whom. Minimally, such a definition should include economic, political and social groups as potential victims. There have been a number of efforts to amend and expand the UN definition of possible victim groups—so far without success.[12]

This lack of success is all the more puzzling since the 1951 United Nations Convention Relating to the Status of Refugees specifies that a refugee is "Any person who owing to well founded fear of being persecuted for reasons of race, religion, nationality, membership of a particular social group or political opinion, is outside the country of his nationality . . ."[13] These two conflicting definitions, arising from the same organization, seem to produce a puzzling paradox: People fleeing from a genocide—as defined below—are being recognized as refugees, while those unable to flee from the same events are not acknowledged as being its victims. So, after many revisions, we have finally adopted the following definition for our own research:

GENOCIDE is a form of one-sided mass killing in which a state or other authority intends to destroy a group, as that group and membership in it are defined by the perpetrator.[14]

The main difference between the United Nations definition and ours is that we have no restrictions on the types of groups to be included. This allows us to include even those groups that have no verifiable reality outside the minds of the perpetrators, such as 'wreckers' or 'enemies of the people'; while such groups may not fall within the usual definition of a group as used in the social sciences, the labelling of such groups by the perpetrator suffices to define them.

HISTORICAL ORIGINS

However, although the term 'genocide' has only been coined in the middle of the twentieth century, it describes a phenomenon that is as old as recorded history. Baillet[15] tells us that genocides were common in predynastic Egypt; the Assyrians[16] claim to have practiced it, if we are to accept their own reports; and there are several cases to be found in the Old Testament.[17]

The Old Testament contains several quite specific descriptions that are of interest to us. The Amalekites are reported to have been annihilated several times, which might raise questions about the historical accuracy of the reports or about the completeness with which the annihilations were carried out. Our interest is not so much in these details as in the style in which they are reported. That style allows us to conclude that the physical destruction of the entire people of defeated opponents was not unusual at that time, nor that it evoked any humanitarian outrage. The victims seemed to have accepted their fate as the usual lot of the losers at the same time as they were lamenting their losses.

The origins of genocide are shrouded in the unrecorded past. But because in antiquity it is always reported in connection with wars, we can make an educated guess about its roots. City states and empires were very small by modern standards; many of them were located in the so-called golden triangle, the modern Middle East. The geo-political dimensions of this area seemed to have been designed to produce almost continuous warfare. The valleys of the Tigris and the Euphrates are very fertile with few natural boundaries. The region lies across the trade routes between Asia, Europe and Africa. Similar criteria apply to the Nile valley. Thus, opportunities for competition and conflicts leading to wars seemed to be ever-present. However, these wars initially did not settle anything; the defeated party went home, recruited and trained another army, produced more and sometimes better weapons, and then returned to fight another war in order to recoup its losses and wreak revenge. It did not take much imagination for someone to decide that the only way to preserve a victory was to annihilate the vanquished enemy entirely—not only the combat forces. Baillet argues that this method of concluding a victorious campaign lasted for about a thousand years in Egypt before it fell into disuse. This change was not the result of any rise in humanitarian concerns, but rather the realization that the victims would be much more valuable alive than dead.[18]

These states in the fertile crescent were extraordinarily labour intensive because their fertile valleys required elaborate irrigation systems, because the large number of gods that they prayed to all required temples, and because few rulers were content with the palaces of their predecessors and therefore spent huge resources on new palaces, or burial sites in Egypt, to glorify their reign. Thus, the new realization that the captives of a conquered enemy were much more useful as slaves than as corpses became widespread in the area.

Genocides continued to be performed by states and empires in order to eliminate a real or perceived threat, in order to terrorize a real or imaginary enemy, or in order to acquire economic resources that were owned by others but could not be carried off as loot and booty. These three motives were usually present at the same time, although one of them tended to predominate in any particular situation. Of course, the further we go back into the past, the more difficult it becomes to obtain evidence of the motives of the perpetrators.

In antiquity it is particularly difficult to account for the fates of peoples. From inscriptions, clay tablets, and parchments we know a great many names of peoples about whom hardly anything else is known. Even when we know something of their history, some of them have disappeared without our knowing what happened to them. The classic illustration is the story of the Hittites[19] who are well known to us from scripture and Egyptian records. We know that they conquered their neighbours and built an empire that competed with Assyria and Egypt. And then they disappeared from history without a trace. In fact, it is only in modern times that the remains of their capital were discovered; it had been burned to the ground and cursed to prevent it from being resettled. Their library contained thousands of clay tablets which were thoroughly baked during that conflagration and thus preserved for the future. Their writing was deciphered, and the peace treaty that they negotiated with Rameses II was decoded. However, we still have no idea what happened to the Hittite people. Were they dispersed to other areas? Did they assimilate into the culture of their conquerors? Or were they slaughtered? Only the development of an archaeology of genocide holds any promise of solving that riddle.

The history of empires, right into the modern period, is punctuated by periodic persecutions, sometimes escalating into genocides, that were performed either to build up an empire or to maintain it. One of the important characteristics of these types of genocides is that the victim groups were always located outside the perpetrator society, physically and socially. The campaigns of Athens against Melos,[20] of Rome against Carthage,[21] of Genghis Khan against several peoples,[22] and of the Crusaders against the populations of Antioch and Jerusalem,[23] may serve as examples.

MODERN GENOCIDES

Starting with the Crusades, a new element appeared that has become the dominant one in the twentieth century: genocides to implement a belief, ideology or theory. The Crusade to reconquer Palestine as well as the Albigensian Crusade in the South of France were early precursors in which the motives to enlarge an empire and to spread a belief were both present. At the end of the eleventh century, the crusaders started out to free the Holy Land from the infidels. When they conquered Jerusalem they slaughtered the entire non-Christian population. But they also stayed to establish kingdoms and acquire wealth. At the beginning of the thirteenth century, the Languedoc (present-day southern France), the most flourishing region of Europe, was devastated by the Albigensian Crusade. Various heresies were quite wide-spread and even found some sympathy among the aristocracy in court circles. The Pope saw this as a threat to the authority of Rome and asked the king of France to organize a crusade to wipe out the heretics. He did this so effectively that the region has never recovered its preeminent status; but, while the heretics and their sympathizers were eradicated, the region was also incorporated into the realm of the king of France.

The first purely ideological genocide probably was the persecution of Christians in seventeenth century Japan[24]. Early Spanish and Portuguese trading ships carried not only merchandise but also missionaries who were surprisingly successful in making converts, both among the upper classes and among the poor peasantry. The Tokugawa court perceived this foreign penetration as a threat that undermined not only traditional trading patterns, but also traditional values governing a quite rigid social order. This resulted first in several so-called exclusion decrees and then in the Shimabara rebellion during which large number of Christians were massacred. These exclusion decrees effectively closed Japan to Western influences for over 200 years.

At approximately the same time Western Europe experienced the Great Witch-Hunts during which mostly very poor people were persecuted for conspiracy with the devil. We are not suggesting that these were genocides—they were not. But the wide-spread persecutions and burnings were meant to eradicate deviations from the dominant belief system. The procedures for extracting damaging evidence developed at that time are still in use by some modern genocidal regimes.

When we get to the twentieth century, all of the major genocides are ideological ones that are perpetrated to enforce some ideological imperative. Here the victim groups are always located within the perpetrator society, both physically and socially. This explains one of the often overlooked differences between genocides that are performed to establish or maintain an empire and genocides that are performed to enforce an ideological imperative: the former produced tangible benefits for the perpetrators in that they did eliminate the threat, or terrorize the enemy, or produce new economic wealth, while the latter are always carried out in spite of great costs to the perpetrator societies in both social and economic terms.[25] This is true whether we examine the Turkish annihilation of the Armenian community, Nazi Germany's destruction of the Gypsies and Jews, Stalin's extermination of several groups, or the Khmer Rouge's killing of the urban third of Cambodia's population.

There are several features that ideological genocides seem to have in common and that ought to provide a clue to ways of preventing future genocides. These types of genocides tend to be performed in the name of theories, beliefs, or ideologies (1) that devalue the individual in favour of the collectivity, (2) that sanctify means in order to achieve ends, (3) that reject the rule of law, and (4) that do not subscribe to or observe The Universal Declaration of Human Rights, adopted by the General Assembly of the United Nations on the 10th December 1948. Each of these points is explored in the following paragraphs.

(1) One of the major ways in which beliefs, ideologies and theories differ is in how they define their subject. In some cases they define as their subject the individual human being, and the collectivity plays only a secondary role. We are most familiar with this kind in the West; in civic matters we believe that individuals should vote to help decide the future of the collectivity, and in religious matters we believe in individual conscience rather than the duty of the collectivity. But in many other parts of the world the individual is of secondary importance and it is only the collectivity that matters. In such countries it will be accepted as a matter of course that individuals must suffer in order to further the good of the collectivity. Their leaders may even look with contempt at the Declaration of Human Rights (or the American Bill of Rights) as a document of an inferior culture.

(2) Beliefs, ideologies and theories also vary in how they interpret the relationship between means and ends. That relationship has produced some very interesting debates and analyses. However, in the present context it will suffice to say that when the ends justify the means, human rights and human lives are seriously at risk.

(3) Although often enough used without specification of what the "rule of law" really means, its meaning is neither obvious nor clear. However, the rule of law is a very important notion in the comparative study of governments. Most simply expressed, 'the rule of law' refers to a type of society where there is only one kind of law and where everybody is subject to that law. In a society governed by 'the rule of law', the lowliest workers and the highest ruling elites are all subject to the same law. When a society exempts certain individuals or groups from that law, it has taken the first steps away from a democratic regime. The idea of democracy is so widespread that we often do not remember what it refers to. Literally, it refers to rule by the people; but that is hardly possible in a large scale society. Instead, we invest the authority to rule in the hands of representatives chosen in free elections. We think it still appropriate to call such government a democracy and we refer to countries that have this kind of an arrangement as republics. Whether that appellation remains appropriate depends on the people's ability to maintain final control. When a government rules in spite of the opposition of the majority, or when it clings to power against the will of the people, then the appellation of democracy becomes inappropriate and the rights of man are at risk.

(4) These three aspects of beliefs, ideologies and theories overlap to quite an extent. Perhaps we can adopt as a short-cut measure whether a country observes the terms of the United Nations Universal Declaration of Human Rights or the related Helsinki accord. Unfortunately, some countries have signed these documents under pressure from some Western powers, but have no intention of applying them to their internal affairs.

4. STATE TERRORISM AND DISSENT (REVOLUTIONARY) TERRORISM

Certainly, the commitment to observe these agreements is the best guarantee that human rights will not be violated—and that includes genocide, the ultimate violation of human rights.

One response to persecution and potential genocide is the attempt to escape. Because there always are some people who manage to escape, there never has been a completely "successful" genocide. In the second half of this century there have been several genocides, and there have been increasing numbers of people who, seeing the danger, managed to escape. The result is that the majority of refugees in the world today are refugees from genocides. They represent two very different kinds of challenges. The first one arises from the fact that these refugees often bring the most accurate and reliable news of an incipient genocide. When they are taken seriously, and not discounted as biased observers, they can be a crucial part of an early warning system. The second challenge taxes the UN High Commission for Refugees and the other humanitarian organizations that are trying to assist these refugees.

NOTES

1. Raphael Lemkin, *Axis Rule in Occupied Europe* (Washington, D.C.: Carnegie Endowment, 1944), chapter IX.

2. Leo Kuper, *Genocide: Its Political Use in the Twentieth Century* (New Haven: Yale University Press, 1981), p. 26, quoting the Polish delegation.

3. United Nations, *Convention on the Prevention and Punishment of the Crime of Genocide*, 9 December 1948 (London: Her Majesty's Stationery Office, March 1966).

4. Frank Chalk and Kurt Jonassohn, *The History and Sociology of Genocide: Analyses and Case Studies* (New Haven: Yale University Press, 1990), pp. 9–23.

5. Pieter N. Drost, *The Crime of State*, vol. 2 (Leyden: A. W. Sythoff, 1959), p. 125.

6. Hervé Savon, *Du cannibalisme au genocide* (Paris: Hachette, 1972), chapter I.

7. Irving Louis Horowitz, *Taking Lives: Genocide and State Power* (New Brunswick, N.J.: Transaction Books, 1980), p. 17.

8. Irving Louis Horowitz, "Genocide and the Reconstruction of Social Theory: Observations on the Exclusivity of Collective Death," *Armenian Review* 37 (1984): 1–21.

9. Helen Fein, "Towards a Sociological Definition of Genocide," a paper presented at the annual meeting of the International Studies Association, St. Louis, Missouri, April 1–2, 1988, p. 9. For a fuller presentation of Fein's definition, see Helen Fein, "Genocide: A Sociological Perspective,"*Current Sociology*, 38, No. 1 (Spring 1990): 23–25.

10. Leo Kuper, *Genocide* (New Haven: Yale University Press, 1981) and *The Prevention of Genocide* (New Haven: Yale University Press, 1985).

11. Leo Kuper, ch. 2, 1981.

12. Ben Whitaker, *Revised and Updated Report on the Question of the Prevention and Punishment of the Crime of Genocide* (United Nations Economic and Social Council, Commission on Human Rights, E.CN.4 Sub.2, 1985.6: 2 July 1985).

13. Frances D'Souza and Jeff Crisp, *The Refugee Dilemma* (London: Minority Rights Group, 1985), MRG Report No. 43, p. 7.

14. Frank Chalk and Kurt Jonassohn, *op. cit.*, p. 23.

15. Jules Baillet, *Le Régime Pharaonique dans ses rapports avec l'évolution de la morale en Egypte*, Tome Premier (Grande Imprimerie de Blois, 1912), pp. 151–152.

16. Frank Chalk and Kurt Jonassohn, *op. cit.*, pp. 58–61.

17. *Ibid.*, pp. 61–63.

18. Jules Baillet, *op. cit.*, pp. 167–168.

19. Frank Chalk and Kurt Jonassohn, *op. cit.*, pp. 60–61.

20. *Ibid.*, pp. 65–73.

21. *Ibid.*, pp. 74–93.

22. *Ibid.*, pp. 94–113.

23. Steven Runciman, *The History of the Crusades*, Vol. I., *The First Crusade and the Foundation of the Kingdom of Jerusalem*, (Cambridge, At The University Press, 1962), pp. 235, 260, 286–87.

24. Frank Chalk and Kurt Jonassohn, *op. cit.*, pp. 139–151.

25. *Ibid.*, pp. 415–421. For an expanded version of this paper see: Kurt Jonassohn, "The Consequences of Ideological Genocides and their Role in Prevention." *The Armenian Review*, 42, no 4/168 (Winter 1989): 1–16.

On Human Rights, Iran Still an Outlaw

John Hughes

While the Bush administration is focused on the menace of Iraq, neighboring Iran remains almost as objectionable and, in its own way, just as dangerous.

Wistful observers look for signs that Iran is moderating. President Hashemi Rafsanjani, goes their argument, is looking for ways to reintroduce Western technology and aid to rebuild Iran's economy; he has been "helpful" in getting American hostages released; he is seeking, in parliamentary elections next month, to curb the hard-line fundamentalists and give parliament a more conciliatory caste.

But the facts are that the Iranian regime is one of the most ruthless oppressors of human rights within its own borders. Abroad it has engaged in terror and murder against its critics and opponents. And it is in the midst of an arms buildup, possibly attempting the acquisition of nuclear capability.

In its latest tantrum, the Tehran government is kicking out the International Red Cross, apparently because the international relief organization has cooperated with the United Nations in pinpointing the torture and execution of prisoners, the ill-treatment of women and religious minorities, and other abuses of human rights in Iran.

Recently the UN Commission on Human Rights issued a tough report on Iran, claiming that the number of executions in that country in 1991, totaling 884, was considerably higher than in the two previous years despite UN protests and Iranian promises of legislative reform.

The UN commission also deplored the Iranian government's endorsement of death threats to author Salman Rushdie and the violence toward those involved in the publication of Mr. Rushdie's book, "The Satanic Verses." Alberto Ettore Capriolo, who translated the book into Italian, was stabbed in Milan last year by a hit squad demanding the location of Rushdie's hiding place. Also last year, the Japanese translator of the Rushdie book, Hitoshi Igarashi, was murdered near Tokyo.

The UN report also cites Iran's involvement in the murder of political opponents in Europe.

Many of the executions in Iran were supposed to be of drug traffickers, but political prisoners were also executed by public hanging. The UN protested some particularly cruel methods of execution, including three alleged cases of stoning to death, and the case of a man reportedly pushed from a cliff top last July.

The UN cited involuntary disappearances and torture to gain confessions from prisoners by means of flogging, whipping, suspension by the wrists, deprivation of sleep, and psychological torture.

With respect to trials, the UN commission found them falling far short of international standards of fairness. Defendants are often denied legal counsel, and the proceedings last only a few minutes. Public and press are barred.

Numerous instances are cited of discrimination against women, particularly for not using full Islamic dress or for wearing makeup. Hundreds of women have been arrested for dress-code "offenses" and others barred from government offices, hospitals, cinemas, and other public places. Revolutionary Guards have beaten some women for being improperly veiled.

Religious minorities fare just as badly. Assyrian shopkeepers are obliged to place signs in their windows identifying their religious faith, a measure designed to hobble their businesses.

Members of the Bahai faith are harassed and discriminated against. They are denied the right of property, access to universities, businesses, employment, public services, cemeteries, and places of worship. Some 10,000 Bahais who lost their jobs in the 1980s are still unemployed. Retirement pensions from the state are denied them. Former public employees have continued to receive demands for the return of salaries or pensions paid in previous years. Many confiscated Bahai properties have been auctioned off without compensation to the owners. The Bahai are barred from joining agricultural cooperatives and are denied credit and use of machinery usually provided by the cooperatives.

In the face of such widespread and calculated lack of civilized behavior, it is ludicrous to accept at face value the Iranian regime's hints and promises of reform.

Egypt's Islamic Extremists Step Up Violent Attacks

Cramped by police in the cities, extremists move to the countryside

Carol Berger

Special to The Christian Science Monitor

ASSIUT PROVINCE, EGYPT

HAMDI MUHAMMAD SULEIMAN lives in the village of Dayrut, more than 180 miles south of Cairo. There, in the lush Nile Valley's small farms and dusty villages, recent sectarian strife has left at least two dozen people dead and as many wounded. "Everyone is living in terror," he says, "the police and the people."

Like most residents, Mr. Suleiman has his own theory about how the bout of violence last month began: an argument over the price of tomatoes, curses exchanged between Muslim and Christian shoppers, and gunfire.

Regardless of the spark, few deny that religion is the catalyst for the worsening conflict between Egypt's Muslims and the minority Coptic Christian population, particularly in the Nile Valley. But Egypt is witnessing a wave of extremist violence in various parts of the country:

■ A senior police officer in charge of a prison holding Muslim fundamentalists just south of Cairo was wounded on Monday by gunmen suspected of being extremists.

■ Late last month alleged extremists mounted an attack near one of Egypt's most renowned Pharaonic sites, the Karnak temple in Luxor. Two homemade bombs exploded as tourists attended the nightly "Sound and Light" show.

■ Farag Fouda, a prominent secularist writer, was gunned down June 7, allegedly by Muslim extremists, outside his Cairo office. Mr. Fouda, a professor of agricultural economy, was one of Egypt's few outspoken critics of the Islamist trend.

SHIRLEY HORN – STAFF

Most extremists in the Nile Valley area belong to the underground Jamiat Islamiya (Islamic Groups) which advocate violence in their bid to impose Islamic law. Egpyt's largely secular government claims that 90 percent of the country's law already conforms to Islamic social, civil, and penal codes.

In the past year extremist Islamic groups have moved out of the urban centers, where security is tight, to the countryside where they quickly take control of village life. The impoverished rural areas have proved a fertile ground for religious zealots. In the mud-brick villages that line the banks of the Nile there are few jobs for a growing population.

Many communities were almost wholly reliant on remittances by relatives working in the Gulf and Iraq. But now even that has been lost in the wake of Iraq's 1990 occupation of Kuwait and the war which followed. Hundreds of thousands of Egyptian men were forced to return home from Kuwait and Iraq, many of them losing not only their work but also their life savings.

As conditions continue to deteriorate, religious extremists are exploiting tensions between Muslims and the more affluent Christian community. The state's response has been to increase repressive measures against suspected Muslim extremists.

For decades the most organized and most intransigent opposition to successive Egyptian regimes has been the Muslim fundamentalist movement. The Muslim Brotherhood, although technically illegal, is tolerated by the regime of President Hosni Mubarak and in recent years its members have been brought into many levels of government – an effort to move them into the political mainstream.

During the same period, however, more radical Islamic parties have been calling for the imposition of Islamic law and supporting the use of violence to achieve it. The recent attacks suggest to many here that extremist movement has reached a new level of organization and effectiveness that poses a greater threat to domestic stability.

Both government officials and police have tried to play down the political implications of the killings in the Nile Valley. Instead they attribute the violence to vendettas between families which lead to revenge killings. But local residents interviewed in Dayrut

and Sanabu, speaking on condition of anonymity, said police have worked hand in hand with Muslim extremists to demand protection money and "taxes" from the Christian community.

The first man to die in the outbreak of violence here, which began in May, was also the first who refused to pay, they assert. Days later extremists assassinated 13 others, one of whom was a Muslim who tried to defend his Christian neighbors. Residents compared the killings to "gangland slayings."

Recent police transfers out of the province may have been a belated attempt by Cairo authorities to end the reported corruption in this long-neglected backwater. But the apparent breakdown in law and order and the large number of arms held by the public has

now forced a heavy-handed crackdown. At least 450 residents have been arrested since the violence began, officials say.

While the rural provinces have been tense for months, Cairo had remained relatively unaffected until earlier this month when columnist Fouda was killed. Leading writers and intellectuals have been put under extra police protection amid fears that still others may be assassination targets.

State officials have blamed Fouda's killing on Islamic Jihad (Holy War), the underground Muslim group which assassinated President Anwar Sadat in 1981. The last major attack blamed on the group was in 1990, when motorcyle-riding gunmen killed Egypt's Speaker of parliament and five others.

The Decline of the Red Army Faction

Hans Josef Horchem

Hans Josef Horchem, former President of the Office for the Protection of the Constitution for the Federal Land of Hamburg, has published Die Verloren Revolution (The Lost Revolution), *a history of German terrorism to 1989.*

The Red Army Faction (RAF) has changed the structure of its organisation several times. This happened usually after setbacks in its operations which were regarded by sympathisers and supporters as defeats. Regroupings in the hierarchy were made in the hope to get new energies for the armed struggle. In the last year difficulties in communications developed, particularly between the command level and the prisoners. The attempt to establish a 'West European Guerrilla' failed.

At the beginning of the 1980s the RAF worked out its 'MIC-strategy' which was aimed at the so-called 'Military-Industrial-Complex'. Meanwhile this conception is replaced by another target. The enemy of the terrorists now is the 'European Superpower'. By creating this new hostile figure the RAF is renewing its attempt to form a 'European Front of the Guerrilla'. But the call for new allies remained without resonance until today.

Between 6 and 18 June 1990 nine former members of the Red Army Faction (RAF) were arrested in the German Democratic Republic (GDR). They had been living under assumed names for years, in part, since 1980, in East Berlin, Frankfurt/Oder, Magdeburg and other places under the former Communist regime. Some had married and had children. All of them were engaged in regular work.

I. THE RAF IN THE EX-GDR

The Ministry of State Security (MfS), Main Section XXII, had had charge of the former terrorists, had given them new identities and arranged employment for them. This led to speculation that the MfS might have made use of actions of the RAF with the knowledge of, or under the instructions of, the government of the GDR, with the aim of destabilising the Federal Republic of Germany.

Arrest warrants for two RAF members, Ekkehard Freiherr von Seckendorf and Sigrid Sternebeck, were in part justified on the grounds that they had participated in RAF actions during 1984 and 1985. Witnesses had stated that they recognised Ekkehard von Seckendorf as one of the robbers at a bank raid on 26 March 1984 in Würzburg. Other witnesses thought they had recognised in Sigrid Sternebeck the woman who had obtained the car that had been used as a car-bomb in the attack on the US airbase at Frankfurt on 8 August 1985.

Zealous researchers had further discovered that Henning Beer had taken a vacation at the time when German terrorists were preparing an attack on the US naval base at Rota near Cadiz in Spain. The shoot-out between the terrorists and the Spanish police, in the course of which the preparation plans were discovered, took place on 18 June 1988. According to his work record, Henning Beer had been away from work from 17 to 20 June. When the car of Federal Finance Ministry top civil servant Hans Tiedtmeyer was shot at by RAF persons on 19 September 1988, Henning Beer once again had time off work. He was absent from his workplace from 17 September until the late shift on 20 September. Likewise when Alfred Herrhausen was murdered on 30 November 1989, according to journalists' reports, Henning Beer did not appear for his work shift for three days.[1]

Ekkehard von Seckendorf and Sigrid Sternebeck have an alibi for the time that witnesses claimed to have seen them participating in RAF actions. It is the experience of investigating officers that statements made by witnesses to violent actions carried out in a short time tend to be of only limited reliability.

Henning Beer will presumably be able to produce facts to clear him during the period in question, exonerating himself from implication in the events he is suspected of having been involved in. Besides, it is quite incredible to proceed on the notion that Henning Beer could have flown out from Neubrandenburg, where he was arrested, to Spain for a day, in order to take part in the preparations of an explosives attack there. Experience hitherto has shown that the RAF has always prepared its actions very carefully and long in advance; for example, the attack on Karlheinz Beckurts on 9 July 1986 was prepared, according to the Federal Criminal Office (BKA), at least three

From *Terrorism and Political Violence*, Vol. 3, No. 2, Summer 1991, pp. 61-74. *Terrorism and Political Violence*, published by Frank Cass and Company, Ltd., England. Copyright © Frank Cass & Co., Ltd., 1991.

months in advance by the 'Mara Cargol Commando' group which was responsible for the attack. The preliminary planning and preparation phase leading up to the murder of Alfred Herrhausen almost certainly took even longer. The preparations for all the RAF actions hitherto were carried out collectively by the commando group concerned. Plans were discussed and decided on collectively, then individual tasks assigned according to the expertise of the appropriately qualified member of the group. In the case of all the actions, the deed was a communal one: successes could be claimed by each and every individual; likewise, an unsuccessful action was a failure for which each individual had to share the blame.

It is completely out of the question that Henning Beer, if he was a member of the commando unit, could have been carrying out his normal work in the GDR throughout the entire preparatory phase and then have only travelled to the Federal Republic on the day of the attack in order just to press the release mechanism of the bomb.

The RAF members arrested in the ex-GDR have given up terrorism; they have renounced violence. The former Head of the Main Section XXII, Lt. Gen. Gerhard Neiber, stated that the former terrorists were granted GDR citizenship and their new cover stories only after they had expressly sworn to desist from any further terrorist attacks and promised to break off any relationship with the RAF.[2] This statement is credible.

The risk of allowing the RAF to use the sovereign territory of the GDR as sanctuary as a safe-haven operational base would have been too great. In the event of any such operation, the Minister for State Security, Erich Mielke, would have had to inform, as well as quite definitely Erich Honecker, probably the entire Politburo, and to have obtained permission for it. The GDR was in the process of gaining an improved reputation in the community of nations. If it had become known that it was carrying out acts supporting terrorists, this process would have been cut short. Furthermore the GDR government would have had to reckon with a cancellation of all West German credits and payments via the Swing agreement, transit fees and preferences involved in their direct access to the EC.

Conversely it is unimaginable that the RAF would have voluntarily subjected itself to the MfS. The RAF always refused, because of its own image of itself, to 'go into action for any other organisation, even as some sort of deal in compensation for services rendered'.[3] The RAF's attempt, from 1984 onwards, to construct a 'West European Guerrilla' was only undertaken and followed up because the RAF hoped to retain a controlling influence over its partners in any such alliance. Cooperation with the Italian Red Brigades became difficult because this key aim was repeatedly called into question by the Italians.

What did the Stasi (GDR State Security) want from the former RAF people? In the first place, every secret service—and the MfS was one of the best secret services—is interested in information about systems which affect politics or could do so. Even retrospective insights into the 1970s structure, operations and goals of the RAF must have been of interest to the MfS. The debriefing of former RAF members at the beginning of the 1980s again allowed the MfS to infer possible alterations in the mode of operations. Inge Viett, for example, was likely to have retained contacts dating back to her stay in Paris, from which information could be gleaned about the prospects of a 'West European Guerrilla'. Other former terrorists—above all Susanne Albrecht—had links in the Near East. Through her links could be established, and this must have been of interest above all for Lt. Gen. Markus Wolf's HVA—the overseas intelligence service. In the Near East the GDR intelligence service was interested not only in information but also in increasing the influence of the GDR.[4]

Likewise the priority interests of the USSR have to be taken into account. The Mfs had to defer to them in the 1980s. For a considerable time the Soviets have been keeping tabs on any developments of a terrorist nature occurring in their sphere. They have to anticipate an expansion of Shi'ite fundamentalist fanaticism in their Muslim provinces. It is possible that the MfS also gave the former West German terrorists asylum in order to be able to give to their KGB partners an explanation of which groups operate using which methods and what links exist between European and Near East organisations.

The fact that several of the terrorists arrested in the GDR have in the meantime had themselves transferred voluntarily to the Federal Republic likewise suggests that the RAF people in the GDR want to have nothing more to do with the actions of their former comrades. Both Susanne Albrecht and Silke Maier-Witt want to make use of the 'state-witness regulations' currently valid in the Federal Republic. Werner Lotze has declared that he expects that the law for Aussteiger (repentant terrorists wanting to abandon terrorism) and the programme developed in the Federal Republic will be applied.[5] According to the 'prescriptions' evolved in the Federal Republic, this also means that it is a precondition that Werner Lotze gives a full account of himself.

In this context the accusation has to be cleared up, which stated that the German security service had indications about the RAF terrorists' residence in the ex-GDR. In the meantime it has emerged that in three cases the BKA (the Federal Criminal Office) had been presented with information to that effect. This however was in the context of hundreds of further items of information suggesting that they were in the Near East. The West German authorities also followed up these leads concerning the GDR, but neither enquiries directed to the GDR authorities nor their own researches led to any clarification.

This naturally does not alter anything as far as the conclusion is concerned, to which experts have now come, namely that the MfS did render assistance for international terrorist attacks on West German and

American targets. Since the trial of Ahmed Hasi and Farouk Salameh on 26 November 1986 in the Berlin Court it has been known that the Syrian secret service, with the knowledge and consent of the MfS, organised and carried out the attack on the German-Arab Society in West Berlin on 29 March 1986. According to documents just discovered it is clear that Libya was responsible for the bomb attack on the West Berlin La Belle Disco on 5 April 1986. The operation was not only sanctioned but also supported by the MfS.

However pronouncements by the SPD (Social Democrat) member of the Federal Diet's Interior Affairs Committee, Wilhelm Nöbel, asserting that a 'totally hermetically sealed-off' group of Stasi-staff not only arranged a new homeland for their RAF pensioners but also gave logistics support to active RAF cadres and composed propaganda proclamations to be left at the scenes of RAF crimes[6] would appear to be speculation. Up till now Nöbel has not presented any corroborating evidence for his assertions.

For the RAF currently still operating the fact that well-known comrades in relatively high numbers abandoned the struggle and demonstrated resignation, represented a propaganda defeat; their arrest is a second defeat. The readiness of some group members to act as witnesses for the state amounts to a virtual admission that the terrorist battle has been lost. A glance back at the years past, and the fact that RAF core members were unexpectedly willing to abandon the RAF and give up in resignation, as has been revealed in the meantime, is a pointer to fractures in the RAF and differences between the individual 'circles' of the organisation. The RAF has on several occasions altered its organisation, in part because it hoped after defeats to gain fresh energies.

II. ALTERATIONS IN THE ORGANISATION

In the first phase of the RAF attacks between 1970 and 1972 the initiative, the power of command and the control lay with the activists of the command-level core. When the group of leaders (Andreas Baader, Gudrun Ensslin, Ulrike Meinhof, Jan Carl Raspe) had been taken into custody in June 1972 the hierarchical centre of gravity centred on the prisoners. The simultaneous development concentrating RAF actions on attempting to free the prisoners in some sort of forced deal meant that the armed struggle was limited.

With the failure of the major operations of the year 1977 (Ponto, Buback, Schleyer murders) the RAF's concept changed. Up to the murder of Hans Martin Schleyer RAF strategy aimed at kidnapping eminent personalities from politics, industry and the economy, in order to put the authorities under pressure and force them to release the imprisoned RAF members. After 1977 the RAF did not carry out any more hostage-taking. All subsequent opera-

tions aimed at killing representatives of the 'Military-Industrial-Complex' (their 'M-I-C' strategy) and killing representatives of the 'apparatus of repression'. This development was accompanied by a restructuring of the organisation.

In the year 1982 the RAF tried for the first time to enlarge the basis of the armed struggle and gave it an ideological foundation. In May 1982 a new RAF strategy paper with the title 'Guerrilla, Resistance and Anti-Imperialist Front'[was presented]. In this paper the RAF declared that it was possible and necessary to unfold a new phase in their revolutionary struggle. Guerrillas, Militants and political fighters should come together as 'integral components'. Guerrillas, they argued, fought the armed struggle based in illegality; the Militants would have to launch their attacks predominantly from the legal part of society; the political fighters should carry out resistance. The common goal was to be the construction of an antiimperialist front. In this organisation there should be no demarcation separating the different lines.

Together with the strategic goals, this paper also clearly showed the RAF's new organisation. Its centre appeared at first still to be, as hitherto, the circle of RAF prisoners. Operations were to be carried out by the 'commandos', command-level units. Then as now this level only comprised 15 to 20 persons. This command-level was encircled by some 200 persons who formed the 'Illegal Militants'. This circle was surrounded by a third ring described in the paper as the 'political fighters'. These form the third wider field or the 'legal arm' of the RAF. At the beginning of the 1980s this circle numbered some 400 supporters and sympathisers.

In 1984 it became clear that the RAF prisoners no longer stood unchallenged on their own at the top of the RAF hierarchy. During the July 1984 arrest of six core members at Frankfurt and Karlsruhe a 'Planning and Discussion Paper' was found. Its contents had obviously been discussed with the RAF members in prison, but only trivial details could be corrected. The agenda was being set for planning future actions and the discussions about future strategy were no longer led by the imprisoned RAF members but instead were decided by the 'commandos'—the command level group.[7] These materials on 'Planning and Discussion' formed the theoretical basis for the '1984/85 Offensive'.

On 4 December 1984 the RAF prisoners began a hunger strike. The 'Illegal Militants' in the meantime carried out 15 explosives attacks and 23 incendiary attacks. Half of these attacks had 'military targets'. The 'Patsy O'Hara Commando' unit killed a German manager in the armaments industry, Ernst Zimmermann, in Munich; after an 'Elisabeth van Dyck Commando' group of the *Action Directe* (AD) had shot General Rena Audran in Paris. After the murder of Zimmermann on 1 February 1985 the RAF prisoners broke off their hunger strike. The transfer of initiative-taking and decision-making to the 'commando'-level persisted for some time. It was last visible in

'Offensive '86'. Earlier however there was already a clear drop in support and loss of sympathy.

On 8 August 1985 the RAF carried out a serious bomb-attack on the American Rhine-Main Air Base at Frankfurt. The RAF exploded a car-bomb which killed two Americans and injured 11 passers-by. On 7 August 1985 two RAF members had murdered US GI Edward Pimental, shooting him in the nape of his neck, in order to steal his ID-card. With this ID-card the RAF were able to sneak in to the sealed-off air base. In the note left behind later the RAF claimed it had been a joint action with *Action Directe*.

The murder of Ernst Zimmermann had already met with a lack of comprehension on the part of the New Left. The murder of GI Edward Pimental led to heated discussions among the 'Legal' RAF supporters. The 'command(o)' level of the RAF saw itself forced to formulate a response to the murder in a special paper: it acknowledged that the murder was—'a mistake'.[8]

The loss of a favourable response from the Left and the desperate attempts to dream up new revolutionary projects led to a blurring of the borderlines between fact and fiction, between political realities and their ideas. The discussions about a forward-looking strategy for the armed struggle and the resultant revolutionary tactics required continued up to the Frankfurt Congress arranged by supporters of the RAF and the Autonomous Left on 1 and 2 February 1986. At this Congress both the Autonomous Left and sections of the RAF sympathisers attacked the murder of GI Edward Pimental. They described the murder as an act of revolutionary 'self-justice'.[9]

Despite this loss of support the RAF held on to its strategic concept. It persisted in its assumption that armed action, the 'propaganda of the deed', could mobilise new recruits. Accordingly even after the peak of the criticism levelled at them by the New Left, the RAF carried out further murders. On 9 July 1986 the RAF began 'Offensive '86' and murdered Karlheinz Beckurts, a board member of Siemens. On 10 October 1986 two RAF members murdered the Bonn Foreign Office civil servant, Ministerialdirektor Gerold von Braunmühl.

The essential message of the RAF note left at the scene of von Braunmühl's murder was the call to establish a 'revolutionary front in West Europe'. At first the impression is given that this front is already in existence. On the other hand the writers of the note repeatedly give reasons why it is a necessity for revolutionaries in West Europe to close ranks. The opponent, the 'bourgeoisie', has, they argue, already lined up its forces: European Political Cooperation (EPC), they argue, is the 'operations centre against the revolutionary struggle' and the 'European pillar of NATO'. The European Community is perceived to be 'the instrument to enforce the power of state apparatuses', pushing them through the whole range of gear changes into overdrive, as it were. Linking the Federal Republic, France, Britain and Italy there has crystallised a coordination (*Vereinheitlichung*)—a process led by France and the Federal Republic. Overall the RAF

note communicates the RAF's recognition that the 'revolutionary potential' in West Europe was still far from having finished constructing this 'revolutionary front in West Europe'.

III. THE WEST EUROPEAN GUERRILLA

The RAF launched its first full-scale attempt to construct a West European Guerrilla with its 'Offensive '84/'85'. The groups the RAF were trying to enlist in this alliance were in the first place the French *Action Directe* (AD) and the Belgian *Cellules Communistes Combattantes* (CCC). From the beginning of 1984 there had been a growing interest evinced among the RAF's circle of supporters in AD operations. The Left terrorists in the Federal Republic evaluated the AD as being the only Marxist-Leninist terrorist organisation in Europe capable of functioning. Notes left by AD and their other publications were read with interest and became topics for internal discussions. This interest eventually led to the cooperation between the RAF and AD culminating in the murders of Rena Audran and Ernst Zimmermann, and the attack on the US Air Base in Frankfurt. The murder of the Director-General of the French Renault Works, Georges Besse, on 17 November 1986, can also be classified as one of these operations of the 'anti-imperialist front in West Europe'. Like General Audran and Ernst Zimmermann, Georges Besse was a symbolic figure representing the 'Military-Industrial-Complex'.

With the arrest of the leading members of the internationally-orientated wing of the AD (Jean-Marc Rouillan, Nathalie Menigon, Joelle Aubron, Georges Cipriani) on 21 February 1987 in a farmhouse near Orleans the 'Front' of the West European Terrorists was, for all practical purposes, smashed.

The CCC only gave the RAF logistical support in one single case. In the farmhouse at which Jean-Marc Rouillan and his three accomplices were arrested there were found explosives which the CCC had stolen through a break-in to a quarry at Eccaussines (Belgium) in June 1984. The RAF had used some of the same explosives in its failed December 1984 attack on the NATO School in Oberammergau.

Already in 1985 the RAF had attempted to get the Italian Red Brigades to work with them. This created difficulties, because from September 1984 the *Brigate Rosse* had split into two 'positions', as they called them. The first 'Position' is termed BR-PCC (Red Brigades for the Construction of the Fighting Communist Party) and it is like the RAF more strongly internationalist and anti-imperialist in its orientation. The second 'position' is called the UCC (the Union of Fighting Communists). This group is more 'proletarian' and geared to the 'class-struggle'.

The RAF published in May 1986 in its underground newspaper, *Zusammen Kaempfen*, No.6, declarations by members of the Red Brigades, some of them in prison, elucidating concepts, without commentary. After the RAF murders of Beckurts and von Braunmühl there were declarations of solidarity by the Red Brigades' internees. Other writing pointed to differences in ideology and conception.

In a declaration by the BR-PCC of 17 February 1987 there is for the first time a comprehensive evaluation of RAF and AD 'revolutionary activities'. It begins with the remark that in an 'objective political sense' the West European Front of the Guerrilla will have to be 'part of the programme of the Communists'. Then it goes on to say that the activities of the Guerrilla in Europe had become 'more specific'. In saying this the BR-PCC was distancing itself from the offer of cooperation being made by the RAF. The UCC exploited this and although till then it had not been 'internationalistic' it joined in open competition. On 20 March 1987 the UCC murdered General Licio Giorgieri who was responsible within the Defence Ministry for the armaments technology of the Italian Air Force. The Italian security forces in the course of 1987 arrested about one hundred UCC members. This was due in no small measure to the willingness to testify shown by witnesses under the Italian *Pentiti* scheme. Further UCC members were captured in France and Spain. The UCC Organisation has still not recovered from this blow.[10]

The 17 February 1987 declaration of BR-PCC remained an isolated case. There were no further support actions on behalf of the RAF either in the form of agitation or far less by any action by the Red Brigades. Nevertheless the RAF tried repeatedly to preserve the vision of a common European guerrilla front by naming its murder hit-squads or 'commandos' after international 'martyrs'.

IV. STRUCTURAL PROBLEMS AND NEW STRATEGY

The RAF developed its concept of attacking the M-I-C, the 'Military-Industrial-Complex', at the beginning of the 1980s. Both in its declarations accompanying the murders it carried out and in the articles of its underground newspaper, *Zusammen Kaempfen*, this concept surfaced with increasing frequency till it reached a climax in the 'Offensive '84/'85' (murders of General Audran and Zimmermann) and the 'Offensive '86' (murders of Beckurts and von Braunmühl) in the media, and was also accepted by wider circles of the RAF. After that this description of the armed struggle levelled off. This decline was accelerated by the discussion between some RAF members and functionaries of the Red Brigades on the question whether the 'industrial re-structuring of West Europe' was already completed or not.[11] During the February 1990 hunger strike there was no further mention of the 'Military-Industrial-Complex'.

At the end of the 1980s the ideologists in the RAF had discovered another 'buzz-word', a fresh strategic concept

to describe what motivated their guerrillas: namely, United Europe. This new definition first appeared in the underground press and in some of the information service editions for relations of the RAF prisoners. This coincided with the recognition by the RAF comrades that their own attempts to build up a West European Guerrilla had failed. The French AD, with which cooperation did exist, had been wiped out for the immediate future. The Belgian CCC, the Fighting Communist Cells, had been smashed. The Italian Red Brigades, split into two 'positions', admittedly proclaimed the existence of cooperation but there had been no joint action. Any solidarity with the Spanish GRAPO has been limited to some hunger-strike actions.

The invention of a new target for their hostility, namely the image of a 'European global power', is intended to boost the RAF's attempt to try once more to form a 'European guerrilla front'. Driven on by this new 'theorem' the RAF carried out two further attacks. On 20 September 1988 a 'Khaled Aker Commando' shot at the official car of the State Secretary Hans Tietmeyer, Permanent Secretary in the Federal Finance Ministry. The RAF attempted to justify the assassination attempt by asserting that Tietmeyer had a crucial role in the 'formulation, co-ordination and implementation of imperialist economic policies'. On 30 November 1989 a 'Wolfgang Beer Commando' murdered the spokesman of the Board of the Deutsche Bank, Alfred Herrhausen. He was Chairman of the Supervisory Board of Daimler-Benz and played a crucial role in the merger of Daimler-Benz and Messerschmitt-Bölkow-Blohm. Herrhausen had repeatedly expressly supported private investment in the GDR in the lead-up to re-unification. He embodied for the RAF not only the links between 'Capital' and 'Armaments Industry', but also symbolised the forces which, supposedly, aim to build up West Europe under the leadership of the Federal Republic into an economic superpower.

European economic policy, by which the Third World is exploited, also affects the agricultural sector, so reasoned the RAF. Accordingly the representative of the 'creation of the Moloch Europe' in this field is the Federal Agriculture Minister, Ignaz Kiechle. A 'Juliane Plambek Commando' unit declared on 2 March 1990 that it had 'attacked Ignaz Kiechle'.[12] In their eyes he represented the 'West European forming processes', moulding and manipulating the European internal market, leading to a 'United Europe of Capital'.[13]

On 3 March 1990 the RAF issued a communiqué spreading the news that 'the goal of the attack on Ignaz Kiechle had not been reached'. They had been forced to break off the action in order not to endanger persons not involved.[14] Meantime it emerged that the RAF prisoners, in contrast to their exclusion from the preparations for the murder of Alfred Herrhausen, were kept informed of the goal of the Kiechle operation and in agreement with the attack. It was only after the failure of the attack that there were discussions as to whether after all Ignaz Kiechle had been a correct target. After the attack on Herrhausen, which had been 'successful', many RAF sympathisers and supporters regarded the choice of Ignaz Kiechle as the next assassination victim as a distinct lowering of revolutionary energy by the RAF command-level and a sign of diminished capabilities.

The 'commando' went into hiding. It took seven and a half weeks for the discussions to be concluded and a response agreed on. No response was issued until 26 April when a new communiqué was put out by the RAF, now denying that any attack had been planned or attempted. Now the RAF asserted that the communiqués of 2 and 3 March 1990 had been part of a disinformation campaign by the Office for the Protection of the Constitution (Verfassungsschutz). The 'Agri-Worm' Kiechle was 'not the sort of target that would have any paradigmatic value', not an action anyone would wish to copy as a model. Simultaneously the RAF announced that it proposed to issue a 'comprehensive text' giving a statement of the RAF's views on the 'revolutionary process'. This was, they stated, necessary in order to bring to an end the 'disorientation and chaos which set in following the declaration fabricated by the internal security forces'.[15]

Alongside these clear dissonances in the organisation, it had previously come to considerable difficulties in communication between the command-level and the RAF prisoners. The hungerstrike from February to May 1989 had begun and had been carried out without the support of the 'commando'-level. The RAF prisoners had adopted a role that was not accepted by the command-level, at best it tolerated it. Helmut Pohl admitted as much when, in his letter of 10 November 1989, he admitted that the RAF prisoners had 'seized the initiative on behalf of others, at this time'.[16] The action started by the prisoners was not supported either by the 'commando'-level or by attacks by 'Illegal Militants'. The prisoners terminated the hungerstrike without any evidence of success. They were no longer involved when it came to planning the murder of Herrhausen. There is in any case no longer any steering of the attacks from the cells, as existed in the 1970s. The RAF prisoners were hardly in any position to judge the situation 'out there' in the outside world.[17]

V. THE RAF: WITHOUT HOPE?

The new concept of the RAF—its struggle against the 'Fascist beast West Europe'[18]—appears to have no prospect of any success. The latest murder attempt, the attack on Secretary of State Neusel which was acknowledged by the RAF, still bore the label. It was planned to kill Neusel, not because he belonged to the 'apparatus of repression' but because he was considered as part of the new strategic target, 'Europe as a global power'. The RAF's paranoid fixation with this target group is shown both in the short communiqué found at the scene of the incident and

in the paper giving a statement of basic principles, the statement that had been promised and awaited since the end of April, which finally appeared, as an extended note claiming responsibility for the attack on Neusel, on 29 July 1990.[19]

The declarations of the 'Jose Manuel Sevillano Commando' unit commenting on the question why the attack had failed (explaining that an inadequate amount of explosives had been used) are feeble, ineffectual, flaccid, lacking in any conviction. The attempt to justify the attack in particular on Neusel on the grounds that the Interior Ministry and by extension the Office for the Protection of the Constitution were opposed to any bringing-together of the RAF prisoners into one prison was an argument that only served to reduce their credibility with their own sympathisers and supporters still further. As these circles round the RAF were aware, the Office for the Protection of the Constitution was declaredly, and is, in favour of a regulated bringing-together of the RAF prisoners.[20] The problem of the 'commando'-level to communicate to the circles of sympathisers and supporters the necessity for the armed struggle to be carried on, is demonstrated by the rather casual treatment of the developments taking place in the states where there was 'real existing Socialism'. Mention is made almost as an afterthought of the 'dissolution of the socialist bloc and thus also the end of its historical function for the processes of liberation in the Trikont'. The fact is noted, but no attempt is made to examine the causes, or indeed the implications for the future.

The 'commando'-level, asserts a revolutionary 'counter-force' could only be built-up in a 'long struggle-phase against the newly arising Pan-German West European global power'. It is also argued that the 'anti-imperialist front in West Europe is composed of a multiplicity of struggles'. This is a call to alliance parties, which have hitherto rejected co-operation, or whose organisations have been shattered.

The RAF is clearly worried that it stands in isolation. The RAF is aware that it has lost the armed struggle if it remains isolated. Many comrades who were involved in the 1970s attacks have meantime dropped out, becoming Aussteiger. The aureole surrounding the guerrilla lost its radiance.

Helmut Pohl attempted to counter this impression of decline in a declaration which was published in a minor left wing Hamburg paper.[21] The letter remained largely disregarded. It only found an echo when a shortened version was published in the Zurich weekly, Wochenzeitung, of 5 October 1990. German publications took it up then, interpreting the declaration as a move away from the 'terrorist basic principle of the RAF', and as a beginning of a 'debate on violence' among the RAF prisoners.[22]

This way of viewing it is not correct. The letter first of all conjures up a 'Unity of the Prisoners'! This was doubtless a necessity after the experiences of the latest hungerstrike, in which not all of the prisoners participated. Next Pohl attempts to 'relativise' the significance of the arrests of former RAF comrades in the ex-GDR and the readiness of some of them to make detailed confessions and statements. Worries felt by the RAF at this development are underlined by the fact that Pohl in this connection expressly claims that he is also speaking about Heidi Schulz, Christian Klar and Brigitte Mohnhaupt. Pohl portrays it as a mistake that the RAF ever recruited these former RAF members, who have now been transferred to prisons in West Germany. The RAF, he suggests, recognised its mistake and 'right from the beginning tried to clarify and solve this'. As a result these people are not genuine *Aussteiger* (or *Pentiti*). The programme to assist *Aussteiger* [to] break free from their terrorist past is, according to Pohl, nothing but a propaganda action designed by the VS, the Office for the Protection of the Constitution, to lure these people to establish contacts.[23]

The offer of reduction in sentences and even release from custody which the VS, the Office for the Protection of the Constitution, held out to potential *Aussteiger*, evidently causes the RAF considerable concern. This is revealed by Pohl's assertion that if the former RAF members caught in the ex-GDR had been arrested anywhere else and any earlier, they would have been put away for life, with no prospect of review, remission or pardon. Pohl's formulation is intended to scare any activists from RAF circles from toying with the idea of abandoning the armed struggle.

But the crucial problem for the RAF is probably the circumstance that they are isolated, as they always have been, in the spectrum of left extremism. This is surely the only explanation for the rather lengthy passages in Pohl's discussion devoted to describing the 'concept debates' and expounding the development of the 'Left' since the mid-1970s. Pohl complains: 'Everybody was against us; the Left waged campaigns against us to break off solidarity with us, "de-solidarisation" campaigns'. The fact that the official argument with the RAF was 'running the same old film', stuck in a groove, was due to the 'positions' held by the 'mid-Seventies Left troop' today. This group was 'saturated', and in their sated state they harked back nostalgically to their 'youthful adventures in the playground'.

The excuse for a lack of 'engagement' or commitment was their inability to accomplish anything in the face of overwhelming odds and the force of the apparatus of the state. But this was no excuse; there were people everywhere willing to do something and also able to do things. This superiority of the apparatus of the state was just a myth, according to Pohl's argument.

The entire political militant Left had to 'get on a new footing' now. Only right at the end of his declaration does Pohl discuss the question of violence. He asserts: 'in revolutionary politics violence plays a definite role; the armed struggle is constrained by how it is politically

defined; the whole development is politically controlled'. In the hungerstrike, everywhere where 'conversations had taken place' (this presumably refers to conversations with representatives of the state authorities) the prisoners had 'laid down the thick-beams-formulation': this 'moves the entire argument in its whole context in the direction of discussion and political process'.[24]

From these sentences it is hard to extract, infer or deduce any rejection of violence. They are rather a sign of the pressure under which the prisoners exist, facing, as they are, long prison sentences. In addition these sentences clearly show the lack of agreement between the prisoners and the 'commando'-level. If the RAF prisoners should decide to make a clearer plea for the channelling of acts of violence, or for the giving up of violence, then the command-level will not be guided by any such plea.

The RAF will continue to perpetrate murders. It believes it is faced by an alternative: either the RAF has lost the struggle and must die; or the RAF has to continue the struggle, even with little chance, and the same risk of perishing. This is the attitude of desperados. The RAF prefaced the paper, which enunciated its basic principles, with a formulation extracted from Holger Meins' last letter: 'People who refuse to end the struggle, they win or they die: instead of losing and dying'.

The RAF only gives the *appearance* of having given up the hope of being able to win the armed struggle.

NOTES

*This article was translated from *Aus Politik und Zeitgeschichte* B46-47/9O by A.M. Stewart (Aberdeen).

1. Cf. 'daily newspaper', *taz*, 22 June 1990.
2. Cf. *Frankfurter Allgemeine Zeitung (FAZ)*, 23 June 1990.
3. Peter-Jürgen Boock, in *FAZ*, 23 June 1990.
4. Ibid.
5. Werner Lotze, in *FAZ*, 12 July 1990.
6. Wilhelm Nöbel, in *Quick*, 30 June and 19 July 1990.
7. Hans Josef Horchem, 'Terrorismus inder Bundesrepublik Deutschland' in *Beiträge zur Konflikforschung 1, (1986)* p.12.
8. 'An die, die mituns kämpfen,' published in the RAF periodical 'Zusammen kaempfen', 5 January 1986.
9. Hans Josef Horchem, *Die verlorene Revolution* (Herford, 1988) p. 162
10. Cf. Alison Jamieson, *The Heart Attacked: Terrorism and Conflict in the Italian State* (London: Marion Boyars, 1989) p. 216f.
11. Cf. Informationsdienst *Terrorismus*, No.2 (February 1990).
12. Note claiming responsibility (*Selbstbezichtigungssehreiben*) of 2 March 1990.
13. Ibid.
14. Cf. Communiqué of 3 March 1990.
15. Communiqué of 26 April 1990.
16. *FAZ*, 2 Dec. 1989.
17. Cf. Christian Lochte, in *FAZ*, 18 Aug. 1990.
18. Communiqué accompanying attack on Hans Neusel of 29/7/1990.
19. Cf. Communiqué of 29 July 1990.
20. Cf. Chr. Lochte (note 17 above).
21. Cf. Declaration by Helmut Pohl in *ak* No 322 of 24 Aug. 1990.
22. *Kölner Stadt Anzeiger* and *Die Welt*, 10 Oct. 1990.
23. Note 21 above.
24. Ibid.

A Travesty of Justice

In denying asylum to a Guatemalan man who fled forced recruitment by guerrillas, the US Supreme Court tied itself into semantic knots

Stephen F. Gold

Stephen F. Gold is a lawyer with the Public Interest Law Center of Philadelphia.

EIGHTEEN-YEAR-OLD Elias Zacarias fled Guatemala and sought refuge in the United States. Several months earlier, two uniformed guerrillas, carrying machine guns and wearing bandanas, told him to join their ranks. Mr. Zacarias refused to join the guerrillas because they were "against the government and he was afraid the government would retaliate." The guerrillas told him to "think it over well" and warned they would return.

Guatemala's civil war has been the bloodiest in Central America. Since the mid-1970s, more than 100,000 civilians have been killed by the military, their bodies left along the roadside. Another 40,000 people are still "missing," probably buried somewhere in mass graves. Nearly 200,000 children are orphans, and 50,000 women are widows.

Disregarding these statistics, the US Supreme Court recently held that Zacarias had not fled his homeland based on a "well-founded fear" he would be persecuted "on account of ... political opinion." The court didn't mention an advisory letter from the US State Department acknowledging that Guatemala's "civil conflict ... has caused various hardships and dangers, including forced recruitment by opposing armed forces."

What kind of proof would satisfy Justice Antonin Scalia and the

When two masked guerrillas with machine guns threaten to return for you, a person either joins or flees – either decision reflects a political reality.

five other justices who made up the court's majority that Zacarias had "well-founded" fear? Maybe living with the urban turmoil in Washington, D.C., has made the court believe that murder and torture are facts of life. Or maybe the court agreed with the Immigration and Naturalization Service's speculation that the guerrillas wore handkerchiefs not to conceal their faces but "because it might have been dusty that day."

Maybe the court thinks Zacarias should have asked the guerrillas to remove the handkerchiefs and identify themselves, so he could be sure his fear was "well-founded." Perhaps Zacarias should have asked for a demonstration of the effectiveness of their machine guns. Or, when the guerrillas were carrying their guns, he should have obtained a notarized affidavit from them that they really meant to return for him (which in fact they did twice after he fled), that his parent would really be killed if he did not join them, and that the guerrillas were not kidding.

Last, maybe he should ask the court to subpoena the guerrillas to come to the US and explain their motives. After listening to them, if the court still thinks no "well-founded" fear exists, the guerrillas could be asked for a demonstration. Maybe they've seen "Treasure of Sierra Madre," and they could point their guns at the court and say, "Badges, we don't need badges."

Besides not proving that the fear was "well-founded," the court held that Zacarias, in resisting the guerrillas recruitment, still had to prove he was "expressing a political opinion hostile to the persecutor...." The court opinioned that people "might resist" joining the guerrillas because of "fear of combat, a desire to remain with one's family and friends, [or] a desire to earn a better living in civilian life."

These may all be true if a person is considering voluntarily enlisting. But when two masked guerrillas with machine guns threaten to return for you, a person either joins or flees – either decision reflects a political reality and a political opinion about "which side are you on."

The court said Zacarias did not show a political motive because he was only "afraid the government would retaliate against him and his family" if he joined the guerrillas. How selective our memories are. During the Vietnam war, if Vietnamese villagers refused to be relocated due to fear of retaliation, the US labeled them "political" and forcibly removed them.

Perhaps the court would have been swayed if Zacarias had used "magic words" with the guerrillas: "I refuse to join your ranks because I do not accept the political ends or means of your political movement. After many years of living in terror, I have formed the political opinion both you and the government be damned." Is asylum a game of words?

Maybe the court has in mind acceptable multiple choice options to demonstrate that resistance is based on political opinions. A multiple choice list could be distributed to persons who might in the future want to seek asylum here.

Whereas the federal court of appeals believed it was necessary to determine if Zacarias resisted kidnapping "because the persecutors' motive [was] political," the Supreme Court ruled that only the victim's – not the persecutors' – political opinion was important to determine why he resisted.

Justice Scalia stated in his opinion: "If a Nazi regime persecutes Jews, it is not, within the ordinary meaning of language, engaging in persecution on account of political opinion." Under this reasoning, once again, Jews could not gain refuge in the US if another Nazi regime arose.

From the victim's viewpoint, political/religious semantic distinctions are irrelevant. For Jews who fled, it was the persecutors' motive and actions that would exterminate them.

The Supreme Court's absurdity will become clear when Zacarias is deported, and we count the days he is able to stay alive. Congress must once again tell the court that our history, humanity, and political will mandate that Elias Zacarias and other similar refugees shall be given asylum here and that Statue of Liberty means what it says.

On My Mind

China's Black Book

A. M. Rosenthal

Long before the extermination camps, the world knew that Hitler's basic instruments of power were torture and murder.

Only shortly after the Germans elevated him to office, "black books" were published in the West—detailed reports of the flogging, genital tortures, deaths by suffocation carried out routinely in Gestapo prisons.

From then on, the nations knew their ambassadors were accredited to a regime from hell and their businessmen were buying its products.

Most people did little or nothing until the war. But some did. They too acknowledged the truth and fought it—with their voices, however, lonely, with whatever economic and political strength they had, however small.

After World War II the underground writings of the Soviet freedom fighters told the world about the Soviet gulag. Most people did little or nothing. But some did. They acknowledged the truth and fought with whatever energy and power they had.

Now, black books are published again. They are about another national system of torture and murder—the Chinese Communist gulag, where every day of every year 16 to 20 million men and women labor and suffer in slavery.

They live—they exist—in a world of torture, starvation and humiliation meticulously planned to create greater profit through greater production for the Communist Government. We are the customers.

Recently I wrote about a report on China's slave laborers—"Laogai: The Chinese Gulag," by Hongda Harry Wu. He spent 19 years in the slave camps. I could not escape that book and cannot escape another on my table. It is about the hundreds of prisons in the huge province of Hunan. "Anthems of Defeat" is reported with documentation, statistical tables, notes and names by Tang Bogiao, a Chinese dissident.

Mr. Tang was moved from prison to prison and has compiled this annotated encyclopedia of evil. It is published by Asia Watch (212-972-8400).

Torture as national policy.

All prisoners received trials—without confrontation of witnesses or pleas of innocence permitted.

Prof. Peng Yuzhang, in his 70's, was sent to Changsa No. 1 jail for backing student sit-ins. He was placed on the "shackle board," a door-sized plank with shackles for hands and feet and a hole for defecation. Chained to the board, he would sing encouragement to student prisoners he could not see. Sometimes he would cry out, "I need a bath."

Professor Peng remained on the board for three months. Then he was sent to a psychiatric asylum. Is he alive?

The shackle board was just one form of punishment. Other commonplaces:

Torture with electric prods. Public whippings to the blood. Forced bootlicking. Chaining, face on cell floor, arms around toilet buckets in use through the night by other prisoners.

A dozen kinds of hand and ankle cuffs, sometimes with iron rods between them to make movement almost impossible. Multiple fetters to shackle prisoners tightly together. "Martial arts"—guards kicking prisoners into unconsciousness.

Solitary confinement in metal boxes so small prisoners can neither lie down properly nor stand up straight. "Electric shackle treatment"—shock applied through hand and ankle cuffs, often while the victim is chained to the shackle board.

Prisoners who do not fill work quotas are punished by all these tortures, by starvation diets, and by extended sentences. By official Communist policy their work is considered an essential part of Chinese export.

So we know—no escape. What can we do? American laws against forced labor imports are sieves. But stockholders can raise the issue at company meetings. Are we selling slave labor goods, or using our pension funds, to help the torturers? Please investigate and report back fully.

Before we buy, we can ask shopkeepers to find out from their vendors what "made in China" means—made where, by whom?

President Bush has vetoed every Congressional attempt to apply mild economic sanctions to the Chinese Communists. This battle will not end, whoever is elected President.

Meantime will all the delegates at the Republican and Democratic Conventions remain mute about slavery and torture in China? Will Ross Perot? Or will they cleanse themselves of silence—at least some of them?

Tibet's Shattered Hopes

The US should join other nations in condemning Chinese repression

Eric Kolodner

Eric Kolodner is pursuing a joint degree at Princeton University's Woodrow Wilson School and at New York University Law School.

The Bush Administration recently demonstrated once again both its willingness to sacrifice human rights and its inclination to acquiesce to Chinese pressure.

In mid-March a broad coalition at the United Nations Commission on Human Rights supported a European Community-sponsored statement condemning the Chinese occupation and oppression in Tibet. When this coalition sought much-needed support from the United States, Washington waited until the final hour and submitted a watered-down version of the resolution that the US knew would fail. As predicted, original supporters defected, and last-minute delay tactics by the US guaranteed that there would be no time to resurrect Tibetan hopes.

As prospects for democracy in Tibet faltered, President Bush emerged from the situation a clear winner on two fronts – both at home and in China. While presenting himself to the Chinese as the force behind the resolution's failure, he can simultaneously confront a Congress critical of his China policy with the assertion that he recently supported a statement condemning Chinese human-rights abuses.

This recent move manifests the cynical premise that drives Bush's foreign policy: that the fate of oppressed people must be subjugated to the maintenance of his domestic popularity and the manipulation of international geopolitics.

Not long ago, Bush was fervently condemning Iraqi atrocities against the Kurds as he rallied support for his Persian Gulf war initiative. Then, when advocating Kurdish freedoms was no longer expedient, he quietly abandoned their cause. Some Tibetans postulate that if the Tibetan plateau were rich in oil, they would have already regained their independence.

The ramifications of the 1950 Chinese invasion of Tibet have been devastating. Over 1.2 million of the 6 million Tibetans have died as a direct result of the Chinese occupation. Meanwhile, the Chinese have decimated the Tibetans' unique culture, destroying all but 13 of Tibet's 6,254 monasteries and murdering or imprisoning an entire generation of Tibetan politicians and religious leaders.

Because monasteries have historically been the centers of power and learning in Tibet, the Chinese have instituted severe re-strictions on religious freedoms. The Chinese Army continues to surround the three Lhasa monasteries that fomented uprisings of 1988 and 1989. Monks require permission before they can leave.

Meanwhile, the Chinese prohibit new monks from joining these monasteries and strictly limit the number of new monks at other monasteries. The Chinese have furthermore forbidden religious leaders from giving large public teachings and have canceled the Tibetans' most sacred religious holiday, the Monlam prayer festival, for the past four years.

Freedom of expression is severely limited for all Tibetans, but monks are granted even less latitude and are punished more harshly than lay people. While publicly advocating independence will certainly lead to imprisonment, monks can also be incarcerated for uttering "forbidden" religious prayer or for carrying a picture of the Dalai Lama, the Tibetans' spiritual and political leader.

According to human-rights groups such as Amnesty International and Asia Watch, monks and nuns suffer inhuman abuse in prison. Prisoners are often crammed into damp solitary-confinement chambers for months. Nuns are raped.

While the Chinese have particularly targeted religious figures in Tibet, their policies ensure that all Tibetans suffer under Chinese occupation. All citizens suffer restrictions on basic civil liberties. Individuals who transgress Chinese rules are tried under procedures known as *xian pan hou shen* (verdict first, trial second). Many people are never formally tried but rather assigned "administratively" to years of "reeducation through hard labor."

The Chinese policy of population transfer is especially alarming, for it promises to make the Tibetans a minority in their own country. The Chinese government offers special incentives to Chinese who settle in Tibet. Already the capital, Lhasa, has more Chinese than Tibetan residents. Beijing calculates that if this population-transfer policy continues, Tibetan cries for independence will soon be muffled under the blanket of new Chinese settlers.

Chinese policies in Tibet affect not only Tibetans, but much of the Asian subcontinent. China's rampant deforestation of Tibet not only contributes to the greenhouse effect but also alters the flow of rivers crucial to the Asian ecosystem. Recent studies have linked deforestation in Tibet with the devastating floods that have swept through Bangladesh and India.

Without concerted and direct pressure on the Beijing government, the Chinese will never change their policies in Tibet. Since the Chinese know the US will never retaliate against their intransigence concerning Tibet, they have no incentive to change.

As Deng Xiaoping once said about a 1970s democracy leader, "we can afford to shed some blood.... Look at Wei Jingsheng. We put him behind bars and the democracy movement died. We still haven't released him, and there has been no international uproar."

The Chinese fear that if they yield in Tibet, other peoples such as the Uighurs and Kazhaks will besiege them with similar claims to independence. Scheduled to regain Hong Kong in 1997, the China's government is also concerned that any reported domestic turmoil would damage confidence in Hong Kong's future and scare away vital investment.

Bush hopes that by fostering capitalism in China, he will concomitantly promote political liberalization there and in Tibet This simplistic formula is doomed to failure. There is no evidence that a mere infusion of capitalism produces greater political freedoms. General Pinochet in Chile brought about remarkable market reforms without compromising his authoritarian rule over that country. Capitalism and apartheid peacefully coexisted for years in South Africa.

It's time for the US to realize that its passivity reaps little reward either for it or for the people of China and Tibet. It's time to make the Chinese realize that they need us more than we need them. And it's time for Bush to demonstrate that he is committed to a vision which comports with his New World Order rhetoric.

India Under Fire Over Rights Abuses

Government denies torture, points to terrorism problem

Cameron Barr

Staff writer of The Christian Science Monitor

NEW DELHI

The human rights organization Amnesty International last week released a 195-page report accusing India's police and security forces of torturing, raping, and killing people during custody. Interior Minister S. B. Chavan immediately labelled Amnesty's work "mere hearsay" and an Indian diplomat in London said the report was part of an international campaign against his country.

The reaction to the Amnesty report seems to exemplify what three human rights observers here say is an unreasonable refusal, on the part of officials in India, to even acknowledge human rights problems. But a government spokesman says the official skepticism of human rights criticism is justified because groups active in India are too partisan in their approach and have served as fronts for terrorist organizations.

The Amnesty report highlights Indian officials' repeated denials that human rights abuses occur here. The document opens with a statement that late Prime Minister Rajiv Gandhi made to a British television interviewer in January 1988:

"We don't torture anybody. I can be very categorical about that. Wherever we have had complaints of torture we've had it checked and we've not found it to be true."

But Amnesty says "torture is pervasive and a daily routine in every one of India's 25 states, irrespective of whether arrests are made by the police, the paramilitary forces, or the Army." The report details 415 cases of custodial death since 1985, and says that in only 52 cases were criminal charges brought following the death. Three cases resulted in the conviction of a police officer, the report says.

"A major cause of the persistence of widespread torture in India," Amnesty adds, "is the failure or unwillingness of leading government officials and representatives to acknowledge that torture even exists, let alone that it needs to be vigorously tackled. The government maintains this position despite the fact that judges, journalists, expert commentators, police officers themselves, and official commissions have attested to its widespread occurrence."

Ravi Nair, a former member of Amnesty's board who has started his own human rights group here, says "any dissent is seen as treasonous" in India's current political climate. The central government in New Delhi has been struggling for years to control separatist movements in the northwestern states of Punjab and Jammu and Kashmir, as well as in the country's northeastern region.

"There's a mood of 'anything goes,' in the name of national security," Mr. Nair says, a mood that breeds little tolerance for the claims of human rights workers.

"The Indian government has always adopted a very cynical attitude toward any discussion or mention of human rights," says George Fernandes, a vocal opposition member of Parliament and a longtime associate of Nair's.

Mr. Fernandes suggests that India's reluctance to heed human rights criticism is culturally and religiously based.

"Indian society is by definition an unequal society," he says, because of the caste system and the country's dramatic economic inequities. The concept of human rights—insofar as it is based on the equality of all men and women—"is not acceptable to the Hindu mind."

One Western diplomat in New Delhi says Fernandes's views are extreme. He notes that several human rights groups have long operated in India and been able to voice their criticisms.

"But there is . . . a sort of reluctance to take [human rights groups] seriously," he adds. "They're all viewed with tremendous suspicion."

"The government feels bad about the totally partisan way of looking at" human rights, says Interior Ministry spokesman D. Mukhopadhyay He says that groups overlook abuses by terrorist and militant organizations in India, and that "everyone forgets about the security forces risking life and limb in service to their country."

The government is now forming an official human rights commission, a step that would fulfill a campaign promise of Prime Minister P. V. Narasimha Rao's Congress (I) Party, Mr. Mukhopadhyay says.

Indian officials have also argued that terrorists sometimes operate as human rights workers. A year ago, police arrested Shahbuddin Gori, a

> *'The Indian government has always adopted a very cynical attitude toward any discussion or mention of human rights.'*
>
> —Opposition member

New Delhi graduate student and a volunteer with Nair's South Asian Human Rights Documentation Center, on charges of engaging in a criminal conspiracy to funnel more than $50,000 to Kashmiri militants. Nair

says he feels Mr. Gori "has been framed in that case."

According to spokesman Mukhopadhyay and Y. P. Chhibbar, a Delhi University economist and the general secretary of the People's Union for Civil Liberties, the government has yet to convict a human rights worker for terrorist activities.

"I think it might be natural that the government defends its own workers" when they are criticized, Mr. Chhibbar says. He also reports that some senior government officials have taken steps to correct human rights problems identified by his organization.

Ethnic Conflict in Sri Lanka and Prospects of Management: An Empirical Inquiry

Gamini Samaranayake

Gamini Samaranayake is a Sri Lankan currently at the Department of International Relations, University of St Andrews, Scotland.

The objective of this article is to examine the background and the pattern of conflict and the management procedure in Sri Lanka. The author examines issues such as state sponsored peasant resettlement schemes, the official language policy, public sector employment and university admission policy as the background of the conflict. The pattern of the conflict began as political terrorism in 1972, gradually expanded and developed into organised guerrilla warfare. Finally the response of the government and the contradictory objectives of the main actors is examined.

The political and government structure of modern Sri Lanka[1] evolved under the successive colonial powers which ruled the country. From the sixteenth to the eighteenth centuries the maritime provinces were first under the Portuguese (1505–1667) and second under the Dutch (1667–1796). From 1815 to 1948 it was a colony of the British Raj. However, unlike most of the other colonial countries, Sri Lanka gained independence by peaceful means in 1948. The whole process of the transfer of power was so smooth that Sri Lanka in 1948 was even described as 'an oasis of stability, peace and order'.[2] Since its independence in 1948 until the 1970s its political processes have been dominated by the westernised elite and some orthodox-left wing parties. Unlike most other new nations Sri Lanka developed a flexible and viable political system in which competitive political parties had the opportunity of forming alternative governments. Consequently, Sri Lanka was cited as the best model of parliamentary democracy within the Third World.[3]

These ideas and myths regarding the political stability of Sri Lanka's democratic process were shattered by the political violence manifested in ethnic separatism led by the Tamil (minority) youth and the revolutionary-motivated violence led by the Sinhalese (majority) youth. Although political violence is a new phenomenon in Sri Lanka's contemporary politics it has posed a decisive challenge to the established institutions. Consequently, during the post 1970s period Sri Lanka has become a good case study of conflict and management in South Asia. The main objective of this article is to discuss the causes and pattern of ethnic conflict and the prospect of peaceful management in Sri Lanka. Therefore, this study shall be viewed from the following perspectives: background, government response organisations and objectives, development of conflict, and management prospects.

BACKGROUND

The background to ethnic conflict in Sri Lanka is deeply entrenched in the competition between the Sinhalese majority who comprise 74 per cent of the population and the major minority, the Sri Lankan Tamils, who comprise 12.5 per cent of the population.[4] The two ethnic communities are divided by differences of race, language and religion. The Sinhalese claim descent from the Aryans of North India, speak Sinhala and are principally Buddhists. The Tamils originate from Dravidian stock of South India, speak Tamil and are essentially Hindus. Both communities have been exposed to the influence of Christianity.

The current ethnic conflict is not a phenomenon of recent origin but could be traced back over the centuries in the historical annals. The Sinhalese and the Tamils have been intermittently involved in power struggles as in the seizure of the Sinhala throne by Tamil adventurers, the contest for parts of the Sinhala kingdom and wars

From *Terrorism and Political Violence*, Vol. 3, No. 2, Summer 1991, pp. 75-87. *Terrorism and Political Violence*, published by Frank Cass and Company, Ltd., England. Copyright © Frank Cass & Co., Ltd., 1991.

between the invading South Indian armies and defending Sinhala kings.[5] The ethnic conflict, in the current context, however, emerged as a result of socio-economic and political transformations during the British period. However, the more pertinent factors for such an ethnic conflict were created by the socio-economic and political changes which came about since independence in 1948.

The Citizenship Act of 1948 was a pretext for certain Tamil political leaders to break away from the Tamil Congress (TC) and form the Federal Party (FP) with the objective of campaigning for a federal state.[6] Since the formation of the FP there have been four major issues which have given an added impetus to the demand for a federal state. These issues are state-sponsored peasant resettlement schemes, language, state employment and university education.

The increasing pressure on land in the densely populated wet zone led to the resettlement of peasants in sparsely populated areas of Sri Lanka, mainly the dry zone. However, when peasant resettlement spread to the northern and eastern provinces, where Tamils constitute 86 per cent and 40 per cent of the population respectively, there was strong opposition from the Federal Party. Thus, the settlement of Sinhalese peasants in Tamil-dominated areas was perceived as a political strategy designed to reduce the Tamils to the position of a minority within their own territorial bases. The crux of the argument was that the resettlement of Sinhalese peasants within the so-called Traditional Homeland would undermine the balance of the ethnic composition.[7]

The issue of an official language was another area of disagreement and discontent. During the 1940s the Sinhala and Tamil politicians had mutually agreed that Sinhala and Tamil would be the official languages instead of English which was the official language of the British. The pressure exerted by the Sinhala Buddhist forces, however, compelled the Sinhala politicians to declare Sinhala as the official language. The Official Language Act of 1956 declared that the Sinhala language should be the only official language of Sri Lanka. This change of policy marked the beginning of another area of grievances and discontent. The opposition to the Sinhala-only act was spearheaded by the FP and culminated in the ethnic violence of 1956 and 1958.

The language issue gradually developed into a protracted and bitter area of dispute and the subsequent measures to establish Tamil as a language of administration was intended to alleviate this development.[8] The Tamil Language Act of 1966 recognized Tamil as the language of administration in the Northern and Eastern provinces where the Tamil population is concentrated. Moreover, the second Republican Constitution of 1978 sought to confer further recognition on the Tamil language by recognising it as an official language. These changes proved to be too late as the roots of disharmony between the two ethnic communities had already taken root.

The issue of language was not an isolated issue but was directly linked to the issue of public sector employment. The conditions in the northern and eastern provinces were not conducive for the expansion of agricultural activity and thereby limited the scope of employment in the agrarian sector. As a result a majority of the Tamils were obliged to seek employment in the state or private sector. Considering the added facilities for English education made available to the Tamils a larger segment of the Tamil people were absorbed into the state sector. The Sinhala-only act thus proved to be a serious threat to the privileges hitherto enjoyed by the Tamils. The Tamils believed that it was a deliberate attempt of the government to ensure that more Sinhalese and fewer Tamils were absorbed into the public sector. What was considered most unjustifiable was the fact that Tamil public servants were required to demonstrate proficiency in a basic knowledge of Sinhala at an examination prior to being considered as eligible for promotion in the service.

This conflict based on language and employment has been accompanied by competition for university education. Until 1970 a salient feature was that university admissions especially to the faculties of medicine and engineering were totally dominated by Tamil students. The Sinhala community perceived this so-called monopoly of university education as a denial of equal opportunities. As a result there was growing agitation for reforms in the system of university selection. By 1971 a system of standardisation was introduced. According to this system the pattern of marking was readjusted according to the media of study combined with a district quota system. The objective of this new system was to give students from areas with reduced facilities an equal opportunity to compete with students from areas with improved facilities. This system marked the beginning of a sharp decline in the number of Tamil students entering the medical, engineering and science faculties. Tamil students who accounted for 40.7, 40.8, and 31.1 per cent of the total admissions to the faculties of engineering, medical and science respectively for the year 1970–71 had declined to 14.1, 17.4 and 21 per cent respectively for the same faculties by 1975.[9] Thus, the competitiveness of university admissions and the constraints laid have doubtless played a significant part in the ethnic conflict.

GOVERNMENT RESPONSE

Given these circumstances, the government response towards the Tamil issues is vital in terms of the management of the ethnic conflict. Prior to 1970 two major efforts were made both by the Sri Lanka Freedom Party (SLFP) (1956–60) and the United National Party (UNP) (1965–70) governments to arrive at a political settlement with the Federal Party which would ease the problem of the ethnic conflict. The first attempt in this regard came to be known as the Bandaranaiake-Chelvanayakam (B-C) pact. This pact included a plan for regional councils empowered to take decisions pertaining to educational and agricultural issues, and on the selection of colonists for state-sponsored colonisation schemes. The pact also aimed to campaign for legislation that would recognise Tamil as the language of the national minority and as the dominant language of the Tamil areas. However, Prime Minister Bandaranaiake was forced to succumb to the pressures by forces within the SLFP led by Buddhist *bhikkhus* (clergy) as well as by the UNP. Finally, the pact was withdrawn.

The Bandaranaiake government made another attempt to address the language issue by ratifying the Tamil Language (Special Provisions) Act No. 28 of 1958. As a result of this act, the use of Tamil in education and public service entrance examinations, and for administrative matters was granted in the northern and eastern provinces. The drawback in these proposals was that they were passed in 1958, but to become effective they had to be gazetted and this was not done until January 1966.[10] Thus, the language concessions only had a limited effect on the diffusion of both ethnic tension and the Tamil agitation.

The second attempt was made by the Prime Minister of the UNP government (1965–70) to negotiate a settlement with the leader of the FP. This pact came to be known as the Dudley Senanayake-Chelvanayakam (D-C) pact. The basic tenets of this pact were to provide specific guarantees pertaining to the status of the Tamil language, and to the establishment of district councils.[11] In accordance with the demands of the D-C Pact the Tamil language was declared an official language in the Northern and Eastern regions of the country in 1966. Follow-up measures were also taken to draft a 'White Paper' comprising the proposals to set up district councils in June 1968. However, this proposition had to be abandoned due to opposition from within the government and the opposition led by the SLFP. In the final analysis it is evident that both pacts were futile because of pressure from the Sinhala-Buddhist chauvinists and political opportunism.

Finally, the Republican Constitution of 1972 which stated that Sinhala was the official language and Buddhism the state religion shattered the hopes of the Tamil people for a federal state. The decline in hopes of achieving a federal state was accompanied by a more intense desire for a separate state. As a result the gulf between the Sinhala and Tamil peoples widened. In 1972 the FP joined with other Tamil political parties such as the Tamil Congress and formed a coalition called, first the Tamil United Front (TUF) and later Tamil United Liberation Front (TULF) to fight for the Tamil cause. In 1976 the TULF demanded a separate Tamil state instead of a federal state.[12] Although the TULF continued to pursue a non-violent strategy, the other breakaway factions mainly comprised of Tamil youth resorted to guerrilla-cum-terrorist tactics.

ORGANISATIONS AND OBJECTIVES

The guerrilla movement is mainly formed by a group of the Tamil youth who call themselves the Tigers. This is a blanket term applied to the many factions of Tamil youth who operate undercover and are responsible for violent activities since 1972. The proliferation of factions has led to the formation of no fewer than 35 splinter groups. Of the many factions which operate five guerrilla groups have achieved dominance over the others. These groups are the Liberation Tigers of Tamil Eelam (LTTE); the Tamil Eelam Liberation Organisation (TELO); the People's Liberation Organisation of Tamil Eelam (PLOTE); Eelam People's Revolutionary Liberation Front (EPRLF); and the Eelam Revolutionary Organisation of Students (EROS).[13] Ideologically the LTTE and the TELO are more nationalist orientated than the other groups. The EPRLF, the PLOTE and the EROS express their own adaptation of Marxist-Leninist ideology.

All groups maintain their own international links. The LTTE maintains close ties with the PLO. Its members have been trained in Lebanon, South India and in camps set up in remote areas of the northern province. The TELO maintains links with the DMK in Tamil Nadu and the central government of India. The PLOT has established contact with the Popular Front for the Liberation of Palestine led by Habash. However, they all maintain a common contact with Tamil Nadu and India.[14]

For the financial support required to acquire arms and train members abroad these groups relied on bank robberies and financial aid from expatriate Tamils, mainly those living in the west and their refugees. Moreover, there is evidence of drug trafficking to raise funds for these groups. However, these groups were competing for supremacy and there was conflict over issues of ideology, strategy and personal leadership. During May 1986 the LTTE was engaged in a bitter feud with the TELO which resulted in more than 200 deaths including that of the TELO leader, Sri Sabarathnam. During June 1990 the LTTE once again attacked and destroyed the entire leadership of the EPRLF including the secretary P. Padmanabha. The LTTE has thus gained supremacy over the other organisations and this development may have a significant impact on the future direction of Tamil guerrilla warfare. The ultimate objective of all these guerrilla groups is to establish a separate Tamil state, which would be named Eelam. The territorial limits of this state comprise the northern and eastern regions of the country.[15] They all agree that the state of Eelam would be a socialist state achieved by means of violence.

PATTERN OF CONFLICT

The Tamil guerrilla movement introduced a new dimension to ethnic conflict in Sri Lanka. At the initial stages these guerrilla groups were confined to carefully pre-planned sporadic attacks on selected targets. But as it expanded and gathered momentum a distinct pattern of violence began to emerge and this pattern is viewed in three stages as following: The first period (1972–87); The second period (1987–90); and The third period (1990 onwards).

At the initial stages the Tamil guerrillas concentrated on assassinating Tamil politicians who collaborated with political parties in office since 1972 and police informers. These assassinations were organised by the Tamil Tigers prior to the break up of factions, [w]ith the specific objective of strengthening the cause of Tamil guerrilla warfare. Of these murders the assassination of the Mayor of Jaffna Alfred Duraiappah gave much publicity to the Tiger movement.[16]

From 1977 onwards there was a change of direction in the attacks which came to be focused on the police and the armed forces. At the initial stages attacks on the police forces were confined to Tamil policemen who conducted inquiries into violent activities. However, their targets later expanded to include Sinhala and Muslim members of the police and armed forces. From 1977 to July 1983, 50 police officers and servicemen, 11 Tamil politicians, 13 police informants and 16 civilians were killed, amounting to a total of 90 deaths.[17] The government maintains that approximately 100 members of the security forces and the army and almost 200 civilians were killed by the Tamil guerrillas between 1977 and 1984. A number of so-called lamp-post killings of Tamil civilians have also taken place. Other than the direct killings from 1981 to 1984, 34 police stations were attacked by the Tamil guerrillas and they were able to capture 473 weapons. The indiscriminate killing of Sinhala members of the armed forces resulted in an inevitable backlash in the south and paved the way for the ethnic violence of 1977, 1981, and 1983.

From 1984 onwards the pattern of violence took yet another turn. Sinhala civilians residing in isolated villages within the northern and eastern provinces came to be vulnerable targets. Gradually these attacks extended to villages and peasant settlements peripheral to the northern and eastern provinces. The attacks on civilian targets increased in their brutality and magnitude from attacks on small civilian targets to large-scale massacres, such as when 65 Sinhalese were killed in the Mullaitivu district on the Kent and Dollar farms in November 1985.[18] During the same year several incidents of violence resulting in the killing of Sinhalese settlers in the eastern province have become known, as in Dehiwatte and Namalwatta. The most serious of these attacks were the massacre in Anuradhapura, the historical capital of Sri Lanka, where more than 200 people were killed in May 1985; the mass massacre in Trincomalee where 175 bus passengers were killed in April 1987; and the bomb blast in Colombo which killed nearly 200 people in May 1987. In 1986 the guerrillas blew up an Air Lanka airliner killing 27 passengers including 16 foreigners.

Attacks on selected economic targets remained an inherent part of their guerrilla strategy. In 1986 the Tamil guerrillas damaged the cement factory in Trincomalee which was jointly owned by Japan's Mitsui Cements Co. and a group of Colombo investors. Bank robberies, damage to government property and tourist hotels were a part of their strategy. Moreover, their propaganda that Sri Lankan tea was poisoned compelled foreign buyers to impose strict testing procedures for Sri Lankan tea and made them more cautious buyers.[19] Thus, the activities of the guerrilla groups which began as singular sporadic attacks on selected targets gradually expanded and evolved as an organised guerrilla movement which challenged the government.

The response of the Sri Lankan government at the early stages was confined to constitutional and legal action to counter and prevent violence. A state of emergency was declared in the Northern Province and in 1979 the Prevention of Terrorism Act (Temporary Provisions) was enacted. This act empowered the police and armed forces to arrest and search persons and places and impose internment. Simultaneously, Brigadier Tissa Weeratunga of the Sri Lanka Army was commissioned by the state as commander of the security forces in Jaffna.

The non-military measures taken by the state included abolishing the standardisation rule, the status of a national language was accorded to the Tamil language in the constitution of 1978 and political decentralisation was introduced by means of the District Development Council (DDC) Act in August 1981. This act intended to decentralise administration and devolve power to the 24 districts in Sri Lanka. Temporarily these measures appeared to take the edge off the Tamil guerrilla movement. However, within two years the implementation of the DDC scheme proved to be a failure due to a lack of finances and an authentic devolution of power. The escalation of violence compelled the government to call for an all party conference in 1984. However, at the end of that year the all party conference dispersed after failing to reach an agreement.[20]

As the guerrilla warfare grew in scope and intensity the government of Sri Lanka turned to foreign countries for assistance. China, Singapore and Belgium were the prime sources of small arms and equipment, and South Africa was the main supplier of armed vehicles. Pakistan not only supplied arms but was also involved in the training of Sri Lankan security personnel and home guards. Israel assisted by providing facilities to the forces. The USA, and the UK too, provided assistance but the Sri Lankan Tamils had stepped up their propaganda campaign and had successfully lobbied in the western countries thereby limiting the overt assistance provided from these sources. Of the foreign countries involved it was India that played a complex and contradictory role in relation to the Sri Lankan ethnic conflict. By this time most of the Tamil guerrilla organisations had sought refuge in India and while harbouring them India sought to intervene as a mediator of the crisis following the ethnic violence in 1983.

Rajiv Gandhi's succession to power in late 1984 eased the tense relations between India and Sri Lanka, and President Jayawardane was able to meet the Indian Prime Minister four times within two years in order to forge a political settlement. The outcome of this new dialogue was the Thimpu, Bhutan talks of August-September 1985 where the government and representatives of the guerrilla groups came together for discussions.[21] These talks too ended in failure but India continued to participate as a mediator. Eventually, the two countries signed an agreement, which came to be known as the Indo-Sri Lanka Accord, to terminate Tamil guerrilla warfare which had killed more than 6,000 civilians and members of the security forces and rendered thousands as refugees in India and Sri Lanka.[22] This accord (July 1987) offered to establish provincial councils within the framework of a unitary state. The northern and eastern provinces would be combined into one administrative unit temporarily subject to a permanent referendum in the east which would finalise a merger. As part of this agreement more than 50,000 Indian troops were stationed in the northern and eastern provinces with the objective of disarming the Tamil guerrilla groups who were fighting to establish an independent Tamil state.[23] The accord and the presence of the Indian Peacekeeping Force indicated to the guerrilla groups that India would not help them to create a separate Tamil state.

MANAGEMENT PROSPECTS

The outcome of ethnic conflict depends on the interplay of actors in the conflict management processes. It is obvious that there is no possibility of a separate Tamil state. The idea of regional autonomy has been discussed as a solution. However, due to the following contradictory perceptions and roles of actors the peaceful management of the conflict is just that much more difficult.

The LTTE is by far the most intransigent Tamil guerrilla group in Sri Lanka. It is not willing to enter into negotiations for a peaceful settlement of the conflict. Due to its self-imposed status as the sole authentic representative of the Tamil people it does not like to share political power with any other Tamil party or group. It has already demonstrated its ability to hinder peace proposals imposed by India or Sri Lanka. Therefore, the LTTE would dismiss the prospect of any solution without its participation.

In order to get a peaceful solution the government has to offer more concessions to the LTTE. The Tamils are likely to give up the demand for a separate state in favour of a high degree of autonomy for the Tamil areas. The provincial council has provided a basic framework for devolution. However, the issues of power sharing between the centre and the provinces and the merger of the northern and eastern provinces remain unresolved. Another problem of implementing the provincial council system is the lack of grass roots institutions.

The Buddhist clergy (Sangha) plays an influential role in the ethnic conflict. They vehemently opposed any sort of devolution and the merger of the northern and eastern provinces of Sri Lanka. The Buddhist clergy's opposition is grounded mainly on fears and suspicions that any form of devolution of power would only lead to a separate Tamil state, which would subsequently be annexed by South India. Moreover, the cultural and social links with South India heightened the doubts that the Tamil demands for greater autonomy would subsequently lead to a separate state which would be an ally of Tamil Nadu. These fears of the Buddhist clergy surfaced when any attempts were made to introduce a system of devolution as in 1958, 1968, 1987 and the failure of any such subsequent attempts.

The disagreement between the SLFP and the UNP over a solution to the ethnic problem undermined the prospects for a political solution. Both parties collectively account for approximately 85 per cent of all the votes cast in any election in Sri Lanka. If the two parties could agree to work together toward a solution to the ethnic conflict, they could bring the majority of the Sinhala-Buddhist people along with them. The problem is that they generally refuse to work together. When one succeeds the other sabotages the negotiations through accusations of collaboration with murderers and terrorists. The problem of political opportunism was that when the SLFP attempted to solve the problem, the UNP vehemently opposed the solution and when the UNP attempted to solve it, the SLFP opposed, in spite of the solutions being similar.

The lack of a moderate Tamil political party as an active participant in Sri Lankan politics makes the prospects of negotiated settlement less likely. The Sixth Amendment to the constitution and the extended parliamentary term through a referendum, which excluded a general election for 11 years, led to the TULF abandoning participation in the parliamentary processes. This expulsion alienated the moderate Tamil politicians from the management process. Although the TULF returned to the parliament in 1989 it was no longer a political force within the Tamil community.

A significant outcome of the ethnic conflict in Sri Lanka is the increasing awareness of Muslim ethnic consciousness and radicalism. It paved the way to establishing a separate Muslim political party called the Sri Lankan Muslim Congress (SLMC). The Muslim Congress vehemently opposed a merger of the northern and eastern provinces and demanded a separate Muslim regional administration in the east.

The Indo-Sri Lanka accord not only failed to disarm the LTTE, but was contributory in the generation of strong anti-government sentiment in the south of the country. These sentiments were polarised in a group—the JVP—

which started the insurgency of 1971.[24] Moreover, the JVP resented the government because they believed that the government betrayed the sovereignity, independence and territorial integrity of the Sinhala people. Voicing the intensity and nature of this resentment they vowed to continue their attacks until the agreement is dissolved and the Indian Peacekeeping Force in the north and east of Sri Lanka was withdrawn. The JVP have embarked on a strategy of assassinating supporters of the Indo-Sri Lanka accord in July 1987.[25] The government was able to defeat the second insurgency (1987–89) of the JVP but failed to bring them into the mainstream of the Sri Lankan political process.[26] Any solutions in favour of the LTTE may lead to a resurgence of the JVP as a champion of the Sinhalese-Buddhists.

India is the only outside power which has an interest regarding the ethnic conflict in Sri Lanka. Basically, the Indian involvement was based on the two factors of Indian security and Tamil Nadu pressure. India does not encourage the Tamil guerrilla groups to establish a separate state in Sri Lanka, nor does it tolerate a complete military defeat of the Tamil guerrillas by the government forces.

CONCLUSION

Thus, the ethnic conflict beset by political violence has become the most intractable national crisis in the country since its independence. Despite the operational validity of the socio-economic factors within the context of the ethnic conflict, it is the political factors which have persistently been at the fore of the conflict. The Tamil youth of the North have resorted to guerrilla warfare to establish a separate state. Both parties have recourse to violence in seeking a resolution to ethnic conflict. Consequently, conditions in Sri Lanka have been more propitious for the containment of Tamil guerrilla warfare than its management. The government efforts at political negotiations and settlement have failed so far. The onus of negotiating a settlement has fallen on the government which has to depend on dialogue and discussion to arrive at a lasting solution which embraces the northern and southern guerrilla wars.

NOTES

1 Until 1972 Sri Lanka was known as Ceylon.

2 K. M. de Silva, 1974.

3 See J. Jupp, *Sri Lanka: Third World Democracy* (London: Frank Cass, 1978).

4 Department of Census and Statistics (Sri Lanka), *Census of Population and Housing, Sri Lanka, 1981*, Preliminary Release No. 1. Colombo, 1981.

5 Of these historical battles the Dutugamunu-Elara war has been integrated into popular Sinhala nationalism as a war which established the sovereignty of the Sinhala people. The Sinhala king

Dutugamunu is almost revered by the Sinhalese as a hero who saved the country from Tamil domination and established a Sinhala kingdom during the second century BC. This event has served as a symbolic manifestation of Sinhala nationlism.

6 The main outcome of this act was that while 140,000 Tamils of Indian origin obtained Sri Lankan citizenship nearly a million of them were stateless and disenfranchised. The Sirima-Shastri (1964) and Sirima-Ghandhi (1974) agreements solved the problem of the Indian Tamils. For details of this subject see S. U. Kodikara, *Indo-Ceylon Relations Since Independence* (Colombo, 1965).

7 See Robert N. Kearney and Barbara Diane Miller, *Internal Migration in Sri Lanka and Its Social Consequences* (London, 1987).

8 For source on the language conflict see Robert N. Kearney, *Communalism and Language in the Politics of Ceylon* (Durham; Duke University Press, 1967) and 'Language and the Rise of Tamil Separatism in Sri Lanka', *Asian Survey*, 18, No. 5 (1978), pp. 521–534.

9 C. R. de Silva, 'Weightage in University Missions: Standardization and District Quotas in Sri Lanka 1970–1975', *Modern Ceylon Studies*, Vol. 5, No. 2 (1974), pp. 151–167.

10 S. U. Kodikara, 1970, p. 197.

11 More details on the D-C pact see S. Ponnambalam, 1983, pp. 257–258.

12 The demand was widely interpreted in Sri Lanka not as a call for an actual separate state, but rather as a tactic to win further concessions.

13 Rohan Gunaratna, *War and Peace in Sri Lanka* (Kandy: Institute of Fundamental Studies, 1987), pp. 18–27, and Sinha Ratnatunga, *Politics of Terrorism: The Sri Lanka Experience* (Melbourne, 1988), pp. 224–271.

14 See 'Island at War', *Time*, 9 June 1986, pp. 11–16.

15 See Appendix 1.

16 T.D.S.A. Disanayake, *The Agony of Sri Lanka* (Colombo, 1984), pp. 29–52.

17 Details of killings see W. I. Siriweera, 'Recent Developments in Sinhala-Tamil Relations', *Asian Survey* (Sept. 1980), pp. 903–913, and Tilak Ratnakara, *Origins of the Ethnic Problem and Separatist Tamil (Eelam) Terrorism in Sri Lanka* (Colombo, 1985), pp. 21–23.

18 Government of Sri Lanka, 'Northern Terrorists Massacre Innocent Farmer Civilians in Sri Lanka' (leaflet, no facts of publication).

19 Eugene Mastrangelo, 'International Terrorism: A Regional and Global Overview, 1970–1986', p. 56 in *The Annual on Terrorism*, Dordrecht: Martinus Nijhoff, 1987).

20 All Party Conference Statement of His Excellency the President and Chairman of the All Party Conference (Colombo: All Party Conference Secretariat, 1984).

21 See Ministry of State (Sri Lanka), 'The Thimpu Talks: The Stand Taken by the Sri Lankan Government', (Colombo: Department of Information, 1985).

22 Figures on casualties cited in this article have been obtained from official statements published in local newspapers.

23 See Appendix 2 for the detail of Indo-Sri Lanka Accord.

24 The JVP is a splinter group of the pro-China Communist Party of Sri Lanka. This group broke away in the 1960s. Their ideological convictions are an admixture of Marxism-Leninism, Maoism, Guarism, and more prominently Sinhal-Buddhist nationalism. The JVP has succeeded in attracting Sinhala-Buddhist rural youth, mainly students and unemployed youth. In 1971 the JVP launched an armed insurrection to capture political power but the insurrection proved to be futile and resulted in the death of 1,200 persons and the imprisonment of 18,000 members. When the United National Party (UNP) came to power in 1977 they granted an amnesty to the JVP and provided an opportunity for them to participate in electoral politics. At the presidential election of 1982 the JVP contested and gained 4 per cent of the vote. However, in 1983 the government proscribed the JVP blaming it for the ethnic violence of 1983.

25 Their programme of assassination came to the fore when they attempted to assassinate the President in August 1987 while he was participating in a parliamentary meeting within the parliamentary complex. The President was uninjured but one of the District Ministers was killed outright and several more people were injured, including the Prime Minister, and the Minister for National Security.

26 The official figure for JVP violence and counter-violence by government security forces from July 1987 to December 1989 totalled over 6,000 deaths. However, unofficial estimates put the number very much higher.

Burmese, After Years of Terror, Hope Things May Soon Change for the Better

Philip Shenon

Special to The New York Times

YANGON, Myanmar, April 27—For many of the people of Yangon, the faded capital of a nation better known to the world as Burma, the best they could muster this week was a muted, wary optimism that maybe something might change.

"We do not know what to believe, whether this junta could ever tell the truth," said a 26-year-old painter, asked about the announcement by the military Government that it would release political prisoners and would allow family members to visit the nation's Nobel-prize winning dissident, Aung San Suu Kyi. "Optimism is a luxury."

After hopes for a democratic Myanmar were brutally crushed by the junta when it ignored election results in 1990 and jailed and tortured many of the winning candidates, optimism, he said, is a thing still easily smothered by fear.

Foreign diplomats in Yangon, formerly Rangoon, admit they are also puzzled by elements of the Government's decree. They say there is great—and justifiable—suspicion over the motives of the soldier who now appears to be running the country, Maj. Gen. Khin Nyunt, the 52-year-old director of Myanmar's secret police.

Pictures of Prisoners

In tea houses and noodle stands along the steamy, tree-shaded side-streets of Yangon, formerly Rangoon, people this week have been hunched over copies of the Government newspaper, The Working People's Daily, to study the grainy photographs of the 19 political prisoners who have been released so far.

"She looks very thin," said a shopkeeper eating breakfast at a noodle stand on Pansodan Street, pointing to the photograph of Mah Theingi, a writer who was Mrs. Aung San Suu Kyi's personal assistant. On Sunday, Ms. Theingi was released from detention in Yangon's notorious Insein Prison.

Between spoonfuls of an aromatic noodle soup flavored with banana stem and a sprinkling of fried garlic, the shopkeeper looked at the photograph again and again.

"Mah Theingi is not smiling in the photograph," he said. "The other political prisoners are smiling. Why isn't Mah Theingi smiling? Perhaps she knows this is a trick. We all hope these developments mean more openness. But we all know this could be a trick."

The shopkeeper and a group of friends stopped their loud chattering—their faces froze, in fact—when a Western reporter, traveling in Myanmar on a tourist visa since journalists are officially banned from the country, asked them about the soldier whose picture appeared on the front page of the newspaper, General Khin Nyunt.

"This man is very powerful," whispered one of the friends, brave enough to say something about General Khin Nyunt but not brave enough to actually utter his name in a place where strangers might be listening. Informers working for the general's secret police are thought to be everywhere.

Several Western and Asian diplomats in Yangon say they believe that General Khin Nyunt engineered the moves that began Thursday night with the announcement that the chairman of the junta, General Saw Maung, had stepped down because of ill health.

His health problems were not specified in the announcement, although diplomats say that the 64-year-old general suffered a nervous breakdown.

Last December, as he was about to tee off at a golf tournament, he reportedly started screaming, for no apparent reason, "I am the great King Kyanzittha! I am great King Kyanzittha!"

Known as Slorc

The junta calls itself the State Law and Order Restoration Council and is better known by Myanmar's large English-speaking population by the acronym Slorc.

"Essentially, Khin Nyunt is running Slorc," said a Western diplomat.

"Saw Maung seems to have been the bottleneck to progress," said another diplomat. "Khin Nyunt is no angel, of course. But he seems to be much more pragmatic, more sophisticated than his colleagues. He knows that something has to be done to prevent Burma from being isolated any further in the international community."

[That isolation eased some on Tuesday when Myanmar's Foreign Minister and his Bangladesh counterpart signed an agreement under which Myanmar will accept the return of thousands of Burmese Muslims who fled across the border since early 1991, charging they were driven out of Myanmar, which is predominantly Buddhist. More than 200,000 Burmese Muslims are now living in squalid camps in Bangladesh.]

Power Believed to Be Shared

Others in diplomatic circles say that General Khin Nyunt's power is still far from absolute, and that his authority is shared with other generals, most notably Than Shwe, who is now the junta's titular chairman, and Ne Win, the architect of the 1962 coup that began three decades of xenophobic authoritarian rule in Myanmar.

Among those free last weekend was the nation's last democratically elected Prime Minister, 85-year-old U Nu, who had been held under house arrest since December 1989. He was reported by his family to be in good health.

To no one's surprise in Yangon, the order did not include Mrs. Aung San Suu Kyi, the charismatic leader of Myanmar's pro-democracy movement and the dissident whom junta members often angrily refer to in their speeches simply as "that woman."

The daughter of Aung San, the nation's founder, Mrs. Aung San Suu Kyi has been held under house arrest in Yangon since July 1989. Last year she was awarded the Nobel Peace Prize for her nonviolent campaign to bring democracy to Myanmar.

On Saturday, it was announced that Mrs. Aung San Suu Kyi's British husband and their two children would be allowed to meet with her for the first time in more than two years.

Could Remain a Prisoner

There has been no suggestion that she will be released anytime soon from her family's gracious lakeside home on Yangon's University Avenue, and diplomats say that unless she agrees to leave Myanmar and renounce politics—something she has refused to do—Mrs. Aung San Suu Kyi could remain a prisoner of the junta for years.

Some are freed, but optimism remains a luxury.

As the head of the nation's secret police, the Directorate of the Defense Services Intelligence, General Khin Nyunt is thought to be well aware of, if not actually directing, the Government-sanctioned torture and killing of junta opponents allied with Mrs. Aung San Suu Kyi.

In its 1991 report on international human rights practices, the State Department found credible evidence "to suggest a number of civilian deaths at the hands of government officials or soldiers" in Myanmar, and that political opponents were routinely tortured by methods that included electric shock, cigarette burns, suffocation and sleep and food deprivation.

Military Operations to Stop

Special to The New York Times
BANGKOK, Thailand, April 28—The military government of Myanmar, formerly Burma, announced today that it would suspend military operations against the nation's best-armed rebel group in hopes of negotiating a peaceful settlement to an insurgency that began more than four decades ago.

The announcement, carried on Myanmar's state radio, amounted to an admission that Government troops would be unable to overrun the ethnic Karen rebels during the dry season, which ends in a few weeks.

Earlier in the year, the junta vowed that it would take the Karen headquarters, Manerplaw, by March 27, Armed Services Day. It missed that deadline, although Government forces did capture several other Karen strongholds in fierce battles.

The Nature of the Genocide in Cambodia (Kampuchea)

Ben Kiernan

Ben Kiernan is Associate Professor of History at Yale University in New Haven, CT 06520.

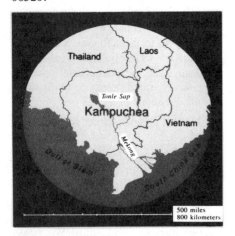

In Cambodia it is rather common to hear the view expressed that "Pol Pot was worse than Hitler." This is because the Nazis killed Jews but not Germans, whereas "Pol Pot massacred his own Khmer people." The first claim is incorrect, but the second is true. The word "auto-Genocide" has since been coined to describe extermination of members of one's own race.

During the Pol Pot period from April 1975 to January 1979, Cambodia was subjected to probably the world's most radical political, social, and economic revolution. The country was cut off from the outside world, its cities were emptied, its economy was militarized and its Buddhist religion and folk culture destroyed, and 1½ million of its 8 million people were starved to death or massacred, while foreign and minority languages were banned and all neighboring countries were attacked.

Background

Cambodia won its independence from French colonialism in 1954. It was ruled from then by Prince Norodom Sihanouk, an autocrat who tried to preserve Cambodia's independence from its neighbors and from the superpowers. This became much more difficult after 1965, when the U.S. massively intervened in the neighboring war in South Vietnam: U.S. and Vietnamese armies soon encroached upon Cambodia's territory and integrity.

On March 18,1969, the U.S. Air Force began a secret B-52 bombardment of Vietnamese sanctuaries in rural Cambodia (Shawcross 1979: 21-3, 31). One year later Prince Norodom Sihanouk was overthrown by the U.S.- backed general, Lon Nol. The Vietnam War spilled across its border, Sihanouk swore revenge, and a new civil war tore Cambodia apart.

The U.S. bombing of the countryside increased from 1970 to 1973, when Congress imposed a halt. Up to 150,000 Cambodians were killed in the American bombardments. Nearly half of the 540,000 tons of bombs fell in the last six months. In the ashes of rural Cambodia arose a Communist Party of Kampuchea (CPK) regime, led by Pol Pot.

Pol Pot's CPK forces (known as the "Khmer Rouge") had profited greatly from the U.S. bombardment. Contemporary U.S. government documents and peasant survivors reveal that the Khmer Rouge used the bombing's devastation and massacre of civilians as recruitment propaganda, and as an excuse for their brutal, radical policies and their purge of moderate and pro-Vietnamese Khmer communists and Sihanoukists (Kiernan 1985, 1989). By 1975 they were in a position of national power.

The Nature of the Genocide

The 1948 United Nations Convention on Genocide applies to the Khmer Rouge regime's persecution and slaughter of *three* categories of their Cambodian victims. These are: religious groups like the Buddhist monks; ethnical or racial groups like the Cham and Vietnamese minorities; and at least one part of the majority Khmer national group, the eastern Khmer population from the provinces near Vietnam (and possibly the Khmer urban population too). All were targeted for destruction as such and are therefore cases of attempted genocide by the Khmer Rouge.

On March 30,1976, a Pol Pot regime memorandum divided up what it called "The Authority to Smash People Inside and Outside the Ranks." Some political killings were held to be the prerogative of the Center, others were delegated to the regime's regions (Boua 1988, 3). Thus the Pol Pot group formally legitimized the murder of perceived opponents. Who were these opponents?

Genocide against a Religious Group

Pol Pot's government tried to eradicate Buddhism from Cambodia. Eyewitness testimony abounds about the Khmer Rouge massacres of monks and the forcible disrobing and persecution of survivors. For instance, out of a total of 2,680 Buddhist monks from eight of Cambodia's 3,000 monasteries, only 70 monks were found to have survived in 1979.

A self-congratulatory note on the subject also survives, in an eight-page Pol Pot Center document dated September 1975. Entitled *"About the Control and Application of Political Leadership in Accumulating Forces for the National Front and Democracy of the Party,"* this document says:

> Monks have disappeared from 90 to 95 per cent. Monasteries . . . are largely abandoned . . . The foundation pillars of Buddhism . . . have disintegrated. In the future they will dissolve further. The political base, the economic base, **the cultural base must be uprooted**.

This clear evidence of genocidal intent was carried through. As Chanthou Boua points out, "Buddhism was eradicated from the face of the country in just one year."

Genocide against Ethnic Groups

The largest ethnic minority groups in Cambodia before 1970 were the Vietnamese, the Chinese, and the Muslim Cham ethnic group. Unlike most other communist regimes, the Pol Pot regime's view of these and the country's twenty other national minorities, who had long made up over 15 percent of the Cambodian population, was virtually to deny their existence. The regime officially proclaimed that they totaled only 1 per cent of the population. Statistically, they were written off.

Their physical fate was much worse. The Vietnamese community, for instance, was entirely eradicated. About half of the 400,000 member community had been expelled by the U.S. backed Lon Nol regime in 1970 (with several thousand killed in pogroms). Over 100,000 more were driven out by the Pol Pot regime in the first year after its victory in 1975. The rest were simply murdered.

In more than a year's research in Cambodia since 1979 it has not been possible to find a Vietnamese resident who had survived the Pol Pot years there. However, plenty of eyewitnesses from other ethnic groups, including Khmers who were married to Vietnamese, testify to the terrible fates of their Vietnamese spouses and neighbours. This was a campaign of systematic racial extermination.

The Chinese under Pol Pot's regime suffered the worst disaster ever to befall any ethnic Chinese community in Southeast Asia. Of the 1975 population of 425,000, only 200,000 Chinese survived the next four years. Ethnic Chinese were nearly all urban, and they were seen by the Khmer Rouge as archetypal city dwellers, and therefore prisoners of war. In this case they were not targeted for execution *because of their race,* but like other evacuated city dwellers they were made to work harder and under much more deplorable conditions than rural dwellers. The penalty for infraction of minor regulations was often death. This was systematic discrimination based on geographic or social origin.

The Chinese succumbed in particularly large numbers to hunger and to diseases like malaria. The 50 percent of those who perished is a higher proportion than that estimated for Cambodia's city dwellers in general (about one-third). Further, the Chinese language, like all foreign and minority languages, was banned, and so was any tolerance of a culturally and ethnically distinguishable Chinese community. That was to be destroyed "as such" (Kiernan 1986).

The Muslim Chams numbered at least 250,000 in 1975. Their distinct religion, language and culture, large villages, and autonomous networks threatened the atomized, closely supervised society that the Pol Pot leadership planned. An early 1974 Pol Pot document records the decision to break up the Cham people, adding: "Do not allow too many of them to concentrate in one area. " Cham women were forced to cut their hair short in the Khmer style, not wear it long as was their custom; then the traditional Cham sarong was banned, as peasants were forced to wear only black pajamas; then restrictions were placed upon religious activity.

In 1975 the new Pol Pot government turned its attention to the Chams with a vengeance. Fierce rebellions broke out. In one case, the authorities attempted to collect all copies of the Koran. The villagers staged a protest demonstration, and Khmer Rouge troops fired into the crowd. The Chams then took up swords and knives and slaughtered half a dozen troops. The retaliating armed forces massacred many and pillaged their homes. They evacuated the area, and razed the village, and then turned to a neighboring village, massacring 70 percent of its inhabitants.

Soon the Pol Pot army forcibly emptied all 113 Cham villages in the country. About 100,000 Chams were massacred and the survivors were dispersed in small groups of several families. Islamic schools and religion, as well as the Cham language, were banned. Thousands of Muslims were physically forced to eat pork. Many were murdered for refusing. Of 113 Cham *hakkem,* or community leaders, only 20 survived in 1979. Only 25 of their 226 deputies survived.

All but 38 of about 300 religious teachers at Cambodia's Koranic schools perished. Of more than a 1,000 who had made the pilgrimage to Mecca, only about 30 survived (Kiernan 1988).

The toll goes on. The Thai minority of 20,000 was reportedly reduced to about 8,000. Only 800 families survived of the 1,800 families of the Lao ethnic minority. Of the 2,000 members of the Kola minority, "no trace . . . has been found" (Kiernan 1990).

Genocide against a Part of the Majority National Group

Finally, of the majority Khmers, 15 percent of the rural population perished, and 25 percent of the urban. The most horrific slaughter was in the very last six months of the regime, in the politically suspect Eastern Zone bordering Vietnam. My interviews with 87 survivors revealed something of the toll. In just eleven villages, the Khmer Rouge carried out 1,663 killings in 1978. In another community of 350 people, there were 95 executions in 1978; 705 executions occurred in another subdistrict; 1,950 in another; 400 in another. Tens of thousands of other villagers were deported to the northwest of the country. There they were "marked" as easterners by being forced to wear a blue scarf, reminiscent of Hitler's yellow star for Jews (Kiernan 1989a), and then eliminated en masse.

A total 1978 murder toll of more than 100,000 (more than one-seventeenth of the eastern population) can safely be regarded as a minimum estimate (Kiernan 1986a). The real figure is probably much higher.

The World's Response

In 1990 the perpetrator of all these massacres remains a member of the United Nations, represented there by Pol Pot's hand-picked ambassador. From 1979, all Western countries refused every opportunity to challenge the Pol Pot regime's right to speak for its victims. Most, including the U.S., have regularly supported it.

Ironically, one last chance derived from this. While still a member state of the UN, *the Pol Pot regime could be held accountable* for its crimes in the World Court. Its overthrow in 1979 also meant that the evidence could be gathered against it. Fellow members of the UN, who have signed the Convention without reservations, could take the case to the World Court. None has done so even though the Pol Pot forces remain the major obstacle to peace in Cambodia. Negotiations have consistently broken down over their role, and because of Chinese and U.S. demands for the ouster of their only Cambodian opponent, the Hun Sen regime.

The chance is unique in the annals of mass murder. Failure to seize it undoubtedly encourages future genocidists in the knowledge that the Convention will never be applied. The long delay has buoyed Pol Pot's forces, now pursuing a war to retake power.

References

Boua, Chanthou, David P. Chandler, and Ken Kiernan, eds. and comps. *Pol Pot Plans the Future: Confidential Leadership Documents from Democratic Kampuchea, 1976-77.* Southeast Asia Studies Monograph no. 33. New Haven, Conn.: Yale University, 1988.

Kiernan, Ben. *How Pol Pot Came to Power.* New York: Routledge, Chapman and Hall, 1985.

_____. "Kampuchea's Ethnic Chinese Under Pol Pot: A Case of Systematic Social Discrimination." *Journal of Contemporary Asia* 16, no. 1 (1986): 18-29.

_____. *Cambodia: Eastern Zone Massacres.* Documentation Series no. 1. New York: Columbia University Center for the Study of Human Rights, 1986a.

_____. "Orphans of Genocide: The Cham Muslims of Kampuchea under Pol Pot." *Bulletin of Concerned Asian Scholars* 20, no. 4 (1988): 2-33.

_____. "The American Bombardment of Kampuchea, 1969-1973." *Vietnam Generation* 1 (Winter 1989): 4-41.

_____. "Blue Scarf/Yellow Star: A Lesson in Genocide," *Boston Globe* (27 February 1989a).

_____. "The Survival of Cambodia's Ethnic Minorities." *Cultural Survival* 14, no. 3 (1990): 64-66.

Shawcross, William. *Sideshow: Kissinger, Nixon and the Destruction of Cambodia.* New York: Simon and Schuster, 1979.

Wadalabhitewad Journal

Violence, Like Punjab's Wheat, Finds Fertile Soil

Edward A. Gargan

Special to The New York Times

Wadalabhitewad, India—Young, knee-high wheat undulated in the hazy sunlight, fields of it stretching away from the Grand Trunk Road, which arrows toward Pakistan. Lakhwinder Singh shuffled out of his farmhouse, a mass of black hair knotted atop his head. Then, with a length of patterned cotton slung over his shoulder, he fashioned a rough turban, tucking in the last corner with the carelessness of habit.

"This road has been manned by security forces for a long time so we do not have much of a problem," he said, gesturing with a farmer's calloused hand. "Still, we cannot go out at night and that hampers us. We used to work at night, but not now."

He looked up as his mother arrived with a tray of glasses filled with the toffee-colored sweet tea drunk everywhere in northern India. "But we have less to fear from the terrorists than the police," he resumed. "They will grab you and suspect you."

A CALAMITOUS DECADE

Mr. Singh, who tills 50 acres with his brother Sukhwinder, dropped his head when he talked of the troubles that have gripped the Punjab for nearly a decade, troubles that have resulted in an attack on and desecration of the Sikhs'

holiest shrine, the emergence of dozens of armed extremist groups and the slowdown in Punjab's economy, the most productive in India.

At the conflict's very roots, Punjabis are consumed by the belief that the central government has discriminated against them since independence in 1947 in terms of development, access to jobs and a voice in national affairs. But over the last eight years Sikh animosities have been solidified by the memory of Prime Minister Indira Gandhi's order to attack the Golden Temple in Amritsar to evict armed extremists, and the memory of the Hindu-led riots that led to the deaths of thousands of Sikhs after Mrs. Gandhi was assassinated by her Sikh bodyguards.

"One thing you have to assume is that all Sikhs are angry with the Government over this," said Khushwant Singh, one of India's great historians, as well as one of its wittiest writers. "Then there is the vision of Khalistan, an independent state. But it is not viable. But it goes on and on. There is still what Toynbee called the consciousness of frontiers."

While from his deeply cushioned chair in his New Delhi study Khushwant Singh surveys India from a more nationalist perspective, in the Punjab it is the memories of death, and the dream of Arnold J. Toynbee's frontiers that rule life.

Since 1984, when 635 people—police officers, civilians, militants—were

killed in incidents ascribed to political unrest, until last year, when the police recorded 4,766 deaths, Punjab has plummeted into a violence that has touched nearly everyone's life. The houses of public officials are guarded by men with machine guns. Civilians traveling on trains or buses run the risk of attack. Funds are extorted from shop and factory owners to finance the activities of separatist militants. Farmers are prevented from working their fields in the coolness of the night by police-imposed curfews.

In New Delhi, successive Governments have struggled to regain control of the Punjab, to weld it firmly into the Indian Union, as equally firmly as some Sikhs try to complete its divorce.

"The Sikhs should be able to rule as they like, not interfered with by the Government," said Harbhajan Singh, a business student at Khalsa College in Amritsar. "The Punjab problem cannot be solved until the boys who picked up arms are called to the table to negotiate."

But as romantic as the idea of an independent Sikh homeland may sound to the ears of the aggrieved, a realism that it is hardly possible, that the future lies with India, is more widely accepted. Reluctantly perhaps, but accepted nonetheless.

Gurpeet Singh, another business student at Khalsa College, summed up the view of many of his classmates. "If the Government adopts a positive attitude, withdraws the army, releases those in prison, we would not necessarily need Khalistan, but we could be an autonomous state," he said.

Every day, a dozen or more people die in violence related in one way or another to militant Sikh separatist activity. Sometimes, it is an attack on the police or army. On other occasions, as happened in late December, militants stop a train and systematically kill all the Hindus aboard. In all cases, the violence seems intended to show that the Punjab is ungoverned and ungovernable.

It is, though, the central Government, dominated almost since independence by the Congress Party, that is blamed by many commentators for the misery of the Punjab. Tavleen Singh, a widely respected columnist, put it bluntly: "In Delhi, we who count ourselves among the liberal press have been bitterly critical time and again of the Congress's role in creating the Punjab problem."

ELECTIONS SCHEDULED

Once again, the Government is trying to fashion a way forward for the Punjab and its heavily Sikh population; of 20 million Punjabis, perhaps one out of three is Sikh. In February, elections for Parliament and the local legislature are to be held, elections that were canceled last year during a spasm of violence that left a dozen candidates dead and hundreds of civilians massacred by militants trying to disrupt the election process.

A bloody conflict drags on between Sikhs and India's Government.

The divisiveness of conflicting personalities and power bases has thrown Sikh political leaders into confusion. Some wish to fight the election, and in the process, they believe, regain control of Punjab's political future. Others, though, regard the entire exercise as a cynical and dishonest ploy by the government of Prime Minister P. V. Narasimha Rao that will result in rigged elections. The numerous extremist groups have declared they will kill anyone who tries to run for office.

Gurjeet Singh Jawanda, an official in one of the main Sikh political groupings, all confusingly called Akali Dal, differs with his political colleagues who do not want to participate in the elections. "My personal view is that we should not run away from elections," he said. "I am pretty sure the people are with us. But many people have lost total faith in the center. Remember, the center has gone back on its commitments to the Punjab time and again."

Here in Wadalabhitewad, an undistinguished village just 12 miles from the Pakistani border, there is, however, a visible weariness with the killings, the curfews, the political chaos that have swept away the certainties of rural life. "The common man will not care if the elections are held or not," said Lakhwinder Singh. "We only care about our problems. Whatever is happening in the Punjab is very wrong. We want peace so that the old prosperity can flourish."

War and Peace Advance in Sudan

Karen Lange

The biggest offensive by the Sudanese government in nine years of civil war has overrun about a dozen towns and driven rebels into the southeastern corner of the country.

But even with their backs against the borders of Kenya and Uganda, the guerrillas of John Garang's Sudan People's Liberation Army (SPLA) are continuing their struggle against a succession of authoritarian governments based in Khartoum, the Sudanese capital.

As troops from the Islamic fundamentalist government advanced against the rebels last month, Khartoum hedged its bets by dispatching delegates to peace talks in Abuja, Nigeria.

While the two sides discussed the conflict in which thousands have died and more than a million have been forced from homes and farms, the shifting fighting has imperiled some 300,000 southerners who the United Nation's Operation Lifeline Sudan estimates are in desperate need of food and medicine.

Relief organizations send most of their emergency aid to southern Sudan overland through northern Kenya and Uganda, the only feasible routes for delivering large amounts of supplies to much of the south. If the war forces relief organizations to operate solely out of Khartoum in the north, the flow of aid to the south will slow to a trickle, because supplies will have to be sent by barge down the White Nile, says Daniel Kelly, executive director of the Nairobi-based Association of Christian Resource Organizations Serving Sudan. The government has denied aid groups permission to fly to most rebel-held areas since the dry season offensive started in March.

The May 27 capture of Kapoeta, a center for relief operations on the road from Kenya, cut the main overland route into southern Sudan, blocking humanitarian organizations' access to most territory east of the Nile, Kelly says. But Operation Lifeline has so far been able to reach parts of southern Sudan west of the Nile and some territory east of the river, including Garang's headquarters of Torit, using overland routes from Uganda, says Detlef Palm, Nairobi-based program coordinator for Unicef, the United Nations Children's Fund.

There are many reasons the government of Lt. Gen. Omar Ahmad Hassan al-Bashir has gained control over relief routes and the battlefield this dry season. Khartoum has benefited from:

- weapons Western diplomats say it bought with hundreds of millions of dollars received from Iran;
- the overthrow in May 1991 of SPLA backer Ethiopian military ruler Mengistu Haile Mariam; and
- a split in the rebel group last August that only began to heal early this month.

But the SPLA guerrillas have a single powerful element on their side—the weather.

The rain that usually marks the end of the government's annual dry season offensive has begun falling already in southern Sudan. And, even if the dry season continues longer than usual, as appears likely, heavy rains almost certainly will make roads impassable by the end of June or early July, Palm says.

The rainy season, which continues through November, will leave government troops stranded on islands in the midst of the bush, controlled by the SPLA.

"As soon as the rains do come, the government troops will be in a vulnerable position," says a U.S. official in Washington, DC. "How are they going to supply these towns? Southern Sudan is huge. You could take all of Vietnam and drop it into southern Sudan and it would disappear. It's not like you can take 20,000 troops and go in there and subdue it."

Garang has vowed the rebels will fight on, even if the government takes every town the SPLA holds.

"What the government is doing is entering towns and saying it has captured them, which is true," says Bona Malwal, a London-based Sudanese journalist who endorses the cause of the SPLA. "But how much territory do these towns represent? I've never seen a guerrilla army defeated this way."

"The rebels haven't fought any big battles and lost," the U.S. official says. "There's been fighting (only) in the sense that the rebels have been harassing convoys and inflicting a lot of casualties."

"I don't think you can say there is a decisive victory by the government against the rebels," says Francis Deng, a former Sudanese foreign minister who is a senior fellow at the Brookings Institution in Washington, DC. "It's very easy to see these forces get back

Reprinted from *Africa News*, June 8–June 21, 1992, p. 7. Copyright © 1992, Africa News Service.

to the bush and continue fighting for years to come."

Even if the government succeeded on the battlefield, Sudan would not be rid of the deep religious, cultural and ethnic rift between north and south, fostered by the British in colonial days and widened in post-independence conflicts, Deng says. The north, which contains about four-fifths of Sudan's estimated 26 million people is predominately Arab-speaking and Muslim. The government in recent years has imposed *Sharia,* or Islamic law, a move resisted by the black Africans in the south, who are predominately Christian and animist. Attempts to unify north and south by force will only fuel the anger that drives the rebels, Deng says.

Estimates of the troop strengths of the government and the SPLA vary. The U.S. official says each side has between 10,000 and 30,000 troops in the south. One press report estimates government forces at 80,000 and the rebels at 40,000.

Whatever their numbers, John Garang's faction of the SPLA, which contains 90% to 95% of the rebel troops, has been in retreat since the government began this year's offensive in March.

When Ethiopian rebels forced Mengistu Haile Mariam from power last year, the SPLA lost bases, a radio station and a source of military supplies. Since the split in the SPLA, government troops have enjoyed free passage through territory held by the break-

away "Nasir" faction, based in the Sudanese towns of Nasir, Akobo and Waat. The government has seized towns long held by Garang's forces, most recently Kapoeta, a crossroads of 45,000 in the heart of the rebel leaders' territory that served as the headquarters for the relief arm of the SPLA, the Sudan Relief and Rehabilitation Association.

In addition to complicating relief efforts, the fall of Kapoeta sent thousands of refugees, including rebel fighters, over the border into Kenya and put further pressure on Garang's headquarters, a town about 90 miles (144 kilometers) to the west. Government forces cut a supply line, leaving Torit open to attack on two fronts.

An SPLA spokesman characterizes the rebel's losses of towns as "strategic withdrawals." But there are indications the setback is more serious.

The government-controlled Sudan News Agency reported that when the army took Kapoeta it captured 29 rebel fighters, including two lieutenants, chased three battalions into Kenya, where they were disarmed as refugees, and seized large amounts of weapons, food and medicine.

Elsewhere in the country, government officials report that hundreds of SPLA fighters, deprived of supplies, are surrendering.

This year's offensive represents the largest government advance into the south since 1983, when the SPLA began the latest in a series of north-south struggles that have divided Sudan since

1955. A 1972 accord granted the south limited autonomy and gave the country a decade of respite from civil war. But fighting began again after the government cut the south into three parts and seized areas containing oil, uranium and fertile land.

The negotiations in late May and early June marked the first time the government and the SPLA have met for peace talks in over two and a half years. The Nigeria talks were attended both by Garang's "Torit" SPLA and by the Nasir group, which split from the main rebel body over what it described as human rights violations, mismanagement and unrealistic objectives.

The government came to the peace talks with an offer of autonomy for the south within a federal system and exemption from *Sharia* for non-Moslem areas. The Torit SPLA came asking for a secular state and an end to Islamic law throughout Sudan, and—if that was not possible—either confederation or self-determination. The Nasir faction came demanding self-determination.

In the midst of talks, the two rebel groups announced they were unifying, at least at the bargaining table, to press for self-determination. When the government refused to discuss an independence referendum, the united SPLA agreed to drop the demand and discuss a Nigerian proposal for power-sharing.

Both sides agreed to meet again in Abuja at a later date.

Terrorism in America

Although the focus on terrorism is usually on overseas developments, there is increasing evidence of both intensification and greater potentialities in the United States. Oliver Revell's essay stresses the U.S. government's role in countering existing groups identified as operating in our jurisdiction. James Stinson's article is more expansive in its survey of indigenous groups as well as enumerating those that are externally supported in their activities here. This additional focus on sponsorship and networking abroad leads to a further discussion of the steps necessary to counter these groups by the American authorities.

"Bombs Over America" provides a frightening picture of the potential for actual violence in the streets of the United States as well as the available instruments for this or other kinds of terroristic activities. The companion piece, "The Plague of Our Cities," depicts all too graphically the connection between drugs, arms, and violence in urban America. Overseas, the attention is often focused on children as products of violent circumstances; now it is also America's turn to wonder and concern itself with the legacy of the street cultures on their eventual behavior.

Looking Ahead: Challenge Questions

What similarities exist between U.S. terrorist groups and overseas terrorist groups? What aspects are unique to the U.S. groups?

What are the prospects and the means to counter terrorism in America? Is terrorism a manageable phenomenon in the United States?

Structure of Counterterrorism Planning and Operations in the United States

Oliver B. Revell

Federal Bureau of Investigation, Washington, DC 20520

INTRODUCTION

Responsibility for managing the federal response to acts of terrorism rests with the attorney general of the United States. As the chief enforcement officer of the federal government, the attorney general coordinates all federal law enforcement activity. The attorney general has designated the Federal Bureau of Investigation (FBI) to be the lead federal law enforcement agency in the U.S. government's fight against terrorism, and, as such, the FBI is responsible for investigating the activities of terrorist groups within the United States and for the investigation of terrorist acts against U.S. citizens abroad.

While the FBI has been charged with this responsibility, there is no all-encompassing federal law concerning the issue of terrorism. The FBI bases its investigative and intelligence efforts on several federal criminal statutes. At present, the FBI has investigative jurisdiction over more than 250 statutes that categorize violations of federal law.

The mission of the counterterrorism program is to detect, prevent, and/or react to unlawful, violent activities of individuals or groups whose intent is to: (1) overthrow the government; (2) interfere with the activities of a foreign government in the United States; (3) substantially impair the functioning of the federal government, a state government, or interstate commerce; or (4) deprive Americans of their civil rights as guaranteed by the Constitution, laws, and treaties of the United States.

Counterterrorism investigations are based on the fundamental duty of government to protect the public against terrorism and criminal violence intended to destroy or manipulate our constitutional system. While it is the responsibility of the attorney general to ensure that every effort is made to protect U.S. citizens

and property, it is also his responsibility to protect the rights of all individuals in the United States. To accomplish this, the attorney general issues investigative guidelines. These guidelines, which are subject to continual review and revision, establish a consistent policy concerning when an investigation may be initiated and what techniques may be employed while conducting the investigation.

The approach taken in counterterrorism investigations is responsive to the need to both prevent incidents where possible and to react effectively after incidents occur. The focus of FBI investigations of terrorist organizations is on the unlawful activity of the group, not the ideological motivations of group members. In the course of conducting investigations, the FBI collects information regarding group membership, associations, movements, support structures, funding, and so forth. This information serves not only as a basis for prosecution, but builds an intelligence data base making possible the prevention of terrorist acts. The reactive phase, on the other hand, consists of effective and timely response to a terrorist incident through crisis management and conventional investigative techniques.

Additionally, in response to the threat posed by terrorists against Americans and their interests abroad, the U.S. Congress passed legislation defining certain criminal acts committed overseas as violations of federal law. This legislation, which is included in the Comprehensive Crime Control Act of 1984 and the Omnibus Diplomatic Security and Antiterrorism Act of 1986, assists the U.S. government's counterterrorism efforts by establishing federal jurisdiction over certain crimes involving U.S. nationals that take place outside the United States. With host country concurrence and close procedural coordination with the U.S. Department of State, the FBI may collect evidence in these international incidents for eventual prosecution in a U.S. court.

The FBI is committed to a program of intensive investigative activity to successfully counter the vio-

From *Terrorism*, Vol. 14, 1991, pp. 134-144. *Terrorism*, published by Taylor and Francis, 1101 Vermont Ave., NW, Suite 200, Washington, DC 20005.

lent intentions of terrorist organizations in the United States. Although the arrest, prosecution, and incarceration of key leadership elements of various terrorist organizations, coupled with successful preventive measures, has significantly contributed to the decline in the number of terrorist incidents committed in the United States, it would be incorrect to conclude from these successes that the pernicious threat of terrorism in the United States has been eradicated. More properly, the reduction in terrorist incidents in the United States closely corresponds to the FBI's and associated law enforcement agencies' acceleration of an all-out counterterrorism effort, which has been characterized by the steady commitment of resources, enhanced counterterrorism training, and more efficient use of an increasingly effective intelligence base.

FBI ORGANIZATION STRUCTURE

Headquarters

The Counterterrorism Section (CTS) at FBI headquarters in Washington, D.C., provides program direction and management to all FBI counterterrorism investigations. Overall program policy and investigative procedures are set and monitored by program managers in the CTS. Because most terrorist activities involve broad geographic areas in the United States, which transcend FBI field division boundaries, it is necessary for headquarters to coordinate investigative activity.

The CTS is a component of the Criminal Investigative Division, which coordinates all criminal investigative programs. The CTS is further organized into several units that manage investigative matters, planning matters, research/analysis projects, training, staffing, and program funding responsibilities.

Field Divisions

FBI field divisions are located in 56 major cities throughout the United States and Puerto Rico. The locations have been selected in accordance with crime trends, the need for regional geographic coverage, and the need to efficiently manage resources.

Within each field division, there exists a squad or a component of a squad that conducts counterterrorism investigations. Counterterrorism personnel conduct these investigations directly from field division locations or from approximately 400 smaller satellite offices known as resident agencies (RA). Investigative information developed at an RA is coordinated through its respective field division and then transmitted to FBI headquarters. There is continual contact between FBI headquarters, field divisions, and RAs, which contributes to effective program management.

Legal Attaches

The FBI maintains legal attache offices in 18 foreign countries. The primary mission of FBI legal attache offices is to establish and sustain effective liaison with principal law enforcement, intelligence, and security services throughout designated foreign countries, thereby providing channels through which FBI investigative responsibilities can be met. The legal attache function also provides for a prompt and continuous exchange of law enforcement information.

Legal attaches and associated liaison activities play a vital role in the successful fulfillment of the responsibilities of the FBI abroad. These activities are maintained in strict accordance with limitations imposed by statutes, presidential directive, attorney general guidelines, and FBI policy. But this is not a one-way street. The FBI assists cooperative foreign agencies with their legitimate and lawful investigative interests in the United States, consistent with U.S. policy regarding "foreign police cooperation" matters.

Special Capabilities

Each of the 56 FBI field divisions maintains a special weapons and tactics (SWAT) capability that is utilized to respond to, contain, and terminate terrorist activity in progress. Each field division also has trained hostage negotiators and technical capabilities. However, in response to extremely high-risk situations, other special abilities, equipment, and techniques, beyond those of local authorities or FBI SWAT teams, are sometimes required.

To provide the president and the attorney general with a civilian law enforcement alternative to the use of military force, the FBI, in 1982, developed the Hostage Rescue Team (HRT). The HRT exceeds the capabilities of a normal SWAT team in the areas of training, communication, command control, and the use of sophisticated weaponry and electronics equipment. HRT personnel have expertise in handling several types of weapons and in using explosives devices for breaching and diversionary tactics. HRT personnel are also trained in emergency medical treatment.

The HRT has been in place at events such as the 1984 Olympic Games held in Los Angeles, California, the 1984 and 1988 presidential conventions and subsequent inaugurations, the 1986 Statue of Liberty rededication, and the Tenth Pan American Games in Indianapolis, Indiana, in 1987, to provide immediate response if a hostage situation would have arisen. The HRT was also used in the November 1987 prison uprising in Atlanta, Georgia, after Cuban refugees seized prison personnel as hostages. Although the HRT was not used to counter the siege, which was eventually settled through negotiations, the team was prepared to take the necessary action to resolve the hostage standoff. The HRT was utilized to resolve the August 1991 uprising at the Talladega, Alabama, Federal Corrections Institute. On August 21, 1991, 121 Cuban detainees scheduled to be returned to Cuba from FCI, Talladega, gained control of a cell block and took 11 Bureau of Prisons officers hostage. Also located within this cell block were 18 American prisoners. On August 30, 1991, after extended negotiations had failed to resolve the hostage situation, the FBI's HRT effected a full-scale rescue operation. The HRT was supported by Bureau of Prisons Special Operations Team and FBI regional SWAT team. All of the hostages were rescued without harm and only one detainee was slightly injured in this operation.

In several arrest situations, the HRT has been used to augment FBI field division personnel because of the unique situation certain fugitives present. The 1984 arrest of top ten fugitive Raymond Luc Levasseur was effected by the HRT. Components of the HRT were involved in the September 1987 arrest, in international waters of the Mediterranean Sea, of Fawaz Younis, an international terrorist who was wanted in connection with the hijacking of a Royal Jordanian Airlines flight in June 1985. The arrest was successfully accomplished by the HRT, which returned him to the United States for prosecution.

The FBI's HRT is an important element of the U.S. government's counterterrorism program. It provides the necessary means for a measured response to serious-risk and crisis situations.

PROGRAMS/COOPERATIVE EFFORTS

Professional law enforcement officials operating in open societies have the important responsibility to develop effective and lawful counterterrorism programs and engage in cooperative relationships to achieve these ends.

Joint Terrorism Task Forces
The FBI's cooperative efforts with state and local law enforcement agencies have been greatly enhanced in recent years. For example, where persistent terrorism problems exist, chiefly in major metropolitan areas, formal joint task force relationships have been created. In 1980, a joint terrorism task force was established in New York City. Since then, similar arrangements have been developed in several other cities. The purpose of these task forces is to maximize interagency coordination and cooperation and create a close-knit, cohesive unit capable of addressing the terrorism problem facing federal, state, and local agencies within a specific geographic area. These units are staffed and supervised by police officers, detectives, state troopers, and FBI agents. All involved agencies participate equally in the formulation and implementation of investigative

strategies. Experience has shown that the pooling of personnel and resources achieves significant results.

Federal Community
On the federal level, cooperation between the various government agencies has been strengthened through interagency policy coordination groups focusing on working relationships. Additionally, federal agencies such as the FBI; Federal Aviation Administration; Bureau of Alcohol, Tobacco, and Firearms; U.S. Customs Service; U.S. Secret Service; Immigration and Naturalization Service; and Departments of Defense, Energy, State, and Transportation work together where mutual jurisdictional interests are involved. Such a cooperative effort was instrumental in the successful September 1987 arrest of Fawaz Younis. This demonstrates the U.S. government's capabilities in and commitment to the fight against international terrorism.

The FBI participates in numerous interagency working groups that deal with terrorism issues. One example is the Protective Security Working Group, which the FBI chairs. This group ensures that federal agencies tasked with protective responsibilities for facilities and individuals are kept abreast of all aspects of the terrorism threat. Another group, the Policy Coordinating Committee on Terrorism chaired by the state department, is responsible for the development of overall U.S. policy regarding international terrorism.

Domestic Threat Warning System
This is a newly developed system, managed by the FBI, that is used to transmit threat warning messages that have been thoroughly coordinated through the U.S. intelligence community. Once coordinated, the message is sent via secure means to appropriate FBI field divisions for appropriate action and local coordination. In addition, FBI headquarters will notify appropriate local police departments through the National Law Enforcement Telecommunications System (NLETS).

The contents of the message will consist of the following: (1) summary of threat information, (2) source of information (if available), (3) characterization of credibility, (4) duration of the threat, (5) target and type of criminal act, and (6) possible identities of alleged terrorists.

This system provides a means for transmitting a coordinated threat warning or alert message to law enforcement agencies, federal agencies, or potential targets, in a timely manner to prevent the crime from taking place.

Both the Protective Security Working Group and the Domestic Threat Warning System were put to the acid test and heavily utilized during the Desert Shield/Storm crisis. The FBI utilized the Protective Security

Working Group to coordinate security procedures and threat assessment activities with all federal agencies involved in providing security against terrorist attacks. The Domestic Threat Warning System was used extensively to provide information, intelligence, and threat assessment data to law enforcement agencies throughout the United States. Through an extremely vigorous and proactive program, the FBI, supported by numerous state, federal and local agencies, was able to prevent any acts of terrorism in support of the Iraqi regime within the United States during this crisis.

Infrastructure Vulnerability/Key Asset Program

In the United States, residents rely heavily on the existence and operation of a complex system of networks to provide essential services: electric power, oil and natural gas, the telephone, interstate highways, railroads, telecommunications, financial transactions, air travel, the shipping industry, and water supply. Stated simply, the United States is a society of intricate networks that are interdependent. Yet, critical service networks are very vulnerable and present prime targets to terrorist groups.

In November 1988, Executive Order 12656 assigned to the Department of Justice coordinating responsibilities for emergency preparedness matters. Principal operational duties in this connection have been delegated to the FBI. Accordingly, the FBI has developed an infrastructure vulnerability/key asset plan. The objective of this plan is to develop, implement, and maintain a national program that addresses potential and actual acts of terrorism directed against key assets of the infrastructure of the United States. The foundation of this plan rests on the tasking of the FBI's field divisions to identify specific key assets, establishment of liaison with the owners and operators of those assets, and the formulation of contingency plans aimed at preventing or effectively reacting to a terrorist attack. This program involves cooperative planning with other government agencies, U.S. military commands, private industry, and independent research groups.

Special Events Management

Another example of substantial cooperation has come in the area of special events management. A *special event*, broadly defined, is any event of such national or international significance that it is: (1) an attractive target for terrorists, and/or intelligence indicates a credible threat that a terrorist act will be committed at the event; (2) of such a nature that the potential for collecting significant classified intelligence by hostile foreign governments exists; or (3) an event of such national or international ramifications that FBI presence would logically be warranted to fulfill its investigative responsibilities.

Elaborate security measures for special events, such as the Olympic Games, World's Fairs, political conventions, presidential inaugurations, and the rededication of the Statue of Liberty, have become obligatory. All elements of the federal government work closely with numerous state and local agencies to ensure that everything is done regarding the security of participants in the events.

In addition, to ensure that the FBI can meet its extraterritorial investigative responsibilities and also to allow foreign governments to draw on the experience of the FBI in the area of special events management, the FBI, in coordination with other U.S. government agencies, has assisted foreign governments in their pre-Olympic security planning. This was done for the 1988 Seoul, Korea Summer Olympics and the Winter Olympics in Calgary, Alberta, Canada. Also, the FBI is currently assisting the government of Spain in its planning for the 1992 Barcelona Summer Olympics and the government of France in its planning for the 1992 Albertville Winter Olympic Games, and the Atlanta Olympic organizing committee and Georgia law enforcement agencies in preparation for the 1996 games.

Training

The FBI provides courses of instruction for law enforcement personnel, both at the FBI Academy at Quantico, Virginia, and throughout the United States at various training facilities, in order to improve administrative, investigative, management, and technical capabilities. In addition to course offerings, FBI Academy faculty conduct research and provide assistance to practitioners on a myriad of topics and investigative techniques relating to counterterrorism matters.

Training is offered to mid-level U.S. and foreign law enforcement officers through an 11-week National Academy program held at Quantico, Virginia. Also, as follow-up for National Academy graduates, periodic retraining sessions are held throughout the United States, as well as in Europe, Asia, and Latin America. Finally, through the Department of Justice initiated International Criminal Investigative Training Assistance Program, training is provided at a professional level to the various components of the criminal justice system in Latin America and the Caribbean.

Publications

The FBI's Terrorist Research and Analytical Center (TRAC) routinely produces a variety of documents available to law enforcement professionals. The most prominent publication is the annual report entitled "Terrorism in the United States." In producing this and other publications, TRAC conducts extensive research on terrorism and analyzes raw reporting to discern trends, determine investigative direction, and support ongoing counterterrorism operations. This analytical capability has greatly enhanced the FBI's counterterrorism program.

Also, in October 1987, the *FBI Law Enforcement Bulletin (LEB)* devoted an entire issue to the subject of terrorism. Other articles on terrorism periodically appear in the monthly *LEB*.

MULTINATIONAL FORA

The FBI supports and actively participates in several international working groups to exchange counterterrorism information and develop joint strategies with cooperating foreign governments. Several multinational fora are available to professional law enforcement personnel to ensure that cooperation among services continues to expand.

INTERPOL

This international law enforcement organization, which was established in 1923 and now consists of nearly 150 nations, provides for rapid transmission of vital information needed by law enforcement authorities throughout the world. INTERPOL originally hesitated to address the issue of terrorism because Article III of its constitution prohibited member countries from intervening in or investigating matters that were considered to be racially, politically, militarily, or religiously motivated. However, at the General Assembly meeting held in 1984, member countries adopted a resolution that determined that, although acts of terrorism may have a political motivation, this motivation is not considered and the acts are determined on the basis of the nature of the crime. This interpretation of the INTERPOL constitution opened the doors for the world law enforcement community to exchange information on terrorists and to use the INTERPOL network to trace and apprehend terrorists charged with criminal offenses. The United States was in the lead in having INTERPOL reconsider its position on terrorism.

Further developments in INTERPOL's effort to combat terrorism resulted in the approval by member countries of a special unit within INTERPOL to deal with information concerning terrorist activity and compile and analyze available data on terrorist groups. The Counterterrorism Unit, established at INTERPOL Headquarters in France, became operational in 1986. One objective of this unit is to conduct symposia on terrorism to foster cooperation among law enforcement agencies in the international fight against terrorism. An FBI agent has been assigned by the secretary general of INTERPOL to head this unit.

TREVI Group

The TREVI Group (TREVI is an acronym for Terrorism, Radicalization, Extremism, Violence International) was established in Luxembourg in 1976. At this initial meeting, ministers of justice and interior of the European Economic Community countries pledged to reinforce their cooperation against organized international crime and, in particular, against terrorism. Since 1986, the United States has actively participated as an observer. TREVI meets semiannually to consider specific measures to combat terrorism through joint international initiatives and cooperation. The attorney general leads the U.S. involvement with the TREVI Group and the FBI director assists by working with counterparts from police and security agencies in Europe to establish programs and cooperative relationships.

Quantico Working Group (QWG)

This is an annual gathering of law enforcement and intelligence agency representatives from several European nations, Canada, Australia, and the United States. It was originally developed in 1979 by the FBI and held at the FBI Academy at Quantico, Virginia. The conference is hosted by member countries on a rotating basis. This group discusses a variety of terrorism-related issues, coordinates investigations and information sharing, and presents topical papers in the terrorism field. Papers presented and working group sessions have concentrated on current areas of interest including, developments/trends/forecasts in Armenian, Croatian, Shi'ite, and general worldwide terrorism, along with effective counterterrorism responses. In addition to multinational gatherings, the FBI has enhanced its bilateral consultations with numerous countries in recent years.

Italian-American Working Group (IAWG)

A good example of productive bilateral cooperation is the existence of the IAWG and its Terrorism Subgroup. Formal meetings of the Terrorism Subgroup are held annually and alternate between Washington, D.C., and Rome, Italy, at which time formal agreements are signed to address initiatives for the coming year. Additionally, meetings are held periodically to accomplish objectives set forth in the formal agreements. The attorney general heads the U.S. delegation to the IAWG and the FBI director heads the American delegation of the Terrorism Subgroup.

The general objectives of the Terrorism Subgroup include: (1) the exchange of operational information on all forms of terrorism; (2) the development of more regular, detailed, and rapid exchange of information at the bilateral level; (3) cooperation in the preparation of trial materials in judicial proceedings resulting from terrorist incidents in which both countries' interests are affected; and (4) mutual training in specialized areas through courses offered in the United States and Italy.

United States and Canada

Another bilateral relationship that has been successfully maintained in the last several years is that of the United States and Canada. The FBI has an established, strong, and effective working relationship with the Royal Canadian Mounted Police (RCMP) and Canadian Security Intelligence Service (CSIS). Information is exchanged on terrorism-related matters through liaison between Canadian officers in Washington, D.C., and FBI headquarters, and liaison between Canadian officers and the FBI's legal attache staff in Ottawa, Canada. Terrorist-related information, which is exchanged, relates to identities of individuals, travel itineraries, group activities, and ongoing operations in which requests for assistance are needed.

The exchange of information is often vital to the outcome of a particular operation and, at the very least, is necessary to trace the activities of subjects of terrorism investigations. The 4000-mile border between the United States and Canada provides such an inviting opportunity for terrorists to escape detection that a close operational and liaison relationship is essential to both the FBI and the CSIS and RCMP.

INTERNATIONAL ASSOCIATION OF CHIEFS OF POLICE (IACP)—COMMITTEE ON TERRORISM

For the past several years, the IACP has taken a leadership role in the fight against international terrorism. In 1986, the president and board of directors of the IACP concluded that international terrorism was of such a concern to the international police community that the IACP should establish a committee on terrorism to examine the issue of cooperative police activities in combating international terrorism. After conferring with IACP executive personnel, it was determined that the committee should be international in scope, and be composed of members with command level responsibilities in the counterterrorism arena.

The membership of the committee on terrorism represents eight countries. In addition to foreign representation, the committee consists of 32 law enforcement professionals from various U.S. federal, state, and local agencies.

The committee on terrorism meets four times annually. One of these is an annual terrorism symposium in Washington, D.C., and at the workshop held during the IACP annual conference. The other two meetings are held at various locations in the united States and Canada and deal with various counterterrorism topics.

In addition to general committee responsibilities, two subcommittees are currently operational to address specific areas relating to counterterrorism training and intelligence assessment issues.

To date, the committee on terrorism has developed initiatives in contingency planning, training, operational capabilities, and information exchange systems. The IACP is proud of the accomplishments of this group and firmly believes that, through this continued and often painstaking work, many problems in dealing with the law enforcement response to terrorism will be solved.

Enhanced cooperation, better sharing of information, improved educational opportunities, and enhanced investigative techniques among law enforcement officials and agencies are the objectives of the IACP committee on terrorism. The leadership of the IACP is of the opinion that through these initiatives the IACP can make its greatest contribution in combating the threat of international terrorism.

CONCLUSION

Throughout the 1980s, terrorism continued to be a pervasive international problem, and it is likely to continue as such in the 1990s. However, through collective efforts there has been a measure of success. This is evidence in the statistical data that shows a decline in terrorist incidents in the United States from 25 in 1986 to 7 in 1990. Also, during the five-year period from 1985 through 1989, U.S. law enforcement was successful in preventing 47 acts of terrorism in the United States. Worldwide as well, the record has shown improvement. In 1990, 455 total incidents were recorded, a substantial decrease from 1988, when 856 occurred.

While these statistics are encouraging, law enforcement authorities must not lose sight of the devastating potential that terrorism poses worldwide. The world has still experienced too many terrorist attacks in recent years. This points to the fact that the international law enforcement community must not become complacent.

The structure of the national counterterrorism program is a sound one. This is largely due to the ongoing cooperation at all levels in the United States and with our foreign counterparts. To be sure, one of the strongest tools in the fight against terrorism is the exchange of vital information and working together to achieve common goals. Cooperation and exchange of intelligence must continue if we are to effectively meet the challenges of terrorism in the 1990s and beyond.

Domestic Terrorism in the United States

James Stinson

James Stinson manages a government research project addressing counterterrorism analysis, planning and response.

Assessing the terrorist threat to the United States always presents a challenge. For years, students of terrorism have debated over *when* international terrorism will hit the United States, and *why* terrorist groups have shied away from attacking Americans on U.S. soil with the same intensity with which they attack Americans overseas.

After the dramatic surge in terrorist incidents worldwide during 1985, any increase during 1986 would have been significant. Such an increase did occur, however. Terrorists conducted 3,801 incidents in 1986, an increase of 35 percent over 1985's total. A total of 5,950 people were killed (up 8.4 percent from 1985) and 6,842 were wounded (up 9.8 percent). Over 14,722 people were victims of terrorist attacks in one form or another, 389 of whom were Americans.

Terrorism remains unchecked internationally. Nations around the globe are struggling with how to handle this complex problem. Groups once thought to be defunct have stymied governments, including our own, with their longevity and destructive capabilities. While our record as a victim of terrorist attacks abroad is well documented and does not need to be addressed here, the ever-present question of how and when terrorism will strike the United States at home remains.

This discussion is divided into three parts. The first explores the indigenous, home-grown groups that currently operate in the United States and also looks at those international groups with operational capability in the United States. The second section deals with the problems facing law enforcement in the investigation and prosecution of such cases. The third focuses on conclusions and recommendations for handling the problem both reactively and proactively.

For the purposes of assessment, groups are divided into three primary categories: indigenous, separatist and international. Those separatist groups operating in the United States against foreign targets, and whose primary target is *not* the United States, will be handled as international groups.

INDIGENOUS GROUPS

Three principal groups operate in this category. Two present an operational threat to government and business targets. The first is the May 19 Communist Organization, the current generation of the old Weather Underground. The second group, the Aryan Nations, is a right-wing supremacist group on the other end of the political spectrum. Both groups have nationwide networks and a long history of violence. Both have also demonstrated sophisticated tactical capabilities and have assassinated law enforcement personnel in the conduct of their actions. The third group in this category that has resurfaced in recent years is the Jewish Defense League, known for its operations against Arab and Soviet targets.

The May 19 Communist Organization (M19CO) defies description. Originating in the 1960s as the Weather Underground Organization, its members have been operating in the underground for over twenty years. In many cases they have greater experience, man-for-man, than the law enforcement agencies investigating them. As a revolutionary Marxist-Leninist terrorist group waging war against imperialism and the United States, M19CO has focused its attention in recent years on support of third world issues, particularly in the areas of Central and South America, Palestine and Africa. They have conducted operations on behalf of the Puerto Rican FALN and Central American groups in El Salvador and Nicaragua. Actions have included operations against U.S. government facilities, such as the bombing of Ft. McNair in Washington, D.C.

The group has expressed solidarity for the Palestinian struggle and has ties to both the Popular Front for the Liberation of Palestine (PFLP) and the West German Red Army Faction (RAF). The M19CO and its predecessor, the Weather Underground, have been proclaimed defunct on four occasions by various federal investigative organizations and each time have resurfaced stronger. Travel in 1986 by over twenty members to a meeting in Frankfurt with the RAF gave the group contact with terrorist organizations throughout Europe and the Middle East, demonstrating the group's desire to develop and maintain its linkages with the international terrorist community.

Domestically, the M19CO has strong ties to groups in the United States, including the Puerto Rican FALN and its front group the MLN; and to the Republic of New Africa and its recent offshoot, the New Afrikan Peoples Organization (NAPO). A most alarming development within the past few years has been M19CO's interest in the disarmament and antinuclear community. The group's most recent publication of "Breakthrough" (Winter/Spring 1987) lists, in its "Prisoner of War" section, members of Ploughshares and other disarmament groups currently incarcerated. M19CO's infiltration into both support groups and main stream disarmament structures poses a difficult situation for law enforcement in investigating these connections.

As one can readily see, the organization is in no way defunct. It would be a serious mistake to assess as dormancy the group's new targeting and quiet rebuilding in the underground.

Aryan Nations may well be the most deadly group operating in the United States today. While its foundations trace back to the 1950s and early 1960s, the group's current structure was organized in 1970 under the leadership of Richard Butler with headquarters in Hayden Lake, Idaho.

Aryan Nations is based on an extremist ideology of racism that is anti-semitic and anti-black. It couches its beliefs under the religious doctrine of "Identity," which states that Jesus Christ was not a Jew but an Aryan, and that the lost tribes of Israel were in fact Anglo-Saxon and not Semitic. Jews are considered to be children of Satan.

Its operational profile is best found in the writings of American Neo-Nazi William Pierce. Pierce authored the "Turner Diaries," a blueprint for revolution in the United States based on a race war. In the book a small racist group begin actions with armored car robberies, bombings of government facilities and assassinations of key Jewish leaders, culminating in the theft of a small man-portable nuclear weapon with which they conduct a suicide operation against the Pentagon in Washington, D.C.

Aryan Nations has used a variety of names for tactical missions, including the Order, the Silent Brotherhood, the White American Bastion and others. It is linked to several armored car and bank robberies, counterfeiting, assassinations and assaults on federal, state and local law enforcement personnel. One of the group's leaders, the head of the Texas Ku Klux Klan movement, proposed a point system to achieve Aryan "Warrior" status. This approach awards fractions of a point for assassinations. Members of Congress are worth one-fifth of a point each; judges and the FBI director one-sixth; FBI agents and U.S. Marshals one-tenth; journalists and local politicians, one twelfth; and the president of the United States one full point and the immediate achievement of the rank of "Warrior."

The group utilizes guerrilla warfare concepts. Training camps have been identified in several states. An annual meeting/training session is held at Butler's Hayden Lake compound roughly every year. Although almost thirty members of the Order have been arrested since 1985, it must be remembered that this group alone has over 150 identified hard core members and a support base of over 1,200 people around the country. With several million dollars unrecovered, the group has stated that it is breaking up into smaller cells and going underground to rebuild.

This group has also been pronounced "finished," only to resurface to conduct several bombings last year in Kootenai County, Idaho. It was later discovered that the bombings were intended as a decoy for a major operation that was not carried out. Earlier the same month (August 1986) the group conducted a bank robbery in Rossville, Illinois. The group presents a viable and distinct threat to law enforcement. Investigations should not be based on the group's last operation but on its status as a group and its planned future actions.

The Jewish Defense League founded by Rabbi Meir Kahane, now the leader of Kach and a member of the Israeli Knesset, is the best known of the Jewish extremist groups. Although various smaller groups are active in parts of the country, none has the national network that the JDL has at this time. During 1985 and 1986, the group was implicated in and claimed a number of bombings around the country, and was suspected in at least two assassinations and several attempts. The group has focused on Nazi war criminals and Arab-related targets. Although not active against government targets and law enforcement personnel, the group should be considered active and operational at this time. This group has made attempts to collect information on Aryan Nations and one can reasonably infer that eventually targeting will move in that direction also.

SEPARATIST GROUPS TARGETING THE UNITED STATES

The primary groups operating in this category are the U.S.-based Puerto Rican FALN and the Puerto Rican-based OVRP, which has begun operations on U.S. soil in the past 24 months. Both groups have deadly backgrounds and a lengthy history of survival.

The **FALN** (Armed Forces of National Liberation) is a Marxist-Leninist revolutionary terrorist organization fighting a "rear-guard" struggle to free Puerto Rico from "imperialist domination." The group has claimed credit for over 150 bombings in the United States. Several lives have been lost in group operations. The FALN has tight organizational and operational ties to the M19CO in the United States and has known connections to the Cuban intelligence apparatus. As a group with international governmental support, it has tremendous potential. It has been dealt setbacks, however, through the use of the grand jury inquiries. The group's refusal to cooperate sent many key members to prison, many of whom are now being released back onto the streets. This group also has a history of over twenty years of covert struggle and will not succumb easily to conventional investigations.

The group is known to utilize training camps in the United States and is well supported with a network of front organizations and underground members. The hard core is thought to number around 120 members, with a support base of over 2,000 members centered in New York, Chicago, El Paso, Denver, Milwaukee, Los Angeles and Washington, D.C. Front groups operate as the Movement for National Liberation (MLN), Crusade for Justice, California Committee Against Repression, Colorado Committee Against Repression, La Raza Unida Party and others. Joint support operations with M19CO are carried out as the "New Movement in Solidarity with the Puerto Rican and Mexican Revolutions." The group is in an underground rebuilding stage and is very much alive. It would be a serious mistake to assess this group as dead or dormant.

The **Organization of Volunteers for the Puerto Rican Revolution** (OVRP) is another Marxist-Leninist revolutionary group, advocating the freedom of Puerto Rico from the United States so it can begin the armed struggle in the homeland. Originating around 1978 and first claiming actions with the Macheteros, this group up until last year had operated solely in Puerto Rico against Puerto Rican and U.S. targets. It is responsible for numerous bombings and assassinations. During 1984 and 1985, the group began to assert in its communiques that it was expanding its struggle to the mainland to "operate in the belly of the beast." Recently, it was uncovered that this group was responsible for the surveillance of several military facilities around the country and a recent threat against a high ranking U.S. military officer. OVRP has a very high operational capability for assassination against protected targets and bombings against "secure" government facilities. The fact that they have not done operations of this type on the mainland should not be factored into the group's threat assessment; it is capable of conducting such attacks at this time. The group is known for its large, well-coordinated joint operations. Given its strong connections to the FALN, it can be expected to use the group's support and operational

network to increase its operational activities on U.S. soil over the next few years.

The **Macheteros,** formerly known as the Ejercito Popular Boricua (EPB), is a third Marxist revolutionary organization based in Puerto Rico. Originating during 1978 with the OVRP, the group has been the most violent and deadly of the Puerto Rican organizations. Machetero actions were limited to the island until September 1983 when it engineered the armed robbery of a Wells Fargo depot in Hartford, Connecticut, escaping with over $7 million dollars. The group used an insider to gain access to the facility, and although the Macheteros claimed the attack, authorities were slow to believe them due to the fact they had never operated on U.S. soil. The group members involved escaped to Puerto Rico and Cuba. Almost $4 million is believed to be in Cuba to pay for training and logistics.

Previous to this the group had conducted extremely sophisticated attacks and a long string of cold-blooded assassinations in Puerto Rico. Its establishment of a base of operations in the United States will definitely breed future CONUS actions. It, like the OVRP, will most likely use previous Puerto Rican underground networks to establish itself. These should be the key collection and surveillance focus of concerned investigative organizations tasked with operating against this group. Two Machetero members were arrested in the United States in 1985; others must be considered as operating in the United States as well.

INTERNATIONAL GROUPS OPERATING IN THE UNITED STATES

Most investigative organizations do not realize how many international groups have operational capability in the United States. This section will briefly discuss those groups that have conducted operations in the last two years or who have active cells in the United States. No attempt will be made to detail the group's operational expertise or current threat at this time.

After the **Armenian Secret Army for the Liberation of Armenia** (ASALA) was pronounced defunct, it conducted one of its most sophisticated terrorist operations against the Turkish embassy in Canada in March of 1985. The group utilized explosive entry techniques and SWAT-type tactics, indicating that it had been trained both in police tactics as well as in specific methods for countering rescue force tactics. This latter element represents probably the most disturbing trend coming out of the analysis of recent group activities.

Headquarters and leadership for the ASALA cell that conducted the Canadian operation is in the United States. The Armenian groups' target in over 70 percent of their attacks is against countries holding their members from previous operations. The United States holds one convicted for assassination of a consul-general. As a result, future attacks against U.S. interests, either at home or abroad, may be expected.

Indian Sikh extremists have used the United States to set up training and logistics operations for use in their war against the Indian government. Several major operations were planned here for international implementation. The suspects in the Air-India bombing that killed several hundred people were based in the United States and received training from a mercenary training camp in the Southeastern United States. This group will continue to expand its domestic operations to use the United States as a safe-haven and base of operations. Operations here, against either Indian or American targets, if called for by the group, are quite plausible, given local strength.

The **Libyan** network has been active in the United States for many years. Originally based out of its "People Bureaus" before they were closed, Libyan action units specialized in tracking anti-Khaddafi dissidents to threaten—and, in some cases, to assassinate—them. One such case occurred as an element of the Wilson-Terpil affair and involved an ex-Special Forces enlisted man who was incarcerated for the attempt. With the recent attacks in Europe against Americans and Khaddafi's desire for vengeance after the April 1986 U.S. air-strike, more CONUS-based activity by this group may be expected, either directly or through surrogate groups they are known to sponsor. The Libyan network in the United States and several European countries represents a classic example of state-sponsored terrorism and demonstrates the high level of capability a group can have when utilizing a state intelligence network for support and operational control. Activity will definitely increase in the future.

Virtually every major **Palestinian** group has representatives in the United States responsible for financial support, logistics and intelligence collection. Several have been operational in the United States since the early 1970s and have well-established infrastructures. The major active groups known to have significant capabilities here include Al Fatah, the Popular Front for the Liberation of Palestine (PFLP) and the Democratic Front for the Liberation of Palestine (DFLP). Principally oriented around intelligence collection, recruitment, logistics and safe-haven activities, an extensive apparatus exists to conduct operations as well. Recently, seven members of a PFLP support apparatus were arrested in Los Angeles after nearly a year's investigation, only to have the judge release the suspects on bail following his refusal to hear closed, classified government arguments against their release. The suspects currently reside in Southern California and have not been deported as of this writing.

Every major terrorist group in Northern Ireland has some representation in the United States. These groups are also dedicated to the logistical support of their Northern Irish sponsors and provide funds, supplies, personnel, safe-havens and propaganda. Groups represented include both the Irish Republican Army (IRA) and the INLA. United States citizens have been identified on numerous occasions as being major suppliers of weapons and money. The supply of funds and logistics is so strong from the United States that it is unlikely that an operation would be attempted on U.S. soil. The one exception would be to target the royal family on a visit here, which either the IRA or the INLA would attempt. Indeed, one such plan to target Princess Margaret on a U.S. tour was uncovered and foiled as far back as 1978.

Iranian groups, both anti- and pro-Khomeini, operate in the United States. Both sets of groups have demonstrated a capability for terrorist operations. Indeed, one left-wing group, the Mujahadeen, is currently conducting operations inside Iran and in the European sector. The pro-Khomeini groups also present the challenge of state sponsorship for terrorist activities. As we have seen in Lebanon and Europe, these groups can be deadly and persistent. The U.S. response in Lebanon was to retreat in the face of attack to reduce or eliminate the risk. This will not be an option within CONUS. Hussein Musawi, leader of the Shiite Islamic Amal and the leader of the Islamic Jihad Organization, claims to have cells of operation in America. Operations have occurred in every other country for which he has made such claims. We would do well to believe him and identify these elements prior to their implementing operations.

The list goes on. Both Cuba and Nicaragua are known to have operatives in the United States capable of initiating terrorist operations. We must also consider the Croatian groups that were active a few years ago, as well as several European groups that have been identified in contact with our domestic groups. This should serve to emphasize that we have in the United States numerous groups that are conducting support operations, and that remain capable of initiating tactical operations at any time. These groups present a credible threat to the law enforcement community, which must keep track of them; they pose, without question, one of the major challenges law enforcement will face in the future.

MAJOR INVESTIGATIVE PROGRAMS

Law enforcement strives to develop conventional methods that work consistently across a broad spectrum and can be easily codified and taught. Such is the nature of the law. Terrorist groups are covert by design, structuring themselves to be difficult to detect and investigate with conventional methods. A dichotomy thus arises when the two meet. Conventional methods will routinely be ineffective against terrorist group structures. When arrests are made, they will generally be for isolated incidents involving tactical members and will rarely target the leadership and underground structure that make the group a viable threat. The first priority for law enforcement must therefore be to educate key investigative and administrative personnel on how groups organize and develop. The inner workings of terrorist ideologies and group structures must be understood before they can be effectively combatted. Next, the issue of proactive versus reactive action must be addressed. The administrator must decide if he is going to wait until an incident occurs and react with tactical responses or develop interdiction capabilities to stop the group before it becomes involved in an incident. Both require different types of teams and different intelligence products. The risk with the former approach is that many groups possess high tactical capabilities and, even with the best counterforce teams, there is the potential for disaster. These types of fast-moving, high-violence activities have a tendency to go sour with the best of intentions. Complicating the issue is the large number of groups identified in 1986 as receiving training in anti-counterforce techniques. With incident success rate for all groups in 1986 remaining above 90 percent for the third straight year, the risk of waiting for terrorist groups to strike first before responding to their threat is made clear.

Proactive approaches hold the best promise for reducing violence and successfully interdicting violent incidents; however, they require a substantially different approach. A number of nations have been shifting to this level of activity over the past few years with a great deal of success. Some important issues must be considered before shifting to the proactive mode, however.

First, dealing in interdiction necessitates working with fragmentary data and requires a dedicated analytical effort. The farther out in front of the problem, the more sophisticated the analytical requirement will be.

Second, there must be some national or international clearinghouse for the exchange and transfer of data. Groups will operate in the shadows and cracks of society. The selection of multiple jurisdictions for group actions is designed to create problems for the investigative teams. This must be understood and channels developed for overcoming these problems.

Third, working to the front of the problem requires unique capabilities in the areas of collection, such as surveillance-countersurveillance, photography, electronic intercept, agent handling and informant control measures. Paramount to this is an analytical team to assemble the fragments into a viable threat assessment product. This directly implies an effective and ongoing intelligence apparatus. Coming out of the 1960s and the Watergate era, intelligence units are still thought of as necessary evils to be avoided at all costs. Adversary groups will exploit this sentiment and use legal support channels and harassment suits against agencies seeking to maintain or develop proactive intelligence capabilities. The adversary knows that such units are the key to working the problem from the front end and will develop an impressive array of tactics—some legal, others not—to combat them. Guidelines for investigative behavior must be established early on as these investigations will be politically charged, complex and hazy. Staffing the unit with outstanding personnel will be essential in these cases, as it is in any complex area. The alternative is to put your resources into tactical response and follow the incidents one after another. In the long run this may not only be more costly, but it is also less effective. While we may win a battle or two, we may lose the war.

PREPARING FOR THE THREAT

Assuming that you choose to operate in the pre-incident and interdiction mode, the first element to consider is whether your region has a threat with which to be concerned. If it does not, consider yourself fortunate. If, on the other hand, you have had a problem of this type, or there are indications of one developing in your area, your first task will be to determine how structured the threat is within the region. Initial questions should focus on each group's identity, regions of operations, key members, ideology, goals, and current tactics and techniques. These must then be matched against available targets within the region to determine their vulnerability. The level of the problem will dictate whether the problem can be handled internally within your agency's resources or requires a regional or task force approach. If the group crosses jurisdictional boundaries, either geographically or legally, then sooner or later a regional effort will be necessary. A lead agency should be established, preferably one where the center of group activity is located.

Intelligence is the determining factor in whether you stop the group pre-start or respond to their incidents. A key issue is a centralized collation and analysis center. Data must be centrally located and shared if the investigation is to be successful. This may not be a problem at local or regional levels; however, in the past it has been a major stumbling block at the federal level. In some cases, lack of cooperation among investigative agencies has worked to the terrorist group's advantage. In nations where this problem has been resolved, the level of response and agency capability against a given group has risen dramatically. Simply put, jurisdictional conflict must be overcome or sidestepped in some way. One viable approach lies with the development of regional intelligence networks with secure membership to support the investigative effort. Without this cooperation, no terrorist group with a national network will ever be effectively dismantled. We will continue to see groups with ten- and twenty-year operational histories time and again.

Along with an effective intelligence apparatus must be defined approaches for dealing with groups when they begin to perform operational targeting. These methods must be clearly defined and understood by all team members. Once incident planning unfolds and groups reach the pre-incident staging phase, there will be little time to develop interdiction responses. If complex and high-risk arrests are to be made, tactical teams need to be apprised of whom and what they are going to face, with sufficient time to equip and train themselves. A breakdown often occurs in this phase as the intelligence apparatus shifts from information collection and analysis to operational support. The problem, however, requires a unit flexible enough to handle both types of activity and able to shift between them with ease. Abuse of authority can be an issue at this point but can be controlled or avoided with adequate checks and balances.

The primary issue in developing counterforce strategies is how an agency without a major threat can justify a highly trained, tactical/SWAT team to handle effectively intermittent terrorist problems. Any region facing an active terrorist group must have this capability or be able to rely on some type of outside team to provide the capability. Any agency that relies on an externally based counterforce team will face accountability issues as well as command and control problems. In addition, the local agency will be left to pick up the pieces within the city after the counterforce team is gone. A viable approach here again would be a regional team made up of members from several agencies to ease the burden on personnel resources. Such interagency teams are built on a daily basis for complex investigations and in such highly technical areas as explosive ordinance disposal and major crime investigations. Advance planning is paramount. You cannot afford to discover your need for tactical response capabilities in the middle of a major incident. A positive correlation exists between the quality of intelligence and interdiction work and counterforce response. Good intelligence and interdiction capabilities will provide for a more effective counterforce response if one is required. The obverse is also true.

The organization or region that prepares its intelligence collection and analysis capabilities and trains its interdiction and counterforce teams to deal accurately and effectively with the threat will achieve the best terrorist response capability a democratic government can have. Effective incident management alone, however, will not solve the problem over the long run, which returns us to the need for effective preoperational group intelligence. Successful control of terrorism begins and ends with successful control of the entity that creates the incident. We will not control the problem until we control the group.

Bombs over America

You name it, they use it. Explosives are a growing menace on the streets

Police in Aurora, Ill., knew they had a problem earlier this year when, in a neighborhood frequented by drug gangs, they discovered a black suitcase crammed with a half-dozen sticks of a dynamitelike explosive. Used by mining companies to pierce huge rocks, the explosives, if properly detonated, could easily have blown nearby homes to bits.

None of Aurora's half-dozen warring gangs ever experimented with those explosives—the suitcase recovery presumably exhausted the supply—but police in the northern Illinois city now fear that gangs are simply turning to bombs that are easier to buy, steal, make and use. On April 29, a local gang lobbed a home-made pipe bomb through the window of a downtown home where a rival gang had converged, blowing a foot-wide hole in the living-room floor. In the ensuing panic, the bombers ambushed a 16-year-old leader of the Latin Kings drug gang and shotgunned him to death. Over the next five days, gangs lobbed Molotov cocktails at two other enemies' homes, torching one gang member's front porch. "If you throw a bomb into a house full of people, you'll hit a lot more people than with an automatic [weapon]," explains Victor Branch, 18, a former "chief" of Aurora's Vice Lords gang until he dropped out this winter. "You'll give a guy a big gash on his leg and that's good for your reputation. It's all about reputation." Aurora police agree that showmanship lies behind the sudden appeal of explosives. "Gang members are into big-time macho intimidation,"

says Sgt. John Dobran, a former member of the city's antigang task force.

Lately, a growing number of drug dealers and gangs nationwide have begun using and stockpiling explosives for their own demonstrations of bravado. Overall, there were 3,541 "explosives incidents" in 1990, the highest number in 15 years and a 20 percent hike from 1989, according to the Federal Bureau of Alcohol, Tobacco and Firearms. Of those, 45 were drug related. Authorities recovered 8,033 pounds of explosives during drug-related investigations last year— or nearly 10 times as much as was collected in 1989. They also brought in a record 185 pounds of stolen military plastic explosives called Composition C-4, just a half pound of which could demolish an average police station or destroy a commercial airliner.

Drug dealers were caught with more hand grenades than ever before, too. Authorities recovered 143 grenades last year in drug-related investigations, more than in the previous three years combined. In Chicago alone, gangs and small-time dealers have tossed World War II-style hand grenades at enemies on four separate occasions in the past 10 months. Chicago ATF agent Jerry Singer says police already have recovered 50 grenades, which had been selling on city streets for $150 apiece. There is even a booming trade in detonators, small explosive devices used to set off much more powerful explosives, with a record 623 recovered by police last year. "When you look at the growth of those numbers, it is cause for concern," says ATF Director

Stephen Higgins. "It's one thing to confront someone with a weapon, but bombers want to intimidate on a larger scale."

Handguns and semiautomatic rifles are still most drug dealers' weapons of choice. Even with the proliferation of bombs on the streets, only one person died in a drug-related explosives incident last year; even that was an accident, ATF agents say, caused when a 24-year-old Detroit crack dealer blew himself up while making a hand grenade he had hoped to sell to area drug dealers. But explosives trouble law enforcement officials nonetheless. Ironically, though, there is little clamor for an enforcement crackdown. Few even got worked up after the spectacular explosion set off last year outside the new U.S. Drug Enforcement Administration office in Fort Myers, Fla., by convicted cocaine dealer Jeffrey Matthews. His bomb was stuffed with 2 1/2 pounds of smokeless powder, .38-caliber bullets and other shrapnel—and taped to a 5-gallon gasoline can. It demolished the 6,000-square-foot building and caused about $4 million worth of damage.

No questions asked. The problem is that virtually anyone can make or buy bombs. Three fourths of all the explosives incidents reported from 1985 to 1989 involved homemade pipe or bottle bombs, many of which were fueled with everyday ingredients like gasoline or even match heads. Corner stores sell much more destructive components. Anyone at least 21 years old can go to a gun shop and buy black powder, a common pipe-bomb ingre-

From *U.S. News & World Report*, July 29, 1991, pp. 18-20. Copyright © 1991, U.S. News & World Report.

HOW UNCLE SAM HELPS MANIACS

The secret of bomb making

When most criminals want to get their hands on explosives, they steal from poorly guarded construction sites or call a black marketeer. But some head instead to their local library. Dozens of books purport to show even a hopeless chemistry-class dropout how to make everything from hand grenades to homemade napalm.

If government officials are disturbed by the publishing trend, they have not said so. And they would only appear hypocritical if they did, since the U.S. Army and CIA publish some of the bestselling bomb books available. Need to blow up a bridge or a major telephone system? Simply turn to the demolition projects section of a widely

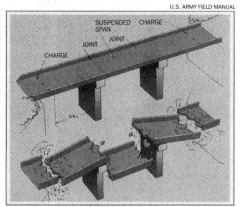

U.S. ARMY FIELD MANUAL

How to . . . *Explosive advice from the Army*

available U.S. Army field manual. Want to learn how to make picric acid, a powerful booster explosive, from 20 tablets of household aspirin? Look it up in the "Field Expedient Methods for Explosives Preparations" manual originally written for the CIA and now sold by a commercial publishing com-

pany for just $6.95. "There's magnificent irony in all this," says Peder Lund, a former Special Forces captain in Vietnam whose publishing company, Paladin Press, markets seven explosives manuals originally written for the government. "Our government provides security and, at the same time, the means by which that security can be breached."

Beyond that, dozens of other titles by nonmilitary authors include "Improvised Explosives: How to Make Your Own" and "Ragnar's Guide to Home and Recreational Use of High Explosives." One classic in the genre, "The Poor Man's James Bond," even illustrates how to booby-trap a building near a church so that, "after a curious crowd has gathered, a second heavy charge [goes] off, seriously damaging or destroying the building and killing or wounding many onlookers."

dient, for about $8.95 per pound, no questions asked.

People with no proven explosives training can go a step further and even buy dynamite—responsible for 8 percent of all domestic bombings—with nothing more than a driver's license in many states, including Tennessee, Arkansas and Mississippi. Although most states make it tougher to buy, federal regulations only require buyers to be 21 years of age or older and reside in the state where the sale takes place. Criminals are on the honor system and simply have to state on ATF forms that they are not convicts, drug users or "mentally defective" to walk home with armloads of ready-made bombs. Most explosives are reasonably priced and easy to find, too. Dealers advertise under the "Explosives" section in the local yellow pages, and sell dynamite to legitimate users such as farmers and construction workers for about $75 per 100 sticks. Blasting caps sell for $1.50 apiece and detonating cord goes for just 20 cents per foot.

Drug dealers and other criminals fear paper trails and attention, however, and find it safer to buy on the black market. Consequently, more than 90,000 pounds of high explosives were

stolen or pilfered from poorly guarded construction sites, quarries and explosives manufacturers and dealers from 1985 to 1989, including 80,000 pounds of dynamite. Most of the thieves simply snipped a lock. Last July, for example, thieves drove two pickup trucks to an unguarded explosives depot in southern West Virginia, cut through locks with a bolt cutter and loaded 3 tons of dynamite into their vehicles. State police, who later recovered the dynamite while searching for marijuana fields on a nearby mountain now suspect that the goods were to be resold for half the list price to small coal-mining companies in the area.

The United States government inadvertently helps stock drug dealers' weapons arsenals every year, too. Security and weapons accounting is loose at many military bases, according to a Federal General Accounting Office investigation, and there often is no way to tell if explosives used in training were actually detonated or pocketed for use or resale by soldiers and reservists. The results can be frightening. In March 1984, for example, members of a Virginia motorcycle gang used gasoline, dynamite and a thermite grenade stolen from the U.S. military to blow

up a drug-addiction clinic in Norfolk, Va. No one was killed, but the resulting fire caused about $700,000 worth of damage to the clinic and two adjoining businesses. Late last month, the danger of improperly securing and accounting for military explosives and arms was brought to life in Florida. On June 25, a U.S. District Court judge sentenced Army Green Beret Sgt. Michael Tubbs to eight years in prison for illegally conspiring to possess a massive arsenal of military explosives and weapons gathered from U.S. Army bases at Fort Bragg, N.C., and Fort Campbell, Ky. "There were enough explosives to blow up the Gator Bowl," one ATF agent said. Authorities say the cache—including some 90 pounds of C-4 and military TNT, Claymore antipersonnel mines, hand grenades and antiaircraft and antitank machine guns—was never intended to be sold to drug dealers. The government claimed that Tubbs, 31 was linked with a white supremacist group, and it produced a charter written by Tubbs calling on new group members to "dedicate [their] blood to this great nation and the white race." Tubbs denies the allegations, and they never were proved in court.

5. TERRORISM IN AMERICA

Land mines, too. The theft of explosives from military bases is hardly new. From 1979 to May 1990, for example, the ATF reported that 3,710 pounds of C-4 had been stolen from bases and 4,913 recovered. From Jan. 1, 1989, to June 30, 1990 alone, Army bomb squads across the country responded to 1,127 calls from local police asking for help in the disposal or disarmament of stolen or abandoned military materiel. The squads recovered some 85 rockets, 400 grenades, 200 pounds of C-4, 45 pounds of TNT and a dozen land mines, according to military documents provided to the *Harrisburg* (Pa.) *Sunday Patriot-News.* Even today, the same problem persists. The ATF reported just last week that local law enforcement authorities recovered 25 pounds of C-4, 117 grenades and 4 pounds of TNT—all presumably stolen off military bases—from January to April of this year.

Despite the mounting evidence, there has been little discussion, much less action, in the government and the law enforcement community to deal with the growing bomb threat. The "big" new reform that will be implemented within a few weeks is this: The Department of Defense has finally consented to tell the ATF when explosive material has been swiped from its bases.

James Popkin

The Plague of Our Cities

The drug epidemic may be waning, but violence is thriving

Guy Gugliotta and Michael Isikoff

Washington Post Staff Writers

Shereker Wilkins died on her ninth birthday in September, killed by a stray bullet fired from the street as she sat in her Milwaukee apartment, combing her mother's hair. In New Orleans the same week, Dorothy Mae Gourrier, 59, was killed on her way to a doctor's appointment. A would-be robber opened fire on her car, shattering the windshield and wounding her in the shoulder and chest.

For the last several years, law enforcement authorities have blamed drug trafficking—especially of cocaine and its derivative crack—for the surge in urban crime. But this year, a new and in some ways more alarming trend is developing: The drug epidemic in many American cities shows signs of abating, but the culture of violence that accompanies it is thriving as never before. After increasing steadily for three years, the number of homicides in 1990 is breaking records in urban areas nationwide.

Cocaine and crack may have encouraged and financed the violence as traffickers bought large numbers of top-of-the-line weapons to replace the cheap, poorly made "Saturday night specials" and rubber-band-powered zip guns of the past. But the ethic of firepower has taken on a life of its own. Guns have become part of the urban landscape, injecting an extra element of fear into everyday life.

"There's a viciousness out there on the street with people with weapons," says New Orleans Police Superintendent Warren G. Woodfork. "They don't care if they live or die, it seems, or if you live or die."

In interviews in 16 cities across the United States, Washington Post reporters and special correspondents spoke to law officers, community activists, criminologists, young people and residents of some of the nation's toughest neighborhoods.

In 15 of the cities, homicide rates have increased over 1989—Boston by 45 percent; Denver, 29 percent; Chicago, Dallas and New Orleans more than 20 percent each; Los Angeles, 16 percent; and New York, 11 percent. In Washington, D.C., which led the nation in number of homicides per capita last year, the rate is slightly ahead of last year's record pace.

Those interviewed mentioned drugs, poverty, television violence, social tension and hopelessness—root causes of violence that have afflicted the inner cities for generations. But they also spoke of guns, gangs and a new street ethic that in many cases almost requires young men to commit murder to prove manhood.

"As kids under 18 got involved in drug dealing, they got armed," says Lawrence W. Sherman, president of the Crime Control Institute, a Washington-based think tank. "Even if drug dealing declines, they still have the guns. Once the guns have been stockpiled, you can expect they will be used in all kinds of disputes."

Gang members, says Dan Cabrera, special senior agent for the Los Angeles office of the Bureau of Alcohol, Tobacco and Firearms, "rule by fear—fear of dying is a strong motivator. If you're trying to get respect and you've killed three or four people, people are going to jump when you given an order."

This year, the new ethic of violence has meant banner headlines for a flood of seemingly senseless, gruesome crimes—the Wilkins and Gourrier killings, the shooting death of a 33-year-old television executive making a telephone call outside his Greenwich Village apartment, the slaying of a 21-year-old Tulane University honor student as she strolled to a bus stop on her way to work.

Even more disturbing for law enforcement, however, has been the increasing use of firearms as the preferred tool for settling disputes from domestic quarrels to schoolyard slights.

In a South Philadelphia apartment in October, Tuan Anh Nguyen, 18, was fatally shot in the chest, arm and stomach when a dance-party quarrel erupted in gunfire. In Brooklyn in September, barber Ferdinand Augustin died when a would-be customer shot him in the head with a .25-caliber pistol after Augustin refused to give him a haircut. In Chicago on one September weekend, 75 people were shot. Of those, 13 died, including Aaron Martinez, 15, an aspiring Olympic boxer shot in the face by a 19-year-old whom he had beaten in a fistfight.

"I see a lot of violence at the slightest provocation—'you stepped on my sneakers, you said something about my mother,' " says Mel Grizer, executive director of the United Community Center in the East New

York section of Brooklyn. "There's a lot of kids getting killed over girlfriends."

There is little argument that drug trafficking has played a crucial role in spawning the rise of violent crime—cocaine in the early 1980s and crack in the last five years. "In the 1960s and '70s, it was heroin, which just makes people lie down and go to sleep," says Richard Bank, a 17-year career public defender in the Philadelphia court system. "Today, the heroin is cocaine, which makes people very excited and nervous. They're much more dangerous."

But most available indicators suggest that, over the last year, even hard-core cocaine and crack abuse has begun to decline in many parts of the country. The number of people being treated for cocaine-related hospital emergencies peaked nationwide at 11,285 in mid-1989. During the first three months of this year, the figure had dropped to 8,135, lowest since 1987.

At the same time, the number of people arrested who test positive for cocaine appears to be declining. In the District of Columbia, inmate urinalysis last July showed 17 percent of juvenile defenders testing positive, down from 35 percent in 1987. For adults, results were almost as pronounced—52 percent tested positive last June, down from 72 percent in 1987.

Statistics available in many other cities have shown slight downward trends, or at least a leveling-off from previous increases in drug use. By contrast, however, the Senate Judiciary Committee projected in August that 23,220 people would be murdered nationally this year, making 1990 the bloodiest on record, although the homicide rate relative to population would still be slightly below that of 1980, when 23,040 people were slain.

"Police are telling us there is more violence that doesn't involve drugs," says Stephen E. Rickman, director of statistical analysis for the office of Criminal Justice Plans and Analysis here. "It's kind of a spillover effect. It's become an acceptable way of settling disputes."

Still, many law enforcement officers do not believe that drug violence is declining. They have noticed, and the Drug Enforcement Administration reported this summer, that cocaine prices have risen over the last year while street purity of the drug has declined, indicating that cocaine is becoming more difficult to obtain.

Many law enforcement officials suggest that a relative scarcity may be fueling the upsurge in violent crime: "Now, with a shrinking market, they have to compete aggressively," Rickman says. "That sparks a certain level of violence."

And no one interviewed disputes the proliferation of guns on America's streets and the willingness of people to use them. Today's street weapon is more sophisticated, more expensive and more deadly than ever.

"They're not using 'Saturday night specials' anymore," says Capt. Donald Curole, chief of homicide for the New Orleans Police Department. "It's MAC-10s and . . . 9 millimeter" semi-automatic pistols. "Ten years ago, a victim would have one or two gunshot wounds at the most. Now you're seeing multiple gunshot wounds—10 to 15 in one victim. . . . There's a tremendous amount of overkill."

Boston Deputy Police Superintendent William Celester says the very availability of guns has changed the nature of street warfare. "I was born and raised in Roxbury," he says, referring to a tough Boston neighborhood. "I was a member of a gang. There were guns, but nothing like this."

In his day, Celester says, youths fought with fists, chains, bats or, rarely, knives. "So you go away with a broken arm, or maybe you got stabbed," he says. "Now you're dead, or maimed for life. Plus, these kids are quicker to fight now. They pull out a gun and BOOM!"

In San Diego, gun seizures have soared from an annual average of 1,700 in 1980–85 to 2,500 from 1986 to 1988 and about 4,000 last year. Mona Vallon, property-evidence manager for the San Diego Police Department, says she gets "carts-full on a daily basis."

"It used to be that they'd go into a house and seize one or maybe two guns," she says. "Now, they're seizing arsenals—10, 15, 20 guns."

The department has filled one gun room, Vallon says, and opened a second while seeking innovative ways to get rid of the swelling inventory. Traditionally, San Diego police have dumped guns in the Pacific Ocean—525 in 1980 but 3,000 projected for this year. The department would like to shred them for scrap but cannot find an adequate facility.

Besides more and better guns, today's violence has other prominent characteristics. One is race. In Boston, the proportion of black homicide victims rose from 41 percent in 1973 to 67 percent this year, and this year Boston police reported that 78 percent of murder suspects are black.

In New Orleans, 203 of 229 homicide victims through Sept. 30 this year were black, 187 of the black victims were male and 266 of 284 murder suspects were black. "Mostly, it is black males who are dying," says New Orleans police spokeswoman Carmine Menchel. "We're seeing black males killing black males."

Early this summer, New Orleans Superintendent Woodfork, who is black, chastised city residents for not paying attention to the city's rising homicide rate. Later, he told The Washington Post that his entreaty was largely ignored until Tulane coed Karen Lynn Knupp, who was white, was killed at a city bus stop in July.

A second characteristic of murder in the 1990s is that it involves young people more than ever. A study by Washington's Center to Prevent Handgun Violence found that the number of youths killed by firearms nearly doubled between 1984 and 1990 from 962 to 1,897.

Yet while the rate of arrests of teenagers for murder also doubled, arrests for other crimes—including rape and robbery—did not increase significantly, the Crime Control Institute study showed. "It's not like kids are going out and attacking more people like you and me," says the Institute's Sherman. "They are shooting each other."

That means that young people are growing up in an increasingly violent atmosphere.

At the Desire public housing project in New Orleans, one of the city's worst, 16 residents have been slain this year. Random shots echo through the neighborhood "every two or three hours," says Barbara Price, whose niece was wounded by a stray bullet on her way to the grocery store in September.

Price, a quiet, soft-spoken mother of seven, ticks off the weapons she sees regularly in Desire: semi-automatic "Uzis, AK-47s, Tech 9s" and even a machine gun or two. "A lot of these kids, they're not into drugs, they're just fascinated with guns," she says.

Carl Bell, a University of Illinois psychiatrist, recently completed a study for Chicago's Mental Health Council that found that 74 percent of 1,000 South Side and Southwest Side children had witnessed a killing, shooting or robbery. Among students from South Side high-crime areas, 24 percent had seen someone killed.

"If you're a victim of violence, you come from a broken home, you're poor . . . and if you've been knocked upside the head a couple of times, then you might think about getting a weapon," Bell says. "It is going to be a whole lot more difficult to teach a kid not to carry a gun when he's been jumped on."

Many youths congregate in gangs because they know nothing else. "They think the world is one long ghetto from sea to shining sea," says public defender Bank in Philadelphia. "They think that everybody lives like they do."

The idea is to survive and prosper in a hostile environment. Power comes from the gang or from the barrel of a gun. "It adds to the machismo," says Lt. Bruce Meyer of the Los Angeles Police Department's gang unit. A gang member willing to commit a gun crime is "sometimes looked up to by other members."

For small children, coping with the violence has become a traumatic burden. "I stay in the house almost all the time," says Malika Mitchell, 10, who lives in Brooklyn's Brownsville section and was interviewed at an East New York community center. Just two or three years ago, she says, "I would go outside and ride my bike. Now it just sits in the corner."

Jeffrey Jones, 10, has another solution: "I want to move to Florida, to Orlando. Every time I visit, when you're watching the news, you don't hear things like, 'He got shot, he's going to jail. He's on America's Most Wanted.' "

Contributing to this report were Washington Post staff writer Gabriel Escobar (Washington) and special correspondents Christopher B. Daly (Boston), Laurie Goodstein (New York), Elizabeth Hudson (Dallas, Denver), Lauren Ina (Chicago, Detroit), Jon Leinwand (Atlanta, Miami) and Jill Walker (Los Angeles, San Diego, San Francisco, Seattle).

Terrorism and the Media

The articles in this section have three main emphases. First, they identify and delineate the critical connection between terrorism and the media that flows from the third factor in the terror triangle—the audience (the public). It is the audience that must be effectively intimidated. Second, the articles point up the particular nature of the problem facing democracies, which, with their free presses, offer the best opportunities as targets for terrorists. And third, they focus on the dilemmas and responsibilities of the various media in regard to this form of political violence.

What is immediately apparent in all the articles is the perception that terrorists have evolved about the use of the media, especially the Western media, for conveying their causes, demands, threats, and attempts at intimidation to a wide audience. The media are so critical to terrorists that they have developed special skills and personnel to handle their interactions with them. The terrorists have gained a sense of the value that the public attaches to high drama at the same time that the media have done so.

All four articles in this section identify the stakes in the terrorist-media interaction for those immediately involved. They also address subsequent ramifications (such as copycatism and media hostaging) of terrorist acts.

"Terrorism and the Media: Lessons From the British Experience" is an instructive essay in how different (but still democratic) societies deal with the relationship between the media and terrorism. The British experience might go against democratic values, in the view of many Americans, but it is one worth serious consideration.

Aside from noting the dilemmas for the media in democratic societies, these articles present some of the more sophisticated arguments from the media's perspective. One subtle argument asserts that refusal to cover a story could be construed as censorship, a self-defeating and antidemocratic proposition. By implication, the terrorist wins if the event is publicized; if the story is not told, on the other hand, democratic values are weakened.

The greatest strength of these articles is the inclusion of numerous examples of situations involving terrorism and the media that actually occurred over the years. These concrete cases help the reader to understand the nature and significance of the controversies that arise in the media coverage of terrorist acts.

Looking Ahead: Challenge Questions

How do we know the difference between a news story and terrorist propaganda?

What are the responsibilities of the media in a terrorist situation?

What have been the more common criticisms by governments and even by journalists of media handling of terrorist incidents?

How much of a priority are media considerations in the tactical operations of a terrorist group?

At what point (if any) can a democratic government draw the line on coverage of terrorist activities by the media?

Unit **6**

UNMASKING TERRORISM

MANIPULATION OF THE MEDIA

Rushworth M. Kidder

A free people needs a free press. But terrorism needs a propaganda platform. So the news media face a dilemma: Is it possible to keep citizens informed of daily events (including the often graphic tragedy of terrorism) without becoming, to some degree, propagandists for the perpetrators?

Belfast

He was out with guests at a restaurant late one evening when the phone call found him.

Rushing back to his office, James Hawthorne, head of the British Broadcasting Corporation (BBC) for Northern Ireland, was met by a slightly white-faced senior editor. The message: A correspondent had just gotten an interview with Evelyn Glenholmes. The question: Should the BBC broadcast it?

Some news executives would instantly have said "Yes!" Ms. Glenholmes was a hot property, a prime suspect in the attempted assassination of British Prime Minister Margaret Thatcher by the Irish Republican Army (IRA) at a Brighton hotel in 1984. Glenholmes had gone underground. Getting her on tape was something of a coup.

But under Britain's Prevention of Terrorism Act, the IRA is an illegal organization. Broadcasting Glenholmes's words might entangle the BBC in legal considerations. Here in Northern Ireland, only the finest of lines separates reporting on terrorism (which is legal) from providing a propaganda platform for terrorists (which is not).

Which was it here? When BBC correspondent Anne Cadwallader had been approached in Dublin by several IRA members, she didn't have time to call Belfast for advice. Her instincts told her to go with them in their car. She was hooded and taken to a house somewhere in Dublin, where she met a young woman who said her name was Evelyn Glenholmes.

Listening to the tape later, Mr. Hawthorne heard a woman's voice protesting her innocence. Was it really Glenholmes? The Dublin correspondent could not have been expected to recognize her. Even if authentic — and even if legal — would the broadcast stir up a hornet's nest of criticism?

In such a case, says Hawthorne, the news executive has

to make "a very, very careful judgment as to where this inherently difficult decision is going to land [him] with public relations and the reputation of the BBC."

"I had a gut feeling that it was proper to do it — an instinct that this was *real* news. I made that decision between 1 a.m. and 3 a.m." Then Hawthorne did his legal duty: He phoned the relevant authorities at 3 a.m. — knowing he would get only a duty officer who would have to wait until morning to refer the information higher — and went home. The story went out with the first morning news.

Is it news or terrorist propaganda?

In the fast-paced world of breaking news, even such apparently simple stories can involve agonizing decisions. Yet when such stories do go out, what is their effect?

Do they contribute to the free marketplace of ideas, helping the citizenry to understand the central issues of their day? Or do they give terrorists a megaphone through which to spread their message of fear to their ultimate target — the public at large?

Do the news media, in Mrs. Thatcher's words, provide "the oxygen of publicity" on which terrorism thrives? Or do they in Hawthorne's words, "allow people of the most seditious views to speak them," so that in the end "they don't have to express them in the hard way?"

Does extensive media coverage lead to what Jerrold M. Post, a psychiatrist with Defense Systems Inc., in Washington, D.C., calls a "Robinhoodization" of the terrorists, inflating them to the proportion of folk heroes? Or does such coverage produce what Paul Wilkinson, a terrorism authority at the University of Aberdeen in Scotland, calls "the outrage effect" — public revulsion of terrorist acts and demands for tougher governmental measures?

Does journalism interfere with official efforts to resolve crises, either by giving away essential information or, as Die Zeit political editor Dieter Buhl notes, by putting "so much pressure on the government" that it acts without due care? Or does it provide needed information to officials, since in hostile situations reporters can sometimes go where government decisionmakers cannot?

Finally, are the media hooked on terrorism? "Terrorism is drama," says Noel Koch, who oversees the Pentagon's counterterrorism efforts. "It's got suspense, it's got grievance, it's got people at risk, it's got the families that are crying; you can't duplicate it in fiction."

So do the media, in an effort to captivate viewers, turn to terrorist incidents whenever possible? Or do they simply report what they find, and try hard, as Alan Protheroe, assistant director general of the BBC, says, to do it "responsibly, accurately, with total care, and with total fairness in the things that [we] do not advocate"?

On these and other points there are vehement disagreements, not only among students of terrorism but within the broader public. On three points, however, there is basic consensus:

• Television is the terrorist's medium of choice. It is far preferable to print or radio as the outlet with the most immediacy and the most terrifying impact.

• Television is no longer simply reporting *about* the story: It has become *part of* the story. Making that point, Lawrence K. Grossman, president of NBC, calls television "the stage on which terrorist incidents are played."

• In the never-ending debate about the role of the news media in a free democracy, television is at the center of an ongoing controversy — and terrorism is Exhibit A.

Terrorists' growing media skills

Paul Nahon, news director at France's second television channel, Antenne-2, has a front-seat view of the terrorists' news-management skills. One of his four-man camera crews is being held hostage in Lebanon. The terrorists have colleagues in France who monitor everything said about the situation and pass it back to the captors.

In deciding how to cover the story, he says, "we have to be very, very careful every day. [The terrorists] are managing all this like professionals — professional politics, professional dramatism."

One of the noticeable developments in recent years, in fact, lies in the increasingly skillful use of publicity by terrorist organizations. "The vice-president for media relations," says Dr. Post, referring only half in jest to the individual within nearly every terrorist group who orchestrates media coverage.

With the growth of inexpensive videotape equipment, these groups are increasingly able to provide news organizations with television-ready footage: messages from terrorist leaders, interviews with captives, and even (in the case of British journalist Alec Collett, who disappeared in Lebanon in March 1985) visual records of executions.

Yasser Arafat's Palestine Liberation Organization now owns a share in an Arab communications satellite, leading one observer to wonder whether the world will soon see a new network, "Television Arafat."

And, as last summer's hijacking of TWA Flight 847 in Beirut showed, terrorists are getting very good at organizing press conferences and handling requests for interviews: A tour of the plane was reportedly offered to the networks for $1,000, and a session with the hostages themselves could be had for $12,500.

While NBC's Mr. Grossman likes to recount figures from a Gallup poll showing that 89 percent of Americans applauded television's coverage of the TWA incident, other observers, especially overseas, where television coverage is more understated, are less approving. "What [the American] media did in Lebanon during the TWA hijacking was disastrous," says Hans Josef Horchem, former head of West German domestic security and a recognized expert on counterterrorism. "It not only hurt the interests of the security forces, it was a question of taste."

In retrospect, says Ari Rath, editor of the Jerusalem Post, the TWA incident "is probably a very good example of very sophisticated use by hijackers and terrorists of the media."

To report or not to report

Mr. Rath, who like all other Israeli editors operates under a carefully organized form of governmental censorship, feels the tug between journalist and citizen.

"When you work as an Israeli journalist, you also have the other part in you, and that is your security awareness." He cites an example of a terrorist bombing several years ago that made use of a new method: a bicycle frame filled with TNT. When his paper reported how the bomb was made, the censor chastised him, showing point by point how his article had hindered both immediate and long-term police work. "It was an eye-opener," says Rath, who remains persuaded that his paper did the wrong thing. "One could have given a very good and grim and realistic description of that particular bombing incident without giving away some details which really did harm the investigation."

■ THE ETHICS OF REPORTING TERRORISM

How do the Western news media see their role in reporting terrorism? Interviews with leading journalists and news executives in Europe, America, and Israel suggest agreement on one principle — the media should be as free as possible. Beyond that, there are widely divergent views.

Eberhard Pilz, commentator, Association of Public Broadcasting Stations (ARD Television), Bonn

"

Is it the role of the press to fight terrorism, or is it the role of the press to report what's going on?

"

■ *"Censorship is to be ruled out, that's not even something we should seriously discuss. [But] I'm not feeling that I am betraying my profession if I say that we have to have self-restraint. There are no imposed regulations [in West Germany], but there is a certain degree of understanding among all the participants. We as journalists need to be aware of the role we are playing, and the risks for society if the journalist lets himself be used by the terrorists to magnify whatever their intentions are. But an event is an event — you can't mute the media. [Instead,] you have to educate the audience to behave differently . . . to get this competition a bit more civilized."*

Nachman Shai, director, Galei Zahal (Army Radio), Tel Aviv

"

[The news media] sometimes seem to create a situation which plays into their own hands. The press is not passive anymore.

"

■ *"If there is a general understanding that we have to fight terrorism, why should we make it harder? In some cases, the media do not represent the public anymore. In some cases the media force the public to know more than it really wants. I don't trust the networks . . . and especially the American networks. They will not lose any picture which shows . . . tragedy, emotions, something which will help them to attract viewers. Afterwards they will be very sorry, and they will send condolences to the families, but when it takes place [another time] they will fight each other [again]. . . . If they have 100 producers, reporters, cameramen, [and other] crew all over, they need to find something to do. They need to show that their mission was not in vain, that they did something."*

Alan Protheroe, assistant director general of the British Broadcasting Corporation, London

"

You're living in a democracy . . . . I believe that the public is entitled to know what and why [terrorists] are doing what they're doing.

"

■ *"[My] journalistic assessment goes like this: Does what I am reporting actually enhance and add to the sum of information available to the viewer so that he may make up his mind? I still have the highest regard for the three [American commercial] networks. I have to say that I'm a great fan of the American technology and a lot of the journalistic practices that you have. [But] I think a national broadcaster of that caliber, of that importance or relevance to the community, has got imposed upon him . . . certain standards and certain concepts and precepts that you don't run from. You draw a line and say, 'No, I am sorry, there are standards of taste and standards of decency and standards of journalistic behavior,' . . . you draw a line and nobody crosses it."*

Ted Koppel, anchor, ABC Television's "Nightline"

> "
> The American media stretch the outer boundaries of what may seem acceptable to our European allies.
> "

"*[American television is] particularly vulnerable to misuse. We are vulnerable to misuse by our own leaders. We are vulnerable to misuse by our international adversaries. And they obviously include terrorists. The fact that terrorism by definition tends to be dramatic, [and] the fact that by definition it tends to involve acts which are pictorial, makes us even more vulnerable. [But] don't make the mistake of jumping to the conclusion that the immediate impact of that day's visual message is the final impact. The American media . . . operate under what ultimately is our basic assumption in this country, a Jeffersonian notion, that if you allow the public access to all the information, no matter how dramatic or devastating it may be at any given point, ultimately they will reach the proper conclusions.*"

WAS IT NEWS OR A BULLY PULPIT?

The decision whether or not to broadcast or publish interviews with admitted terrorists brings journalists to the fine line between news and a forum for propaganda.

On one point, there is basic consensus: Television is the terrorists' medium of choice.

It is far preferable to print or radio as the outlet with the most immediacy and the most terrifying impact.

Should known terrorists be interviewed on television?

Wherever that question arises in the West, it provokes emotional discussion. Yes, say those who defend free and uncensored journalism. No, say those who complain that the news media are little more than collaborators in spreading terrorist propaganda.

When the question arose in Britain last August — over a BBC television interview with Irish Republican Army leader Martin McGuinness (which was pulled at the last minute by a skittish board of governors) — the furor rose to the prime minister's office before the program was eventually allowed to run.

This sort of flap has now crossed the Atlantic, in the form of two-minute interview on NBC News May 5. The subject: Abul Abbas, the alleged mastermind behind last October's seajacking of the Italian cruise liner Achille Lauro. According to Mr. Abbas, his 1,200-strong Palestine Liberation Front now plans to bring its campaign of terrorism to the United States, to "respond against America, in America itself." Abbas also noted that "[President] Reagan has now placed himself as enemy No. 1."

The interview caused an outcry. Ambassador Robert B. Oakley, head of the State Department's counterterrorism office, accused NBC of being an accomplice to terrorism by giving Abbas publicity. A State Department spokesman noted that NBC's action might "encourage the terrorist activities which we are all seeking to deter."

What galled many observers, however, was not what Abbas said but the circumstances under which he said it. Terrorists, whose central tactic is to inspire fear, typically bluster and threaten. But should they be allowed their bully pulpit during America's prime-time news? And was NBC right to have agreed, as a condition of getting the interview, not to disclose the name of the "Arabic-speaking country" where Abbas was interviewed?

New York Times foreign editor Warren Hoge noted that his paper refused to interview Abbas under similar conditions, since "the most important news was his whereabouts" and "not being able to say where he was, was just unacceptable."

NBC officials, however, defended their decision on classic freedom-of-the-press grounds: Abbas, they said, was a newsmaker, and the American people have a right to know about terrorism. Cable News Network's Ted Turner, quoted in Broadcasting magazine, sided with NBC. "Once you start not running interviews [with controversial personalities], where do you stop?"

"What is more important," muses Rath, "to have the one-time scoop or save lives?"

Should the media, then, not publicize full details of terrorist incidents? Ambassador Robert B. Oakley, director of the US State Department's Office of Counter-Terrorism and Emergency Planning, thinks not. "There's a long history of what you might call copycatism [and] competitiveness, [especially] among Middle East terrorist groups."

His point was substantiated when the Feb. 28 assassination of Swedish Prime Minister Olof Palme was followed less than 36 hours later by the assassination of Zafer Masri, the mayor of the West Bank city of Nablus, under almost identical circumstances.

Observers also call attention to the news media's reporting of counterterrorism measures taken by security forces. During the siege of the Iranian Embassy in London in 1980, recalls the BBC's Mr. Protheroe, journalists were puzzled when a Thames Gas Board van came through police cordons, parked very close to the building, and produced several men with jackhammers who drilled up the street.

At the time, journalists were told it was to shut off the gas in case of an explosion. Later, they learned that the jackhammers provided noise cover for the Special Air Service commandos, who were drilling peepholes through the embassy walls from the building next door.

"I think you've got to report that," says Protheroe, although he would not want it reported while the incident was under way. His reason: to keep the electorate as fully informed as possible.

Censorship vs. self-regulation

Throughout the debate on the media's role, one call stands out: the need for journalistic self-regulation and not censorship. First, censorship would clearly violate one of the treasured cornerstones of democracy: a free press. "One of the biggest victories terrorists could ever achieve," notes NBC's Grossman, "would be to force democracies to adopt the repressive press restrictions of dictatorships."

But there is a second and more subtle reason: Given the pace of today's technology, censorship simply would not work. The anticipated threat: satellite television, beamed from any part of the world and receivable by viewers anywhere. In Europe, where some of the state-run television networks have worked out (1) fairly high standards of taste and (2) agreements with national security forces to withhold or delay broadcasts in certain cases, there is broad concern about the effect of general access to the major US networks.

If European television had to face pressure from American television, says Peter Goebel of West Germany's second television channel, ZDF, "I'm almost sure [the European stations] won't be able to keep their principles."

Nachman Shai, director of Israeli Army Radio and a former television journalist, finds the situation doubly difficult in Israel, where foreign television crews are a constant presence. However much Israeli journalists might choose not to broadcast certain pictures, he says, "there is such competition it is almost impossible to stop pictures from getting out."

Is such competition good or bad? How free should the media be? Again, there is serious disagreement.

"The disadvantages of the public not being accurately informed, or being informed only by administration spokesman, are too severe in our society," says former Central Intelligence Agency chief Stansfield Turner. "While I decry the media releasing secrets as much as they do, I would never think of trying to organize a government censorship bureau."

But Rand Corporation scholar Paul B. Henze sees a need for greater controls on the media. "What has been gained by all of the minute media reporting on terrorism? Whose interests have been served? Who has learned something? I find it very hard to think very readily of what good has been done by just simply tantalizing people."

But, putting the problem in another perspective, he notes that the criticism may well be overblown. "If the media had had as much deleterious impact as many critics of the media think," he quips, "we'd all be finished."

The Media Dilemma and Terrorism

Barry Rosen

For weeks during the summer of 1985, a daily crescendo of television news bulletins, specials, and newscasts brought the American people the drama of the hijacking of TWA Flight 847. Network morning news programs were full of the subject, and when there were no updates, they always had someone to interview. As is so often the case, the media became part of the story. Were the networks used by the terrorists? Were they undermining America's interests and weakening the government's ability to deal with the crisis? Did the network anchors cross the line separating journalism from diplomacy? To what extent did network competition affect the story?

These questions have been asked before—during the massacre of Israeli athletes at the 1972 Munich Olympics, the kidnapping of Patricia Hearst in 1974, the Hanafi Muslim takeover of three buildings in Washington in 1977, and, of course, during the captivity of the American hostages held in Iran from 1979 to 1981. Those questions will certainly be asked again when another incident occurs.

A replay of the debate over the proper place of television in the coverage of terrorism took place in the aftermath of the TWA incident. Prime Minister Thatcher urged news organizations to restrain their coverage of terrorism and remarked that television must "find ways to starve the terrorist . . . of the oxygen of publicity." United States Attorney General Edwin Meese endorsed the prime minister's comments and took her proposal a step further. He said that the U.S. government might ask news organizations to adopt a code of restraint and that broadcasters might be asked to agree to "some principles reduced to writing."

Any meeting between government and the Fourth Estate may provoke mixed emotions. The prospect of the government determining how television journalists should meet their responsibilities conjures up a vision of state control of information, perhaps leading to the British D-Notices. In Great Britain, the government formally notifies the press about security issues, and requests that information be withheld from the public. This is certainly not a system that I believe can work in the United States.

Subsequent to TWA Flight 847, a number of prominent news organizations, including UPI, the *Chicago Sun-Times*, and CBS News, independently drafted guidelines for the coverage of terrorist incidents and hostage-taking. These policies read something like "We should avoid providing an excessive platform for the terrorist," "there should be no live coverage of the terrorist," and "our coverage will not sensationalize a story beyond the fact of it being sensational." The guidelines attempt to shape responsible coverage and acknowledge that no specific rules can exist for coverage of stories where facts and circumstances vary. To quote Dan Rather of CBS Evening News, "Journalism is not a precise science. . . . It is a crude art even on its best days."

Nevertheless, the inevitable relationship between TV and terrorists should not embarrass television news people or make them defensive. Terrorism is a product of modern life and as Russell Baker of the *New York Times* says, "It is not surprising that malcontents all over the world who believe they have just causes should spend their lives scheming to get a piece of the camera action."

The argument that television has become the terrorists' ultimate tool states that the granting of airtime to terrorists and to the events they stage-manage is akin to giving a credit card to assassins and bomb-throwers with which to shop the free world for sympathy and support. My wife, Barbara, who spent many hours appearing on television, articulates this view in an article she wrote for the *Wall Street Journal*:

Have [U.S.] television journalists forgotten they are Americans? Everyone knows that terrorists want publicity for their cause, yet no less do they want to inflate their own personal status in their communities. . . . Therefore, each time the media afford the right to speak, they award them a victory!

I would, however, differ with my wife and the general argument. The drive to be first, combined with television's remarkable technology, is what makes for disturbing viewing. The most serious charge, therefore, is not really targeted toward television itself. A major reason

From chapter 5 of *Terrorism and the Media: Dilemma for Government, Journalists and the Public*, edited by Yonah Alexander and Robert Latter, Brassey, VA, 1990.

that television was, for example, present in Beirut, is just that television exists; it has become a condition of being. Tom Wicker, the American columnist, made this point in 1985:

It may on occasion be inconvenient, intrusive, even harmful; but if because of government censorship or network censorship the hostage crisis had not been visible, *real*, on American screens, the outrage and outcry would have been a thousand times louder than what's now being heard, and rightly so; for we depend on television for perception as we depend on air to breathe.

Much of the criticism of the media's hype of terrorism should be directed elsewhere. Although terrorists may in some respects dictate the script of an event that they have staged and determine in yet other ways the priorities of news coverage, the administration in Washington can also stage-manage much of the coverage. According to Hodding Carter III, the State Department spokesman during Jimmy Carter's presidency, "The government is not without resources to hold off or encourage a media presence." Six years after the Iran hostage crisis, he recalled that during a period of quiet negotiations with Latin American countries aimed at freeing us, he was ordered to stop talking about the hostages, and he said, "The story all but vanished." The Reagan administration, I suggest, raised the ante of the media coverage during the 847 incident, when it announced the president's vacation had been canceled and assigned presidential spokesman Larry Speakes the job of telling reporters—and through them, West Beirut's Shiites—that Reagan was considering the option of a blockade of Lebanon or of shutting down Beirut's airport. A signal was being sent.

What of the criticism that the media reports U.S. military movements and thus provides information that might be useful to hijackers and terrorists? Michael Burch, a Pentagon spokesman, has said, "For the price of a 19-inch television, a group of hijackers who only represent the back pew of some mosque have a very elaborate intelligence network." This issue was raised in 1985 in relation to media reports of the movement of the Delta Force from its U.S. base. From what I can gather in reading accounts of that incident, virtually all news organizations received information regarding military and diplomatic moves from government officials who provided it with the understanding that it was to be revealed. Network heads maintain that the reports were accurate and were promoted by the administration to send a message to Shiites. Unless the United States was prepared to take direct military action in Beirut, the U.S. military presence was a symbol more than a threat, and symbols need to be appreciated.

Again, as the media reacts to charges of exploitation, the question is, Who is exploiting whom? Are the media furthering terrorist aims by providing extensive coverage? What's more, the public may be unduly alarmed and frightened, perhaps undermining its faith in the government as an institution that can ensure security and stability. In this case, the media face the possibility of becoming, in the public's view, unwitting allies of the terrorists. On the flip side, exclusively following the government line and interpretation opens the media to the charge of being the stooge and propaganda tool of the government. The media are damned if they do and damned if they don't.

Are the families truly exploited, or are the media, particularly television, helping to transmit information to families, to other Americans, and even to the U.S. government about how hostages are being treated? Are reporters keeping the issue alive for families who fear it will disappear in a diplomatic muddle? Indeed, many hostage families feel that the media, instead of invading their privacy, serve as a link to millions of sympathetic Americans and help make the crisis as important to others as it is to them. Peter Jennings, ABC's anchor, says that psychologists have told his staff that in some cases "there is actually a cathartic effect" for hostage families when they are interviewed. He recalls that when the Marine compound was bombed in 1983, "people telephoned me and said, 'My son was killed, and why haven't you called me?'"

Nevertheless, a problem exists here. News executives, anchors, commentators, and correspondents skirt the issue. Many journalists and broadcasters embrace a philosophy that assumes a reality in the world that their job is to mirror accurately and recapture in all its detail so that an objective representation of the real world gets presented to their audience. The content of news broadcasts, however, at times suggests something else. This "reality" is filtered through an elaborate gatekeeping mechanism that screens and edits news content. Some news is, in effect, better than other news. Broadcast networks always keep an eye on ratings, on their competitors, and on the changing tastes of the audience. Crime news in the states has always done well, and terrorism, with its dramatic visual effects, is perfectly suited for television. That the media pursue their own self-interest and seek to sell the big story as effectively as they can is not surprising, even if, in some circumstances, this entails the gloss of melodramatics.

The dilemma the media face is real and pressing, with no palpable solutions at hand. If the media censor terrorist news, the decision may infringe on the public's right to know. In fact, the audience doesn't necessarily know what restraints journalism—television, radio, or print—may be imposing on itself. For instance, Lou Cannon of the *Washington Post* has pointed out that the press did not report that one hostage on Flight 847 was a member of the National Security Agency, which would have endangered him. On a local level, Lieutenant Robert T. Louden, the commanding officer of the New York City Police Department's Hostage Negotiating Team, echoes Cannon's remarks. Louden praises members of the media who respond to authorities' private pleas not to cover stories or aspects of stories that might result in harm to hostages or interfere with plans to take terrorists into custody.

Clearly, "objectivity" is, at best, difficult to approximate, much less to achieve. As the U.S. government has faltered in developing a policy for fighting terrorism that is grounded in both coherent and comprehensive principles yet still flexible enough to allow for effective response, so too has the media. Perhaps all that is possible to expect is that journalists make intelligent choices that require a sense of perspective. Perhaps less extensive and repetitive coverage that gives less airtime to terrorists is a beginning. Nevertheless, although the issues raised by terrorism are complex, they must not become a stalking-horse for depriving American citizens the access to a full account of events that affect their lives and their nation.

Media Coverage of Political Terrorism and the First Amendment: Reconciling the Public's Right to Know with Public Order

John E. Finn

The topic is large and unwieldy: the First Amendment and media coverage of political terrorism. Such discussions commonly proceed fairly quickly to an examination of possible restraints upon media coverage and then to whether those restraints should be imposed by governmental authorities or should instead be voluntarily adopted by a responsible and disciplined press. The former proposal immediately and properly evokes fears of censorship, the latter doubts about utility and feasibility.

These questions are important and contentious. For now, however, they are premature. They rest upon a set of assumptions that the literature on terrorism too easily takes for granted. Foremost among these unexamined assumptions is the fairly routine claim that the media somehow promote terrorism, either as an active, gullible, or naive partner or by providing an irresistible forum for publicity and propaganda. We are all familiar with claims about the symbiotic nature of the relationship between the media and terrorism: violence sells and violence is newsworthy; terrorism is theater and terrorism entertains.

Freedom of speech and association hold a privileged constitutional position in democratic states. This position does not mean, as some seem to argue, that freedom of speech is an absolute and inviolable value. As discussed later in this chapter, the constitutions of most democratic states contemplate times when commitment to civil liberties must be sacrificed in the name of security. The most difficult issues terrorism raises in democratic states are not questions of physical integrity but rather of spiritual integrity, of the strength of our commitment to two or more positive values that appear irreconcilable. The apparent conflict is between our commitment to unhindered public discourse and the need for public security. This conflict is only one aspect of a much larger conflict between security and democratic aspiration. It does mean, however, that in a constitutional democracy those who advocate the need for and the legality of media restraints, whether voluntary or mandatory, as do those who oppose them, have an obligation first to examine those assumptions and the empirical claim upon which they rest.

A series of straightforward but thoroughly contentious questions must be examined. Answers to these questions are an essential precondition to an intelligent discussion of whether the media in constitutional states should voluntarily adopt certain restraints or whether governmental authorities should impose certain constraints on media coverage of terrorism. A minimum set of concerns exists that the advocates of restraints must satisfy if they are to make a persuasive case for their position. The concerns are specified without supposing that they can or cannot be satisfied. Opponents of media regulation should be required to address a similar set of questions.

MEDIA COVERAGE AND THE FREQUENCY OF TERRORIST EVENTS

First we need to establish precisely what the relationship, if any, is between aggressive media coverage of terrorist spectaculars and terrorist incidents. In other words, does media coverage influence terrorism and, if so, how? In addressing this question, we must be careful to distinguish between two distinct issues. The first is a matter of frequency. Proponents of restraints typically claim that media coverage of political violence encourages additional terrorist acts. Commonly known as the "contagion effect," the argument proposes that media coverage of terrorism inspires repetition in the group that undertook the violent act and subsequently profited from the coverage, as well as imitation and emulation by other groups. In the former case, media coverage "reinforces the terrorists' sense of power and . . . may contribute significantly to the prolonging of the incident or to an increase in its serious consequences."[1] Imitation and emulation by other groups are a consequence because

From chapter 4 of *Terrorism and the Media: Dilemma for Government, Journalists and the Public*, edited by Yonah Alexander and Robert Latter, Brassey, VA, 1990.

they learn that terrorism is a powerful currency with which to purchase publicity. Moreover, excessive media coverage may teach in other, more direct ways, perhaps by providing these groups with tactical or strategic information that they can later use to advantage.

The contagion effects of terrorism have been the subject of rigorous research, much of which has shown that it "is a demonstrably contagious phenomenon."[2] However, these findings should be interpreted carefully. The media may play an important structural role in determining the highly imitative character of terrorism, a point addressed below, but the larger and more important case that media coverage has substantially increased the frequency of terrorist incidents is very difficult to make, at least as measured by absolute increases in political violence. Indeed, the last few years have seen much talk about how the frequency of terrorist incidents has seemed to decrease recently. The question arises as to what may have caused this recession in the economy of violence. Of course, some measure other than absolute increases in violence could be chosen for all sorts of good reasons, not least of which is the unreliability of such data, but the proponents of media restraints have yet to suggest what that other measure should be or why it is more appropriate than others.

Another possibility is that the prospect of publicity through media coverage serves to encourage opposition groups to employ violence as a tool for political change, as opposed to less violent and hence less newsworthy methods of political action. In this case, the issue is less one of distributional frequency than of proclivity; media coverage lowers the threshold. Much interesting work needs to be done here. Unfortunately, however, the literature on decision-making within terrorist organizations is still in its infancy.[3] We cannot yet conclude that excessive media coverage acts as an incentive in the strategic choices terrorist organizations make.

The second question is not of frequency but of form. Whatever the effects of media coverage on the frequency or distribution of terrorism, the media—in particular, the electronic media—might affect the specific forms that terrorism takes. Terrorism often appears faddish. Diplomatic and commercial kidnappings were especially common in Latin America in the 1960s and 1970s. Aircraft hijackings and car bombings were frequent throughout the 1970s; hostage-taking characterized the 1980s.

As indicated earlier, scholarly research demonstrates the imitative character of political terrorism, and undoubtedly the media glamorization of spectacular terrorist acts helps make such imitation possible. No doubt terrorist organizations learn in much the same ways that other organizations do. Nevertheless, this process is hardly novel and not unique to terrorism. The subject has bedeviled criminology for decades. All that can be said is that the media *may* influence the form and specific character of terrorist strategy—quite a different claim and a much weaker one than the argument that media coverage

actually encourages or promotes terrorism. The first claim about the relationship between the media and political terrorism, if it can be demonstrated, might support restraints upon media coverage. The second claim is much less certain a foundation.

MEDIA INVOLVEMENT IN TERRORIST INCIDENTS

A second set of issues involves not so much the relationship between media coverage and the frequency of terrorism as the effects of coverage during an ongoing terrorist incident. Critics often complain that the media have improperly interfered during the course of an incident, perhaps by broadcasting sensitive information or by involving themselves in negotiations. This charge is not frivolous, but again we must take care to distinguish between things that are not alike.

On one level, media coverage of terrorist incidents necessarily affects how the participants act. Something very much like the Heisenberg uncertainty principle operates in such circumstances, as observation remakes and changes what is observed. (Some version of this truth explains much of the faddish character of terrorist violence. Hijackings lose their glamour and interest through repeated exposure and must then be replaced with some other, novel form of violence.) Of course, the media can be cautioned not to sensationalize, but how this influence can be avoided without an expansive form of censorship is unclear. Why censorship would be appropriate for this reason alone is also not certain. That the mere presence of the media affects the conduct of terrorist incidents is one claim, and that media presence *necessarily* hampers the successful resolution of such incidents is quite another claim. Instances can be recalled in which the media's presence caused problems, but at times it has helped as well.

The task, then, is to identify with greater precision the areas in which media involvement has been troublesome and, if they are thought to be exigent, to tailor restraints to just those situations. Two areas are of particular concern here. In some cases, the media have publicized sensitive information and intelligence that may have handicapped the efforts of authorities to cope with terrorist incidents, especially hijackings and other hostage situations. In what is perhaps the most serious case, radio broadcasts alerted the hijackers of a Lufthansa jet that the plane's captain was transmitting information to ground authorities. The hijackers subsequently killed the captain. Americans may also recall the Hanafi Muslim case, in which radio and television broadcasters went so far as to conduct live interviews with the Hanafis. [With regard to] the media's involvement in the 1985 hijacking of TWA Flight 847, after the incident ended, the London *Times* wrote that "the behavior of the American television crews and companies was a disgrace." Excessive television coverage, including, as in this case, stage-managed news conferences with some of the hostages, may act as an incentive to terrorists to prolong the incident and may thus hinder the efforts of governmental authorities to resolve it.

These incidents clearly indicate the need for discretion and discipline in how the media actually cover terrorist incidents. Once again, however, whether anything more is required here than what the media typically demand of themselves in reporting nonterroristic hostage situations is not clear. The appeal must be to the professional integrity of journalists; respect for those professional values, coupled with cooperation between authorities and media representatives, does more to avoid difficulties of the sort outlined than would legal regulation. Mandatory restraints inevitably invite deliberate violation, especially among what is commonly called the popular press. They promote an environment of continued antagonism between the press and security officials. The antagonism would be most unfortunate for, as indicated before, the presence of the press in such cases is not necessarily negative. Moreover, instances of cooperation occur. Several American police departments, including that of New York City, as well as the FBI, now invite media representatives to training sessions for hostage negotiators.

Another point should not be ignored. Security forces often claim, with good reason, that they have learned over time how best to cope with terrorist situations and that their sophistication increases with experience. American media representatives now make a similar claim that should not be dismissed out of hand. With experience, the press came to honor requests for restraint in the reporting of criminal kidnap cases. The press also chose not to report that one of the hostages on TWA Flight 847 was a member of the National Security Agency.

MEDIA RESTRAINTS, THE FIRST AMENDMENT, AND CIVIL LIBERTIES

The foregoing leaves open the question of support for opposition to legal restraints upon media coverage of political terrorism. The imposition of restraints without first specifying the reasons why they are necessary and under what conditions they are tolerable is, however, to be opposed. The proponents of restraints have not yet satisfied these requirements. The burden of such justification is a heavy one. Some will respond that such a burden is too stringent and that it substantially underestimates the threat terrorism poses for democratic states and the role the media play in making that threat effective.

As indicated earlier, however, the threat that terrorism poses for democratic societies is greatly overstated, notwithstanding repeated warnings in scholarly and popular literature that democratic states are especially and unusu-

ally vulnerable to political terrorism. Much of that vulnerability is attributed to the freedom such states guarantee the media. Nevertheless, the cases in which terrorists have posed a truly substantial threat to the physical integrity of Western democracies are in truth quite infrequent, if indeed they have happened at all.[4]

Far more common and far more troublesome are the hazards terrorism poses to the spiritual integrity of Western democracies and to their commitment to democratic and constitutional principles. Widespread terrorism, like other forms of political violence, typically evokes claims in democracies that we cannot adequately protect ourselves if we strictly adhere to constitutional limitations upon governmental power, limitations we freely adopted in less troublesome times. Claims of this sort have led many to conclude that the real danger is not terrorism but rather how we choose to respond to it. Indeed, one prominent student of terrorism has concluded that the "consequences of terrorism have a great deal to do with the limits each society imposes on the civil liberties of its citizenry to secure its survival,"[5] and Paul Wilkinson warns that "the real danger of resorting to sledgehammer methods to cope with the relatively low intensities of political violence . . . in most Western countries is that they would extinguish democracy in the name of security."[6] This concern, above all others, counsels caution in the legal regulation of media coverage of terrorism. However, these concerns constitute just one aspect of the larger problem.

These fears should not be dismissed; indeed, they are quite real and terribly important. Nevertheless, they tend to proceed at a level of generality not unlike claims about how the media promotes terrorism, and for this reason, as well as some others, they are just as unsatisfactory. As Martha Crenshaw has noted, remarkably few studies "document the concrete effects of policies against terrorism on individual freedoms."[7] Only a few studies describe the content of antiterrorist policies in any detail, and we know even less about the operation and implementation of antiterrorist legislation.[8] That neglect is really quite surprising, for every major Western democracy has either proposed or enacted special antiterrorist legislation to respond to terrorism. In the Republic of Ireland and in Northern Ireland in the United Kingdom, for example, the police possess expansive powers of arrest and detention, and in both states special courts are charged with jurisdiction over terrorist offenses. These courts sit without juries and operate under substantially relaxed rules of procedure and evidence. The constitutions of Italy and the Federal Republic of Germany explicitly prohibit special courts, but both countries have enacted legislation that grants authorities sweeping powers of arrest and detention. France, Canada, the Netherlands, Denmark, and Belgium have all enacted antiterrorist legislation as well. Frequently these efforts include restrictions on press coverage of terrorist incidents. Section 3(1) (a) of the Canadian War Measures Act, for instance, provides that the governor in council may issue regulations concerning "censorship and the control and suppression of publications, writings, maps, plans, photographs, communications and the means of communication."

Perhaps the most notable example is Section 31 of the 1960 Broadcasting Authority Act in the Republic of Ireland. Acting under this section in 1972, then Minister of Posts and Telegraphs Conor Cruise O'Brien banned state radio and television networks from broadcasting interviews with Irish Republican Army officials or known sympathizers. In 1976 the government expanded the prohibition to include interviews with members of Sinn Fein (the political counterpart of the IRA) or with members of any organization proscribed under the Northern Ireland Emergency Provisions Act of 1973. Sinn Fein is a legal political party in Britain and routinely runs candidates in general elections in Northern Ireland.

Concerns have been expressed in Great Britain as well. Prime Minister Thatcher has spoken repeatedly about the media's responsibility to deprive terrorists of the "oxygen of publicity," and of late the D-Notice system has received renewed criticism. Moreover, critics of the Prevention of Terrorism Act of 1976 have charged that Section 10, which creates a number of criminal offenses that generally concern "support" for terrorist organizations, has led the British media to decline to televise some documentaries on the Northern Irish problem for fear that they might "encourage support" for the IRA and other banned organizations. In the summer of 1980, for example, the BBC refused to televise two documentaries presented by the British Film Institute because they "lacked balance."

More recently, BBC broadcast journalists went on strike after the BBC's Board of Governors, under pressure from the home secretary, overruled management's decision to televise a documentary on Northern Ireland, *Real Lives: At the Edge of the Union*, because it featured interviews with Martin McGuinness of Sinn Fein and Gregory Campbell of the Democratic Unionist Party. Both men held elective office.

Claims are frequently made that such problems are not possible in the United States because the First Amendment absolutely prohibits governmental regulation of the news media and their coverage of terrorism. Although individual justices have insisted that the First Amendment absolutely prohibits governmental restraints upon the media, that position does not accurately reflect First Amendment jurisprudence. President Lincoln took rigorous measures against certain editors of Confederate newspapers during the Civil War. As recently as 1971, a probable majority of the justices of the Supreme Court, although they could not agree upon a common opinion, could agree in the Pentagon Papers case[9] that in extraordinary circumstances, such as those occasioned by war or some other emergency, governmental restrictions upon the media might be warranted under some notion of constitutional necessity.

In 1971 the *New York Times* and the *Washington Post* gained access to stolen copies of the Pentagon Papers, a governmental study of American policy decisions in Vietnam. After the newspapers began to publish excerpts of the material, the Department of Justice sought federal injunctions against further publication. One federal court granted a temporary injunction, and a second refused to issue one. The Supreme Court accepted the case, heard oral arguments, and issued an opinion just four days later.

In his concurring opinion, Justice William Brennan wrote:

Our cases . . . have indicated that there is a single, extremely narrow class of cases in which the First Amendment's ban on prior judicial restraint may be overridden. . . . Such cases may arise only when the Nation is "at war," . . . during which times "no one would question but that a government might prevent actual obstruction to its recruiting service or the publication of the sailing dates of transports or the number and location of troops."

Likewise, Justice Harry Blackmun agreed in dissent that "the First Amendment, after all, is only one part of an entire Constitution. . . . First Amendment absolutism has never commanded a majority of this Court.' "[10]

The First Amendment notwithstanding, then, governmental restraints upon the media may be both necessary and constitutionally permissible in a crisis of sufficient severity. The burden of justification is a heavy one, however, and as suggested earlier the proponents of mandatory restraints have yet to produce anything like the evidence necessary to make the case persuasive.

The case is strong enough, however, to warrant voluntary self-regulation. Many people have offered numerous proposals that are quite interesting and generally thoughtful, but they do not substantially improve upon or differ from those presented in the Report of the Task Force on Disorders and Terrorism (1976). Among the more prominent proposals are the following:

1. Limitations on interviews during hostage incidents
2. Delays upon the release of inflammatory or sensitive information
3. Minimum intrusiveness in the course of terrorist incidents
4. Balanced and noninflammatory coverage of such incidents

Several news organizations have promulgated their own standards. These rules often coincide with the recommendations of the task force, but differences exist as well. The best known of these guidelines are those of the CBS News Division. . . .[11] These too call for balanced coverage, avoiding "the use of inflammatory catchwords or phrases," and avoiding the provision of "an excessive platform for the terrorist/kidnapper."

Occasionally, some media representatives oppose even self-regulation; they claim that it is only a more subtle form of censorship. At best, this claim is spurious. Although proposals for self-regulation vary in particulars, all essentially amount to little more than exhortations to practice responsible and balanced reporting. They appeal, in other words, to the standards of ethical and responsible behavior that inhere in journalism as an honorable profession.

Skeptics will deny that such values exist, and nothing written here is likely to disabuse them of their doubt. Realists will insist that the competitive structure of the news industry, at least as it functions in the United States, forces even the most responsible of news organizations and journalists to compromise those values. If so, such compromise is a cost of our commitment to democratic values. Democracy *is* a messy business. Our commitment to it and to the protection of civil liberties is often inconvenient, inefficient, annoying, and profoundly costly.

SOME CONCLUDING THOUGHTS

As mentioned in the introductory remarks, the topic—reconciling the public's right to know in cases of terrorism with the demands of public security—is large and unwieldy. The topic is also but a specific example of a much larger and older problem: what the framers of the American Constitution called "good government" can be established upon the basis of reason and deliberation or, in the words of Edmond Cahn, upon the promise "that persuasion and free assent can triumph over brute force and build the foundations of a happier commonwealth."[12] The widespread use of political terrorism in a democratic state casts doubt upon and challenges that promise, but failure to respond to terrorism in a fashion consistent with democratic ideals calls into question our commitment to those ideals and in that respect challenges our very identity.

The larger problem, then, is one of conflicting objectives. Responding to terrorism exposes a conflict between our need for survival, the most urgent objective, and our commitment to democracy, our highest purpose. In this one respect, the oft-repeated charge that democratic societies are especially susceptible to terrorism contains an element of truth. However this claim obscures as much as it illuminates. The founders of constitutional democracies are generally aware of the historic frailty of such communities, and they typically include provisions in their constitutions that acknowledge the occasional necessity for expansive powers of self-defense. Article I, Section 9 of the U.S. Constitution authorizes suspension of the writ of habeas corpus in cases of "rebellion or invasion" and when "the public safety may require it." Section 8 empowers Congress to declare war and raise armies and to provide militia to suppress insurrections, and we have already seen that First Amendment guarantees are not absolute. Among the less explicit provisions for crisis government are Article II, which provides that executive power is vested in the president, and Section 3 of the

same article, which requires that the president faithfully execute the laws.

European constitutions are generally more precise. The Irish Constitution of 1937, for example, expressly authorizes special emergency laws and sanctions the creation of emergency courts. Moreover, Article 28(3) states:

Nothing in this Constitution shall be invoked to invalidate any law enacted by the legislature which is expressly to be for the purpose of securing the public safety and the preservation of the State in time of war or armed rebellion.

The Basic Law of the Federal Republic of Germany sets forth in Article 115 and various other provisions a detailed catalog of procedures the German government must follow in declaring and coping with states of emergency. In direct contrast to the Irish Constitution, Article 101 of the Basic law prohibits extraordinary courts. An amendment, Article 155g, further provides that the "constitutional status and the exercise of the constitutional functions [of the Federal Constitutional Court] must not be impaired."

Most democratic states, then, have constitutionally sanctioned powers of emergency. Therefore, attributing the vulnerability of democratic states to political terrorism to an imagined constitutional incapacity is a gross mistake. The means to protect ourselves against the physical threat exist; only resolution wards off the greater threat to our identity.

NOTES

1. Grant Wardlaw, *Political Terrorism: Theory, Tactic, and Countermeasures* (Cambridge: Cambridge University Press, 1982), p. 77.

2. Martha Crenshaw, ed., *Terrorism, Legitimacy, and Power: The Consequences of Political Violence* (Middletown, Conn.: Wesleyan University Press, 1983), p. 17. See also Manus I. Midlarsky, Martha Crenshaw, and Fumihiko Yoshida, "Why Violence Spreads: The Contagion of International Terrorism," *International Studies Quarterly* 24 (1980): 262.

3. See, for example, Kent Layne Oots, *A Political Organization Approach to Transnational Terrorism* (Westport, Conn.: Greenwood Press, 1986).

4. See, for example, Yehezkel Dror, "Terrorism as a Challenge to the Democratic Capacity to Govern," in Martha Crenshaw, ed., *Terrorism, Legitimacy, and Power.* One might argue about Uruguay.

5. Irving Louis Horowitz, "The Routinization of Terrorism and Its Unanticipated Consequences," in Martha Crenshaw, ed., *Terrorism, Legitimacy, and Power,* p. 50. See also Irving Louis Horowitz, "Can Democracy Cope with Terrorism?" *Civil Liberties Review* 4 (1977): 29.

6. Paul Wilkinson, *Terrorism and the Liberal State,* 2d ed. (New York: New York University Press, 1986), pp. 38–50.

7. Crenshaw, *Terrorism, Legitimacy, and Power,* p. 14.

8. There are exceptions. See, for example, Ronald D. Crelinsten, Danielle Laberge-Altmjed, and Dennis Szabo, eds., *Terrorism and Criminal Justice* (Lexington, Mass.: D. C. Heath, 1978); Christopher Hewitt, *The Effectiveness of Antiterrorist Policies* (New York: University Press of America, 1984); Yonah Alexander and Allan S. Nanes, eds., *Legislative Responses to Terrorism* (Boston: Martinus Nijhoff Publishers, 1986); and Kevin Boyle, Thomas Hadden, and Paddy Hillyard, *Ten Years On: The Legal Control of Political Violence* (Nottingham: Russell Press, 1980).

9. *New York Times v. United States,* 403 U.S. 713 (1971). See also *Near v. Minnesota,* 283 U.S. 697 (1931).

10. "The Pentagon Papers Case," *New York Times Company v. U.S.* 403 U.S. 713 (1971).

11. These are discussed and reprinted in Wardlow, *Political Terrorism,* pp. 193–194.

12. Edmond Cahn, "The Consumers of Injustice," in Ephraim London, ed., *The Law as Literature* (New York: Simon and Schuster, 1960), p. 590

Terrorism and the Media: Lessons from the British Experience

Abraham H. Miller

Abraham H. Miller is a Bradley Resident Scholar at The Heritage Foundation and Professor of Political Science at the University of Cincinnati.

In war, truth is the first casualty. In terrorism, truth never makes it to the casualty list. Its death silently precedes the first act of violence.

Warfare is about taking political power through force of arms. Terrorism is about seizing political power through force of propaganda. Terrorist violence is a facade behind which is concealed political and military impotency.

A terrorist leader is in a sense a dramatist. He produces violent spectacles designed to create the illusion of power through horror. What the terrorist lacks in real power, he compensates for in the production of attention-riveting visuals. Terrorism is theater played on the world stage to an audience of eager journalists—preferably those holding a camera.

The relationship between terrorists seeking publicity and journalists seeking news is at times called symbiotic, as the purveyors of violence-laced propaganda and the disseminators of news feed off one another.

It is this relationship—this production of violence for the camera—that presents the media with difficult ethical choices. Terrorists push the media into that grey area where distinctions blur between reporting the news and becoming part of the news, and frequently journalists have to ask themselves whether certain terrorist events would occur if not for the media's willingness to report them.

To ask that question, however, is not to suggest, as some regrettably have, that if the lens were to be capped, terrorism would somehow miraculously cease. Although terrorists do covet publicity, that is not their only motivation for violence. Terrorist violence is used for vengeance and as an instrument of negotiation.

Live Drama. Beyond that, capping the lens, even if legally permissible, is increasingly becoming bureaucratic whimsy. The same technology that makes contemporary terrorism live drama increasingly puts that drama beyond the effective reach of the censor—a fact that is underscored by recent events in Eastern Europe.

If there is any doubt as to terrorists' ability to function without the media, one only need be reminded that two of the most effective terrorist organizations on record, the Sicarii and the Zealots, functioned in the first century A.D. (And as even most American high school students know, that was before Dan Rather came to CBS.) These groups did rely on the propaganda of the deed, which they achieved by killing their victims in broad daylight on holy days amid large crowds, whose word-of-mouth accounts spread fear.

FRAMING THE ISSUE

Properly framed, the issue before us is not whether the media should cover terrorism, but how it should report it. The corollary question, of course, is who should decide how the media goes about its business.

If we are justifiably horrified at what havoc government can wreak with economic policy, contemplate momentarily what the bureaucracy could do if unleashed on the media. We might find that the media's rights under the First Amendment resemble nothing so much as First Amendment rights at some of our universities.

There would be the First Amendment hour, where freedom of speech would not be infringed if it did not run beyond prime time. Or there might be freedom of speech zones, the West coast on alternate Tuesdays and the East Coast on Mondays and Fridays.

And of course there would be decency rules, which would prohibit negative comments about both government-approved terrorist groups and state sponsors of terrorism. As the approval list would change frequently, it would be appropriate to check for updates with the State Department to see which terrorists were "in" and which were "out."

For those who believe the bureaucracy is incapable of such machinations, I suggest a short visit to the closest university that has adopted a so-called "decency standard."

Disregard of Ethics. Although I strongly believe that we conservatives do not desire to take the government out of the economy and put it into the newsroom, I also know that the risk of that tragic occurrence is the result of the media's own reckless disregard of basic journalistic ethics. Journalists of every stripe appear to learn ethics in the classroom and forget that they were meant to apply to something other than the final examination. As one thoughtful news expert put it, when we get discussions of ethics out of the classroom and into the boardroom, we will know then that ethics will have some influence on behavior.

The media is its own enemy. Nothing has been a greater threat to the media's continued access to its Constitutional rights than its coverage of terrorism and most notably its coverage of the hijacking of TWA Flight 847 to Beirut (June 1985). This event brought into focus, more than did any prior event, the media's general unwillingness to distinguish its rights from its responsibilities.

Whatever the media might have learned from its earlier coverage of the Iranian hostage crisis was quickly lost in the drama and competition of this new event. In their quest to beat the competition, the networks sent their superstars to Beirut, a device known as "bigfooting," where the resident and knowledgeable local correspondent is squashed into oblivion by the presence of a network's superstar.

TWA 847 became a media circus, and at one dramatic point Shiite gunmen had to discharge their weapons to preserve order at a press conference that had all the decorum of a school of ravenous barracudas encountering dinner in the open sea. But if that scene was the most dramatic and most memorable, it was so only because it came to symbolize the media's excesses. The media showed poor judgment at a number of points throughout the episode.

"Ratings Be Damned." As in the Iranian hostage situation—where in exchange for an interview with Marine Corporal William Gallegos, NBC permitted a fanatical spokeswoman called "Mary" to launch a five-minute tirade against America—all the networks gave airtime to people forcibly holding innocent Americans at gun point. The Iran hostage episode which became a soap opera for ratings so angered *TV Guide* (Dec. 22, 1979) that it published an editorial—which later appeared as an advertisement in the *Wall Street Journal*— noting, "We have seen enough unwashed Iranians chanting their slogans and waving their fists on cue to last a lifetime. . . . Let the ratings be damned."

TV Guide was alluding to an 18 percent rise in the size of the network news audience as a result of the coverage of the hostage crisis. Wild-eyed Shiites and captive Americans pushed up advertising revenue. Cloaked in the First Amendment, the networks showed us that captive Americans could be comfortably exploited for revenue.

If this exploitation of the hostages is infuriating, it seems to me that it is less so than the twisted rationale the media used to justify such interviews. Robert Siegenthaler, of ABC, [testifying before the House Subcommittee on Europe and the Middle East (July 1985)] claimed that his correspondent about to film an interview with a TWA hostage was able to say surreptitiously to the hostage that ABC would pack up and leave if the hostage did not want to be interviewed. Undoubtedly, this example will give new meaning to the concept of "informed consent."

Forget, if you can, that the networks are in a sense partners in this crime where Americans are being held in captivity because they are Americans and because they provide entree to the American media. Does anyone really believe that this hostage could have said to ABC, "Go home," and not suffered at the hands of his captors?

That a vice president of the network would use this episode to justify ABC's exploitation of the situation for "entertainment" purposes (it certainly is not news), indicates at best a certain sense of unreality and at worst a disdainful arrogance.

Congressman Thomas Luken in his outrage at Siegenthaler's response said, "This is so palpably offensive to me. He [the reporter] is still talking to people who are under complete control. He is still talking to people who had been given an indication by their captors as to what they should say. . . . You wouldn't even [have] had them on if the captors didn't deliver them to you. And you don't have the sophistication to recognize that the captors would have told them what to say? Privately or publicly?"

Cult of Objectivity. Charles Krauthammer writing in *Time* (July 15, 1985) refers to the media's arrogance as deriving from its cherished belief in the cult of objectivity. This doctrine is summed up for Krauthammer by veteran correspondent Sam Donaldson's remark, "It's our job to cover the story . . .we bring the information."

The act of observing and transmitting, however, even in the best of circumstances, alters the story. Every schoolboy learns that once he stains a slide to enhance its reflection under the microscope, he has intervened in what he observes. The media would have us believe that the camera does not alter the characteristics of events, even events staged by the propagandists of the deed.

Krauthammer finds the doctrine of objectivity to be little more than a self-serving rationale. I would argue, however, that the problem is not the doctrine of objectivity, for properly exercised it is as appropriate to the media as it is to science. The problem is that the media, unlike science, claims objectivity to conceal the intrusiveness of the process of observation.

One wonders if ABC would concede that David Hartman's solicitation of Nabih Berri—the good Shiite in this drama of good Shiite and bad Shiite—"Any final words to President Reagan this morning?" was something more than reporting the story?

It prompted enough reflection at ABC to put Hartman's, "Good Morning America," under the aegis of the news division the following day. Some said that this was done to make the program more sensitive to news guidelines. More cynical observers saw this as an attempt to wrap the program more tightly in the protection of the First Amendment.

Highjacking the Networks. TWA 847 presented us with other examples of the media becoming part of the story. The continual updates from Lebanon gave the appearance that the Shiites had not hijacked an airplane but had hijacked the networks. And all the lessons that were supposed to have been learned from the Iranian hostage situation were lost as TWA 847 was conducted like some instant replay of the Tehran soap opera. The media was not simply reporting the news; it was making the news. When Dan Rather asked one of the hostages what he would have President Reagan do, Rather demonstrated the ability of the media to be intrusive.

There was also the networks' subtle editorializing through the use of the doctrine of moral equivalence. Shiite gunmen held captive in Israel were portrayed as hostages, with tearful mothers and concerned families, no different from the mothers and families of the innocent Americans whose only crime was their citizenship. It would not be inappropriate to be reminded that one of the "equivalent" Shiites, subsequently released by Israel, was reported to have been involved in another act of terrorism, one which took place over Lockerbee, Scotland with the disintegration of Pan Am 103. So much for "objectivity" as applied to news analysis.

My concern here is not to excoriate the American news media for its reporting of TWA 847. As Jody Powell noted in testimony before the Congress (July 1985), the problem is not so much that the media will bring down the government or society, but that its excesses do damage to itself. And if the media wounds itself, we all suffer, for a free society is impossible without a free media.

It is one thing to depict media excesses. It is far and away another to prescribe an effective solution. Some have suggested that the media would act more responsibly if the media saw terrorism as threatening the social and political foundations of the society itself. How does the media report terrorism in a democratic society under siege? And would those experiences provide lessons for the American media's conduct of its business? To explore those issues I examined the behavior of the media in the United Kingdom.

THE BRITISH EXPERIENCE

Britain's experience with media coverage of terrorism casts these concerns against a backdrop where terrorist violence threatens the very integrity of the political system. For that reason, the British experience which tugs and pulls between concerns of freedom and order in a society that is directly under siege, might provide us with lessons about our own strengths and vulnerabilities. After all, media excesses might be tolerated when the reporting is from Beirut and the threat is to hostages and not to the very viability of the social and political system.

Cherishing Independence. To Americans, the British media appears to be only half free, for the British media can be subjected to prior restraint. But the similarities between the American and British media far overshadow their differences. Both function in liberal democracies that cherish as a primary value the media's independence from government intrusion—even if that value is sometimes practiced in the breach. For Britain, as for America, the major issue has been television coverage of terrorism. The intimacy, immediacy and reality of the electronic media elicits both a mental and visceral reaction that the print media cannot duplicate. And it is the impact of this that has greatly concerned British governments since "the troubles," as they are called, began in Northern Ireland in the late 1960s.

All British governments—and not just the Thatcher gov-

ernment—have attempted to influence the British Broadcasting Corporation (BBC) through either its Director General or the Chairman of its Board of Governors, generally, albeit not exclusively, to prevent the broadcast of televised interviews with terrorists involved in the conflict in Northern Ireland. There is, however, little concern about interviews with terrorists whose targets do not involve the integrity of the United Kingdom as a political structure. The Director General of the BBC never need fear that his phone will ring over a forthcoming program on SWAPO, the PLO, or even the dreaded Abu Nidal's Black June.

The BBC, an independent but government-funded corporation, is seen as more vulnerable to such influences than the IBA, the Independent Broadcast Authority which awards commercial franchises. But the IBA too is pressured to use its legal power to prevent networks from broadcasting programs, or, more commonly, to edit those it sees as being in conflict with the public interest. The government has pressured the IBA from time to time, but governmental concern is widely perceived as disproportionately directed against the BBC, which is seen as conveying a special legitimacy on those it interviews.

By American standards, the British government's intrusiveness into the media's conduct of its own affairs is appalling. From the government's perspective, however, the argument against interviewing terrorists is that a terrorist is an advocate of murder and such interviews are an incitement to commit murder in the future as well as a reward for having done so in the past.

For their part, the British media argues that such interviews enable the public to see the advocates of violence for what they really are and that the average viewer is revolted by terrorists' arrogant justifications of murder.

THE INLA INTERVIEW

These disparate perceptions clashed dramatically after a little-known Republican group calling itself the Irish National Liberation Army murdered Member of Parliament Airey Neave (March 30, 1979) as he drove toward the exit in Parliament's garage. In Dublin, the BBC televised an interview with an INLA spokesman. The INLA member not only admitted to the group's responsibility for the murder but reveled in it, calling Neave an advocate of torture. This charge was quickly challenged and disproved in the broadcast.

On the floor of Parliament the BBC was denounced. Prime Minister Thatcher said that she was appalled by the incident, and Lady Neave, the MP's widow, wrote to the *Daily Telegraph* (July 12, 1979) to express her distaste for the BBC's lack of sensitivity. Yet, 80 percent of the British public supported the broadcast, and despite Parliamentary pressure, Sir Michael Havers, the Attorney General, refused to prosecute the BBC.

On the floor of Parliament, Havers advised his colleagues that since the BBC interview had taken place in Dublin, the appropriate aspects of Britain's Prevention of Terrorism Act would be difficult to enforce. Some observers within Britain's law enforcement community suggested that a more compelling reason was that Britain as a society had to weigh the damage of prosecuting the BBC against the damage done by the broadcast. Even they acknowledged that Britain could live better with the consequences of the interview than the consequences of an attack on the media in the courts.

American vs. British Media. The idea of dragging the media before the courts for interviewing a terrorist is as appropriate a topic of discussion for the British as it is frightening to Americans. Nothing so separates the American media from the British as a common misperception of what "freedom of the press" means.

In January of 1972, for example, the *Times* (London) lavished praise on Ben Bradlee, editor of the *Washington Post,* and the *New York Times'* Abe Rosenthal for their vigorous defense of the press against, what the *Times* (London) called, the savage attacks against the media launched by Vice President Spiro Agnew. Mindful of a controversy surrounding the BBC's defense of journalistic freedom against the British government, as the government attempted to quash a televised program on Ulster, the *Times* concluded that freedom of the press might be good for the Americans but not for the BBC. The BBC, the *Times* reasoned, was a public corporation and thus had an obligation not to challenge the government.

But the BBC was challenging the government and persisted in doing so. Long before the INLA episode, in January of 1972, a BBC public affairs program, which openly debated the Ulster issue and in which the government refused to participate, drew strong condemnation on the floor of the Parliament and open threats to withdraw the BBC's charter when it came up for renewal. Lord Hill of Lutton, the Chair of the Corporation, took umbrage at this intrusion and lashed back at the government. In contrast to the BBC, the commercial authority refused permission to Granada Television to transmit a program for its "World in Action" series also depicting the conflict in Ulster.

But it is too facile to conclude from this juxtaposition that the BBC stood firm against censorship and that the commercial authority easily capitulated. Broadcast journalists continually complained of an atmosphere of self-censorship that permeated the industry, and the BBC was alleged to have imposed a series of restrictions that amounted to censorship. Journalists who broke ranks with the Corporation on this issue were said to have had their tapes blocked from transmission and their contracts dropped at renewal time.

NEW MEASURES IN RESPONSE TO TERRORISM

As the conflict in Northern Ireland crossed the Irish Sea and landed on the shores of Great Britain and IRA bombs took their toll on British soil, Parliament, in 1974, responded with legislation that its advocates called "draconian" and "unprecedented in peace time."

Initially this legislation, known as the Prevention of Terrorism Act, appeared not to be directed at the media. As terrorism escalated so did the legislation, and in 1976 two sections were added that originally were not directed at the

media but ultimately came to have strong consequences for how journalists went about their business. The two new Sections were titled 10 and 11.

Section 10 prohibited anyone from giving aid that resulted in contributing to terrorism. Section 11 required everyone with knowledge of the whereabouts of actual or potential terrorists to bring that information to the police.

Threat to Civil Liberties. In 1978, in response to growing concerns about the Act's implications for civil liberties, Lord Shackleton was appointed to review the Act. Lord Shackleton's review showed no linkage between these sections and the media, but Section 11 was found to be threatening to civil liberties. Lord Shackleton recommended that it be dropped, but it was not.

When the BBC interviewed the INLA spokesman in Dublin, they exposed themselves to Section 11. In the aftermath of this broadcast, the attorney general entered into an exchange of private letters between the government and the corporation concerning the INLA broadcast. On the floor of Parliament, Conservative members wanted the letters disclosed, and in the process showed strong concern over the BBC's violation of the Prevention of Terrorism Act's Section 11. Here for the first time, and in contrast to the conclusion of Lord Shackleton, the attorney general interpreted Section 11 to apply to the media.

The BBC was unyielding. It argued that Section 11 if so interpreted would in effect prevent journalists from going about their business and subject them to terrorist retribution if they did comply with the government's order.

Clearly the issue was now framed in terms of civic obligation. Did a journalist have a civic obligation as a citizen first or as a journalist? And how could he function as a journalist if the two obligations were incompatible?

It is impossible in the context of this lecture to present each and every dispute between the British media and the government. If one were to look at the most important of those conflicts, one would be presented with an image of a society under siege attempting to cap the lens and a media attempting to go about its business weighing its journalistic responsibilities against its sense of civic obligation, with journalistic responsibilities in ascendance.

One might also see—as I have elsewhere—a society committed to basic journalistic freedom going through an elaborate ritual of lashing out at the messenger when it is incapable of lashing out against terrorism. Such perceptions are not inaccurate, but I no longer believe they totally describe the situation.

RETHINKING THE OBVIOUS

In thinking about the struggle between the British government and the media and how to analyze it, I am reminded of an episode that took place in a philosophy of science class of Abraham Kaplan's some twenty-five years ago. Kaplan began making a case for the intelligence and compassion of dolphins, by pointing out that almost as long as man has kept records there have been episodes of sailors being led to shore by schools of dolphins. Kaplan would cite evidence from different points of history and different points of geography. The accumulated account, which spanned both time and earthly space, seemed to make an impressive case.

Seeing how he had convinced his students, he then—as he often did on such occasions—would turn to them and present one crisp question. In this case, he asked, "Now what about the sailors who had been led out to sea?"

Too frequently we confront what might appear to us to be the zealotry of the media to commit excesses and to defend those excesses in terms of traditional values of freedom of inquiry. What we forget to consider is—the other side of the issue—the harm that comes from the zealotry of government censorship wrapped in the garb of the public interest.

For every widely-publicized episode where the media and the British government have come into conflict over a program on terrorism that the media aired over strong government objection, there are numerous, less publicized episodes where programs are not produced, not aired or severely edited because exchanges of letters, the threat of the Prevention of Terrorism Act, and Parliamentary criticism. All of this results in a creeping and insidious censorship.

THE MEDIA AND DEMOCRACY

A society under siege, in many ways, needs a critical and, yes, objective media more so than a society whose viability is not threatened. For siege itself produces societal reactions that are not in keeping with respect for individual liberty.

The policy of internment without trial in Northern Ireland; the sensory deprivation interrogations in Castlereagh and other prisons; and the British Government's attempt to obstruct the investigation of John Stalker into the RUC's (Royal Ulster Constabulary's) alleged shoot-to-kill policy are all grave threats to the integrity of a free society on both sides of the Irish Sea.

British society is best served by the continued vitality of its free media so that these issues—and the more recent ones concerning the killings at Gibraltar and the alleged collusion between the British Army and Protestant terrorists—see the light of public debate both within the halls of Westminster and across British airwaves.

In the face of such controversial issues that tear at the democratic fabric of Britain, she has been better served by their vigorous debate in the media than by those who would ultimately seek to censor these topics from public discussion. To the extent that the unions of broadcast journalists are correct in their accusations that an atmosphere of intimidation and censorship surround the production of television programs on Northern Ireland, terrorism has taken a strong toll on Britain.

In response to the BBC's initial refusal to air the controversial program, "The Edge of Union," Professor Paul Wilkinson, one of Britain's most respected authorities on terrorism, put the issue this way: "[A]ny suggestion that any external body is bringing pressure to bear and altering editorial judgement as a result of political considerations undermines not only the credibility of the media, but the credibility of democratic government. And there is plenty of evidence that the overall impact of good professional media reporting in democratic societies has been to harden the will of the decent majority against any submission to terrorist blackmail."

LESSONS YET TO BE LEARNED

The primary lesson for the American media is that as terrorism increasingly becomes a direct threat, there will be those in government who will desire some American version of the Prevention of Terrorism Act. It might start out innocuous, but like the Prevention of Terrorism Act, its interpretation will become more severe and its impact more insidious as the threat grows.

To restrict the media's freedom is to concede a victory to the terrorists. For ultimately, a society under siege will have all sorts of attacks on its basic liberties, and it will need a free—and yes responsible—media to make the public aware of the costs to balance freedom with order.

Terrorism and freedom do not exist well side by side. Few societies, even the most democratic, are going to avoid taking vigorous action and sometimes short-cutting civil liberties to defend themselves. Yet, such actions can be as threatening to democratic viability as the acts of terrorists.

Exploiting Hostages. I would prefer not to see an American television journalist conducting an interview with another American who is being held hostage, has a gun held to his head while he responds to questions, and is then forcibly yanked around the neck when the answer is not to his captor's liking. This is precisely what did happen to the captain of TWA 847. Such a scene is obscene. It exploits the hostage for perverse entertainment value. Equally insidious, it threatens the very freedom that enables the journalist to conduct the interview.

If journalists do not have more common sense and more ethical restraint than this, then the media's freedom—and ours as well—is in grave danger. American journalists might find themselves struggling as the British do to balance the responsibilities they have to their craft and to democratic traditions while evading the threat of an ever-intrusive government. What the journalist loses in this process fades in comparison to the price the rest of us will pay in the coin of individual liberty.

Freedom has to be tempered with responsibility. It is best tempered with the responsible exercise of journalistic ethics and not with the intrusiveness of government bureaucracy. Britain's bureaucratic intrusiveness into the media's conduct of its affairs has created the ridiculous situation where the Provisional IRA have less difficulty running for Parliament than getting on the BBC.

It is a situation that causes anguish in Britain. It is a situation that those in the American media who least desire it may through their own recklessness cause to occur. Let us hope that the American media can remember Mark Twain's advice on the issue—if I may interpret with some liberty— the blessing of freedom of the press was given to the American people with the corresponding blessing of the good sense to know when not to abuse it.

Tactics, Strategies, and Targeting

Terrorist tactics, strategies, and targeting provide a common basis for disparate terrorist groups. Different groups often exchange information and express sympathy with one another's goals. Many terrorist organizations have identical or very similar targets even if their motivations are quite different. Hence, it is easy for the Libyan government to help the IRA since it upsets the British, whom Muammar Qaddafi dislikes for being an ally of the United States and occasionally helping Israel.

Terrorism is not an inexpensive activity. Terrorist organizations usually require and even compete for assistance from supportive governments in the form of training and protection. Most of all, though, they are consistently in need of financial assistance. In Bradford McGuinn's study of burgeoning Iranian-Sudanese relations, we see both the strategy and finances of state-sponsored and state-supported terrorism at work. Iran's new frontier of coercive threats and activities extends itself to North Africa and black Africa, a major jump in overseasmanship.

"Hidden Threat" raises both a long- and short-term concern about the implications of the demise of the Soviet Union for worldwide prospects of terrorism. Particularly ominous are the possibilities of theft or sale of nuclear weapons to other regions of the world. Given the scramble for nuclear capacity in the Middle East and North Africa, the implications are both regional and extraregional. Attached to the essay are charts pertaining to Saddam Hussein's past (and current?) efforts at developing a nuclear threat capability for war and terror purposes.

In the next four essays, we get some insight on narco-terrorism as practiced in two Latin American societies—Peru and Columbia. The sophistication of gaining control and intimidating the farm growers of coca leaf has placed the Shining Path in the position of destroying the entire national economy or running the only viable aspect of it. The finances are so assured that the prospect of the terrorist group's collapse is hard to foresee. The Colombian economy has also thrived on the narcotics business and forced a weakened government to accept former terrorists into the political mainstream and to reject extradition of drug lords abroad. Authorities and privateers have ended up practicing terrorism as a way of life.

In "Fugitive Leader of Maoist Rebels Is Captured by the Police in Peru," James Brooke reviews the capture of the rebel Abimael Guzmán Reynoso. For over 12 years the Peruvian government has hunted Guzmán, the leader of the Maoist Shining Path group—the largest and most violent insurrection group in Latin America.

Whether terrorists will at some point resort to using weapons of mass destruction is explored in "Will Terrorists Use Chemical Weapons?" Nuclear weapons are not yet a plausible choice at this stage, but chemical or biological weapons may very well be.

Terrorism is a complicated subject and, therefore, it is not unreasonable to suspect that, even where it has been applied, it is not uniformly condemned. As "Terrorism and Public Opinion: A Five Country Comparison" indicates, public opinion and even support for terrorism can differ dramatically from society to society, especially when specifically targeted by the terrorists.

Looking Ahead: Challenge Questions

What are some of the important ways that terrorist organizations finance their operations?

How do the sometimes varying interests and goals of terrorist groups coincide? How do they on occasion compete against one another? What do terrorist groups representing the extreme Left and Right have in common?

What advantages are there in hostage-taking? What circumstances make it so easy?

What is the relationship between drug trafficking, drug users, and terrorism?

What are some weapons that may be used by terrorists in the future?

How is terrorism regarded in different societies and what accounts for the differences?

Unit 7

The Emerging Iranian-Sudanese Relationship: Implications for the New Islamic Politics of North Africa

Bradford R. McGuinn

Bradford R. McGuinn, is a professor in the Department of International Relations at Florida International University in Miami, Florida.

• • •

The Sudanese Connection: Preliminary Speculations

Sudanese society is bifurcated between the Muslim Arab northern population and the Christian or animist Black African sector in the south. Stability and national "integration" thus hinge on the promotion of a type of rule that does not privilege the status of one group over the other. However, ever since Jafar al-Numeryi's attempt in 1985 to impose Sharia (Islamic) law as the legal basis of the Sudanese state a violent civil war has existed between Black and Arab-Islamic forces.[4] Of course, this is really a very old conflict, just as the legacy of fundamentalist Islam in the Sudan enjoys an old and distinguished pedigree. Since Numeryi was deposed in 1986 the governments of Sadiq al-Mahdi and General Umar al-Basir have been informed greatly by the fundamentalists for whom the advancement of Islamic law is of cardinal importance.[5]

The leading figure of Sudanese fundamentalism is Shaikh Hassan al-Tourabi, a Sunni Pan-Islamic leader. A supporter of Khomeyni, al-Tourabi has been considered a "leading Islamic fundamentalist theoretician and advocate of establishing Islamic regimes in all Arab countries".[6] Tourabi was also a critic of the American-led military effort against Iraq and was, presumably, a factor in Sudan's support for Saddam Hussein, a posture which, of course, put the country at odds with its much stronger neighbor to the north, Egypt.[7]

What motivation could be assigned to Iran for its cultivation of relations with Sudan? In a recent article in **The New York Times** Youssef Ibrahim speculated that it reflected a basic shift in Iran's focus from Lebanon to Sudan.[8] In his view, the shift was necessitated as Iran's room for manoeuvre in Lebanon decreased. Presumably, this shift was undertaken because Sudan seemed the most fertile ground for Iranian influence. Yet, it could also be argued that the Sudanese connection is vital if Iran seeks to have any influence over the new politics of Egypt and the North African region.

At present, little is precisely known about the depth of Iranian-Sudanese relations. To date, most of the information emphasizes the military and political nature of the ties. For example, a report in the Saudi **Al-Sharq Al-Awsat** on November 29, 1991, detailed a large-scale arms deal in which Iran was serving as the intermediary between the Sudanese government and China.[9] This report indicated that the deal involved some $300 million in arms and fighter aircraft. It included as well the dispatch of a "team of Chinese Air Force experts". This deal was apparently signed during the rule of Sadiq al-Mahdi. Bashir, then, found it difficult to make the payments and requested Iranian financial assistance.[10]

In another report, Ibrahim suggests that Iran has sent between 1,000 and 2,000 Revolutionary Guards to the Sudan from Lebanon.[11] Citing "Western and Arab intelligence officials" Ibrahim claims that "at least a dozen training camps have been

established". The purpose of these facilities, he asserts, is to train Islamic fundamentalist activists from Algeria, Tunisia, Egypt, and the Persian Gulf region to engage in "subversive activities". To this end, according to Ibrahim, Iran has furnished Sudan with "at least 17 million [dollars] worth of military equipment".[12]

In a more general sense, Sudan's relations with Iran stem logically from the revisionist posture it has assumed over the past several years. It will be recalled that Sudan was one of the countries which evinced support for Iraq during the Gulf Crisis. In fact, there has been some speculation that it was during the run-up to hostilities, in December of 1990, that the Iraqi regime sought to employ its Sudanese ally as a mediator with Iran, with whom Iraq sought a rapid rapprochement in the face of regional and international isolation.[13]

A good deal could be said regarding the Iraqi-Iranian competition for influence in the general North African area. It might be argued, for instance, that in its connection with Sudan Iran is energetically filling a vacuum created by Iraq's defeat in the Gulf Crisis. Iraq had, after all, developed strong relations with many regimes in the region. The **London Sunday Times** has recently reported, for example, that Iran and Algeria had engaged in nuclear cooperation. The purpose of this cooperation was, according to this report, the creation of an "Islamic Bomb".[14] For its part, the Algerian government has recently issued strenuous denials regarding th

From *The Political Chronicle*, Vol. 4, No. 1, Spring 1992, pp. 21-29. Reprinted by permission of *The Political Chronicle* (Journal of Florida Political Science Association) and Bradford R. McGuinn.

existence of any such program or weapons capability.[15] No doubt, the prospect of a nuclearized Tehran-Khartoum-Algiers axis is a major source of concern for the United States and its regional allies.

Rafsanjani of Khartoum

The emerging Iranian-Sudanese relationship was given tangible expression in the second week of December after the Islamic Conference Organization meeting in Dakar, Senegal. Returning from Dakar, Iranian President Hashemi-Rafsanjani stopped for an official visit to Khartoum. He was accompanied by a host of Iranian officials including Foreign Minister Velayati, Minister of Defence and Armed Forces Logistics Akbar Torkan as well as Ministers for Construction, Commerce, Information, and Budget.[16] It was reported also that Sudan's Army Chief of Staff held meetings with Major General Mohsen Reza'i, commander of the Islamic Revolutionary Guard Corps.[17] The presence of these figures has prompted a great deal of speculation regarding the Sudanese role in the "export" of Islamic revolution throughout North Africa. The visit was, incidentally, the first by an Iranian head of state to Sudan since 1956, the year of Sudan's independence.

During Rafsanjani's visit he met with key Sudanese officials as well as with religious leaders such as Hasan al-Turabi. Through these meetings and his public appearances Rafsanjani emphasized several major themes.[18] First, he stressed that Sudan merited the respect of Iran inasmuch as it has sought to faithfully apply an Islamic model. "What we have seen", Rafsanjani asserted, "shows that the Islamic revolution in the Sudan has reached all aspects of life in the country".[19] He praised the regime's efforts toward the "Islamization" of the Sudan. Second, Rafsanjani discussed the common threats faced by both countries. The main threat, he asserted, emanates from the nature of the post-Cold War international order which is viewed by Iran as one characterized by American hegemony.[20] In his view, the demise of the Soviet system and its motivational basis means that an ideological and power vacuum has been created. It is imperative, from his perspective, that this vacuum is not filled by American "arrogance" or by the designs of its regional allies, notably Israel. Indeed. a great deal of support was evinced for what might be termed the "rejectionist" position on the Arab-Israeli equation. In this sense, both Iran and Sudan advocate a "maximalist"

and "Islamic" solution to the Palestine question.[21]

Iranian officials also noted that attempts by outside powers to assist Black rebels in the south constituted an attempt to thwart the spread of Islam. Indeed, there has been recent speculation that the forging of Iranian-Sudanese ties implies a new threshold of violence on the part of the al-Bashir regime against Black oppositionists in the south.[22] And, third, Rafsanjani advocated an increasingly activist approach by Islamic forces amidst the radical reconjugation of international politics over the past several years. This may not be activism of the same sort as was identified with the "export of revolution" approach of the 1980s. Rather, it could represent an attempt to project Iran's influence through less violent means. In some remarks made in Sudan Rafsanjani noted that the Islamic Umma consisted of some 50 countries, one fourth of the world's population, over fifty percent of its natural resources, and enjoys control over key geo-strategic points.[23] Hence, Iran's relationship with Sudan represents an attempt to join together Islamic forces and project Muslim power in the Arab world as a coherent balancing force to the power of the United States.

The London-based **Sawt al-Kuwayt Al-Duwali** has disclosed what it claims to be the substance of a "security accord" between Iran and Sudan.[24] It cited four main provisions. First, Iran agreed to supply Sudan with about 2 million tons of oil annually at no charge "...to meet the Sudanese Army's needs until the problem of the South is over".[25] Second, "Iran will finance a 260 million Sudan-PRC arms deal under which Khartoum will receive 18 Shenyang F-7 and F-8 fighter planes, 140 T-54 and T-59 tanks and 20 T-70 tanks, 27 military trucks and armored vehicles, a number of multiple rocket launchers, and medium range guns".[26] Third, "Iran will send a group of military experts to help the Sudanese forces in the fields of scientific training and defence industries.[27] It agrees also to admit a number of Sudanese officers to Iranian academies, especially the Air Force Academy attached to the Revolutionary Guard where modern training takes place under the supervision of Chinese and North Korean advisors".[28] And, fourth, it seems that a joint security committee has been formed between the two countries whose primary function it is to "supervise all efforts to strengthen ties ...".[29] It is further indicated that many of the National Salvation Front Members have received training in Qom and other Iranian

religious centers. It appears as well that Iranian military advisors have assisted the al-Bashir regime in the creation of a Sudanese Revolutionary Guards Corp, modelled after the Iranian units.[30] This action was taken, it is speculated, because Iran has come to fear for the stability of Sudan's Islamic government.

The **Sawt al-Kuwait al-Duwali** report provides some contextual information from the Iranian policy perspective. It mentions that this relationship had been in the works for some time. Yet, Iran had moved slowly because it was concerned about the level of internal opposition to the al-Bashir regime.[31] It was reluctant also because of the perception that his regime was becoming increasingly subject to international isolation. Indeed, it will be recalled that the Khartoum regime was severely criticized over the past year for its mishandling of relief efforts in the south. Furthermore, Iran was apparently concerned about deepening its relations with Sudan for fear of antagonizing Egypt and key Gulf states.[32]

Have these concerns been abandoned? This would seem doubtful. One of the salient trends in recent Iranian Middle East policy has been its rapprochement with two sets of actors. The first are the GCC states, notably Saudi Arabia. Indeed, it was at the Dakar Summit that Rafsanjani met with Saudi Foreign Minister Sa'ud Faysal and it was agreed that the two heads of state must soon meet.[33] This is a vast departure from the type of real animosity evinced between these states only several years ago. There have also been some signs of improvement in the relations between Iran and Egypt.[34] This has been expressed in the comparatively benign Iranian response to the activities of the "Damascus Declaration" group of Saudi Arabia, Syria, and Egypt. And, atop all this, of course, is the noticeable lowering of tension between Iran and the United States.[35]

What then is the purpose behind Iran's exertions in Sudan? No doubt as a Middle Eastern actor Iran seeks to improve its state-to-state relations with other countries in the region. To this end, it has enhanced its formerly tense relations with a host of "moderate" regimes in the Gulf and the Middle East as a whole. Yet, the Sudanese connection suggests a somewhat different pattern. It indicates, one may speculate, a desire on the part of Iran to play a critical role in the new politics of North Africa. And, it may be argued, that from the Iranian perspective, North Africa now represents the most promising area for the advancement of Islamic fundamentalism.

Sudan and Islamic Terrorism

There is now considerable evidence to suggest that the Sudanese regime is actively promoting Islamic as well as Palestinian terrorist activities. This process began, apparently in 1989, upon the accession of the al-Bashir regime.[36] At that time, contacts were made within the international Muslim Brotherhood movement, the purpose of which was to establish Sudan as a major base of Islamic activism.[37] Three such facilities were immediately created: on the Red Sea coast, in the town of Kaduqli, and in the suburbs of Khartoum.[38] At these and subsequently developed facilities, Islamic militants from a host of Middle Eastern and African countries are presently undergoing training.[39]

The recent Gulf War marked a critical juncture in this process. During the course of hostilities, meetings among fundamentalists were held in Khartoum, Amman, and Lahore.[40] A key issue for these activists was the location of a suitable base for Islamic activist operations since movement in Lebanon has become increasingly restricted.[41] For his part, al-Tourabi apparently travelled to Afghanistan and Iraq, obtaining support from Afghan Islamic forces and Saddam Hussein.[42] According to one report, an agreement was reached whereby Sudan would "...receive weapons as well as members of the Arab religious groups that travelled before to fight in the Afghan war".[43]

In Sudan, the proliferation of terrorist training camps continued apace during 1990 and 1991. They were placed under the overall command of Colonel al-Hadi 'Abdallah, a high-ranking Sudanese military official with close ties to al-Tourabi.[44] These camps have provided assistance to such figures as the Tunisian fundamentalist leader Rashid Ghannouchi, head of the Ennahda movement.[45] It has been claimed that these facilities host various Palestinian fundamentalist groups, notably Hamas and Islamic Jihad.[46] It has been asserted that al-Tourabi's organizations have "...recruited approximately 500 personnel from the extremist Palestinian groups to take part in assassinating leaders and security figures inside the Arab region".[47] To these Palestinian activists may be added Islamic militants from a variety of states including Algeria, Morocco, Saudi Arabia, Libya, Uganda, the United Kingdom, Kuwait, Bahrain, Mauritania, and India.[48] Through its connection with Iran, Sudan has been

also active in assistance for Shi'i groups now operating in Tanzania, Kenya, Uganda, Burundi, and Zaire.[49]

This "Shi'i connection" has also involved close relations between al-Tourabi's group and the Lebanese Hizballah.[50] From Hizballah's perspective, the Lebanese theater is no longer as attractive as it was during the 1980s. Israel and Syria, the two great powers of that area, share a mutual desire to reduce the influence of pro-Iranian Islamic forces such as Hizballah. This convergence was given tangible expression recently when the Israeli air attack which resulted in the death of 'Abbas al-Musawi failed to elicit any Syrian response. It is not unlikely, therefore, that given this new environment, Hizballah will seek to base more of its operations in the relative safety of Sudan. . . .

The Iranian-Sudanese Nexus and North Africa

It is possible to point to serious Islamic challenges to all of the regimes of North Africa, including Egypt. In terms of the Iranian-Sudanese connection most of the available information centers on Tunisia, Algeria, Libya, and Egypt. Yet, the implications of this Islamic challenge extend, of course, well beyond North Africa.

Tunisia

From the time of its independence in 1956 until 1989 Tunisian politics was dominated by President Habib Bourguiba and his Neo-Destour Party. In theory, Bourguiba's rule was one of Arab nationalism and mild socialism, influenced largely by French political thought.[65] In practice, Tunisia was run as a single-party dictatorship, albeit a relatively benign one. By the late 1970s, however, an organized Islamic opposition emerged. Throughout the 1980s its main expression, the Islamic Tendency Movement, served as a critical source of potential instability for the secularist Bourguiba regime.[66] In an attempt to deny the Tunisian character of this Islamic challenge, the regime and its defenders depicted the Islamists as "Iranian-sponsored" extremists. While Iran did indeed provide the inspirational model for these forces and evidence exists to support the theses that a measure of tangible cooperation occurred, there can be no denying the authenticity of Tunisia's Islamic movement.[67] In fact, it was out of fear of the rising popularity of these forces coupled with the poor economic performance of the regime that precipitated the

downfall of Bourguiba and the ascent of President Zine al-Abidine Ben Ali. It has been his chief aim to engineer a successful Tunisian **Perestroika**. But his task is a difficult one. As Mr Gorbachev discovered to embark upon such a course is to solicit forces which once turned loose are impossible to control.

The recent tension in Tunisia's relations with Sudan are symbolic of Ben Ali's predicament and vulnerability. A recent report in the Tunisian **Al-Sharq** suggests that these relations may be near the breaking point. The cause celebre of this tension is, apparently, Sudan's support for the Tunisian Islamic group called "Ennahdhah" or "Al-Nahda".[68] Specifically, it is claimed that Sudan providing false passports to Rachid Ghannouchi the leader of Al-Nadha so that he might travel to France and elsewhere.[69] More ominously, it is asserted by this and other sources that Sudan (and presumably Iran) is provided training and logistical support for Tunisian Islamic forces seeking to overthrow the government.[70] According to an **Al-Sharq** report, Hasan al-Turabi as secretary-general of the Khartuom-based Arab-Islamic People's Conference serves as a focal point for the training of Islamic activists from Tunisia, Algeria, Egypt, and the Palestinian movement, Hamas.[71]

A report from the Egyptian **Al-Wafd** described, in detail, the workings of the Sudanese support for Tunisian fundamentalists. It asserted that a group of 16 Tunisians recently left Sudan for "Paris and Tunis".[72] The group was "one of several assassination squads entrusted to kill 14 Tunisian security men, described by the Ghannouchi group as "the Formidables".[73] According to this report, this group has trained "at the al-Ma'aqil camp, which is attached to the Sudanese Armed Forces northern command near Shandi, about 170km north of Khartoum".[74] These squads were, the paper continues, the outcome of an agreement between Turabi and Ghannouchi.[75] In addition to Ben Ali, the group's "hit list" includes a number of key Tunisian government officials.[76]

The **Al-Wafd** article describes an ever more ambitious Sudanese strategy. It quoted, for example, a member of the Bulgarian parliament who stated that Sudan has "become a world center for the Islamic movement".[77] At a variety of training facilities, the Al-Kadru Camp, the al-Kamilin Camp, the Jabal al-Awiya Camp and the Sawba Camp, Sudanese officials train cadres from a number of "hardline world religions".[78]

The Tunisian regime is unequivocal in its assertion that Sudan is currently playing a de-stabilizing role in the region. This is expressed clearly and not without a note of panic in the Tunisian press. **La Presse,** for example, contends that Sudan presently maintains "more than 30 training camps for . . . terrorism".[79] It states further that "the aim of National Islamic Front leader Hasan al-Turabi . . . is to provide active assistance to various fundamentalist movements in other Arab and Islamic states".[80] The Tunisian press also gave wide circulation to stories of the involvement of Sudanese officials at the gathering of Palestinian rejectionist forces in Tehran.[81] No doubt much of this reflects a measure of desperation in Tunis. It may reflect as well a measure of "tactical" alarm. That is to say, by evoking images of Iranian-sponsored "terrorism" the Tunisian regime automatically garners the support of various "moderate" actors who, in turn, are able to solicit the services of the United States in their efforts to promote "stability" both domestically and regionally.

Algeria

Since 1962 Algeria has been ruled by the Front de Liberation Nationale (FLN). For a generation of Third World politicians and their Western admirers the FLN symbolized the anti-Colonial struggle. Indeed, along with Cuba and Vietnam, Algeria has occupied a privileged place in the theory and praxis of Third World revolution. The works of Franz Fanon, for example, are known to have exercised a great influence over Iran's Islamic revolutionaries.[82] Over the past decade, however, the allure and moral legitimacy of the FLN has faded for many younger Algerian activists. Increasingly, their critique of the "old order" is framed in Islamic terms.[83] And, in the past two elections, in June 1990 and December 1991, the vast majority of the votes went to the Islamic parties, notably the Islamic Salvation Front (FIS).[84] In fact, the victory of the FIS in the recent elections raises the real possibility that Algeria will join Sudan and Iran in imposing Islamic law on the state. Concomitantly, there is some evidence to suggest that Sudan and Iran are not assuming a passive position regarding developments in Algeria.

A report in **Al-Wafd** suggests that Sudan is currently sponsoring key fundamentalist groups from both Tunisia and Algeria.[85] According to the report, Algerian Islamic Salvation Front extremists who "carried out an armed attack against an Algerian post near the Tunisian border in late November were trained at a Sudanese camp used to train fundamentalist groups:.[86] Members of

this group "secretly arrived on the Algerian-Tunisian border via a European capital.[87] This apparently coincided with the arrival of the Tunisian terrorists previously mentioned. According to **Al-Wafd,** Tunisian authorities seized some of the Al-Nahdah militants and discovered papers linking them with Khartoum.[88] This account makes two additional key points. First, it is asserted that the figure in charge of the Sudanese effort is Hasan al-Turabi.[89] Apparently he is in charge of preparing fundamentalists in North Africa.[90] Second, this effort has been assisted by Afghan Islamic fundamentalists or North Africans who gained experience in the Afghan war.[91]

In the run-up to the December elections there was an incident in Guemar, in northeast Algeria, in which Islamic fundamentalist groups reportedly attacked a border, army outpost. The Algerian government assigned culpability to the FIS, perhaps in an effort to discredit it before the elections, and engaged in a highly publicized effort to "wipe out" these "subversive forces".[92] A great deal of attention was given, in this connection, to the activities of the Tayeb el-Afghani Group, an organization perhaps linked to the FIS and led by an individual who fought with the Afghan resistance.[93] For their part, the leadership of the FIS denied any involvement in the Guemar affair, but claimed that it simply reflected the "revolutionary situation" which now prevails in Algeria.[94] It could be noted as well that an important figure in the FIS participated in the recent Tehran conference. In his view, "Algeria has found a sibling in the Islamic Republic".[95]

For its part, Iran has responded favorably to the recent course of events in Algeria. It has been argued in the Iranian media that Algeria's Islamic victory was the natural result of the country's recent political evolution.[96] These sources are also critical of the "somber prediction" offered by Western observers regarding the outcome of the election.[97] They are, indeed, critical of the general perception in the West of Islam as a "threat" to the well-being and stability of the region. One commentary pointed to a contradiction in the American concept of positive political change. Whereas the dramatic shifts in Eastern Europe, the demise of totalitarian orders and the emergence of nascent democracies, has been viewed as positive by Western observers, a similar transition away from one-party authoritarian regimes is considered "dangerous" when applied to North Africa.[98] For Iran, then, the developments in Algeria as in the Muslim ex-Soviet Republics, represent a real political windfall. The Sudanese connection, therefore, represents

an attempt to strengthen Iran's position in this area of Islamic ascendancy.

The resignation of President Chadli Benjedid and the creation of a "State Council" led by Mohammad Boudiafe and military elements signals a reaction to the democratization process in Algeria. In what must be seen as a panic induced move, this State Council has nullified the results of the recent elections and canceled the next round. This move came after several weeks of disarray following the victory of the FIS. The FIS and its leader Abdelqader Hashani had, prior to the coup, declared that Algeria would now follow an Islamic path, a notion antithetical to the country's socialist parties and Western-oriented urban populations, including much of the military. After the coup FIS officials declared that the Islamic forces will resist this anti-democratic development. Parallels may, of course, be drawn here with the Soviet coup attempt in August 1991. In Algeria today, as was the case in the USSR, a dynamic exists in which organized elements within the new civil society are steadily gaining ground on state structures increasingly devoid of ideological legitimacy and the ability to instill fear in the populous.

The Algerian situation is, therefore, a very fluid one.[99] Should open resistance and armed conflict ensue the Islamic elements will presumably be able to receive assistance from Iran through Sudan. Of course, the Iranian leadership can make the effective case that the West has no right to be "alarmed" at such a prospect because if it really stood behind its democratic rhetoric the United States and its allies in the "New World Order" would demand the restoration of democracy in Algeria. The Iranian government has indicated that it will support Algeria's Islamic forces at the expense of its bilateral relations with the Algerian regime.[100] Sid Ahmed Ghozali, Algeria's Prime Minister, has gone so far as to accuse Iran of "providing direct financial and logistical support to the fundamentalists".[101] Other reports have, indeed, suggested that Iran is providing financial assistance to Algerian fundamentalists through its Revolutionary Guards stationed in Sudan.[102] Iran's position could, therefore, be critical as the Algerian's new rulers head toward conflict with their Islamic critics.

A consensus of sorts has emerged among moderate and secularist Arab regimes to condone the "anti-democratic" actions of the Algerian government. This alone must give pause to those who see signs of "democratization" in such countries as Egypt.[103] In fact, the Egyptian government seems eager to assist the Algerian regime in its efforts against the fundamentalists. There have been reports of Egyptian security specialists who are advising Algerian authorities as well as stories of possible coup attempts by the FIS. In this connection, the primary supporter of the FIS is said to be the Sudanese regime.[104]

Libya

There have been indications that Libya's Colonel Mu'ammar al-Qadhdhafi has recently voiced concern regarding the nascent Sudanese-Iranian connection. According to the London based **Al-Hayah**, Qadhdhafi has "ordered the transfer to remote military zones of a number of senior army officers accused of making contacts with Sudanese military elements".[105] It notes also that with Iranian funding Sudan has acquired Iranian and Chinese-made "silkworm missiles".[106] There are other indications that a "crisis" presently exists in Libyan-Sudanese relations over the Islamic activism of al-Turabi.[107] In this sense, it is suggested that Qadhdhafi has embraced the Egyptian position on the deleterious nature of the Sudanese-Iranian linkage.[108] There have, in fact, been indications that the Libyan-Egyptian relationship is growing more intimate, especially in the areas of military and security cooperation.[109] Qadhdhafi's domestic problems, coupled with the difficulties his regime faces with the United States in connection with the Pan Am 107 bombing, render him more vulnerable before the Iranian-Sudanese Islamic challenge and Egypt's desire to enlist Libya into its generally pro-American regional order. Of course, the notion of a Sudanese-based threat to the Libyan regime is quite ironic in light of Qadhdhafi's long history of subversive involvement in the politics of Sudan.

The Egyptian Response

The fate of Sudan is, by virtue of its geography, of paramount concern to Egypt. Indeed, whether it was during the period of British control or the subsequent eras of independence Egypt has generally exercised a measure of hegemony over its Southern neighbor. Egypt's desire to dominate Sudan stems from Sudan's control of the Nile River, Egypt's lifeline. Anything that compromises Egypt's access to the Nile must, from Cairo's perspective, be viewed as a direct security threat.

It is, then, in this context that Egypt has reacted to the emergence of the Sudanese-Iranian relationship. Indeed, this apprehension has been energized still further by the fact that the nexus of this nascent relationship is Islamic fundamentalism, a force which represents, arguably, the chief internal challenge to the Mubarak regime.[110] It is, therefore, not difficult to fathom the sources of Egypt's opposition to any Iranian involvement in Sudan.

To these factors must be added a third. In the post-Gulf War regional environment Iran and Egypt have emerged as the two key Arab or Islamic Middle Eastern powers. Indeed, they vie for ascendancy on several levels. Ideologically, Iran's fundamentalism challenges the essentially secular basis of the Mubarak regime. Politically, Egypt's close relations with the United States gives them an advantage over Iran amidst the new regional "Pax Americana". Moreover, the emergence of the "Damascus Declaration", an alliance between Egypt, Syria, and the GCC states, provides Egypt with a "legitimate role" in the security of the Persian Gulf, a role which Iran views as threatening to their primacy.[111] One reading of Iran's involvement in Sudan is, then, its attempt to gain some leverage over Egypt by projecting Iranian influence to Cairo's southern periphery.

It has been reported that Egypt has communicated its displeasure to Sudan regarding the Iranian connection. Apparently, "...information has already reached the Egyptian capital that an agreement signed by Sudan and Iran during ...Rafsanjini's visit to Khartoum stipulates that about 5000 Iranian fighters would be stationed in Sudan".[112] The report indicates as well that the Egyptian government "...has formed a special team..." to monitor the situation.[113] Mubarak has apparently instructed al-Turabi, that insofar as the Sudanese fundamentalists were giving assistance to their Egyptian partisans he was "playing with fire".[114] There have, in fact, been recent reports of tension on the Egyptian-Sudanese border.[115] In one instance the Egyptian Air Force launched a mock air raid in northern Sudan which forced the evacuation of several hundred foreign oil workers and the dispatch of Sudanese air defense personnel.[116]

The nature and implications of this relationship were explored in further detail by Ibrahim Nafi, the Editor-in-Chief of **Al-Ahram**. In his view, Sudan's decision to invite an Iranian presence reflects the isolation which the al-Bashir regime presently faces.[117] This stems from the repressive nature of the regime which has earned the scorn of the international community during the time of Sudanese drought conditions and its pro-Iraqi stand during Gulf hostilities. According to the **Al-Ahram** piece, the al-Bashir regime is in desperate shape, destined to go the way of Mengistu's in Ethiopia.[118] The recent success of the SPLA and the oppositionists in Darfur are suggestive of the government's vulnerability. For Nafi then, Sudan's involvement with Iran is tied primarily to Iran's ability to furnish arms to be used against the regime's opponents.[119] The Chinese deal was also cited in this connection.[120]

Yet, in Nafi's view the "more dangerous aspect" of this relationship is the training role of the Iranian Revolutionary Gaurds. "It is known", Nafi asserts, "that the Revolutionary Guards were directly or indirectly responsible, together with the Lebanese Hizballah party, for the hostage crisis in Lebanon".[121] "It is", he continues, "the political-military establishment that reflects the most hard-line aspect of the Iranian regime and is used to export the revolution".[122] Here again it should be noted that this "alarmism" and demon-ologizing is not devoid of tactical utility. To conjure up the "Islamic threat" is, of course, to legitimize efforts taken against it by the Mubarak regime and its allies.

Mr. Nafi then proceeds to offer an analysis of Iranian intentions in Sudan and the region. He makes six general points. First, Iran is, in his view, seeking to become the dominant power in the Gulf area.[123] Second, it is seeking closer ties with Pakistan and Afghan resistance groups in an effort to "...strengthen its links with the Asian Islamic republics in the Soviet Union to cordon off the Gulf Region".[124] It is moreover "...attempting to build a network of extensive relations with western Asia as part of a new Middle Eastern order and as a substitute for the Arab order".[125] According to this view, then Iran is seeking to "breakoff" the Gulf from the "Arab" Middle East.[126] In this sense, Iran emerges as the "Super Power" of a new Southwest Asian order, of which the Gulf represents the strategic prize.

Third, much of this is motivated, M. Nafi asserts, by Iran's concern over the rising influence of Egypt and Turkey as dominant forces in the area.[127] Hence, a link with Sudan serves to challenge Egypt in its own "back yard". It acts also to challenge Saudi Arabia within its critical Red Sea sub-region. This challenge has recently taken the form of joint Iranian-Sudanese-Eritrean mili-

tary exercises in the Red Sea.[128] The participation of Yemen as an "observer" in this
alliance must add to the Saudi unease.[129]
Fourth, support for Turabi and Sudanese
fundamentalists furnishes a base for radical
Islamic activities throughout North Africa.
Fifth, Iran's efforts in this connection stem
as well from its desire to offer a "balancing"
force to what it sees as an American hegemony.[130] That is, Iran's Islamic approach
challenges the basically moderate and pro-
American Egyptian and Saudi approach.
And, having lost its position in Lebanon,
activism in Sudan represents a way of exercising some leverage over the Americans and
their allies. Sixth, in the bigger picture, Iran's
activity in Sudan may be seen as part of a
larger Middle Eastern strategy. According to
this view, Iran seeks to fashion a coalition
comprised of Sudan, Afghan resistance
movements, " . . . and Islamic movements
in numerous Arab countries such as Sudan,
Algeria, and Yemen".[131] There are also
indications that Egypt is concerned about
Iran's exploitation of the Ethiopian situation.
With increased autonomy upon the downfall
of the Mengistu regime Eritrean and Tigrean
forces are, apparently, providing support to
the Iranian-sponsored Sudanese army in its
fight with the SPLA.[132] In this connection, it
has been reported by Sudanese oppositionists
that 18,000 Iranian troops have been sent to
southern Sudan and that Iranian naval vessels
have been based at Eritrean ports.[133] For its
part the Egyptian government cannot but
look with unease at the formation of a pro-
Iranian coalition comprised of Sudan and the
independence-minded Muslim provinces of
the old Ethiopian state.[134]

On a number of levels, then, Iran's
Islamic assertion represents a direct
challenge to Egypt in the new Middle
Eastern balance of power. Domestically,
as the death of Anwar Sadat revealed, the
most potent source of instability is to be
found in the numerous Islamic radical
groups. The growth of the Islamic
movement among the intelligentsia,
students, professional classes, and newly
urbanized elements must be viewed with
alarm by a regime unable to come to terms
with Egypt's massive social and economic
problems. Within the North African and
Red Sea sub-regions the spread of "militant"
Islam and the enhanced Iranian role
challenges Egypt's traditional hegemony.
Iran's long-standing Islamic activism in
Sub-Saharan Africa also threatens Cairo's
historical centrality in African Islam.
Further afield, in the Middle East as a
whole, Iran's way challenges Egypt on a
range of questions from the Arab-Israeli

equation to the security of the Persian Gulf
to the legitimate role of the United States
in the region. . . .

Notes
• • •

4   For an account of Sudan's civil war see Lesch,
    A.M. "The Republic of Sudan" in Ismael, T. and
    J. Ismael. **Politics and Government in the
    Middle East and North Africa.** (Miami: FIU
    Press, 1991). Also see Holt, P.M. and M. Daly.
    **The History of Sudan from the Coming of
    Islam to the Present Day.** (Boulder: Westview
    Press, 1989).

5   See Voll, J. "Political Crisis in Sudan". **Current
    History.** (Volume 89, 1990).

6   See Ibrahim, Y. "Iran Shifting Its Attention From
    Lebanon to Sudan." **The New York Times.**
    (December 13, 1991).

7   Sudan was generally supportive of Iraq during
    the recent Gulf Crisis.

8   Ibrahim, Y. op. cit.

9   See the translation in **Foreign Broadcast and
    Information Service-Near East and South Asia.
    [hereafter FBIS-NEA]** (December 3, 1991) pp.
    11-12.

10 See **FBIS-NEA.** (December 13, 1991) p. 31.

11 See Ibrahim, Y. op. cit.

12 Ibid.

13 See **FBIS-NEA.** (December 30, 1991) p. 16.
    Also see al-Bashir's comments in **FBIS-NEA.**
    (January 9, 1991) pp. 9-11.

14 See **FBIS-NEA.** (January 7, 1992) p. 6.

15 Ibid.

16 For details of Rafsanjani's visit see **FBIS-NEA.**
    (December 16, 1991) pp. 24-29.

17 This was reported by Ibrahim, Y. op. cit.

18 These were taken from his remarks as translated
    in **FBIS-NEA.** (December 16, 1991) pp. 24-29.

19 Ibid. p. 29.

20 This theme has been articulated forcefully by
    Rafsanjani and other Iranian leaders since the
    demise of the bi-polar international order.

21 A comprehensive critique of the "peace process"
    and the Madrid Talks was presented at a series of
    meetings in Iran attended by a variety of regional
    rejectionist forces.

22 See, for example, the analysis presented by
    Barbara Crossette, "U.S. Aide Calls Muslim
    Militants Concern to World" in **The New York
    Times.** (January 1, 1992) p. 3.

23 See **FBIS-NEA.** (December 16, 1991) p. 26.

24 See the translation in **FBIS-NEA.** (December 19,
    1991) p. 39.

25 Ibid. p. 39.

26 Ibid. p. 39.

27 Ibid. p. 39.

28 Ibid. p. 39.

29 Ibid. p. 39.

30 See **FBIS-NEA.** (February 10, 1992) p. 23.

31 Ibid. p. 39.

32 Ibid. p. 39.

33 See the news accounts in **FBIS-NEA.** (December
    9, 1991) p. 21.

34 See the statements by Egypt's Foreign Minister
    Amr Musa in **FBIS-NEA.** (February 6, 1992)
    p. 11.

35 Of course, movement on the hostage issue and
    the return of frozen Iranian assets represent areas
    of improvement in the relationship.

36 See **FBIS-NEA.** (February 14, 1992) pp. 16-18.

37 Ibid. p. 17.

38 Ibid. p. 17.

39 Ibid. p. 17.

40 Ibid. p. 17.

41 Ibid. p. 17.

42 Ibid. p. 17.

43 Ibid. p. 17.

44 Ibid. p. 17.

45 Ibid. p. 17.

46 Ibid. p. 17.

47 Ibid. p. 18.

48 Ibid. p. 18.

49 Ibid. p. 18.

50 Ibid. p. 18. . . .

• • •

65 See, for example, Moore, C. ed. **Tunisia Since
    Independence: The Dynamics of a One-Party
    Government.** (Berkeley: University of California
    Press, 1965).

66 On the Islamic Tendency Movement see Wright,
    R. **Sacred Rage.** (New York: Simon and Shuster,
    1985). For a discussion of the fundamentalist
    issue in contemporary Tunisia see Boulares, H.
    Islam: The Fear and the Hope. (London: Zed
    Books, 1990).

67 Some of the linkages between Iran and Tunisian
    Islamists are explored in Schechterman, B. and
    B. McGuinn. Linkages Between Sunni and Shi'i
    Radical Fundamentalist Organizations: A New
    Variable in Recent Middle Eastern Politics?" in
    Schechterman, B. and Slann, M. eds. **Violence
    and Terrorism 90/91.** (Conn: The Dushkin
    Publishing Group, 1990).

68 On "al-Nahda" see **FBIS-NEA.** (November 21,
    1991) pp. 20-21.

69 See **FBIS-NEA.** (December 9, 1991) p. 33.

70 See **FBIS-NEA.** (November 21, 1991) pp. 20-21.

71 See Ibid. pp. 20-21.

72 See **FBIS-NEA.** (December 19, 1991) p. 15.

73 Ibid. p. 15.

74 Ibid. p. 15.

75 Ibid. p. 15.

76 Ibid. p. 15.

77 See FBIS-NEA. (December 9, 1991) pp. 41-42.

78 Ibid. pp. 41-42.

79 See **FBIS-NEA.** (December 29, 1991) p. 14.

80 Ibid. p. 14.

81 Ibid. p. 14.

82 See, for example, Shari'ati, A. **What Is To Be
    Done?** (Houston: The Institute for Research and
    Islamic Studies, 1986).

83 See Mortimer, J. op. cit.

7. TACTICS, STRATEGIES, AND TARGETING

84 For recent reaction to the Algerian election see **FBIS-NEA**. (December 30, 1991) pp. 6-10.

85 See FBIS-NEA. (December 19, 1991) p. 15.

86 Ibid. p. 15.

87 Ibid. p. 15.

88 Ibid. p. 15.

89 Ibid. p. 15.

90 Ibid. p. 15.

91 For more on this "Afghan connection" see **FBIS-NEA**. (December 2, 1991) p. 11.

92 See FBIS-NEA. (December 9, 1991) p. 30.

93 See FBIS-NEA. (December 2, 1991) p. 11.

94 See FBIS-NEA. (December 9, 1991) p. 31.

95 Ibid. p. 31.

96 See FBIS-NEA. (December 30, 1991) p. 42.

97 Ibid. p. 42.

98 Ibid. p. 42,

99 By late January 1992 the new Algerian regime had arrested Hachani and had moved to ban all Islamic political activity. See Ibrahim, Y. "Algeria Arrests a Senior Islamic Leader." **The New York Times**. (January 23, 1992).

100 See Ibrahim, Y. "Iran Usets Algeria by Backing Muslims." **The New York Times**. (January 19, 1992).

101 See Ibrahim, Y. "Algeria Arrests a Senior Islamic Leader." **The New York Times**. (January 23, 1992).

102 See **FBIS-NEA**. (February 19, 1992). p. 59.

103 See, in this connection, Al-Sayyid, M. "Slow thaw in the Arab World." **World Policy Journal**. (Fall 1991).

104 See **FBIS-NEA**. (February 4, 1992) p. 14.

105 See **FBIS-NEA**. (December 12, 1991) p. 16.

106 Ibid. p. 16.

107 See **FBIS-NEA**. (November 18, 1991) pp. 12-13.

108 Ibid. pp. 12-13.

109 See **FBIS-NEA**. (February 24, 1992) p. 21.

110 The depth of Islamic fundamentalism in Egypt is discussed in Dkmejian, R. H. **Islam in Revolution**. (Syracuse: Syracuse University Press, 1985). There are indications that recent events in Algeria have triggered demonstrations among Egyptian fundamentalists in such arcas as Asyut. See **FBIS-NEA**. (February 11, 1992) p. 23.

111 This concern stems from Egypt's involvement in the Damascus Declaration bloc and its involvement in Gulf security.

112 See **FBIS-NEA**. (December 23, 1991) p. 11.

113 See **FBIS-NEA**. (December 24, 1991) pp. 15-18.

114 See **FBIS-NEA**. (February 4, 1992) p. 2.

115 See **FBIS-NEA**. (February 19, 1992) p. 18.

116 Ibid. p. 18.

117 See **FBIS-NEA**. (December 24, 1991) pp. 15-18.

118 Ibid. p. 15.

119 Ibid. p. 15.

120 Ibid. p. 16.

121 Ibid. p. 16.

122 Ibid. p. 17.

123 Ibid. p. 17.

124 Ibid. p. 17.

125 Ibid. p. 17.

126 Ibid. p. 17.

127 Ibid. p. 17.

128 See **FBIS-NEA**. (February 6, 1992) p. 16.

129 Ibid. p. 16.

130 See **FBIS-NEA** (December 24, 1991) p. 17.

131 Ibid. p. 17.

132 See **FBIS-NEA**. (February 24, 1992) p. 27-28.

133 Ibid. pp. 27-28.

134 See **FBIS-NEA.** (February 27, 1992) pp. 22-23. . . .

● ● ●

HIDDEN THREAT

Gerald Steinberg considers the scenarios that could be created by the theft of thousands of small and largely unmonitored nuclear weapons

Gerald Steinberg is a senior lecturer in political science, and a research director of the Center for Strategic Studies at Bar-Ilan University.

The breakup of the Soviet Union was accompanied by great concern over who would control its nuclear arsenal, estimated to include 28,000 warheads and bombs. The attempted coup in August, and the transfer of power from Gorbachev to Yeltsin, focused attention on the nuclear "codes." Whoever controls these codes (called permissive action links) can send intercontinental missiles, submarine-based missiles, and long-range strike bombers hurtling towards targets in North America and Western Europe.

While the world's attention focused on these strategic nuclear weapons, and most of the arms control negotiations between the US and the Soviet Union dealt with them, the majority of nuclear weapons take different forms. Nuclear land mines, artillery shells, short-range missiles, surface-to-air missiles, cruise missiles, torpedoes and "free-fall" bombs dropped from aircraft constitute almost two thirds of the total arsenal. These are known as theater, battlefield, or tactical nuclear weapons.

Unlike strategic weapons, which travel thousands of kilometers and can destroy cities on the other side of the world, tactical nuclear explosives are intended for relatively close military targets. Thousands of nuclear land mines were manufactured to block a large-scale invasion in Central Europe. The Soviet military also produced approximately 7,000 nuclear artillery shells with ranges of from 10 to 30 km. These were produced in order to destroy tank formations on the battlefield.

In contrast to strategic nuclear weapons, which are restricted to Russia, Ukraine and Kazakhstan, tactical arms are scattered in bases in other republics that were formerly part of the Soviet Union.

Until two years ago, these weapons were also deployed with Soviet troops in Eastern Europe (including East Germany), and the Baltic republics. The coded command and control procedures used for missiles and other strategic weapons are often absent or far weaker in the case of nuclear land mines and artillery shells. In addition, while American reconnaissance satellites keep a close watch on the strategic nuclear forces, the locations of thousands of small tactical nuclear weapons is impossible to monitor from such a distance.

All of this makes the prospect of the theft or transfer of tactical nuclear weapons from a military base in one of the former Soviet republics a frightening possibility. With the pressures of starvation, and without other sources of hard currency, the temptation to sell or trade a "small" tactical nuclear bomb for food or oil might prove irresistible. As countries in the Middle East, including Iraq, Algeria, Libya and Iran, scramble for a nuclear capability, these former Soviet republics might present a source for off-the-shelf weapons.

In addition to the relatively easier access to such weapons, their small size makes the prospect of nuclear smuggling even more plausible. Nu-

Iraq's Lethal Plants

Inspectors have uncovered more than a dozen Iraqi nuclear facilities since the gulf war.

Al-Sharqat Calutron enrichment plant

Al-Jazira Uranium-processing plant

Tarmiya Calutron enrichment plant

Al-Qaim Uranium-extraction plant

Akashat Phosphate mine and uranium extraction

Tuwaitha Calutron test facility and plutonium-separation lab

Falluja Military base and equipment storage

Al-Furat Centrifuge factory

Abu Ghraib Military base and fuel-rod storage

Al-Musayyib High-explosive test site

Al-Atheer Manufacturing base for implosion device to detonate bomb

Baghdad

IRAQ

SOURCE: NUCLEAR CONTROL INSTITUTE AND INTL. ATOMIC ENERGY AGENCY

Reprinted from Newsweek, October 7, 1991, p. 33.

Reprinted from *The Jerusalem Post Weekly English Edition,* February 15, 1992.

157

The Evidence: How Saddam Planned to Build a Bomb

Iraq's extensive nuclear-weapons program survived the gulf war. Saddam Hussein was much closer to producing a workable nuclear bomb than experts had realized. Following is some of the most important evidence uncovered by U.N. inspectors.

Plutonium

Where it was found: At a reactor in Tuwaitha, U.N. inspectors identified three grams of illegally produced plutonium, an element capable of setting off a massive chain reaction in a fission bomb.

How it was processed: Weapons-grade plutonium-239 is produced in reactors by irradiating uranium, then separating it by chemical means. The International Atomic Energy Agency has identified Tuwaitha as a site of plutonium separation.

Uranium

Where it was found: U.N. inspection teams turned up small amounts of weapons-grade uranium-235 and evidence of uranium extraction in Akashat. To be used in bombs, naturally occurring uranium—containing 0.7 percent U-235—must be enriched in one of several ways:

Calutron: A method of uranium enrichment used in the Manhattan Project, the calutron takes ionized uranium-laden gas and separates fissionable U-235 from non-fissile U-238 by means of an electromagnet. Iraq has 23 calutrons at Tarmia and Al-Sharqat, as well as calutron component and assembly plants at Al-Dijjla, Al-Dura, Al-Rabesh and Augba bin Nafi.

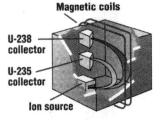

Magnetic coils

U-238 collector

U-235 collector

Ion source

Centrifuge: A centrifuge factory at Al-Furat, damaged in the gulf war, confirms Iraq's ability to enrich uranium via this method, which separates gaseous isotopes by passing them through a high-speed rotating cylinder. U.N. inspectors say Iraq planned to build 600 centrifuges, based on European designs.

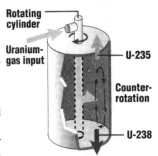

Rotating cylinder

Uranium-gas input

U-235

Counter-rotation

U-238

Other methods: Iraq may have experimented with chemical enrichment—developed by Japan and France—which relies on catalysts to speed up exchanges between U-235 and U-238.

Reprinted from *Newsweek*, October 7, 1991, pp. 34–35.

The Bomb

Gun type: A fuse sets off an explosive, which drives a uranium wedge through a gun barrel into the uranium target. No evidence of such an Iraqi device has yet been found.

Explosive   Gun barrel   Uranium wedge   Uranium target

Implosion type:

1 A conventional explosive surrounds a sphere of uranium or plutonium that will be compressed into a high-density, supercritical mass.

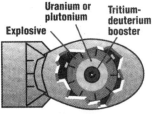

Explosive   Uranium or plutonium   Tritium-deuterium booster

2 As the core of fissile material implodes, an initiator releases neutrons which accelerate the fission reaction.

Detonators trigger implosion   Neutron initiator

3 Implosion creates a supercritical mass and a chain reaction resulting in a nuclear blast. Iraq's importation of explosives and electronics suggests development of an implosion-type bomb.

Super-critical mass

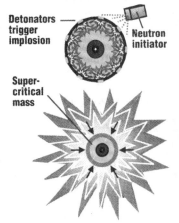

Equipment

Casings: Iraq imported quantities of high-grade metals that could be used to encase a bomb device.

Charges: U.N. inspectors have found quantities of HMX, an explosive that can compress uranium cores in a fission reaction.

Capacitors and krytrons: A joint U.S.-British sting operation in 1990 intercepted Iraq-bound capacitors, which control charges. The sting also netted krytrons, switches that set off implosions.

Delivery

Scud: The Al-Abbas, a type of Scud-B missile with a maximum range of 560 miles, could be modified to carry a small nuclear device. The Scud was notoriously inaccurate during the gulf war.

Planes: Just about any of Saddam's attack planes and fighter jets could be fitted with a nuclear bomb.

Supergun: Designed to fire 350-mm shells at a range of 437 miles, the Supergun (barrel: 172 feet long) could, with modification, fire off a nuclear device.

SOURCES: GARY MILHOLLIN, WISCONSIN PROJECT ON NUCLEAR ARMS CONTROL; STEVEN DOLLEY, NUCLEAR CONTROL INSTITUTE; LEONARD SPECTOR, THE CARNEGIE ENDOWMENT FOR INTERNATIONAL PEACE; THE BULLETIN OF THE ATOMIC SCIENTISTS; THE NUCLEAR ALMANAC

clear land mines are small enough to fit into a suitcase, and eight-inch nuclear artillery shells are externally indistinguishable from conventional shells of the same size and shape. Three thousand nuclear-capable tactical aircraft are also scattered throughout the republics of the former Soviet Union, and with some assistance, a pilot could conceivably fly an aircraft and its nuclear payload to a neighboring country.

While such possibilities are scary, it is important to note that the vast majority of tactical nuclear weapons have small yields. Because they were designed to be used on the battlefield at relatively short ranges, the explosive force had to be limited. Nuclear artillery shells, for example, can be as small as one tenth of a kiloton, and nuclear land mines on the order of $1/100$ of a kiloton. (A kiloton is the equivalent explosive force of 1,000 tons of conventional explosives.)

By way of comparison, the nuclear weapons that were used against Japan in 1945 were about 15 kilotons. City-destroying strategic nuclear weapons, in contrast, range from hundreds of kilotons to megatons (millions of tons of conventional explosives). In other words, even if a country like Iraq obtains a nuclear land mine or artillery shell, such a weapon is not on the same scale as a large strategic device. Still, even a "small" nuclear bomb can do tremendous damage.

The threat posed by unauthorized access to tactical nuclear weapons has been recognized in the past year. Immediately after the attempted coup in August, President Bush announced that the US would slash its stockpile of such weapons. Shortly afterwards, Gorbachev made a similar announcement. (These are the only two countries which are known to have produced battlefield weapons.)

Since then, however, the Soviet Union has collapsed, and Moscow's central control ended before the tactical and battlefield weapons could be destroyed or neutralized—a process requiring sophisticated and careful handling.

The US has continued to focus attention on the safeguarding of these weapons until they can be dismantled, and arms controllers are aware of the dangers of this quick route to proliferation. Some of the funds already transferred to the newly independent republics are earmarked specifically for the strengthening of controls on the tactical as well as strategic nuclear arsenals.

In many weapons, depending on the design, the radioactive material inside will decay independently and become less powerful over a period of 10 to 20 years. The other less sophisticated weapons, however, will maintain their explosive potential for many years or perhaps decades unless rendered inoperative. As political control over these weapons weakens, the danger will continue to grow. If certified destruction does not take place soon, no one will know how many still exist and where they are located. The result will be nuclear chaos.

Peru's Maoist Drug Dealers

Stephen G. Trujillo

Stephen G. Trujillo, a former Army Ranger and Green Beret, is writing a book about his work for the Drug Enforcement Administration in Peru. The views expressed in this article are his own.

Some well-meaning analysts still ignore the truth about Shining Path, the Maoist revolutionary movement terrorizing Peru. While the guerrillas may be ruthless, those who romanticize them claim they are untainted by the drug trade that poisons Peruvian society. This is a myth.

I know from my experience working for the Drug Enforcement Administration in Peru that the guerrillas are systematically involved in all levels of the drug trade in the Upper Huallaga Valley, where most of the world's coca is grown.

This state of affairs is important for the U.S. to keep in mind as it reevaluates its policy toward Peru in light of this week's military-backed crackdown. The Peruvian military, itself implicated in drug corruption, has argued that fighting Shining Path is the key to stabilizing Peru. The U.S., which temporarily suspended assistance on Monday, has emphasized the war on drugs. As we will see, the two fronts are intricably linked.

On July 2, 1990, I was advising a detachment of the Peruvian drug police southwest of the village of Nuevo Progreso in the Upper Huallaga. We torched a drug laboratory owned by a Shining Path cell called Los Tigres.

Plates of rice on the table were still warm, the cocaine base residue in the drying filters was moist, and there were fresh notations on Maoist lesson plans left in the house. More important, ledgers were found with up-to-date payments to coca farmers and income from Colombian-dominated trafficking organizations. The guerrillas escaped into the jungle.

I have direct knowledge of other labs and secondary knowledge of many more. This and other evidence directly implicates Shining Path in the Peruvian cocaine industry.

Its control of the Upper Huallaga is such that it can force farmers to plant coca. Other peasants, called cocaleros, are ordered to grow less or more coca or to plant other crops altogether. The farmers defy the rebels at their peril.

Evidence about the guerrillas' links to the middle tiers of the Peruvian cocaine industry—notably, the traffickers—is more oblique. The Upper Huallaga town of Uchiza, the cocaine capital of the world, is dominated by the Peruvian Army during the day, but is surrendered to Shining Path after nightfall. The guerrillas have respected Uchiza's status as an army town, but only after they made the point that they can enter it at will and punish "enemies of the people." Traffickers who export from Uchiza's airfield and other army-controlled airstrips, give both military officers and Shining Path cadres sizable sums of money.

The local police pose no obstacle to this arrangement. One night in March 1989, the guerrillas attacked the Uchiza police post and publicly beheaded its corrupt police commanders. The police station remains vacant today. The commanders there had unwisely cheated the drug traffickers, who appealed to the only other source of justice in the Upper Huallaga Valley—Shining Path.

Whether through arrangement or cowardice, the Peruvian Army unit about a half-mile down the road did nothing, though the soldiers must have heard the echoing gunfire and jeers of hundreds of Uchiza citizens who gathered to watch.

The Colombian cocaine syndicates prefer dealing with the Peruvian Army, because, unlike Shining Path, it does not complicate its corruption with ideology. But the narcos have to deal with the rebels, who decided nearly a decade ago to align themselves with coca farmers and regulate drug commerce in areas they control.

The country depends on the cocaine trade, which is run by Shining Path.

Indeed, Shining path has succeeded in intimidating the Columbian-dominated drug mafias, or firmas. The rebels have enforced limits on the number of Colombian narcos working in Upper Huallaga and imposed strict rules of behavior. The guerrillas kill those who displease them, as they did in late 1988 when they butchered 19 Colombian narcos.

Upstart revolutionary rivals have been similarly treated. Shining Path fought a rare pitched battle with elements of the Tupac Amaru Revolutionary Movement outside Tochache in July 1987. Shining Path's victory banished the smaller revolutionary movement to the Northern Huallaga.

Shining Path's domination of the firmas enables it to tax all levels of the cocaine industry in the Upper Huallaga: subsistence farmers, speculators, middlemen and lab owners, firmas and Colombian traffickers. In addition, the rebels process and refine cocaine in their own drug labs.

It is clear that Shining Path is financing its revolution with cocaine. According to conservative estimates, the rebels' annual revenue ranges from $15 million to $35 million. One Pentagon source thinks the amount might be as much as $100 million.

Revolutions are expensive, and very little foreign money reaches Shining Path, which is highly xenophobic. Yet the revolutionaries manage to finance "people's committees," which supplant legal government in many Peruvian villages and city neighborhoods, as well as their armed component, the Guerrilla Army of the People. They can mobilize thousands of sympathizers with little notice. Without cocaine revenues, the inexorable growth of the movement would have been slower.

Shining Path's involvement with drugs is opportunistic. The rebels, unlike the military factions, are not corrupted by greed. And they will turn on the cocaine mafias one day.

Cocaine is crucial to the Peruvian economy, which is essentially bankrupt. It accounts for a conservative 35 to 45 percent of export earnings. The central bank is estimated to take in $4 million to $5 million daily in narco dollars from the streets of Lima alone.

Given Shining Path's control of drug commerce in the Upper Huallaga, the rebels could precipitate the collapse of the country's economy. The gross domestic product shrank by 22 percent from 1988 to 1990, and catastrophic inflation has wiped out what legal income the country has.

Yet Peru has not missed one payment on its international debt since the summer of 1990, when Alberto Fujimori was elected President. Even the resumption of foreign aid to Peru may not have accounted for its return to solvency. Many experts believe the country's creditors are being paid in narco-dollars, a prospect that inevitably undermines counter-narcotics efforts in Peru.

We must anticipate the impact a possible Peruvian economic collapse may have on its Andean neighbors, not to mention its creditors. In Peru, such a catastrophe could presage a seizure of power by the rebels. The Shining Path is undoubtedly the most ferocious revolutionary movement in the world, and it controls the valley producing most of the world's most lucrative cash crop.

There are some people who think that the military-backed state of siege declared this week in Peru is the only way to fight Shining Path. But it is clear that a regressive military approach will not work. In 1983 and 1984, the Peruvian military killed thousand of suspected guerrillas in Ayacucho, the cradle of the revolution, and declared a victory. But Shining Path simply went underground and migrated up the Andean spine of the country. After only a brief period, the rebels had managed to infiltrate nearly all provinces.

Today, the Peruvian military may make the mistake of unleashing a new regional "dirty war." The United States, as it weighs what to do next in Peru, must realize that the war on drugs, as it has been waged, may only abet this repression.

Kidnapping and 'Taxes' Transform Guerrilla Inc.

James Brooke

Special to The New York Times

LIMA, Peru, July 23—Hunched over computers confiscated from a guerrilla group here, detectives recently discovered a surprising electronic file: a list of 239 Peruvian businessmen forced to contribute "war taxes" and a directory of 2,500 additional candidates for extortion or kidnapping.

With the collapse of the Soviet Union and the near-bankruptcy of Cuba, South America's orphaned guerrilla groups survive by honing their skills at local fund-raising. Several groups in Peru and Colombia might rightfully be named "Guerrilla Inc." And the sophistication of their intelligence-gathering apparatus testifies to the seriousness of their pursuits, with some keeping detailed files on the finances, personal lives and movements of local executives.

"The guerrillas lose their ideological coloring and become a bureaucracy," said Gene Mastroangelo, manger of risk information service at Pinkertons's Security and Investigation Services in Van Nuys, Calif., which tracks politically inspired incidents around the world and advises companies on such risks. "They take on a corporate structure and have to finance it."

Companies Pay Ransoms

In Colombia, guerrillas are considered responsible for a third of the 375 kidnappings that take place in the first three months of 1992. In the last year, multinational companies paid guerrilla ransoms for the release of one American geologist, two Japanese engineers and three American oil engineers. Natco, an oil services company in Tulsa, is reported to have paid $1 million for the release of the three engineers.

The guerrillas' refusal to release 300 kidnapping victims—largely ranchers and rural businessmen—was a big reason that peace talks with Colombia's Government broke down in June.

Originally supplied by Cuba, Colombia's two main guerrilla groups, the National Liberation Army and the Revolutionary Armed Forces, have been fighting the state for more than 25 years. Today, to keep their fighters fed, clothed and armed, the groups extort "war taxes" from rural businesses and provide armed guards for cocaine laboratories and plots of opium poppies.

In Chile, police officers investigating the arrest this week of two central committee members of the Lautaro Youth Movement, a leftist guerrilla group, announced that the pair received salaries five times Chile's minimum monthly salary of $100, a level that allowed the urban guerrilla leaders' families to maintain middle-class life-styles.

Double Drag on Peru's Economy

In Peru, guerrilla activity by the Tupac Amaru Revolutionary Movement and by the more radical Shining Path cost Peru's economy about $500 million in the first half of 1992, according to Senator Enrique Bernales, who tracks the human and financial cost of the violence. In a second drag on the economy, guerrilla violence is frightening foreign investors away from an ambitious Government plan to privatize most of Peru's state enterprises, from telephone companies to copper mines.

A recent series of police raids against the Tupac Amaru here laid bare the modern financing techniques of this largely middle class, pro-Cuban guerrilla group.

Cellular telephones, facsimile and photocopying machines, American and South Korean computers, and a basement "people's jail" in a comfortable neighborhood were all part of a smoothly efficient Tupac Amaru kidnapping and extortion operation uncovered by the police.

"They had files on most Peruvian businessmen, where they lived, where they worked, where their children studied," said Julio Favre Carranza, a leader here of business resistance to extortion demands. According to Mr. Favre's group, the Confederation of Peruvian Industries, companies here spend more than $150 million a year on security protection against terrorists.

Working on a tip from a Lima businessman forced to pay Tupac Amaru "war taxes," the police on April 15 arrested Peter Cárdenas Schulte. Described as operations director for the guerrillas, Mr. Cárdenas had $237,500 in United States currency in his apartment at the time of his arrest.

Well-Organized Ring

In June, police arrested the group's top leader, Victor Polay Campos, while he was dining in a restaurant in an upper-middle-class neighborhood here. The police have issued an international warrant for the arrest of the group's financial director, María Luisa Benza Pflucker, who may have fled to the Netherlands, her mother's native land.

Studying documents and more than 50 computer diskettes seized at Optimisa S.R.L., a front company run by Miss Benza, detectives pieced together details of a well-organized kidnapping and extortion ring.

"We found information relating to economic and financial movements, company directories, addresses and telephone numbers of different public and private businesses—all designed to be used for extortion and blackmail for subversive activity," said a spokesman for Peru's National Anti-Terrorism Police Directorate.

The police said that bank clerks either sold or supplied free of charge financial and personal information about bank executives and holders of large accounts. Police found photo albums filled with newspaper clippings and snapshots of potential kidnapping victims. A small library of private school yearbooks provided more photos and residential addresses of potential victims.

Studying computer printouts, antiterrorist police officers said that the 239 companies that regularly paid "war taxes" included mining companies, pharmaceutical makers, soft drink bottlers and printers. To prevent double billing by common criminals, Peru's guerrilla extortionists gave printed receipts, which they call "war bonds."

The police speculate that the Tupac Amaru hid millions of dollars in overseas accounts. But when a judge in late June asked Mr. Polay to list his assets, the guerrilla leader responded defiantly, "All I own in the world are the clothes on my back."

Grenades and Phony Passports

At one news conference here, the police displayed materials purchased with extortion money: falsified passports and passes for official cars,

---

Leftist bureaucrats with detailed files fit for extortion.

---

immigration stamps, infrared binoculars for night vision, sophisticated radios, pistols, grenades, antitank weapons and ammunition for automatic weapons. Police said they also found plans to dynamite the Camino Real, Lima's largest shopping center and the site of several multinational companies' local offices.

Peru's more radical guerrilla group, the Shining Path, is thought to finance its activities through the collection of as much as $40 million a year in "war taxes" from Peruvian coca leaf growers and Columbian cocaine traffickers.

In early July, the anti-terrorist police released a document that they said was seized during a recent raid on a Shining Path cell in Lima. According to this document, the Shining Path committee in Peru's principal coco leaf-growing area, the Upper Huallaga Valley, promised to turn over to the party

half of the protection money raised from coca leaf growers and laboratory operators.

Addressing landing fees collected from planes arriving from Colombia, the documents' signers promised to devote 5 percent to the maintenance of airstrips and to deliver the rest to the central committee of the Shining Path, formally known as the Communist Party of Peru.

Big Profits From Drugs

Analyzing this and other documents, Caretas magazine, Peru's largest-selling news weekly, estimated this month that the Shining Path earned $250 million from the drug trade over the last six years. The magazine speculated that most of the money had been spent on domestic operations or had been deposited in overseas accounts.

Recognizing that continued terrorism is preventing Peru's economic revival, President Alberto K. Fujimori issued an emergency decree in May that establishes life sentences for most major terrorist crimes.

But with guerrillas firmly established as extortionists in the public mind, businessmen are now plagued by freelancers trying to piggyback on the guerrillas' fearsome reputation.

In Peru's second-largest city, Arequipa, police in late June freed a kidnapped textile executive, breaking up a gang that had extorted "war taxes" from local businesses since 1985. These "guerrillas" turned out to include one active-duty policeman and two retired police officers. Their leader, Carlos Corso Portocarrero, was a well-known businessman who frequented the city's most exclusive club, Club Arequipa, apparently to select his victims.

Fugitive Leader of Maoist Rebels Is Captured by the Police in Peru

Dozen Seized in Stunning Blow to Shining Path

James Brooke

Special to The New York Times

RIO DE JANEIRO, Sept. 13—In a stunning blow to the guerrilla insurrection that has paralyzed much of Peru and shaken its Government, the Peruvian police have captured the movement's leader, Abimael Guzmán-Reynoso, after a 12-year manhunt.

The capture of Mr. Guzmán on Saturday night is seen as Peru's greatest victory in a war that has cost 25,000 lives and an estimated $22 billion in damage.

"My turn to lose," Mr. Guzmán, the head of the Maoist Shining Path group, reportedly said when the police arrested him at a house in the middle-class Surco neighborhood in Lima.

A Dozen Others Captured

The police said that in that raid and in another nearby, they had captured about a dozen high-ranking members of a group formally called the Communist Party of Peru but more widely known as Sendero Luminoso, or Shining Path.

The group's 12-year insurrection is by far the largest and most violent in Latin America. Its challenge to the Peruvian Government has provoked widespread concern in the region, and its control of coca-growing regions in Peru has complicated anti-drug efforts by the United States and other countries.

The movement, which has an estimated 5,000 fighters and thousands of other supporters, was born in 1970 in the Andean city of Ayacucho, where Mr. Guzmán was a philosophy professor in the 1960's and 70's. In 1980 it began its armed insurgency.

It has spread to all of Peru's provinces in 12 years of almost uninterrupted growth, fed in part by the wide gulf between rich and poor and its emphasis on giving power to indigenous people at the expense of the elite of Spanish heritage.

Several analysts predicted today that while the arrests would increase President Alberto K. Fujimori's short-term popularity, they would not spell the end of the insurgency.

Within Shining Path, Mr. Guzmán enjoys virtually godlike stature. His followers acclaim him as "the fourth sword of Marxism" and his writings are held to be on a par with those of Marx, Lenin and Mao.

"They have captured the godhead—it is like capturing an Inca," Paul L. Doughty, a University of Florida anthropology professor and expert on Shining Path, said by telephone today.

Rebel Attacks on the Rise

In Lima, which bears the scars of repeated Shining Path attacks, including a car-bombing campaign in July, there was jubilation today.

"Public Enemy No. 1 Arrested" read a headline in a special edition of the newspaper Expreso. "Abimael Guzmán is captured; the most wanted murderer of the century arrested."

Expreso said that Mr. Guzmán was captured as he met with other members of Shining Path's central committee to plan an October bombing campaign named "Operation Conquer Lima."

Guerrilla attacks on Lima and elsewhere in the nation of 23 million people have intensified this year. Mr. Fujimori cited the conflict when he suspended constitutional rule on April 5. He made the capture of Mr. Guzmán a top priority.

"The arrest is going to greatly strengthen Fujimori politically," Nelson Manrique, a Lima sociologist who has studied Shining Path, said today. "If the Government capitalizes on this success, it could win a majority in the Assembly."

Mr. Fujimori hopes that two slates he is backing will win the Nov. 22 election for a new Congress, a body that is also to function as a constitutional convention.

In April, Mr. Fujimori closed Peru's courts and Congress, charging that they were obstacles to his war on terrorism. In public opinion polls, his popularity surged to 85 percent, and then fell back to about 60 percent last week.

"His popularity is fragile," Mr. Doughty, the University of Florida professor, said. "If Fujimori makes too much of this, it could be disastrous. Where is he going to come up with one million jobs? He is not out of the woods by any means."

Peru is in deep recession and its economic problems have been compounded by the cost of the war against Shining Path and the damage the group has inflicted. Bombing targets often include bridges, rail lines and power installations.

Mr. Guzmán's capture was the second major anti-insurgency victory for the Government this year. Three months ago the police arrested Víctor Polay, the leader of Peru's other guerrilla group, the Cuba-inspired Túpac Amaru Revolutionary Movement.

The elusiveness of Mr. Guzmán, whom officials said was being held in Lima at the headquarters of the anti-terrorist agency, had become legendary in Peru over the last decade.

In June 1990, he was nearly captured at a Lima safe house, but slipped away. When the police broke in, they found only his reading glasses and medication.

A History of Violence

In another raid in Lima, in January 1991, the police found a videotape showing the Shining Path leader mourning at the funeral of his wife, Augusta La Torre. He and 14 other Shining Path leaders were dressed in collarless jackets of the type popular in China under Mao Zedong.

The movement has been marked by a high degree of violence, which

Path of Terror: 22 Years of Revolution

1970 Abimael Guzmán Reynoso, a philosophy professor in the poor Andean region of Ayacucho, founds Sendero Luminoso, or Shining Path, devoted to the most orthodox Marxist-Leninism.

May 18, 1980 Shining Path begins its armed insurgency when a band of youths burn ballot boxes and voting lists in Chuschi, a village in Ayacucho. The rebels, mostly Quechua-speaking Indians, set out to conquer Peru with a Maoist strategy of overcoming rural areas and strangling the cities. Mr. Guyzmán goes underground.

May 1983 Government sends troops to crush the rebels after conceding that Shining Path is now active near the capital.

1984 Government antidrug operations show that Shining Path is working with coca growers.

April 1985 Alan García Pérez is elected President. Shining Path is estimated to have 2,000 to 4,000 soldiers and thousands of collaborators.

July 1986 Guards at a Lima prison kill 124 prisoners accused of belonging to Shining Path.

1988 Shining Path strengthens its presence in urban areas.

May 1989 One million people obey a Shining Path call for a three-day armed strike. In an election year, the rebels mount their strongest campaign of terror, killing more than 120 mayors and other local officials by year's end.

June 1990 After a new terror campaign, the García Government captures 31 suspected rebels and tons of Shining Path pamphlets. Alberto K. Fujimori is elected President. He vows to continue the fight against Shining Path, but he also offers to negotiate.

April 1992 President Fujimori suspends constitutional rule.

Sept. 12, 1992 The police arrest Mr. Guzmán and other Shining Path members.

in turn has provoked the harsh measures by the security forces.

In a recent example, seven people were killed at a gasoline station near Lima on Sept. 5. Eight guerrillas robbed the station, apparently to draw the police. When they fled, they left behind a van. When the police arrived and opened the door of the van, a bomb exploded, killing the 7 and seriously injuring 13.

Car bombings in Lima this summer, in response to Mr. Fujimori's crackdown, caused scores of casualties and widespread damage.

Although Shining Path followers revere Mr. Guzmán, they have said that the struggle will survive him.

"This will demonstrate to the world that what we have in Peru is a peoples' war, not a central committee's war," said Adolfo Olaechea, a director of the Sol Perú Committee, a London-based group that supports the rebels. "The war has more to do with a class struggle than with personalities."

'Further Action' Predicted

"The upper class is opening champagne bottles for this criminal action against the chairman, but the masses will be spurred to further action," Mr. Olaechea, a Peruvian exile, said today by telephone.

Several analysts said the Government had strengthened its hand by capturing the Shining Path leader alive, rather than dead.

"Peru is a country with martyrs, not with heroes," Mr. Doughty said. "All the national icons are martyrs. The Government has to take care of his capture, in order not to martyr him."

"We don't know if there is a well-thought-out succession," he added.

"Is it like Fidel Castro's Cuba, where there is no visible successor?"

Mr. Manrique, the sociologist, said: "The fact that Guzmán fell alive, without offering resistance, is

---

A stunning blow for rebels, but they are expected to fight on.

---

key. If he fell in combat, he would have been more important dead than alive."

The police said today that the house where Mr. Guzmán was arrested had been under surveillance for five months. Starting in June, Mr. Fujimori imposed a 10 P.M. curfew on vehicles and had begun a publicity campaign urging residents to report suspicious people and activity.

"It's a great success that you cannot deny the Fujimori Administration," said Luis Cisneros Vizquerra, a retired army general and former Minister of Interior who has been a critic of the Fujimori strategy against terrorism.

Colombia's bloodstained peace

FROM OUR SPECIAL CORRESPONDENT IN BOGOTA

A N EX-MINISTER arrives for tea in an armoured limousine, with six gun-toting plug-uglies. The bullet-scar on his chin shows that such protection can be penetrated. Bogota, a handsome, friendly city, is a dangerous place to make enemies in. On every corner of the smarter districts one, two or three armed men in various uniforms or none lounge with miscellaneous light weapons. In the poor quarters the police go in by squads, and get out as fast as they can.

Unofficial armies beset Colombia. Ranchers, plantation-owners, miners of emeralds and less glamorous minerals, employ gunmen for "protection"; the richest gangs work for cocaine traders, in the loose alliances known as cartels. The government's own army, ill-paid and ill-equipped, hires freelances for some quasi-military operations. Four guerrilla movements are at work around the country; as their leaders' left-wing faith fades, the fighters get their pay from extortion, kidnapping and theft. Ministers and mayors, judges and tax-collectors—and many journalists, academics, priests and people of reason—bravely denounce the terrorists who threaten them.

President Cesar Gaviria and his startlingly young ministers and advisers are on the side of the angels. They want to reform everything at once. But the government's powers have not kept up with the country's growing wealth.

Through the 1980s, while Latin America rocked motionless in the trough of its own debt, Colombia grew at a steady 3.5% a year, more than twice the regional average. Unrecorded exports of cocaine eased the economy through its import booms, and smoothed the way for legitimate exports. Entrepreneurs did nicely out of freer trade, especially with their bigger, oil-rich neighbour, Venezuela. Despite the collapse of coffee, once their staple export, Colombians have developed new farm exports, such as winter flowers for North America. Foreign investors lust for the country's oil, coal and other minerals.

The economy grew stronger, but the state stayed weak. Colombian politics were frozen in the late 1950s, at the end of the ghastly episode known as *la violencia*, in which some 300,000 people died in civil strife between the two main political parties, Conservatives and Liberals. In a deal to end the slaughter, the parties agreed to divide power. However the people voted (and not many bothered), ministries, and patronage, and the profits of economic protection, were shared between the parties. But with rising prosperity, outsiders started the fight to get in: successful businessmen, restless leftists, landless malcontents, men with vast cocaine fortunes.

Virgilio Barco, the Liberal president of 1986-90, began to open up both the country's economy and its politics. He cut a swathe through the licences, quotas and other barriers that protected the country's old-established businesses, thus enabling new ones to thrive. He joined the United States in its war on drugs, to which the narco-terrorists reacted with extra violence. And he strove to coax the extremists of the far left into normal politics.

Mr Barco persuaded the largest and least extreme guerrilla group, the May 19th movement (M-19), to become a normal political party and run in the 1990 election. But he could not protect its candidates. Dozens were murdered during the campaign, including Carlos Pizarro, running for president. Nobody is sure who ordered his murder. It was drug gangsters who killed the Liberals' much-loved presidential candidate, Luis Carlos Galan.

Mr Gaviria, the 42-year-old Liberal who won the 1990 election, had not been his party's first choice. But his ambitions, backed by a new political generation, were grandiose: to open the economy to the outside world, and to reform Colombia's own government institutions from top to bottom. At the outset of his presidency a constitutional convention reformed the system of political patronage and introduced new judicial procedures, with safeguards for human rights. In particular, Colombia wanted better judges, better protected against threats and bribes.

The amended constitution also sheltered the drug barons against the fate they most fear, which is extradition to the United States. The most notorious of them promptly surrendered; Pablo Escobar, said to be the boss of the "Medellin cartel", is now rather comfortably in prison, awaiting trial. The main rival drug ring, based in Cali, continues to prosper, but less violently than the Medellin lot. Colombians reckon the trade will thrive as long as export demand for drugs continues, but welcome the decline in narco-terrorism.

Ordinary terrorism goes on. Mr Gaviria's government runs sporadic peace talks with the various guerrilla movements, grouped for this purpose into a loose co-ordinating council; since the council fails to co-ordinate its political demands, the negotiations would be hard even if not interrupted by atrocities.

The security forces, fighting ferocious opponents, too often misuse their powers. The minister of defence, Rafael Pombo, argues that repression alone cannot defeat terrorism—particularly not terrorists hired for better pay than the soldiers and policemen they fight against, and much more than the unemployed from whose ranks they are recruited. Ministers acknowledge that economic growth, and the drift to the towns, have created real grievances about jobs, housing, education and health care. Defeating the bandits is going to require massive social spending, as well as stronger and cleaner policing.

Nobody loves taxes

But all Colombia's public services are inadequate. The deficiency was dramatised in recent months, when most sizeable towns spent up to 12 hours a day without electricity. The dams that produce 70% of Colombia's power have dried up in the drought that has struck all northern South America. Competent management could have avoided the fiasco.

Even if it were better organised, the Colombian state lacks the resources to provide the minimum that people expect of their rulers: justice, peace, roads, water, education. The government collects and spends about 15% of GNP. For comparison, the government of Chile, Latin America's most successful privatiser, spends 32% of GNP. Non-governmental organisations cannot begin

to fill the gap. Some are admirable charities paid for by the rich; others are mere fronts for terror groups, extorting contributions in exchange for not blowing up pylons or pipelines.

In the 1960s Colombia was overwhelmingly rural, almost without roads and railways. It has grown to be a largely urban, rapidly industrialising society, and needs a correspondingly stronger, richer and more active government. But its most effective modernising policy has deprived the government of much of the revenue it used to collect.

Until the early 1980s, taxes and duties on foreign trade brought in almost 20% of the government's revenue. Free trade has boosted growth, but cut state revenue just when state spending needed to rise. Privatisation cannot fill the gap, since the state owns little worth selling except for a profitable and efficient telecommunications company. The national airline, Avianca, is famously unreliable—and privately owned.

If Colombia's government is to bring off its peaceable revolution, it must raise more money by taxes. Nobody likes that. Value-added tax, recently introduced at 12%, was unpopular enough at that level. Proposals to raise it to 15% have raised howls of protest; VAT hits the poor fastest. The political diffi-

culties of taxing the rich are even greater. Most of Colombia's prosperous firms and farms are owned by the families (overwhelmingly, in a Latin-American way, of Spanish descent) that also provide the country's political leaders, control the two big party machines and hold patronage in most congressional districts. They want reform, to be sure, but not taxes.

In January this year the president had seemed unchallengeable, with 70% support in the polls. His tax proposals turned people against him, even before the power cuts. Faced in late May with a proposal for higher tax rates and—worse still—better tax collection, Congress vetoed it, and voted instead for a tax on oil companies that would, if carried, drive off potential foreign investors. The most recent polls show his popularity at around 40%, and falling.

With tax plans stuck in Congress, chances of real change sink below the horizon. Drug money and revolutionary extortion offer Colombians the hope of a better life than any civilised alternative. If peaceable reform peters out in the country that supplies more than half of the world's cocaine, and an increasing amount of its heroin, the damage will be felt far beyond the Andes.

Will Terrorists Use Chemical Weapons?

Yonah Alexander

Yonah Alexander, an authority on international terrorism, is a research professor at George Washington University's Elliott School of International Affairs and senior fellow of the U.S. Global Strategy Council.

News stories about Libya's Rabta Plant, which the United States believes produces chemical weapons, and the warning by President Saddam Hussein that Iraq will destroy half of Israel with chemical weapons if the Jewish state preemptively attacks his country, have refocused attention on the threat of unconventional warfare.

Development of chemical and biological weapons is easier than that of nuclear explosives. There are no insurmountable technical impediments in the use of chemical agents such as floroacetates, organophosphorous compounds and botulinum toxin.

They are relatively easy to obtain, their delivery systems are manageable and dispersal techniques are efficient. In fact, terrorists desiring to make nerve gases rather than obtain them directly from Libya, Iraq or even the commercial market, can still find the formulas at some libraries despite attempts by various governments, including that of Great Britain, to remove them from public access.

Once in possession of such information, a terrorist with some technical know-how could synthesize toxic chemical agents from raw materials or intermediates. In fact, many chemical toxins (e.g. Cobalt-60 and TEPP insecticides) are commercially available. They could be bought or stolen.

Also, covert and overt options for dispersing chemical agents are virtually limitless, including poisoning of water systems, contamination of food supplies, generation of gases in enclosed spaces with volatile agents, generation of aerosols in enclosed spaces with nonvolatile agents, and dispersal with explosives.

Early Attempts

There is no accurate statistical data on the number of chemical- and biolog-ical-related terrorist incidents because not all of them have been reported by governments and the news media. But there apparently are more than 100 known cases.

- In 1975, German authorities were threatened that mustard gas—stolen from an ammunition bunker—would be used in Stuttgart unless all political prisoners were granted immunity. Only some of the stolen canisters were found later.
- In 1978, an Israeli citrus fruit export to Europe was contaminated with liquid mercury. Israel had to cut back its orange exports by 40%. A similar incident on a smaller scale occurred in 1989.

As in the case of chemical violence, biological terrorism—the use of living organisms to cause disease or death in man, animals or plants—is technically possible. Warfare agents such as bruceliosis (undulant fever), coccidioidomycosis (San Joaquin Valley or desert fever) and psittacosis (parrot fever) are easy to acquire, cultivate and disseminate. The poison Ricin, for example, is developed from castor beans; about half a milligram is fatal.

Terrorists evidently have considered resorting to biological terrorism:

- In 1970, members of the Weather Underground planned to steal germs from the bacteriological warfare center at Fort Detrick, Maryland, for the purpose of contaminating a city water supply.
- In 1975, technical military manuals on germ warfare were found in a San Francisco hideout of the Symbionese Liberation Army.

To be sure, such forms of technological terrorism have been rare in comparison to the approximately 40,000 domestic and international incidents during the past 20 years. Terrorist operations typically have been limited in scope and not indiscriminate—owing to the perpetrators' desire to demonstrate their tactical capabilities rather than to commit a major violent act for its own sake.

Better-Trained Terrorists

However, technological developments offer new capabilities and targets.

Terrorists today are better organized, more professional and better-equipped than those in the 1970's. They are likely to take greater operational risks in the next decade. A few sophisticated terrorist groups could use higher leverage tactics to achieve mass disruption or political turmoil.

For example, Force 17, a terrorist body with special operational responsibility in Yasir Arafat's Fatah—the major constituent of the Palestine Liberation Organization (PLO)—had been trained in chemical weapons. Similarly, the Hezbollah (Islamic Jihad or the Party of God), operating with the support of Iran, might employ chemical terrorism against Western interests in the Middle East or against other adversaries such as Iraq or Saudi Arabia.

In addition to some of the Middle Eastern terrorist groups, some European extremists including Direct Action (French), the Irish Republican Army, and Red Army Faction (German) are likely candidates for unconventional terrorism.

Biological and chemical weapons have many advantages for terrorists. These include low cost, ease and speed of production, and the fact that they can be developed by individuals with limited education. Weapons production requires only a minimum of tools and space, and equipment can be improvised or purchased without arousing suspicion.

Other advantages include the reliability and availability of such weapons. Also, they are easier to disguise and transport than conventional arms.

Since chemical and biological weapons also are the "weak" states' answer to lack of nuclear arms, their proliferation, particularly in the third world, is disturbing. Libya and Iraq provide recent examples of this challenge.

In the longer term, nuclear terrorism—explosion of a nuclear bomb, use of fissionable material as radioactive poison or seizure and sabotage of nuclear facilities—also is plausible. And if only one terrorist group succeeds in achieving its goals through the use of weapons of mass destruction, then the temptation for other extremists to escalate will grow.

Reprinted from *JINSA Security Affairs*, June/July 1990, p. 10.

Terrorism and Public Opinion: A Five Country Comparison

Christopher Hewitt

This article examines public attitudes towards terrorism in five countries: Uruguay, Spain, Italy, Germany and Northern Ireland. It analyzes public concern over terrorism, images of the terrorists, support for the terrorists' goals, and public approval of anti-terrorist measures. There are significant differences between nationalist and revolutionary terrorism. Nationalist terrorists have a high degree of support from an ethnic constituency, while revolutionary terrorists attract a much smaller degree of support primarily from the educated young. It is concluded that public opinion towards terrorism is a product of complex historical situations, and that public attitudes are unaffected by the terrorist campaign itself.

The goal of insurgent terrorism is to alter the political situation by changing public opinion. The relationship between terrorism and public opinion is, therefore, an important issue that needs to be examined.

One purpose of terrorism is to draw attention to some cause or grievance. Schmid and de Graaf go so far as to claim that

> the genesis of contemporary insurgent terrorism ... (can be seen) primarily as the outgrowth of minority strategies to get into the news. The choice of this strategy to get grievances vented and redressed is ... probably due to the fact that the significance of parliaments as an intermediary between people and the executive has declined.[1]

Getting noticed is one thing – being understood is another.[2] Governments threatened by political insurgents usually dismiss them as common criminals, and, among the general public in England and the United States, terrorists are often seen as psychologically disturbed. For the terrorists, one of their initial problems is simply to be taken seriously, to be considered as having realistic political goals.

Even if the public regards terrorists as politically-motivated revolutionaries or nationalists, it still does not follow that they will support them or their goals. Those who advocate an urban guerrilla strategy believe, however, that terrorism itself can create a revolutionary situation. Two processes supposedly produce revolutionary consciousness. In the nineteenth century, many anarchists and social revolutionaries believed that the masses would be inspired by the 'propaganda of the deed' to rise up against oppression. The Narodnaya Volya's manifesto claimed that 'terrorist activity ... aims to undermine the prestige of the government, to demonstrate the possibility of struggle against the government [and] to arouse in this manner the revolutionary spirit of the people and their confidence in the success of their cause'. Kropotkin said that one terrorist act could 'make more propaganda than a thousand pamphlets. Above all, it awakens the spirit of revolt.' This view was echoed a century later by Latin American revolutionaries. Regis Debray wrote that 'the destruction of one troop transport truck is more effective propaganda for the local population than a thousand speeches'. According to the Tupamaros, 'revolutionary action in itself ... generates revolutionary consciousness, organization and conditions'.[3]

An alternative view of how to create a revolutionary situation is the 'provocation-repression' theory. By attacking the establishment and the security forces, the insurgents provoke the state into mass repression which alienates the general public, and increases support for the rebels.[4]

The Basque insurgent group ETA believed that by attacks against the Spanish military and Guardia Civil, they would

> provoke Spanish authorities into an overreaction that would inflict heavy damage on the civilian Basque population. In attempting to stop ETA, Madrid would aggravate already strong but latent hostility against its policies among the Basques, and the previously inert civilian population would then commit itself to support ETA's armed struggle.[5]

In addition to mobilizing and radicalizing their own supporters, terrorists seek to destroy the morale of their enemies. To revolutionaries, the enemy is the ruling class and their agents, to nationalists, the enemy is the nation oppressing them. This produces markedly different campaigns, where revolutionaries selectively attack politicians and businessmen, while nationalists try to raise the costs to the foreign occupiers by killing large numbers of soldiers.[6]

Most counter-insurgency writers deny that terrorism produces support for the insurgents' goals, and argue that the strategy is actually counter-productive. According to Moss, 'in most cases, urban guerrillas are dangerous less for what they do than for what they inspire: the erosion of the consensus, a hardening of the political battle lines and a backlash that strikes back too hard and too indiscriminately', and he goes on to suggest that 'the usual response to terrorism is revulsion'.[7] Clutterbuck claims that, in both Germany and Italy, killing policemen with consequent 'TV pictures of their tearful working class families ... created widespread anger'.[8]

In the case of Uruguay, the consensus holds that public perceptions changed as the Tupamaro campaign became more deadly. Originally the Tupamaros carefully avoided unnecessary violence and attacked only the rich and elite. During Christmas they hijacked a food truck and distributed the groceries in the slums of Montevideo. They robbed the casino, but returned that share which would have gone to the employees. They broke into a financial institution and publicized its corrupt and illegal practices (which implicated a cabinet minister). When one of their kidnap victims had a heart attack, they kidnapped a specialist to treat him, and then released their prisoner when his condition worsened.

Such tactics created a favorable image for the Tupamaros, but the public supposedly turned against them once they began to murder people. 'They lost their original Robin Hood image as imaginative student pranksters who pilfered from the rich to give to the poor, by systematically murdering policemen as well as an American hostage, Dan Mitrione.'[9] This is a common view, usually supported by citing polls which show a dramatic decline in those thinking the Tupamaros were 'motivated by a concern for social justice' from 59 percent in 1971 to four per cent in 1972.[10]

There has, however, been no systematic cross-national analysis of the relation between public opinion and terrorism. This article attempts to remedy the omission by examining five societies, Uruguay, Germany, Italy, Spain/Basque provinces and United Kingdom/Northern Ireland, where significant terrorist campaigns have taken place. Since these cases do not constitute a representative sample, and were selected primarily

From *Terrorism and Political Violence*, Vol. 2, No. 2, Summer 1990, pp. 145-170. *Terrorism and Political Violence,* published by Frank Cass and Company, Ltd., England.

because of data availability, I shall discuss later the extent to which the findings can be generalized.

Insurgent terrorism has taken two forms. In Northern Ireland and the Basque provinces of Spain, nationalist terrorism by the Irish Republican Army (IRA) and Euzkadi ta Askatasuna (ETA) aims to drive out the British and Spanish, and to inspire the local population to support Irish unity or Basque independence. The Tupamaros in Uruguay, the Red Army Faction/Baader–Meinhof group in Germany, and the Red Brigades in Italy sought to bring about a revolution.

Terrorist groups see the public divided into two main categories: their constituency and their enemies. Their constituency consists of potential and actual supporters. For nationalist terrorists, their core constituency is defined by ethnicity: Catholics in Northern Ireland, ethnic Basques in Spain. Politically their support is organized in the militantly nationalist parties such as Provisional Sinn Fein (PSF) and Herri Batasuna (HB) or Euzkadiko Ezkerra (EE). Moderate nationalists such as the Social Democratic and Labour Party (SDLP) and the Partido Nacionalista Vasco (PNV) represent potential supporters, who hopefully can be won over to a militant position.

The revolutionary constituency is less clearly defined. Supposedly it is the proletariat, but *de facto* revolutionary terrorists draw their support from the educated young. Politically they lack an organized base, but are sympathetically, if critically, regarded by the extreme left. In a general sense their appeal is aimed at the left, whether communist, socialist or even social-democratic.

The available survey data are unfortunately, but not surprisingly, short of being ideal. On some topics we lack any information at all. If we wish to make comparisons between countries, the questions are rarely asked in the same form. Although we are interested in whether terrorism changes public attitudes, on several matters survey data exist for only one point in time.[11]

However, we do have sufficient information to consider four topics in some detail: the level of public concern, the image that the public has of the terrorists, the degree of support for the political goals of the terrorists, and public attitudes towards government anti-terrorist policies. Furthermore, although fragmentary, the data allow us to make comparisons between countries, as well as over time, and between groups within the same country. Thus we are able to suggest why people hold the opinions that they do and to link the description of public opinion to the theoretical literature on terrorism.

Terrorism as a Problem

The first question that needs to be asked about public opinion is to what extent terrorism is seen as a problem. One standard survey question asks what is the most important problem facing the country. In Table 1 the percentage selecting terrorism or a related topic is shown.

The answers are obviously affected by the list of topics suggested and by the wording of the topic. In so far as the question forces a single choice on respondents, it does not take account of those who see terrorism as a significant but not the most important problem. In Spain, if we include those who selected terrorism as the second most important problem, the number is much higher. Furthermore, for certain groups terrorism may be more important. In Northern Ireland, Protestants were more likely than Catholics to see terrorism as the most serious issue (41 per cent and 24 per cent).

The simplest explanation for the degree of public concern is that it is directly linked to the amount of terrorism: the more terrorism the more concern. This interpretation is supported by two pieces of evidence. First, cross-national differences in the proportion saying that terrorism is the most important problem do correspond to variations in the level of terrorism. If we consider terrorism-related deaths, for the period prior to when the polls were taken, the rank order is correct. Northern Ireland has the most deaths followed by Spain and then Italy with Uruguay and Germany having far fewer, and this corresponds to the concern expressed.

Second, within Spain, the changing level of concern is closely linked to the monthly death totals. Indeed, it is striking how quickly public attitudes change in respect to short-term fluctuations in the numbers killed (see Figure 1). Unfortunately, in none of the other countries are there a sufficient number of observations to examine changes over time.

Clearly, however, the amount of violence is not the only factor operating on public opinion. In the case of Spain, we can also examine regional differences to see whether there is more concern where terrorist

TABLE 1
TERRORISM AS A PROBLEM

	Most Important Problem (%)		Deaths from Terrorism
(1) Northern Ireland 1982	Terrorism	34	2,340
(2) Spain 1979–82	Terrorism/public order	22	414
(3) Italy 1972–79	Public Order	16	227
(4) Great Britain 1971–2	Northern Ireland	13	678
(5) Uruguay 1968–69	Disorder/subversion	4	14
(6) Germany 1976	Public Order	8	12

Sources: *Attitudes to the Northern Ireland Assembly* (Survey conducted for BBC by Ulster Marketing Surveys, Oct. 1982).
Revista Espanola de Investigaciones Sociologicas (1972–82).
Gallup Political Index (London: Gallup Poll).
Indice Gallup de Opinion Publica (Montevideo: Gallup Uruguay).
Karl Cerny, *Germany at the Polls* (Washington: American Enterprise Institute, 1978), p.137.

violence is highest. Contrary to expectations, it is those areas with the highest levels of violence which are the *least* likely to see terrorism as a significant problem (see Table 2). This can be explained by considering the role of ethnicity in Barcelona and the Basque provinces, where most violence has taken place. Basques and Catalans have strong regional and ethnic identities, and sizeable minorities support separatist parties.[12] Terrorism is directed primarily not against fellow ethnics but against the Guardia Civil who are – as a deliberate policy – drawn from other regions of Spain.[13]

A similar explanation can be offered to explain the Northern Irish situation, where Catholics feel much less concern about terrorism than Protestants. By 1982 (when the survey was taken) the victims of terrorism were disproportionately Protestant.[14] On the other hand, the Catholic rate of unemployment was much higher than the Protestant rate. Not surprisingly Protestants rated terrorism the main problem facing Northern Ireland with unemployment the second ranked problem, while Catholics reversed the order.

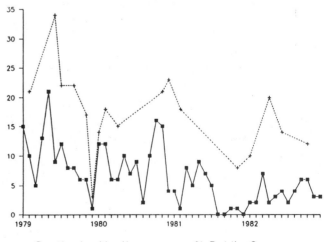

FIGURE 1
TERRORISM AND THE LEVEL OF PUBLIC CONCERN IN SPAIN (1979–82)

■ Deaths by Month   + % Public Concern

Source: *Revista Espanola de Investigaciones Sociologicas* (1979–82).

7. TACTICS, STRATEGIES, AND TARGETING

The importance of Northern Ireland to the British public can also be explained by considering who was being killed. During 1971–72 British concern reached a peak, with 13 per cent on average saying it was the most

TABLE 2
PUBLIC CONCERN IN SPAIN OVER TERRORISM BY PROVINCE AND DEATH RATE

	Terrorist killings/ m. population	Terrorism main problem (%)
Basque Provinces	191.9	10.5
Madrid	18.1	14.2
Barcelona	7.0	10.1
Galicia	1.8	16.5
Catalonia	0.8	15.7
Andalucia	0.8	18.4
Canaries	0.7	19.9
All other provinces	1.4	21.9

Source: Revista Espanola de Investigaciones Sociologicas (1979–82).

important problem for the country. The salience of the Northern Ireland issue was lower than would have been predicted given the number of deaths during the period (678). However, if we focus on the number of *British* soldiers killed (177), the concern expressed is at about the expected level. Since the early 1970s British interest in Northern Ireland has diminished considerably, paralleling the decline in the number of British soldiers killed.

How the Public Views Terrorists

In most of the cases that we examine, survey data are available on public perceptions of the terrorists. In Uruguay, respondents were asked whether the Tupamaros were well-intentioned revolutionaries or common delinquents. In Italy, the public was asked to choose one or two phrases that best applied to the Red Brigade members. Three phrases were negative (instruments controlled from on high, dangerous assassins or crazy), but the others were ambivalent (pursuing a just end with the wrong means) or very positive (fighting for a better society). In Germany the question was whether the Baader–Meinhof gang acted out of political conviction or if they had become true criminals. In the Basque provinces, surveys have asked whether terrorists are patriots, idealists, madmen, criminals or individuals manipulated by outside forces. In Northern Ireland, respondents were asked whether they agreed or disagreed with statements about the IRA and the loyalist paramilitaries. (Were the IRA basically patriots and idealists? Were the actions of the loyalist paramilitaries a justified reaction to what has happened in Northern Ireland?) Given that the form of the question varies and furthermore that the answers change over time, somewhat procrustean procedures are necessary to compare the different cases. Table 3 shows the percentage of the public holding positive images of the different terrorist groups, and reveals that a significant proportion acknowledge the political nature of their actions.

TABLE 3
PERCENTAGE OF PUBLIC HOLDING POSITIVE IMAGE OF TERRORISTS

1.	Basque Provinces (ETA)	47.3
2.	N. Ireland (IRA)	38.6
3.	Uruguay (Tupamaros)	38.6
4.	N. Ireland (Loyalists)	37.6
5.	Italy (Red Brigades)	27.6
6.	Germany (Baader-Meinhof)	18.0

Sources: Juan Linz, *Conflicto en Euskadi* (Espasa Calpe: 1986).
E. Moxon-Browne, 'The Water and the Fish: Public Opinion and the Provisional IRA in Northern Ireland', *Terrorism*, Vol. 5 (1981), 41–72.
Indice Gallup de Opinion Publica (1967–72).
L'Espresso (10 Jan. 1982).
Allensbacher Jahrbuch (Institute für Demoskopie Allensbach, 1971).

Some groups are more likely to hold a favorable image of the terrorists. This is particularly true with regard to nationalist terrorists who are regarded very sympathetically by their fellow ethnics. In the Basque provinces, those who consider themselves as Basque are much more likely to see ETA as patriots and idealists than those who consider themselves to be Spanish. In Northern Ireland, Catholics and Protestants disagree significantly in how they view both the IRA and the Loyalist terrorists.

Revolutionary terrorists lack such a clearly defined constituency. Their Marxist rhetoric suggests that their support should be concentrated in the working class; yet, in fact, the Tupamaros and Baader–Meinhof are viewed most sympathetically by those of higher socio-economic status, although the differences are small. Demography rather than class is a differentiating factor with men somewhat more sympathetic than women, and the young noticeably more so than the old.

Political ideology is correlated with attitudes towards the terrorists.

TABLE 4
PERCENTAGE HOLDING POSITIVE IMAGE OF NATIONALIST TERRORISTS BY ETHNICITY

	By Fellow Ethnics	By Other Ethnics
Positive Image of ETA	65.9	15.5
Positive Image of IRA	46.3	34.7
Positive Image of Loyalists	43.9	25.0

Sources: Calculated from Clark, *The Basque Insurgents*, p.181; Moxon-Browne, 'The Water and the Fish ...', pp.41–72.

TABLE 5
PERCENTAGE HOLDING POSITIVE IMAGE OF REVOLUTIONARY TERRORISTS BY CLASS AND DEMOGRAPHIC CHARACTERISTICS

	Baader-Meinhof	Tupamaros
Men	20	36
Women	16	33
Young	25	47
Middle Aged	16	35
Elderly	13	27
Educated	18	37
Less Educated	17	31
Upper Class		37
Middle Class		35
Lower Class		32

Sources: Allensbacher Jahrbuch (1971), Indice Gallup de Opinion Publica (1967–72).

In the Basque provinces, supporters of the extremist Basque nationalist parties (HB and EE) hold very positive views of ETA, and in Northern Ireland, supporters of PSF hold very positive views of the IRA. Moderate nationalists like the Basque PNV and Catholic SDLP hold ambivalent but far more sympathetic attitudes than non-nationalists. A similar ideological polarization is seen in Uruguay, where supporters of the leftwing Frente Amplio were much more likely to view the Tupamaros as well-intentioned revolutionaries than were the center-left Blancos or center-right Colorados. In Germany, however, partisan differences were very slight between the conservative Christian Democrats and the Social Democrats. The Free Democrats, a middle class liberal group, were the most sympathetic.

Although plausible, the view that terrorists will damage their image by killing people is not supported by the evidence. Indeed, it is those groups that kill the most, like IRA and ETA, that have the most positive ratings, while the Red Brigades and the Baader–Meinhof gang, groups that have killed far fewer, have the most unfavorable images.

Only in the Uruguayan case are survey data available that allow us to examine how public attitudes actually changed over time as a result of terrorist violence. Three questions were asked repeatedly: whether a specific action was a legitimate revolutionary act or a crime; whether the Tupamaros were well-intentioned revolutionaries or common delinquents; and, whether there was any justification for the Tupamaros 'under the political conditions of our country'.

Some evidence does suggest that a soft-line campaign helps maintain a more favorable terrorist image. For example, the proportion of respondents who believed kidnappings to be legitimate revolutionary acts, increased *after* the victims were returned unharmed, as happened in the cases of Fly and Jackson.[14] When Fly was first kidnapped only 18 per cent of the individuals surveyed thought it a legitimate revolutionary act, but 32 per cent saw it as such after he was released. In the case of Jackson the figure rose from 30 per cent to 36 per cent. On the other hand, the killing of Mitrione brought about a dramatic decline in those thinking his abduction was justified. The week before his death, the public was evenly divided between those who thought it a legitimate revolutionary act (34 per cent) and those who considered it a crime (34 per cent). After his murder the division became 18 per cent and 44 per cent, respectively.

However, terrorist violence clearly has only a temporary effect. Figure 3, showing the proportion considering the Tupamaros 'well-intentioned revolutionaries' and their actions 'justified under the political conditions of the country', does not suggest any deterioration of their public image. The first killings of policemen were not until July 1969, but the public perception of them as well-intentioned revolutionaries averaged 38.7 per

FIGURE 2
PERCENTAGE HOLDING POSITIVE IMAGE OF TERRORISTS BY PARTY

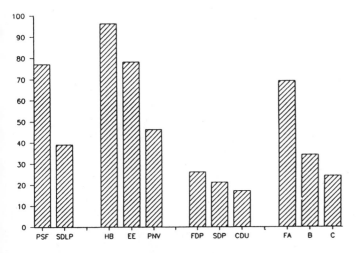

Sources: From the Shadow of the Gun (MORI, 1984).
W. Phillips Davison and Leon Gordenker, *Resolving Nationality Conflicts* (New York: Praeger, 1980), p.47.
Allensbacher Jahrbuch (1971).
Indice Gallup de Opinion Publica (1967–72).

cent before that date, compared to 38.9 per cent afterwards. Mitrione's murder had no discernible impact on public opinion either. Nor does the actual number of killings appear to be a negative factor. The percentage of respondents thinking the Tupamaros justified under the political conditions of the country increased substantially during the period when terrorist killings were at the their highest.

The often cited poll, showing a decline in public support for the Tupamaros, is doubly mistaken. Richard Clutterbuck erroneously cited statistics from an earlier article by Brian Crozier in the London *Times*.[16] Crozier, citing Gallup Uruguay, referred to the percentage who thought the Tupamaros 'well-intentioned' as dropping from 52 per cent to four per cent over the year. He compared this statistic to the proportion thinking that the armed forces were doing a good job, which had increased from 33 per cent to 59 per cent. Clutterbuck mixed up the two figures when he spoke of the decline being from 59 per cent to four per cent. However, Crozier also had gotten his figures wrong, since the actual July 1972 figure, approving the Tupamaros, is not four per cent but 36 per cent. The source

of Crozier's four per cent is uncertain, but appears to be the July 1972 Gallup Uruguay poll. This poll also asked what *caused* the Tupamaros to appear, and reported that there was a decline from 11 per cent to four per cent in those who mentioned a 'lack of social justice'. Presumably this is the original source of the erroneous figure.

FIGURE 3
ATTITUDE TO TUPAMAROS

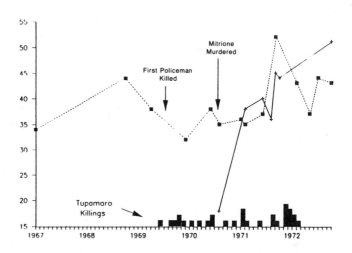

■ *Well-intentioned Revolutionaries*
+ *Justified*
Source: Indice Gallup de Opinion Publica (1967–72).

It seems, therefore, that a high level of violence does not in itself alienate the public. What appears crucial in creating a positive image of the terrorists as 'sincere patriots' and 'revolutionaries' is that they should behave like patriots and revolutionaries, and that such roles are understood within the society. Thus, the IRA operates within the context of a militant nationalist tradition deeply rooted in Irish history, and 'contemporary events so often evoke vivid and bitter memories'.[17] Basque nationalism and ETA's image are also the result of memories of past oppression by the Franco regime and popular resistance to it. In their campaigns the IRA and ETA usually behave like patriots fighting a national liberation struggle. Their targets are predominantly military, and they usually try to avoid killing innocent civilians.[18] Nationalist terrorists enjoy more legitimacy than do revolutionaries, particularly among their fellow ethnics, perhaps because revolutionary ideology is less easily understood by the general public. Even in Italy, a country with a well-established Marxist tradition, the Red Brigades had a much lower approval rating than the IRA or ETA.[19]

German political culture offered even less ideological support for revolutionary activity and Marxism has been largely supplanted by revisionist social democracy.[20] Pridham comments that 'it is difficult to measure the ideological dimensions of German terrorism' since the terrorist language 'has been both confused and confusing as a means of communicating ideas'.[21] Unlike Italy, the German system was working well, and hence demands for its revolutionary transformation were largely incomprehensible to the great majority of Germans.[22]

Attitudes Towards Revolution and Nationalism

Survey data are available for Uruguay, Italy, Germany and Spain on general ideological orientations and their changes over time. In Uruguay the population was asked whether they believed the solution to the country's problems lay in 'armed revolution' or 'law and order'. In Germany and Italy the options were 'radical change by revolutionary action', 'gradual improvement by reforms' and 'valiant defense against all subversive forces'. In Spain respondents were asked to locate themselves on a continuum from extreme left to extreme right. Figures 4 and 5 show the changes over time in the proportion supporting the various positions.

Does urban terrorism generate revolutionary consciousness? If it does, there should be an increase in the proportion of those defining themselves as revolutionaries or extreme leftists, but obviously this did not happen. In Uruguay and Italy, where major left-wing campaigns were mounted, the

7. TACTICS, STRATEGIES, AND TARGETING

number favoring revolution declined steadily throughout the period of terrorist activity. In Germany and Spain, where leftist terrorism was conducted at a much lower level, the proportion of revolutionaries and extreme leftists remained virtually unchanged at a trivial level.

Does terrorism generate a backlash, with increased support for tough law and order measures? In Uruguay, Germany and Italy there is clear evidence of such a relationship. In Uruguay, the number of terrorist acts rose each year during 1968–72, and this is matched by a steady increase in the law and order category. The worst years for terrorism in Germany

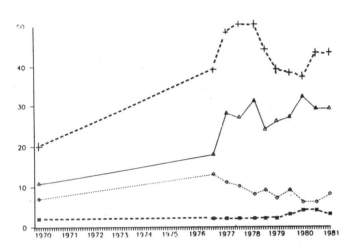

FIGURE 4
POLITICAL ATTITUDES IN GERMANY AND ITALY

■ Germany Revolution
+ Germany Defense
△ Italy Defense
◇ Italy Revolution

Source: *Index to International Public Opinion* (1981–82).

were 1977 and 1980 and in Italy 1978 and 1980, and during these years the percentage of the population favoring a 'valiant defense of society' reaches a maximum.

These shifts in Italy and Germany can be compared to those found in the EEC bloc as a whole to see whether the trend is due to a general change in political climate in the 1970s. In fact, the trend in the other EEC countries is different. From November 1976 to April 1981, the average of the other EEC countries (excluding Germany and Italy) shows a slight increase in

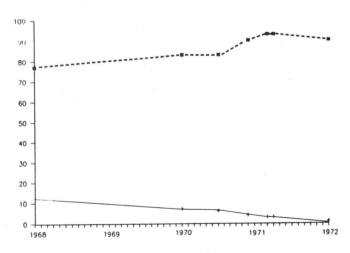

FIGURE 5
POLITICAL ATTITUDES IN URUGUAY

■ Law and Order
+ Armed Revolution

Source: *Indice Gallup de Opinion Publica* (1968–72).

the proportion of revolutionaries (six per cent to seven per cent) and no change in the proportion favoring a valiant defense against subversion (27 per cent at both dates).[23]

Support for nationalism reveals a very different pattern from that for revolution, and seems unaffected by the level of violence. The people of Northern Ireland have been asked repeatedly for their views on 'the best solution to the Northern Irish problem' or their 'long-term constitutional preference', etc. Despite the fact that the options and the form of the question varies somewhat between the different polls, the answers can be compared over time. (Only a handful or respondents refuse to answer or have no opinion.) There is no sign that attitudes to Irish unity have changed within either the Catholic or Protestant community since the troubles began. Among Catholics, a united Ireland is usually favored by a plurality but not a majority, and there is no clear trend in the level of support. (The low point in nationalist sentiment coincides with the attempt at 'power sharing' during 1973–74.) Of equal significance is the fact that Protestants show no sign of accepting the desirability of Irish unity, and continue overwhelmingly to support the British connection.

For the Basque provinces, Clark presents data from a large number of surveys on support for Basque independence. Unfortunately, as he notes, many respondents 'simply refuse to answer questions about ETA, terrorism, or politics in general'. There is no clear trend in the proportion that wanted full independence, although as the table points out the proportion seems to have declined after the granting of autonomy in 1979.[24]

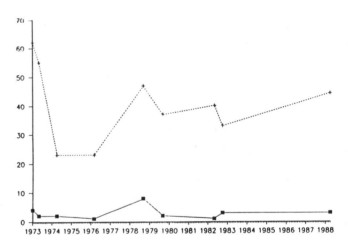

FIGURE 6
SUPPORT FOR IRISH UNITY IN NORTHERN IRELAND BY RELIGION

■ Protestant Support
+ Catholic Support

Sources: 'What Ulster Thinks', *Belfast Telegraph* (19 Feb. 1973).
'Ulster 1973', *Carrick James Market Research.*
'Seven Out of Ten Back Power Sharing', *Belfast Telegraph* (19 April 1974).
ORC *Report* (5 June 1974).
Moxon-Browne, 'The Water and the Fish'.
'What the People of Ulster Think', *New Society* (6 Sept. 1979).
'Public Reaction in N. Ireland to Aspects of the Prior Proposals', *MRBI (Irish Times)* May 1982.
Fortnight (July–Aug. 1982).
Attitudes to the Northern Ireland Assembly.
From the Shadow of a Gun (MORI, 1984).

The social characteristics of revolutionaries and nationalists are shown in Tables 6 and 7, and it is clear that the pattern corresponds to that found in the previous section. Those who have a positive image of each terrorist group are similar to those who agree with the group's goals. Nationalism is strongly linked to ethnicity, and, whatever class differences exist, can be explained by the class composition of the different ethnic groups. Thus, Northern Irish Catholics are disproportionately working class, so Irish nationalists are more likely to be working class, but ethnic Basques are disproportionately middle class so Basque nationalists are more likely to be middle class. As would be expected, those favoring Herri Batasuna or Sinn Fein are usually nationalists. The lack of a definable class base for revolutionary ideology is again apparent, although revolutionaries are disproportionately young males.

TABLE 6
PERCENTAGE SUPPORTING NATIONALISM BY ETHNICITY AND PARTY

	Basques/ Catholics	Other Ethnics	HB/PSF
Basque Provinces	45	5	61
N. Ireland	33	3	69

Sources: Richard Gunther, Giacomo Sani and Goldie Shabad *Spain After Franco* (Berkeley, CA: University of California Press, 1986), pp.325–58.
Attitudes to the Northern Ireland Assembly.

TABLE 7
CHARACTERISTICS OF NATIONALISTS AND REVOLUTIONARIES

	Sex		Age			Class		
%Supporting Revolution in:	Men	Women	Young	Middle Aged	Older	High	Middle	Low
Uruguay	3.3	2.6	5.3	2.9	1.4	2.9	2.4	3.7
Italy			14.4	7.2		9.0		9.0
Germany			3.2	1.6		2.0		2.0
% Supporting Nationalism in:								
Basque Provinces						26.0	26.0	18.0
N. Ireland	18.0	10.0	17.0	12.0	13.0	13.0	15.0	

Sources: *Indice Gallup de Opinion Publica* (1968–72).
 Ronald Inglehart, *The Silent Revolution* (Princeton, NJ: Princeton University Press, 1977).
 Commission of the European Communities, *The Young Europeans* (Brussels, 1982).
 Clark, *Basque Insurgents*, p.183.
 Attitudes to the Northern Ireland Assembly.

Public Opinion on Anti-Terrorist Policies

Faced with political violence, governments often respond with repression. People are arrested, shot by police or soldiers, stopped and questioned on the street, their houses searched, and their civil liberties and political rights restricted. Some survey data on attitudes towards anti-terrorist policies are available for all five countries, but the amount and quality vary significantly. The data for Northern Ireland, Germany and Uruguay are good, but those for Spain and Italy are fragmentary. Although precise comparisons between countries are difficult since questions are rarely asked in the same form, the data in Table 8 do suggest certain conclusions.

Usually, majorities or pluralities in all countries support getting tough with terrorists or rioters, and favor specific hard line policies. Cross-national comparisons reveal that public attitudes are more hard-line in Northern Ireland and Germany than in Uruguay, Italy or Spain. In Northern Ireland a large majority believe the Government 'should take a tougher line with the IRA', but in Uruguay those favoring a 'hard-line' approach are outnumbered three to one by those who favor a 'soft-line'. Taking a tough or hard-line approach can mean several things. Punishing terrorists is certainly popular in most countries. In Germany and Italy, there are majorities favoring more severe penalties for terrorist offenses, and in Northern Ireland, Italy and Germany for the restoration of the death penalty for terrorist murders. Uruguayans are obviously less enthusiastic about either policy. Terrorists who go on hunger strikes receive scant sympathy. More than three-quarters of those in Northern Ireland were against making any concessions to them, and in Germany, after Holger Meins starved to death, a similar proportion thought the authorities 'could not be held responsible'. Increasing the strength of the police is favored by a majority in both Northern Ireland and Germany, while a plurality is also willing to have them 'shoot to kill'. In Italy, a majority thought the police should intervene 'with force and decision' when political violence took place.

Restrictions on the legal rights of suspected terrorists are generally accepted. In Uruguay, most people approved the use of military courts, and in both Germany and Northern Ireland most thought that terrorists got a 'fair trial' despite special procedures. In Germany, measures such as supervision of defence lawyers, separating suspects and lawyers by glass panels, etc. were approved by overwhelming margins.

Attitudes towards preventive detention and internment show a reversal of the normal cross-national pattern. In Germany a proposal that terrorists who had served their sentence could be held in police custody 'when it

TABLE 8
SUPPORT FOR ANTI-TERRORIST POLICIES BY COUNTRY AND TYPE OF POLICY

	N. Ireland	Uruguay	Germany	Spain	Italy
PERCENTAGE SUPPORTING:					
Tougher/hardline policies in general	81	22	-	48	-
More severe penalities	-	43	85	-	87
Death penalty	53	21	61	43	54
Strengthening police	73	-	63	-	65
Shoot to kill policy	43	-	49	-	-
Trial procedures	53	48	60	-	-
Preventive detention/ internment	37	48	57	-	-
Hardline with hungerstrikers	77	-	78	-	-
Giving up civil liberties in interest of security	-	50	64	-	-
Censorship	-	38	77	-	-
ID checks	-	70	60	-	-
House searches	-	19	50	-	-
Positive rating of security forces	86	45	22	40	31

Sources: 'Public Attitudes to Internment', *Fortnight* (6 Sept. 1974).
 Moxon-Browne, 'Water and the Fish'.
 'What the People Think about Supergrasses', *Fortnight* (Nov. 1984).
 'Opinion Poll', *BBC Spotlight* (May 1985).
 Belfast Telegraph, 6 Feb. 1985.
 John Finn, 'Public Support for Emergency Legislation in Northern Ireland: A Preliminary Analysis', *Terrorism*, Vol. 10 (1987).
 Indice Gallup de Opinion Publica (1968–81).
 Index to International Public Opinion (1979–81).
 Allensbacher Jahrbuch (1968–81).
 Revista Espanola de Investigaciones Sociologicas (April/June 1978).
 'Imagen Publica de la Policia', *Revista Espanola de Investigaciones Sociologicas* (April/June 1982).
 Cambio 16 (7 Jan. 1979).
 L'Espresso (10 Jan. 1982).
 Piergiorgio Corbetta, 'Perche piu indulgenza per i terroristi?' *Cattaneo*, Vol. 3 (June 1983).
 Fabris, *Il comportamento politico degli italiani*, pp.225–6.

appears that they will commit other terrorist acts' was strongly supported and near majorities in Uruguay thought detention 'justified and well-handled'. However, those agreeing with internment in Northern Ireland, never constituted more than a substantial minority.

Throughout the period, the great majority of Germans declared themselves willing to give up 'some of their personal freedom in order to fight crime and terrorism', and in Uruguay a majority supported 'the suspension of individual guarantees' (that is, civil rights guaranteed by the constitution.) On specific issues, the Germans were willing to submit to identity checks and house searches by police, and to news blackouts for security reasons. On the other hand, Uruguayans, although conceding the necessity of identity checks, did not believe that censorship or house searches were justified.

There were noticeable differences between countries in how the public rated the conduct and competence of the security forces. By large majorities, both army and police were seen to be 'doing their job well' in Northern Ireland. In Uruguay throughout the period, almost half of those surveyed said their conduct was either good or very good. However, most Italians saw police measures to combat terrorism as both 'inefficient and insufficient', and only 31 per cent saw them as efficient or adequate. The German police were judged even less positively with only 22 per cent saying they 'took good care of security'. In Spain, public perceptions of the police were mixed. A majority thought they 'treated the public correctly' and 'protected and defended them'. However, almost half said they felt fear when coming into contact with the police, and only a minority thought the police had improved with democracy, had adapted to political change, or respected individual rights and liberties.

7. TACTICS, STRATEGIES, AND TARGETING

One might anticipate that support for tough policies would be greatest in those countries where terrorism poses the greatest threat, but this is not the case. German public opinion is as hardline as that of Northern Ireland, while Spaniards and Italians are no more hardline than Uruguayans. Historical factors may explain these cross national differences.[25]

An alternative view, that harsh security measures will alienate the public, is widely held. In the case of Uruguay, Moss claims that 'emergency measures alienated public opinion'.[26] Porzecanski says that the police 'became well known among the population for extensive and routine use of torture, as well as for heavy-handed citywide search operations'. These massive searches 'conducted clumsily at all hours of the night … created great resentment among Montevideo's population'.[27] Labrousse describes how 'the population was incensed by the continual police controls'.[28] In the case of Northern Ireland, Moxon-Browne and Finn argue that harsh measures have 'alienated' public opinion and 'eroded' public confidence.[29] This view can be tested by examining differences in attitudes to security policies between groups, and also by examining changes over time.

Whether or not harsh security measures alienate the public seems to depend upon how selectively they are applied. In Northern Ireland, those arrested, interned, or shot by the security forces have been predominantly and disproportionately Catholic. Within Catholic areas, routine identity checks and house searches affect all the inhabitants, regardless of their politics or involvement in political violence. A similar situation obtains in Spain where the Basque provinces have experienced the full rigors of Spanish counter-insurgency policies. The result is widespread alienation among Catholics and Basques, and a polarization of attitudes towards security policy between Catholics and Protestants, Basques and non-Basques.

In Italy and Germany, security measures affect the general public only temporarily and during clearly defined crises, such as the Moro and Schleyer kidnappings. At other times 'since the terrorists proclaim themselves to be revolutionary leftists, radical left wing groups are naturally suspect and become targets of intensive investigation and sometimes harassment by the security forces'.[3] In Uruguay from mid-1970 onwards, mass searches and roadblocks affected the public at large, but most of those arrested and brutally interrogated were members of the radical left party, Frente Amplio. Table 9 compares attitudes towards security policy between those groups who were the targets of repression and the rest of the population. Without being overly cynical, one would conclude that those unaffected by government repression support it, while those who experience repression resent it. Indeed, there are indications that if the categories could be fine-tuned, the polarization would be even greater. Within the Basque provinces, for example, Basque nationalists are most likely to suffer detention and arrest, and are also the most hostile to hardline policies.[31]

Do public attitudes become more negative when repression continues over a long period, or when it is at a maximum? Sufficient data are available for Uruguay and Northern Ireland to explore this question. In Uruguay, four questions concerning security were asked repeatedly: should emergency measures remain in effect, should individual guarantees be suspended, did the public favor a hard-line towards terrorism, and how was the conduct of the security forces rated?

Security force activity intensified in mid-1970 and extensive house searches were conducted in Fall 1970 and Spring 1971. There was a significant increase in the level of repression in April 1972, when a state of 'Internal War' was declared, and thousands were arrested. However, a comparison of attitudes towards security shows no sign that the public was alienated by the intensification of security activity.

In Northern Ireland, although several surveys have asked about security policies, they have not used the same questions. It is possible, nevertheless, to consider the differences between Catholics and Protestants in their support for security policies as a crude measure of Catholic alienation. Taking into account the number of civilians shot by the security forces, the number interned, and the number of houses searched, it appears that repression reached a peak during 1971–76, then declined erratically. However, the degree of Catholic alienation seems to be unrelated to the level of repression, and shows no obvious trend.[32]

Conclusion

The relationship between terrorism and public opinion is not a simple one. Terrorism seems as much a consequence of public opinion as it is a cause of changes in public opinion. Since there are important differences between nationalist and revolutionary terrorism, they will be discussed separately.

Nationalist terrorism emerges where there is a strong, historically-derived sense of nationalism linked to ethnicity. Nationalist ideology legitimates terrorist action and generates a positive image of the insurgents as long as the campaign follows proper tactics and does not lead to the killing of fellow ethnics. Support for militant nationalism does not decrease because of terrorist atrocities against the ethnic enemy.[33]

As a strategy for breaking the will of the occupying force, nationalist terrorism has had mixed results. The IRA's campaign has been greatly successful in affecting public opinion in Great Britain. Since 1974, the proportion favoring troop withdrawal has remained stable, with a clear

TABLE 10
CHANGING ATTITUDES TO SECURITY MEASURES IN URUGUAY (%)

Table 10: Changing Attitudes to Security Measures in Uruguay (%)	Mild Repression (1968–Jun 1970)	Increasing Repression (Jul 1970–Mar 1972)	Intense Repression (Apr 1972–Oct 1972)
Favor Emergency measures	44	41	56
Favor Hardline		24	19
Approve Suspension of Guarantees		46	56
Conduct of security forces good	44	51	50

Source: Indice Gallup de Opinion Publica (1968–72).

majority favoring withdrawal and a plurality favoring a united Ireland.[34] The metropolitan Spaniards have been far more resistant and the most recent poll reveals that only 14 per cent favor giving in to terrorist demands or negotiating with the terrorists.[35]

Within the Basque provinces and within Northern Ireland, terrorism has reflected and exacerbated ethnic polarization. The different ethnic groups not only disagree about nationalism, but also about who is to blame for violence and what should be done about the situation.

Revolutionary terrorists usually start off with a much lower degree of popular sympathy than nationalists. Most people find their goals incomprehensible, and dismiss them as common criminals. Revolutionary terrorism does not increase revolutionary sentiments, either by 'propaganda of the deed' or by provoking repression. The revolutionaries are unable to broaden the basis of their support, which remains restricted to a small sector of the educated youth. Given their isolation, it is possible for the authorities to repress terrorist sympathizers, without alienating the public at large. The most obvious political consequence of revolutionary terrorism is a law and order backlash, which appears to benefit the conservative parties.

Attitudes towards political violence, whether revolutionary or nationalist, depend primarily upon structural-historical features, and are, therefore, little affected by either terrorist actions or by government policies. Those who advocate terrorism as a means of generating revolutionary consciousness are clearly following a false strategy, but those

TABLE 9
POLARIZATION OF ATTITUDES TOWARDS SECURITY POLICIES

% (Supporting Hardline Policies)

	Affected Group	Rest of Population
N. Ireland (Catholics)	27	73
Spain (Basque Provinces)	30	67
Italy (Proletarian Democrats)	11	66
Uruguay (Frente Amplio)	19	60

Sources: Same as Table 8. (Average of all polls which give breakdowns by relevant variables).

who assume that terrorist sympathizers will be alienated by atrocities are equally deluded.

As noted, the data are fragmentary and it is hoped that additional material can be collected to fill in the lacunae, and to provide information on other terrorist groups in other countries. Whether this would lead us to modify our conclusions is uncertain. Israeli–Palestinian attitudes for example, seem very similar to those found in the nationalist conflicts in Spain and Northern Ireland.[36] On the other hand, our interpretation does not seem to be compatible with those cases where insurgencies were successful (for example, the Irish Rebellion of 1916–21, Algeria, Irgun in Palestine, Castro in Cuba), and where participants and observers argue that public attitudes did change dramatically as a result of terrorism and government repression.[37] Is the impact of terrorism on public opinion different between successful and unsuccessful campaigns? I trust that this attempt at a comparative analysis of public attitudes to terrorism will lead future studies to standardize their questions, so that cross-national comparisons can be made, and to replicate past questions, so as to allow an examination of changes over time.

NOTES

The author would like to thank the following organizations and individuals for providing me with survey data: Allensbach; Institut für Demoskopie, Zentral Archiv für Sozialforschung, Universitat zu Koln; Instituto di studi e richerche Carlo Cattaneo; Belfast Telegraph; Irish Times; BBC Northern Ireland; Professor Robert Clark, George Mason University; Professor Richard Rose, University of Strathclyde; Professor Juan Linz, Yale University; Professor Edward Moxon-Browne, Queens University of Belfast. The author is also grateful to the University of Maryland Baltimore County for purchasing the polls of Gallup Uruguay. The research for this article was partially funded by the United States Institute of Peace. The opinions, findings, and conclusions are those of the author and do not necessarily reflect the views of the United States Institute of Peace.

1. Alex Schmid and Janny de Graaf, Violence as Communication (Beverly Hills, CA: Sage, 1982), pp. 215–66.
2. David C. Rapoport, 'Fear and Trembling: Terrorism in Three Religious Traditions', American Political Science Review, 78, #3 (Sept. 1984), p. 665.
3. Schmid and de Graaf, pp. 13–14. Robert Moss, Urban Guerrillas (London: Temple Smith, 1972), p. 218. David C. Rapoport, 'The Politics of Atrocity', in Yonah Alexander and Seymour Finger (eds.), Terrorism: Interdisciplinary Perspectives (New York: John Jay Press, 1977), pp. 47–51.
4. The Brazilian revolutionary, Carlos Marighella, advocated this strategy in 'Mini Manual of the Urban Guerrilla', Tri-Continental, Vol. 6, (June 1969).
5. Robert Clark, The Basque Insurgents: ETA 1951–80 (Madison, WI: University of Wisconsin Press, 1984), pp. 40–41.
6. For a discussion of the differences between nationalist and revolutionary terrorist campaigns, and the government policies used against them see Christopher Hewitt, The Effectiveness of Anti-Terrorist Policies (Lanham, MD: University Press of America, 1986).
7. Moss, pp. 247–8.
8. Richard Clutterbuck, Kidnap and Ransom (London: Faber, 1978), p. 38.
9. Moss, p. 223.
10. Richard Clutterbuck, Protest and the Urban Guerrilla (New York: Abelard Schuman, 1973), p. 230; Anthony Burton, Urban Terrorism (New York: Free Press, 1976), pp. 95–102; Stephen Goode, Guerilla Warfare and Terrorism (New York: Franklin Watts, 1977), p. 80; Bard O'Neill, Insurgency in the Modern World (Boulder, CO: Westview Press, 1980), p. 178.
11. In the tables following, when more than one survey is cited, a single statistic represents an average.
12. A statewide survey by J. Jimenez Blanco, La Conciencia Regional En Espana (Madrid: Editorial Cuadernos, 1977), on regional consciousness found that Barcelona and the Basque country expressed the most acute grievances over administrative centralization, were most likely to support independence, and were the most likely to vote for separatist parties.
13. On the basis of names, only 30 out of 403 victims of terrorism in the Basque provinces appear to have been ethnic Basques.
14. In the five years before the survey (1978–82), 61 Catholics and 199 Protestants, were victims of terrorism. Thus, Protestants, who make up 63 per cent of the population, suffered 77 per cent of the deaths.
15. Claude Fly, an American agricultural expert, was kidnapped in 1970 and Geoffrey Jackson, the British consul, in 1971.
16. See Clutterbuck, Protest, pp. 230, 239.
17. Moxon-Browne provides a good discussion of the historical factors which explain Catholic support for the IRA. 'The Water and the Fish: Public Opinion and the Provisional IRA in Northern Ireland', Terrorism, Vol. 5 (1981), 41–72.
18. Legitimate military or political targets constitute approximately 80 per cent of ETA's victims, and 65 per cent of the IRA's victims. See Hewitt, Effectiveness of Anti-Terrorist Policies, p. 29.
19. The attitude of the Red Brigades to the PCI (Communist Party of Italy) was ambivalent. They saw the party leadership as having abandoned the goal of revolution, but hoped to win over the rank and file. Yet, among PCI supporters, 83 per cent were in 'total disagreement' with the actions of the extreme left (L'Espresso, 30 Oct. 1977).
20. Sympathy for the Baader–Meinhof gang was concentrated among students, but even in this group only 18 per cent agreed that 'terrorists are freedom fighters.' See Yonah Alexander and John Gleason (eds.), Behavioral and Quantitative Perspectives on Terrorism (New York: Pergamon, 1981), pp. 266–7.
21. Juliet Lodge, Terrorism: A Challenge to the State (New York: St. Martin's Press, 1981), pp. 24–5.
22. Questions on satisfaction with the way that 'democracy is working in my country' show consistently high levels of satisfaction in Germany and consistently low levels in Italy. In 1978, Germans had the highest satisfaction of all EEC countries and Italians the lowest. Survey Research Consultants International, Index to International Public Opinion 1978–79 (Westport, CT: Greenwood Press, 1980), p. 287.
23. Index to International Public Opinion 1981–2, p. 582.
24. Clark, pp. 168–84.
25. The simplest explanation may be that Germans support law and order because they fear the emergence of a Weimar-type situation in which a weak government allowed extremist violence to flourish, while Spaniards fear a resurgence of Francoist repression.
26. Moss, p. 217.
27. Arturo Porzecanski, Uruguay's Tupamaros (New York: Praeger, 1973), pp. 55–6.
28. Alain Labrousse, The Tupamaros (Harmondsworth: Penguin, 1973), p. 130.
29. E. Moxon-Browne, 'Alienation: the Case of the Catholics in Northern Ireland', Journal of Political Science, Vol. 14, (Spring 1986), pp. 74–89. John Finn, 'Public Support for Emergency Legislation in Northern Ireland: A Preliminary Analysis', Terrorism, Vol. 10, No. 2 (1987), pp. 113–124. 30. Andrew Mack, 'The Utility of Terrorism', Australian and New Zealand Journal of Criminology, Vol. 14, (Dec. 1981), 218.
31. See Richard Gunther, Giacomo Sani and Goldie Shabad, Spain after Franco (Berkeley, CA: University of California Press, 1986), p. 362. Their study found that nationally 88 per cent favored moderate-to-hard antiterrorist policies, but this position was held by only 43 per cent of the Basques and only 16 per cent of those supporting HB and EE. In Italy, the young and the educated are less likely to support the death penalty for terrorists. Piergiorgio Corbetta, 'Perche piu indulgenza per i terroristi', Cattaneo, Vol. 3, (June 1983), 21–35.
32. As measured in this fashion, Catholic alienation averaged 87 per cent in 1974, 83 per cent in 1982, and 73 per cent in the most recent 1985 survey.
33. A 1984 poll found 48 per cent of Catholics agreeing that the IRA are patriots and idealists (virtually the same as in Moxon-Browne's 1978 survey; see From the Shadow of the Gun, London: MORI, 1984). Even the bombing of a Remembrance Day memorial ceremony at Enniskillen produced only a five per cent decline in those saying they sympathized with the IRA. (Fortnight, April 1988). Within the Basque provinces, surveys carried out during the 1978–80 period show no trend, and those seeing ETA as 'patriots or idealists' constituted 48 per cent in 1978, 41 per cent in 1979, and 50 per cent in 1980. (Linz, Conflicto en Euskadi).
34. From 1974–1977 those favoring troop withdrawal averaged 57 per cent, and from 1978–81 those wanting to withdraw the troops immediately or within five years also averaged 57 per cent. Richard Rose, Ian McAlister and Peter Mair, Is there a Concurring Majority about Northern Ireland? (Glasgow: Centre for the Study of Public Policy, University of Strathclyde, 1978). For attitudes subsequent to 1977, see Index to International Public Opinion.
35. See Gunther, Sani and Shabad, p. 362. Earlier polls by Linz in 1978 and 1979 show a decline in those supporting negotiation or acceptance of terrorist demands from 24 per cent to 17 per cent. Leon Gordenker (ed.), Resolving Nationality Conflicts: The Role of Public Opinion Research (New York: Praeger, 1980), p. 48.
36. Palestinian support for anti-Israeli terrorism is certainly comparable to Catholic support for the IRA, or Basque support for ETA. A 1986 poll in the occupied territories found that 78 per cent believed violence to be justified. Meron Benvenisti, West Bank Data Base Project: 1987 Report (Jerusalem Post, 1987), pp. 45–6. See also Mohammed Shadid and Rick Seltzer, 'Political Attitudes of Palestinians in the West Bank and Gaza Strip', Middle East Journal (Winter 1988), 16–32.
37. Begin, for example, claims that Irgun attacks against the British produced an upsurge of support among the Jewish population. The Revolt (New York: Nash Publishing, 1977), pp. 193–6.

Countering Terrorism

The articles in this section focus on counterterrorist measures ranging from legalistic (and, by inference, moralistic) responses to retaliation by means of force. Some approaches are at the unilateral end of the response continuum, and others at the multilateral (or collaborative) end. Suggestions or discussions of combinations and mixed approaches abound in the articles as well. It is important to remember that countering terrorism is at least as complicated and certainly more difficult to apply than terrorism itself. After all, terrorists do not really worry much about interfering with the sovereignty of states. Governments are bound by international law to consider one another's sovereignty, however. Moreover, as we now know, terrorism is not a monolith. Different and flexible strategies are required to successfully thwart terrorism.

Implicit in countering terrorism is the admonition that international terrorism cannot fully or finally be stopped unless there is international cooperation against it. But how can this be done? This unit's essays consider possibilities that include dealing firmly with states that are directly involved in terrorism, supporting the advocacy of human rights, the exchange of intelligence between governments, and exploring all reasonable possibilities to anticipate and discourage terrorist acts.

"10 Steps Against Terror" suggests a counterterrorism strategy for the 1990s from a former CIA director. "Terrorism and World Order" depicts what we were up against in the 1980s, and it will prepare students of terrorism for what the 1990s may offer.

While acknowledging the limitations of economic models, the authors of "Economic Analysis Can Help Fight International Terrorism" do raise some interesting possibilities, including the one of whether terrorists behave in a rational (and therefore somewhat predictable) fashion.

The question of whether democratic governments avoid disconcerting facts on those occasions when they require assistance from governments normally labeled as terrorist is discussed in "Closing Our Eyes." The possibilities are far from pleasant and do not add to the viability of counterterrorism.

Articles 51–54 provides insights about several components of counterterrorism. These include the avenues of exerting pressure on governments to live up to their commitments to human rights, collecting intelligence and using it to maximum benefit, the place, conditions, and timing of negotiation with terrorists, and overall responses to terrorist acts.

Looking Ahead: Challenge Questions

What are the basic problems a government encounters in trying to direct its efforts against a terrorist group?

What are the hindrances in an international law approach to countering terrorism?

What are the political, legal, and ethical constraints on American use of military force against terrorists?

Unit 8

10 STEPS AGAINST TERROR

From assassinations to doing deals—the admiral who headed the CIA tells what works, what doesn't, and what new threats may come in the battle with terrorists.

Admiral Stansfield Turner

Admiral Stansfield Turner, US Navy (ret.), former Director of Central Intelligence, is the author of "Secrecy and Democracy" (1985).

I N THE FALL OF LAST YEAR I CALLED ON the chairman of the KGB, Vladimir A. Kryuchkov, in Moscow.

Chairman Kryuchkov told me that the KGB had made many mistakes in its past, but that he was intent on operating it in a manner compatible with a democracy. When I asked whether there were any prospects for cooperation between the KGB and the CIA against terrorists, he responded that the Soviet Union was willing to go to great lengths to cooperate with the US. He was interested not only in exchanging intelligence but in undertaking joint operations against terrorism.

While Chairman Kryuchkov made no acknowledgment of any Soviet involvement with terrorists, he was forthright in saying that the reason he wanted to work with the US was that terrorism has become a serious problem inside the Soviet Union. He noted that today's terrorists are well organized, professional, and adept at new technologies. He was worried about the possibility of nuclear terrorism.

I believe he was saying the Soviets realize that, if they hope to control domestic terrorism, they cannot ignore terrorism abroad. For instance, in December 1988 Soviet terrorists, using 30 schoolchildren as hostages, commandeered an Aeroflot aircraft and had themselves flown to Israel. With the United States facilitating communications, the Israelis disarmed and arrested the hijackers when they arrived in Tel Aviv. The price for continued assistance of this sort will be reciprocity and cooperation.

Kryuchkov also suggested that the Soviet Union and the United States promote a consensus within the United Nations on standard punishments for terrorism. I pointed out that the UN had never been able to agree on a definition of terrorism and suggested that perhaps at least our two countries could do that, now that we no longer were competing in the third world. He agreed.

Meanwhile, the potential for terrorism to increase is there, but terrorists are not invincible; the bygone Zealots, Assassins, and others were suppressed in time.

Today many countervailing strengths come from the very fact that the United States and more and more other countries have democratic systems. But this means that governments need public understanding of the options for curtailing terror—and the wisdom to avoid actions that might undermine the democratic process they are defending.

I have searched US history for common threads, which, it turns out, go all the way back to the founding of American government. I was not surprised to find that much of the common wisdom about dealing with terrorism does not accord with what presidents have actually done.

There are 10 options that I call pro-legal or pro-active. Presidents and public must understand the strengths and the pitfalls of each one. My views on these are:

1. Assassinations are neither an appropriate nor an effective counterterrorist tactic.

The lure of assassination is that it seems surgical and final. In reality, it is neither. If US authorities attempted to kill a foreign leader, they would logically turn to foreigners to do the deed or to help their own people get away safely; thus the Americans would lose control. Because an assassination would be a major foreign policy choice, it would require an order by the president, who would then be embarked on a game of dirty tricks in which America's opponents are likely to be far more ruthless and persistent than Washington.

Assassination is morally repugnant to the majority of Americans. It is always dangerous to counter terrorism with terrorism. A nation can lose what it is defending in the process of defending it.

Still, most US administrations, when frustrated beyond measure by a Khomeini in Iran or a Qaddafi in Libya, will be tempted to consider assassination. I believe the US needs a law, not just the present presidential executive order, prohibiting assassination. The rationalization that the deliberate killing of an individual can be classed as "justifiable homicide," not assassination, would be more difficult to maintain against a law than against an executive order.

I believe, though, that such a law should be limited to peacetime. Targeting specific leaders in wartime, when the country has determined openly that widespread killing is justified, is quite different from a president's making a secret political decision to take someone's life.

2. Punitive military attacks are a remedy to be used, but sparingly.

It is futile, even irresponsible, to advocate consistent use of force against terrorists. The record shows the American people will not accept it. For instance, Ronald Reagan unleashed only one attack—the one against Libya in 1986—despite repeated provocations.

A principal inhibition on Reagan was the reluctance to take human life outside the due process of law or war. Even the advocates of punitive force tacitly acknowledge concern about the killing of innocents when they talk of employing "surgical attacks." But we know how low is the probability of punitive attacks being surgical. In Libya, though the US employed a particular aircraft because of its accurate bombing system, some bombs hit the French Embassy.

Perhaps the best argument for exercising the punitive option is that doing so reinforces all other options. Allies, for instance, are more likely to be cooperative if they believe a country really will turn to the use of force. Terrorists are more likely to come to terms for the same reason.

In short, between "never" and "always" there is some ground for the occasional use of punitive force.

3. Judicious covert actions should be undertaken, even

though the probability of success is low.

There are a number of covert techniques that can be effective against terrorists, such as infiltrating an organization and making its plans go awry; feeding disinformation to groups to mislead them and perhaps cause them to terrorize one another; and toppling governments that sponsor or provide support to terrorists. Maneuvers like these present formidable challenges: Jimmy Carter's efforts to change the complexion of Iran's Khomeini government never made headway; Reagan's attempt to use arms to advance the position of moderates in that same government ended in a giant con game.

We must take into account that these actions come under even less scrutiny than other secret government operations. Who, for instance, will make the judgment that the people Washington supports to overthrow a government will do so within Washington's bounds? Who will determine the cost if Washington's disinformation feeds back into America's own media? Washington should not ignore covert actions just because there are such risks, but it must weigh the prospects for success against the threat to American values.

4. Rescue operations must be readied, but will continue to be highly risky for the United States.

A government that values its citizens will try to maintain a capability for rescuing them if they are taken hostage. And a rescue operation will be tempting because, if it is successful, it will solve the problem instantly.

But rescue operations carry high risks. Many former hostages say they were afraid of being killed during a rescue attempt, either deliberately by their captors or accidentally by the rescue forces.

Because such operations are complex and often demand feats approaching the heroic, they can fail through (1) poor execution, as with the 1975 US assault on Koh Tang Island (to search for the crew of the hijacked merchant ship Mayaguez) and the 1980 Desert One operation (to rescue hostages in Iran); or (2) bad timing, as with TWA 847 that had been hijacked to Beirut in 1985 and the ship Achille Lauro that was hijacked in the Mediterranean in the same year.

Maintaining competent rescue forces will always be difficult for the US military, because it is expected to have such a wide range of capabilities. At one end it must deter thermonuclear war, and at the other outwit a handful of 20-year-olds who have seized an airliner. Presidents and secretaries of defense would do well to make periodic inquiries about the readiness of rescue forces and to order unannounced tests of them, as a modest amount of such high-level attention to low-level operations will advance the day of readiness.

5. Improved intelligence, especially by human means, is always desirable but seldom achievable.

There is a danger that overemphasis on improving human intelligence as an antidote to terrorism could lead to the neglect of technical intelligence systems. Satellite photos revealed who was probably behind the third terrorist bombing in Beirut. National Security Agency electronic intercepts produced the clinching evidence about the terrorist bombing in Berlin that sent US bombers over Libya in 1986.

When President Bush's Commission on Aviation Security and Terrorism recommended more attention to human intelligence, it called intelligence the "first line of defense." This was misleading. The number of times US intelligence has given operationally useful warning of impending acts of international terrorism is so low that it can hardly be termed a line of defense. At most it is a soldier in the battle.

That is not to say Washington should not sustain a major intelligence effort against terrorism, but if a president counts too heavily on it, he will be disappointed and may ignore important alternatives. Washington must also be careful that agencies, in their zeal to track down terrorists, do not intrude on the privacy of Americans except as provided by law.

6. Restraint of the media could be helpful, but very modest self-restraint is the most to be expected.

Publicity for their cause is usually one objective of terrorists. Almost any media coverage plays into their hands. There are also situations in which counterterrorist efforts are hurt by reporting, as when the hijackers of TWA 847 were tipped off that Delta Force was on the way to the Mediterranean; or when too many details are printed about hostages.

But erring on the side of the openness that keeps government accountable is preferable to governmental control of sources of information. The media face difficult decisions. Would publication of the information harm the national interest? Or is an administration attempting to bury a political embarrassment or to use secrecy to do something the public might reject?

Administrations that appreciate the media's dilemma will think carefully before attempting to manipulate them. (It is not only terrorists who attempt manipulation of the media.) In building credibility and understanding about terrorism, administrations would do well to conduct simulations of terrorist incidents with media participation. Each side could learn to appreciate the other's considerations.

7. Economic sanctions should be used against state sponsors of terrorism, even though they will be effective only after a considerable time, if at all.

Unilateral economic sanctions can have only limited effect. Someone else will usually fill whatever gap the US creates and take the business away from Americans besides. The Congress in 1985 strengthened the hand of presidents by authorizing them to bar imports from or aid to countries that harbor or otherwise support international terrorism. Such measures are useful tools.

Americans tend to believe there must be something they can do to solve any problem, and just forcing other nations to decide whether to honor or reject US requests for sanctions can help. These countries must evaluate what they believe to be their responsibilities; over time, their assessment can help make them more reliable.

8. Defensive security is unlikely to receive sufficient attention or money.

Recent history in Beirut shows how difficult it is to persuade Americans to take security overseas seriously. Within 17 months Americans were struck by three bombings, largely because of lack of physical preparedness. Once the Congress and the administration became committed to the construction of better physical defense in Beirut and elsewhere, the bombers lost interest.

In 1985, in the wake of TWA 847, Congress passed the Foreign Airport Security Act, directing the secretary of transportation to assess periodically the security of 247 foreign airports. President Bush's Commission on Aviation Security and Terrorism noted, though, that "severe FAA [Federal Aviation Administration] personnel shortages generally limit the depth of these assessments to interviews and observations....Inspectors do not substantively test the operational effectiveness of security procedures." A modest increase in resources would allow for rigorous inspections and make useful a provision of the 1985 act that permits the suspension of air services to any airport where conditions threaten the security of aircraft, crews, or passengers.

9. Deals are an option that Washington must be ready to employ.

The platitude that no one should ever make deals with terrorists because doing so inevitably leads to more terrorism is factually incorrect. We have seen deals that did not lead to a repetition of events; for example, Lyndon Johnson's gaining release of the crew of the USS Pueblo in 1968 by agreeing to a false confession when the North Korean captors demanded a confession that the ship had intruded into their waters on a spying mission. Except for Gerald Ford, every president since Johnson has been involved in at least one deal.

In the wake of the political explosion that followed the exposure of Reagan's arms-for-hostages deals with Iran, politicians have become leery of any talk of deals. The reality is that presidents will make them, so Americans had better learn to differentiate between a deal that is acceptable and one that is not.

And presidents, instead of stating categorically that they will never cut a deal with terrorists, should stimulate discussion of all possible alternatives. Then, if a deal provides clear advantages for the United States, they would be in a better position to accept it without appearing weak.

10. Legal recourse is the option most compatible with American societal values.

Legal recourse against terrorists falls into two categories: apprehending terrorists, and isolating states that support terrorism. Apprehending the terrorists themselves serves as a warning to would-be terrorists that they are likely to be caught. Despite the examples of suicide drivers, most terrorists prefer not to be killed or jailed.

Isolating a nation by means of political condemnation can be telling over the long run, though it seldom has an immediate impact. For instance, in October 1980, when the Iranian prime minister visited the United Nations to seek that body's denunciation of Iraq's invasion of his country, he found a total lack of sympathy, because for 11 months Washington had been reminding the world that Iran was holding US diplomats hostage. That must have given impetus to the pragmatists in Iran who wanted to put the hostage issue behind them.

Legal means are by far the preferable way of dealing with terrorism. They do least violence to democratic values, even if some efforts to arrest suspected terrorists violate legal principles.

When Americans forced down the aircraft carrying away the hijackers of the Achille Lauro, they broke international law against air piracy. In my view that was reasonable, as the rights of the culprits would have been only slightly abused had they been innocent.

The secret of dealing with terrorism lies in selecting the option or mixture of options, both pro-legal and pro-active, that will have the greatest impact on the terrorists while minimizing the intrusions into societal values.

My appraisal of the effectiveness and the risks associated with each of the ten options will certainly not be shared by everyone. No individual's judgment is necessarily right and another's wrong; it depends on one's view of the seriousness of the threat.

It is all too easy to be misled by an immediate threat. Jimmy Carter's fear for the American hostages in Tehran led to unwarranted optimism about the rescue mission. Ronald Reagan's concern over the US hostages in Beirut led to a flouting of the Constitution. In each instance, the responses of the president damaged America's national interest. Noel Koch, a former Pentagon official involved with countering terrorism, stated, "Most of the damage to US interests done by terrorism has been self-inflicted."

But there may be times when Americans choose to pay a high price. They might do so in response to two forms of terrorism they have not had to face: widespread terrorism at home, as the West Germans and the Italians experienced in the 1970s and 1980s with the Baader-Meinhof gang and the Red Brigades, and nuclear terrorism.

Fortunately, international terrorists have hardly ventured onto US soil—because of the excellence of the FBI and the law enforcement system, and because they found it easier to attack Americans abroad. Terrorists may move to the US out of desperation if America and its allies close in on them. Washington would then have to rely on more difficult measures. One would be stringent inspections at international airports and other points of entry, with all the inconvenience that involves for Americans who travel abroad. Another would be intrusion into citizens' private lives by law enforcement officials ferreting out terrorists who had slipped by. Much the same would be the case with nuclear terrorism.

However, thus far, terrorist groups have not shown great interest in acquiring nuclear weapons or materials. Governments must be concerned, though, with countries that support terrorism, like Libya and Iraq, and also aspire to nuclear capabilities. Again, tightening entry inspections at airports, ports, and border crossings would be one recourse. Military defenses against delivery by aircraft or missiles would be another.

The major effort, though, should be directed toward preventing the acquisition of nuclear capabilities by such nations. This will require worldwide, highly intrusive controls and inspection procedures, something possible only with the wholehearted support of all responsible nations, large and small.

That returns us to the importance of Washington's working for heightened international cooperation against all forms of terrorism.

Americans should set their sights high in the hope that the burden of terrorism they are currently carrying will be a blessing in disguise by helping usher in a new era of world cooperation that will reach well beyond the suppression of terrorism itself.

TERRORISM AND WORLD ORDER

GEORGE A. LOPEZ

George A. Lopez is Associate Professor of Political Science and convenor of the Peace and Global Studies Program for Earlham College. He has written on political economy, terrorism and conflict resolution, having articles in CHOICE, Peace and Change, *and* Terrorism: An International Journal. *With Michael Stohl he is contributor and co-editor of* The State As Terrorists: The Dynamics of Governmental Violence and Repression. *(Greenwood Press, 1983)*

Introduction

The period 1968-1978 witnessed a number of fundamental changes in world politics. The U.S. involvement in a protracted Asian war ended and the Soviet-American Cold War moved to detente. Power took on new meaning as a group of militarily weak states in the Middle East brought the mighty industrial West to its knees by turning down the petroleum faucet.

It was also a time of large scale violence. In particular, it was a decade of terror, as self-styled revolutionaries adopted a new set of tactics, victims, and arenas for making war on governments. The names and acts of the Palestine Liberation Organization, the Basques, South Moluccans, Tupamaros, and Liberation Front of Quebec comprised weekly news.

Similarly, the period witnessed a dramatic increase in the use of government terror against citizens. Death squads operated freely in Brazil and Argentina. The government of West Pakistan undertook the massive extermination of over one million West Bengalis (Bangladeshis), Idi Amin of Uganda used massacres as standard policy, and Chile's General Pinochet practiced "disappearances" and torture of political foes.

With this contradictory cluster of events, it is no surprise that scholars, policy-makers and citizens have

Portions of this paper were delivered under the titles, "Terrorism & Alternative Worldviews" and "Terrorism & World Order: A Policy Approach," at the 1982 and 1983 meetings of the International Studies Association respectively. The author would like to thank Michael Stohl for his numerous substantive comments on both earlier essays and Pat Mische for her substantive and editorial assistance in this final version.

been examining new theories and perspectives for helping us understand the complex world in which we live. Recently, our thinking about international relations has been challenged by a new and distinct paradigm, self-proclaimed the world order approach. While a number of thorough studies (e.g., Mische and Mische, 1977, Falk, 1975; Mendlovitz, 1975), of the underlying assumptions, goals and methods of the approach have appeared and world order theorists are beginning to focus more directly on particular policy issues (e.g., Christensen, 1979, Galtung, 1980; and, Mazrui, 1980), no direct application of world order approaches has been undertaken for the issue of terrorism in global affairs. This paper is an analysis of terrorism in light of the goals, methods and values prevalent in world order approaches to global affairs. The paper presents three general arguments:

•that the study of terrorism has been dominated by two general perspectives on the nature of the problem called terrorism and that this has led to particular policies which have proven inadequate in dealing with the full contours of the global problem of terrorism;

•that the substantive and methodological orientations of the world order approach provide a third and richer perspective on the problem of terrorism, in large part because they focus on state, as well as insurgent, terrorism; and,

•that world order thinking produces a set of strategies, institutions and normative goals which speak directly to the underlying causes rather than merely the symptoms of global terrorism.

Dealing With Terrorism: The Legacy of the Dominant Views

In a recent study Lopez (1982) has demonstrated that

From *Whole Earth Papers*, No. 18, 1983, pp. 1-8. *Whole Earth Papers*, Global Education Associates, Suite 1848, 475 Riverside Drive, New York, NY 10115.

the study of terrorism in U.S. scholarship has been dominated by two distinct but mutually re-inforcing perspectives on global affairs. On the basis of these worldviews, the state-centric and the surrogate warfare perspectives, scholars and policy-makers have postulated the definition of the problem called terrorism *and* the logical ordering of all information under this definition in a set of causes and sustaining factors which explain its increased appearance in world affairs. As with other areas of international relations, from such definitions of the problem and assessments of the causes emerge a series of policy prescriptions for the deterrence, if not total elimination, of the problem. Both perspectives are summarized on Table 1.

State-Centric View

In the state-centric perspective on the world, nation-states, and by extension, their national governments, are considered the primary units of analysis. In this approach, all international events are considered in light of their place vis a vis the state. Occurrences within borders involve domestic affairs; happenings between entities in two countries comprise international relations. Most

TABLE 1

Statement of the Problem:	State-Centric Perspective	Surrogate Warfare Perspective	World Order Perspective
Terrorism is:	a strategy of the weak aimed at revolution by direct or indirect attacks on government. It is arbitrary, inspires fear, is designed to provoke government repression.	a strategy of predominately Marxist revolutionary groups and their allies. It is the new tactic of the cold war aimed at the vulnerabilities of western democracies and those states struggling to be democratic. It is a coordinated effort across targets and designs and fueled by the aid of Cuba, Libya and the Soviet Union.	a form of political violence used by governments and groups outside of government to accomplish aims not possible in the existing social, legal or political order. It is a manifestation of a lack of institutionalization of grievance procedures, social change and law and order.
The Causes of Terrorism are:	— failure of "revolutions" of the 60s — vulnerability of the west — availability of technology — success of terrorism — national and international tolerance	many of State-Centric factors but interpreted in a particular light: — inability of Soviets or internal revolutionaries to mobilize support — willingness of various groups, like SWAPO and PLO, to be coopted — ease of inter-group connections	1. for *non-government* groups: a. the *absence* of: — effective political voice for non-national actors — effective human rights machinery — international arms treaty — new international economic order — regional and international mediation/court structure b. the *presence* of widespread social injustice 2. *for government* as terrorist: — international arms sales — rise of national security ideology — cooperation of actors like MNCs, IGO and US programs — government success
The Treatment of the Problem Must Involve:	— policies of national, regional and international actors aimed at deterrence. — policies which deal out quick and effective punishment when deterrence fails.	— policies as with State-Centric view but with additional pressures on Cuba, Libya, Soviet Union and those who will deal with them. — increased foreign aid to governments trying to deal with insurgency — greater police power to deal with inter-group connections, arms sales, etc.	the creation of regional and international agencies and norms to: a) correct above "absences" b) promote greater social justice c) provide effective international legal mechanisms for dealing with terrorism.

international relations textbooks and research journals employ this state-centric approach as the sole lens through which patterns of political, economical and social activity can be understood.

Given the contours of the state-centric model, we are not surprised that in the past decade there was a major convergence on the "definition of the problem" called terrorism. One of its major analysts of the seventies, David Fromkin, defined terrorism as a strategy of psychological war by direct and indirect attack on a national government. In such a strategy, the weakness of the terrorist's position would always be apparent, while governments, possessing the key attributes of power in the nation-state, had the upper hand. Fromkin pointed this out to decision-makers and citizens:

> Those who are the targets of terrorism — and who are prepared to defend themselves by doing whatever is necessary in order to beat it — start with a major advantage. The advantage is that success or failure depends upon them alone. Terrorism wins only if you respond to it in the way that the terrorists want you to; which means that its fate is in your hands and not in theirs. If you choose not to respond at all, or else to respond in a way different from that which they desire, they will fail to achieve their objectives.
>
> The important point is that the choice is yours. That is the ultimate weakness of terrorism as a strategy. It means that, though terrorism cannot always be prevented, it can always be defeated. You can always refuse to do what they want you to do. (1975:697)

Thus terrorism in a state-centric perspective was seen as a new but rather deviant form of anarchy (at worst) or revolt (at best). It was essentially arbitrary, designed to inspire fear in the population and to provoke repression from the government, thus setting the scene for societal discord. In some sense, the horrifying methods of the non-governmental terrorist group were paralleled only by their daring attempt to attack the integrity and authority of the state.

But how were we to explain such a form of political discontent? Given this perception of terrorism as revolt emanating from non-governmental actors, the causes or conditions for the increase of terrorism were read through the lenses of governmental-subnational group dynamics. They constituted a neatly arranged, and in some sense logically-related set of factors. From reading the literature on terrorism in the seventies, we can isolate features of the political, social and economic order which posit a clear relationship between their appearance and the dynamic of political terrorism. These features include the failure of the democratic and economic revolutions of the early sixties in developing countries; the increasing bureaucratization of western society; improvements in technology; increases in the development of and group identification with diverse ideologies; increased toleration of terrorism in international affairs; and strong indications of likely success for terrorist operations. (Lopez, 1982: 3-7)

Given the importance of the national government in this state-centric worldview, it is not surprising to see scholars and policy-makers who adhere to this view opt for a dual stategy to treat the problem of terrorism:

1. the *deterrence* of non-governmental terrorist activity through policies of a bi-lateral, regional and international character.

2. Quick, hard and effective *punishment* when deterrence fails.

International activities aimed at deterrence include:

1. the three successive agreements on skyjacking undertaken by the members of the International Civil Aviation Organization (ICAO) from 1963-1971. The three accords, signed as conventions at Tokyo, the Hague and Montreal respectively, increased the severity of punishment and the cooperation of states in the matter of air terrorism;

2. the Council of Europe legislation of the late 70s on adjudication of terrorists and state co operation on a number of anti-terrorist dimensions. Examples of the punishment rubric included both the no-negotiation posture of the U.S. and the counter-terrorist strike forces of Israel and West Germany. That full scale agreement at the U.N., especially on crucial definitional issues, did not emerge from member states indicates that a number of policies are yet to be put in place.

Surrogate Warfare View

In the late seventies there was a convergence of two distinct but mutually reinforcing trends in the interpretation of terrorism in world affairs. The first trend centered on concern about the linkages of terrorists across national boundaries. It became obvious that the state-centric perspective for viewing terrorism might have been too narrow or might have become outdated. The second trend focused on the extent to which certain nations, particularly those interested in being a major thorn in the side of the United States, had been training and exporting terrorism as a new mode of attack on western democracy.

The Terror Network by Claire Sterling (1981) and Kupperman and Trent's *Terrorism: Threat, Reality and Response* (1979) coalesced quite nicely with the development in the Reagan administration of an effort to focus on the terrorist activities of Cuba, Libya and the Soviet Union. Due to these developments, the worldview accepted as the most recent perspective for considering terrorism and its surrounding conditions became the surrogate warfare perspective. It defined terrorism as a strategy of predominately Marxist revolutionary groups and their allies. In this view terrorism is seen as the new tactic of the cold war aimed at the vulnerabilities of western democracies and those states struggling to achieve democracy and economic growth. It is seen as a coordinated effort by the Soviet Union with strong support from Libya and Cuba in particular.

In postulating the causes and sustaining factors of terrorism, the proponents of the surrogate warfare view have relied heavily on the factors articulated in the state-centric approach but have added a number of new variations on the theme. Whereas the state-centric worldview characterized the increase in terrorism as the perceived failure of the western model of evolutionary development (i.e., economic progress and increased political participation), the surrogate warfare perspective maintains that it is the Soviet and Cuban revolutionary models which have failed.

The surrogate warfare view suggests that a second casual factor for the increase of terrorism within states is the willingness of a number of groups attacking their governments or other governments to be coopted by the Soviets. Strong and condemning cases have been made against the IRA, SWAPO and the PLO in particular. It is not historical conditions nor the range of local disagreements, but rather the alliance between the group and the surrogate warfare benefactor which is seen as the explanation for the continued resort to this type of violence. The ease of inter-group connections contributes to the surrogate warfare view. Further, the vulnerability of the west, not as a condition in and of itself, but as a point to be exploited by the Soviets due to the failure of their other cold war strategies, is seen as a major support.

What policy prescription emerges from the surrogate warfare perspective? First, one must deal with the issue at its perceived source. Thus a policy of direct challenge to the Soviet Union is seen as a necessity. Second, and directly related to the direct, frontal attack on the source, is a major campaign against key surrogates such as Cuba and Libya. Third, not deterrence, but the countering of the terrorist threat in local arenas is seen as imperative.

Two distinct arenas come to mind here. In the primary group are those nations which are in a dynamic state of internal change and who are therefore especially vulnerable to external intervention and terrorist attack. These states, the El Salvadors, Chiles, South Koreas, etc., must receive large amounts of development and military assistance to shore them up against the mobilization of an effective terrorist campaign which would be directed by the Soviets.

Continuous and strong relationships in areas likely to be "targets" due to historical conditions, but not yet in flux, are necessary. South Africa and Chile are exceptionally susceptible to terrorists of a variety of persuasions and locales. Such forces, once begun, might be uncontrollable as was the case with Iran and Nicaragua. Anti-terrorist policy must work with foreign aid and diplomatic support to not isolate, through human rights policy or some other manner, future targets of Soviet design.

Finally, within this view, if counter-terrorist policy is to have a fair chance of success, the linkage among groups must be discovered and disrupted. Such an approach demands a major effort of intelligence gathering, better control of the movement of international persons, and the ability of international and national law enforcement personnel to be unencumbered by inappropriate restraints on their operation. The movement for greater police power grows as one can demonstrate (through new ways of collecting data on the amount of terrorism) the increasing levels of the problems.

World Order View

It is clear that the state-centric worldview constituted the reigning framework in the U.S. for considering terrorism in the bulk of the seventies and has been challenged as the "legitimate" worldview by the surrogate warfare perspective.

This paper suggests there is yet another perspective from which to assess the spread of events and the changing dimensions of the problem we call terrorism. This is the world order view. Its focus yields a differing definition of the problem, statement of causes and especially a distinct set of policy treatments.

In the 1970s the field of international relations began to be critically assessed by some specialists within the field. They saw that the new facts of increasing global interdependence required inter-*national* perspectives to give way to *trans*-national or *global* perspectives. Championed by Kaiser (1971) and Nye and Keohane (1971, 1977) the transnationalists suggested that: (1) to focus international relations solely on national governments as the units of analysis was too narrow; the examination of non-state actors such as Inter-Governmental Organizations (IGOs), Non-Governmental Organizations (NGOs) and Transnational Corporations (TNCs), and of sub-national groups was essential; (2) theories of international affairs which suggested only struggles of peace and war missed the changing nature of the world as a global bargaining environment in which diverse actors negotiated across a number of specific issues; and, (3) the task of international relationship of various and changing actors to various issues and policies.

Developing parallel to this challenge was the world order critique exemplified by the World Order Models Project. Sponsored by the Institute for World Order, this project enlisted the scholarship of eight academic teams in different world regions. These teams assessed the policies and trends emanating from the existing state-centric system and developed various models of a preferred future from diverse cultural perspectives. They did this in the framework of agreed on values of peace, social justice, economic well-being and ecological balance. Books and materials were produced which contributed to a growing body of world order materials. Authors included Falk (1975), Mendlovitz (1975), Kothari (1975), Galtung, Sakamoto, Mazrui (1976), Lagos and Godoy (1977) and others.

Initially such work was considered too "normative" or "applied" to be "mainstream international relations." Not only was the critique of policies and models according to preferred values a challenge to traditional international studies, but the world order analysts also challenged some of the basic working assumptions of international studies. They claimed that the state-centric system that emerged from the ashes of Feudalism and was given expression in the Treaty of Westphalia in 1648, was now itself undergoing large scale transformation under the pressures of increasing interdependence. Thus the policy task of the present and future must be the development of new, global institutions and structures to manage problems that were transnational.

8. COUNTERING TERRORISM

It Is Clear That The World Order Approach To Policy Formation With Regard To Terrorism Poses New and Intriguing Challenges To The Global Community

The implications for these perspectives, when layered one on top of the other, are noteworthy for the study of world affairs in general and for terrorism in particular. This worldview entails more thorough investigation of issues and actors. It focuses new attention on the institutional processes and potentials of the international system. It rejects as the singular perspective for determining policy, only the elimination of "observed causes." It suggests that part of the policy task is to invent solutions to this unprecedented mixture of problem issues.

Under such a schema for analyzing international affairs, the definition of the problem called terrorism as outlined in Table 1 becomes much more complex. Its focus is less on the actor dynamic and more on the act of terrorism. The assessment of causes and sustaining factors varies according to the terrorist actor under analysis. The prescriptions for treatment focus less on deterrence and punishment and more on preventing the conditions that produce terrorism.

The world order view would yield a definition of the problem which states that terrorism is a form of political violence used by actors in political systems (subnational, national or transnational) to accomplish goals and objectives not possible in the existing social, legal or political order.

The world order framework distinguishes between two types of terrorist acts:

1. those perpetrated by non-state actors against national governments;

2. those perpetrated by governments against non-state groups and individuals. This distinction is of utmost importance because the government acts are not considered terrorist in the state-centric and surrogate war worldviews. Thus an important set of events, literature and policy perspectives, mostly held by third world analysts, has been excluded from a consideration of the definition, causes and treatment of terrorism.

State Terrorism

Specifically, a world order analysis acknowledges that state terror, rooted in the tradition of the Reign of Terror, Hitler and Stalin, may be the oldest form of such violence and appears in a variety of modes in contemporary international affairs. It is, as Dallin and Breslauer define it:

> ... the arbitrary use, by organs of political authority, of severe coercion against individuals or groups, the credible threat of such use, or the arbitrary extermination of such individuals or groups ... it is a form of coercion which is a form of control. (1970: 1)

The process of state-sponsored terror is one in which the initial victims may have importance in themselves but their fate is also meant to spark new forms of political behavior on the part of other societal groups. Thus a government may arrest all the nation's union leaders for two reasons: (1) to break the power of the unions; and, (2) to show journalists, intellectuals, and others that they may comprise the next group of prisoners if their activities do not change.

What is unique to this analysis of terrorism is the variety of forms that state terror may take. In a number of situations, national governments employ assassins or deploy their own secret police to execute enemies of the state. Such enemies have usually fled their home territory and are exterminated in the territory of another nation, thus raising serious questions of international law. Two of the most famous "executions" have been those of Georgi Markov, a Bulgarian defector assassinated in London in 1978, and Orlando Letelier, former Chilean ambassador to the U.S. in the Allende government. Letelier, killed in Washington in 1978, was a victim of the Chilean secret police. In a similar fashion, the Mossad, the Israeli secret police, and a number of assassin units under the direction of Iraq and other governments, appear on the rise in Western Europe (*The Guardian,* January 14, 1979: 4, 5).

Further, the state may direct or simply overlook the activities of internal groups who employ terror tactics against anti-government terrorists or insurgents. Some of these government-sanctioned groups have been labeled "Death Squads" in Uruguay, Brazil and El Salvador. Others, such as the Argentine Anti-Communist Alliance, have acquired an identity a bit more independent of the government. At least in their early phases of operation, membership in such groups is usually limited to para-military personnel of the government.

Finally, governments may engage in terror activities in their own borders under the wider rubric of human rights violations. This is an issue of substantial importance in the world dialogue about the causes of and control of terrorism. A number of global citizens and governments cite the record of regimes in Johannesburg and evidence gathered by Amnesty International on practices in Brazil, Argentina and Chile to point out that the daily and systematic violence of national rulers constitutes terrorism. Other governments will stop short of applying the terrorist distinction to these violations, even while acknowledging their occurrence. This disagreement poses serious stumbling blocks in the formation of effective and global law to deal with terrorism.

The causes of terrorism as perpetrated by national governments vary from the causes for non-national actors. Three major factors can be cited as important to the rise of governments as terrorist. First, in much the same manner that the sub-national or transnational terrorists have available to them sophisticated technology for carrying out their deeds, so too do national governments. International arms trade increases the potential for governments to torture and exterminate their enemies. In particular, counterinsurgency training and devices, as part of military assistance pacts between states, increases significantly the ability of small governmental groups to conduct "operations" against segments of a population. (See Wright, 1978.)

Closely related to this arms issue, and a dynamic force for government terrorism in the third world, is the rise of national security ideology. As articulated by Mische and Mische (1977) at a general level and by Comblin (1981) Herrera (1980) and Child (1979 and 1980) in the context of Latin America, national security is often used as a rationale to justify state repressing and terror. Thus statesmen in countries undergoing rapid economic change can, with the longview in mind, "temporarily" control and constrain political and social freedoms in order to maintain the viability of the state and these freedoms for the future. In practice, such an ideology permits the state to label any dissident a terrorist and to suspend liberties in the short term under the unchallengeable claim of preserving them in the long run. (Lopez, 1983).

In much the same way that Milbank (1976) and others have documented the success rate of non-governmental terrorists as a sustaining factor in their continued activities, so too, although with less precision, can we cite success as a factor in state terror. Despite attempts by NGOs such as Amnesty International, by IGOs such as the International Labor Organization and the UN General Assembly, and even national human rights policy efforts to curtail state terror, the gains from pursuing internal repression policies in South Africa, Brazil or Chile far outweigh for these regimes the costs of such criticism. The international community, out of a respect for the notion of sovereignty, simply will not directly challenge "internal affairs" of other states. Such a practice of looking the other way sustains state terror.

Insurgent Terrorism

What of the causes and sustaining factors of non-governmental terrorism? The world order perspective, when applied to the actors previously listed as primary perpetrators of terrorism against governments, would tend to focus less on a search for direct observables as is the hallmark of the two other worldviews. Clearly world order thinkers would point out that a direct cause of insurgent terror can be found in the large gaps which exist between ruling groups and those undertaking political change via error.

With its bent toward bargaining processes and institutional analysis, the world order approach would suggest that group terrorism is not simply a result of a number of other causes. Terrorism as a strategy of political change over time is directly related to the absence of institutions for political expression by other means. In particular, where states lack mechanisms for demand-making, grievance procedures for ethnic minorities, institutions for effective human rights monitoring and adjudication, terrorism will develop (as opposed to "be caused").

Dealing With Terrorism: World Order Policies

In light of the definitional dimensions and the diverse causes for terrorism outlined above, it should come as no surprise that policy prescriptions from a world order theme do not focus on deterrence, counterterrorism or police power. Rather, approaches to solving the terrorist nexus, in developing nations in particular, call for the creation of a number of regional, transnational and international institutions. Although no specific plan for such institutions yet exists, it is clear that these would include those with human rights monitoring and adjudicating ability; with mediation capacities between dissidents and regimes, and between ethnic minorities and majority populations; with structures for political grievances of non-governmental entities, and with arms control procedures and structures which would control the level of violence should it break out.

Below we briefly outline eight particular policy approaches which would respond to the form of political violence called terrorism in both its governmental and insurgent form. These include:

1. *The establishment of an international criminal court,* either as a separate entity or an adjunct to the International Court of Justice. Such a legal structure, which was originally proposed in the early 1950s, would be able to hear cases for non-governmental actors as well as states. It would have jurisdiction to hear cases brought against individuals, such as hijackers, assassins, etc. and lighten the burden often felt by national governments that fear to bring a particular terrorist to trial in their national court because it identifies them as the next target of the terror group. Such a judicial structure might also be empowered to bring charges, filled by citizens of a state, against a former head of state, i.e., the Shah of Iran or Somoza, for very particular kinds of offenses, such as genocide or violations of the Universal Declaration of Human Rights.

2. *The increased inclusion of non-governmental political actors,* particularly those with a clear and homogeneous identity, into some form of dialogue with national actors in regional and international organizations. Here we are referring to the plight of ethnic minorities, stateless people and refugees resident in another state. Such an arrangement provides means for airing grievances and increasing the international status of such actors. It also increases their stake in appropriate behavior because they are now part of its structure rather than being systematically ostracized from it. The inclusion of the PLO in an "Observer" status in a number of UN organizations serves as an example.

3. *The establishment,* through the U.N., regional organizations or private international consultants and arbitrators, *of a grievance agency* to act as a low-level intervenor in disputes and also to provide a redress procedure for forms of state terror. Such an agency might have played a large role in the quagmire which was the US-Iranian hostage situation. The success of such impartial facilitators in a number of domestic political systems is well known and can spillover as an international approach.

4. *The development of an International Mediation Agency,* similar to that called for by many at the original UN Charter conference, and functionally similar to the U.S. Community Relations Service or Federal Mediation and

8. COUNTERING TERRORISM

Conciliation Service. Whereas observer status (#2 above) provides a continuous route to make claims and a grievance committee (#3 above) a vehicle for seeking redress, the mediation approach would attempt to resolve disputes such that states and citizens might not "need" to resort to violence as a means of conflict resolution.

5. *The creation of a UN High Commission and High Commissioner for Human Rights.* Given the success which the UN counterpart has had in the refugee area, the structural precedent is established, but the reality depends on the willingness of states and others to directly acknowledge the existence of state terror and to provide means for holding leaders accountable for violations of the Universal Declaration of Human Rights. Such an official might have investigated the crimes of the Shah of Iran and presented a fair and effective recommendation which may have changed the course of U.S.-Iranian affairs.

6. *The development and enforcement of a Code of Behavior for multi-national corporations* in the area of terrorism and human rights. This might entail those codes treating the relationship between the direct support of state terror systems, such as South Africa, because governments purposely control minimum wage laws for purposes of creating favorable business conditions. Also, such an ethical scheme might question the policy of corporations paying ransom to insurgent terrorists regardless of the advice or policy of the government not to do so. In light of the successful work of the UN in establishing its Centre on Transnational Corporations and its work on codes of conduct in financial aspects of foreign investment, this may not be too difficult to attempt.

7. *The development of an international arms sales treaty* which would control both the access which insurgent groups might have to sophisticated weaponry *and* the transfer across international borders of those police and interrogation technologies which provide the tools for repression. While this treaty, in and of itself, will not prevent terrorism, it clearly would influence the character and parameters of terror.

8. *The development of some form of a new international economic order* which would place state leaders much less in a position of needing to so tightly control their economy that they generate a condition of war against their citizens in order to maximize economic performance. Similarly, new rules for trade and finance might create the conditions whereby those insurgent groups might have greater control of their own economic quality of life, without government acting as the enforcer of a particular mode of development.

While these recommendations need to be further articulated and discussed, it is clear that the world order approach to policy formation with regard to terrorism poses new and intriguing challenges to the global community. The task which lies ahead is to examine short term transition stages which can move us beyond the narrow policy confines generated by the state centric and surrogate warfare perspectives on terrorism to the realization of these world order policies.

Conclusion

This paper has presented three distinct worldviews which yield three distinct assessments of terrorism, its causes, and viable policies for its treatment. While a number of the issues internal to each position were not fully explored, it is clear that each worldview, when used as the screening and interpretative device for examining terrorism, maintains across the dimensions discussed a certain internal and logical consistency.

What questions for the future analysis of terrorism does this exploratory analysis raise? Three critical areas of future inquiry come to mind. First, the postulating of alternative worldviews which produce different perceptions of terrorism begs for a discussion of the true nature of evidence. Some of this has been undertaken in the debates about the accuracy of the surrogate war perspective but the issue is much broader than even this crucial argument. What does the presence of Soviet hardware in the hands of Palestinians or Basque separatists mean for assessing "causes" of terrorism? Can we, short of appealing to our own worldview, verify and generalize from such evidence?

Second, how can the methodological challenge of the transnational/world order approach with its focus on observable *absences* carrying equal importance to social and political causes, be better utilized in preventing and dealing with terrorism? From such an assessment might emerge a challenge in other areas of cause-effect thinking in international affairs.

Finally, unless scholars and citizens continue to analyze and debate these alternative worldviews and the questions they generate, policy-makers may continue in singular perspectives out of tune with the variety and dimensions of the events we call terrorism. We will be left not much further along than we were a decade ago, when it became clear that for some, "one man's terrorist was another man's freedom fighter." Now that questions of human rights and dignity, national security policy and a host of other issues are seen as much more entwined with perspectives on terrorism than they were before, we can develop broader, more far-reaching policies and strategies to treat this growing worldwide problem.

References

Christensen, Cheryl. *The Right to Food: How To Guarantee.* (WOMP Working Paper, 1980).

Child, John. "Strategic Concepts of Latin America: An Update," *Inter-American Economic Affairs* (Summer, 1980). pp. 61-82.

Child, John. "Geopolitical Thinking in Latin America," *Latin American Research Review,* 14, 2 (Summer, 1979) pp. 89-111.

Comblin, Jose, "Latin America and the National Security State," *The Whole Earth Papers,* No. 14, Global Education Associates, East Orange, New Jersey, 1980.

Dallin, Alexander and George W. Breslauer, *Political Terror in Communist Systems.* Stanford, California: Stanford University Press, 1970.

Falk, Richard A., *A Study of Future Worlds.* The Free Press, 1975.

Fromkin, David, "The Strategy of Terrorism," 53, 4 *Foreign Affairs*, (July 1975), pp. 683-698.

Galtung, Johan. *The North-South Debate: Technology, Basic Human Needs and the New International Economic Order.* (WOMP Working Paper, 1980).

Galtung, Johan, *The True Worlds: A Transnational Perspective.* New York. The Free Press, 1975.

Herrera, Genaro Arriagada. "National Security Doctrine in Latin America" (trans. H. Richards), *Peace and Change*, VI, 1-2 (Winter, 1980), pp. 49-60.

Kaiser, Karl, "Transnational Politics: Towards A Theory of Multinational Politics," *International Organization* (Summer, 1971), pp. 790-817.

Kothari, Rajni, *Footsteps into the Future: Diagnosis of the Present World and a Design for an Alternative*, New York, Free Press, 1975.

Kupperman, Robert H. and Darrell M. Trent. *Terrorism: Threat, Reality and Response.* Palo Alto: The Hoover Institution Press, 1979.

Lagos, Gustavo and Horacio Godoy, *Revolution of Being.* New York: Free Press, 1977.

Lopez, George A. "A Scheme for the Analysis of Government As Terrorist" in M. Stohl and G.A. Lopez (ed.). *The State As Terrorist: The Dynamics of Governmental Violence and Repression.* Greenwood Press 1983.

Lopez, George A. "Terrorism and Alternative Worldviews," A Paper Presented at the 1982 Annual Meeting of the International Studies Association, Cincinnati, Ohio, 1982.

Mazrui, Ali. A. *The Barrel of the Gun and the Barrel of Oil in the North-South Equation.* (WOMP Working Paper, 1981).

Mazrui, Ali. A. *A World Federation of Cultures: An African Perspective.* New York: Free Press, 1976.

Mendlovitz, Saul H. (ed.) *On the Creation of a Just World Order.* The Free Press, 1975.

Milbank, David L. "International and Transnational Terrorism: Diagnosis and Prognosis," Washington, D.C.: Office of Political Research, Central Intelligence Agency, PR 76 10030, April 1976.

Mische, Gerald and Patricia. *Toward a Human World Order: Beyond the National Security Straitjacket.* Paulist Press, 1977.

Nye, Joseph and Robert Keohane (eds.). "Transnational Relations and World Politics." *International Organization,* (Summer, 1971) Special issue.

Nye, Joseph and Robert Keohane. *Power and Interdependence.* Boston: Little, Brown and Company, 1977.

Sterling, Claire. *The Terrorist Network.* New York: Holt, Rinehart and Winston, 1981.

Wright, Steve, "The New Police Technologies," *Journal of Peace Research,* No. 4, Volume XV; (1978): pp. 305-332.

Economic Analysis Can Help Figh International Terrorism

Choice-theoretic models describe economic behavior of individuals who maximize benefits and minimize costs. Analysis leads to the testable behavior of terrorists, while government policy can raise the costs and reduce the benefits.

TODD SANDLER, WALTER ENDERS,

and HARVEY E. LAPAN

Todd Sandler, Walter Enders, and Harvey E. Lapan are members of the Department of Economics, Iowa State University. This article is based on research funded by the National Science Foundation (SES-8907646). The views expressed here are solely of the authors and should not be attributed to NSF.

Recent events in the Persian Gulf, including the Iraqi invasion of Kuwait and Operation Desert Shield, increase the threat of international terrorism against U.S. forces and interests worldwide. In the last twenty years, a significant number of international terrorist events have had their roots in the Middle East. Terrorism is the premeditated use, or threat of use, of extranormal violence or force to gain a political objective through intimidation or fear. The political objectives of terrorists may involve nationalism, separatism, nihilism, religious freedoms, ideology, or issue-specific concerns. Although the underlying motivations for terrorist acts are varied, terrorist tactics are similar among groups, and include bombings, kidnappings, assassinations, threats, hoaxes, and skyjackings. By targeting a large audience, often not directly involved in the decision-making process, terrorists attempt to apply pressures to bear on government officials in charge of policies. Thus, on October 23, 1983, a Mercedes truck, packed with two thousand pounds of plastic explosives, was driven into the lobby of the Battalion Landing Team building, hous-

ing some of the U.S. Marines at Beirut International Airport. The resulting blast created a crater 30 feet deep and 120 feet across and caused the four-story building to collapse, killing 241 American servicemen and injuring over eighty. This incident and other terrorist attacks in Lebanon during 1983-84 caused the United States and other nations to reassess their policies; many foreign troops were subsequently withdrawn as the terrorists had demanded.

Since the legitimacy of any government depends, in large part, on its ability to safeguard the life and property of its constituency, terrorist groups that can strike at will, aided by surprise, pose a serious threat to political stability. If terrorists exert sufficient pressures on a duly elected government to capitulate to their demands, democratic principles are compromised, inasmuch as an unelected minority has altered policy without a voters' mandate. A democratic government must respond with care: if it appears to use too much force to repress the terrorists, then the government may lose popular support. But it may also lose that support if it uses too little force to gain control of the situation.

Growth of terrorism

As advances in technology, transportation, and communication in recent decades have made the world a global community, terrorism has become transnational. In other words, terrorist incidents involve perpetrators, institutions, boundaries, civilians, or government participants from two or more nations. The kidnappings of Americans and other Westerners from the streets of Beirut by groups such as the Hezbollah, Islamic Jihad for the Liberation of Palestine, and the Revolutionary Justice Organization are examples of this. The downing of Air India Flight 182 over the Atlantic Ocean on June 23, 1985 and the downing of Pan American Flight 103 over Lockerbie, Scotland, on December 21, 1988, are transnational events with great loss of life. Three hundred twenty-nine people died in the 1985 crash, and two hundred seventy died in the 1988 tragedy.

Recent statistics published by the U.S. Department of State indicate that the threat of transnational terrorism escalated in the middle 1980s: from 1980 to 1983, 1,990 transnational terrorist incidents were recorded; from 1984 to 1987, that number had jumped to 2,989. In 1988, 856 transnational terrorist events resulted in the death of 658 persons and the injury of 1,131. Since the late 1960s, the start of the era of transnational terrorism, terrorist events have become dramatically more lethal: 1,741 people died in transnational attacks during 1968-77, while 4,925 people died in such attacks during 1978-87. Though recent figures for 1989 indicate a decline of nearly 38 percent in transnational terrorism to 528 incidents , most experts view this as a temporary lull, permitting terrorist groups and sponsors to prepare for the next wave of events.

Dramatic changes in the relationship among the superpowers in the late 1980s brought hope for an era of world peace. But recent events in the Persian Gulf have shown that world stability may be threatened by smaller nations that seek other nations' resources. The Iraqi invasion of Kuwait and the subsequent deployment of U.S. troops and materiel to the Persian Gulf have dashed hopes for a peace dividend. Since the late 1960s, a sizable portion of transnational terrorist events has either taken place in the Middle East or else has been caused by terrorist groups operating from that region. Noteworthy examples are the bombing of the U.S. embassy in Beirut on April 18, 1983, the hijacking of the *Achille Lauro* on October 7, 1985, and the simultaneous attacks on the Rome and Vienna airports on December 27, 1985. With U.S. intervention in the Persian Gulf, the United States and the other nations supporting the United Nations resolutions against Iraq are potential targets for a new wave of terrorism. This vulnerability is underscored by the taking of Western hostages by the Iraqi government for use as human shields.

Terrorism may become more prevalent in the 1990s, since it is a cost-effective means to create political instability. The covert nature of terrorism allows state sponsors to destabilize a regime while remaining anonymous.

Applying economic methods

In recent years, we and other researchers have applied methods derived from economics to study the threat of transnational terrorism and to analyze the policies that might work best to curb this threat. Economics can help shed light on many questions people have about terrorism. Are terrorists rational? What antiterrorist policies work best? Why are international agreements on terrorism ineffective? Why do governments negotiate with terrorists after pledging not to do so? Will the threat of terrorism worsen during the 1990s? This article attempts to answer these questions.

Of course, economic methods have their limitations. We do not claim that they provide the only technique for understanding terrorism; rather, we would argue that economics has something to add to the study of terrorism, especially when used in conjunction with insights gained from other disciplines. No economic theory is meant to explain all forms of terrorism or to apply to all incidents. Since an economic theory is necessarily an abstraction, based on simplifying assumptions, the theory applies only to those cases which satisfy the assumptions under which the generalization has been drawn. After a theory is formulated, rigorous empirical testing is needed to evaluate whether the facts are consistent with the theory's predictions.

There is no universally accepted method to measure the threat of terrorism. In Figure 1, the number of transnational events per quarter is depicted for 1968-88. The time series displayed are derived from a data set, *International Terrorism: Attributes of Terrorist Events* (ITERATE), developed by Edward Mickolus, Todd Sandler, Jean Murdock, and Peter Fleming, using newspaper reports on terrorist events. This coded data set is the most comprehensive one currently available to the public. The U.S. Department of State and the U.S. Central Intelligence Agency maintain more comprehensive data sets, but have not made them available to researchers. Hence, Figure 1 is an understatement of the

Figure 1   **Terrorist Incidents: Bombings & Totals**
(quarterly data)

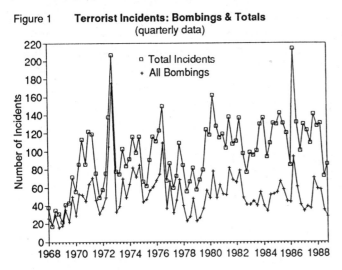

Source: International Terrorism: Attributes of Terrorist Events.

Figure 2   **Terrorist Incidents: Other Types**
(quarterly data)

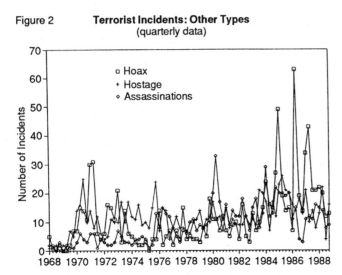

Source: International Terrorism: Attributes of Terrorist Events.

true level of transnational terrorism. Figure 1 also depicts the time profile for bombings during 1968-88, while Figure 2 displays the time profiles for three other types of terrorist events—hostage missions, assassinations, and threats and hoaxes—during 1968-88. Hostage missions—kidnappings, skyjackings, barricade and hostage-taking attacks—are the most risky acts and are the most apt to capture media attention. Terrorists have used kidnappings and skyjackings to gain freedom for jailed comrades and to finance operations. Threats and hoaxes are incidents that attempt to intimidate without real action and the expenditure of resources.

Clearly, the overwhelming number of incidents involve bombings. The shape of the bombing series is a prime determinant of the shape of the time series for all events. Bombings remain the terrorists' favorite tactic, with approximately half of all transnational events tak-

ing this form. Two noteworthy peaks in transnational terrorism were reached in late 1972 and early 1986: the former followed a series of conflicts, including the War of Attrition between Israel and its Arab neighbors, while the latter followed the U.S. retaliatory raid on Libya. The escalation of transnational terrorism came after the Six Day War between Israel and its neighbors in June 1967. This upward trend in total incidents ended temporarily after the Yom Kippur War in 1973. Middle-East-inspired terrorism has greatly added to transnational terrorism since the late 1960s. We also note that logistically complex hostage taking incidents are a small portion of the total. Moreover, increased fortification of potential targets in the 1980s (airports, embassies, public buildings, for example) has apparently forced terrorists to resort more often to threats, hoaxes, and assassinations in recent years.

Each type of terrorist event displays a cyclical pattern with an upward trend. Eric Im and Jon Cauley of the University of Hawaii-Hilo and Todd Sandler have used spectral analysis to show that cycles characterize transnational terrorist events: all events display a 28-month periodicity, while hostage missions display periodicities ranging from 4.1 months (skyjackings) to 72 months (barricade missions). These cycles are thought to arise from alternating periods of attack and counterattack by the terrorists and the authorities, respectively.

Choice-theoretic models

In economics, individual behavior is characterized as a choice-theoretic situation. Individuals attempt to maximize some goals (utility or profit, for example), subject to one or more constraints. As such, an economic agent is depicted as a rational being who maximizes beneficial returns and minimizes costs, while responding to constraints which denote scarcity. If the constraints change, then predictable alterations in behavior follow. Economists judge rationality based not on one's goals but on the appropriate response to constraints in the achievement of these goals. Thus terrorists, who skyjack planes and leave bombs in crowded marketplaces, are viewed as rational provided they react appropriately to their constraints as they attempt to achieve some objective.

A terrorist group must allocate its scarce resources, such as labor and time, between terrorist and nonterrorist activities in order to maximize its well-being, which depends, among other things, on the attainment of some political objective. The allocation process might further involve the assignment of resources among the various modes of attacks—kidnappings and assassinations, for example. The terrorist group's resource constraint equates the value of expenditures and its income (resources). For any given terrorist activity, expenditures include the per-unit price times the number of units of the activity. In the case of a terrorist attack, the "price" reflects the additional costs, in terms of resources and risks, of performing each event. Since hostage events are far riskier and more logistically complex than a bombing, hostage events have a higher per-unit price than most bombings. This, in turn, explains the relative scarcity of hostage missions vis-à-vis bombings (see Figures 1 and 2). Risks associated with one type of terrorist event would increase when a government took actions, installing metal detectors or increasing security at embassies, to harden one type of target. Such actions would increase the relative costs of one attack mode as compared with the costs of another attack mode that had not been influenced by the government's policy.

The choice-theoretic model leads to some testable behavior with respect to terrorists. If a government policy increases the relative cost or price of one kind of terrorist mode of attack, then the terrorists will merely choose those modes whose prices are unchanged. The overall level of terrorism need not decline. If the government intends to curb terrorism in general, then it must either reduce terrorist resources or else raise the cost of all terrorist operations relative to nonterrorist activities. Piecemeal policies, aimed at one or two modes of attack, will not necessarily curb terrorism.

Terrorists have high success rates. Using the ITERATE data for 1968-88, we find that terrorists are logistically successful (that is, they complete the mission as planned) as follows: threats and hoaxes, 97 percent success; bombings, 87 percent; hostage missions, 76 percent; and assassinations, 75 percent . Logistical success in the case of hostage missions does not mean that they negotiate successfully. It only means that they secure their hostage(s) without mishap.

Like the terrorists, the government also faces a choice-theoretic problem as it allocates its scarce resources, generated from taxes and bonds, to meet social goals and to curb terrorism. Just as the terrorists must make optimizing decisions based on government actions and their beliefs about future government actions, the government must make its own optimizing decisions based on past terrorist acts and its beliefs about future acts.

In particular, the government attempts to minimize the costs or impact associated with a terrorist campaign when it decides upon deterrence, intelligence gathering, and responses to terrorist demands. Both the terrorist group and the government must choose strategies based on how they *anticipate* the other side will react to its optimizing choices. Since strategic interactions between opposing agents are crucial, game theory can be used to link the opposing sides' choice-theoretic models. When several nations face a terrorist threat from the same group (Abu Nidal Organization targets Israeli, Jordanian, and American interests, for example), strategic interactions between governments regarding deterrence, crisis management, and intelligence become relevant. Intergovernmental strategic interactions are especially germane to transnational terrorist incidents.

Governmental responses

In fighting terrorism, a government can choose between two general responses—passive and active. Passive or defensive responses include erecting technology-based barriers (metal detectors at airports, bomb-sniffing devices), fortifying potential targets (embassies), instituting stricter laws, augmenting intelligence, and enacting international agreements. Active responses involve retaliatory raids (especially against state sponsors), preemptive strikes, group infiltration, and covert actions.

To examine the effectiveness of some specific terrorist-thwarting policies as well as the reactions of terrorists to these policies, we apply an econometric forecasting technique known as interrupted time series analysis. We first determine the impact on skyjackings attributable to the screening of airline passengers. On January 5, 1973, metal detectors were installed in U.S. airports. Shortly thereafter, similar screening devices and procedures were instituted at foreign airports. Figure 3 displays the number of U.S. skyjackings (plus attempts) per quarter between 1968 and 1988. An abrupt drop in the number of skyjackings occurred immedi-

Figure 3   **Domestic Skyjackings**

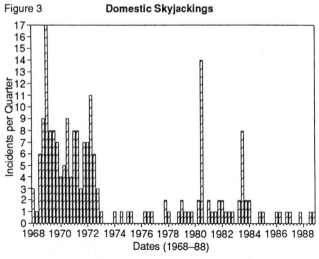

Source: International Terrorism: Attributes of Terrorist Events.

8. COUNTERING TERRORISM

Figure 4 **Non-U.S. Skyjackings**

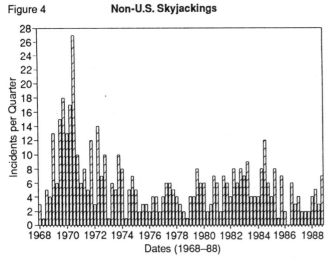

Source: International Terrorism: Attributes of Terrorist Events.

Figure 5 **All Non-Skyjacking Hostage Incidents**
(Kidnapping and Barricade Missions)

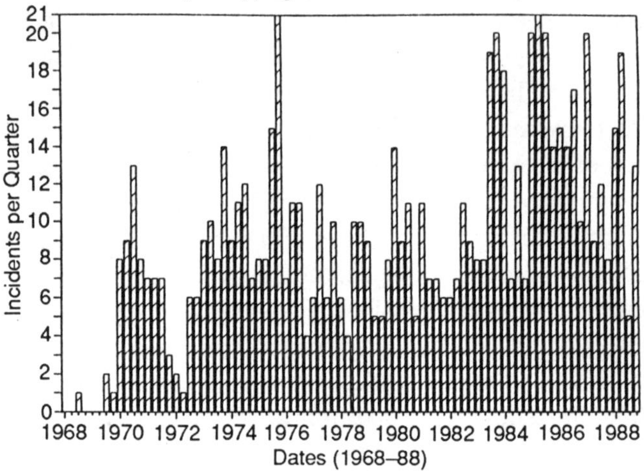

Source: International Terrorism: Attributes of Terrorist Events.

ately after screening devices were installed. We have calculated that prior to the installation of these devices, approximately seven skyjackings occurred on average per quarter in the United States. Afterwards, skyjackings averaged about one per quarter. The two spikes in 1981 and 1983 involved hijackings to Cuba. In many instances, the hijackers claimed to have a flammable liquid in a plastic bottle. Stiffer penalties announced by Cuba eventually curbed these incidents. Figure 4 shows the number of nondomestic skyjackings. A more gradual, but significant, reduction took place once these devices were installed abroad. In the long run nondomestic hijackings dropped, on average, from almost 10 per quarter to just under 2.5.

We also found that starting in 1973, terrorists switched their hostage missions to kidnappings and barricade attacks, which were not protected by metal detectors. The increase in nonskyjacking hostage missions is evident in Figure 5. We have calculated that, after 1972, all skyjackings dropped in the long run by almost 11 per quarter, while other kinds of hostage events increased by just under 11 per quarter. Clearly, terrorists have responded to the increased risks posed by screening devices by changing the type of hostage mission. A clear substitution effect has resulted from the change in relative costs.

Using a more advanced forecasting technique, we can investigate the interrelationships between two or more terrorist modes over time. When vector autoregressive techniques are combined with intervention analysis, we can ascertain the impact of multiple policies on more than one terrorist mode of operation. This combination of techniques allows us to give further evidence of terrorists' proclivity to respond to government actions by substituting one mode for another.

Substitutions

In Figures 6 to 8, the forecasted or predicted patterns (estimated using vector autoregressive techniques) are displayed for five attack modes—skyjackings, assassinations, other hostage incidents, threats and hoaxes, and bombings and related incidents. Three policy impacts are studied: metal detectors (January 5, 1973), the fortification of U.S. embassies (October 1976 and beyond), and the U.S. retaliatory raid on Libya (April 15, 1986). The installation of metal detectors is associated with a decrease in hijackings as well as threats and hoaxes, but is also associated with increases in other hostage incidents, bombings, and assassinations. The fortification of embassies and other potential targets beginning in 1976 meant a decrease in bombings and hostage missions (especially the takeovers of facilities) but an increase in assassinations. Diplomats and others were less at risk in protected facilities, but were more at risk when outside.

Figure 6 **Bombings and Hostage Missions**
(Predicted 1970–88)

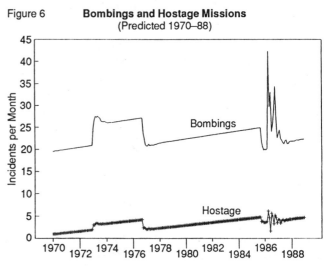

Source: Authors' data and calculations.

Figure 7 **Skyjackings and Assassinations**
(Predicted 1970–1988)

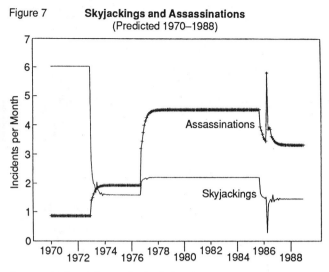

Source: Authors' data and calculations.

Figure 8 **Threats and Hoaxes**
(Predicted 1970–88)

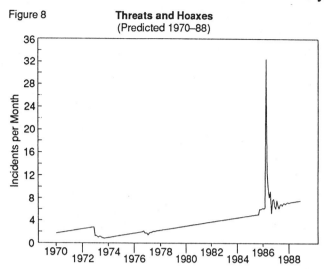

Source: Authors' data and calculations.

The retaliatory raid on Libya increased threats, hoaxes, assassinations, and bombings immediately following the event, but had no long-term influence on the level of terrorism. We have estimated that the raid incited increased attacks against the United States and the United Kingdom by almost 39 incidents in the first post-raid month. Within about three months, attacks returned to pre-raid levels. Retaliatory attacks seem merely to fuel fervor. Any decline in attacks following the immediate post-raid increase was probably due to an intertemporal substitution effect, in which terrorists move planned future attacks into the present to express outrage.

The predicted series indicates that the time profiles for the various modes of attack are related. Hostage missions have a similar profile to that for bombings and related incidents, such as arson. This implies that these modes are influenced in similar ways by government policies aimed at thwarting terrorism. In response to metal detectors, skyjackings and assassinations have reacted in opposite ways (the former decreased, while the latter increased). However, in response to increased security of diplomatic and military facilities, the two series have reacted in a similar manner. The choices of modes by terrorists are clearly related to government actions to secure potential targets. This insight should be kept in mind when policies are designed to thwart terrorism.

Other passive responses by government have had no discernible effect. For example, the so-called Reagan get-tough policy on terrorism, expressed in two public laws, signed in October 1984, had no measurable influence on terrorism directed at U.S. interests. These laws augmented penalties against convicted terrorists, and offered rewards for information leading to the apprehen-

sion of terrorists who target U.S. interests. Apparently, terrorists do not view these laws as threatening.

United Nations conventions and resolutions condemning hostage-taking, crimes against protected individuals, such as diplomats, and skyjackings, have had no discernible influence when scrutinized with econometric techniques. The failure of these conventions and others, like the 1971 Montreal convention outlawing acts of aviation sabotage, has puzzled experts. If it is in every nation's collective interest to abide by these agreements, then why do nations, when confronted with terrorist events, renege time after time on their responsibility? Simple game theory can offer an answer.

Game theory and the behavior of nations

Here is a hypothetical situation typical of the payoffs associated with an international agreement pledging to punish sponsors of terrorism. Suppose three nations sign an agreement to retaliate against a known state sponsor of terrorism. Each signatory would confer a benefit of 5, from deterrence, to itself and to the other

Table 1 **Game Matrix:
Listing Payoffs to Nation *i* under
Various Compliance Scenarios**
(three-nation case)

| | | Other Two Nations' Strategies | | |
		Other Two Nations Abides	One Abides and One Does Not	Neither Abides
Nation *i*'s strategies	Abide	5	0	–5
	Does Not Abide	10	5	0

nations in the agreement. If all three abide by the agreement, each nation receives total benefits (before costs) equal to 15 (= 5 x 3). Each signatory, however, faces a private cost of 10 to make good on their commitment. These costs would arise, in part, from resources assigned to retaliation. Other private costs may arise from retribution by the targeted sponsor.

In Table 1, we list the payoffs to nation i based on its own strategy and those of the other two nations. Each nation has two potential strategies: abide and not abide. For three nations, six possible scenarios can occur. If all nations abide, then nation i receives a *net* payoff of 5—the difference between private benefits of 15 and private costs of 10. If, however, nation i does not abide while the other two nations abide, then nation i receives 10 (5 times the number of abiders), since it has no private costs to pay. When nation i and one other nation abide, nation i receives 0—the difference between private benefits of 10 (from two abiders) and private costs of 10. If nation i does not abide but one nation of the remaining two abides, then nation i receives 5, since it has no private costs. The other two payoffs are computed similarly. For nation $i,$ the dominant or best strategy is to not abide, since the payoffs in the bottom row exceed those in the top regardless of the other nations' actions. Since all nations view the game as does i, none abides when needed and the payoff to each nation is zero. Each nation hopes in vain that it can get away with reneging, while the others support the agreement. Collective irrationality results because each nation could receive 5 in net benefits if all were to cooperate. The payoff scheme above is characteristic of an n-player Prisoner's Dilemma and is behind the failure to achieve many international agreements, including preserving tropical forests, saving the ozone layer, and ending an arms race.

A potential escape from the dilemma materializes if the agreement provides for an enforcement mechanism that punishes defecting nations with sanctions that exceed the individual gain of 5 associated with defecting. If, for example, a penalty of 6 is imposed on the defector by the other nations, then the payoffs from abiding will dominate. If, moreover, the parties view the game as being repeated from one period to another, so that gains from defecting must be weighed against losses from others defecting in future periods, then cooperation may be fostered. Tit-for-tat strategies, based on the threat of future defections, may elicit cooperation in repeated Prisoner's Dilemmas. Cooperative strategies for a Prisoner's Dilemma may evolve when the endpoint of the game is unknown. However, once the players know that the game is about to end, threats are no longer a deterrent, and players revert to defector strategies. A

lame-duck administration is especially vulnerable to defecting from a commitment, since it will not suffer the costs associated with defection. This may explain the Reagan Administration's willingness to barter arms for the release of three hostages—Rev. Benjamin Weir, Rev. Lawrence Jenco, and David Jacobsen—during 1985-86.

The application of game theory can explain why governments that precommit never to negotiate often renege on their pledge when confronted with an actual hostage crisis. This behavior characterizes governments that may or may not have a known endpoint. Even the staunchest supporter of the no-negotiation strategy, Israel, has made noteworthy exceptions in the case of the school children taken hostage at Maalot in May 1974, and during the hijacking of TWA flight 847 in June 1985. It is conventionally expected that if a government precommits never to capitulate, then potential hostage takers will have nothing to gain from holding hostages. Consequently, no hostages will be taken. This expectation rests on a number of crucial implicit assumptions: (1) the government's pledge is fully credible to would-be hostage takers; (2) there is no uncertainty concerning payoffs; (3) the terrorists' gains from hostage taking only derive from the fulfillment of its demands; and (4) the government's expenditures on deterrence will stop all attacks. Each of these assumptions is suspect.

There are two sets of players in the game—the terrorists and the government; hostages are pawns. The game is modeled with multiple periods so that reputation costs are included. First, the government chooses its expenditure on deterrence; second, the terrorists decide whether to attack; and third, the government determines whether to negotiate in the event of a logistical success for the terrorists. In each period, the above sequence of actions is relevant. The optimal strategy for each agent depends on its payoff in each state and the beliefs that it holds as to the likelihood attached to each contingent state.

If the terrorist group realizes a gain from either a logistical or negotiation failure, as it may if it values media exposure or martyrdom, then the government's statements and its level of deterrence cannot necessarily forestall an attack. Consequently, hostages may still be taken. If hostages are taken, then the government must compare the expected costs of not capitulating with those of capitulating. Situations may consequently arise where a government views the cost of not capitulating as too high, even when accounting for lost reputation, and, hence, reneges on its pledge and trades with the terrorists. If would-be hostage takers believe that they may be able to impose costs sufficient for a government to renege on its stated policy, then they will take hostages, since the credibility of the government's pledge depends on an uncertain outcome. Whenever the government caves in, the terrorists will update or raise their beliefs about future capitulations. In other words, learning based on past actions allows terrorists (and the government) to update their beliefs in an interactive fashion. Constitutional constraints or congressional hearings, which impose huge perceived costs on those officeholders who capitulate, may be the only means of raising the costs of capitulation sufficiently to make precommitment a policy without regrets once hostages are taken. Moreover, the failure of nations to act in a united way also raises uncertainty about the outcome associated with the holding of hostages. This uncertainty inhibits conventional expectations from working.

Game-theoretic considerations also impede efficient actions when two or more nations are targeted by the same terrorist group. If each nation decides its deterrence independently, then each may allocate too many resources to inducing terrorists to switch their area of attack, rather than to curbing overall terrorism. This follows because the nations do not take into account the negative influence (by inducing terrorists to operate on another nation's soil) that their deterrence choices create for others. In consequence, too much may be spent on controlling terrorism as each nation tries to force the terrorists to stage their events elsewhere. If these nations were to share intelligence concerning the group's true preferences for attacking alternative targets, then the overdeterrence problem would be aggravated as nations are better able to calculate what it takes to make the terrorists go elsewhere. Piecemeal policy, in which intelligence but not deterrence decisions are shared, may make everyone worse off. A grand strategy for coordinating policy on all fronts is required to handle transnational terrorism.

From theory to practice

What can policymakers gain from this study? We would argue that technology does work to harden targets and should be applied to protect against a wide range of terrorist attacks. Authorities must be ever vigilant to anticipate terrorists substituting into alternative events when new technologies are applied to thwart specific modes of attacks. Governments need to develop policies that impede multiple modes of terrorist attacks, while anticipating substitution into those modes not affected by new policies. Any policy or technology designed to thwart all forms of terrorist activities—such as cutting channels of supplies— would be immune to the substitution phenomenon. Retaliatory raids appear to impose short-run costs with no apparent long-run benefits and hence are best avoided.

Unless a central enforcement mechanism is instituted, international conventions are expected to have little real impact owing to incentives that induce nations to renege on agreements. Resources may be better spent on bilateral agreements where all parties consent to an enforcement procedure. Transnational terrorism gives rise to scenarios where nations may work at cross-purposes when confronting a common threat. Unless nations coordinate a wide range of anti-terrorist policies, nations may not make true gains in the fight against terrorism.

On My Mind
CLOSING OUR EYES

A. M. Rosenthal

About the downing of Pan American 103, only two major questions remain to be answered. This is the first:

Will the truth be disclosed to the world—the full truth, not just the part being recited at the United Nations?

The answer is yes, someday—it's a matter of time. Too many people were involved in the crime, from too many countries, for the U.S. and the U.N. to be able to hang the bombing only on the Libyans and then just walk away forever from the rest of the story, the heart of it.

And too many people have been part of the investigation—intelligence agents, technicians and magistrates from America, Europe and the Middle East.

Among those I have talked to over the past years, I have found none who believed only Libya alone paid for, planned and carried out the crime—exactly none.

Steven Emerson, the Washington journalist who, with Brian Duffy, wrote "The Fall of Pan Am 103" in 1990, provided me with this updated summary:

"The undisputed intelligence shows that Syria-based and -supported terrorists, led by Ahmed Jabril, head of the Popular Front for the Liberation of Palestine—General Command, planned and organized multiple airplane bombings against U.S., European and Israeli airlines in October 1988.

"The money and orders for the oper-

Pan Am 103: the full story.

ation came from Iran, seeking revenge for the shooting down of the Iranian airbus that summer by the U.S. According to intelligence officials, Iranian officials traveled to Germany to oversee the operation and to personally witness the transfer of explosives and bombs.

"But the plan went awry when Syrian-based terrorists were arrested by German police in late October 1988. Jabril, who had received funding from Libya for at least the previous two years, handed off the operation to Libya, which had its own terrorist infrastructure in place."

In any inquiry as long and complicated as the Pan Am investigation there are differences among investigators as to timing and importance of details. I quote the Emerson summary because among professional investigators I found no quarrel with its basic outline:

The Iranians paid for the operation. The Syrian-based terrorists planned it. Libyans were brought in for the kill—the physical planting of the bomb.

Vincent M. Cannistraro headed the C.I.A.'s investigation in the first years, until he left the agency in 1990. He says that the Jabril group was central to the operation.

Ahmed Jabril is a former Syrian army officer. It is in Syria that his troops are barracked and trained. He also has close ties, financial and political, to Iran. As for the Libyans, some of the Jabril group fly planes for them, and fought with them in the war with Chad.

Mr. Cannistraro says that after scouting the field for a target, the Jabril group settled on Pan Am because it found that in Frankfurt the airline was not "reconciling" baggage fully—not making sure that every piece of baggage was identi-

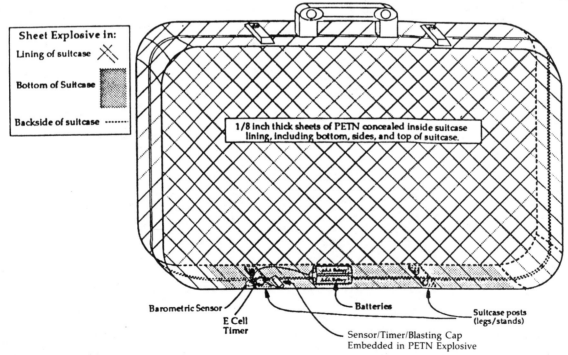

Figure 1. Suitcase Bomb with PETN explosive, barometric sensor, E cell timer, and blasting cap concealed inside lining on bottom, top, ends, and sides of suitcase

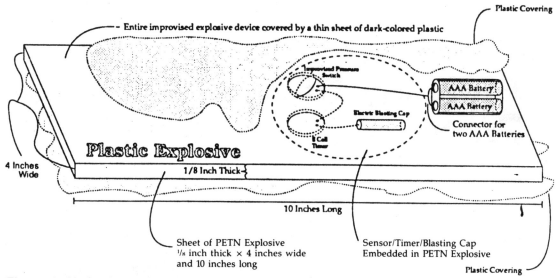

Figure 2. Under-the-seat-cushion bomb used against Pan Am.

fied directly with a passenger before being taken on board.

Then came the arrests by the Germans, and the handoff to the Libyans. Mr. Cannistraro thinks it likely that the Libyans were part of the operation from the beginning.

Until 1991 the U.S. made it no secret that Ahmed Jabril was at the center of the web, thus involving Syria. Then evidence was found that also pointed to

two Libyans. President Bush thereupon stunned the intelligence world by saying that Syria had received a "bum rap."

So now we are expected to believe that two Middle Eastern terrorist gangs, paid by the same masters, comrades in previous actions, were carrying out separate bombing operations against the same U.S. airline at the same time in the same city, all unknown to each other. Separately, two intelligence spe-

cialists came up with the same description of that idea: total barnyard epithet.

Now the second question—why the refusal of the U.S. to indicate that Syria and Iran are, at the very least, guilty accomplices?

Sometimes relatives of the 270 Pan Am victims ask if Mr. Bush is guilty of cover-up. I say no but he is closing his eyes to what he does not wish to see. We all do that, I said to one relative and she said yes but we are not all Presidents, are we?

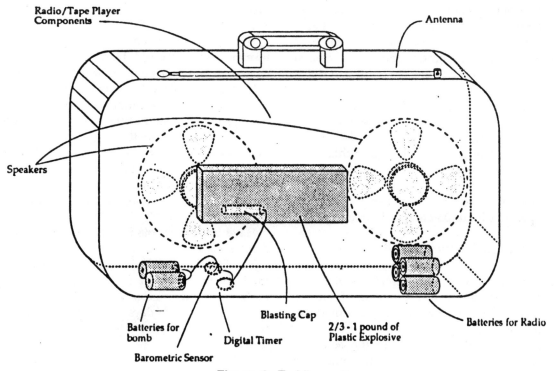

Figure 3. Toshiba radio

Amnesty Head Urges More Pressure on Human Rights

BOSTON

I an Martin, secretary-general of Amnesty International, met with Monitor staff on March 23, a day before the release of a report on human rights violations in India. He spoke of Amnesty's work around the world.

What do you see as your mission and what is it you do that changes the situation?

Any ordinary person can do something that can affect the human rights conduct of governments. [When it was first proposed,] that seemed like a pretty crazy idea. But over the years, that's exactly what has happened.

In the last five or six years access has opened up to a lot of places that were closed off to us before, obviously, but it's still not all the world. Some people are surprised to know that [India] is one [nation] that won't give us visas to go and do research, as well as the more obvious cases like China, Syria, and Iraq, etc.

We have, I think, largely gotten away from the case where there's any resonance for the argument that human rights criticism is interference in internal affairs. We still get that a bit from the Chinese government. But it sounds more and more anachronistic each time you hear it. Even the Chinese are beginning to shave that position and to say, yes, we are going to engage in human rights dialogue.

What's particularly important . . . is that people don't give up on human rights as an issue because they think it's sort of taken care of, with the trend to democracy, with Western governments making human rights more central in their foreign policies.

Because, positive as those things are, it's not very hard to see that democracy from elections is only the beginning . . .of improving the protection of human rights.

How do you function on the ground?

Information collection is very hard to generalize about because you have such a spectrum of situations. You have the really open situation: If you're talking about the Philippines, or if you're talking about Peru or Colombia, there is no obstacle to our going there.

So you've got that on the one hand. I suppose North Korea would be the ultimate example at the other end now, but a few years ago I would have included Burma, for example, in the case of countries [that do not allow access to Amnesty workers. In Burma, that changed in] 1988, when students fled into Thailand. But there we can only go to the borders where there are refugees and interview them.

How big a factor is Amnesty's letter-writing campaign in addressing human rights abuses?

It's real. It's not just keeping members feeling involved. Take the kind of report we release. If I were a government and a human rights organization was publishing a report, I'd be unhappy about it. But if it was a [matter of a] week's publicity, I wouldn't be that worried. I'd sort of keep my head low and let it blow over a bit. . . .

[The India] report would be the beginning of an international campaign, which means that Amnesty members in all our 47 sections would be going to see ambassadors in their countries. . . . I think our strength is in . . . the publicity around the fact-finding and its results with sustained action, and our membership base gives us that possibility.

What happens when a country gets letters about its human rights record? Does it reform because of a change of heart or because of international pressure?

It's both. Perhaps it is overwhelming embarrassment. But I don't think one should underestimate the extent to which sometimes at the other end [there] are people with a conscience. Or, more than that. We all know no government is monolithic, and there are apt to be very different attitudes, and there are balances of power within it. Perhaps what we're doing is strengthening the hands of the better people within the systems of governments.

Have improvements in technology had any effect on Amnesty's work?

Yes. One of our researchers in Guatemala said—I don't think she was exaggerating—that today we get faxes from indigenous Indian groups who five years ago just sort of walked in for three days to give information to a contact who would then post it to us. Now they're sending us faxes.

-Scott Baldauf

INTELLIGENCE AND THE WAR

DIMINISHING

AGAINST TERRORISM

THE THREAT

Meir Amit

The author is a retired major general who served as director of IDF military intelligence and as head of the Mossad. He has also held senior positions in both government and industry. He is currently chairman of General Satellite Corporation, which is developing the Amos communications satellite in conjuction with IAI.

A ided by advances in technology, communications, transportation, and even diplomacy, a new plague has cursed the family of nations: terrorism. There are few activities today which require as much thorough and monotonous preparation as anti–terror campaigns. As the attacks themselves become increasingly sophisticated, the counter–measures must respond in kind, using first–class professionals who are well–trained to pinpoint their target.

Public relations is an important part of anti–terrorist activity. The enemy must be exposed, and the public must be convinced of the need for the steps to be taken against them.

Range of Measures

When determining what means to use against a particular terrorist threat, operational intelligence is of primary importance. Defensive measures, such as fencing off an area, can be combined with preventive measures, such as keeping weapons from being smuggled into a given area.

Preventive measures on the political level include detention, which aims to prevent potential trouble makers from being involved in expected operations. In addition, "agents of influence" are effective in shaping opinions, especially among youth who may be inclined to join terror organizations.

Retaliatory actions and punishment, of course, are always possible responses to a terrorist action. It should be emphasized that collective punishment is less effective than isolating those who are really responsible for a particular act. In addition, punishment doesn't really prevent terrorism. At best it can delay it, which is an important factor in a continuous struggle.

The retaliatory steps taken against Jordan in the late 1960s and early 1970, in response to terrorist actions emanating from that country, provide an interesting case in point. In September 1970, the Jordanian government decided to restore order. In one week, more Palestinian terrorists were killed in Jordan than had been killed by Israel during the preceding 20 years. There was no international reaction. The incident showed that sometimes pressure on others brings them to achieve your goals for you.

Another very important measure is education: preparing the public to behave correctly before, during, and after a terror attack. No matter how many agents the authorities place in areas sensitive to attack, there is no replacement for an alert public.

Cooperation, encompassing various possibilities from international cooperation to inter–service cooperation, is a component of the overall struggle against terrorism. Sometimes there are differences of opinion between the various services, a problem faced by Israel until the responsibilities between the different services combating terror were very clearly defined. It was not easy, and ideal results can never be achieved. Cooperation also means the flow of information, shared doctrine, and the coordination of retaliation and counter–terrorist activities.

Crucial Weapon

Intelligence is the most crucial weapon against terrorism. Only those anti–terror activities based on good intelligence can be effective.

With advance knowledge, we can be sure that 80–90 percent of terrorist incidents will be prevented. The majority of hostile actions within Israel do not take place at all because of early intelligence information. They are prevented before they begin. Reliable intelligence allows the authorities to concentrate on sensitive or suspected areas, which makes them more effective and saves a lot of resources.

While the intelligence community is active 24 hours a day, 365 days a year, its achievements cannot be publicized.

Reprinted by permission of the *IDF Journal* (Israel Defense Forces Journal), Fall 1989, pp. 8-10.

Only mishaps, fiascoes, and failures receive public attention. The large majority of intelligence actions are successful, but nobody knows about them.

Intelligence is also vital for effective retaliation. In 1973, three of the key Fatah terrorists in Beirut were killed. They had been personally involved in planning and executing terrorist acts. They had been the brains behind the operations. In planning retaliation against them, they were followed, and **their habits and those of their families,** whom we did not want to harm, were carefully studied. Intelligence played a decisive role not only in providing the information, but during the operation itself. Israeli agents went into Beirut and found their targets simultaneously in their homes in different high–rise buildings. Without very specific information these kinds of operations would be impossible to carry out.

Anti–Terrorist Planning

The first task is to set up a static network that collects data on a continuous basis, thereby establishing a database. This is not an easy job and it is not the most interesting work. On top of this static network you have to superimpose a dynamic network that supplies information in real time. ·

The next step is to establish priorities, which amount to warning lights or *Important Information Indicators.* To avoid a constant state of alert, priorities must be established for the collection agencies as well as for those who evaluate the information. There is an ocean of information and, although there are computers that use sophisticated processing methods, it is very difficult to cope with so much data. That is why it is necessary to set priorities and define important items.

Subsequently, information has to be processed, edited, and disseminated. Information that is not sent to the right people at the right time and in the right form is worthless. There is a dilemma here. Political leaders and decision makers want raw information. They want to feel the flavor, they don't want sterile processed information. This can be very dangerous.

When Moshe Dayan was Minister of Defense, he liked to *feel* information, to *sense* it. The danger was that he would draw conclusions from one set of facts, against all the rules. We worked hard to find the right way to present the information while also satisfying his need to be close to the raw input. This was not unique to Dayan, and whenever it occurs, it creates a real problem for intelligence officers.

The next step is to build a communications network that connects all the parties concerned. This is intended not only to establish links, but to keep them open and to see to it that the information will flow in real time. Even the best information, the best processing, and the best analysis will produce no results if they are not communicated to the decision–makers at the proper time.

International cooperation is also vital, including databases, exchanges of information, and open communication. There is a need to define a clear and unified terminology. Each country must decide its own order of priorities, which makes it difficult to combine efforts.

Decision–Making

There must be an efficient and quick decision–making process on both the national and international levels. Adequate resources must be allocated for in-

telligence, including money, people, organization, and even definition of areas of responsibility. There is no better investment than intelligence. It gives the best results, even better than any other investment in defensive or offensive activity.

Finally, the need for very close cooperation between intelligence and operations must be stressed. The operations staff must understand intelligence, while intelligence personnel must understand the operation.

As opposed to other modes of warfare, terrorism is irregular. It is a partisan war, and is highly compartmentalized. Terrorists operate in small mobile units. They are flexible and have almost no hierarchy. It is very difficult to mix in their crowd, as closed groups know one another. Any stranger who appears on the scene is immediately suspect, therefore, collecting information about terrorists in their own milieu is very difficult.

There are ethical problems as well. In conventional war, the rules of the game are different. But terror activity takes place in peacetime, when these rules are not applied. Martial law cannot be imposed, and the courts must be respected.

Finally, we face the problem of false alarms, since no chances can be taken when combating terror. Repeated diversions of false alarms add up to a major imposition which diminishes the reliability of intelligence.

Anti–terror activity is a continuous war. Although terrorism does not present a danger to our very existence, its cumulative effect has been a major drain on our resources, as well as on our national spirit. In the future, terrorists may turn to nuclear or chemical weapons, and the threat they pose will increase. We must be constantly vigilant. I do not think terrorism can be stopped altogether, but it can be diminished.

Terror and Negotiation

Martin Hughes

This article considers the claim that we should never negotiate with terrorists. The author argues that, although it may always be wrong to let terrorists dictate to us, negotiation may still be acceptable since to negotiate and to submit to dictation are different things. A ransom agreed in negotiation is a ransom which can be afforded and so should not be withheld. The claim that to ransom some victims is to endanger others is commonly exaggerated to the point of treating existing hostages as unconditionally expendable; a certain barbarism is reached at that point. Turning to the argument that negotiation concedes legitimacy to illegitimate political forces the author argues, firstly, that to deny that an opponent has any legitimacy is to risk brutalizing oneself and, secondly, that to seek legitimacy in opponents who have been evil hitherto is a useful means of securing peace. He concedes that the search for legitimacy in evil people may fail for years or even fail indefinitely and that during those years negotiations are useless; which makes ruthless repression on our part the only reply to terrorism which, during those years, is of any use. But this concession does not elevate 'Never negotiate with terrorists' into an absolute moral principle.

It is always wrong, according to the convictions of many people, to negotiate at all with terrorists because this always makes them stronger materially and – what is worse – confers legitimacy upon them. In opposition to this I argue that readiness to negotiate, though not readiness to accept any terms asked, is, in general, right. Refusal to negotiate means that we resolve to use force as our only means of dealing with certain enemies; to use force only, even against opponents of undeniably evil nature, is corrupting. This is a general moral point: I refer to particular cases but offer no manual for negotiators; I suggest only that the special features which each case is likely to have make it hard to find any maxim which is morally compelling every time. The maxim that a firm policy of refusing terrorist demands should be firmly followed,[1] a maxim which seems to rule negotiations out, except perhaps negotiations on such temporary matters as food supplies for the hostages, has a stark simplicity which I cannot accept and moral consequences which disturb me.

The consequence which most concerns me is falling into the trap noticed by Joseph Conrad in *The Secret Agent*. Conrad portrays a terrorist called 'the Professor'[2] whose aim is to put himself beyond arrest by carrying explosives which he will detonate when any attempt at arrest is made – he means to force the police to shoot him down illegally. He believes that by forcing the police into illegality, that is forcing society to rely on force alone, he can strike the heaviest blow against society, corrupting its soul rather than simply shedding some of its blood. Before arguing that he was right in this belief I offer some definitions and indicate the background in political philosophy from which I argue.

By 'terrorists' for present purposes I mean those who take and threaten hostages, using their hostages' lives as a bargaining counter. By 'anti-terrorists' I mean those who oppose terrorists, by 'counter-terrorists' those who try to oppose them by some equivalent threat, if necessary in disregard of legal restrictions. 'Hostages' may refer, in a narrow sense, to captives in a dungeon or a hijacked plane but also there are hostages in a wider sense: whole populations who must run their lives with an eye on on the shadowy presence of a private army, hostile to the legitimate government, in their midst. Plainly, hostages in the wider sense may be sympathizers with the terrorist cause or potential recruits to it; so, sometimes, may hostages in the narrow sense if the emotional circumstances are right. Terrorists may be able to create these circumstances – 'the Stockholm syndrome'[3] – by the manipulation of language.

Although not all brutality counts as terror it is possible under my definition for brutal methods used by governments to be counted as terror against the people and it is possible both for unofficial terrorists and for governments to terrorise their own supporters. Rulers in crisis, desperate to modernize their countries or to prepare for war, sometimes treat those supporters who are entrusted with any office or responsibility as hostages: if they do not fulfil the Plan they pay with their lives. But in current usage the term 'state terrorism' refers less to such domestic management by terror as to support by one state for terrorists operating against another state. In this paper I do not discuss international negotiation where one government is currently terrorist in either sense. Although I do mention negotiation with governments whose past is terrorist my main concern is with terror as part of internal or civil conflict.

I assume that terrorists are ruthless servants of a big idea and ruthless manipulators of language in the cause of their idea. Accordingly they belong to a category of people whose appearance in civil conflict is incisively described by Thucydides[4] and angrily discussed by Hobbes, who is much influenced by Thucydides and is the greatest philosopher of conflict, in Part IV of *Leviathan*,[5] where the perversion of ideas, particularly of Christian ideas, is the main topic. This topic has remarkable contemporary importance. The acrimony and fanaticism of the old religious wars has found rebirth in the terrorism of today: increasingly we find religion as a motive and terrorism as a means.

From *Terrorism and Political Violence*, Vol. 2, No. 1, Spring 1990, pp. 72-82. *Terrorism and Political Violence*, published by Frank Cass and Company, Ltd., England.

8. COUNTERING TERRORISM

But Hobbes comes to the conclusion that it was a fault in the government of Charles I to repress people whose political ideas were perverted. So it was wrong, at least according to this phase of Hobbes' philosophy, to treat these dangerous people as if they had no legitimacy, wrong even though they had in truth no legitimacy: and this phase of Hobbes' philosophy is what I attempt to explore and apply in this article. Refusal to negotiate is the logical expression of the belief that the other side has no legitimacy and so should not be treated as if it had. From noticing why people refuse to negotiate we can see what negotiation truly is.

To understand the idea of negotiation we should first distinguish negotiation from dictation. If one side has no choice except the choice between its own destruction and the acceptance of dictated terms then the situation is a different one from those we consider here, where we presuppose that the choice between negotiation and hostilities (with some chance of success) is always open. Negotiation envisages compromise and therefore presupposes that the other party has, or can acquire, some predictable character: if that other party is completely unstable he cannot compromise or take any definite position. We can, of course, use negotiation to create the character we want. Facing a man who had seized a gun in desperate rage we might try to talk, offer him ways out and so calm him down: a minor but significant example of negotiation and of the search for common ground where people can converse without threats.

The aim of negotiation is to remove threats and so must be a search for legitimacy in the other party. This is exactly why some say 'Never negotiate with terrorists'. They say this because they demand absolute fidelity to our original principles: these were right and we should stick to them; the other side, who rejects our principles, is and always was hopelessly corrupt and should be treated accordingly. If we accept that there is any legitimacy in them we commit moral treason.

The tactical maxim of the upper hand, which says 'Never negotiate except from great strength and to great advantage' is rather different and concentrates on the material strength of the enemy, which, by this maxim, must never increase either directly or through any form of political gain which may recruit more supporters or increase morale. Thus even legitimate demands should be refused, once they have been pressed by terrorist means, unless you are already sure of victory over the terrorist forces. Postponing the central question of legitimacy, I consider first the practical arguements against letting the terrorists gain advantage in any way, even for a time.

II

Against the idea of negotiating with terrorists the 'more hostages' argument – that is the argument that negotiation to release actual hostages 'merely puts others at risk' – usually prevails. Furthermore it is argued that, if there is a ransom, the enemy will use the ransom to buy more arms which will bring more hostages within his reach; I call this the 'more guns, more hostages' argument. Still more important, if part of the ransom is release of captured terrorists, they will feel they can operate with impunity. We will have made them a present of renewed morale. I call this the 'impunity argument'. All these arguments are variations on one theme, that the terrorist enemy must be denied all material and tactical advantages.

These arguments do not really have anything like the decisive force that people imagine. The 'more hostages' argument treats a contingent risk as if it were ineluctable. It is extraordinary that Western governments refuse or pretend to refuse to negotiate with terrorists who seize Western hostages on the streets of Beirut, a place where armed gangs, each based in a few crowded and impenetrable streets, have sometimes been the only power.[6] The refusal is justified because others must not be put at risk. But why not take the simple precaution of keeping our people out of Beirut and the tiny areas where the terrorists' writ runs? The fear of more hostages in the future loses its force completely if there other means sure to cut off the hostage supply; and it loses its force not completely, but significantly, if there are means simply likely to cut off that supply.

Here I might be challenged by people with better factual knowledge than I can claim of the situation in Beirut, who might scorn my remark that there is a 'simple precaution'. It may be that there will always be Westerners who cannot avoid venturing into the danger zone or that success in Beirut will tempt Lebanese terrorists to try their hand abroad, even in Western countries. But the conclusion is the same even if these objections are correct.

If the danger zone is not avoidable and there will always be people who are potential hostages but who must venture there, then the most important point is that there is no reason to think that refusal to negotiate over previous hostages protects them: the terrorists may take great satisfaction in creating impotent anger and gnawing fear in those whom they especially hate and they can achieve this by adding more victims to their collection, emphasizing once again the impossibility of rescue. Furthermore, even if there must be some venturers into the danger zone it is obvious that there cannot be many: only extreme commitment, necessity or folly will bring flies to the spider's web. So there is no serious fear that the number of hostages might become so high that the terrorists' bargaining position, should negotiations happen, will be unbearably strong.

Again, it may be that Lebanese terrorists will release present British hostages but then take more, not in Lebanon if none are available there, but in other countries, even in Britain itself. But then the battle would be on much better ground. The present hostages have languished for years: in Beirut no rescue is thinkable, elsewhere it would be. So, even if keeping our people out of Lebanon is not as complete a precaution as I believe it is, the future risks do not prohibit the negotiated release of the present hostages.

Another form of the argument I oppose suggests that, even if there are no more physical hostages, we can by negotiation make our sovereignty and government policy a hostage. Those who say this forget the distinction between negotiation and dictation. Of course, no government can accept dictation of policy by anyone else. But is it an inflexible principle that policy never changes in any respect to save the lives of our citizens? Surely there is neither fairness nor fidelity to the social contract in protecting some others from a hypothetical risk by means which submit the present hostages to real, unending misery. Moreover there is a certain barbarity in treating any individuals as utterly and unconditionally expendable, which is what this principle insists that we do to the present hostages.

Similarly, a few more guns and a bit more money are not too worrying if their effects can be neutralized by the enormous arsenals and treasuries of the anti-terrorists. The 'more guns, more hostages' argument treats an absolute increase in terrorists' power as if it were important; in reality it is the increase relative to the power of the anti-terrorists that matters and that relative increase, even when the absolute increase is substantial, may be completely trivial. My argument presupposes that the ransom will not be too great: which, I suggest, is a rational presupposition. No money ransom is likely to bring the overall armament of the terrorists to a point anywhere near that of the anti-terrorists: if it were it would not be paid. The central point is that ransoms by definition are set, if they are negotiated rather than dictated, by what the donor can afford. Ransom in kind, if it were (say) nuclear weapons able to turn the whole balance of power between terror and anti-terror, would not be granted.

If we turn to the impunity argument we should note that 'impunity' either refers to freedom from due and legal punishment under a social contract or to freedom from revenge by aggrieved people, including aggrieved governments.

Freedom from punishment outrages us in proportion to our commitment to protect the social contract which protects us all: to grant impunity is to strike a blow at the heart of the social contract. There is no question but that unrestricted impunity for terrorists would be a mortal blow but we cannot instantly conclude that lesser degrees of impunity have the same drastic effect. It is clear that not all demands, however extreme, made in negotiation can be met but not clear that negotiation should not start.

Terrorists have often seized hostages to secure the release of their own friends imprisoned for previous terrorism. The result of negotiation has sometimes been – as in the recent hijack involving Iran, Kuwait and Algeria in various roles, against which British opinion reacted very strongly – that the imprisoned terrorists stayed in prison but that the free terrorists stay free in exchange for the hostages' lives.[7] If – and it is a big if – an outcome on these terms is acceptable it follows that impunity is acceptable, at least impunity to a certain degree.

British government and public opinion had strong reservations about accepting even this degree of immunity for those who had perpetrated the Iran–Algeria hijack, which was hideously protracted and brutal. But this understandable movement of opinion may have been wrong. If we refuse to end any terrorist incident with immunity to the terrorists, and maintain this refusal even if we can see no other way to release the hostages, our refusal amounts to the absolute assertion that, as a matter of principle, the outcome in which hostages and terrorists all die is preferable to the outcome in which all live. But surely – to expand slightly on a point made above – the idea of social contract is to protect innocent lives and to create rulers, armed forces, courts of law and punishments, as means for this protection. The absolute, exception-free assertion demands that we sacrifice the end, protection of life, to the means, victorious use of armed force: which is illogical.

Punishments are a substitute under the social contract for the natural right of revenge, which is personal vindication of honour and reputation and which any social contract severely limits. But it is possible for governments or individuals to treat revenge as more important than punishment in extreme situations. They may think that contracts are meaningless unless the government can defend its honour. This is not necessarily a vainglorious idea: it appeals to the idea of honourable behaviour, meaning firm and consistent defence of what we believe in. That means, they suppose, no advantage to terrorists of any sort: all they deserve is retribution. This retribution or revenge must be claimed at all costs, since anything else dishonours and subverts government. Justice, on this view, becomes summary. The right to fair trial and treatment which ordinary criminals have is simply an advantage which terrorists will (as they so often have done) shamefully exploit. Terrorists have no rights.

But this at-all-costs retributionist view, adopted in the name of consistent and honourable moral effort, is disastrous to rulers, partly but not only because of the catastrophic loss of support that may occur if 'all costs' are willingly paid. The classic example is the excessive repression after the 1916 rising in Ireland.

But even apart from this kind of catastrophe, campaigns of all-out retribution and repression against terrorists are always, but for one exceptional class (which is the worst), fought inconsistently and by two kinds of force. First there are those genuinely under the control of the government and thus with rules of engagement that apply some limits to what they can do; secondly there are irregular forces who find these limits irksome. Irregular military forces are not necessarily mere scum or social outcasts transformed into mindless death squads. If the regular forces are weakened then good people may have to consider saving society by private means; if the regular forces are expensively strengthened and wear totalitarian trappings then there will be some who want to assert their independence of spirit by doing their job for them, quickly and cheaply. In the mind of Ulster Protestantism,[8] ever since it emerged as a political force, there have been appeals to both principles: the British government and its armed forces sometimes seem too weak, therefore in need of private citizens' help, and sometimes too overbearing, therefore in need of correction by true patriots. This is a necessary development. Governments can scarcely remain governments if they do not insist on controlling their supporters and in a violent scene this means serious tension: the government has wider policy questions to think of, its local supporters have an overwhelming concern with immediate problems and fears – with face-to-face enemies who may be waiting with a gun round the next corner. The immediate fear turns local loyalists into vigilantes, persons with a self-awarded licence to kill.

When the government calls for victory and retribution against the enemy at all costs it means victory for its own authority: when the vigilantes call for victory over the same enemy they mean that their right to self-defence (by attack if necessary) must be vindicated, even at a cost to the authority of the government which it would be self-defeating for the government to pay. Government restraint on vigilantes – which probably means painful restraint on the keenest members of the regular forces as well – is therefore a concession to the terrorists: they are to be treated as if they had rights after all. And that cancels the policy of retribution at all costs.

For example, de Gaulle was put into power by French Algerian forces that were, because they had decided to keep Algeria French at all costs, escaping constitutional control; once in power, he had, if he was truly to exercise government, to control them. It is plain that his decision to negotiate with the native Algerian terrorists led to a bloody conflict with French Algerian forces. The converse is just as true: his need to be genuinely in power forced him into conflict with his former supporters. Because he was fighting them he had to abandon their policy: so he, once the chosen representative of those who cried for victory at all costs, had to negotiate with the terrorists. This example illustrates how the policy of victory and retribution at all costs does not lead to a consistent effort but raises two forces, potentially in serious conflict, on what was once the same side.

There is, as mentioned, an exceptional and worst case typified by El Salvador: here the government is not genuinely in power[9] but formally in office while vigilantes – now official stormtroops and the only effective anti-terrorist force – act in their own way, the way of people trained only for violence. This is a recipe for barbarism. No one in this situation stands on a moral plane higher than that of the terrorists. We simply find a range of armed factions contending for victory at all costs. The only moral distinction between them now is in policy for the future. If we have to choose between them only on these grounds we might well hope for negotiation and compromise, so that after the fighting there will

be some scope for policy rather than victory in a desert. Once again it is a mistake to think that refusal to compromise is the only sign of a consistent and honourable mind.

This completes my case as far as it concerns material and tactical advantages. The arguments I oppose overestimate the material advantages to be gained by the terrorists from negotiation and underestimate the costs paid by the government by refusing to negotiate, including the costs of vigilantism. I now turn to the question of legitimacy.

III

The slide from anti-terrorism to counter-terrorism and stormtroop behaviour is the slide by government to the same moral plane as the terrorists occupy. My argument above shows, I believe, that 'the Professor' was right: that to induce this slide is a most important objective for terrorists because it splits their opponents into vigilantes and legitimists. The opposite process is the one in which terrorists are raised above their original plane – that is, acquire legitimacy. Even though this may take generations to complete, or seriously to begin, it is the more desirable process. It demands entry into negotiations by representatives of non-terrorist traditions; the latter are bound to have suspicions which they need to keep within bounds if the process is ever to be completed. By far the most important example is that of the Soviet Union, a society that once attempted modernization through terror and whose rulers, heirs of the terror, now appreciate that further modernization requires the removal of the substantial remains of the system by which terror was inflicted. I accept that the example of the Soviet Union, now an established world power, raises rather different questions from those raised by my general topic, terrorist civil wars. But the differences do not make the example irrelevant. It should encourage us to believe that, even where there is not the slightest short-term prospect for negotiation, we should not rule it out on principle: the right time may come.

My central contention is that the best and most prudent thing we can do with terrorists or the heirs of terrorists is give them legitimacy, thus enabling them to abandon and leave behind the methods of terror: the means to this is negotiation, because negotiation is a search for legitimacy in the other side. If they will not accept the gift then, of course, the hostility must continue – and this may be the case for several generations. By parity of reasoning we on our part should refuse to offer the gift only if we ourselves want to ensure that the conflict or battle continues and so are ready to commit ourselves to the necessary campaigns of repression and to pay the price that these entail.

I support my contention as follows. I have already argued that repression 'at all costs' in the name of absolute fidelity to our original principles is detrimental in practical terms. I now suggest it brings with it a fundamental moral problem. Governments facing this problem may find their own legitimacy lost. The root of that problem is this, that to deny legitimacy to any group of human beings is to commend highly the job of controlling them and to condemn bitterly all their objections to our control. The more consistently we affirm these values and the more we embody them in the law the more we commit ourselves to a double standard and so become, after all, unfaithful to our original principles.

An example is to be found in certain events which form part of British dealings with Irish terror. In the 'Birmingham Six' judgement, recent at the time of writing, the Court rejected an appeal, mentioning among other points that those concerned were known IRA sympathizers, had 'signified approval'[10] of the IRA. There has been immense debate about the facts of this case; for the purposes of this argument I assume that the Court was right in every disputed matter of fact. Behind the apparent factual dispute there lies something quite different, in truth a dispute over the legitimacy of Irish nationalism.

Nothing could be more rational than the opinion that known sympathisers with a terrorist cause are more likely, in comparison with known opponents, to be terrorists themselves. This remains true however widely the word 'sympathy' is defined: Irish nationalism, which is support for the objectives of the IRA, is obviously more likely, compared with opposition to those objectives, to issue in active IRA membership. The sympathy makes the action more probable. Thus there is a valid inference: given his opinions he can reasonably be suspected of crime. From this there is a further inference: the opinions of Irish nationalists are illegitimate because of their criminal tendency. Because Irish nationalists reject this conclusion they reject the whole train of inferences and accuse the Court, in its assessment of facts, of gross unfairness and of travesty. These accusations are themselves unfair; all the same the Court's proceedings were one part of a picture which should give us grave concern.

8. COUNTERING TERRORISM

At about the same time as the 'Birmingham Six' case a British soldier, convicted of murder in the course of service in the Northern Ireland terror zone, was pardoned and reinstated in the Army: he was, on an official view, merely involved in a 'tragic error'.[11] We may have no difficulty at all in sympathising with a young man under the intense pressure of war against lurking gunmen. But the official attitude (supported by public opinion) to this case was the logical counterpart to the attitude to terrorist sympathisers just described. From the fact that someone has dedicated himself against terrorism there is an inference to his essential justice and innocence, bestowed by the goodness and legitimacy of the cause.

These two cases taken together apply, if we consider the reasons given and the words used, a double standard to the idea of guilt, double because the essential question is 'Which side is he on?' We might imagine the opposite double standard applied to the two cases in the hardest Catholic areas of Belfast:

> A brutal army of occupation officially declares that this murder is an error rather than an evil: so we can conceive of patriotism only as violent opposition to those who so despise the Irish. Meanwhile British courts insult the Irish by using as evidence of guilt of violent crime simple belief in the nationalist cause, belief which is nothing but elementary patriotism.

From a British point of view we would readily see that the Thucydidean process, whereby the beautiful words of moral discourse become stupefying weapons of propaganda, was at work here. But I suggest that the examples show that the same process is also at work, though it may not be so advanced, in the British body politic.

The trains of thought underlying both the Court of Appeal judgment and the pardon for the soldier can readily be understood by anyone with British patriotic loyalties, the loyalties which I share. Indeed I believe public opinion supported both, with major protest only from those with Irish sympathies. But acceptance of both is very disturbing. Even if one of the two trains of thought is fully justified morally, it is impossible that both should be. We cannot approve of both unless our thought is dominated by the question 'Which side is he on?' But if that question is dominant we are no longer thinking in a moral spirit, since a moral spirit demands impartiality and impartiality is just what this question excludes. Not to think in a moral spirit is to lose integrity.

But this loss of integrity is hard to avoid if we insist that we are a legitimate political force and that others, with whom we are in conflict, are not legitimate. Then the question of which side someone is on, ours or theirs, must be of supreme importance when we judge his actions. To claim exclusive legitimacy is to lose moral integrity because it is to abandon impartial judgement, and to lose moral integrity is to put our claim to legitimate political authority at risk, perhaps to lay the foundations of tyranny or some other serious moral decline.

This problem connects with the problems of negotiation with terrorists because it arises from the claim to exclusive legitimacy, the claim which is most often advanced by those who rule out negotiation with terrorists completely and on principle. The moral danger inherent in making this claim is very serious, akin to the dangers of excessive zeal which Hobbes saw in the religious policy of Charles I: excessive even against people whose religious ideas were dangerously perverted.

Perhaps there are some people in whom we can never find good or even the shadow of some legitimate purpose. Still, I oppose the idea that we should, as a matter of principle, refuse to look for good in the other side during protracted years of conflict. The refusal to look is the rejection of the very idea of negotiation, the process by which we seek for legitimacy in opponents or seek to create it in them.

The practical alternative to negotiation is the apparatus of repression – blazing guns, bleak prisons, intrusive surveillance – always evil in themselves. I have never questioned that these means may have to be used, even intensively and over long stretches of time. I am aware that negotiation has been tried in Northern Ireland and has always failed abysmally. But the awareness of that failure should not make us nail our colours to the claim of exclusive legitimacy. This claim is corrupting. 'Never negotiate with terrorists' is a false moral principle.

NOTES

1. P. Wilkinson, *Terrorism and the Liberal State*, 2nd ed. (London: Macmillan 1986), p.301.
2. See E.K. Hay, *The Political Novels of Joseph Conrad* (Chicago, 1L: University of Chicago Press, 1963), pp.251–63.
3. M. Connor, *Terrorism: The Solutions* (London: Paladin Press, 1987), pp.127–9.
4. Thucydides, *Histories*, Book III, para.82.
5. T. Hobbes, *Leviathan*, especially Ch. 47.
6. J. Laffin, *The War of Desperation* (London: Osprey Publishing, 1985), p.204.
7. *The Times*, 21 April 1988.
8. S. Nelson, *Ulster's Uncertain Defenders* (Belfast: Appletree Press, 1984).
9. *The Economist*, 21 Nov. 1987.
10. *The Times*, 29 Jan. 1988.
11. *The Times*, 24 Feb. 1988.

RESPONSES TO TERRORISM

Peter C. Sederberg
● ● ●

When the United States bombed Qaddafi in April 1986 in reprisal for his supposed sponsorship of a terrorist attack in West Berlin, many commentators cheered because America was finally getting tough with terrorists. Ironically, the people who plotted the raid on Qaddafi were, at about the same time, carrying out secret negotiations with Iran for the release of American hostages in Lebanon. These negotiations culminated in a major scandal for the Reagan administration, and the number of Americans in captivity increased. The different consequences of these two policies seem to demonstrate that military reprisal, not conciliation, is the proper approach to terrorism. Some skeptics (Kaldor and Anderson, 1986; Hersh, 1987), to be sure, pointed out that Syria, not Libya, appears to have been the primary sponsor behind the Berlin attack, but Syrian air defenses are rather potent. Moreover, the attack failed in its objective of killing Qaddafi. Finally, the goal of assassinating a head of state with indiscriminate means (2000-pound bombs) resembles the terrorism it purports to be combating and, in fact, resulted in dozens of noncombatant deaths.

Attachment to a particular line of response to terrorism impoverishes our understanding of the range of policies actually available and discourages a more thorough analysis of what might be appropriate and when. These options, varying from extreme repression to systematic conciliation, arise not from a definitive theory of counterterrorism so much as reactions to different situations and opportunities. The absence of any encompassing theory of terrorism, after all, should lead us to expect similar diversity when it comes to policies to combat it.

One theme in the literature of response agonizes over the peculiar vulnerability of democracies to dissident terrorism as well as their institutional incapability of responding effectively against it (Dror, 1983; Lasser, 1987; Netanyahu, 1986; Wilkinson, 1986). Relatively open societies present more opportunities for attack; open borders facilitate the travel of radicals and their weapons; and, the commitment to the rule of law restricts the police but has no effect on those willing to use terrorism. Finally, special attention has been paid to the role of the free media in amplifying the effects of terrorism, thereby unwittingly serving the perpetrators' objectives (Livingstone, 1986; Miller, 1980; Wardlaw, 1982, 1990). On the other hand, critics (Chomsky, 1988; Herman and O'Sullivan, 1989) suggest that the United States is implicated in supporting establishment counterterrorist campaigns around the world and, moreover, is able to manipulate the media at home to support such policies.

Dror (1983) qualifies his discussion of the problems terrorism poses for democracies by arguing that *weak democracies* are the most vulnerable. His point should be taken one step further. *Weak states*, whether fragile democracies or narrowly supported autocracies, are most vulnerable to terrorism. Not only will dissident groups find the space to operate in a weak state but such regimes are more likely to succumb to the temptation of establishment terrorism, whether private or official, when confronting widespread dissent. The general prescription against terrorism of all kinds is to strengthen the institutional foundations of the state, and democracies have demonstrated that relative openness, representativeness, responsiveness, and commitment to the rule of law have proven generally superior to authoritarian prescriptions for institutional development.

Of course, long-term prescriptions do little to meet short-term challenges, and specific policies have been developed in response to immediate threats. When faced with an outbreak of dissident terrorism, many countries devise new laws to strengthen the ability of governments to manage more effectively. Among the measures approved in Western nations since 1970 are harsh penalties for acts defined as "terrorist," creation of special courts and prosecutors, restrictions on freedom of movement both internally and across national boundaries, and restrictions on the media (see country studies in Gutteridge, 1986 and Lodge, 1981b; see also Miller, 1982). Domestic legal remedies for establishment terrorism, however, appear almost irrelevant. Vigilante terrorism, after all, often develops precisely because the existing legal institutions are perceived as ineffective. Once the regime itself engages in terrorism, the notion of legal remedies, short of some kind of regime transformation, becomes moot.

8. COUNTERING TERRORISM

Given the transnational dimension of some terrorism, international legal remedies have also been sought. Despite the political difficulties encountered in defining terrorism to the satisfaction of all interested parties, some success has been achieved with respect to specific offenses such as air piracy, hostage-taking, and attacks on diplomats (Levitt, 1988; Wardlaw, 1982, 1990). Efforts to develop international prescriptions on establishment terrorism also have yielded only limited success. Numerous declarations of human rights have not stopped widespread abuses, often protected by the principle of noninterference in internal affairs. One formal success, however, is the Convention on the Prevention and Punishment of Genocide, a compact to which the United States finally agreed after forty years (Kauffman, 1990). With this treaty, as with all international agreements, effective enforcement remains a problem.

When confronted with dissident terrorism, regimes often turn to specifically coercive responses, either within or beyond the law. Coercive measures can also be directed at countries engaging in establishment terrorism (see, for example, Livingstone and Arnold, 1986; Merari, 1985; Montana, 1983; Rivers, 1986; Wolf, 1989). A variety of techniques of varying intensity, have been tried or advocated. First, nonmilitary pressure can be brought against those engaging in or sponsoring terrorism, ranging from public condemnations, diplomatic expulsions, and complete diplomatic ruptures to arms embargoes and economic sanctions. Second, security and intelligence can be improved in an effort to deter terrorist attacks. Third, military reprisals in retaliation for specific offenses can be undertaken. Those unwilling to wait for an attack to occur advocate a fourth alternative, preemption. Finally, the most severe coercive reaction to terrorism is a comprehensive antiterrorist campaign, sometimes involving military invasion, such as that of Israel's of Lebanon (Yaniv, 1987) or Vietnam's of Cambodia (Etcheson, 1984). The former was in response to Palestinian dissident terrorism; the latter was partly rationalized as a way to stop the terrorism of the Pol Pot regime.

Legal and coercive responses to dissident terrorism, especially as they increase in harshness, pose certain obvious and not so obvious problems. Obviously, such acts run the risk of being costly, provocative and more damaging to the institutions of the country undertaking them than the terrorism they purport to combat. Moreover, insofar as successful antiterrorist policies require international cooperation they probably encounter problems of free riding—nonparticipants hoping to benefit from the antiterrorist activities of other countries, thereby undermining policy effectiveness—and "paid riding"—where some countries compromise with radical groups in the hope they take their terrorism elsewhere (Lee, 1988; Lee and Sandler, 1989).

Despite their potential risks, coercive policies against terrorism appear to be overvalued in the literature. More conciliatory alternatives are often dismissed without review of their merits, with the argument that any such response would only encourage further terrorism. Despite rejectionist rhetoric, however, various conciliatory actions have been undertaken. Negotiations with hostage takers have occurred, and even Wardlaw (1982), who rejects making substantive concessions, recognizes that some flexibility here is required. Concessions have also been made and ransoms paid to gain the release of hostages. A major issue involves knowing when to bargain (Laplan and Sandler, 1988). Beyond short-term concessions, some left-wing commentators call for the consideration of substantive reforms to address the justifiable grievances of dissident groups using terrorism (Falk, 1988; Hippchen and Yong, 1982; Rubenstein, 1987). Interestingly, the debate over the appropriateness of concessions also enters into the consideration of penalties for those who engaged in establishment terrorism in a previous regime, such as in Argentina, Brazil, Uruguay, or Chile (Weschler, 1990).

The notion that the demands of groups engaging in terrorism might be met may initially seem absurd and even immoral. Yet, over the past several decades, such policies have been enacted for what appear to have been good reasons. For example, nationalist movements in Kenya, Algeria, Cyprus, and elsewhere were accused of terrorist tactics but ultimately their demands for independence were met. Similarly, in Uruguay, Argentina, and more recently Chile at least partial amnesty has been granted to those involved in establishment terrorist campaigns in order to preserve the political stability of new civilian democracies.

A key area for further policy-oriented research would involve specifying the conditions that should shape the character of the anti-terrorist policies. Blanket recommendations for unrelenting retribution or automatic concessions should be viewed with considerable reservation. Among the factors that could affect the character of the response to dissident terrorism are (1) the ideological aims of the dissident group(s); (2) their relative isolation/representativeness; (3) the role of terrorism in the overall dissident strategy; and (4) the significance of external sponsors. Among the factors to be considered in responding to establishment terrorism might be (1) the nature of the challenge to which the terrorism is a response; (2) the representativeness of the regime; (3) the degree of institutionalization of the program of establishment terrorism, and (4) the susceptibility of the establishment/regime to external pressure.

In a world of perfect justice, those who indiscriminately attack noncombatants, whether in the name of the revolution or the regime, would not gain from such tactics. In an imperfect world, cycles of retribution and revenge should probably be shunned. In the case of the concessions described, the terrorism was placed in the context of a wider political struggle, and the response to terrorism weighed with respect to broader political objectives. In a perfect world, moral choice is clear; in our world, moral dilemmas are real.

A NOTE ON FURTHER RESOURCES

This article only samples the rather substantial body of material on terrorism in order to illustrate some of the major themes of research. The most thorough introduction to the literature, as well as a bibliography of nearly six thousand citations is Schmid and Jongman, *Political Terrorism* (1988). This volume, in ad- dition, provides a review of the more significant statis- tical data packages available, although those contem- plating using such statistics should be sensitive to the kinds of contamination problems arising from the absence of a clear conceptual consensus. Further cau- tionary advice is contained in Laqueur (1987). Other reasonably current bibliographies are Lakos (1986), Mickolus (1988), Otiveros (1986), and Signorielli and Gerbner (1988).

Schmid and Jongman also provide the most compre- hensive, annotated directory of groups associated with terrorism and other forms of violence, both establish- ment and dissident. Other directories of groups are Janke (1983), Rosie (1987), and Thackrah (1987). Cordes et al. (1985) develop a framework for analyzing dissi- dent terrorist groups.

Trends and Projections of Terrorism

In many respects, attempting to see into the future of terrorism is as difficult as defining terrorism or setting its boundaries. None of these articles, all written by specialists in the field, is encouraging about checkmating or eliminating terrorism in the world today or in the future. They all seem to share the perspective that terrorism is a phenomenon that has persisted throughout human history and will continue to do so.

The first article in this unit, "Terrorist Threat to Commercial Aviation," provides an explanation as to why terrorists are fond of targeting commercial airliners. While this form of terrorism is declining, the danger is still relevant—as the activities of aviation security companies can attest.

In a two-part listing, Bernard Schechterman provides a summation of lessons presumably learned and expectations and projections derived from the wisdom of the many specialists in the terrorism field. Bruce Hoffman concretizes some critical aspects of the trends and projective analyses with his special focus on terrorist groups in the United States in the 1990s. Dennis Pluchinsky does the same for Western Europe, adding the viewpoint that

what transpires there will eventually spread to newly emancipated Eastern Europe as well. Again the noteworthy point is made that most Middle Eastern terrorist activity occurs in Western Europe and represents a greater impact than Marxist-Leninist or separatist groups.

The general thread running through all of these articles is the point that the United States needs to develop insight and perspective in regard to the direction of terrorism. A key factor will be the speed and effectiveness of America's adjustment to and anticipation of developments.

Looking Ahead: Challenge Questions

What are the basic trends in present-day terrorism, and what trends are projected for the future?

What factors explain the specific dynamics of terrorism today?

What factors explain any recent and perhaps temporary downturns in terrorist activity?

How is orthodox religion influencing the conduct and ethical codes of terrorists?

Unit

9

TERRORIST THREAT TO COMMERCIAL AVIATION

Brian Michael Jenkins

The author is an expert on aviation security for the Rand Corporation in Los Angeles.

On July 22, 1968, an El Al Boeing 707 flying from Rome to Tel Aviv was hijacked by three members of the Popular Front for the Liberation of Palestine. The hijackers ordered the plane flown to Algiers, where they demanded the release of an unspecified number of Arabs imprisoned in Israel, in return for the release of the passengers and crew. The Algerian government removed the hijackers to a nearby army camp but kept the hostages and took over the negotiations. The non-Israeli passengers were released, and later the three female flight attendants and the women and children passengers were also let go. The 12 remaining Israeli crew members and passengers were held until September 1, when Algeria released all of them. On the following day, Israel announced the release of 16 Arab prisoners as a humanitarian gesture. Clearly, a deal had been struck.

The 1968 hijacking set a tactical precedent. There had been hijackings before, to be sure, but this was the first terrorist hijacking in which political demands were made. From the terrorists' point of view, it was a success. An El Al plane had been seized. That would never happen again. It had not been necessary to kill any of the hostages. In future episodes, hostages would die. The Israeli government had yielded. When faced with future hostage incidents, Israel would take a harder line. Other groups imitated the Palestinians, and by 1970, hijacking had become a well–established terrorist tactic.

The 1968 hijacking was also a strategic innovation. With it, terrorists defined commercial aviation as part of their battlefield. In this episode, the hijackers justified their action on the grounds that El Al had carried spare parts for the IDF during the Six Day War and therefore was a legitimate target. Later, terrorist hijackers ceased to offer any justifications. The world would spend the next 20 years trying to keep commercial aviation off the terrorists' battlefield. How well has it succeeded?

Why Choose Airliners?

Commercial airliners attract terrorists for both political and operational reasons. Airlines are symbols of nations, almost as much so as embassies and diplomats, and certainly as much so as big corporations with brand names. Statistically, these are the two favorite targets of terrorists. Airlines are not only symbols of nations, they are scepters of nationhood.

On the operational side, airplanes are convenient *containers* of hostages. They can be seized and controlled by a few people. They are *portable* and can be flown anywhere in the world. On international flights, the majority of the hostages will usually share the nationality of the carrier, thus providing a direct challenge to that government. The presence of hostages of other nationalities will involve other governments as well and will complicate things, often to the terrorists' advantage.

Hijackings account for half of all terrorist attacks on commercial aviation.

Terrorist attacks on commercial aviation – hijackings, sabotage of aircraft, attacks at airports, and bombings of airline ticket offices – account for 13 percent of all international terrorist incidents. But, because of the heavy casualties resulting from airline bombings and the bloody terminations of some hijackings, they account for 34 percent of all fatalities.

Looked at another way, the 2,015 deaths resulting from terrorist attacks on commercial aviation over the past two decades account for nearly 10 percent of all commercial aviation deaths.

In response to the wave of hijackings and airline bombings that occurred in the late 1960s and early 1970s, airport security measures were increased. In 1973, passenger screening was introduced on all flights in the United States. El Al adopted even more rigorous search procedures. Analysts developed *profiles* of the types of passengers who were most likely to hijack planes: persons to be watched more carefully. For a while, some countries, including the United States, also deployed armed security guards on the planes themselves, a practice that a number of airlines continue. Pilots are divided on the use of these air marshals. Some consider their presence a significant deterrent to hijackers, while others worry more about the safety of the passengers and the aircraft if a gunfight should erupt while the plane is in flight.

International Cooperation

The physical security measures have been matched by efforts to put pressure

Reprinted by permission of the *IDF Journal* (Israel Defense Forces Journal), Fall 1989, pp. 11-12, 14, 16, 18.

on countries granting asylum to hijackers. During the 1968 El Al incident, the International Federation of Airline Pilots Associations as well as several airlines threatened to suspend flights to Algeria if the hostages were not released. A prerequisite to progress on the international front was a change in attitude. Until terrorists adopted the tactic for their own ends, hijackings were often seen in a positive light, as a means of escape from behind the Iron Curtain. The spate of hijackings to Cuba in the 1960s, however, caused people to review their thinking, and the later terrorist hijackings accelerated the shift. All hijackers had to be punished. If that meant people had to find another way to escape Communism, it was the price the West would pay to achieve international cooperation.

New conventions to guarantee the trial and punishment of terrorists who hijack or place bombs aboard airliners were negotiated and signed. They have been widely ratified and now represent one of the few areas where there is considerable international cooperation. A 1988 protocol extends the measures to cover airports as well as airliners. Governments also exerted direct pressure on organizations like the PLO to abandon hijackings and bombings of aircraft as a component of their armed struggle.

What were the results? Hijackings declined from 151 incidents, whether successful or not, between 1968–1970, to 56 incidents between 1971–1973, to 17 between 1974–1976. This represents an overall drop of nearly 90 percent. Most of the hijackings were still getaways in which the hijackers wanted only to change the destination of the airplane. Only 20 percent of the ostensibly politically–motivated hijackings were carried out by actual terrorist organizations. These declined too, from 27 in 1968–1970, to 25 in 1971–1973, to 13 in 1974–1976. This is an overall decline of nearly 50 percent. Terrorist hijackings remained at this level until the second half of the 1980s, when there was another drop.

Attack at Ben–Gurion

At the same time that terrorist hijackings were declining, terrorists were altering their tactics and shifting to easier commercial aviation targets. Terrorist attacks at airports began in

1972 with the bloody assault on passengers at Ben-Gurion Airport near Tel Aviv by Japanese terrorists, allies of the Palestinians. Twenty-five people were killed, and more than 70 were wounded, many of whom turned out to be Puerto Rican pilgrims on their way to visit the Holy Land. This episode shocked the world both by its ferocity and by its international character. How is it, people asked, that Japanese come to Israel in the name of Palestinians to kill Puerto Ricans? Terrorist assaults at airports increased during the following years. During the next decade (1973–1982), terrorists carried out 39 such attacks. Terrorist bombings of airline offices also increased beginning in 1974, and for 10 of the next 15 years, bombings at ticket offices outnumbered terrorist attacks on airliners. Overall, terrorist attacks of all types against commercial aviation increased, reaching a high point between 1980–1982. There has

been another decline since 1983.

Despite the decline, hijackings remain a serious problem. They can be divided into two types: those in which terrorists hijack an airliner as a means of escape and perhaps to obtain a moment's publicity for their cause (41 percent of all terrorist hijackings), and those involving political demands and sometimes lengthy negotiations (59 percent). As security measures have required would–be hijackers to make a greater investment and take greater risks, terrorists want more in return. In recent years, hijackings have become more likely to involve demands beyond destination changes. Of the 13 terrorist hijackings in the last five years, 11 have involved demands beyond asylum or publicity.

Terrorist hijackings are also somewhat more likely to involve bloodshed than ordinary hijackings. Fatalities occurred in 23 percent of the terrorist hijackings, compared with 16 percent of the non–

Israeli Aviation Security Companies

The need to provide adequate security in Israel has resulted in the establishment of a number of Israeli security companies, including those specializing in aviation security. Three such companies are ICTS, ISDS, and MIPHA.

ICTS – Established in 1982, ICTS (International Consultants on Targeted Security Ltd.), is a world leader in providing security consulting services. The company's objective is to help corporations, organizations, government facilities, and individuals face and respond to terrorism, white collar crime, kidnapping, and other actions that may threaten them. The company was founded and is headed by a select group of former military commanding officers, veterans of government intelligence and security agencies, and business people.

ICTS is a specialist in aviation security. Due to the complex nature of airports and commercial airliners, they require special security measures and procedures that allow them to conduct daily operations without interfering with critical time schedules. In order to meet these demands, ICTS bases its security plans on a *screening* principle that focuses on the potential problem passenger, cargo shipment, etc. This method, when used in passenger security checks, is known as the *profile* method.

ICTS serves clients worldwide, and among their clients are three of the largest U.S. airlines with international routes.

ISDS – Established in 1982, ISDS (International Security and Defense Systems) offers consulting services in aviation security and provides training for security officers and personnel. ISDS's objective is to provide integrated security consultancy to public and private bodies through a security concept that stresses the prevention and deterrence of threatening acts. The company also supplies clients with a complete security package that includes equipment, manuals, training, and project establishment.

ISDS also offers a course entitled "Air Transport Protection for Security Officers." The course, held in Israel three times a year, covers a variety of areas of concern to aviation security officers including developing strategy in countering terrorist actions, gathering and protecting information and intelligence, and using air transport protection equipment.

ISDS has set up security systems in 17 countries throughout the world, and developed the security concept for the 1992 Summer Olympics to be held in Barcelona, Spain.

MIPHA – MIPHA International Ltd. specializes in a broad spectrum of security services including comprehensive consulting and training services as well as joint ventures covering every aspect of effective security. In aviation security, the company offers expertise in upgrading current airport security procedures, inspecting passengers and objects, conducting training programs for airport personnel, and providing aircraft security both on the ground and in the air.

---

terrorist hijackings. This is somewhat misleading, however. In ordinary hijackings, it is often the hijacker who is killed, while in terrorist hijackings, passengers are more likely to be counted among the casualties. It seems that terrorist hijackings are getting bloodier. Of the 13 hijackings carried out by terrorists during the past five years, seven incidents (53 percent) resulted in fatalities.

Crash of Pan Am 103

The crash of Pan Am flight 103 in Lockerbie, Scotland in December 1988 underlines the second major component of the terrorist threat to commercial aviation. Sabotage of aircraft is the biggest terrorist threat today. Since 1969, terrorists have placed or attempted to place bombs aboard commercial airliners on at least 46 occasions. Eleven of these have caused crashes, resulting in the deaths of 1,016 persons. However, not all the planes crash. In 1986, four passengers, including a mother and her infant daughter, were blown out the side of a TWA airliner over the Adriatic Sea. Despite the damage to the hull, the pilot was able to bring the plane down safely, but the incident still resulted in four fatalities.

In all, 1,128 persons have died during the past 20 years as a result of bombs going off aboard airliners in flight or in cargo containers on the ground. This represents 20 percent of all of the deaths in international terrorist incidents during the past two decades. There is a large number of fatalities in each incident: 329 were killed by a terrorist bomb on an Air India flight in 1986, and 115 were aboard the Korean Airlines flight brought down by a bomb in 1987. The fatalities attract intense media coverage and cause public alarm. Eleven of the 25 worst incidents of international terrorism, measured by the number of fatalities, resulted from terrorists planting bombs on commercial airliners. The other episodes were mainly car bombings. The threat of bombings, more than hijackings, now drives airline security.

The passenger screening procedures developed in the 1970s do not provide adequate protection against terrorist bombs. Standard X-ray machines and metal detectors will not necessarily alert operators to the presence of explosives. However, research into explosives-detection has accelerated during the last few years, and several technologies are being developed. One depends on the characteristic vapor emissions made by certain explosives. A machine using this technology can detect the most minute trace of explosives in luggage or on a person. Another device analyzes the unique *backscatter* patterns created when different materials are bombarded with neutrons.

Detection Technologies

The challenge has been to develop technologies that can accurately indicate the presence of explosives and that are still reliable and practical, given the tremendous volume of passengers and baggage that must be inspected at every major airport. The current vapor-detection machines require up to one-and-a-half minutes to detect the presence of explosives. At that speed, even with two machines, it would take several hours to check the passengers and baggage on a single Boeing 747 jumbo jet. Canadian officials look forward to an improved model that will require only three seconds per passenger, but even with a prototype in hand, deployment of bomb detection technology at airports around the world is still several years away. In the meantime, although improved X-ray machines can now alert operators to the possible presence of explosives in a suitcase, the most reliable procedure remains the tedious hand search of all luggage.

We may also want to think about additional ways to secure aircraft against bombs, for example, by hardening cargo holds to sustain or deflect explosions or by shielding vital controls to reduce the chances of an explosion resulting in loss of control and the crash of the airliner.

Bombings of airline ticket offices may be viewed as a substitute for attacks on airliners, a "poor man's" hijacking, a way to make a political point without running the risks. In contrast to airline sabotage, bombings of airline ticket offices are mainly symbolic forms of attack. Of 267 bombings, only eight incidents, or 3 percent, involved fatalities.

Bombings provide an indirect indicator of the threat to commercial airliners. They tell us which airlines terrorists would attack if security measures were less stringent. Terrorists, for example, have difficulty getting near El Al airliners, but they frequently attack El Al ticket offices. This is not to say that all terrorists planting bombs in front of airline ticket offices would hijack or blow up airliners if they could. One of the attractions in setting off a bomb at a ticket office is that casualties can be avoided. But these bombings do reflect grievances, anger, a willingness to resort to violence, and in some cases, a willingness to cause casualties. Thus, it could be argued that those airlines whose ticket offices are bombed most frequently are those whose aircraft are at greatest peril.

Who Gets Hit?

Who gets hit most often? Ten airlines account for 57 percent of all airline ticket office bombings. In descending order of frequency, these are Aeroflot, Pan American, Air France (and affiliated French carriers), El Al, THY (Turkish Airlines), Lufthansa, British Airways, Saudia, TWA, and Swissair.

How does this profile compare with attacks on airliners? Counting both terrorist hijackings and incidents of aircraft sabotage over the past 10 years (1979–1988), there have been 62 incidents, which point to some differences. First of all, the threat is diffuse. Thirty-two airliners from 30 countries have been attacked by terrorists. Air India heads the list, followed by Middle East Airways, Pan American, Air France (and other French carriers), Shasa (Honduras), THY, and American Airlines, the last four with two attacks each.

Looking at both terrorist and ordinary hijackings, plus incidents of aircraft sabotage during the past five years, the 64 incidents give a somewhat different picture. Here, Middle East Airways heads the list, followed by Aeroflot, Iranair, Air India, and Air France. American carriers were targeted in one of the 64 incidents, or 14 percent of the total.

Security consultants sometimes advise their clients to avoid certain carriers, certain routes, or certain airports to decrease their risk of becoming a victim of terrorism. To the extent that this advice is based on the historical record, I tend to be somewhat skeptical. As one can see from the preceding discussion, how secure an airline appears to be depends a great deal on how far back one wants to count and on how one counts. Does an unscheduled detour to Havana count the same as a terrorist hijacking to Beirut? Merely counting how many times an airline has been hijacked or bombed, without taking into account the number of its flights, may also give a misleading impression.

With these limitations in mind, and looking only at the period 1981–1988, one could safely tell frequent flyers to try to avoid, if they can, domestic flights in Iran, Poland, the Soviet Union, China, and Central America. Since 1981, eight flights out of Miami have been diverted to Havana. Flights from airports in Beirut, Athens, New York (another jumpoff point for hijackings to Cuba), and Frankfurt have each been targets of more than one terrorist attack. Attacks on U.S. carriers account for 19 percent of the total number of incidents, most of them being non-terrorist hijackings.

Who Hits Them?

Who are the adversaries? Individuals, groups, or persons not known to be affiliated with any terrorist group account for the largest share: 32 percent of all attacks on airliners since 1968. Arabs operating on behalf of various Palestinian groups and other Middle Eastern groups account for about 22 percent of the total. Various Latin American groups account for about 10 percent. The remaining attacks have been carried out by diverse European and Asian groups.

Focusing on terrorist hijackings and sabotage of aircraft yields a different picture. Various Palestinian organizations have claimed responsibility for 24 percent of all terrorist hijackings. Shi'ite extremists account for 12 percent. Other Middle Eastern groups account for another six percent. Together, they account for 42 percent of all terrorist hijackings. Palestinian, Shi'ite, and other Middle

East organizations account for 45 percent of the sabotage incidents.

What are we likely to see in the future? Perhaps fewer, but deadlier and more sophisticated terrorist hijackings. The 1988 hijacking of Kuwaiti Airlines Flight 441 illustrates the problem. In that case, the hijackers were familiar with the cockpit and ground procedures and apparently even the tactical ploys used by negotiators, which they took steps to counter. The challenge, then, will be how to deal with hijackers who know accepted procedures and tactics.

Sabotage of aircraft is the most serious problem today. Even though it accounts for relatively few incidents, these incidents cause great numbers of casualties and widespread alarm. As their sophisticated devices show, terrorists are familiar with current security measures, and their bombs are becoming increasingly sophisticated. If the frequency of incidents like the crash of Pan Am 103 increases, passengers, particularly business flyers, may seek safe travel in corporate aircraft, or *membership* flights chartered by consortiums of companies that will vet and clear passengers beforehand.

Publicize the Problem?

Threats against airlines will remain a major problem. Should they be publicized? I think not. The fact is, airlines receive hundreds of threats. All are scrutinized. When they are specific, a flight may be delayed while the aircraft is searched. When they are general, security measures may be increased, depending on an assessment of credibility. We probably need to devote more attention to how to do this. But to publicly post threats would only inspire the pranksters, the fanatics, and the lunatics,

thus multiplying the number of threats, increasing the noise level, and making it more difficult than it already is to assess credibility. Publicizing threats would tell passengers everything, but would provide them with no information. It's a bad idea.

Increased scrutiny of passengers and luggage will make it more difficult to smuggle weapons or explosives aboard aircraft through the *front door.* In some of the recent incidents, terrorists are suspected of having had confederates among the ground crew or of posing as members of flight crews or ground staff. We will have to pay more attention to locking the *back door,* that is, to controlling access to planes and cargo. This poses a major challenge. Major airports may have 25,000 to 50,000 workers. Aircraft cannot easily be sealed. Unlike boarding passengers, there are few obvious chokepoints.

With these trends in mind, we come to the most pressing question. Just how safe is air travel? More than 200 million passengers flew internationally in 1987. Two hundred fifty-nine of them died in the crash of Pan Am 103. The 2,015 fatalities since 1968 would give us a probability range of one chance in a million to several million of being killed by terrorists while flying on a commercial airliner or passing through an airport. One is in greater danger of being killed by a falling object. Several hundred million persons fly domestically each year in the U.S. alone. The odds against death at the hands of terrorists there would be even more remote. The best advice to frequent business flyers is still, drive carefully on the way to the airport.

This article was presented at the First International Seminar of Aviation Security.

Specific Trends and Projections for Political Terrorism

Professor Bernard Schechterman

We are in a relatively new era of emphasis on "low-intensity warfare," which includes guerrilla warfare, liberation movements, and terrorism. This is due, amongst many things, to:

1. The decentralizing tendencies in regional and world politics. We appear to be in a transitional stage in the distribution of power and await the development of new equilibriums, including blocs, alliances, and hegemony. A vacuous situation provides great opportunities for lesser actors.

2. Ethnic nationalism has emerged from behind its submerged status over many years. With its full and open expressions come demands for autonomy, separatism, coequality, self-determination, etc. The range of options for implementation includes peaceful to extremist violent modes of behavior.

3. Most dissident movements include advocates of extremism, especially if there are early successes and growth in size.

4. The less developed world continues to have the greatest potentialities because their dissidents seek political participation, either which is denied or not achieved programmatically so far because of the primordial (conflict) nature of the society's culture, the lack of maturity and experience in arranging and managing a pluralist society, and the demographic availability of an extensive youthful population for manipulation and recruitment.

5. The nature of the dissident elements as well as the establishment elites in most Third World countries—not liberal democrats making revolution or rebellion against tyrants or paternalistic rulers, but often "degenerate elements" with no norm of decent and humane behavior before and after ascending to power. With available technological/communication capabilities, these corrupted elements can wreak greater carnage in the future, i.e., airplane bombings, chemical, and biological warfare.

6. Even before the demise of the Soviet Union and its bloc of states, socioeconomic ideological groups were declining in favor of ethnic and religious extremists, more closely associated with North-South relations and Third World intraregional political dynamics.

7. There has been an overall decline in the concept and unit called the nation-state because of globalistic and subnationalistic tendencies. Weaker states represent both vulnerabilities to terrorism as well as the inability to respond effectively.

Summary Lessons and Expectations for International Terrorism

Professor Bernard Schechterman

1. Does not respect national boundaries.

2. Terrorists have significant relations with other terrorist organizations, rarely remaining isolated.

3. Terrorists may be supported by a state (state's choice), especially by a state that practices terrorism at home.

4. Modern communication systems give added importance to the phenomenon because terrorists' demands and actions are seen and heard around the world. They are known to affect distant actors.

5. Terrorists pose a crisis for democratic governments because of a limited ability to respond to them overseas.

6. An issue for which no consistent or easy international response has been formulated—whether viewing the United Nations or international law. It tends to split the North and South politically.

7. The mass media gives added significance to terrorism by providing an audience, which is essential to terrorists' plans.

8. Proves that state boundaries can be penetrated easily by hostile forces without a state's consent.

9. In world politics, small groups have the ability to harm state interests with minimum effort and cheaply.

10. Terrorism remains a disruptive phenomenon for the international system—raising by other means the issue of stability vs. instability prospects.

11. Terrorism has clearly gained international recognition and attention.

12. Terrorism tends to demonstrate the limitations and ineffectiveness of strategic power.

13. Terrorism further demonstrates interdependency in the international system.

14. Terrorism can and often does undermine the authority of the state.

15. Terrorism often affects foreign entities, in particular, functional activities, i.e., corporations, tourism, etc.

16. Terrorism demonstrates the vulnerability of a technologically dependent world, i.e., airplanes, shipping, communications, energy.

17. Terrorism demonstrates that a state-centric or global-centric view of world politics is inadequate to explaining and analyzing all its dynamics, i.e., the importance of subnationalist groups.

18. The study of ordinary diplomacy and military conflict yields little information about the significance of nonstate actors.

TERRORISM IN THE UNITED STATES:

RECENT TRENDS AND FUTURE PROSPECTS

Bruce Hoffman

RELATIVELY FEW TERRORIST incidents occur in the United States each year, compared with the number of attacks on Americans overseas, and terrorism is in fact statistically insignificant compared with the domestic nonpolitical violence in this country.

While the total volume of international terrorist activity has generally increased, the number of terrorist incidents in the United States has remained relatively constant—in fact, it declined slightly in 1986. The RAND Chronology of International Terrorism recorded 360 incidents in 1983; 386 in 1984; 481 in 1985; and 412 in 1986. The RAND Chronology of Terrorist Incidents in the United States recorded 49 incidents in 1983; 52 in 1984; 52 in 1985; and 39 in 1986.

In contrast to the small number of *politically motivated* violent incidents in this country (three killings in 1986, three in 1985, one in 1984, and eight in 1983), more than 1.3 million acts of nonpolitical violence occurred in the United States in 1986, including nearly 19,000 homicides.

Nevertheless, the United States is not immune to terrorism within its own borders. There are a variety of ethnic/emigre groups and other terrorist organizations that are committed to the use of violence in pursuit of their political objectives. In recent years the United States has experienced attacks from Puerto Rican separatists, Jewish radicals, and militant opponents of legalized abortion. Right-wing extremist groups have increased their activities, and foreign drug dealers have committed terrorist acts on American soil. There is evidence that a black Chicago street gang sought to make a deal with a foreign government to initiate terrorist operations in the United States, along with indications that Middle Eastern elements within this country have been involved in planning and executing terrorist acts. The threat of terrorism in America can by no means be discounted.

CHARACTERISTICS OF TERRORIST ORGANIZATIONS IN THE UNITED STATES

There are three types of domestic terrorist organizations in the United States:

- Ethnic separatist and *emigre* groups.
- Left-wing radical organizations.
- Right-wing racist, anti-authority, survivalist-type groups and anti-abortion militants.

In the past, the *emigre* groups have generally been the most persistent and violent (e.g., they have inflicted the most casualties) of the three types of groups. Their causes and grievances often have little or nothing to do with domestic American politics; the United States is simply the battleground where their quarrels are fought. These groups also spawn successor generations of younger terrorists. However, despite their potentially wide appeal within their own communities, these organizations focus on parochial, ethnic-centered causes, which limits their political constituency to other ethnic/emigre groups in scattered, tightly knit communities around the country.

In contrast, left- and right-wing groups and other issue-oriented terrorists (such as those opposed to U.S. military involvement in Central America, South Africa's apartheid policy, or legalized abortion) have a much broader constituency. Indigenous, left-wing terrorists and issue-oriented groups at both ends of the ideological spectrum are generally less lethal than their ethnic/emigre counterparts. They engage primarily in symbolic bombings to call attention to themselves and their causes, but they seldom undertake actions that could cause widespread, indiscriminate casualties that might alienate potential or perceived supporters. Although some of the leftist groups justify their existence and operations with vague references to Marxist-Leninist dicta, others are quite specific in their reactions to contentious political issues.

The right-wing terrorists appear to embrace the respective traits of both the ethnic-separatists and left-wing terrorists. They are extremely violent, have no reservations about killing, spawn successor generations, and are often oriented toward particular political issues. Right-wing groups can be divided into specific, issue-oriented terrorists (e.g., anti-abortion crusaders in amorphous entities like the "Army of God") and traditional hate groups. Several racist and reactionary groups have recently surfaced, including anti-federalists, anti-Semites, racists, survivalists, and Christian fundamentalists.

From *TVI Report*, Vol. 8, No. 3. Excerpt from *Recent Trends and Future Prospects of Terrorism in the United States*, The RAND Corporation, May 1988, Santa Monica, CA.

PERPETRATORS OF TERRORIST ACTS
IN THE UNITED STATES

While there was little change in the total number of annual terrorist incidents in the United States between 1983 and 1986, there were significant fluctuations in the numbers of incidents attributed to different types of terrorist organizations. Armenian and anti-Castro Cuban terrorists have had no violent acts attributed to them since 1984, and the number of attacks committed by left-wing terrorists has also declined steadily, from nine in 1983 to none in 1986. The level of violence perpetrated by militant opponents of legalized abortion in the United States soared in 1984, remained at about the same level in 1985, but declined appreciably in 1986.

The number of incidents attributed to Jewish extremists declined in 1984, increased in 1985, and declined again in 1986. In contrast, the number of violent acts committed by both Puerto Rican separatists and right-wing extremists increased dramatically in 1986. Only five terrorist incidents were attributed to Puerto Rican groups between 1983 and 1985, but during 1986, these groups were responsible for 10 attacks. Throughout the same period, right-wing extremists committed only six terrorist acts, but during 1986 they were responsible for 11 incidents.

Ideologically motivated terrorism—e.g., terrorist acts by white supremacist and anti-federalist groups or anti-abortion militants—has largely supplanted ethnic-centered domestic terrorist activity. Between 1974 and 1984, ethnic separatist and *emigre* organizations committed more than 75 percent of all the terrorist incidents in this country, whereas during 1985 and 1986, they were responsible for only 32 percent of the incidents. By comparison, right-wing and anti-abortion terrorists were responsible for 53 percent of the terrorist incidents that occurred in the United States in those two years.

The up-and-down incidence of attacks by individual terrorist movements may be explained by the fact that periodic outbursts of concentrated violence are frequently followed by a dramatic decline in terrorist operations because of heightened attention from federal and local law enforcement agencies. Thus there appears to be a cyclical pattern to terrorism in the United States.

TACTICS USED BY TERRORISTS IN THE
UNITED STATES

Bombings accounted for 47 percent of the terrorist incidents in the United States between 1983 and 1986. Armed attacks and acts of arson were the second most common tactic, accounting for 32 percent of the incidents during this period. Whatever tactic is used, however, most terrorist attacks are "symbolic," i.e.,

intended primarily to draw attention to the terrorists and their causes. This is further evidenced by the small number of persons killed by terrorists in the United States. Most terrorist operations in this country have been directed against structures—government offices, military installations, businesses, airline or tourist offices, and the like—and not against people.

The reliance on bombing by terrorists in this country is not surprising: Bombings account for approximately 50 percent of all the terrorist attacks committed annually throughout the world. They provide a dramatic means of drawing attention to terrorist causes that is relatively easy and risk-free. Preference for bombings usually indicates that a terrorist group is at an early stage in its development and lacks the organizational expertise, logistics, or knowledge to engage in more complicated operations.

At the same time, however, in the bombings committed and attempted by right-wing extremists and Puerto Rican separatists during 1986, the construction and placement of the explosive devices themselves seems less significant than the characteristics and prior activities of the perpetrators. Indeed, these two terrorist movements have demonstrated an ability to mount more complex and sophisticated terrorist operations than many of their domestic counterparts. Moreover, the weapons skills and training in guerrilla warfare of the right-wing groups, coupled with their racial and religious intolerance and their apocalyptic vision, bring to bear a potential not only to engage in more sophisticated types of terrorist operations, but to undertake attacks that deliberately cause widespread casualties and destruction.

RECENT TRENDS IN TERRORIST ACTIVITY

The main reason for the overall decline in terrorist incidents in the United States during 1986 is the decrease in activity by many previously highly active terrorist organizations, including anti-Castro Cuban, Armenian, and left-wing groups between 1983 and 1985, and Jewish and anti-abortion groups in 1986.

Any optimism that might be engendered by the decrease of activity among some terrorist movements must be tempered by the increases recorded in the activity of others. The growing violence of right-wing extremists and Puerto Rican separatists, the contract killing of a federal informant by Colombian "hit-men" employed by drug traffickers in that country, and reports that a Chicago street gang sought to make a deal with Libya to perpetrate terrorist attacks in the United States in return for money are all cause for concern.

Despite widespread arrests of right-wing and Puerto Rican terrorists in 1985, the threat posed by these groups has not abated. Right-wing extremists carried out only four terrorist attacks between 1983 and 1985, and Puerto Rican separatists committed only three. But during 1986, right-wing extremists were responsible for 11 terrorist attacks or attempts, and Puerto Rican separatists carried out 10 attacks. Right-wing groups accounted for 29 percent of the terrorist incidents in the United States in 1985, and Puerto Rican groups accounted for 26 percent.

RIGHT-WING TERRORISM

The growth of right-wing extremism in the United States has prompted increased concern among federal, state, and local law enforcement agencies, government officials, racial and religious minority groups, and civil rights organizations. Organized hate groups such as the Ku Klux Klan and different incarnations of Hitler's National Socialist (Nazi) party have existed in this country for decades, but extremist, white supremacist paramilitary groups oriented toward "survivalism," outdoor skills, guerrilla training, and outright sedition are a new phenomenon.

Although these groups have relatively few *active* members (a recent report by the Anti-Defamation League of B'nai B'rith estimates membership in these groups to be between 400 and 450 persons), they have an estimated constituent base of 15,000 to 20,000 supporters. Moreover, the magnitude of the threat the groups pose is clearly demonstrated by the wide-ranging geographical dimensions of the movement, the diversity of its adherents' causes, and their overlapping agendas. The movement has constituents, followers, and sympathizers from Idaho, California, and Arizona in the west, to North Carolina and Georgia in the east; they are found from Texas to Canada and in the Midwestern states as well.

The aims and motivations of right-wing extremists span a broad spectrum of anti-federalist and seditious beliefs and racial and religious hatred, masked by a transparent veneer of religious precepts. They are bound together by their shared hostility to any form of government above the county level; their vilification of Jews and non-whites as children of Satan; their obsession with achieving the religious and racial purification of the United States; their belief in a conspiracy theory of powerful Jewish interests controlling the government, banks, and the media; and their advocacy of the overthrow of the U.S. government, or the ZOG (Zionist Occupation Government), as they call it.

The unifying thread in this patchwork ideology is the so-called Christian Identity movement. The basic tenets of the Identity movement include the beliefs that Jesus Christ was not a Jew, but an Aryan; that the Lost Tribes of Israel are not composed of Jews but of blue-eyed Aryans; that white Anglo-Saxons and not Jews are the true Chosen People; and that the United States is the Promised Land. In this context, Jews are

viewed as imposters and children of Satan, who must be exterminated.

Unlike the isolated, crudely unsophisticated pipe-bomb manufacturers who dominated most of the U.S.-based terrorist groups in the past, the right-wing extremists are well-trained in the use of arms and explosives, they are skilled armorers and bomb-makers, and they are adept at guerrilla-warfare techniques and outdoor survival.

THE ARYAN NATIONS

At the center of the right-wing extremist movement is an organization called the Aryan Nations, a fanatical, anti-Semitic, New-Nazi group of white supremacists, survivalists, and militant tax resisters. Its headquarters is on a secluded, fenced-in 40-acre site at the edge of the Coeur d'Alene National Forest in Hayden Lake, Idaho. The group was founded in 1974 by Richard Girnt Butler, a 69-year-old former aeronautical engineer from California who moved to Idaho in 1973. Butler is also head of the Church of Jesus Christ Christian, which has its headquarters on the Aryan Nations compound. The church is based on the white supremacist dogma and aggressive anti-Semitic beliefs espoused by the Identity movement.

The Aryan Nations is an umbrella-type entity that coordinates a variety of different, but similarly oriented organizations. One of its purposes is to further the ties between members of various like-minded hate groups. To this end, Aryan Nations congresses have been held every year since 1973, with the exception of 1985, when widespread arrests of members of The Order dealt a stunning, albeit temporary blow to the white supremacist movement. The congresses bring together members and representatives from white supremacist anti-Semitic, racist, anti-federalist, and survivalist organizations throughout the United States and Canada.

Beyond any doubt, the Aryan Nations congresses and related ceremonies and events cement ties among a variety of like-minded right-wing extremists and fuel the seditious campaign for the establishment of an independent white homeland in the Pacific Northwest. Their legacy is perhaps most clearly borne out by the activities of The Order during 1983 and 1984 and the fact that during the following year, members of that group were arrested in 12 different states, where they had sought refuge and assistance from persons affiliated with similarly oriented groups.

BRUDER SCHWEIGEN STRIKE FORCE II

Six of the terrorist incidents attributed to right-wing extremists in 1986 were perpetrated by a radical splinter group of the Aryan Nations called the Bruder Schweigen Strike Force II. This group was responsible for a series of bombings in Coeur d'Alene, just a few miles from the Aryan Nations compound in Hayden Lake, between August and September 1986. The most serious incident was the nearly simultaneous explosion of four bombs at a department store, a restaurant, the local federal building, and an armed forces recruiting station. Three members of the Aryan Nations were charged with the attacks—David Dorr, Edward Hawley and Robert Pires—and Dorr and Hawley were also charged with counterfeiting.

Pires cooperated with authorities and described a conspiracy orchestrated by Dorr to terrorize residents of the area into leaving so that members of right-wing groups could take advantage of low real estate values and set up a racially pure "Aryan" bastion. Dorr also compiled a hit list targeting federal judges, FBI agents and community leaders, in addition to Richard Butler, founder of the Aryan Nations, because he was considered too moderate.

Pires, Dorr and Hawley were all subsequently tried and sentenced for a variety of activities associated with the bombings and counterfeiting. This latter endeavor has figured prominently in the financing of right-wing terrorism, and Dorr claimed that he planned to finance yet another, more violent, movement to promote a race war.

THE POSSE COMITATUS AND THE ARIZONA PATRIOTS

The Posse Comitatus (the Latin phrase is translated as "Power of the County") and its offshoot, the Arizona Patriots, both have ties with the Aryan Nations. These groups reject any form of government above the county level and specifically oppose federal and state income taxes, the existence of the Federal Reserve system, and the supremacy of the federal judiciary over local courts. They decry federal and state income taxes as "Communist and unconstitutional" and advocate a return to the gold standard and the abolition of the Federal Reserve Bank.

Throughout the 1970s, local chapters of the Posse Comitatus were founded in almost every state in the country.

Originally, Posse Comitatus activities focused on passive tax resistance, but in recent years it has become increasingly violent, particularly in the Midwest and Northwest. The seventh and eighth right-wing terrorist incidents during 1986 were non-fatal bombing attacks against a federal judge who had presided at the trial of one of the group's members, and a local post office. It is presumed that the Posse Comitatus was retaliating for the earlier prosecution, but no arrests were made for these bombings.

The ninth right-wing incident of 1986 was a conspiracy of Arizona Patriot members to bomb several federal offices and Jewish organizations throughout various western states, and to rob an armored car. Federal informants and investigators infiltrated the

group, and six of its members were arrested and indicted before they could initiate any attacks.

THE WHITE PATRIOT PARTY

The tenth right-wing incident of 1986 occurred on the East Coast and involved the White Patriot Party, another group linked to the Aryan Nations. Three members of this group—Stephen Miller, Robert Jackson, and Anthony Wydra (Jackson's half-brother)—were arrested in North Carolina and charged with plotting to rob a fast-food restaurant to obtain money with which to purchase explosives. The explosives were to be used to bomb the offices of the Southern Poverty Law Center in Montgomery, Alabama. Two other members of the organization, Wendell Lane and Simeon Davis, were also subsequently arrested and charged in the plot.

One of the most militant offshoots of the Ku Klux Klan, the White Patriot Party was founded in 1985 by Frazier Glenn Miller (no relation to Stephen Miller), a former U.S. Army Green Beret who served two tours in Vietnam and was a "longtime activist" in the American Nazi Party.

According to a federal indictment, Miller and his associates conspired to train and equip a paramilitary group committed to white supremacy, and they were charged with receiving weapons stolen from a federal armory, to be used to attack the Southern Poverty Law Center and to assassinate its director.

On April 13, 1987, Stephen Miller was convicted of conspiracy charges, and Lane and Davis avoided prosecution by testifying against him. Wydra was acquitted of all charges. (Jackson failed to appear in court but was later apprehended.)

PUERTO RICAN SEPARATISTS

For more than 30 years, Puerto Rican separatists have waged a sporadic, but persistent, terrorist campaign against U.S. possession of their island. Most of this activity has been carried out by either the FALN (*Fuerzas Armadas de Liberacion Nacional,* or Armed Forces of the National Liberation), which is based in the continental United States, or by the *Ejercito Borican Popular* (Popular Army of Borica, the island's name before Spanish colonization), more commonly known as the *Macheteros* (Spanish for "machete-wielders"), which thus far has operated only in Puerto Rico.

Throughout the seventies and early eighties, the FALN was responsible for 125 bombings, primarily in New York, Chicago, and Puerto Rico, killing five people. The FALN suffered a serious blow, however, with the 1985 arrest of many key members.

The *Macheteros* first surfaced in 1979, when they carried out eight bombing attacks in Puerto Rico in coordination with four FALN bombings in New York and Chicago. Subsequently the *Macheteros* undertook

9. TRENDS AND PROJECTIONS OF TERRORISM

a largely independent campaign on U.S. Government targets in Puerto Rico. In 1979, they ambushed a Navy bus, killing two sailors and wounding 10, and the next year they attempted to assassinate three Army officers. In January 1981, the *Macheteros* mounted one of the most costly terrorist atacks in history, destroying nine jet fighters worth $40 million.

The *Macheteros* were responsible for nine of the 10 incidents attributed to Puerto Rican terrorists during 1986. On October 28, the group bombed three U.S. military facilities, with one injury, and another six explosive devices were found at other military targets on the island. The group's stated purpose in embarking on its terrorism campaign is to focus attention on its cause, publicize grievances and educate fellow Puerto Ricans about the alleged inequities forced on them by U.S. domination.

Though several important members of the *Macheteros* were arrested in 1985 (along with those of the FALN), the group has continued its violent assaults. Their tactics demonstrate less sophistication than in earlier years, but they tenaciously cling to demands for independence and are still willing to mount terrorist attacks on behalf of that cause.

The remaining terrorist incident attributed to Puerto Rican separatists was the murder of a former police undercover agent who had been involved in the deaths of two revolutionaries in a 1979 incident. The Volunteer Organization for the Revolution (OVRP) claimed responsibility and expressed intentions to kill other police officers tied to the execution-like slaying of the two separatists after they had surrendered.

The OVRP had been dormant for the most part until the murder of the former policeman; the stated goal of killing yet more policemen indicates that the group is still a threat despite its general inactivity.

DRUG-RELATED TERRORISM AND TERRORISM FOR HIRE

Two other terrorist incidents that occurred in 1986 are cause for concern. In February, a three-man Colombian hit-team killed Adler (Barry) Seal, a pilot who had been working for the Drug Enforcement Administration, on behalf of a Colombian drug cartel. The second incident came to light in August, and linked a Chicago street gang to plans to engage in domestic terrorism in the United States of behalf of Libya.

Principals in both criminal endeavors were arrested and prosecuted, and the incidents do not seem to constitute a trend. They do, however, indicate the dangerous potential for links between common crime and political terrorism.

SOURCES OF CONCERN AND FUTURE PROSPECTS

Despite the overall decline in domestic terrorism in 1986, several trends are cause for concern. Foremost is the continued activity of right-wing extremists and Puerto Rican separatists, together with the possibility of terrorist attacks being committed by Islamic elements in this country on behalf of either radical Middle Eastern countries or militant Palestinian terrorist organizations.

RIGHT-WING TERRORISM

The most serious threat is undoubtedly posed by the right-wing extremist groups. Although one might be inclined to dismiss the members of these groups as intemperate hot-heads, country bumpkins, or mentally unstable alarmists, they have demonstrated that they are serious in their beliefs and dedicated to their causes—and that they are willing to use violence in pursuit of their goals. Moreover, under the Aryan Nations umbrella, the first truly nationwide terrorist network has been established in this country.

The right-wing terrorist movement has also demonstrated remarkable resilience to pressure from heightened attention by federal, state, and local law enforcement agencies, to rebound from setbacks (such as the widespread arrests of members), and to continue attempts to carve out a whites-only homeland in the Pacific Northwest.

In April 1987, indictments were handed down against 14 white supremacists by a Federal Grand Jury in Fort Smith, Arkansas. The indictments alleged a conspiracy to carry out assassinations and bombings, destroy utilities, establish guerrilla camps, pollute water supplies, and procure false identification. These activities were to be financed by armed robbery and counterfeiting.

Among targets of the indictments were Richard Girnt Butler, founder of the Aryan Nations, and Louis Beam and Robert Miles, two leading members of that organization. The 14 accused included some of the most influential and active proponents of right-wing violence.

Despite that fact, the 14 were acquitted of the charges a year later because the jury doubted the veracity of the government's main witness, James Ellison. A founder and leader of The Covenant, The Sword, and The Arm of the Lord, still another extremist group with ties to the Aryan Nations, Ellison's testimony was compromised by the suspicion that his testimony was tainted by a desire for lenient treatment and a lower sentence for his own activities.

Shortly after the Fort Smith indictments, U.S. attorney Sam Currin announced that white supremacist groups had been dealt a fatal blow. However, given the diverse constituencies of white supremacists and the nationwide network of supporters, adherents and sympathizers, the blow proved not fatal at all. In fact, it may well incite increased terrorist activity in reprisal.

During the year interim between the indictments and acquittals, white supremacist organizational and recruitment efforts continued unabated. In July 1987, the Aryan Nations sponsored its fourteenth annual congress, bringing together 200 members of like-minded groups to its headquarters near Hayden Lakes, Idaho (as it did again this year), and in October of that year, 200 white supremacists attended a strategy session at the Michigan farm of Robert Miles, one of those indicted at Fort Smith.

Meanwhile, the Aryan Nations has embarked on an ambitious campaign to attract new recruits and supporters. Added to outreach centers in Thompson Falls, Montana, and Toronto and Alberta in Canada, is another in Utah and two more in Texas and Washington. Besides continuing to target its traditional rural constituency, the Aryan Nations is attempting to recruit members of ''skinhead'' gangs, who comprise a small, violent youth movement located in urban and suburban areas.

The groups have their roots in Great Britain, wherein the early seventies shave-headed, tattooed youths from the lower classes began to appear. Militantly patriotic, xenophobic and racist, they have a history of association with English neo-Nazi groups and distinguish themselves by an attitude of nihilistic violence. They are credited with much of the hooliganism between fans of rival soccer teams that has led to deaths on occasion, and indiscriminate attacks on Pakistanis and other Asian immigrants in England.

There are probably less than a thousand skinheads in the United States, but their ranks appear to be growing, and members of these gangs have been arrested on charges of assault, arson, robbery and narcotics violations in Michigan, Illinois, Ohio, Texas, Florida and California.

The Ku Klux Klan has not been idle either in recent years, and it has stepped up efforts to increase visibility and recruitments. Beginning in 1987, Klan rallies, attracting hundreds of supporters in some cases, have been staged in Georgia, North Carolina, Ohio and Maine. This resurgence of Klan activity and militancy seems to have led to increasingly bold violent attempts or acts, including a plot to assassinate presidential candidate Jesse Jackson.

Despite vigorous prosecution by federal and state authorities, with many notable successes, right-wing movements reveal a disturbing ability to mutate and reconstitute themselves in new forms. Appealing to diverse constituencies with overlapping agendas and the ability to network on a nationwide scale, these groups show no prospect of giving up their violent strategies in the near future.

PUERTO RICAN SEPARATISTS

The arrest and imprisonment of Puerto Rican separatist members and leaders has also had only an ephemeral effect, if any, on their commitment to violence. Since the sixties, several groups have been identified, their members effectively prosecuted, only to be replaced by new revolutionary underground organizations. A formerly unknown group, for example, the Guerrilla Forces for Liberation, planted eight bombs on May 25, 1987, to protest U.S. domination of Puerto Rico. The threat posed by separatists there has not abated and is likely to persist for many years.

ISLAMIC EXTREMISTS

There are indications that Islamic elements may be preparing to carry out terrorist attacks in the United States for anti-American Middle Eastern countries or Palestinian terrorist organizations. Although such attacks have not materialized, at least four state-sponsored incidents have taken place in this country allegedly at the behest of either Libya or Iran, and a purported terrorist plot by foreign nationals with Middle East connections was recently thwarted.

Vigorous monitoring of suspected Middle Eastern radicals has severely limited the potential of the threat in this country. That situation, however, should not be seen as ending the danger of terrorist acts mounted by such groups. The recruitment of domestic, apolitical criminal gangs to engage in political violence has been attempted once, and it highlights the continued intent of radical foreign elements to commit acts of terrorism in the United States.

CONCLUSION

The increase of terrorism worldwide and of attacks against American targets overseas has focused attention on the threat posed by international terrorist organizations to U.S. interests, citizens, and government and military personnel. At the same time, however, the United States is not immune to politically motivated violence within its own borders. Indigenous terrorist organizations are active in this country, and they are committed to the use of violence to achieve their political objectives. The targets of their attacks are other American citizens and residents, American businesses, and U. S. government and military personnel and property. The dangers of complacency are all too apparent, given the periodic eruptions of violence by ethnic and *emigre* groups in this country, the continuing attacks against abortion clinics and family planning services by opponents of legalized abortion, and the increasing scope and dimensions of right-wing terrorist activity. The emerging predominance of right-wing terrorism in this country during the past two years represents a significant trend in domestic terrorism.

FOOTNOTE

1. This article is excerpted from the author's *Recent Trends and Future Prospects of Terrorism in the United States* (Santa Monica, CA: The RAND Corporation, May 1988, R-3618).

Middle Eastern Terrorism in Europe: Trends and Prospects

Dennis A. Pluchinsky

Office of Intelligence and Threat Assessment, Bureau of Diplomatic Security, U.S. Department of State, Washington, DC 20520

Abstract *Europe has been the preferred operational area for Middle Eastern terrorist groups—some 418 attacks from 1980–1989. Unlike European Marxist revolutionary or separatist terrorist groups, the Middle Eastern groups present Europe with a regional security problem. The most dangerous element in this Middle Eastern terrorist threat is the state-sponsored activities of Iran, Libya, Syria, and Iraq. These countries provided the fuel for a decade of Middle Eastern terrorist bloodshed in Europe. Given the problems of solving the various political conflicts and feuds in the Middle East and the continuing attractiveness of Europe as a substitute battlefield for Middle Eastern terrorist elements, the threat of Middle Eastern terrorist activity in Europe should continue into the 1990s.*

Keywords Europe, Middle Eastern terrorism, state-sponsored terrorist activity, Iran, Syria, Libya, Iraq.

Three major strains of terrorist activity have been active in Europe over the past decade: indigenous/ Marxist-Leninist, indigenous/separatist, and Middle Eastern terrorism. The security and political effects of the first two strains have generally been contained within individual countries. Marxist-Leninist terrorist groups like the Red Army Faction (RAF), Red Brigades (RB), Direct Action (DA), the Communist Combatant Cells (CCC), and the Revolutionary Organization 17 November (17N) have only caused problems for Germany, Italy, France, Belgium, and Greece, respectively (their countries of origin). None of these groups has ever posed a major threat to a neighboring country. Their terrorist activities have been restricted primarily to their primary targeted countries. In 1985 and 1988, several of these groups attempted to form an "anti-imperialist front" of West European terrorist groups, a potential regional problem. However, both attempts failed because not all of the Marxist-Leninist groups agreed with the ideological foundation of the front and

The opinions expressed in this paper are solely the author's and should not be interpreted in any way as representing the views or policies of the U.S. government.

those that joined were subsequently neutralized by police arrests. None of the European separatist groups such as the Irish Republican Army (IRA), the Corsican National Liberation Front (CNLF), the Basque Fatherland and Liberty group (ETA), or the Catalan Free Land (FL) showed any interest in joining this anti-imperialist alliance.

Like the Marxist-Leninist groups, the European separatist groups also had a limited impact on the European security environment. Their activities were generally focused within their respective ethnic regions. Most of the terrorist activities of the ETA have been limited to the Northern Basque region of Spain. The CNLF has focused its operations on the French island of Corsica. The FL has restricted its terrorist activities to the Northeastern Catalan region of Spain. However, the ETA and CNLF have occasionally carried out terrorist operations outside their ethnic regions, in the capitals of the targeted countries, Madrid and Paris, respectively. Of all the European separatist groups, only the IRA has demonstrated a consistent willingness and capability to operate outside its targeted country. Over the last decade, the IRA has attacked British targets in Belgium, the Netherlands, and Germany. In these instances, the IRA problem has spilled over into these countries. Some of these IRA attacks have caused injuries to citizens of these countries. Moreover, several IRA cells have been arrested, tried, and jailed in these countries. Generally speaking, however, the impact of the European separatist groups, like that of the Marxist-Leninist groups, has been geographically limited, first to their respective ethnic regions, and second to their primary targeted country or country of origin.

It is the third strain, Middle Eastern terrorist activity, that has had a security and political impact that has affected not only individual European countries, but the region as a whole. Of the three types of terrorist strains found in Europe, only the Middle Eastern strain can be considered a regional problem. This article presents a brief survey of Middle Eastern terrorist activity in Europe over the last decade and offers some projections concerning the Middle Eastern terrorist threat in Europe in the 1990s.[1]

From *Terrorism*, Vol. 14, 1991, pp. 67-76. *Terrorism*, published by Taylor and Francis, 1101 Vermont Ave., NW, Suite 200, Washington, DC 20005.

226

The 1980s: Themes and Variations

There are two characteristics of Middle Eastern terrorist activity in Western Europe that differentiate it from the operations of the European Marxist-Leninist and separatist groups. The first characteristic is that Middle Eastern terrorist activity in Europe includes attacks on public facilities, such as aircraft, airports, trains, train stations, discos, restaurants, hotels, buses, subway stations, cruise ships, shopping malls, department stores, outdoor cafes, and tourist attractions. The second characteristic is that Middle Eastern terrorist attacks often involve indiscriminate tactics, such as machine gun and grenade attacks, firing antitank weapons, bombs aboard aircraft, car bombs on crowded public streets, and so forth. These targeting and tactical tendencies of Middle Eastern terrorist operations in Europe assure that innocent civilians will be killed or injured. They form the leitmotif of Middle Eastern operations in Europe over the past decade, operations that have taken place on battlefields named Paris, Brussels, Rome, London, Bonn, Berlin, Madrid, Istanbul, Vienna, Nicosia, Frankfurt, Geneva, and Athens.

Europe, more precisely Western Europe, has been the preferred operational area for Middle Eastern terrorist groups operating outside the Middle East since 1968, when these groups first decided to operate outside their region. To the author's knowledge, there is no publicly available data base that has tracked Middle Eastern terrorist incidents outside the Middle East since 1968.[2] However, to support the proposition that Western Europe is a preferred operational area for Middle Eastern terrorist groups (Palestinian and Islamic revolutionaries), the following statistical snapshots are offered. According to the Jaffee Center for Strategic Studies' Project on Terrorism, from 1968 through 1989 there were 723 international terrorist incidents carried out by Palestinians, including attacks in the Middle East.[3]

Fifty-eight percent (418) of these incidents took place in Western Europe. The Jaffee statistics do not include terrorist attacks carried out by pro-Iranian, Islamic revolutionaries who only entered the international arena in 1980. The French terrorism expert, Xavier Raufer, in his 1987 book *La Nebuleuse: Le Terrorisme du Moyen-Orient* (The Nebula of Middle Eastern Terrorism), records a total of 396 Middle Eastern terrorist incident worldwide from 1968 through 1987.[4] His total includes attacks carried out by Islamic revolutionaries and attacks carried out in the Middle East. According to Raufer, 62% (245 attacks) of these incidents occurred in Western Europe. It is obvious that the Jaffee and Raufer data bases use different criteria to define a "Palestinian" or "Middle Eastern" terrorist incident; thus the large discrepancy in their totals. However, both data bases come to the same conclusion—that Western Europe has been the site of more Middle

Eastern terrorist incidents than any other region. Both data bases also indicate that Middle Eastern terrorists were more active in Western Europe in the 1980s than in the 1970s.

The author has developed a data base that has recorded Middle Eastern terrorist activity outside the Middle East from 1980 through 1989.[5] This data base includes incidents in Western Europe that can be attributed to Palestinians, Islamic revolutionaries, Middle Eastern states, and independents (the Carlos group, the Japanese Red Army, etc.). According to this data base, of the 418 Middle Eastern spillover incidents that have taken place outside the Middle East during 1980–1989, 87% have occurred in Western Europe. These 365 incidents in Western Europe took place in 16 West European countries and caused over 518 fatalities and some 1933 injuries. Forty percent of these fatalities were Americans. A large majority of these incidents were carried out for the following three reasons: (1) to silence or intimidate exiled political dissidents from Libya, Iran, Iraq, and Syria; (2) to modify the policies or actions of European and Middle Eastern states; and (3) to avenge actions carried out by Israel, the United States, and certain Middle Eastern states.

In reviewing Middle Eastern terrorist activity in Western Europe in the 1970s, it is clear that the dominant theme was the quest for world recognition of the Palestinian cause. This was accomplished by focusing Palestinian terrorist activity on Israeli and Jewish targets in Western Europe, where the publicity spotlight was much wider and brighter. The 1970s was the decade of hijackings and attacks on diplomatic facilities. It was a decade of terror, of which Carlos, George Habbash, Yasir Arafat, and Waddi Haddad were the primary architects. The PLO assault on the Olympics in Munich and the Carlos-led attack on the OPEC Ministerial Meeting in Vienna were the most notorious Middle Eastern terrorist operations in Western Europe during the 1970s. It was also a decade in which the role of Middle Eastern state sponsors was less prevalent than in the 1980s.

The most dominant theme in Middle Eastern terrorist activity in Western Europe in the 1980s was the support and sponsorship role of Middle Eastern states like Syria, Libya, Iran, and Iraq. The author estimates that 152 terrorist incidents, or 42% of all Middle Eastern terrorist activity in Western Europe during the 1980s, can be evidentially or analytically linked to these four states. Most of the more bloody Middle Eastern terrorist operations in Western Europe during the 1980s can be attributed to state sponsorship: the attacks on Rome and Vienna airports in 1985, the bombing of the La Belle disco in Berlin in 1986, the bombing campaign in central Paris in 1986, and the midair bombing of Pan Am 103 in 1988. Libya, Iran, and Syria primarily provided the fuel for this decade of indiscriminate violence. In the mid-1980s, there was also a clear shift in

9. TRENDS AND PROJECTIONS OF TERRORISM

Middle Eastern targeting in Western Europe: toward Western targets, in particular the United States. This explains the large number of American casualties caused by Middle Eastern terrorist attacks in Western Europe over the last decade. While it is difficult to synthesize the many complex motives behind the attacks on American targets in Western Europe into one broad, dominant motive, there does appear to be a correlation between the degree of U.S. involvement (perceived or real) in Middle Eastern developments and terrorist attacks on American targets in Western Europe.

To illustrate this targeting shift by Middle Eastern terrorists in Western Europe beginning in 1985, the following statistical support is offered. The author's data base indicates that from 1980–1984 there were 161 Middle Eastern terrorist incidents in Western Europe. Ninety-eight or 61% were directed at other Arab or Palestinian targets, and 29 or 18% were aimed at Israeli or Jewish targets. The number of incidents directed at Western targets was 34 (including 9 against the United States) or 21%. However, from 1985–1989, there was a significant increase in the number and percentage of Middle Eastern attacks against Western targets. Of the 204 incidents during this period, 95 or 46% were directed at other Arab or Palestinian targets, and only 22 or 11% were aimed at Israeli and Jewish targets. Incidents directed at Western targets increased to 87 or 43% of the total number of Middle Eastern terrorist incidents during this period. Also of interest is that 33 of these 87 anti-Western incidents were directed at U.S. interests in Western Europe—an almost 275% increase in anti-American terrorist incidents from the previous period.

While Carlos, Habbash, Arafat, and Haddad were the main architects of Middle Eastern terrorist activity in Western Europe in the 1970s, in the 1980s they were Abu Nidal, Mu'ammar Quaddafi, Ayatollah Khomeini, and Hafez al-Assad. The bloody scroll of Middle Eastern terrorist incidents in Western Europe increased in the 1980s with the names of Rue Copernic, Jo Goldenberg, El Descanso, TWA 847, Cafe de Paris, *Achille Lauro*, Rome and Vienna airports, Galerie Claridge, TWA 840, La Belle disco, Neve Shalom synagogue, Tati Clothing Store, City of Poros, and Pan Am 103. It was also in the 1980s that, for the first time, a Western government carried out military retaliation against another government because of its support for international terrorism. In terms of Middle Eastern terrorist activity in Western Europe, the 1980s was marked by a rise in incidents, increased targeting of innocent civilians, the expansion of state sponsorship, the emergence of Islamic revolutionary terrorist elements, and small but significant technological advances by terrorists.

The 1980s also marked the first time that a Middle Eastern state had unofficially declared a terrorist war against a European state. From December 1985 until September 1986, pro-Iranian terrorists carried out an extensive bombing campaign in central Paris to force the French government to reduce its support for Iraq in the Iran-Iraq war and to modify its policies toward Iran. This state-sponsored terrorist campaign consisted of 15 terrorist incidents, which together caused the deaths of 13 people and injured over 300. The low fatality toll was due more to luck than design. This was a serious, lethal terrorist campaign that was intended to cause mass casualties in the streets of Paris. Most of the attacks took place during the daylight hours. Consider the targets of the attacks: two department stores, three shopping malls, the Eiffel Tower, a bookstore, a train, two metro stations, the city hall, a cafeteria, a restaurant, a police station, and a clothing store. The bombs on the Eiffel Tower and in the two underground metro stations were discovered and defused. Both of the bombs in the underground metro stations were timed to detonate at rush hour and would have easily caused over 150 fatalities. Another bomb was found in a crowded restaurant and removed by two policemen who later died when the bomb detonated outside the restaurant. In the author's opinion, the 1985–1986 bombing campaign in Paris was the most striking, serious, and disturbing example of state-sponsored terrorism ever to infect the European continent.[6]

During the 1980s, France was the site of the largest number of Middle Eastern terrorist incidents. Sixty attacks took place on French soil. Italy and Great Britain were next with 42 each, followed by Greece (41), Spain (39), Cyprus (31), Turkey (25), Germany (25), Austria (23), and Belgium (13). The remaining incidents took place in Switzerland, Denmark, Malta, Sweden, the Netherlands, and Portugal. Only Luxembourg, Ireland, Norway, Iceland, and Finland were free from any Middle Eastern terrorist attacks in the 1980s. From the above list, it is easy to see why Middle Eastern terrorism was a regional problem for Western Europe in the 1980s. Many of the groups that carried out these operations were smuggling weapons and explosives from one European country to another. It was important for the security and intelligence services of the various European countries to share terrorist-related intelligence with other European countries. It took regional cooperation to counter this regional terrorist problem. A group like the Fatah Revolutionary Council (FRC), popularly known as the Abu Nidal organization, carried out attacks in Great Britain, France, Germany, Spain, Greece, Turkey, Cyprus, Austria, Belgium, Portugal, Italy, and the Netherlands. Each attack was a piece of a puzzle and the only way to see the whole picture was to share all the pieces. In this way, the European security services increased their understanding of this Middle Eastern group.

This was the same, necessary approach that was used to counter the Islamic revolutionary terrorist

The 1990s: A Prognosis

threat in Western Europe in the 1980s. Islamic revolutionaries carried out attacks in Spain, France, Austria, Turkey, Cyprus, Germany, Great Britain, and Belgium. Like the Abu Nidal group, these terrorists were a regional problem. One of the major lessons learned from all of the Middle Eastern terrorist activity that occurred in Western Europe during the 1980s was that this activity was not only a threat to the individual countries in which these operations took place, but also to the region as a whole. The response of the "front line" states (Germany, Italy, France, Spain, and Great Britain) was to increase cooperation among themselves in order to counter this growing Middle Eastern terrorist threat. It was this cooperation, at both the political and security levels, that contributed to the decline of Middle Eastern terrorist incidents in the region during the late 1980s, as Table 1 indicates.

Table 1
Middle Eastern Terrorist Incidents in Western Europe (1980–1990)

Year	No. of Incidents	Year	No. of Incidents
1980	35	1985	79
1981	22	1986	41
1982	34	1987	40
1983	26	1988	21
1984	44	1989	23
		1990	9

In the author's opinion, of all the Middle Eastern terrorist developments that took place in Western Europe during the 1980s, the most significant development was the increased activity of certain Middle Eastern states in supporting and sponsoring terrorist activity. Iran was the most active, followed by Libya, Syria, and Iraq.[7] As previously stated, these four states were responsible for or facilitated 152 incidents, or 42% of all Middle Eastern terrorist incidents in Western Europe during the 1980s. Some of the bloodiest terrorist massacres that took place in the region during the 1980s can be linked to these states. It was the involvement of these states in terrorist activity during the 1980s that caused Great Britain to break diplomatic relations with Libya, Iran, and Syria and forced France to sever relations with Iran. Moreover, it was Libya's involvement with terrorist attacks against U.S. interests in Western Europe from 1985–1986 that compelled the United States to conduct retaliatory air strikes against Libya in 1986. It was this potential to affect state-to-state relationships that has made Middle Eastern state-sponsored terrorist activity in Western Europe the most significant and dangerous terrorist development in Western Europe over the past two decades.

There are four factors that unfortunately argue for continued Middle Eastern terrorist activity in Western Europe in the 1990s. First, it appears likely that the controversial political issues and intra-Palestinian and inter-Arab feuds that trigger Middle Eastern terrorist activity are a long way from being resolved. This includes the question of a Palestinian homeland, the scope and direction of Middle East peace discussions, the political stability of Lebanon, the role of Islamic fundamentalists in Lebanon, the post-Gulf war situation in Iraq, the current and future role of the United States in the Persian Gulf, and internal political adjustments in Iran. All of these developments have acted as major triggers for Middle Eastern terrorist activity, not only in Western Europe, but in other parts of the world. Moreover, a corollary of many of these issues is that they produce disagreements and feuds among various Arab states and within the Palestinian movement. Keep in mind that 53% of all Middle Eastern terrorist activity in Western Europe in the 1980s was directed at other Arab and Palestinian targets. There is clearly a propensity for militant Palestinians and radical Arab states to resort to political terrorism against each other when the need arises.

A second factor is the continued existence of Middle Eastern personalities like Yasir Arafat, Ahmad Jibril, Abu Nidal, Mu'ammar Quaddafi, Saddam Hussein, Hafez al-Assad, Abu Abbas, and so forth. If the previously mentioned controversial political issues in the Middle East are potential terrorist powder kegs, then these are the men who light the fuses. All have used terrorism to accomplish their personal goals and the objectives of their respective groups and states. While they will occasionally sheathe their terrorist swords, these swords still remain within reach. History has shown that not one of these men has permanently rejected the use of the sword of terror. The above-mentioned Middle Eastern political issues and personalities will unfortunately ensure that Middle Eastern terrorist activity will continue into the 1990s. Why will Europe continue to be a preferred operational area for this activity? This question leads us to the third factor: the attractiveness of Europe as a theater of operations for Middle Eastern terrorist groups.

There are five attributes that Europe possesses that have made it an attractive operational area for Middle Eastern terrorists since 1968. First, Europe contains many large Arab and Palestinian communities. Moreover, it has a large Arab student population and is frequently visited by Middle Eastern businesspeople and tourists. All of this facilitates the building and maintenance of a terrorist logistical infrastructure—a network that can provide surveillance data, conspirative apartments, arms caches, false documents, escape routes, and cover to a terrorist hit team. Second,

Europe is a geographically compact area with excellent transportation facilities, and, as a result of the open borders policy mandated by the European community to begin in 1992, will have no internal border controls. Third, Europe offers Middle Eastern groups an abundance of Arab, Palestinian, Israeli, Jewish, European, and American targets. Fourth, Europe offers Middle Eastern terrorist groups a broad and bright publicity spotlight to convey the propaganda messages of their attacks. Last, Europe offers these groups a substitute battleground for their inter-Arab and intra-Palestinian feuds. Middle Eastern groups that desire to attack Syrian, Libyan, Iranian, and Iraqi targets would find it easier and less risky to hit these targets in Europe than inside these authoritarian states. All of these five attributes will continue to exist in the 1990s. Hence, Europe should continue to be the primary operational area for Middle Eastern terrorist groups operating outside the Middle East.

The removal of the communist regimes in Eastern Europe in the summer of 1990 may make Europe a more attractive area than before. Middle Eastern terrorist groups rarely carried out attacks inside the Eastern Bloc countries when they were under communist rule. It was generally believed that Middle Eastern terrorist groups restricted their offensive operations in and against Eastern Bloc countries because these communist regimes were providing support (rest and recreation facilities, weapons, explosives, false document, finances, training, and transit privileges) to Middle Eastern groups.[8] Soviet and Eastern Bloc support to Libya, Iraq, and Syria also precluded these states from sponsoring terrorist activity against and in the Eastern Bloc countries. This symbiotic relationship between the communist regimes and Middle Eastern terrorist elements was in effect throughout the 1970s and 1980s. It should also be noted that there were some isolated incidents in the Eastern Bloc by Middle Eastern terrorists. The author has recorded only five incidents in the 1980s, occurring in Yugoslavia, Poland, and Romania. Almost all of these incidents have been attributed to the Abu Nidal organization. The last incident took place in December 1984, when the Abu Nidal group assassinated a Jordanian diplomat in Bucharest. It is clear that Middle Eastern terrorist elements believed it would be counterproductive to attack Israeli, Jewish, or American targets in Eastern Europe and risk offending and embarrassing their patrons.

With the fall of the communist regimes in Eastern Europe, Middle Eastern terrorist elements may take a second look at this region. The support that these terrorist elements received from the Eastern Bloc countries has apparently been disrupted. Soviet and Eastern Bloc aid to Libya, Iraq, and Syria has also been curtailed. The factors that restrained Middle Eastern terrorist elements from operating in Eastern Europe have been removed. Moreover, from the terrorist's

perspective, there are some attractive conditions that are now developing in Eastern Europe. First, because Middle Eastern terrorists have traveled this region and spent time there, they are familiar with the area. Moreover, there are still Middle Eastern students attending universities in Eastern Europe, and their presence could be the foundation for a terrorist support network. Second, there are many Eastern Bloc intelligence agents who are out of work. Some of them have most likely worked with these Middle Eastern terrorists. These former intelligence agents could also contribute to the terrorists' support network in Eastern Europe. Third, the security and law enforcement agencies in the Eastern Bloc countries have reportedly been weakened by purges, dismissals, and resignations. The effectiveness of these agencies to counter Middle Eastern terrorist activities is questionable. Last, with the rising threat of ethnic violence in some of the Eastern European countries, the governments may be more preoccupied with local problems than with Middle Eastern terrorists. It would appear that the current conditions in Eastern Europe are ideal for Middle Eastern terrorist elements to install a logistical support network in Eastern Europe. It is likely that there could be a significant increase in Middle Eastern terrorist activity in Eastern Europe in the 1990s. One could also envision Middle Eastern terrorist attacks against East European countries that develop anti-Arab, anti-Palestinian policies.[9]

One development that will most likely have a major impact on Middle Eastern terrorist activity in Western Europe in the 1990s is the involvement of the United States in the Persian Gulf conflict and the subsequent military defeat of Iraq. Even though the feared Iraqi-sponsored terrorist activity during Operation Desert Storm did not take place, the Persian Gulf war has initiated a political metamorphosis in the region, especially in Iraq. Such changes or adjustments in Middle East alliances or regional power equations have usually triggered terrorist activity in the Middle East and in Europe. Iraq may decide to settle accounts with Arab and Western members of the Allied coalition, which inflicted a humiliating military defeat on its armed forces. Defeated on a conventional military battlefield, Iraq may take its revenge on the terrorist battleground, especially if Saddam Hussein remains in power. Hussein has a history of settling scores during his rise to power in Iraq, and there is no reason to believe that he will abandon this tendency in the post-Gulf war years.

Iraq has twice been involved in terrorist "wars" on the European continent. In 1978, the Iraqi-backed Abu Nidal organization struck at Palestine Liberation Organization (PLO) targets in Western Europe and the Far east. PLO representatives were assassinated that year in London, Paris, and Islamabad. In retaliation, the PLO attacked Iraqi targets in Brussels, Paris, London, Karachi, Tripoli, and Bonn. In 1980, Iraq became involved in another terrorist war, this time with Iran. Iranian targets were attacked in Kuwait City, London, Athens, and Vienna. In retaliation, Iraqi targets were hit in Rome and Abu Dhabi. All of these incidents were a prelude to the Iran-Iraq war, which broke out in September 1980. Iraq has consistently demonstrated its willingness and capability to engage in political terrorism to settle feuds and disputes. Iraq may also become the target of Middle Eastern terrorist attacks, especially by Iranian-backed Shi'ite fundamentalists who are seeking more political power in Southern Iraq. The Persian Gulf war has not only upset the balance of power equation in the Gulf, but it has also created new antagonisms, feuds, and enemies. Historically, this has been the fuel of Middle Eastern terrorist activity in Europe.

For over two decades, Western Europe has been a major battlefield for Middle Eastern terrorists. It is an operating environment with which they are totally familiar. During these two decades they have constructed efficient logistical networks in Western Europe to support their operations there. Periodic discoveries of their support cells by European security agencies has only damaged, not destroyed, these networks. Those groups that operate on behalf of a Middle Eastern state also have the advantage of being able to plug into the support network of a state intelligence agency and gain access to the benefits offered by diplomatic facilities.

An objective analysis of the current Middle Eastern terrorist situation in Europe strongly suggests that, given the continuing inability to solve key controversial political issues in the Middle East and the current willingness and capability of Middle Eastern terrorists to act in Western Europe, Middle Eastern terrorism in Europe will continue to be a major security problem for Europe and the United States in the 1990s. The level of this activity will fluctuate between temporary lulls and periods of intensified activity. The lulls should not disarm us, and the intensified activity should not alarm us.

NOTES

1. For additional articles by the author on Middle Eastern terrorist activity in Western Europe, see "Political Terrorism in Western Europe," in *Terrorism in Europe*, eds. Yonah Alexander and Kenneth Myers (London: Croom Helm, 1982), pp. 40–78; "Middle Eastern Terrorist Activity in Western Europe: A Diagnosis and Prognosis," *Conflict Quarterly* (New Brunswick, Canada) 6(3) (Summer 1986): 5–25; "Middle Eastern Terrorist Activity in Western Europe in 1985," in *Contemporary Research on Terrorism*, eds. Paul Wilkinson and A. M. Stewart (Great Britain: University of Aberdeen Press, 1987), pp. 164–78; and "Middle

Eastern Terrorist Activity in Western Europe in the 1980s: A Decade of Violence," in *European Terrorism: Current Threats and Future Prospects*, Yonah Alexander and Dennis Pluchinsky (Washington: Brassey's Terrorism Library Series, 1991), ch. 1.

2. Middle Eastern terrorist activity is defined as incidents carried out by Palestinian, Arab, Islamic revolutionary terrorist groups, or other groups working on behalf of these groups (Carlos, the Japanese Red Army, etc.), and by Middle Eastern states. It does not include terrorist incidents carried out by Kurds, Armenians, or Israel.

3. Personal correspondence with Anat Kurz of the Jaffee Center for Strategic Studies, Project on Terrorism, Tel Aviv University, July 1990.

4. Xavier Raufer, *La Nebuleuse: Le Terrorisme du Moyen-Orient* (The Nebula of Middle Eastern Terrorism) (Paris: Fayard, 1987).

5. All statistics used in this chapter are based on the author's chronology of Middle Eastern terrorist incidents in Western Europe 1980–1990. This chronology is a product of information extracted from publicly released U.S. government documents, press and academic sources, conversations with various terrorism experts in Western Europe and the Middle East, and publicly released judicial documents. It must be emphasized that this chronology is an ever-changing one. New information is always surfacing which may cause a reevaluation of certain incidents, especially in regard to the perpetrators of an incident.

6. For additional information on this 1985–1986 bombing campaign in Paris, see "The Terror, Why France, Why Now," *New York Times Magazine*, Oct. 19, 1986; "Hostages, Attacks . . . Operation Satan," *L'Express*, Feb. 3, 1989; *Le Figaro*, Oct. 28–29, 1989; and *Newsweek*, September 29, 1986. The terrorist cell responsible for the bombings was discovered in Feb. 1987 by French police. This cell consisted of some 20 people, but only 10 were arrested. In 1990 they were tried and convicted of lesser charges such as possession and transportation of explosives and planning the bombing attacks. In 1991 they are scheduled to be tried for the actual bombings and the fatalities and injuries they caused. See also *New York Times*, Jan. 30, 1990, p. 2.

7. Iran can be linked to 78 incidents, Libya to 53, Syria to 15, and Iraq to 6.

8. For recent information concerning East Bloc support for Middle Eastern terrorists, see the *Washington Post*, Nov. 14, 1990; the *Washington Times*, Aug. 24, 1990; the *New York Times*, Aug. 2, 1990; the *Washington Times*, July 9, 1990; and the *New York Times*, July 15, 1990. On Jan. 3, 1991, the ABC News program "Prime Time" aired an informative 25-minute documentary on the relationship between Carlos and East Germany, Hungary, Czechoslovakia, and Romania. The French news weekly, *L'Express*, Dec. 20, 1990 issue also contained an informative article on Carlos and Eastern Europe. Revelations in late March 1991 also suggested that the East German secret police had provided logistical aid and training facilities to West Germany's Red Army Faction (see the *Washington Post*, March 27, 1991).

9. Some Middle Eastern terrorist elements were critical of the Polish government's decision in early 1990 to increase its commercial flights to Israel and to transport Soviet Jewish emigrants to Israel. On March 6, the Polish trade office was bombed in Beirut. In April, a Middle Eastern group calling itself the General Command of the Front for the Islamic Army for the Liberation of Palestine issued communique number 2, in which it threatened "to blow up Polish embassies and to physically liquidate the ambassadors and employees of these embassies . . ." if the Polish government continued to aid the emigration of Soviet Jews to Israel. In June, the Hungarian airlines also received threats from Middle Eastern elements if it continued to transport Soviet Jewish emigrants to Israel. It would appear that the Middle Eastern terrorist elements will no longer give "special treatment" to the Eastern European countries. They will now be treated like the Western European countries have over the past 21 years: as potential targets and an ideal operational area.

Appendix

Worldwide Historical Evolution of Terrorism Since World War II

Bernard Schechterman
University of Miami

State or Area	Terrorism by the State		Terrorism Directed Against the State	
	Targets Within the State	Targets Outside the State	Outside Supporter of Terrorism (State Supported Terrorism)[a]	Domestic Revolutionary Terrorist Organization[a]
Afghanistan	Muslim rebels, tribal groups			
Algeria			Ahl al-Dawah/Al-Qiyam (People of the Call, Muslim Brethren)—Egypt, Tunisia, Morocco; Jamaat al-Islamiyyah (Islamic Society)—Muslim Brethren, Egypt National Liberation Front (FLN)—Egypt	Ahl al-Dawah/Al-Qiyam (People of the Call, Muslim Brethren); Jamaat al-Islamiyyah (Muslim Brethren); National Liberation Front (FLN)
Argentina	Communists, the left		Ejercito Revolucionario del Pueblo (ERP)—Cuba, Trotskyites, USSR, Revolutionary Coordination Junta	Ejercito Revolucionario del Pueblo (ERP), Monteneros, Tacuara, Fuerzas Armados, Rebeldes (FAR), Movimento Argentino Nacional Organisacion (MANO), Argentine Anticommunist Alliance (AAA)
Bahrain			Jabhat al-Islamiyyah Lil-Tahrir al-Bahrain (Islamic Front for Liberation of Bahrain)—Iran, Iraq, Gulf States	Jabbat al-Islamiyyah Lil-Tahrir al-Bahrain (Shi'a)
Belgium			Fighting Communist Cells (CCC)—Direct Action	Fighting Communist Cells (CCC), Viaamse Militante Orden
Bolivia			Ejercito de Liberacion National (ELN)—Colombia, Peru ELN's, ERP	Ejercito de Liberacion National (ELN)
Brazil			M-19—Cuba, Nicaragua	Acao Liberidora Nacional (ALN), MR-8, Vanguardia Popular Revolucionaria (VPR), Vanguardia Armada Revolucionaria Palmares (VAR)
Bulgaria	Muslims	Italy		
Burma				Shan State Army
Cambodia	peasants (under Khmer Rouge)			
Canada				Front de Liberation du Quebec (FLQ)
Central African Republic	Tribal groups and individuals			
Chile	Communists, Socialists, the left		Movimento de Liberacion Nacional (MLN)—Tupamaros, Movimiento de la Izquierda Revolucionaria (MIR)—Peru, Venezuela MIR's, Manuel Rodrigues Patriotic Front)Libya	Movimento de Liberacion Nacional (MLN), Movimiento de la Izquierda Revolucionaria (MIR), Manuel Rodrigues Patriotic Front
Colombia			M-19—Cuba, Nicaragua; Ejercito de Liberacion Nacional (ELN)—Peru, Bolivia ELN's, Cuba; Fuerzas Armadas Revolucionarias de Colombia (FARC)—USSR	M-19, Ejercito de Liberacion Nacional (ELN), Ejercito Popular de Liberacion (EPL), Fuerzas Armadas Revolucionarias de Colombia (FARC), Quintin Lame (Indian)

State or Area	Terrorism by the State		Terrorism Directed Against the State	
	Targets Within the State	Targets Outside the State	Outside Supporter of Terrorism (State Supported Terrorism)[a]	Domestic Revolutionary Terrorist Organization[a]
Cuba	Batista elements and dissidents	Nicaragua, Dominican Republic, Colombia, Venezuela, Angola, Mozambique, Grenada		
Cyprus			Ethnki Organosis Kypriakou Agoniston (EOKA)—Greece	Ethniki Organosis, Kypriakou Agoniston (EOKA)
Czechoslovakia			Libya, Palestine Liberation Organization	
Dominican Republic			Macheteros—Cuba	Macheteros Partido Revolucionario Dominican (PRD)
East Germany		West Germany, Ethiopia		
Ecuador				Alfaro Vive, Carajo
Egypt (There are between 50–60 opposition groups, but only some use terrorism)		Israel (Gaza Strip), Lebanon	Hizb Allah (Party of God)—N. Yemen; Hizb al-Tahrir (Liberation Party)—Arab countries; Ikhwan al-Muslimim (Muslim Brethren)—Gulf States, Syria, Jordan, Maghrib, Europe, Saudi Arabia; Jamaat al-Harakiyyah (Society of Action)—Libya; Jamaat al-Islamiyyah (Islamic Society)—Saudi Arabia; Jamaat al Shariyyah (Society of Islamic Law)—Gulf States; Jamaat al-Tabligh (Society of Islamic Law)—Gulf States; Jamaat al-Tabligh (Society of Transmission)—Gulf States; Munazzamat al-Tahrir al-Islami (Islamic Liberation Organizational/Technical Military Academy Group)—Syria, Sudan, Jordan, West Bank; Takfir wal-Hijrah (Denouncement and Holy Flight or Society of Muslims)—Kuwait, Gulf States, Turkey, Jordan, Libya, Pakistan, Syria, Saudi Arabia	Hizb Allah (Sunni), Hizb al-Tahrir (Sunni), Ikhwan al-Muslimim (Muslim Brethren), Jamaat al-Ahram (Pyramid Society), Jamaat al-Fath (Society of Conquest), Jamaat al-Haq (Society of Truth), Jamaat al-Harakiyyah (Society of Action), Jamaat al-Islamiyyah (Islamic Society), Jamaat al-Shariyyah (Muslim Brethren), Jamaat al-Tabligh, Jamaat al-Khalifah (Caliph's Group), Jamaat al-Muslimin lil-Takfir (Society for Accusation of Disbelief), Jamaat al-Muslimin (Muslim Group), Jamaat al-Takfir (Society of Denouncement), Al-Jihad (Holy War), Junud Allah (Soldiers of the Compassionate), Mukaffaratiyyah (Denouncers of Infidels), Munazzamat al-Tahrir al-Islami (Islamic Organizational/Technical Military Academy Group), Munazzamat al-Jihad (Jihad Organization), Qif wa Tabayyin (Halt & Prove), Qutbiyyin (Followers of Qutb), Samawiyyah (The Heavenly), Shabab Muhammad (Youth of Muhammad), Takfir wal-Hirah (Denouncement and Holy Flight), Usbah al-Hashimiyyah (The Hashemite League)
Ethiopia	Urban Leninists, Menarchists, Tribal Groups, and Individual Dissidents	Sudan		Ethiopian People's Revolutionary Party (EPRP)
France			Direct Action—Fighting Communist Cells (Belgium), Corsican Front—Libya Breton Liberation Front/Breton Liberation Army (FLB-ARB)—Spanish ETA, Irish IRA	Direct Action, Corsican Front, Breton Liberation Front/Army
(West) German Republic			Baader-Meinhof or Red Army Faction (RAF)—PLO, Western European Marxist and Anarchist Groups; Revolutionare Zellen—Marxist and Anarchist Groups, Hoffman Military Sports Group—PLO	Baader-Meinhof or Red Army Faction, Bewegung 2. Juni, German Action Groups (Neo-Nazis), Revolutionare Zellen, Hoffman Military Sports Group
Great Britain			Provisional Irish Republican Army (PIRA)—Ireland and No. Ireland, Irish National Liberation Army (INLA)—Ireland and N. Ireland, Palestine Liberation Organization—Fatah, rejectionist factions, Iran-Iraqi officials, dissidents, Libyan dissidents	Provisional Irish Republican Army (PIRA), Irish National Liberation Army, Angry Brigade, Cadwyr Cymru (Keepers of Wales), Mudiad Amddiffyn Cymru (Movement for Defense of Wales)
Greece			International Solidarity/Christos Kassimis—Anarchists in West Europe	International Solidarity/Christos Kassimis, November 17 Movement

State or Area	Terrorism by the State		Terrorism Directed Against the State	
	Targets Within the State	Targets Outside the State	Outside Supporter of Terrorism (State Supported Terrorism)[a]	Domestic Revolutionary Terrorist Organization[a]
Guatemala	Indian Tribal Groups		Movimiento de Liberacion Nacional (MLN)—Tupamaros	Movimiento de Liberacion National (MLN), Fuerzas Armados Rebeldes (FAR), Mano Blanco (MANO), MR-13, Nueva Organisacion Anticommunista (NOA)
Gulf States			Ansar al-Dawah (Supporters of the Call)—Pakistan, India, Gulf States	Ansar al-Dawah (Supporters of the Call)
Haiti	Christian Sects and Individual Dissenters			
Holland			South Moluccans—Ambonese Indonesians	South Moluccans (Ambonese Indonesians)
India			Naxalites—Red China	Naxalites Sikhs
Indonesia	Timor Tribes			South Moluccans (Ambonese Indonesians)
Iran	Bahai, Jews, Mujahadeen, Shah supporters, Dissidents, Tudeh Communists, Kurds	Great Britain, Iraq, Saudi Arabia, Lebanon, Kuwait, Gulf States, France	Siakhal—Iraq, Libya, PLO; Kurdish Democratic Party (KDP)—USSR	Siakhal, Mujahadeen, Kurdish Democratic Party (KDP)
Iraq	Kurds, Shi'a, Communist Party, Tribal Groups, Islamic Groups	Iran, Syria, Lebanon, Kuwait, Bahrain, Saudi Arabia	Hizb al-Dawah al-Islamiyyah (Islamic Propagation Party)—Iran, Gulf States, Kuwait, Dubai, Lebanon, Bahrain; Rabitat al-Mara al-Muslimah (Muslim Women's Assn.)—Iran, Gulf States; Hizb al-Fatimi (The Fatima Party)—Iran, pro-Shah elements; Zaynab (Women's Assn.)—Iran; Hizb al-Thawri al-Islami (Islamic Revolutionary Party)—Iran; Ikhwan Muslimin (Muslim Brethren)—Egypt, Syria, Jordan, Saudi Arabia; Ijtihad al-Islami li-Talabat al-Iraqi (Islamic Iraqi Students Union)—Iran, Gulf States, USA, West Europe; Jamaat al-Ulama (Society of Ulama)—Iran; Majlis al-Thawra al-Islamiyyah (Islamic Revolutionary Council)—Iran; Mujahadeen (Fighters)—Iran; Munazzamat al-Amal al-Islami (Islamic Action Organization)—Iran; Rabitat al-Islamiyyah (Islamic Assn.)—Iran	Hizb al-Dawah al-Islamiyyah (Islami Propagation Party), Zaynab (Women's Assn.) Rabitat al-Mara al-Muslimah (Muslim Women's Assn.), Rabitat al-Islamiyyah (Islamic Assn.), Hizb al-Fatimi (the Fatima Party); Hizb al-Thawri al-Islami (Islamic Revolutionary Party), Ikhwan Muslimin (Muslim Brethren), Ittihad al-Islamic li-Talabat al-Iraqi (Islamic Iraqi Students Union), Jamaat al-Ulama (Society of Ulama), Majilis al-Thawra al-Islamiyyah (Islamic Revolutionary Council), Mujahadeen (Fighters), Munazzamat al-Amal al-Islami (Islamic Action Organization), Kurdish Liberation Movement (Barzani)
Ireland, North			Provisional Irish Republican Army (PIRA)—Ireland, PLO, Libya, USA; Irish National Liberation Army (INLA)—Marxist Groups, Ireland	Provisional Irish Republican Army (PIRA), Irish National Liberation Army (INLA), Ulster Freedom Fighters (UFF), Ulster Volunteer Fighters (UVF), Ulster Defense Association (UDA), Protestant Action Force
Israel		Lebanon	Palestine Struggle Front (PSF)—PLO; Popular Front for Liberation of Palestine (PFLP)—Syria, PLO, Iraq; Al Fatah-Jordan, Syria, Iraq, Egypt, Libya, Algeria, Saudi Arabia	Stern Gang (Lehi), Irgun Zvi Leumi (Jabotinski), Terrorists Against Terrorism (TNT)—West Bank, Ma'atz (Council of Young Delinquents), Palestine Struggle Front (PSF), Popular Front for Liberation of Palestine (PFLP), Al Fatah (Arafat), Usrah al-Jihad (Family of Jihad)
Italy			Red Brigades—Marxist/Anarchist Groups West Europe; League of Fighting Communists (LFC)—Marxist/Anarchist Groups West Europe	Red Brigades, Valpreda, Futurist Movement, League of Fighting Communists (LFC), Armed Proletarian Nuclei, NAR (Neo-Fascist), Ordine Nero (Neo-Fascist), MSI (Neo-Fascist)
Jordan	Al Fatah (PLO)	Israel, West Bank	Ansar Harakat Asna al-Quran (Supporters of the Sons of the Quran)—PLO; Harakat al-Tawhid (Movement of Unicity)—Anti-Arafat Palestinians, Iran; Hizb al-Tahrir al-Islami (Islamic Liberation Party)—Lebanon, Libya, Turkey, Palestinians; Al Fatah (Arafat)—Egypt, Syria, Iraq, Algeria, PLO, USSR, E. Europe	Ansar Harakat Asn al-Quran (Sons of The Quran), Harakat al-Tawhid (Movement of Unicity), Hizb al-Tahrir al-Islami (Islamic Liberation Party), Al Fatah (Arafat)
Korea (North)		South Korea		

State or Area	Terrorism by the State		Terrorism Directed Against the State	
	Targets Within the State	Targets Outside the State	Outside Supporter of Terrorism (State Supported Terrorism)[a]	Domestic Revolutionary Terrorist Organization[a]
Kuwait			Dar al-Tawhid (Unicity Publishers)—Iran, Iraq, Revolutionary Organization/Forces of the Prophet Muhammad—Lebanese Shi'a	Dar al-Tawhid (Unicity Publishers), Revolutionary Organization/Forces of the Prophet Muhammad
Laos			Pathet Laos—N. Vietnam	Pathet Laos
Lebanon		Israel	AMAL (Hope)/Afwaj al-Muqawamah al-Lubnaniyyah (Lebanese Resistance Detachments)—Syria, Iran; Al-Jamaah al-Islamiyyah (Islamic Society, Muslim Brethren)—Syria, Jordan, Egypt; Jihad al-Islami (Islamic Holy War)—Syria, Iran; Hizb Allah/Islamic Amal (Party of God)—Iran, Syria; Arab Knights (Tripoli)—Arafat PLO; Saiqa (Vanguard)—Syria; Popular Front for Liberation of Palestine (PFLP)—Syria, Iraq, USSR; Popular Democratic Front for Liberation of Palestine (PDFLP)—Syria, Iraq, E. Europe, USSR; Al Fatah—USSR, Syria, Algeria, Iraq, So. Yemen, Egypt; Palestine Liberation Front (PLF)—Syria; Fatah Uprising (Abu Musa)—Syria; Fatah Revolutionary Council (Abu Nidal)—Syria, Iraq; Arab Liberation Front (ALF)—Iraq; Palestinian Popular Struggle Front (PPSF)—Syria; Popular Command (Jabril)—Syria; Palestine Liberation Front Breakaway (Muhammad Abbes); Lebanese Armed Revolution Faction (LARF)—Syria, PLO, Algeria; Lebanese Communist Party—Syria, USSR; National Syrian Social Party—Syria	AMAL (Hope); Al-Jamaah al-Islamiyyah (Islamic Society, Muslim Brethren); Jihad al-Islami (Holy War); Hizb Allah/Islamic AMAL (Party of God); Saiqa (Vanguard); Al Fatah (Arafat PLO); Lebanese Armed Revolution Faction (LARF); Arab Democratic Party; Nasserite Organizations (Sidon and Beirut); Lebanese Communist Party; National Syrian Social Party (NSSP); Arab Socialist Union
Libya	Dissidents among students, businessmen, and military	Egypt, Nicaragua, Great Britain, Sudan, Lebanon, Malta, USA, Greece, West Germany, Tunisia, Algeria, Philippines, Jordan, West Bank, France, Israel, Morocco, El Salvador, Guatemala, Pakistan, Portugal, New Caledonia, Thailand, Chile, Colombia, Turkey		Holy War
Mexico				Frente Urbano Zapatista (Zapata), Southern Liberation Army (ELS), Fuerzas Revolucionarias Armadas del Pueblo (FRAP)
Morocco			Ikhwan al-Muslimin/Shabibah al-Islamiyyah (Muslim Brethren)—Egypt, French Brethren	Ikhwan al-Muslimin (Muslim Brethren), Shubban Islamiyyah (Islamic Youth)
New Caledonia			Kanak Socialist National Liberation Front—Libya	Kanak Socialist National Liberation Front
Nicaragua	Miskito Indians	El Salvador, Honduras	Frente Sandinista de Liberacion Nacional (FSLN)—Cuba, USSR, Libya, East Europe; Contra Groups—USA, Honduras, Costa Rica; Miskito Indians	Frente Sandinista de Liberacion Nacional (FSLN); Contra Groups; Miskito Indians
Oman			Omani Liberation Front (OLF)—USSR, So. Yemen	Omani Liberation Front (OLF)

State or Area	Terrorism by the State		Terrorism Directed Against the State	
	Targets Within the State	Targets Outside the State	Outside Supporter of Terrorism (State Supported Terrorism)[a]	Domestic Revolutionary Terrorist Organization[a]
Peru			Ejercito de Liberacion Nacional (ELN)—ELN in Bolivia, Colombia; Movimiento de la Izquierda Revolucionaria (MIR)—MIR in Chile, Venezuela	Ejerecito de Liberacion Nacional (ELN), Movimiento de la Izquierda Revolucionaria (MIR), Sendere Luminoso (Shining Path—Maoist), Tupac Amaru
Pakistan			Al-Zulfigar—Libya	Al-Zulfigar
Philippines			New People's Army—Libya, Saudi Arabia, Moro National Liberation Front—Libya	New People's Army, Moro National Liberation Front
Portugal			April 25 Movement (FP-25)—Libya	April 25 Movement (FP-25)
Puerto Rico			Macheteros—Cuba	Macheteros, Movimiento Independista Revolucionario Armado (MIRA), Commandos Armados de Liberacion (CAL), Fuerzas Armados de Liberacion Nacional (FALN)
El Salvador			Ejercito Revolucienario del Pueblo (ERP)—ERP Argentina, Farabundo Marti National Liberation Front (FMLN-5 groups)—Nicaragua, Cuba	Ejercito Revolucionario del Pueblo (ERP); Farabundo Marti National Liberation Front (FMLN)
Saudi Arabia			Hizb al-Tahrir al-Jazirah (Liberation Party of Jazirah)—Iran, Gulf States, Iraq, Bahrain; Al-Ikhwan (Muslim Brethren)—Egypt, Yemen, Pakistan, Gulf States; Jamaat al-Masjid (Mosque Society)—Gulf States, Oman; Munazzamat al-Thawrah al-Islamiyyah Shubuh fi al-Jazirah al-Aribiyyah (Islamic Revolutionary Organization in Arabian Peninsula)—Iran; Hejaz Liberation Front—Iraq	Hibz al-Tahrir al-Jazirah (Liberation Party of Jazirah), Al-Ikhwan (Muslim Brethren), Jamaat al-Masjid (Mosque Society), Munazzamat al-Thawrah al-Is!amiyyah Shubuh fi al-Jazirah al-Arabiyyah (Islamic Revolutionary Organization in Arabian Peninsula), Hejaz Liberation Front
Senegal			Centre Social Islamique—Lebanon, Iran	Centre Social Islamique
South Africa	African National Congress, Black dissenters, Black unions	Southwest Africa (Namibia)	African National Congress (ANC)—OAU, Black African States, USSR; Umkhonto we Sizwe (MK)—Cuba, Angola, E. Germany	African National Congress, Afrikaner Weerstandbewegung (AWB-Neo-Fascist), Umhkonto we Sizwe (MK), Azarian People's Organization (AZAPO)
Southwest Africa (Namibia)			Southwest Africa People's Organizations (SWAPO)—Cuba, Angola	Southwest Africa People's Organization (SWAPO)
South Yemen (PDRY)		Oman, North Yemen, Lebanon		
Soviet Union (USSR)*	Volga Germans, Tartars, Jews, Baltic Catholics, dissenters	Afghanistan, East European regimes, PLO (Arafat, rejectionist factions), some Communist parties in less developed countries		
Spain			Euzkadi ta Askatasanu (ETA V, VI)—Libya, PLO, French Basques; ETA VI-Liga Communista Revolucionari (LCR)—Anarchist/Marxist groups; Warriors of Christ the King—Italian, South American Fascist Groups; Call of Jesus Christ—Lebanese Maronites	Euzkadi ta Askatasanu (ETA V, VI); ETA VI—Liga Communista Revolucionari (LCR); Frente Revolucionario Anti-Fascista y Patriota (FRAP); GAL; Anti-Terrorism ETA; Anti-Communist Apostolic Alliance (AAA); Spanish Basque Battalion (Neo-Fascist); New Force (Neo-Fascist)
Sri Lanka			Tamil Groups—India Tamils	Tamil Groups
Sudan			Sudanese People's Liberation Army/Anya Nya II (SPLA)—Ethiopia, Libya	Sudanese People's Liberation Army/Anya Nya II (SPLA)
Sweden			Kurdish Workers Party (KKK)—Kurds in Iran and Iraq; Croation Ustasha—Yugoslavia Croats	

*Now referred to as the Commonwealth of Independent States (C.I.S.) since the dissolution of Soviet Communism in December 1991.

State or Area	Terrorism by the State		Terrorism Directed Against the State	
	Targets Within the State	Targets Outside the State	Outside Supporter of Terrorism (State Supported Terrorism)ᵃ	Domestic Revolutionary Terrorist Organizationᵃ
Syria	Muslim Brethren groups	Lebanon, Israel, Jordan, Egypt, Iraq	Ikhwan al-Muslimin (Muslim Brethren)—Egypt, Iraq, Jordan, Gulf States; Ikhwan al-Muslimin (Political Solution Group)—Egypt, Gulf States, Iraq; Kataib Muhammad (Muslim Brethren of the Interior)—Egypt; Salafiyyah (Puritans)—Egypt; Tahririal-Islami (Islamic Liberation Party)—Jordan; Talia al-Muqatila lil Mujahadeen (Combat Vanguard of Fighters)—Iraq, Egypt	Ansari (Supporters); Ikhwan al-Muslimin (Muslim Brethren), Ikhwan al-Muslimin (Political Solution Group), Al-Jihad (Holy War), Junud Allah (Soldiers of God), Kataib al-Haq (Phalanges of Truth), Khulasah (Puritans), Salafiyyah (Puritans), Tahrir al-Islami (Islamic Liberation Party), Talia al-Muqatila lil Mujahadeen (Combat Vanguard of Fighters)
Tanzania	Zanzibar Arabs, Tribal resettlement (Ujamaa villages)	South Africa		
Thailand			Muslim Groups—Libya	
Tunisia			Amal al-Islami/Khawanjia (Islamic Action/Muslim Brethren)—Egypt; Hizb al-Islami (Islamic Party)—Egypt	Amal al-Islami/Khawanjia (Islamic Action), Progressive Socialist Gathering, Djihad Islamique, Ittijah al-Islami (Islamic Orientation), Jamiyyat Hifz al-Quran (Quran Preservation Societies), Hizb Allah al-Muktar, Parti de la Liberation Islamique (PLI) (Islamic Liberation Party), Movement of Popular Unity
Turkey	Kurds		Turkish People's Liberation Army (TPLA)—PLO, Syria, E. Germany, North Korea, USSR, Czechoslovakia; Armenian Secret Army (ASA)—USSR; ASALA (Armenian)—PLO, Libya, Syria, Greece	Nationalist Action Party, Turkish People's Liberation Army (TPLA), Armenian Secret Army (ASA), ASALA (Armenian), Kurdish Groups
Uganda	Tribes out of power			
United States			Aryan Nations—Neo-Nazis in Germany, Movimiento Independista Revolucionario Armado (MIRA)—Puerto Rico MIRA	Weathermen; Movimiento Independista Revolucionario Armado (MIRA); Symbionese Liberation Army (SLA); Aryan Nations; Covenant, Sword and Arm of the Lord (CSA); Posse Comitatus; The Order; White Aryan Resistance; White Patriot Party (WPP); National Alliance; Hanafi Muslims
Uruguay			Movimiento de Liberacion Nacional (Tupamaros)—Guatemala, Chile, Argentina Groups, USSR	Movimiento de Liberacion Nacional (Tupamaros)
Venezuela			Communist Party—Cuba, Movimiento de la Izquierda Revolucionaria (MIR)—Peru and Chile MIR's	Communist Party, Fuerzas Armados de Liberacion Nacional (FALN), Bandera Roja (Red Banner)
Vietnam (South and North)	South Vietnam officials (reeducation camps)	South Vietnam, Laos, Cambodia	Viet Cong—No. Vietnam	Viet Cong
Yemen (North)			Hizb Allah (Party of God)—Saudi Arabia, Gulf States	Hizb Allah (Party of God)
Yugoslavia			Croation Ustasha—USSR	Croation Ustasha
International			Muhammad Boudia Commando (Carlos)—Anarchist/Marxist Groups, PLO, Libya	

State or Area	Terrorism by the State		Terrorism Directed Against the State	
	Targets Within the State	Targets Outside the State	Outside Supporter of Terrorism (State Supported Terrorism)[a]	Domestic Revolutionary Terrorist Organization[a]
International[c]			Fatah (Arafat)—USSR, Arab League, Egypt, Libya, Syria, So. Yemen, Tunisia, Algeria, Lebanon, East Europe States, Jordan, Iraq, Iran, Sudan, Saudi Arabia, Kuwait, Gulf States; Arab Liberation Front (ALF)—Iraq; Palestine Liberation Front (PLF)—Iraq, Tunisia; Fatah Uprising (Abu Musa)—Syria; As Saiqa (Vanguard)—Syria; Palestine Front for Liberation of Palestine (PFLP) (Habash)—Syria, USSR; Palestine Front for Liberation of Palestine, General Command (Jibril)—Syria; Palestine Struggle Front (PSF)—Syria; Palestine Liberation Front (PLF)—Syria; Democratic Front for Liberation of Palestine (DFLP) (Hawatmeh)—Syria, USSR; Fatah Revolutionary Council (Abu Nidal)—Syria, Libya; Palestine Liberation Front Breakaway—Syria; PALM—Syria; May 15th Movement—Syria; Palestine Front for Liberation of Palestine, Security Command—Syria; Palestine Front for Liberation of Palestine, General Command Breakaway—Syria	

[a] It is not uncommon for a group to qualify under the heading of a domestic organization and also receive support from abroad. The domestic aspect indicates there is an indigenous basis for the origin and sustenance of the group apart from the overseas help.

[b] The Islamic Holy War and The Party of God operate by means of various subsidiary groups often brought into being for specific operations by members or by the leadership. Examples would be Organization of the Oppressed on Earth, Organization of Revolutionary Justice, etc. Many of the groups, particularly secular ones, are organized as part of the Lebanese National Democratic Front.

[c] The various Palestinian groups operate by means of various subsidiary groups often brought into being for specific operations by the leadership. Examples would be the Black September, Black June, Organization of Revolutionary Justice to Liberate Palestine, etc. The Palestinian groups most committed to "armed struggle" are also organized under the Palestine National Salvation Front. All are technically part of the larger organization popularly referred to and organized as the Palestine Liberation Organization.

Appendum

1990 Appendum: Survey of Worldwide Terrorism Since World War II (Political Form)

State or Area	Terrorism by the State		Terrorism Directed Against the State	
	Targets Within the State	Targets Outside the State	Outside Supporter of Terrorism (State-Supported Terrorism)[a]	Domestic Revolutionary Terrorist Organization[a]
Afghanistan		Pakistan		
Angola			UNITA-So. Africa, USA, Zaire Movimiento Popular Para a Liberacio de Angola (MPLA)—USSR, E. Europe, Cuba	UNITA, MPLA
Argentina			Motherland Movement-Nicaragua	Motherland Movement (MTP)
Botswana			Black Consciousness Movement (BCM)—PLO	Black Consciousness Movement (BCM)
Bolivia				Zarate Willca Fuerzas Armadas de Liberacion (ZWFAL), Commando Alejo Calatayno (CAC), Frente de Liberacion Nacional (FRELINA), Bolivian Labor Federation (COB), Commando Guerrilla Simon Bolivar (CGSP)
Canada			Direct Action—W. Europe Groups	Direct Action
Cape Verde (Portugal)				Portuguesa des Ilmas de Cape Verde

| State or Area | Terrorism by the State | | Terrorism Directed Against the State | |
	Targets Within the State	Targets Outside the State	Outside Supporter of Terrorism (State-Supported Terrorism)[a]	Domestic Revolutionary Terrorist Organization[a]
Central African Republic			Ubangui Patriotic Front (MCLN)—Libya, Cuba, PLO, Angola	Ubangui Patriotic Front
Chad			National Liberation Front (FROLINAT)—Libya, PLO	National Liberation Front (FROLINAT), People's Revolutionary Movement (MPR)
Chile			Manuael Rodrigues Front (MPFR)—Cuba	Movimiento Juvenil Lautaro (MJL)
Colombia			American Battalion—Nicaragua	Extraditables (Narco-Group), American Battalion
Denmark				BZ (name not fully known)
Djibouti				Troops of Revolutionary Resistance (TRRF)
Dominican Republic				Maximiliano Gomez Revolutionary Brigade (MGRB)
Ecuador			American Battalion—Nicaragua	American Battalion
Egypt			Nasserites—Libya	Nasserites Egyptian Revolution
Ethiopia			Eritrean Liberation Front (ELF)—Saudi Arabia, Iraq, Other Arab States	Eritrean Liberation Front (ELF)
Fiji				Talkay Movement
France				Corsican Revolutionary Action
Greece			Popular Initiative Front—PLO	Social Resistance (SR), Popular Initiative Front, Revolutionary People's Struggle (ELA), Christos Tsoutsouris
Guadeloupe (France)			Caribbean Revolutionary Alliance—Cuba, Libya	Caribbean Revolutionary Alliance, Guadeloupe Liberation Army (GLA)
Guatemala				Guatemalan National Revolutionary Unity (URNG)
Guinea (Portugal)				Partido Africano da Independencia Guinea
Holland			Red Resistance Front—PLO Rode Hulp—W. Europe Anarchists/Syndicalists/Marxists	Revolutionary Anti-Fascist Action (RARA), Red Resistance Front, Rode Hulp
Honduras			Chinchonero People's Liberation Movement (CPLM)—Cuba, Contra Assassination Squads—Nicaragua, Lorenzo Zelaya—Cuba, Nicaragua	Chinchonero People's Liberation Movement, Lorenzo Zelaya Popular Revolutionary Force (LZPRF)
India			Dal Khalsa—PLO	Hizbul Mujahideen (Kashmir), Jammu and Kashmir Liberation Front, United Liberation Front Assam, National Socialist Council Nagaland, United Liberation Front Manipur, Dal Khalsa
Indonesia			Suma Ram (IRB)—Libya, FREITLIN (E. Timor)—PLO, Angola	Suma Ram, FREITLIN (E. Timor)
Iran		Spain, W. Germany, Turkey (Kurds, Islamic Fundamentalists)		
Israel		West Bank Gaza Strip	Japanese Red Army—PLO, Libya, Abu Nidal, Islamic Resistance Front—Muslim Brethren	Arab Freedom Front, Fatah Revolutionary Council (Abu Nidal), Sicarii, Rafik Salmi Bloc (Gaza Strip), Islamic Resistance Front, Keshet/Sicarii
Italy				Autonomia Operaia, Prima Linea, Third Position
Japan				Chukaku-Ha (MiddleCore)
Lebanon	Shi'i Factions (Amal vs. Hizballah), Maronites vs. Shi'i Factions	Spain, France, W. Germany, Great Britain	Islamic Liberation—Iran; Committee for Solidarity with Arab & Middle East Political Prisoners—PFLP-SC (LARF); Islamic Jihad for Liberation of Palestine—PLO	Progressive Socialist Party (Jumblatt), Islamic Liberation, Anti-Khomeinist Front, Vengeance Party, Tanyus Shahin Armed Unit (LARF)
Lesotho/Swaziland				Pan African Congress of Azania (PAC), Basutoland Congress Party (Lesotho Liberation Army)
Libya		Chad, Kenya, Panama		Arab Nationalist Youth Organization (ANYO)

State or Area	Terrorism by the State		Terrorism Directed Against the State	
	Targets Within the State	Targets Outside the State	Outside Supporter of Terrorism (State Supported Terrorism)[a]	Domestic Revolutionary Terrorist Organization[a]
Malawi				Malawi Freedom Movement
Mexico				Movimiento de Accion Revolucionario (MAR), Commando International Simon Bolivar (CISB)
Rio de Oro (Morocco)			Saguiat el Hamra and Rio de Oro (SARIO)—Libya, Algeria	Polisario (People's Front-Western Sahara), Saguiat el Hamra and Rio de Oro (SARIO)
Mozambique			Frente Liberacion de Mozambique (FRELIMO)—USSR, East Europe	Frente Liberacion de Mozambique (FRELIMO), Mozambique National Resistance Movement (Renamo)
New Guinea				Papua Rebellion
Nicaragua		Colombia, Puerto Rico, Dominican Republic		Nicaragua Democratic Front
Panama				La Tendencia
Salvador			Central American Revolutionary Workers Party—Cuba, Nicaragua	PRTC, Clara Elizabeth Front, ARDE (Anti-Communists)
Somalia			Somali National Movement (SNM)—Ethiopia	Somali National Movement (SNM)
South Africa				White Wolves
Spain			October 1st Anti-Fascist Resistance Group (GRAPO)—Direct Action, Red Brigades	Iraultza (Basque Armed Revolutionary Workers Organization), Grupos Antiterroristas de Liberacion (GAL), Primero de Octubre Catalan Red Liberation Army (ERCA), Iparratarrek Terra Lliura (TL), GRAPO
Sri Lanka				Janatha Vimukhti Peramuna (JVP), Tamil Liberation Tigers
Surinam				National Liberation Union (NLU)
Thailand				Pattani (Shi'i) Rebellion, Patani United Liberation Front, Barbisan Revolusi Nasional
Tunisia			Islamic Trend Movement (MTI)—Iran, Libya	Islamic Trend Movement (MTI)
Turkey	Islamic Extremists		National Liberation Front of Kurdistan—Syria, Iran; Gray Wolves—Bulgaria Justice Commandos of the Armenian Genocide (JCAG)—Overseas Armenians Kurdish Workers Party (PKK)—Bulgaria	Armed Peoples Units, Jundallah (God's Warriors—Shi'i), Warriors of the 16th June, National Liberation Front of Kurdistan, Partiya Karkeren Kurdistan, JCAG, Der Sol, PKK, Apoist/Apocular (Kurds), Gray Wolves
Uganda			*National Resistance Council—Libya	Uganda People's Army, *National Resistance Council, National Liberation Front (UNLF)
United Arab States				National Democratic Front (NDF)
United States			Japanese Red Army—Abu Nidal, Libya	United Freedom Front; Ku Klux Klans, Black Liberation Army, Jewish Defense League
West German Republic			Partiya Karkeren Kurdistan-Turkish Kurds	
Zimbabwe				Zimbabwe African People's Union (ZAPU), Zimbabwe African National Union (ZANU)
International (Japanese Red Army)	Japan (Factional Killings)	USA, Israel	Anti-Imperialist International Brigade—PFLP-SC, Japanese Red Army—Abu Nidal, Libya	
International (Abu Nidal-Fatah Revolutionary Council)	Fatah (Yasir Arafat)	Israel, Americans, Egypt, Jordan	Japanese Red Army—Abu Nidal, Libya; Arab Revolutionary Cells; Revolutionary Organization of Socialist Moslems (ROSM)—Syria; Black September—Syria; Palestine National Salvation Front—Syria; Fatah Revolutionary Council—Syria, Libya, Iraq	

*State-run terrorist organization directed against internal tribes but organized and sponsored from abroad.

Credits/ Acknowledgments

Cover design by Charles Vitelli

1. Concept of Terrorism

Facing overview—United Nations photo by Contact.

2. Causes and Scope of Terrorism

Facing overview—United Nations photo.

3. Terrorists: International, State-sponsored, and State-supported

Facing overview—United Nations photo by Milton Grant.

4. State Terrorism and Dissent (Revolutionary) Terrorism

Facing overview—United Nations photo.

5. Terrorism in America

Facing overview—UPI/Bettmann Newsphoto.

6. Terrorism and the Media

Facing overview—The Christian Science Monitor.

7. Tactics, Strategies, and Targeting

Facing overview—United Nations photo by John Isaac.

8. Countering Terrorism

Facing overview—U.S. Navy photo. 200-201—Reprinted from uncopyrighted student paper, source unknown.

9. Trends and Projections of Terrorism

Facing overview—United Nations photo.

ANNUAL EDITIONS ARTICLE REVIEW FORM

■ NAME: _____ DATE: _____

■ TITLE AND NUMBER OF ARTICLE: _____

■ BRIEFLY STATE THE MAIN IDEA OF THIS ARTICLE: _____

_____

_____

_____

_____

■ LIST THREE IMPORTANT FACTS THAT THE AUTHOR USES TO SUPPORT THE MAIN IDEA:

_____

_____

_____

_____

_____

_____

■ WHAT INFORMATION OR IDEAS DISCUSSED IN THIS ARTICLE ARE ALSO DISCUSSED IN YOUR TEXTBOOK OR OTHER READING YOU HAVE DONE? LIST THE TEXTBOOK CHAPTERS AND PAGE NUMBERS:

_____

_____

_____

_____

_____

_____

■ LIST ANY EXAMPLES OF BIAS OR FAULTY REASONING THAT YOU FOUND IN THE ARTICLE:

_____

_____

_____

_____

_____

■ LIST ANY NEW TERMS/CONCEPTS THAT WERE DISCUSSED IN THE ARTICLE AND WRITE A SHORT DEFINITION:

_____

_____

_____

_____

_____

*Your instructor may require you to use this Annual Editions Article Review Form in any number of ways: for articles that are assigned, for extra credit, as a tool to assist in developing assigned papers, or simply for your own reference. Even if it is not required, we encourage you to photocopy and use this page; you'll find that reflecting on the articles will greatly enhance the information from your text.

We Want Your Advice

ANNUAL EDITIONS:
VIOLENCE AND TERRORISM, Third Edition
Article Rating Form

Here is an opportunity for you to have direct input into the next revision of this volume. We would like you to rate each of the 58 articles listed below, using the following scale:

1. **Excellent: should definitely be retained**
2. **Above average: should probably be retained**
3. **Below average: should probably be deleted**
4. **Poor: should definitely be deleted**

Your ratings will play a vital part in the next revision. So please mail this prepaid form to us just as soon as you complete it. Thanks for your help!

Annual Editions revisions depend on two major opinion sources: one is our Advisory Board, listed in the front of this volume, which works with us in scanning the thousands of articles published in the public press each year; the other is you—the person actually using the book. Please help us and the users of the next edition by completing the prepaid article rating form on this page and returning it to us. Thank you.

Rating	Article	Rating	Article
	1. Defining Terrorism		33. Bombs Over America
	2. Editor's Introduction: Is Symbolic Violence Related to Real Violence?		34. The Plague of Our Cities
	3. Unmasking Terrorism: The Fear of Fear Itself		35. Unmasking Terrorism: Manipulation of the Media
	4. Violence Against Violence: Islam in Comparative Context		36. The Media Dilemma and Terrorism
	5. Unmasking Terrorism: The Terrorist Mentality		37. Media Coverage of Political Terrorism and the First Amendment: Reconciling the Public's Right to Know With Public Order
	6. The Terrible Toll of Human Hatred		
	7. Explaining Terrorism		38. Terrorism and the Media: Lessons From the British Experience
	8. What Constitutes State Support to Terrorists?		
	9. The Terrorists' Payoff in the Hostage Deal		39. The Emerging Iranian-Sudanese Relationship: Implications for the New Islamic Politics of North Africa
	10. Horn of Misery		
	11. Israel's Deadly Game of Hide-and-Seek		
	12. The Abu Nidal Organization		40. Hidden Threat
	13. Europe's New Right		41. Peru's Maoist Drug Dealers
	14. The New Sound of Hate		42. Kidnapping and 'Taxes' Transform Guerrilla Inc.
	15. A Triangle of Ethnic Struggle: Northern Ireland's 'Troubles' Become a Fact of Life		
	16. Peru's Rebels Buck Trend as Troop Strength Grows		43. Fugitive Leader of Maoist Rebels Is Captured by the Police in Peru
			44. Colombia's Bloodstained Peace
	17. The State as Terrorist		45. Will Terrorists Use Chemical Weapons?
	18. Genocide: An Historical Overview		46. Terrorism and Public Opinion: A Five Country Comparison
	19. On Human Rights, Iran Still an Outlaw		
	20. Egypt's Islamic Extremists Step Up Violent Attacks		47. 10 Steps Against Terror
			48. Terrorism and World Order
	21. The Decline of the Red Army Faction		49. Economic Analysis Can Help Fight International Terrorism
	22. A Travesty of Justice		
	23. China's Black Book		50. Closing Our Eyes
	24. Tibet's Shattered Hopes		51. Amnesty Head Urges More Pressure on Human Rights
	25. India Under Fire Over Rights Abuses		
	26. Ethnic Conflict in Sri Lanka and Prospects of Management: An Empirical Inquiry		52. Diminishing the Threat: Intelligence and the War Against Terrorism
			53. Terror and Negotiation
	27. Burmese, After Years of Terror, Hope Things May Soon Change for the Better		54. Responses to Terrorism
			55. Terrorist Threat to Commercial Aviation
	28. The Nature of the Genocide in Cambodia (Kampuchea)		56. Specific Trends and Projections for Political Terrorism and Summary Lessons and Expectations for International Terrorism
	29. Violence, Like Punjab's Wheat, Finds Fertile Soil		
	30. War and Peace Advance in Sudan		57. Terrorism in the United States: Recent Trends and Future Prospects
	31. Structure of Counterterrorism Planning and Operations in the United States		
	32. Domestic Terrorism in the United States		58. Middle Eastern Terrorism in Europe: Trends and Prospects

(Continued on next page)

ABOUT YOU

Name_____ Date_____

Are you a teacher? ☐ Or student? ☐

Your School Name _____

Department _____

Address _____

City _____ State _____ Zip _____

School Telephone # _____

YOUR COMMENTS ARE IMPORTANT TO US!

Please fill in the following information:

For which course did you use this book? _____

Did you use a text with this Annual Edition? ☐ yes ☐ no

The title of the text? _____

What are your general reactions to the Annual Editions concept?

Have you read any particular articles recently that you think should be included in the next edition?

Are there any articles you feel should be replaced in the next edition? Why?

Are there other areas that you feel would utilize an Annual Edition?

May we contact you for editorial input?

May we quote you from above?

ANNUAL EDITIONS: VIOLENCE AND TERRORISM, Third Edition

BUSINESS REPLY MAIL

First Class   Permit No. 84   Guilford, CT

Postage will be paid by addressee

The Dushkin Publishing Group, Inc.
Sluice Dock
DPG **Guilford, Connecticut 06437**

No Postage
Necessary
if Mailed
in the
United States